The Pursuit of Southern History

The Pursuit
of Southern History

PRESIDENTIAL ADDRESSES
OF THE SOUTHERN HISTORICAL ASSOCIATION
1935–1963

Edited by

George Brown Tindall

Louisiana State University Press
BATON ROUGE 1964

Copyright 1964 by
Louisiana State University Press
Library of Congress Catalog Card Number: 64–21595
Manufactured in the United States of America by
Kingsport Press, Inc., Kingsport, Tennessee
Designed by E. S. Diman

FOUNDERS

OF THE SOUTHERN HISTORICAL ASSOCIATION

---

*Notices of the organizational meeting
were signed by:*

THOMAS P. ABERNETHY, *University of Virginia*
PHILIP M. HAMER, *University of Tennessee*
BENJAMIN B. KENDRICK, *Woman's College of the University of North Carolina*
CHARLES M. KNAPP, *University of Kentucky*

*Present at the organizational meeting in Atlanta,
Georgia, November 2, 1934, were:*

KATHRYN T. ABBEY, *Florida State College for Women*
KATHLEEN BRUCE, *Hollins College*
JOHN B. CLARK, *Mercer University*
E. MERTON COULTER, *University of Georgia*
PHILIP DAVIDSON, *Agnes Scott College*
EDWIN A. DAVIS, *Louisiana State University*
DOROTHY DODD, *Tallahassee, Florida*
JONATHAN T. DORRIS, *State Teachers College,
Richmond, Kentucky*
FLETCHER M. GREEN, *Emory University*
PHILIP M. HAMER, *University of Tennessee*
THEODORE H. JACK, *Randolph-Macon Woman's College*
CHARLES M. KNAPP, *University of Kentucky*
ROSS H. MCLEAN, *Emory University*
C. LISLE PERCY, *Piedmont College*
GEORGE PETRIE, *Alabama Polytechnic Institute*
WALTER B. POSEY, *Birmingham-Southern College*
AUXFORD S. SARTAIN, *State Teachers College,
Troy, Alabama*
WENDELL H. STEPHENSON, *Louisiana State University*

Acknowledgments

THE EDITOR and publishers are deeply indebted to the members of the Executive Council of the Southern Historical Association, the editors of the *Journal of Southern History,* and the former presidents of the Association for permission to reprint the presidential addresses; to Secretary-Treasurer Bennett H. Wall for supplying necessary information; and to the Institute for Advanced Study, the Firestone Library of Princeton University, and the Department of History of the University of North Carolina at Chapel Hill for other assistance.

Contents

x   *Contents*

Introduction

WHEN a small group of eighteen pioneers met in Atlanta on November 2, 1934, to launch the Southern Historical Association, their enterprise came at a fortuitous time for its success. Since the expiration of the old Southern History Association in 1907 after only a decade of existence, scholarship in regional history had established a much broader foundation on which to build a professional association. Beginning with the first generation of academic historians from Johns Hopkins and Columbia who had populated southern colleges at the turn of the century, the intellectual offspring of Herbert Baxter Adams and William A. Dunning had sired new generations of historical scholars in their turn. The collection of source materials, the establishment of archival depositories, the development of a monographic literature in the field had established southern history by the 1930's as a discrete field of research and study. From 1907, when William K. Boyd offered the first course in southern history at Trinity College (later Duke University), the number of colleges offering such courses had increased to six by 1913 and to thirty or forty in the 1920's. By 1940 there were nearly a hundred.

It was a time of maturation in many fields of regional scholarship; other landmarks were established about the same time by the organization of the Southern Economics, Southern Political Science and South Atlantic Modern Language Associations in the late 1920's and the Southern Sociological Society in 1935. What is more significant, the 1930's were a decade of regional rediscovery, the period of depression and the New Deal and the identification of the South as "the nation's No. 1 economic problem"; a time of agricultural reorganization and renewed industrial growth, of beginnings in the Negroes' drive for equal opportunity, and rising sectional consciousness in politics; a time of literary renaissance, the Historical Records Survey, the WPA state guide books, the Vanderbilt Agrarians, and the Chapel Hill Regionalists, a decade at the end of which John Temple Graves said the

South had become "more aware of itself as a region than it had been since 1861."

Representing one aspect of the renewed regional consciousness, the Southern Historical Association flourished and grew rapidly from the beginning. Its major purposes, as stated by the founders, were to promote interest and research in southern history, to collect and preserve southern historical records, and to encourage state and local historical societies, but it had a secondary purpose to foster the teaching and study of all branches of history in the South. Its membership was not limited to the South, either by residence or by professional interest. The first annual meeting in 1935 included a discussion of the freshman survey course and after 1940 the meetings regularly included sessions on European history, and on other fields of world history after World War II. In its thirtieth year a specialist in European history for the first time became president of the Association. Well before the first annual meeting, *The Journal of Southern History,* dedicated to the Association's major purpose, had become firmly established under the editorship of Wendell H. Stephenson. Probably few of the members are any longer aware that Huey P. Long was indirectly and probably unconsciously godfather to their *Journal,* but it was out of the riches he pumped into the Louisiana State University that it was first subsidized, moving later in succession to Vanderbilt, Kentucky, and Rice. The first annual meeting at Birmingham, October 25–26, 1935, attracted a registration of 109, 140 to the opening session, and 122 to the annual dinner for President E. Merton Coulter's address. Membership climbed steadily thereafter. Nearly two hundred new members were added in 1936, and more than a hundred in each subsequent year, except 1938, to the end of the decade. At the end of 1940 there were 983 members. After some decline during World War II, the upward trend was resumed; at the beginning of 1964 there were 2,554 members.

The chief activities of the Association have been its annual meetings and publication of the *Journal.* Since the basic logistics of these operations fall mostly to functionaries other than the president, he is left with one inexorable responsibility—to celebrate the yearly ritual of a presidential address after the annual dinner. Only three presidents have been deprived of the opportunity to deliver their messages, in each case because meetings were canceled during World War II, but each of them was granted an extension of remarks in the *Journal.*

No standard recipe or formula has been devised for the message, and none has been evolved by precedent. The presidents are presumably free to dish up whatever intellectual nutrition they please, but most of them have held to a staple diet—if sometimes liberally seasoned.

When H. C. Nixon reviewed the earliest presidential addresses on the Association's fifteenth anniversary, he found them somewhat short of "the sedate wine of philosophy" although "pretty well spiked with the hard liquor of polemics. . . ." No president of the regional association has yet seized this opportunity to formulate a personal credo of his craft, except Francis Butler Simkins, who gave Nixon's metaphor a surprising turn by blending its ingredients. The sedate wine of his philosophy—that the historian ought to take the past on its own terms— was heavily spiked with the polemics of his thrust at southern historians who tamper with tradition. But aside from Simkins' unique presentation, most of the polemics have been aimed north of the Mason-Dixon line— at least until very recently—and certain basic Nixonian categories established in 1949 still apply to the subsequent presidential addresses. They are digests of a book or books written or planned (but several stand alone as miniature monographs), or they undertake to sum up the learnings of a lifetime. The president may turn publicist (Nixon might even have said preacher) for an hour. He is likely to emphasize the evidence or significance of an age of transition or of a process of revision.

Taken seriatim, the heterogeneous essays published in this volume may seem a stubbornly unrelated miscellany, held together only by the incidental fact that they have been part of the same perennial rite. They defy classification, and some of them totally escape it. There is, of course, no logical or compelling reason why they should conform to a pattern, but upon closer scrutiny most of the presidential addresses may be found to fall, or may at least be arbitrarily placed for the reader's convenience in three basic categories: southern historiography, sectionalism (including the Civil War and the frontier), and life in the Old South and the New. Approached thus systematically, they can offer the reader a more coherent and profitable experience.

It was appropriate if not inevitable that in the first years of the Association a lively concern with its antecedents and with the evolution of southern history as a field of research and study should be reflected in the presidential addresses. The burden of the very first message by E. Merton Coulter was a survey of what the South had done about its history, with emphasis upon the emergence of a state and regional historical consciousness and the development of the state and regional historical societies that had preceded the new Association. Inaugurating a theme that would be echoed by his successors, Coulter deplored the neglect of southern history while other sections had magnified the minutest details of theirs, and called upon the profession to mobilize. "Historical workers," he declared, "should march together no less surely than soldiers, and ammunition should be garnered, stored, and used with as much precision." In this battle formation, Presidents Hamer and Hamilton fell into the category of ordnance specialists, detailing the movements to collect and store the source materials of southern history, retailing horror tales of priceless manuscripts lost through fire, vermin, and neglect, and summoning the troops to renewed efforts in gathering and preserving the records, whereas Wendell H. Stephenson undertook to examine the broader strategy in the advance of southern academic historiography through its first half century. Taken as a group, the four annual messages of Presidents Coulter, Hamer, Hamilton, and Stephenson provide a remarkably comprehensive introduction to the origins of southern historiography.

It will occasion no surprise that issues of sectionalism enter nearly every one of these addresses and constitute the central theme of many. They were close to the heart of the Association's very reason for existence and were undergoing a substantial revival on the public scene as well as in the concerns of scholars during the decade of the Association's founding. Two academic schools of thought, the Vanderbilt Agrarians and the Chapel Hill Regionalists, provoked a great deal of comment and debate in the period. Although their differences seem not to have agitated the Association in its early years, there was a session on Agrarianism at the 1936 meeting and Agrarian attitudes were expressed especially by Presidents Owsley and Kendrick. The traditional themes of sectional conflict were more congenial to the Association's historical interests, and they had been given a significant boost by the publication of Frederick Jackson Turner's *The Significance of Sections in American History* in 1932.

What is more, nearly every problem touched by the New Deal raised some sectional issue with a resultant crescendo in sectional tensions, just as the nation entered a new war. Most of the sectional issues, not even excepting racial tensions, revolved about the economic plight of the South, and much of the literature and public discussion of the time centered upon what came to be called the "colonial economy" of the South. Antagonism to the allegedly oppressive policies of an imperial Northeast provided a common meeting ground for southerners who differed on a variety of other questions, and the feeling was focused by southern governors and congressmen upon a drive to eliminate discriminatory freight rate differentials.

A remarkable display of sectionalist pyrotechnics that burst over the Southern Historical Association at the beginning of the 1940's was at least partially an outgrowth of these contemporary developments. Frank L. Owsley, the only historian who bore the credentials of an original Agrarian, ignited the fireworks in 1940 with a message that identified the causes of the Civil War—as well as subsequent regional ills—with an "egocentric sectionalism" of the Northeast that sought to remake the nation in its own image and to drag the variant regional cultures down to the dead level of its own common denominator. B. B. Kendrick, the following year, added an even longer historical perspective to the literature of the "colonial South." He sketched the profile of a region that since the first settlements had never been able to escape a tributary relationship first to Great Britain and then to the North, and had become so completely hog-tied that not even a future escape was conceivable. What was even worse, the South provided "a paradox more amazing and ironical than any ever conjured by the imagination of Gilbert and Sullivan. The people of the South, who all their lives had suffered deprivation, want, and humiliation from an outside finance imperialism, followed with hardly a murmur of protest leaders who, if indirectly, were nonetheless in effect agents and attorneys of the imperialists." A. B. Moore, somewhat less concerned with economics but more race-conscious than his two predecessors, took a more traditional point of departure from the evils of Reconstruction to explain how the South had acquired "a colonial status" not only in economics but in psychology, sentiment, culture, and politics.

A more optimistic frame of reference was supplied by Ella Lonn, a native Yankee and naturalized southerner, in her 1946 address. Undertaking to trace the theme of reconciliation between the South and North from the point where Paul Buck's *The Road to Reunion* had dropped it in 1900, she perhaps only aggravated the worst fears of the unreconstructed—and even she was forced to recognize three not inconsequential areas of nonreconciliation: the churches, politics and economics, and regional sentiment or prejudice both North and South. A unique approach was undertaken by Lester J. Cappon, who read the Association a lesson in both the rewards and the dangers of provincialism. William B. Hesseltine, on the other hand, by-passed the issues of sectionalism for a stimulating new synthesis of the American character in terms of four basic traditions: the Trustees, Squires, Artisans, and Yeomen.

Perhaps the most surprising discovery that the reader will make in this volume is that relatively few of the presidential addresses focus upon the Civil War. It is a common experience of southern historians that laymen conceive of their field primarily in terms of the Confederacy and, maybe, Reconstruction. To be sure, the Civil War, its antecedents and its consequences, constitutes the very point of origin for the idea of regional history, as E. Merton Coulter has indicated.

These addresses, however, offer striking evidence of the extent to which the field has broadened away from its origins. What is even more noteworthy is the prospect that the Association will pass the entire centennial observance of The War without a single presidential address on the subject.

Insofar as the subject is considered, the drum and trumpet school of history appears not at all in these pages. Bell I. Wiley came closest to military history, but not in the traditional sense. His summary of impressions gained from two decades of service with the rank and file of the Union and Confederate armies lies in the realm of social history. On the other hand, Kathryn Abbey Hanna's treatment of the South's role in the Mexican adventure of Napoleon III is a unique exercise in diplomatic history in a collection that for the most part neglects the international bearings of southern history.

The other three messages that deal with the Civil War treat its causes and consequences in terms so broad that they fall logically under the larger category of sectionalism. All of them follow the current of interpretation that was most prevalent when the Association was founded: that it was an unnecessary war; that however complex its causes, they all came down finally to an excess of passionate emotion; and that its consequences were more harmful than otherwise. Charles W. Ramsdell concluded his very judicious summary of Civil War interpretation by asking if reflection upon the Civil War would "enable us to attack our present problems with less of emotion and more of cool reason than we frequently display? That, at any rate *should be* one of the lessons of History." And Avery O. Craven capped several decades of studying sectional conflict with a cogent warning against interpretations whereby "a nation's conscience has been soothed to accept four bloody years of battle and ten years of civil enslavement as necessary and beneficial steps toward a sounder future." The price of union, he reminded the assembled members, included the ascendancy of "twisted, unbalanced, vindictive men," an age of hate and social irresponsibility, the corruption of government and business, the economic ruin of southern and western farmers. If the triumph of big business was preordained by the great forces ushering in the modern world, the great American tragedy lay in the way in which the changes were brought about through ruthlessness, waste, and corruption. Owsley's thesis of "egocentric sectionalism," already mentioned, closely resembled the interpretations of Ramsdell and Craven.

Paralleling the group of presidential addresses that treat sectionalism in terms of North and South are three that treat the original Turnerian theme of the West. Thomas P. Abernethy drew upon his extensive knowledge of the southern frontier to shatter some of the cherished images of the frontier legend. The typical frontier, he argued, did not embody the idealized pattern of the independent yeoman; it was instead a remote area of valuable lands whose exploitation required extensive resources of capital and political influence that could be commanded only by the speculator, not by the ordinary settler. Kentucky and Middle Tennessee were cited as typical frontier areas of land speculation where the landless settlers were offered a liberal suffrage but seldom favored in economic policy. The movements for western states during the Revolutionary period "were engineered and controlled by land speculators," and western democracy began to advance only when they had moved on. Moreover, Abernethy asked, were all the effects of the frontier beneficent? While lessening class distinctions, did it not fail to lessen the power of the strong over the weak? Did it not stress the practical at the expense of cultural achievement, despoil natural resources, neglect the social amenities, assume an exaggerated individualism that was more a disregard of authority than a determination to think out one's problems for himself?

The other two addresses on the western theme tackle the question of the South's influence on the West. William C. Binkley was impelled by the publication of Stewart Holbrook's *The Yankee Exodus* to raise the issue of the part the South had in peopling the West and influencing its culture. His pioneering foray into a new frontier of western history, however, by its very scope could only be suggestive of further explorations into southern contributions to the economic, social, and cultural development of the West, but his statistics of southern migration and his evidences of southern leadership in the area point to new perspectives not yet fully achieved. What might have happened, he asked, if the earlier southern historians of the Dunning Reconstruction school had turned their faces instead to Wisconsin and Turner? Robert S. Henry, in turn, went Binkley one better, if in different terms, by suggesting that there might have been no West at all but for such southern leadership as that provided by George Rogers Clark, Jefferson, Jackson, the Austins, and Polk, "as America moved, west by south, to its appointed destiny."

If the Civil War does not loom large as a subject for presidential addresses, it thrusts up repeatedly in considerations of other subjects. It also functions, in H. C. Nixon's phrase, as the "great calendarial dam across the stream of Southern history." Robert S. Cotterill's address, the shortest of them all, was a timely reminder that water had flowed over the dam, but several presidents chose to discourse on certain special aspects of southern life either above or below the dam.

Glimpses into the life of the Old South were provided by Sydnor, Green, Patton, and Posey. A helpful insight into the southern mind was contributed by Charles S. Sydnor, who found that the "planter simply went through life under the assumption that a relatively large number of his deeds had to be performed out past the margin of written law. . . ," under the unwritten code of honor. While the southerner's attitude toward the law was only a secondary characteristic, not a unifying principle or central theme of southern history, it contrasted so strongly with attitudes prevalent in the North as to constitute a serious factor in sectional misunderstandings.

Sydnor contended that the peculiar unwritten code of the planter evolved in part out of southern domestic history, out of the struggle of an aristocratic social order to maintain its position against the enlarging power of the democracy. Fletcher M. Green several years later offered a corrective to the vision of the Old South as primarily an aristocratic order by tracing the evolution of white manhood suffrage and the democratic urge in the politics of the Old South. Drawing upon his studies of constitutional development, he traced the "establishment of white manhood suffrage, the abolition of property qualifications for office holders, the election of all officers by popular vote, . . . the apportionment of representation on population rather than wealth," the rise of public education, and the emergence of political leaders from the small farmer and yeoman classes—in short, "a progressive expansion in the application of the doctrine of political equality" from 1776 to 1860. His findings in the political sphere reinforced the incidental comments of Owsley and Kendrick on the significance of small propertyholders in the Old South.

Out of his broad acquaintance with the sources, James W. Patton added some glimpses of antebellum southerners who, like men in other times and places, had preoccupations other than slavery and politics. Plagued with diseases, they were obsessed with the state of their health. Mostly orthodox Protestants, they were absorbed in their religion, and when they travelled abroad they were inclined to a parochial attitude toward unfamiliar customs and conditions. Walter B. Posey, finally, pursued one group of the Protestants, the Episcopalians, through the difficult tasks of surviving disestablishment and the westward movement.

Working below the "calendarial dam" of the Civil War, Thomas D. Clark beckoned the august historians into the richly human resources of the country weeklies for a closer acquaintance with what the people were thinking, and Rembert W. Patrick reminded an audience in the highly appropriate surroundings of a Miami Beach hotel that tourism, long since a major southern industry, had been almost totally ignored by the region's historians.

Once again in the early 1960's as in the early 1940's, the tensions and spirit of the times have thrust up into the presidential addresses, but in a framework of self-analysis rather than sectionalism. Clement Eaton in 1961 seized upon the experience of Professor James Woodrow, who was dismissed from the Columbia Theological Seminary for his views on evolution, as a useful lesson on the timely issues of academic freedom. Exhorting his colleagues to emulate the moral courage of Woodrow, Eaton challenged them to a bolder stand on the racial issues of their own day. The gage was picked up in 1963 by James W. Silver, who cast off academic caution for a headlong assault upon entrenched credos. "Mississippi: The Closed Society" set forth an arresting and frightful bill of particulars to document the charge that "the totalitarian society of Mississippi imposes on all its people an obedience to an official orthodoxy almost identical with the proslavery philosophy. . . ." It is unique among the presidential addresses for the extensive coverage it got in the nation's press—outside of Mississippi—and it is one of the few (with those by Kendrick and Moore) that constitute in themselves original documents of their times.

Taken as a group, these essays touch upon points in a wide spectrum of their field. It would be too much to ask, perhaps, that they collectively represent any fundamental trends in southern history; too much certainly to demand that they cover the whole scope of southern history. One might more appropriately wonder that they have not more frequently risen to a loftier plane of generalization and philosophizing. Perhaps they confirm the frequent observation that the southern mind is not devoted to introspection and analysis. Given over to a heavy emphasis on sectional conflict in American history, sometimes with an element of belligerence, few of the addresses envision the South as an integral part of a larger culture. There is much on the South's ills at the hands of the North, much complaint at the imposition of northeastern patterns on the South; but little consideration of the idea of the South or the nature and meaning of the South's cultural distinctiveness. What contribution the South may have made to the overall national development and character the presidents say not, except for an unmeasured impact on the West and in Owsley's passing treatment of the South's own "egocentric sectionalism" in the Jeffersonian era— which viewed the nation as a rural Arcadia writ large.

What contribution the southern experience may offer to an understanding of the larger problems of a later day was the subject of only one very thoughtful address, C. Vann Woodward's "The Irony of Southern History," which drew a cogent analogy between the sectional "cold war" of the nineteenth century and the global "cold war" of the twentieth. The habit of defining loyalty as conformity and the increasing identification of the American cause with a particular economic system, he argued, had their parallels in the southern defense of slavery, and postures of moral righteousness in the antislavery attack. From the unique perspective of their region's experience, he suggested, southern historians could bring a sense of irony to bear upon national legends of success and victory, innocence and virtue. They could "reveal the fallacy of a diplomacy based on moral bigotry, . . . the futility of erecting intellectual barricades against unpopular ideas, . . . of imposing the ideas of the conqueror upon defeated peoples by force of arms." They could teach "that any nation that elects to stand or fall upon one ephemeral institution has already determined its fate." Except for Simkins, Woodward is the only president to have contemplated the identity and role of the southern historian.

One is drawn to ponder some other striking omissions. H. C. Nixon's comment on the Association's fifteenth anniversary still retains its validity:

> If all these presidential papers were put together in one volume, the general pattern of interpretation would be a far cry from the picture as set forth by V. O. Key or Gunnar Myrdal. A foreigner reading the volume and also Myrdal's *An American Dilemma* without external identifications would assume that the two works deal with different lands and different peoples. Perhaps they do.

The composite president in the second fifteen years of the Association still falls under Nixon's stricture that he has given a peculiar twist to U. B. Phillips' "Central Theme of Southern History": "Unlike Phillips, he has sought to conceal the southern Negro in a woodpile of constitutional abstractions, ignoring him statistically and spiritually" —one might almost say, entirely. Even Eaton and Silver have concentrated upon the white man's reaction to racial issues.

Nixon's invocation of V. O. Key's *Southern Politics* has become somewhat less pertinent with the delivery of T. Harry Williams' spirited and vigorous evocation of Huey Long. But Williams' address still stands in solitary splendor as a treatment of the tremendously important subject of internal conflicts in southern politics or as an analysis of that celebrated but still undefined figure, the southern demagogue. And Long was, after all, as he said himself, *sui generis*.

One experiences at least a mild surprise that the subject of Reconstruction, while it appears in one of the titles, is considered only briefly in a broader treatment of sectionalism; that economic development of the region, except for tourism, falls into a similar subdivision; that intellectual development, except for historiography, is neglected; and that the international bearings of southern history figure in only one address.

These and other omissions may be summoned to mind, but the fact remains that as they stand these essays constitute a remarkably broad and distinguished cross-section of southern historical scholarship over a period of three decades. They are liberally sprinkled with new insights, stimulating interpretations, and original syntheses. All suggest areas for further exploration; many reach a high level of felicity in expression. Collectively the Association's presidents in its first thirty years have set a standard of excellence that will challenge severely the craftsmanship of their successors.

The Pursuit of Southern History

Chapter I

What the South
Has Done About Its History

E. MERTON COULTER

THE SOUTH has often been referred to as a virgin field for the historian.* Other sections of the country have written almost the minutest details of their history or suffered others to do it, even to magnifying the Boston Tea Party and Paul Revere's Ride into an importance which has permeated the national consciousness, while the South has permitted its history to lie unworked and many of its major figures and movements to remain to this day "unhonored and unsung."

There are certain factors which enter into the growth of a new nation and a civilization, which operate rather uniformly, and which must apply, therefore, somewhat equally to the South, the East, the North, and the West—or to whatever sections we may choose to include in our sum total. It is a truism that a country without a history cannot write it, and, of course, the younger a country is, the less there is to write about or to be interested in. The writing of a nation's history is reminiscing for that nation, and it is a well-known fact that only old and oldish people do much reminiscing. As *De Bow's Review* said in 1853, "It is not in the buoyancy of youth that men or nations look back on the past."[1]

Yet the North, and New England especially, early began to look back on their short past and they soon discovered that it was heroic and that there were giants in those days. They set to work writing about them. Realizing that in union there is strength, individuals early joining forces, organized historical societies, which first being state-wide, multiplied until scarcely a town in New England did not boast of such an organization. Histories accumulated until there was scarcely anything left to

*Presented in Birmingham, Alabama, October 25, 1935.

3

be written about. It is not necessary here to inquire into the reasons for these activities, hasty though entirely laudable. It is sufficient to say that the compact settlements made it possible, that the character of the people led them early to begin looking backward (as well as forward), and that their occupations developed a store of community spirit and a wealth of money.

In comparison with New England and the North, the South early fell behind in its historical consciousness, not because it was less old or had a less interesting or important past, but for reasons that will soon appear, some of which, apart from the comparison, operated everywhere to retard historical activity. Though racially the North and the South cannot be so simply described as Puritan and Cavalier, there were nevertheless important differences in the people who settled the two sections. A great many southerners were Scotch-Irish or of Scotch-Irish descent, and it may not be held to the discredit of other strains to say that the Scotch-Irish exercised an influence in the South out of proportion to their numbers. These people and many other southerners were individualistic and greatly lacking in self-consciousness. They had little of that introspection which characterized the New Englander and made him busy himself not only with his own affairs but also with the affairs of others. The southerner was not community-minded, for he did not as a rule live in communities.

This fact suggests that the South developed a rural population and a civilization based almost entirely on agriculture. The people busied themselves in clearing the land and tilling the soil, largely isolated one from another. They thought in terms of their own problems and had little inclination to get interested in or to seek to examine what had gone before. There long remained in the South many elements of the frontier, and no frontier can become much interested in its history, however long or short it may be. Only with that conservatism that comes with the long occupation of a region and the long association of people in communities, does the historical spirit assert itself.

Also a certain amount of leisure is requisite, and an attitude of mind untroubled and serene helps. The South has had little of either, despite a great deal of romancing to the contrary. Not until 1840 was the South rid of its Indian problems; the slavery issue was not settled until 1865; and then there followed the race question which is yet a matter of some concern. Much of the writing proclivities of southerners in antebellum times was absorbed in a defense of slavery against northern attacks. Without this disturbance it is conceivable that Calhoun might have written learnedly on the philosophy of history and Simms might have become a southern Bancroft.

The restlessness that was bred by these conditions made the people prefer action to contemplation. Their genius sought expression, therefore, more in the excitement of politics. The embryo historians and history readers became politicians and statesmen. As a southerner diagnosed the situation in 1853, "When the offices of the federal and state governments were filled, few men of distinguished abilities were left unemployed." Days of action and fame loomed up ahead. "Who would sit down in his quiet study, and endeavor with toil and pain to extract truth out of a mass of contradictory authorities, when the same energies directed in another channel might make him the ruler of a continent, the arbiter of the world?"[2] The apathy of Virginians toward their history was partly explained by a writer in 1847, who said, "We have seen it summarily accounted for by the fact, that the gentlemen and higher classes of Virginia are so much occupied with the duties of self-government and of governing others, that they have no time to spend over the records of past ages—that they who are acting history themselves, care not to read the histories of other men."[3]

But those who did attempt to write the South's history were immediately confronted with a situation which could be counted on to wither the keenest zeal.[4] The records of the past were scattered and many of them had been destroyed. A people not much interested in their past will take few pains to preserve their current records and even fewer to save old documents. Why should those with little self-consciousness, who want no heroes to worship, and who think objectively care to save the musty records of the past out of which unwanted heroes could be made? Not looking for heroes in the past, they were not even interested in making heroes out of themselves; therefore, there was no passion to preserve family archives. The progression of plantations westward led families to discard their old papers as the least desirable impedimenta. And what was even worse, this unconcern for the past led to a woeful carelessness in public officials in preserving the records of the government. After the current value of documents had passed, they were discarded to an attic or basement, there to rest undisturbed until accumulating in such quantities they became a nuisance. This problem was then solved either piecemeal by some janitor using them as a store of fuel for kindling fires, or all at once, like Tennessee, which cut the Gordian knot as late as the twentieth century by selling them as waste paper.[5]

Aiding this carelessness of private individuals and of governmental officials were forces which could not easily be controlled. Wars, fires, and migrating state capitols wrought sad havoc with the South's records. The South has suffered two wars of invasion, which scattered and destroyed state archives. In the Revolution, Georgia was able to carry part of her records to a place of safety, but so far away that she was unable to recover them for some years afterwards; and in the Civil War she saw many of her records pillaged and carried away by Sherman's soldiery, and even to this day their conscience-stricken descendants are returning the plunder. But it has been from fires more than from wars that the South has suffered. The flames that destroyed the capitols of Texas and Louisiana deprived succeeding generations of many priceless records and consigned to darkness much that was important. Pathetic is the story of county and parish archives, the records that come nearest the lives of the people. Chronically suffering from the carelessness of local officials, they have gone up in smoke from one end of the South to the other. North Carolina has had no fewer than thirty-three court-house fires.[6] For many years the moving population of the South carried state capitols not far behind. The instability of all material things long characterized the South. There is not a state in the South today which has not changed the site of its first capitol. Georgia has had no fewer than five separate state capitols, migrating from Savannah, on the coast, to Atlanta, on the edge of the mountains. It is not difficult to imagine what happened to the state archives when capitols were moved.

This recounting of the South's historical apathy and woes, happily is not the whole story. With all these handicaps, there has been appreciation and progress, and flashes of an historical outlook equal to the best. The South has written histories, collected documents, organized historical societies, and published historical articles and magazines. The South of colonial days had few incentives to be interested in its history; it had no nationalism or even a spirit of nationalism, and it had only a short past, which had no special appeal. Yet Virginia could have a feeling of some age and a desire to look back upon it, for she had lived longer as a colony of England than she has as a part of the American Union; and this historical spirit was felt by Robert Beverly in 1722 and William Stith in 1747, when each brought out his history of Virginia. No other southern colony had a history sufficiently heroic to lead to its being written.

The Revolution came, American nationalism was born and established, the age of heroes arrived, and the first widespread impulse in the South to write its history began. But it was to be state history, for though the South might early have had a sectional feeling of unity, it was not strong enough to break over state lines in the concept of its history until after the Civil War. In every southern state, the generation following the Revolution saw its history written, and though these histories naturally included colonial times, the Revolution was the heart and the impulse. These histories were written because there were, of course, heroes to be honored, but also because justice must be done to the state in the part it played in the struggle; and those states that had been arrogating too much to themselves must be corrected. In 1804–1805 John Burk published his *History of Virginia, from its First Settlement to the Present Day,* in three volumes; in 1812 Hugh Williamson published his *History of North Carolina,* in two volumes; in 1809 David Ramsay published in two volumes his *History of South Carolina, from its First Settlement in 1670, to the Year 1808.* In Georgia, scarcely had the Revolution ended before Edward Langworthy was busily planning his "Political History of the State of Georgia. From its First Settlement. With Memoirs of the Principal Transactions which Happened therein during the late Revolution." He wrote because "he could no longer silently observe several respectable writers, either through misinformation or ignorance, injuring the reputation of his Country—a country though not generally known yet of no small importance in the American Revolution."[7] Unfortunately this work was never completed and the valuable collection of historical material assembled by Langworthy disappeared; but Hugh M'Call in 1811 and 1816 published in two volumes *The History of Georgia, Containing Sketches of the most Remarkable Events up to the Present Day.*

Most of these men wrote their histories under great difficulties, and when their work was finished they felt that they received no rewards in an appreciative public. For some years there was none so bold as to make further attempts. The next histories to appear were for the newer states, which had not yet been honored with a written history. In 1823 John Haywood's *Civil and Political History of the State of Tennessee* appeared, and the next year Kentuckians were presented their history in two volumes by Humphrey Marshall,[8] to be followed ten years later by the work of Mann Butler.[9] The French-born François Xavier Martin, impartial in his interests, wrote in 1827 the first pretentious history of Louisiana[10] and two years later wrote another history of North Carolina.[11] Maryland waited until 1837 for her first formal history, written by L. L. Bozman.[12]

For the two decades preceding the Civil War, there was considerable activity in state history writing. William H. Foote, born in Connecticut, wrote his *Sketches of North Carolina* in 1846 and in 1850 his *Sketches of Virginia, Historical and Biographical.* In the 1850's two more histories of North Carolina appeared, one by Francis L. Hawks and the other by John H. Wheeler.[13] The novelist, poet, and historian, William Gilmore Simms, presented his state in 1840 with a new *History of South Carolina.* Aided by the state government, Joseph V. Bevan in the

1820's set about collecting historical material for a history of Georgia, but he died without producing tangible results; and in the early 1830's Alexander Jones sought to succeed where Bevan had failed, but nothing came of it.[14] It remained for William Bacon Stevens to bring out the next history of Georgia, which appeared in two volumes in 1847 and 1859.[15] The other antebellum Georgia historian was George White, an Episcopal rector, who brought out in 1849 his *Statistics of the State of Georgia* and in 1854 his *Historical Collections of the State of Georgia*. Albert J. Pickett was Alabama's most famous historian of early times, and it was he who in 1851 brought out the first history of the state.[16] The first native historian of Louisiana and the most famous was Charles Gayarré, who brought out in 1846, in two volumes, his *Histoire de la Louisiane*. Texas, late in the field as an American state, found two historians in the 1840's in Henry S. Foote and H. Yoakum.[17] Following Tennessee's historian Haywood was J. G. M. Ramsey, who in 1853 brought out his *Annals of Tennessee to the End of the Eighteenth Century*. Lewis Collins produced his *Historical Sketches of Kentucky* in 1848. In Florida, Mississippi, and Arkansas no historians arose to favor those states with their histories. Not all of these historical works on the antebellum South were produced by native southerners, though most of them were residents of the states whereof they wrote. Most of the historical writing in the antebellum South was in the form of state histories; there were few biographies and no sectional histories. Indeed, up to this moment there has been published no complete history of the South as a region. None of these histories was received with the enthusiasm desired or expected by their authors; and there may be partly an explanation for the historical apathy in the South in the reason given by a southerner in 1847, that is, the absence "of any well-written narrative of any readable book."[18]

These writings were not unaccompanied and unaided by other historical activities. The "Miraculous Thirties" saw the beginning of the state historical societies in the South. Starting with the organization of the Massachusetts Historical Society in 1791 the movement spread throughout a half-dozen northern states before the first society grew up in the South. The honor of being first goes to Virginia, which set up in 1831 the Virginia Historical and Philosophical Society; in 1847 it was reorganized and given its present name. In 1833 the North Carolina Historical Society was organized and was reorganized in 1844 as the Historical Society of the University of North Carolina and again remade in 1875. The Louisiana Historical Society began in 1836; two years later the Kentucky State Historical Society was incorporated, and the next year the Georgia Historical Society was founded.

Thus, the 1830's saw the organization of five historical societies in the South. Five more were set up during the next two decades: the Tennessee Historical Society in 1849, which was the successor to the Tennessee Antiquarian Society founded in 1819; the Alabama Historical Society in 1850; the South Carolina Historical Society in 1855; the Historical Society of Florida in 1856; and the Historical Society of Mississippi in 1858. The other southern states were to wait until after the Civil War to begin organized historical activities. With a slight variation, the age and strength of these societies were closely related to the age of the state.

Immediately the question arises: Why were these societies formed and what purpose did they serve? A definite and direct cause for the organization of some of them may be seen in the reason for the writing of the first state histories: The states should conserve and defend their reputation in the Revolution. It also should be noted that the states were beginning to feel oldish and they would take some pride in their past. But more directly there appeared to be an important and immediate work to be done in order more effectively to secure the general purpose. These societies would collect and preserve the historical records of the state and they would even send agents to European archives for copies of relevant documents not in America, they would publish documentary collections, and through this work and by other means they would encourage the writing of histories.

Despite the apathy and carelessness of the South in general in preserving its records, there were in antebellum times those farseers who had all the zeal of a present-day collector for conserving documents. A history-minded southerner in 1843 bemoaned the waste and loss of historical material and observed that if earlier efforts had been made, "how much, that is now irrevocably lost, would have been preserved to enrich and augment" his country's annals.[19]

There were notable examples of individuals who made historical collections, such as I. K. Tefft, A. A. Smets, and George Wymberley Jones De Renne and his son Wymberley Jones De Renne, in Georgia; but it was felt that the most successful and most desirable work of this sort should be carried on by historical organizations. So, it became the first interest of these historical societies to gather up the scattered records of the state. How inclusive were their wants and how thoroughly they understood the records on which history should be based are illustrated by this call sent out by the Georgia Historical Society at its organization in 1839: legislative journals; proceedings of conventions, committees, and councils, statutes of the colony and the state; Indian treaties; medical journals, statistics of births, deaths, and records relating to the blind, the deaf, and the dumb; accounts of epidemics; catalogues of medical colleges and of other schools; histories of towns and counties; maps, surveys, and charts; meteorological observations; reports of geological and mineralogical surveys; records of the Indians, their manners, customs, battles, traditions, and their place names; sketches of all the eminent people who have lived in the state, and genealogical records; educational records and minutes of scientific and literary associations, sermons, tracts, essays, pamphlets, poems, magazines, almanacs, and newspapers from the earliest times; military records of every nature; every sort of religious record, such as proceedings of conventions, assemblies, synods, conferences, and the histories of individual churches. The appeal was closed with the following reminder: The committee should "solicit contributions of books, manuscripts, pamphlets, newspapers, and everything which can elucidate the history of America generally, as well as Georgia in particular; and they sincerely hope that this call upon the liberality of all who love the honor of our commonwealth, and desire to perpetuate the faithful records of her existence, will be responded to, with an ardor that will ensure the complete success of the GEORGIA HISTORICAL SOCIETY."[20]

The service rendered by these societies in the collection and preservation of historical documents has been outstanding, and this work alone has amply justified their existence. In their zeal to secure everything that might illustrate state history, they sent their agents to England, France, and Spain to secure copies of documents in the archives of those nations. The most notable example of promoting this sort of work in antebellum times is to be seen in the case of the Louisiana Historical Society. The Georgia Historical Society became the custodian of the copies of many records which the state government had secured in England.

Though these societies felt that their first duty was to collect historical material, they also believed they should publish selections from it. The state of historical fermentation in antebellum times did not suggest or make possible the publication of a review or a magazine, after the modern-day methods. The desirability of publishing something was evident to all these societies, but as some were weak and none was very strong, only three published before the Civil War material of any consequence. Virginia was the most prolific. She published in 1833 a volume of *Collections*; from 1848 to 1853 six volumes of the *Register*; and from 1854 to 1860 two volumes of the *Reporter*. Georgia published three volumes of her *Collections,* beginning in 1840; and South Carolina brought out three volumes of *Collections* from 1857 to 1859. By making available their libraries to the historical investigator, these societies promoted the writing of better histories. The Georgia Historical Society soon after its organization, realizing the inadequacy of M'Call's history of the state, requested one of its members, William Bacon Stevens, to prepare a new and complete history. In its rich stores of material Stevens worked and largely as a result of the Society's patronage he produced a history which is considered a classic on the period covered.

In antebellum times these historical societies had no connection with the state governments, which were too much busied with political affairs to care much about promoting such impractical undertakings as historical societies advocated. Most of the states did not have the vision to preserve properly even their own official records; but there are some instances where the value of historical undertakings was recognized. South Carolina seems to have been more liberal than any of the other southern states. From the earliest times the Carolina government had taken care to preserve its official documents, and it gave at various times specific monetary aid to certain historical publications. It appropriated two thousand dollars to aid B. R. Carroll in bringing out his *Historical Collections of South Carolina,* and it also afforded financial aid to R. W. Gibbes for his *Documentary History of the American Revolution,* and to the South Carolina Historical Society for its *Collections.*[21]

Though there were no strictly historical magazines in antebellum times, there were, nevertheless, literary periodicals which gave much attention to history and to the cultivation of the "historical spirit." Some were of only local importance, but there were others which circulated throughout the South, and in this fact is to be discerned a development which would lift history out of its state pockets and give it a wider significance. The *Orion,* published in Penfield, Georgia, gave considerable attention to history, and various other local publications did likewise, but the influence and importance of such journals as *De Bow's Review,* the *Southern Literary Messenger,* the *Southern Quarterly Review,* and the *Southern and Western Monthly Magazine and Review* were widespread. Here was an outlet not only for regular historical narrators, but also for those who would philosophize about history. There was not a total lack of interest and thought in the South in the interpretations of history that were being pronounced by European historical philosophers, and in the writings of historians everywhere. In 1843 a contributor to the *Southern Quarterly Review*[22] noted at length Frederick von Schlegel's *Philosophy of History; in a Course of Lectures,* the occasion being the publication of a translation in 1841. C. S. S. Farrar, of Louisiana, in 1848, taking as his starting point Victor Cousin's *Introduction to the History of Philosophy,* discussed through a half-dozen numbers of *De Bow's Review*[23] the question whether history was a science. Farrar found it difficult to agree with Cousin that history was a positive science instead of being "lawless and arbitrary." Neither Guizot's *General History of Civilization in Europe,* nor George Bancroft's *History of the United States* escaped general notice in the South, and the latter came in for severe criticism in some quarters.

But what did those people in the South who cared to have an opinion think about history, apart from whether it be a science or not? What should be its content and what its purpose? There was some difference of views then as now, but there was much said then which many people unwittingly think is modern. The tendency then as now among the less erudite was to assign to history the chief purpose of making the past grand and glorious and all of its figures heroes, and therefore it should make the present and future have occasion for loving their country.[24] Among the more thoughtful a revolt was developing against the practice of making of history only a heroic story of kings and battles. S. Henry Dickson, of Charleston, South Carolina, in "An Essay on the Difficulties in the Way of the Historian," said in 1846:

By the tradition and history of former years, while the deeds of the gentle and the lofty are loudly sung and fondly repeated, the lowest classes of every nation have been unnoticed, unless to be numbered, as by David, and taxed, as the whole world was by Augustus Caesar.

While we peruse the writings of past ages, we ask involuntarily and ask in vain, where are the people?—here is a phantasmagoria of kings and nobles —priests and councillors—knights, and merchants, and squires—and the immediate retainers and dependents of these, as soldiers and servants; but where are the millions?—how do they live, and in what offices are they employed?[25]

Twenty years later this philosophy was being preached:

For instance, from reading the histories extant of Egypt, Greece and Carthage, one might suppose that these powers did nothing but wage war and plot each other's downfall. ... It should be the object of the historian to present a clear, distinct and vivid picture of the times concerning which he writes. He should portray the home life of the common people as well as the ceremonies and pageants of courts. He should tell us what were their means of support, what comforts they enjoyed, and what were their pleasures. No circumstances should be deemed too trivial which will in any wise illustrate the subject. Such homely themes some consider beneath the dignity of history; but the main springs of national action lie in the character, habits and wants of the common people, and no one who disregards these can hope to have an understanding of the causes from which greater events proceed.[26]

Yet there were those who much earlier perceived a spirit in history that was becoming broad and philosophical. In 1837 in "An Address

Delivered before the Virginia Historical and Philosophical Society," Thomas W. Gilmer said, in a manner that sounds very modern:

History is now associated with philosophy; with that philosophy which scans with microscopic severity the deep current of public events; which traces out moral effects to their causes and their consequences; which analyzes the mysterious and complex fabric of society; which investigates and establishes truth; which discriminates justly between the transient prejudice of an hour and the enduring sentiment of ages.[27]

But with all the thoughts and actions of the antebellum South, practical historical activities and developments never got far beyond state lines. The slavery system and the attacks of the North upon it, welded the southern states into a spiritual unity on that subject, but they still thought of their history largely within state lines. They wrote much to defend southern institutions and southern civilization, but no one thought of writing a southern history or of organizing a southern historical society. In 1861 civil war came and then the people forgot all about the writing of history; instead, they began making history. They lost the war and their nationality, but they went through an experience which touched profounder depths and involved more fundamental principles than had come into their lives since the planting of Jamestown. Here in the course of four years enough history had been made to keep many generations busy investigating and writing it; and here was something for those who liked heroic history and much for those who liked to philosophize on cause and consequence. But there was even more; for here was the great task to see that the truth be told and the record kept straight. Out of the crucible of war there was born a sense of unity in their history; and so now, their history could become regional instead of state, just as their feelings in antebellum times had become sectional instead of state.

The most immediate effect the war had on the historical consciousness of the South was the writing of the lives and war experiences of the heroes by the heroes themselves and by others and the recounting of the campaigns by the leaders. Writers produced lives of "Stonewall" Jackson even before the end of the war, but no one could have planned much earlier the history of the conflict than James B. McCabe, Jr., who said, "In May, 1861, I commenced to collect such papers and documents, both official and unofficial, relating to the war, as I could procure." By the end of the struggle he had on hand more than fifteen thousand papers and documents, and in 1866 he brought out the *Life and Campaigns of General Robert E. Lee.*[28] Immediately after the war General Lee considered writing a history of his campaigns, solely as a last tribute to his men, and he asked other leaders to write their campaigns. For a time Lee set about systematically collecting reports and documents; but he found it very difficult to secure some necessary material. It is said that he was refused by the war department the use of documents which it had, but no positive proof has been found so far that Lee ever applied.[29] Lee gradually gave up his intention of writing his history, but many of the other Confederate leaders, following his advice, wrote their accounts, some for glory, some for money, some to defend their reputations, and some only for the love of it.

Most of the writings by the war generation were deeply tinged with the defense element, and especially was this so with those who wrote civil and political history. Alexander H. Stephens wrote two volumes in his *Constitutional View of the Late War Between the States*[30] to show the justice of the South's course, and Jefferson Davis wrote his volumes on the *Rise and Fall of the Confederate Government,* largely for the same purpose.[31]

The North, having won the war on the battlefield, immediately set out to win it again and consolidate victory on the printed page. A flood of books appeared, and the South took umbrage at most of them. A new invasion was on, and the South must meet words with words—but words based on historical facts. Said Edward A. Pollard in 1866, "All persons in the South who assist in getting the true testimony of their unfortunate struggle, perform a last, but most important office of faithful love, and do a noble work in rescuing the name of a lost cause from the slanders of those who, having been our accusers and executioners in this present time, would also be our judges at the Bar of History."[32] And ten years later R. Randolph Stevenson was saying, "The Southern actors in the great struggle would be recreant to the duty which they owe to their posterity, were they to permit the false allegations of the Northern historians to be accepted as true without attempting a refutation and vindication."[33]

History now took on for southerners a more practical character than had ever appeared before in all the annals of the South. It was the last stronghold of the South not for the defense of its nationality but for the protection of something more dear and sacred, its reputation. Defeated on the battlefields, it was again suffering in Reconstruction the defeat of its reasonable expectations of an honorable peace. With Jefferson Davis destined never to be tried, and the Reconstruction Acts withheld from the judges, it was denied the right of that vindication in the courts which it had reason to expect. For years unrepresented in the halls of Congress, and then misrepresented there by Scalawags and Carpetbaggers, the South had only one tribunal left—the bar of history. As Benjamin H. Hill said: "Thus, denied by our enemies the opportunity of silencing, by the solemn judgments of their own courts, the fierce accusations of criminality in secession; and denied, by our enemies and the follies of our own people, the glorious chance of vindicating our cause in high debate, and face to face with the chosen champions of our accusers, we have but one resource left us for our defense or vindication. That resource is history—impartial, and unpassioned, un-office-seeking history." And further, "We owe it, therefore, to our dead, to our living, and to our children, to be active in the work of preserving the truth and repelling the falsehoods, so that we may secure, for them and for us, just judgment from the only tribunal before which we can be fully and fairly heard."[34] Benjamin M. Palmer said, "Sir, there is a tribunal before which even nations must appear—a tribunal before which old causes shall be retried and the final verdict be rendered which can never again be reversed."[35]

In this new struggle, cooperation was no less desirable and necessary than in the war just ended. Historical workers should march together no less surely than soldiers, and ammunition should be garnered, stored, and used with as much precision. Thus, there was enacted the splendid spectacle of erstwhile warriors turned historians and conservers of history. Generals now became scholars.

On May Day, 1869, in the city of New Orleans, there was founded "by a number of gentlemen" the Southern Historical Society. The organization of this society was suggested by General Dabney H. Maury, and among the gentlemen who participated in the first meeting were General Maury, General Braxton Bragg, General S. B. Buckner, General P. G. T. Beauregard, and Reverend Benjamin M. Palmer. They might well have called their organization the Confederate Historical Society, for so it was and always remained. Benjamin M. Palmer, an eminent Presbyterian devine, was elected president, and the work of collecting documents was started.[36]

It was soon seen that the location of New Orleans was unfavorable to the success of the venture, and so in 1873 the executive committee issued a call for a meeting of the Society to be held on August 14 at Montgomery White Sulphur Springs in Virginia. Here delegates from twelve southern states met, "embracing some of the most distinguished soldiers and civilians of the Confederacy," and unanimously agreed to reorganize the Society. A grand confederation of historical societies was planned. The parent society should be located in Virginia and all of its officials should be residents of that state, with the exception of its vice presidents. The latter should each be president of a state society, and throughout the states were to be organized federated local societies. Voting in the parent society should be by states and each state should have two votes. General Jubal A. Early was elected president of this reorganized Southern Historical Society and the Reverend J. William Jones, secretary-treasurer. The vice presidents for the various states were as follows: R. M. T. Hunter for Virginia, General Isaac R. Trimble for Maryland, Governor Zebulon B. Vance for North Carolina, General M. C. Butler for South Carolina, General A. H. Colquitt for Georgia, Colonel W. Call for Florida, Admiral Raphael Semmes for Alabama, General William T. Martin for Mississippi, General J. B. Hood for Louisiana, Colonel T. M. Jack for Texas, Governor A. H. Garland for Arkansas, Governor Isham G. Harris for Tennessee, General J. S. Marmaduke for Missouri, General S. B. Buckner for Kentucky, and W. W. Corcoran, a Washington philanthropist, for the District of Columbia.

Little was ever done to give life to the state branches, though the ones in Kentucky, Louisiana, Georgia, and North Carolina seem to have existed for a time. In 1879 Buckner resigned from the presidency of the Kentucky branch and was succeeded by General William Preston; Benjamin M. Palmer soon became president of the Louisiana branch with Hood, Beauregard, and others as vice presidents; Benjamin H. Hill helped to organize the Georgia branch; and the North Carolina branch seems to have bespoke its existence more becomingly than any of the others, in publishing four volumes (1874–76) of a periodical called *Our Living and Our Dead; Devoted to North Carolina—her Past, her Present, and her Future.*[37]

The general purpose of the Southern Historical Society has been stated, but to be more specific, it set out to collect, classify, and preserve "all the documents and facts bearing upon the eventful history of the past few years, illustrating the nature of the struggle from which the country has just emerged, defining and vindicating the principles which lay beneath it, and marking the stages through which it was conducted to its issue." Its work should not be "purely sectional" nor of a "partisan character."[38] No time should be lost; the South was standing "upon the outer verge of a great historical cycle, within which a completed past will shortly be enclosed." Southerners must discharge a duty to their fathers whose principles they inherited and "to the children, who will then know whether to honor or dishonor the sires that begot them," and pay a debt to the dead on the battlefields from the Susquehanna to the Rio Grande.[39] The two greatest perils were time and the Federal government. Each day that passed saw documents lost, discarded, or accidentally burned; and the Federal government was systematically gathering all Confederate records possible. Added to the many documents it had captured at the end of the war, it had just recently bought for seventy-five thousand dollars from Colonel John T. Pickett five trunks of important Confederate archives. The policy of the government toward the use of this historical material by southerners was most illiberal. Though the Secretary of War was anxious to get copies of all documents owned by the Society, he consistently refused to allow representatives of that Society to have copies of Confederate records in his possession or even to see them.[40]

The Society immediately spread throughout the South its appeal for papers and documents. It wanted everything which could illuminate the history of the South—books, newspapers, manuscript material of all sorts, military reports, maps, charts, speeches, sermons, economic and social material, poetry, ballads, songs, and anything else that the people would send. It was as much an act of patriotism now to send in this material as it had been in 1861 to join the Confederate army. The appeal did not go unheeded. There was a great outpouring of historical material throughout the former Confederacy, and within two years the Society was able to report that it expected soon to have accumulated "a complete arsenal from which the defenders of our cause may draw any desired weapon."[41] To guarantee the safety of this material, the Virginia legislature gave the Society quarters in the state capitol, where its archives would be as safe as those of the state government.[42]

As for the publication of a definitive history of the Confederacy and of the war, there was a general feeling that such an undertaking should wait for a future generation. In writing his *Rise and Fall of the Confederate Government* Jefferson Davis said that he had "sought to furnish material for the future historian, who, when the passions and prejudices of the day shall have given place to reason and sober thought, may, better than a contemporary, investigate the causes, conduct, and results of the war."[43] And John B. Gordon declared as late as 1903, "The man capable of writing it with entire justice to both sides is perhaps yet unborn."[44]

The Society disclaimed any intention of promoting a history of the war; its great task was to make available the material on which the future historian must rest his account. The Society, however, was not to forego all publication activities. It decided to publish various documents for the interest they would have for the contemporary generation, and as a complete guarantee against the loss of the material itself. The necessity was further heightened by the fact that in 1874 Congress had ordered the beginning of the publication of the official records of the Union and Confederate armies, which work ultimately ran into one hundred and twenty-eight volumes and cost almost three million dollars, being the well-known *War of the Rebellion: A Compilation of the Offi-*

cial Records of the Union and Confederate Armies. At first there was a deep suspicion among southerners, born not entirely without reason, that the Confederate records and dispatches would not be faithfully reproduced. Here was an immediate task for the Southern Historical Society; it should begin the publication of its Confederate records. Beginning in January, 1874, and continuing for a year and a half the Society, under contract with the Messrs. Turnbull of Baltimore, published twenty pages each month in the *Southern Magazine*.[45] This arrangement, being a makeshift, was naturally unsatisfactory, and so in January, 1876, the Society began a monthly journal of its own, which it called the *Southern Historical Society Papers.* The editor announced this policy: "We shall publish nothing which does not bear directly on the War Between the States, and proper understanding of the measures, men and deeds of those stirring times."[46] He hoped "that those who are interested in vindicating the truth of Confederate History will sustain the enterprise and make it a complete success."[47] This publication for fourteen years ran as a monthly, it then became annual, and within recent years it has appeared only occasionally. It has included a great many valuable documents.

The success of the *Papers* in the beginning was greatly aided by a yearly contribution of five hundred dollars made by W. W. Corcoran of Washington. Depending upon such donations and upon the sale of its publications, the Society after a few years was much encumbered with debts, and there was for a time danger that it might be forced to hand over its valuable collections to its creditors, and disband. J. William Jones, the secretary of the Society and the editor of the *Papers,* made heroic efforts to save the situation; Confederate leaders took to the lecture platform to raise money for an endowment; and Jefferson Davis was asked to tour the South in the interest of the Society. Though not entering onto a speaking trip, the former Confederate president spoke in New Orleans in 1882 before a meeting which raised for the Society more than fifteen hundred dollars.[48] After Jones had passed on, the Society became somewhat inactive, though it has never disbanded in name. Its president now is Douglas Southall Freeman, the author of the recent biography of Robert E. Lee.

All of the historical activity in the South following the Civil War was not predicated upon or bound up with that unfortunate struggle. In the period from 1865 to the end of the century, able scholars set to work in every southern state to rewrite state history or to bring up some of the lagging states like Mississippi and Arkansas. To name only a few: J. T. Scharf in Maryland, Philip A. Bruce and John Esten Cooke in Virginia, Stephen B. Weeks and Samuel A. Ashe in North Carolina,

Edward McCrady in South Carolina, C. C. Jones, Jr., in Georgia, George R. Fairbanks in Florida, William Garret Brown, Peter J. Hamilton, and Thomas M. Owen in Alabama, J. F. H. Claiborne, Robert Lowery, and W. H. McCardle in Mississippi, Charles Gayarré and Grace King in Louisiana, George P. Garrison in Texas, John H. Reynolds in Arkansas, W. R. Garrett and A. V. Goodpasture in Tennessee, and Richard H. Collins and Z. F. Smith in Kentucky. The historians since 1900 are too numerous to mention and it would be invidious to make selections.

The historical societies went into eclipse during the Civil War, but since that time all of them have been revived, new ones have been organized, and the tendency has been within the last half century for these organizations either to become state historical commissions or to enter into arrangements whereby state aid is given. Thus have most of the state governments at last awakened to the necessity of taking care of their historical records. The most satisfactory developments along this line have taken place in North Carolina, Mississippi, and Texas. Texas and Arkansas, which had no historical societies in antebellum times, organized respectively the Texas Historical Association in 1897 and the Arkansas Historical Association in 1903.[49] Another evidence of progress in this newer age was the appearance of historical magazines in practically every state, issued either by the state historical society or the state historical commission. The publications of these organizations are now voluminous.

State governments have shown their interest in historical activities not only by the organization of historical commissions, but many of them have financed the copying of their records in Europe and provided for their publication. North Carolina, South Carolina, and Georgia are notable examples of states engaging in this work.

The activities of individuals in writing histories and of states in carrying on the work of historical commissions showed that there was ample enthusiasm for history other than that based on the Confederate War. It was inevitable that the Southern Historical Society should be forced to broaden its interests or another society would be organized to cover the non-Confederate aspects of southern history. The Southern Historical Society was born Confederate and it has always remained so; therefore, a new historical society grew up for the South, not for another southern state. And since Confederates ran the Southern Historical Society no less than they had run the war, it was to be expected that nonparticipants in the war would have much to do with the new society.

The election of a Democrat in 1892 to be president of the United States seems to have been an adventitious cause for the founding of a new southern historical society, for President Cleveland brought to Washington into the government service many able southerners. With the driving force coming from this source, there was sent out from Washington in 1896 an invitation signed by nearly a hundred names, calling for a new southern historical organization. The people represented in the call were widely scattered and represented various professions. There were the inevitable Confederate generals, such as Wade Hampton, M. C. Butler, and George Washington Custis Lee; there were college professors such as Woodrow Wilson of Princeton University and Kemp Plummer Battle of the University of North Carolina; and such other able leaders as Jabez L. M. Curry, Walter Hines Page, Richard Malcolm Johnston, and Stephen B. Weeks. Also six college presidents signed the call. This was not considered to be a movement of hostility against the Southern Historical Society, for the secretary of that organization, Colonel R. A. Brock, signed the call.[50]

The first meeting was held on April 24, 1896, at Columbian University in Washington (now George Washington University), with Stephen B. Weeks in the chair. Jabez L. M. Curry was chosen temporary president, and after various remarks, including a speech by General Butler on the backwardness of the South in preserving its historical records, a constitution was adopted. The name first suggested was "An Association for the Study of Southern History," but its manifest clumsiness led to the adoption of the title, "Southern History Association." William L. Wilson of West Virginia, Cleveland's postmaster general, was elected president; and among the vice presidents were Jabez L. M. Curry, Marcus J. Wright, Thomas Nelson Page, and Woodrow Wilson.[51]

The purpose of the new organization was "the encouragement of original research, discussion, and conference among members, the widening of personal acquaintance, publication of work, and the collection of historical materials."[52] This association embraced the modern ideas of historical activities. According to the old traditions, historical societies should have a set of officers and a library and there should be a membership, not too widespread, and there should be annual meetings, at which orations should be delivered but at which, as time went on, it often happened that nothing was done more exciting than reading the official reports. This new society had got inspiration from the American Historical Association, which had been organized in 1884, and which in 1895 had started a historical periodical, the *American Historical Review*. There were to be annual meetings at which carefully prepared papers should be read, which should later be published in a journal. The first annual meeting was held on June 12, 1896, papers were read, and seventy-nine members were enrolled. In January following, the first issue of the Association's journal appeared, called *Publications of the Southern History Association.*[53]

This Association started out with the resolution that there was much work to be done. Stephen B. Weeks, in a paper "On the Promotion of Historical Studies in the South," said, "In no respect, perhaps, has the South been more silent, more careless of her own duty to herself, than in the matter of history writing and book collecting. We complain that Northern men and foreigners misunderstand and misrepresent us. Who is responsible for this misunderstanding and misrepresentation but ourselves?"[54] This Association seems never to have made a collection of its own as did the Southern Historical Society; but it published in its journal a number of valuable historical articles and conducted for the South its first modern historical magazine. Papers on all periods of southern history were published, documents were included, and books were reviewed. This publication never came under the domination of college professors and educational institutions, and, perhaps, in that fact its life was shortened. Indeed, it came to look upon the type of history the college professor taught and wrote as almost useless. By the coming of the new century, there was much being said about scientific history and objective history writing. The editor of the *Publications* was downright against both. Concerning the former, he said in 1907, "The one distinguishing and inevitable mark of scientific history thus far is dullness, deep, dense, supreme, unrelieved by glimpse of nature or spark of life."[55]

But the Southern History Association never succeeded in making itself much more than a society of southern gentlemen residing in Washington. Its days, too, were numbered. With the coming of the Republicans in 1897, Postmaster General William L. Wilson, president of the Association, retired from office and left Washington. Jabez L. M. Curry was elected president and served until his death in 1903, when Marcus J. Wright was elected to succeed him. Soon the annual meetings dwindled in importance until they were held in the office of the president, and in 1907 the last issue of the *Publications of the Southern History Association* appeared. The membership of the Association never grew far beyond two hundred.[56] The dictum seemed to be fixed and final that historical societies of broader interests than state lines could not be properly nurtured by generals, editors, diplomats, and governmental employees alone. Something more seemed to be needed.

And then the era of the college professor and of the educational institution arrived. The stabilizing influences produced by these factors have led to the organization and continuance of many learned societies, whose days may also be numbered, but the end is not yet in sight. The scientific objective history of the college professor has been tempered in recent years with more artistry. The old saying that "if it is interesting it is not history" no longer holds. The college professor today is beginning to see that there is art as well as science in history-writing, and this discovery may add many cubits to the size of historical societies and many days to their life. We may all hope with reason that this newly organized Southern Historical Association will live for many years to perform a work that has long waited to be done.

Chapter II

The Changing Interpretation
of the Civil War

CHARLES W. RAMSDELL

No OTHER event in American history has produced such a flood of controversial historical literature as has the Civil War.* The reasons for this are plain. The very complexity of the interwoven social, economic, religious, psychological, and political factors, some of them very obscure or elusive, all of them difficult of quantitative analysis, has baffled even the most impartial investigators. No other event in our history caused such widespread suffering or aroused such partisan feeling. Finally, since the conflict was primarily sectional, mass opinion in each section, reinforced by common memories and prejudices, hardened into a tradition which was all but impervious to criticism.

Contemporary writers, inevitably partisan, explained the steps which led up to hostilities in the terms of the party conflicts of thirty years. Since the belief was common in the North that the secession leaders had attempted to break up the Union because they could not control it, there was little difficulty in joining to this thesis the idea that they had sought control in order to force the institution of slavery not only into the territories but also into the free states. Secession, it was asserted, was the result of a treasonable conspiracy, conceived long before and aided and abetted by northern "doughfaces" like President Buchanan. The settlement of Texas by slaveholders, the Revolution by which unscrupulous men tore that vast area from Mexico in order to annex it to the United States, the war with Mexico for more slave territory, the Fugitive Slave Law of 1850, the Kansas-Nebraska Act, the judicial conspiracy of the Dred Scott case and, finally, the effort to break up the Union—

*Presented in Nashville, Tennessee, November 20, 1936.

23

all (and more) were but links in the chain which bound the slave-owning aristocracy to parricidal treason. Most of these charges had been the peculiar contributions of the abolitionists and as such had been laughed at by conservative northerners for years; but under stress of the war psychosis they quickly came to be accepted by the majority of the people. Then the final step was to make this the official version of the origins of the desolating conflict.

In the South the explanation was equally simple and fully as veracious. Northern manufacturers and capitalists had joined with fanatical abolitionists to overthrow the constitutional rights of the southern states, the one in order to subject southern agriculture to heavy burdens for the promotion of northern wealth, the other to break down the beneficent southern social-racial system and, by inaugurating a war of races, destroy white civilization and elevate the African to a position for which he was not fitted. The southern states, exercising their sovereign rights, had withdrawn from fellowship with the free states in order to protect their people from destruction by a hostile sectional majority. For them it was a war of defense against wicked aggression and threatened subjugation. Thus, in the main, ran the arguments.

For the most part the earliest histories followed these assumptions. Horace Greeley, writing the preface to his *American Conflict* in April, 1864, while men were fighting and dying all the way from northern Virginia to the borders of Texas, could see no cause for this carnage but the efforts of arrogant slaveholders to destroy a government which they could not control. Even the philosophical scientist, Dr. John W. Draper, whose three-volume work[1] was begun in the midst of the war and who endeavored to get at the fundamental differences between the sections by a study of geographic and climatic influences, could see nothing in the immediate causes of the dreadful scourge but the tyranny of the slave power and the treasonable ambitions of the southern leaders. And so it was with a host of lesser men. One able northern writer, George Lunt, whose *Origins of the Late War* appeared in 1866, held that "slavery, though made an occasion, was not in reality the cause of the war," but that northern politicians had made use of the slavery issue as an avenue to power and had forced war upon the South as a means of maintaining their control. But Lunt, a conservative Massachusetts Whig who had turned Democrat and had been a consistent opponent of the abolitionists, was a lone voice in New England.

The most prolific wartime southern writer, Edward A. Pollard, in his *First Year of the War*[2] declared that the conflict had been brought about by unscrupulous northern politicians and business men who had consolidated the numerical majority of their own section on the pretext of staying the advance of slavery but with the real design of destroying the constitutional rights of the southern states and subverting the Constitution itself in order both to seize upon supreme power and to rob their southern opponents of their property. In short, he turned back upon the free state leaders the same accusations that they had made against the southern slaveowners. In his more famous postwar book, *The Lost Cause,*[3] Pollard softened his tone but in substance reiterated the charges.

As the war years receded, books and articles dealing with various aspects of the great conflict flowed from the presses in a steady stream. While most of them were concerned with the story of military operations, a considerable number continued the controversy over the responsibility for the waste of life and property. Time does not permit the mention of more than a few of these contributions to the wordy warfare.

In 1868 Alexander H. Stephens of Georgia, a Unionist on grounds of expediency until his state seceded, published the first volume of his *Constitutional View of the Late War Between the States* and followed it with the second in 1870. Stephens defended the right of secession on the basic theory of the absolute sovereignty of each individual state, the doctrine first clearly set forth by John C. Calhoun. In 1872 Henry Wilson, abolitionist senator from Massachusetts and later vice president of the United States, published the first of his three volumes on the *History of the Rise and Fall of the Slave Power in America,*[4] the title of which sufficiently indicates the argument. In 1881 Jefferson Davis finished *The Rise and Fall of the Confederate Government,* a defense of the southern cause and of his administration of the Confederacy. Like Stephens, Davis held that slavery was merely incidental to and not the true cause of the war. The southern states had only exercised the sovereign right of self-determination in withdrawing from the Union in which they could no longer expect protection of their rights under the Constitution, and war had then been forced upon an independent southern people by an aggressive and imperialistic government at Washington. The Davis-Stephens argument was legalistic and therefore limited, but it was so strongly stated that it appealed to southern readers who were seeking for some fundamental principle in the line of the southern tradition upon which to justify the cause for which they had suffered so much. In the middle eighties two eminent Republicans, James G. Blaine and John A. Logan, gave to the public political memoirs[5] which, while adding nothing of importance to the nationalist dialectics, were widely read and served to strengthen the familiar tenets of their party and section.

Meanwhile, no less effective work in the formulation of the rival traditions was being done by thousands of men of lesser prominence—

editors, politicians, preachers, teachers, and platform lecturers. In the North the "Union-savers" and the abolitionists had joined forces early in the war. The abolitionists, strong in the churches, had been able to add religious and moral sanctions to the cause of unionism, thereby adding immeasurably to the popularity of their interpretation of the conflict. In fixing the war guilt upon the secessionists and especially upon the "slaveholding aristocracy," the conviction that religion and morality were on the side of the victors induced a pleasing sense of righteousness; while the evidence that through God's will the nation most favored by Him of all this modern world had been preserved in its territorial integrity, and the most conspicuous outpost of Satan's dominion had been eliminated from America, was a crowning satisfaction. (The equally religious southerner, accustomed likewise to rely upon the workings of the Divine Will, had some difficulty in adjusting himself to this mysterious manifestation, except when he agreed with the pious old North Carolinian that there had been "a temporary interruption of the workings of Providence.") But the growing northern tradition gathered strength from other advantages. The Northeast especially enjoyed an amazing prosperity during the early postwar years, and eager business men, having quickly learned how useful government could be to business, looked back to the war as the beginning of a better and brighter day. Thousands of others, who had shared neither in the righteous exaltation nor in the new profits, settled down into the opinions of their neighbors. As society adjusts itself to revolutionary change and proceeds to build or extend its institutional edifice upon the new plan, it displays an irresistible impulse to accept and justify the established order. Success justifies itself; in the long run the victor is always right. Again, the literary dominance of New England, where for years most of the histories were written, enabled "the New England point of view" to permeate the thinking of the greater part of the country. Northern textbooks in use throughout the nation fixed ever more firmly in the popular mind the nationalist and antislavery interpretation of the causes and character of the war.

The southern cause was as much on the defensive in this battle of interpretations as ever the Confederacy had been on bloodier fields. While many families doubtless resented the loss of their slaves, most southerners professed to be entirely satisfied that the peculiar institution was gone and insisted that they had gone to war to protect their homes from invasion, not to save the property of the slaveholders.[6] Those who were in public life and were looked upon as the spokesmen of the stricken South saw that it was essential to the welfare of their people, in both business and politics, that reconciliation between the sections be effected as quickly as possible and that the Democratic party should be able to recover its strength in the dominant North. Therefore, they had powerful motives for accepting the results of the war without further recrimination and for stilling controversy by saying as little as possible about the causes. This last consideration, however, had little weight with the masses of the people who saw no improvement in their condition by reason of the triumph of the North. While conceding that secession had proved a mistake in expediency, they stubbornly insisted that it had been justified in principle and by the dangers which had threatened them in 1861.

Long before the survivors of the Civil War had finished giving the public their versions of the great convulsion, a new group of historians had begun to attract attention. In 1876, 1880, and 1883 appeared the initial volumes of the series projected by Hermann von Holst,[7] James Schouler,[8] and John B. McMaster,[9] respectively, who had severally undertaken to explain the history of the country from the Revolution to the Civil War. That their eyes were fixed upon that struggle as the climax of the story attests their belief in its overwhelming significance. Von Holst and Schouler, holding to the older conception of history as past politics, confined their narratives almost exclusively to political contests and constitutional questions and used as their sources the published writings of the early statesmen, governmental documents (Federal and state), and the debates in Congress. McMaster, whose interest was in social history, added the files of old newspapers to his sources. It would be unfair to these men to reproach them for the narrow range of their source materials, since they had access to no such vast collections as are available to the historical worker today. But in other respects the limitations of Schouler and von Holst are clear enough to anyone who looks into their nearly forgotten volumes. James Schouler was a New England lawyer, thoroughly imbued with the nationalist-antislavery conception of the background of the secession movement and wholly incapable of understanding the point of view of any section other than New England. Von Holst, a German scholar who had suffered much for liberal principles before he came to New York as a penniless immigrant in 1867, looked upon slavery with horror as the very embodiment of evil and upon the proslavery southern leaders as wicked men. The outbreak of the war in 1861 was the consequence of a long-laid and carefully executed plot of the "arrogant slavocracy." Von Holst had accepted the antislavery tradition *in toto* and had added some embellishments of his own. Both he and Schouler had relied chiefly upon the debates in Congress and on the political hustings and in them they found the southern arguments already answered to their satisfaction. Although McMaster ranged much farther afield, he was content to set down both facts and arguments as he found them with little attempt at criticism or analysis. That he, too, was thoroughly indoctrinated with the nationalist tradition is shown by the fact that, although his eighth volume on the decade of the fifties did not appear until 1913, it still reflected the older point of view.

In 1890 John G. Nicolay and John Hay completed their *Abraham Lincoln: A History* in ten stately volumes. This work not only contributed powerfully to the growing Lincoln legend, which was ultimately to displace Washington for the "rail-splitter" as the American folk hero, but also gave additional sanction to the nationalist and antislavery interpretation of the war by linking it with the apotheosis of the great war president. In 1892, the year in which von Holst's last volume came from the press, appeared the first two volumes of James Ford Rhodes covering the ten years from the Compromise of 1850 to the election of Abraham Lincoln to the presidency. In 1895 came the third volume which carried the story to the spring of 1862. Rhodes had a broader and sounder conception of the subject matter of history than either Schouler or von Holst and he was far more judicial in handling controversial questions. But he was hampered by an initial lack of understanding of the South and by the generally antisouthern character of his sources, and he was also clearly influenced by the traditional attitudes of his native Western Reserve district of Ohio and of his later home in Boston. Nevertheless, while he ran true to form in holding that slavery was the sole cause of secession and, therefore, of the war, he made some advance toward middle ground by testifying to the high personal character of southern leaders and by rejecting the theory that secession was the fruit of a "conspiracy" of the southern senators in Washington.[10] His lucid and attractive style and his authoritative manner gave his work great popularity and influence.

In 1897 was published *The Middle Period, 1817–1858,* the work of John W. Burgess, Dean of the Faculty of Political Science of Columbia University and a great figure in the academic world of political science and constitutional history. This book was followed in 1901 by his two volumes entitled *The Civil War and the Constitution.* Burgess was a Tennessean who had served in the Union army and whose nationalist proclivities had been strengthened by study in the universities of Germany. Now a thoroughgoing nationalist, dogmatic in opinion and strongly prone to regard every political issue from the standpoint of what he habitually called "the correct principles of political science," he was nevertheless a close student of American constitutional and political history as it was revealed in the arid pages of the *Congressional Globe.* In the preface to *The Middle Period* Burgess defined his attitude very clearly when he said that the history of the United States should be written by a northerner and "from the northern point of view . . . because the northern point of view is, in the main, the correct view," and that, while sincerity must be allowed the southern people and their leaders, "not one scintilla of justification for secession and rebellion must be expected. The South must acknowledge its error as well as its defeat." But Dean Burgess did not uphold all of the northern tradition. For instance, he did not admire William Lloyd Garrison or John Brown; he did not regard the settlement of Texas or its revolt against Mexico as a proslavery plot nor the war with Mexico as proslavery aggression. But he held that the policy of the southern Democrats with respect to slavery in the territories was aggressive, not defensive; that the theory of state sovereignty was unjustifiable either by the Constitution or by "sound political science"; and that the southern people and their leaders, by refusing obedience to the Federal government, became responsible for the war. His elaborate analysis of the constitutional aspects of the sectional controversies was the most powerful answer yet made to the state sovereignty arguments of Stephens and Davis and made a deep impression on his contemporaries.

We must pass over the contributions of scores of less conspicuous writers of the years before 1900. It is enough to say that at the end of the century the historical scholars, with few exceptions, agreed that the Civil War had been the overshadowing event of all American history and that most of them accepted the orthodox northern version of the causes and character of that conflict. No convincing presentation of the southern cause had caught the popular attention for twenty years. All the great histories had been written in the North. The old antagonisms had died down as the North became more and more absorbed with the problems of its expanding economic life, as the once-desolated South began to feel the thrills of returning prosperity and the sons of Union and Confederate veterans rallied together under the flag in the brief war with Spain. While tradition lingers long among the common folk, there were signs that among those of the South the old defensive traditions were slowly disintegrating or changing form. Left without learned assistance in replying to the northern historians, affected by the nostalgic reminiscences of the aged for the "good old days before the war," they turned to the romances of Thomas Nelson Page and other southern novelists and recreated the Old South for themselves in terms of moonlight and roses, tall white-pillared porches, minuets, mint juleps, and happy darkies frolicking in the "quarters."

But the historians were not through with this question. By 1900 the growth of the great graduate schools had reached the point at which the historical seminars were beginning to force the complete rewriting of American history. Doctoral dissertations and the flood of other monographs inspired by great teachers began to attack directly and indirectly the assumptions of the older historians both as to the forces which had influenced our history and its traditional interpretations. Frederick J. Turner at the University of Wisconsin and William A. Dunning at Columbia had begun the seminars which were to have such revolutionary consequences upon the interpretation of the whole nineteenth century in America. Turner set his students to work upon the growth and inter-relations of the varied geographical provinces of the United States and he neglected no aspect of the sectional scene—social, economic, religious, political, psychological, or topographical. Dunning first directed his students to the study of Reconstruction and then led them skillfully back through the war into the antebellum situation. McMaster at the University of Pennsylvania and Edward Channing at Harvard set dozens of graduate students to work searching for new light on problems they had encountered in their own notable volumes. At Johns Hopkins, Yale, Chicago, Michigan, and other universities young men and women were being trained in the techniques of historical investigation and writing and were being introduced to profitable fields for research. It was inevitable that many of these youthful enthusiasts who turned eagerly to digging out new material in this fertile and unworked field should be southerners with a consuming desire to study the history of their own section. They had been sufficiently well trained to appreciate the necessity for an objective attitude, but doubtless many of them along with the thrill of discovery found a keen pleasure in overturning the theories and assumptions of von Holst, Schouler, Rossiter Johnson, and Rhodes. Some of the most important contributions in this new activity came from students of northern birth who found fascination in southern history as well as in northern. They searched through dusty and forgotten official archives, examined old files of long neglected newspapers, and unearthed hitherto unknown collections of private papers. It is not surprising that they found many of the assumptions of the elder historians defective through lack of accurate or sufficient information.

Time does not permit the mention of all who made important contributions to the revision of this phase of American history, but a few must be noted. In his studies of the plantation and the regime of slave management, Ulrich B. Phillips[11] thoroughly exploded the abolitionist charge that the slave was systematically or usually overworked or otherwise treated with brutality. His findings, based upon the examination of countless plantation records and related documents and thoroughly objective (for he neither defended nor condemned the system), are so conclusive that it would be impossible for any reputable historian today to describe the institution as did von Holst or Rhodes. Phillips also made it clear that the mass of the southern people were far less concerned about property rights in slaves (since three-fourths of them owned none) than in the underlying racial-social problem involved in emancipation. To put it in another way, they opposed the abolition program because they feared it would ruin the South as "a white man's country." A northern student, Arthur C. Cole, in his *Whig Party in the South*[12] proved that, contrary to northern belief, the slaveholders were mostly Whigs who for the sake of party unity as well as for safety discountenanced agitation over abolition, generally opposed aggressive tactics for the extension of slavery, and were rather consistently Union men who flouted the theory of state sovereignty although devoted to the constitutional rights of the states. It was the Democrats, few of whom owned slaves, who were the more aggressive party. Eugene C. Barker's authoritative studies in the field of Texas colonization[13] made it clear that slavery extension had nothing to do with the Anglo-American colonization of Texas or the revolution against Mexico. Justin H. Smith, a northern historian, after elaborate study came to the conclusion that Mexico, not the United States, was responsible for the war in 1846.[14] Chauncey S. Boucher, of northern birth, in a notable article[15] pointed out the fallacies in the theory that a united and "aggressive slavocracy" had brought about the annexation of Texas, the war with Mexico, and the seizure of a large portion of that distracted country for the purpose of creating more slave states. Boucher held, as did other investigators, that the southerners were on the defensive instead of the offensive throughout the whole slavery controversy. Elaborating this point, Jesse T. Carpenter[16] showed how southern men, always in the minority and conscious of danger to their interests, had erected one defense after another under the Constitution and had finally taken refuge in independence as a last resort when all the others had broken down. Dwight L. Dumond in a careful analysis of the secession movement[17] showed that, from evidence then available, the southern leaders had ample reason in 1860 to believe that the South was in real danger from an increasingly hostile majority in the free states, but that even in the face of this situation they had great difficulty in uniting on any course of action. Other investigators have directed their attention to the economic life of the Old South with the result that some of our earlier ideas about that subject have had to be revised radically. But as many of these studies were not directly concerned with the causes of the war, only one will be mentioned here. Robert R. Russel's *Economic Aspects of Southern Sectionalism*[18] shows how southern discontent over the losing battle which southern agriculture

was waging with the rising northern industry and capital induced attempts
to develop similar industries in the South and contributed to the idea of
political independence.

Meanwhile, there has been considerable revision of earlier beliefs
about the relation of certain groups in the North to the sectional controversy. One of the most interesting is the rehabilitation of Stephen A.
Douglas who had been disparaged in the mistaken idea that this belittling
added to the stature of Lincoln. Several writers have contributed to this
new understanding of the Little Giant—among them Allen Johnson,
Albert J. Beveridge, William O. Lynch, Frank H. Hodder, and George
Fort Milton—but space permits the mention of the work of but one.
The late Professor Hodder showed conclusively[19] that Douglas' introduction of the Nebraska bill in 1854 was not a part of any bargain with
the South and that his acceptance of the amendment to repeal the
Missouri Compromise was not a bid for the presidency. Hodder also
proved that the famous *obiter dictum* of the Supreme Court majority
in the Dred Scott case was not the result of collusion with the proslavery
leaders but was, in a measure, forced by the two minority justices.[20]

Thus, one by one, these old partisan charges of conspiracy and
corruption, once accepted by credulous historians as proven facts, are
deleted from the page of History. In this connection it may be recalled
that abundant evidence has shown that the entire quarrel over the
question whether slavery should be permitted in the territories had no
basis in fact, but was a mere jockeying for strategic advantage, since
no possibility existed that the institution could maintain itself in those
regions. Indeed, it becomes more and more apparent that certain of the
statesmen of that day were more concerned with immediate political
prospects than with the eternal principles of truth which they professed
to serve.

Perhaps some of the most fruitful of the newer studies have been
those which have re-examined the growth of the antislavery movement
and its springs of action. For instance, the recent book of Gilbert H.
Barnes, *The Antislavery Impulse, 1830–1844*,[21] and the related two
volumes of *The Weld-Grimké Letters*,[22] edited by Barnes and Dumond,
throw a bright light upon the origins and character of the abolition
crusade. Here we see the movement as the outgrowth of the humani-
tarian-religious revivals of the early nineteenth century, spreading far
wider and becoming far more influential than has been supposed. Formerly we were told that only a small proportion of the northern people
were abolitionists. These studies show that most of the members of the
powerful evangelical churches became committed to the program. Some
of their leaders, at least, looked forward with pious exaltation to the

prospect of civil war with "the stealers of men." They laid the foundations for the organization of the Republican party in 1854 and they provided the votes which elected Lincoln in 1860. The fears of the southerners in that fateful year seem to have been less unreasonable than we have been taught to believe.

Thus, the monographic attack upon the older history has forced reversal or revision of judgment upon almost every important point. The resulting damage to the traditional interpretation of the break between the sections is even greater than has been indicated, for it must be obvious to every member of this Association that many other very significant studies have not even been mentioned. Time has not permitted their inclusion. But there are two other interesting contributions to the subject which cannot be passed over.

In their brilliant work, *The Rise of American Civilization,* first published in 1927, Charles and Mary Beard have questioned the commonly accepted belief that the institution of slavery was chiefly responsible for the clash between the sections. In their view the war resulted from a desperate rivalry for control of the powers of the general government between the southern planting "aristocracy," committed to a colonial economy, and the rising capitalist-industrial interest which had originated in New England and the Middle Atlantic states and was spreading rapidly during the 1850's into the Old Northwest. At bottom it was the old conflict between the principles of the Hamilton-Webster and the Jefferson-Jackson schools, and it was concerned with the demands of business enterprise for protective tariffs, a national bank for the regulation of currency, and Federal subsidies for shipping interests. This program was repeatedly defeated by the planters through their control of the Democratic party until the southerners became embroiled with the northern laborers and northwestern farmers whose demands for free homesteads on the western public lands they also opposed. When the Kansas-Nebraska Act opened the new territories to slaveowners the free farmers and mechanics, greatly alarmed lest they should be excluded by slave competition, formed a new political organization, basing it upon Jeffersonian principles and calling it Republican. These original Republicans in 1856 demanded only that slavery be kept out of the territories; they would leave it alone in the states. This quarrel, therefore, was over the western lands; it was fundamentally economic and the right or wrong of slavery was not the basic issue. Moreover, the Beards say, the abolitionists were too weak numerically to have much political influence.[23] The original Republicans were not strong enough to win in 1856, were in danger of dissolution by 1859, and were able to win the election of 1860 only after they had effected a combination with the old Whigs of the East on a platform which joined the business program with that for free home-steads in the West. The southern planters, finding their economic order threatened by their loss of political power, resolved upon secession; but they appealed to the fellow southerners to support them on the ground that the constitutional rights of the states and the safety of their local institutions were in danger. The Beards claim that there was no danger since Lincoln received only about 40 per cent of the total votes and his party platform contained no threat of attack upon slavery within the states. With more recent evidence before us, it seems clear that these authors underestimated the strength and the strategic position of the antislavery forces; and it would be easy to raise objection to some of their statements on other points. But there can hardly be any doubt that they have made an extremely valuable contribution to the solution of this vexing problem by their emphasis upon the economic rivalries which to a very great extent motivated sectional antagonisms from 1820 to 1861.

In a recent article[24] Avery O. Craven has brilliantly presented the thesis that the clash of the sixties was the result of emotional appeals carefully nurtured, joined with sublimated economic motives, and clev-erly developed into intersectional hatred. From the side of the North it came, he thinks, from the fusion of three ideas: (1) the religious-humanitarian movement which began early in the century and gradually centered upon slavery as the most grievous of sins; (2) the conviction which grew up among the hard-pressed farmers and mechanics that the realization of democratic ideals was being thwarted by a selfish aris-tocracy, which came to be identified with southern planters living in luxury off the labors of hapless slaves; (3) the belief that the economic progress of the North and Northwest—protective tariffs for the benefit of labor, internal improvements for both farmers and tradesmen, and free homesteads in the West for farmers and mechanics—was being checked by these same aristocratic and sinful planters. God's plan for an ideal democratic America, in which His elect were to be sure of profits and free homesteads, was being thwarted by these southern agents of the Devil whom it was a Christian duty to hate and over-throw. In the South, on the other hand, the leaders, relying upon a strict construction of the Constitution to protect their staple-producing agriculture against the northern demands for tariffs and national banks, had been unable to arouse any emotional response from the masses of farmers. While the rise of the slavery issue had made the nonslave-holders as well as the planters uneasy, because it threatened racial and social disturbance, it was not until the John Brown raid and the startling evidence of wide northern approval of his enterprise had convinced them that they were on the brink of racial war and social chaos that the masses of the southern people began on their own account to conjure up devils in the form of abolitionist Black Republicans. Then they were ready to fight if necessary to preserve their homes against this threatened danger. Men on both sides had "associated their rivals with disliked and dishonorable symbols and crowned their own interests with moral sanctions."

Whether or not we have approximated to something like the final verdict on the general causes of this greatest tragedy of the American people, it is evident that we have come a long way from the explanations of such postwar historians as von Holst and Schouler. Perhaps one day the textbook writers will perceive the change. If one may dare to forecast, it seems likely that, allowing for individual variations, historians will come to agree that the break between North and South came from emotional disturbance over moral convictions (without reference to the essential quality of those convictions) and from economic rivalries, while politicians, intent only upon the immediate objective, fomented for their own ends the emotional forces which they could arouse but could not check when the crisis came. Slavery was a primary cause, but not in the sense that the older historians have made familiar. It was, as the Beards well say, no simple, isolated phenomenon.

Thus far we have considered only the newer interpretations of the forces which brought the two sections face to face in the late winter of 1860–1861 with rival governments in Washington and Montgomery. There is still much investigation to be done on the question of how the war actually came about, a matter which is likely to undergo as radical a revision as that to which the antebellum period has been subjected. For the present, however, this subject may be dismissed with the observation that the popular fear of war which had accompanied the secession of the cotton states in December and January had subsided to a marked degree by the last of March, 1861, and that the mass of the people, North and South, then seemed confident that hostilities would be avoided, in spite of the activities of a war faction in each section; and, further, that if secession were inevitable—there are strong reasons for so thinking—the war itself was not inevitable, unless those whose official positions gave them the power to choose war or peace were obliged to choose war for reasons of policy.[25] It is sufficient here to call attention to the difference between the causes of the first crisis, which resulted in the secession of the cotton states, and the handling of the second crisis which immediately precipitated the war.

Since the purpose of this paper is only to trace the changes in the interpretation of the causes of the Civil War, its consequences and its place in American history, nothing will be said of the progress or conduct of the struggle itself. We may now consider what it has meant to the people of the United States.

When northern people began to consider the fruits of the four years of warfare, it was natural that they should think in terms of what they believed they had fought for. One large group had regarded the preservation of the Union as the main purpose, while another had insisted that the destruction of slavery was the most important aim. Before the end, President Lincoln had managed to combine both purposes. Other and minor considerations were either kept in the background or were overlooked by the majority of the people. After it was over, these two things were held to be the great achievements, worth all the cost of life and property. They had acquired in the course of the conflict an immense emotional appeal, so that a great political party, for more than twenty years after the surrender of Lee, made its appeal to northern voters for further tenure of power upon the plea that it had saved the Union and struck the shackles from the helpless slave. It was but human nature that a people, after a successful war, should prefer to interpret it as something glorious, reflecting honor and credit upon themselves. Somewhat later, as opportunities arose for the commercial exploitation of southern agriculture and natural resources, beneficent consequences to the South itself began to be pointed out. The "poor whites" of the southern hinterlands had been freed as well as the slaves, and fresh currents of energy had been turned into the stagnant pool of southern economic life. And these things are repeated unto this day. Deferring for the moment other consequences of the great intersectional conflagration, let us consider briefly these claims.

The Union was preserved, if we mean that the people of the southern states were forced into subordination to the government at Washington. But it was twelve years after the last ragged Confederate laid down his arms before all of these people were permitted to govern themselves again, and even then the old Union had not been restored. The harshness of the victors to the conquered had aroused resentments that lasted for a generation and are traceable even now. Fortunately, however, a general reconciliation was effected in the course of time. Southern political leaders in Congress found it necessary to proclaim not only their loyalty to the nation but also that the results of the war were "all for the best." Partly out of sheer weariness of the long wrangles, partly out of a sort of fatalism, and partly because of their absorption in material interests, an increasing number of the southern people acquiesced in the verdict. In the North, while the war feeling was periodically revived by political waving of "the bloody shirt," this appeal gradually lost its force. Prosperity and political power turned the thought of the people away from the past and made forgiveness easier. Some southerners remained "unreconstructed"; some northerners never gave up their suspicions of all things southern. But the flowing years smoothed the rough edges of mutual distrust.

But there are other considerations which the historian should take into account. Some of them were examined not long ago by Professor Richard H. Shryock in a very thoughtful paper entitled "The Nationalistic Tradition of the Civil War."[26] Why was this Union so valuable that it was worth the lives of more than half a million men to preserve it, aside from the vast amount of wealth destroyed and the untold suffering left in its train? Americans have been prone to boast of the size of their country. Is there some mystical, imponderable but precious quality in mere bigness? Or was it the danger (as argued by Lincoln) that the successful withdrawal of the southern states would lead to the secession of other states, so that the once mighty Union would have been broken up into a group of petty, mutually jealous and possibly warring little countries? Of that there seems to have been no great danger, for the free states were already bound closely together by economic ties, as well as by blood relationships. The most that could have been expected was that two or three of the border slave states would have decided to join the cotton Confederacy, or that adjustments of boundary or customs lines might have given trouble for some years after 1861. While it is clear that the political unity of all the states has been an economic blessing to those who have found their best markets within the United States behind a high protective wall, it would be hard to prove that these benefits have been shared by all sections, or by all economic groups. As for the assertion so often made that mutual jealousy and fears would have made huge standing armies necessary, we have in refutation the example of our happy relations with Canada. Furthermore, who can say that, had no war been made on the seceded states, there would not have been quicker reconciliation and reunion on a firm and mutually satisfactory basis?

But some may say, "Would not slavery have remained to plague them all, to keep alive reproaches and bitterness, to endanger peace? And could the Confederacy have prospered with its agriculture and industries hampered by a system so outworn and wasteful?" We can all agree that not merely the Negro but the southern white man and the South as a whole is better off with slavery gone. But this admission does not precisely meet the question: Was this the only or the best way to get rid of the institution? And was the manner of it worth the cost?

There can be little doubt that the institution of chattel slavery had reached its peak by 1860 and that within a comparatively short time it would have begun to decline and eventually have been abolished by the southerners themselves. The extraordinary expansion of cotton acreage would almost certainly have resulted in overproduction and lower prices, and the rapid introduction of laborsaving machinery in every step of cotton production except picking would have made slaveholding too expensive for the great majority of planters. Only those who could be surest of continued profits—the sugar planters, perhaps, and the owners of the most fertile cotton lands—could have afforded the expense of rearing their full supply of labor; they would almost certainly have discovered that it would be cheaper to hire labor as needed. And the problem of controlling the freed Negro could have been worked out on the basis of the existing laws. But it is not profitable to speculate too minutely upon these probabilities. The prospect of social evolution was not given a chance.

Chattel slavery was destroyed in the roar of cannon and the murderous rattle of musketry. But the central problem, the adjustment of two intermingled but dissimilar races, was not solved. It remained to plague not only that generation but future ones, and was made far more difficult by the alienation of the races which resulted from the political and social experiments of radical reconstruction. Nor can we overlook the actual suffering from disease, malnutrition, and the other ills which befell the unfortunate blacks during the tumultuous period of transition from slavery to freedom. Beyond question the Negroes have made substantial progress since 1865, but that their condition is better now than it would have been had a more orderly process of social and economic change been followed is not so certain. No thoughtful friend of the Negro will affirm that the economic freedom of the race is yet in sight. The results but illustrate anew the truth that every radical reform in our complex society brings new problems in its train.

It is a favorite dictum of many writers, more especially the northern historians, that the emancipation of the African also set free the "poor whites" of the South. Usually these writers seem to regard as "poor whites" all who were not slaveowners. For something like a hundred years southerners have been trying to make clear to northerners the falsity of this definition and the difference between "poor whites" and the great middle class of nonslaveholders. For some reason the misapprehension survives and it would be too wearisome to explain the distinction again. But is it true that the "poor whites" of the South (as southerners use that term) have been appreciably uplifted in the economic and social scale by the Civil War? That the descendants of some of those who lived in the lower fringe of the social order in the Old South have greatly improved their condition is unquestionable; but that many of this class have furnished leaders to the New South would be extremely difficult to prove. While thousands of sons and daughters of poor families have risen to prominence in business and the professions (as others did before 1861), very few of them came of what the southerner has always called "poor white trash." This submerged class remains submerged. We have but to look at the white share-croppers throughout the cotton country and the white casual laborer and ask ourselves whether these people are appreciably better off than were their ancestors in 1860. It would not be difficult to show that in these submerged groups are many families descended from the independent yeomanry of 1860 who have sunk to their present status under the pressure of adverse economic conditions. The condition of the white farm tenants lends little support to the thesis that the Civil War was a boon to them.

But, it is said with the fervor of conviction, at least the breaking of the power of the planting aristocracy opened the way for industry and commerce and the economic regeneration of the region. Look at the industries which have spread along the piedmont from Virginia around through the Carolinas, Georgia, Alabama, and up through Tennessee and Kentucky. Look at Atlanta and Birmingham and the scores of other thriving cities which remained but small towns as long as cotton was king! The obvious retort is that the destruction of war hindered rather than helped this development. The researches of the younger historians are making it clearer every year that, while southern industry was in its infancy in 1860, the infant was a very healthy one and gave promise of rapid growth. The war destroyed most of what had been built and the capital of the builders was, in most cases, wiped out. When the new start was made railroads, mines, and factories recovered slowly and painfully except where northern capital was available; and the price of northern assistance was usually the surrender of control and of the larger share of the profits to residents of New York, Boston, and other northern centers.

We are told that the defeat of the secessionists not only kept the Union intact but welded the people of the United States into a nation; and in an age when the trend to nationalism throughout the world has been so strong this achievement has seemed very important. The Federal armies destroyed the Calhoun theory of the sovereignty of the states and gave the sanction of victory to the Webster-Lincoln conception of national sovereignty. More specifically, the three "war amendments" to the Constitution enlarged the powers of the general government at the expense of the states. Of special significance has been the "due process of law" clause in the Fourteenth Amendment which, as interpreted by the courts, has hampered the states in their efforts to tax and regulate the great corporations. But while we grant all this, must we assume that civil war was necessary to achieve nationality or to bestow needed authority upon the general government? Are there not plenty of evidences that before 1860 powerful factors were already working toward greater economic and social unity, even though obscured by the sectional quarrel? The railroad, the telegraph, the press, and technological advances were extending business enterprise into wider fields. Farmers, business men, and even laborers were becoming conscious of their group interests. Shall we deny that this movement would have gone on in the same general direction that it has taken since 1865? Would not the Federal government have been called upon eventually to deal with the problems raised by these groups, expanding its powers to that end by interpretation and amendment of the Constitution, as it has done?

Considerations such as these have led some scholars, chiefly of the Turner school, to doubt whether, after all, the Civil War changed the course of American history as much as we have been accustomed to think. They point out that the fundamental forces shaping American life were neither changed nor greatly affected by the war. The frontier line continued to roll westward, railroads were already tending to consolidation, cheaper transportation, and to plotting their courses toward the Pacific. The colonial economy of the southern planters was destined to decay in any case; the slaves must have been emancipated in the course of time. The armies of industry and labor were gathering their forces in textile, steel, coal, oil, and a hundred other camps before the raw troops of McDowell and Beauregard met on the Plains of Manassas; the rise of the mechanical industries to a dominant place in our national economy was as inevitable here as it was in Western Europe. On the other hand, Charles and Mary Beard are of the opinion that only the destruction of the political power of the obstructive planter class gave room for the rising new business enterprise which, directed and controlled by the ruthless captains of industry, proceeded to change the whole structure of our economic, social, and political institutions. But the two views are not irreconcilable. Is it not possible to agree that the swing to industrialism was inevitable and to agree also with the Beards that by suddenly sweeping away the impediments to business enterprise, and by preventing for forty years effective control of individualism-run-mad, the war helped to create a host of intricate problems which we have not yet been able to solve? In short, did not the Civil War, indirectly perhaps and at long range, help to get our own generation into its preplexing predicament?

Now that we look back with the advantage of more than seventy years' perspective to the great conflict in which our fathers and grand-fathers fought and seek to analyze the causes and appraise the con-sequences of the desolating struggle, what conclusions seem finally tenable? The forces that swept toward the disruption of the old Union were far more complex than contemporary observers or the early his-torians perceived. The slavery issue remains a prime factor, but not in the simple terms set down by von Holst, Schouler, and Rhodes. It was in itself a very complicated issue and it was interwoven with a mass of other complexities. Clashing economic interests, and, to an extent, political ambitions played their part. And not merely stubborn differences of opinion on trivial or fundamental policies made adjust-ment difficult, but likewise the emotions aroused by mutual misunder-standing and the fear of responsible political leaders lest they, by concessions, lose the confidence of those whose emotional support they had enlisted. The statement that the war was "to save the Union" ignores all the forces which had brought the two sections into hostility. The phrase "to destroy slavery" is either a confession or an afterthought. And what have been the consequences which, after all, must give the conflict its place in the story of American development? Making all necessary allowances for our inability to weigh accurately the impon-derables in the history of a great people, can we say with conviction that this war accomplished anything of lasting good that could not and would not have been won by the peaceful processes of social evolution? Is there not ground for the tragic conclusion that it accomplished little which was not otherwise attainable? Had the more than half a million lives and the ten billions of wasted property been saved, the wealth of the United States and the welfare of the people would not likely have been less than they are now. Perhaps some of the social and economic ills that have bedevilled us for the past fifty years would have been less troublesome.

Will such reflections enable us to attack our present problems with less of emotion and more of cool reason than we frequently display? That, at any rate *should be* one of the lessons of History.

Chapter III

Democracy
and the Southern Frontier

THOMAS PERKINS ABERNETHY

THE FRONTIER is a subject of perennial interest in American history.* Our traditions attribute to it the distinctive social order which grew up in the New World. So readily does the subject lend itself to generalization, that it would seem well, in an attempt to discover how nearly these traditions approximate the truth, to classify several different types of border development which took shape in different areas and at different times. The peculiarities of the frontier were due primarily to its contact with nature in the raw and to its isolation from the main currents of civilization. All frontiers were essentially alike in sharing the first characteristic. In regard to the second—that of isolation—there were considerable differences according to time and place, and these differences make it possible to distinguish at least three special types of border development.

The first frontier, located upon the Atlantic seaboard at the beginning of the period of settlement, differed from any which followed. This peculiarity was due largely to the fact that it was never entirely out of touch with European civilization, and it was never entirely self-sufficient economically. Staple crops were produced even in the earliest years, and trade with Europe was the lifeline by which the settlements sustained themselves. Since they were dependent upon England likewise for their governmental institutions, their social ideas also came largely from across the sea. Distinctions of rank were made even on the fringes of civilization, and within less than a generation the more fortunate pioneers were able to imitate in many ways the lives of the upper classes in

*Presented in Durham, North Carolina, November 19, 1937.

the mother country. The earliest houses surviving in Virginia are of an orthodox English type, as are the furnishings which they contained.

But it was inevitable that the frontier should make a difference. There were no great fortunes, and, though many poor, there were no paupers. There was plenty of land and plenty of work to be done, but an indentured servant on obtaining his freedom did not find it easy to acquire an estate. In order to secure land, money or its equivalent was necessary, and money was scarce. Lacking it, the freedman had his choice of three expedients: he could hire himself as a laborer, assume the status of a tenant, or he could become a "squatter." Now it is well known that neither hired servants nor agricultural tenants were ever numerous on any frontier, but there were numerous squatters on all of them. And this brings us to the second type of border development.[1]

There was much land which was of little value to the producers of staple crops. Poor tracts in the neighborhood of settlements and lands too far removed from the rivers to permit the transportation of crops always furnished a refuge for the man who could not acquire a title by purchase or headright. There he could produce by the sweat of his brow the necessary food and even the necessary clothing for his family. He lived a very nearly self-sufficient existence because he was forced to improvise the necessities which he could not purchase. He learned to make clothes from peltry in the Indian manner and to build his house from the materials at hand. This is the frontier of free land and social equality, of the hunting shirt and the log cabin, which we are accustomed to visualizing as our fundamental and typical American institution—the frontier from which our democracy developed; but it existed only where the land was of little value and the people of little importance. It is not the typical frontier, and its annals have been neglected.[2]

It is the third type which was in reality the typical frontier, and it developed where land was potentially valuable and where competition for its possession was keen. It was often far removed from settlements and its exploitation required considerable resources. These included, in many cases, not only financial capital but political influence, skilled woodsmen, and experienced Indian fighters. No ordinary settler possessed such means; it was the land speculator who was able to command them.

The piedmont region of Virginia, the settlement of which started near the beginning of the eighteenth century, furnishes one of the earlier examples of this type of frontier. Since there was no Indian menace to cope with here, there was a gradual infiltration rather than an organized movement into the area, but men of wealth and influence, often from leading colonial families, took a conspicuous part in the process. Many of the earliest patents called for immense tracts, bought either to extend the operations of some tidewater planter whose older lands were wearing out, to enable a son to set up his own establishment, or for speculative purposes. Though the population was augmented in the second quarter of the century by settlers who crossed the Blue Ridge from the Valley, and though most of the farms were of modest size, it is yet true that the large landowners from tidewater dominated the scene. They filled most of the important local offices, organized the churches, and set the tone of piedmont society. All institutions were modeled along lines already established in the tidewater region, and though the Scotch-Irish who came over from the Valley were numerous, they exerted no great influence as anyone may discover by observing the relative strength of the Anglican and Presbyterian congregations of eighteenth-century piedmont. Social distinctions and aristocratic ideas were coeval with settlement.[3] Thomas Jefferson belonged to the second generation of piedmont society, and was a fairly typical representative of eastern Virginia culture. His ideas of democracy came from European philosophy rather than from frontier equalitarianism, whatever our historians, steeped in the Jacksonian and Lincolnian traditions, may have said to the contrary. Even Patrick Henry's Hanover was no farther west than the fall line; and Henry himself, despite his social simplicity, was no frontiersman. The manner in which some historians have tried to make westerners out of these two popular leaders is an interesting illustration of how we write history from the point of view of our convictions. They had to be frontiersmen because democracy was a frontier product.

Even the Valley was not notably democratic. Though Jefferson looked upon its inhabitants as "wild Irishmen," the region belonged to the third rather than to the second type of frontier. Its pioneer exploiters carried on their operations on a large scale even as compared to the land barons of the piedmont area. The Fairfax, Van Meter, and Hite holdings in the northern end of the Valley, the Beverley and Borden tracts in the center, and the Patton and Loyal Land Company domains in the south were princely estates; and these speculators and their associates— the Campbells, the Lewises, the Prestons, William Christian, William Fleming—dominated the political scene in the early days. The humble settler, with his "tomahawk" rights, stood little chance against these magnates.

Across the North Carolina line in what is now East Tennessee the situation was peculiar. Settlers penetrated the country before it was cleared of the Indian title and before speculators had had opportunity to fasten their hold on it. As in the case of the Pilgrim Fathers, they organized their first government without authority from above; but when the Revolution broke, North Carolina gave them an official political status. The pioneers retained control of local affairs and with such men as Jacob Brown, John Sevier, Evan Shelby, and the Robertsons at their head, they became an important factor in the early development of the Old Southwest. Thus, because of unusual conditions, we have here a frontier which approximates the picture commonly drawn by theorists. Though the leaders were not averse to taking advantage of bargains in land—some of them developing into speculators of note—they held their positions primarily because of their personal popularity and their skill as Indian fighters. This frontier, therefore, falls somewhat between the second and third categories, and it by no means embodies a typical situation.[4]

Going still farther west into Kentucky and Middle Tennessee, we find a more normal development. In Kentucky, Lord Dunmore's agents led by Thomas Bullitt and the deputies of William Preston, surveyor of Fincastle County which included what is now the state of Kentucky, were the first to mark out choice tracts for those who had political influence. Actual settlement did not begin until two years after the first surveys, and by that time other great speculators, Richard Henderson and his copartners, had appeared upon the scene. The real pioneers and Indian fighters, such as Benjamin Logan, the Harrods, and the McAfees, were never of much political consequence, and though George Rogers Clark exercised considerable influence for a time, he was presently supplanted by General James Wilkinson and a group of capitalistic speculators who accepted him as their leader. Kentucky lands fell largely into the hands of absentee investors, Robert Morris at one time owning more than a million and a half acres and Alexander Wolcott more than a million.[5] Virginia law did much to protect the claims of actual settlers; consequently the speculators were the principal backers of the movement for a forcible separation of Kentucky from the Old Dominion.[6]

In Middle Tennessee, as in Kentucky, the speculator in the person of Richard Henderson preceded the actual settler, and when Henderson passed out of the picture William Blount arose to take his place. As the extreme western frontier of North Carolina, as territory and as state, the Tennessee Country, both politically and economically, was controlled by Blount and his friends and henchmen. These speculators made good all land claims which they had secured by a flagrant manipulation of North Carolina legislation.

Alabama and Mississippi received their first substantial influx of population after the Federal government had come into control of their lands, which were surveyed and sold to the highest bidder. This resulted in intense competition, with the best lands falling into the hands of those who could command the greatest capital, leaving the poorer people to settle without leave in the back country where the surveyor had not yet penetrated. In this manner an economic segregation was brought about at the beginning, and simple equalitarian democracy had no place in the picture.

Thus the prevalent idea that the frontier furnished, as long as it existed, a constant refuge for the poor and the oppressed, provided a safety valve for the growth of American society, and discouraged the development of social stratification and class consciousness, is only partially correct. It is true mainly in the case of the second type of frontier as classified above, but to a lesser degree in the case of the first and third types. This fact is forcibly brought out in a recent article which shows that the periods of greatest migration to the frontier were periods of prosperity rather than of depression, as would have been the case if the safety valve thesis were altogether sound.[7] A fair amount of capital was usually necessary in order to go to new country and break new ground —rarely to be acquired without purse and without scrip. Thus people migrated when money was relatively plentiful, not when it was relatively scarce.

While we must distinguish between different types of border development growing out of varying economic conditions, we must also take into account certain chronological factors which influenced political development in all frontier regions but which apply more especially to the third type. When new country is to be explored, surveyed, and settled, especially when it is distant from existing settlements, the population is ordinarily made up of a minority of powerful speculators and their associates, and a majority of poor men who are seeking fortunes but who have no titles to land. The political institutions established at such times are controlled by the powerful minority, but this minority lacks the traditional prestige and assured position enjoyed by ruling minorities in older communities. It must convince the masses that it is to be trusted, and this it does by employing devices which have become all too familiar in our democracy. It declares for the equality of man, liberalizes the suffrage, and apportions representation according to population. But it sees to it that the land is made safe for the speculator, and the actual settler, with small means at his command, is like a hare among the hounds. Seldom indeed were the landless settlers favored by the economic policy of frontier communities. The object of the capitalistic interests which opened the frontier was profit. Their operations were characterized by exactly the same methods which have exploited most of our other national resources. Permitting the humble prospector with a small "grubstake" to share in the proceeds was not among their propensities. Preemption and homestead laws were never popular among the magnates of the frontier.

This was the situation existing in Middle Tennessee and in Kentucky during the early period of settlement. Though the country in the neighborhood of Pittsburgh which Virginia claimed and the settlements in East Tennessee differed from these areas in some respects, they too were controlled by small groups with large landed interests, and their democracy did not extend into the economic field. The movement for the creation of new western states during the Revolutionary period is usually looked upon as a fine example of the spirit of freedom supposed to be so rampant in the region toward the setting sun. But from the inception of the Westsylvania scheme in 1776 to the last gasp of the state of Franklin, these movements were engineered and controlled by land speculators for the promotion of their own particular interests. Moreover, the land policy of the Franklin government was altogether favorable to the speculator and detrimental to the interests of the simple settler.[8]

It was easy to control majorities made up of a shifting population, scattered through an undeveloped country and lacking means for obtaining information and enlightenment. Few had any facilities for gaining knowledge of public business except such as came to them through the political agitator who was not likely to be disinterested. But as time went on, conditions improved. As soon as the country was reasonably safe and good titles could be acquired in an open market, a more stable element began to augment the population, and, land values having reached something of an equilibrium, more daring speculators moved on to greener fields. Political leadership fell into the hands of men who had grown up with the country and who actually had something in common with their constituents. But there were no really old families who controlled by right of tradition, and there was sharp competition for office. It is usually assumed in America that unrestricted competition brings the best men to the top. That is far from being the case. The greedy and unscrupulous are conspicuous among pioneering promoters, and when they enter the political field, they lack such restraints as an older society is apt to have established.

Nevertheless it was during this second phase of the frontier that our typical western democracy began to take shape. Competition for the favor of the people necessitated concessions to popular views. Demagogic methods were the rule, and the gains made by the masses did not often extend into the economic field, yet the common man did increase in political importance and power.

A good illustration of these tendencies is to be found in the first two constitutions of the state of Kentucky. That of 1792 provided for manhood suffrage and representation according to population, yet it provided also that all cases involving titles to land should go directly before the supreme court, that being the only original jurisdiction enjoyed by that body.[9] It has been stated that George Nicholas, a prominent land speculator, was responsible for this provision, and its object cannot be mistaken.[10] There was hardly a man in Kentucky who had enough legal training to justify his appointment to this court who was not connected in some way with land speculation. The county courts would naturally contain few trained lawyers and many plain farmers. The speculators could not hope to control them so easily, and thus it was important from their point of view that cases involving land titles should go directly to the higher tribunal.

When Kentucky framed a new constitution in 1799, this provision was stricken out. Democracy made a further advance when it was enacted that the governor and members of the Senate were henceforth to be elected directly by popular vote instead of indirectly through an electoral college, as had been provided in the first constitution.[11] Many other illustrations could be given to show that the first phase of border development was one in which the masses were peculiarly subject to political and economic exploitation, and that what we recognize as western democracy really developed after the actual frontier stage had been passed.

Yet this process of putting the government more directly into the hands of the people was not confined to the West. It went on more slowly in the East because the colonial period had developed a tradition of upper-class government; but the poor constituted a majority in all sections, and with the growth of education, newspapers, and means of communication, they were gradually able to make their voices heard in both East and West. For instance, in 1808 South Carolina liberalized her constitution by abolishing the property qualification for voting and by apportioning representation in the lower house of assembly according to population.[12]

Though it is generally believed that western democracy achieved its first great triumph in the Jacksonian period, it is certainly true that many of the ideas of that regime were not of western origin. Jackson's strict-constructionist policies were better suited to the needs of the seaboard planters than to those of the undeveloped West, as Henry Clay well understood. And it is doubtful whether an unrestricted suffrage, rotation in office, instruction of representatives by their constituents, and popular election of judges constituted any real advance along the road to sound self-government. In fact, they tended strongly in the direction of mass government, with all its attendant evils. Enlightened leadership and certain checks upon the unrestrained will of the majority are necessary in a democracy. The Colonial and Revolutionary liberals were concerned about the equality of man before the law, not his equality before the ballot box, and the Jeffersonian idea that government should improve the people before they can improve the government would seem to be a good one even today.

More has been said of the political than of the social effects of frontier conditions, yet the latter are probably more important. If contact with the forest tended to break down class distinctions, did it lessen the power of the rich over the poor, or of the strong over the weak? Why do Americans put more stress upon practical and less upon cultural and intellectual achievements than do most other civilized peoples if it is not because the frontier did so? Why have we in the past despoiled our natural resources with a ruthless hand if it was not because the frontier encouraged it? Perhaps it is not so unfortunate that we pay less attention to the amenities of social intercourse than do most nations, but it is hardly a virtue and the frontier is largely responsible. After all, did the frontier develop individualism? If disregard of established authority constitutes individualism, the frontier bred much of it. If a more admirable tendency to rely upon one's own resources is meant, assuredly the frontier encouraged it. There was also produced a certain goodnatured assumption of equality with all men, especially with one's superiors. But if individualism means that one should face each intellectual problem of life with a determination to think it out for himself, the frontier did not promote it. Intellectual independence is rare in these United States, and the uncultured frontier, which made one man's opinion as good as that of any other man, must bear most of the blame.

In the development of our ideas and habits of popular government, at least three forces have combined to produce the present-day result. The philosophical doctrines of seventeenth- and eighteenth-century Europe, as expounded by Locke, Rousseau, and others, played a leading rôle during the period of the War for Independence. The frontier was a mighty force during a succession of generations, and, lastly, the Industrial Revolution which so powerfully affected the development of democracy in nineteenth-century England has not been without its weight on this side of the water. The Jeffersonian regime developed under the influence of the first of these; the Jacksonian under the second; and the New Deal under the third. It is true that Europe had the leading part in shaping the first and last of these forces, but is there any reason why we should make such disproportionate ado about the second, or frontier, influence just because it was peculiarly American?

Chapter IV

The Records
of Southern History

PHILIP M. HAMER

THE preservation and study of the records of southern history is a problem with which all persons who have a real interest in the South's past and care for its present and its future should be concerned.* Such persons are justly proud of much of the South's peculiar heritage and of the notable progress which has been made in building a new South; but they realize that in many respects the South of today falls below their exacting ideal of it, and they hope that they can participate in the creation of a future South in which there will be a maximum of well-being and civilized living for all southerners. They believe it to be of fundamental importance in the building of this future South that intelligent judgment and will, based upon knowledge and understanding, be applied to the solution of its problems.

To this building of the future South the historian can be an important contributor. He can assist in making known the realities of the past in order that those of the present may be understood and that the future may be wisely planned; he can assist in developing in the South a collective memory and a social consciousness which will contribute to a realistic orientation with the present and to a reasonable foreseeing of the future. For history has no meaning and its study has no purpose unless knowledge of the past makes understandable the present which continuously absorbs the future and quickly becomes itself the past. If this be not so, historians must feel that their professional lives, collectively and individually, are ones of complete frustration. The modern historian, however, looks backward in order that he may look forward,

*Presented in New Orleans, Louisiana, November 4, 1938.

and he thereby identifies himself significantly with the society in which he lives.

But the historian can know the past, and can make it known, only to the extent that records of that past have been preserved and can be used by him. What, then, are these records, the materials which the historian needs for his re-creation of the past of that portion of the United States which we call the South? In the broadest sense they are the sum total of those things which, upon examination at any time after they have been made, enable the examiner to re-create the lives of the people who made them, the society of which these people were a part in all of its significant aspects, and, over a period of years extending to the present, trace the development of that complex of human relationships which has produced the present and seek to find some meaning in it.

These records of southern history are of many kinds. They are such products of man's handiwork as the primitive implements of warfare and of domestic life which the archaeologist unearths from aboriginal mounds and town sites. They are the clothes, the house furnishings, the farm implements, the weapons, and other products of human industry which have been gathered into our museums or ought to be preserved there. They are the results of the creative aspirations of southern artists. They are photographs of southern men and women and of places and events—some historic, in the commonly accepted sense of that word, many commonplace, but each depicting in some respect an aspect of southern life which is, or in the future will be, of value to the student of a broadly conceived history of the South. They are the motion picture films on which is made a visual record of events, and sound recordings which make it possible for future historians to hear the songs we sing, the speeches we make, and the radio programs to which we listen. They are such records as are made of the ballads of the southern mountaineers, the songs of Negroes in the cotton fields or on the wharves or on the chain gang, and even the swing music of our modern "jitter-bugs."

Among the records of southern history, by way of further example, are the buildings of the Vieux Carré, with their iron gates and balconies and their secluded patios, and other structures throughout the South which assist us in our study of the history of southern architecture or otherwise help us to understand the lives of those who have built and have occupied them. They are restaurants such as Antoine's in which we dine this evening, itself an institution in which history has been made and itself a part of history. They are the printed records of man's thoughts and actions, books, newspapers, magazines, pamphlets, broadsides, etc., the earliest imprints, today's newspaper, and such fugitive items as campaign posters and leaflets. They are such unprinted records as letters, diaries, memoranda, and other documents which record the multiplicity of our activities in the religious, economic, political, and social phases of our life. Important among them are the records created by our national, state, and local governments.

Neither age, nor autograph, nor association with names of distinction or with unique events is the sole measure of value of the records which our historians need. No peculiar sanctity attaches to a document solely because now it is yellow with age, the ink so faded that it can scarcely be read. Its value is to be measured in terms of its informational content. Many of those which were created only yesterday are of greater potential value to the historian than inconsequential scraps of paper which date from earlier centuries. For the historian, a document which bears the signature of George Washington, Jefferson Davis, Robert E. Lee, or even Button Gwinnett is valuable only to the extent that there is information in it which adds to our understanding of the past. Of far more value may be some letter, or diary, or account book bearing the signature of a man who individually was unimportant but who has left a record which significantly throws light on an otherwise unknown or incompletely understood phase of southern life. Of greater value than accounts of many unique and spectacular events which delight the antiquarian or the episodic historian are plantation diaries, census schedules, court proceedings, case histories of millions on relief, and other records which are individually commonplace for the most part in themselves but can assist greatly in our attempted reconstruction of the past.

In the past, regrettably, we have not been careful to preserve those records which today would enable us to know our history as we should like to know it. "There hath been a great neglect in keeping the records," was the complaint of Virginia's lawmakers as early as 274 years ago. Such today is the complaint which historians still make. Many of those who have had records in their custody have failed—whatever the reason —adequately to preserve and to make accessible much of our basic source material.

As regards our public records, those made by agencies of government, they have, on the whole, been more carefully preserved than those which can be described as nongovernmental. There have been some legal requirements that they be kept; some of them have administrative value or are basic documents for the establishment of title to property. However wide the gap between legal requirements and actual practice, law and administrative necessity have had some influence making for the preservation of records which would otherwise have been lost. Nevertheless, the record of their destruction is appalling.

In the course of years fire has taken a heavy toll; but reference can here be made only to a few of the major catastrophes caused by fire. In Alabama the state capitol was burned in 1849; and though records on the lower floors were saved, the state library with its valuable collection of documents was destroyed. In Virginia the capitol was burned in 1676, 1698, and 1748; and in 1865 fire destroyed the state courthouse in Richmond, resulting in the loss of many valuable records including those of the old general court from about 1619, of the court of appeals, and of many county courts which had been brought to Richmond for safekeeping during the war. In Texas in 1855 fire destroyed all the records of the adjutant general's office, and tradition has it "that certain wayward citizens had a lively interest in some of the criminal records in the office which they desired expunged, and that the fire was not accidental." In North Carolina many of the state's early records were lost when the capitol burned in 1831. In South Carolina fire in the statehouse destroyed records in 1788, and in 1865. In Kentucky the capitol was burned in 1813 and 1824, and in 1865 fire in the offices of the governor, the secretary of state, and the clerk of the court of appeals created serious gaps in important series of records.

War has twice been a major instrument of destruction of records in the South. Here again a few illustrations must suffice. During the Revolution many of Georgia's records were destroyed by the British and others were lost as they were hurriedly carted to Charleston, South Carolina, then to New Bern, North Carolina, and finally as far as Maryland to keep them from the British. In Virginia, upon the advance of the British, the records at Williamsburg were removed to Richmond and subsequently were tumbled into wagons and carted away to the upper James River country. Many of them had to be collected later from private residences along the route, and many were lost. The Civil War also caused much destruction. Many valuable records were destroyed when state capitols or courthouses were burned or sacked by Union troops; often records were hastily shipped from one place to another in the attempt to protect them from the invading armies with the result that many were never returned. In Jackson, Mississippi, for instance, Union troops destroyed many records of the state and wantonly mutilated others, frequently writing across the pages "Remember Grant," "Remember Sherman," etc. In 1862 Confederate troops, occupying the quarters of the Alabama State Historical Society, used its collection of valuable old newspapers to start their fires. In Arkansas report has it that when paper became scarce some of the state records were used for cartridges.

The major causes, however, of the destruction of the records of our history have been, in addition to fire and war, custodial and public ignorance and negligence and carelessness and indifference. In the old state capitol in Little Rock, Arkansas, the overflow of records from state offices was dumped for decades into "the catacombs" in the basement, the province of the state library, where the rooms were described as late as 1906 as "damp, dismal, and disagreeable." In Georgia "many valuable, even priceless documents of the state have served on occasion to kindle fires in the capitol." In this state also, it has been said that every change of personnel resulted in a house cleaning in which records not immediately required were thrown away. This statement is substantiated by the fact that a resurvey of the state's archives made fifteen years after Ulrich B. Phillips' report on the public archives of Georgia revealed that "any number of valuable records" he listed "had entirely disappeared." In Kentucky, when the state offices were moved into the new capitol, great quantities of records were sold as waste paper. Here also in 1900 troops which were quartered in the capitol during the Goebel-Taylor conflict "made their beds of documents and lighted their pipes with leaves from the files." In Virginia, just after the Civil War, practically all extant state records are reported to have been thrown "in a confused heap into one of the garrets of the capitol," from which they were not removed until 1891. In South Carolina, it is said, practically all the records of the adjutant general's office "were destroyed during the World War by an army sergeant who wanted to use the boxes for shipping purposes." In Mississippi inactive state records were consigned to prison; having been accumulated on the third floor of the capitol, "in hopeless confusion," it was feared that the weight of them endangered the lives of the members of the supreme court who sat in the room below, so the records were removed to the penitentiary. In Tennessee, as offices in the state capitol became crowded, the inactive records were dumped into a crypt in the basement. Here, one observer reported, they "lay piled in masses on the stone floors, among old paint barrels, ashes, trash of every description, dirt and grime. They were wet and rotting, and . . . the janitor . . . burned up several cartloads because of the fact that they were 'wet and nasty and smelled bad.' " Quantities were sold, without legislative authorization, as waste paper. In Florida, about thirty years ago, an investigator found that some of the records of the office of the secretary of state had recently been recovered from a coal bin and that others in the garret were "loose and in great confusion," many of them lying on the floor so thickly that it was literally covered with them.

One might continue at considerable length to cite specific instances of the destruction or mistreatment of the public records of our states. And it is probable that records of our counties have suffered even more severely from war, fire, neglect, theft, dampness, vermin, dirt, etc., than those of our state governments. The fate of the records of our munici-palities has been worse, on the whole, than that of our county records. Descriptions of their condition are meager, but it seems fair to assume that the following account, written in 1903, of the records of a former capital of Georgia is characteristic of far too many of them: "They are in no arrangement, and no care is taken of them. Some of them have been damaged by mice, and all of them . . . are exceedingly dusty and disagreeable to use."

As regards nonpublic records, their preservation has been even more fortuitous, more the result of chance and less the result of foresight than the public ones. We have little of the tradition of preserving family archives. Personal papers have been destroyed deliberately, often by descendants who had no conception of their value. Many have been preserved for a time and then destroyed by fire. One is impressed, and disheartened, as he reads, for example, in the reports of the surveys published by the historical commissions of Alabama and Mississippi more than thirty-five years ago that when attempts were made to locate the papers of prominent citizens of those states, frequently it was re-ported that they had been destroyed by fire or otherwise lost. Too often when they have been preserved, their present possessors are disinclined, for a multitude of reasons, to place them in institutions where they will be kept safely and made available for the use of scholars. Little attempt has been made to preserve business records by the owners thereof. Usu-ally they have been destroyed when they have ceased to be of administra-tive use; little attention has been paid to this type of record by collecting agencies. Records of our social and religious organizations are indiffer-ently kept and often carelessly misplaced or deliberately thrown away.

The underlying reason for most of the destruction of our official records has been public and legislative indifference and a consequent failure to establish in each state an agency of government with sufficient authority and adequate funds to concern itself solely with the preserva-tion, care, and administration of those records. In all of our states, of course, it has been provided by law that certain records must be kept by certain administrative governmental agencies, but such legislation has been based primarily upon consideration of administrative necessity rather than upon any consideration of historical needs, and practice has often and regrettably varied widely from the law. It should not be for-gotten, of course, that during the nineteenth century there were spas-modic evidences of governmental interest in records from the historical as distinguished from the administrative point of view. More often than not this represented the results of the influence of individuals or of local historical societies upon legislative authorities. Notable, in this connection, was the action of North Carolina in securing transcripts of records in Great Britain for the Colonial period of her history and the publication of them in *The Colonial Records of North Carolina,* the first volume of which came from the press in 1886; and this example has been followed in varying degree by other southern states.

The early years of the twentieth century, however, saw a decided improvement in the attitude of legislative authorities in a number of states. This appears to have been a result of the efforts of a relatively small number of men who had not only an understanding of the desirability of preserving the records of our history but those combinations of personality characteristics which enabled them to secure legislative action.

Alabama was the first state in the South to establish a state agency, financed by public funds, whose purpose was to preserve and make available for use the state's noncurrent archives, to collect other historical records, and otherwise to promote the study and increased knowledge of the state's history. The man who was almost solely responsible for this was Thomas M. Owen, a young lawyer, untrained in history as such training is known today but interested in history since childhood, intelligent, resourceful, energetic, and enthusiastic, with a vision of a state supported archival and historical agency, and with the ability to make this vision a reality. In 1898 he virtually assumed control of the moribund Alabama Historical Society and gave it new life; he became its secretary and soon secured for it a state appropriation to finance an annual publication. From the legislature he secured also the appointment of an Alabama History Commission, empowered to make a comprehensive survey of the records of Alabama's history "whether in domestic or foreign archives or repositories, or in private hands." As chairman of this Commission, Owen planned its work and was largely responsible for its report which was submitted in 1900 to the governor and by him to the legislature. The report contained not only the results of an excellent preliminary survey but also a recommendation that a state Department of Archives and History be established. The recommendation was approved by the legislature with the result that in 1901 the department came into existence with Owen as director. Its purposes were declared to be "the care and custody of official archives, the collection of materials bearing upon the history of the State, and the territory included therein, from the earliest times, the compilation and publication of the State's official records and other historical materials, the diffusion of knowledge in reference to the history and resources of the State, the encouragement of historical work and research, and the performance of such other acts and requirements as may be enjoined by law."

Alabama's action had a marked influence upon other states. In Mississippi, in 1900, the legislature provided for the establishment of an Historical Commission similar in purpose to that which Alabama had created two years earlier. With Professor Franklin L. Riley, member of the faculty of the state university and for many years secretary of the Mississippi Historical Society, as its chairman, the Commission issued a report similar in character and recommendations to that of Alabama's Commission. In 1902 the legislature approved a bill which Professor Riley had drafted, providing for the creation of a state Department of Archives and History, and Dunbar Rowland was chosen to be its director. In Arkansas, influenced by the action of Alabama and Mississippi and by the work of Professor J. H. Reynolds of the state university, the legislature provided in 1905 for the appointment of a History Commission to make a survey of the records for the history of the state. With Professor Reynolds as secretary, the Commission completed and published a report similar in character to those of Alabama and Mississippi. In 1909 the legislature provided for a reorganized History Commission, with a secretary as its administrative officer, similar in power and duties to the departments of archives and history in Alabama and Mississippi, but it failed for four years to appropriate money even for the payment of the secretary's salary, and has never provided adequate financial support.

Meanwhile, in 1905, West Virginia's legislature created its Department of Archives and History, with an historian and archivist in charge; and South Carolina established an Historical Commission, with an administrative secretary, to serve as the archival and historical agency of that state. Two years later North Carolina's legislature took similar action. It enlarged the powers and duties of an Historical Commission which had been established in 1903, making it the archival and historical agency of the state. Mr. R. D. W. Connor became the first secretary of this new Historical Commission, as he had been of the old one, and was largely responsible for making it one of the recognized leaders in state archival and historical work in the United States. Recently the North Carolina legislature has enacted laws which place that state in the forefront of southern states in archival legislation as well as accomplishment. In Georgia provision was made for the office of Compiler of State Records in 1902, with the result that a number of volumes of valuable documents relating to the Colonial, Revolutionary, and Confederate periods of Georgia's history were published, but it was not until 1918 that a Department of Archives and History was established. Maryland, with its Hall of Records, is the latest addition to the group of states which have separate state agencies in which are combined the functions of an archival establishment and an historical society.

In Virginia, in 1906, a Department of Archives and History was organized as a unit of the state library. In Tennessee, by the Reorganization Act of 1923, provision was made for a Division of Library and Archives in the Department of Education. Kentucky has a Department of Library and Archives. In Texas responsibility for the preservation of the records of Texas history is vested in both the state library and the University of Texas, the former in practice giving its chief attention to state archives and the latter, with some notable exceptions, to other types of records. Two years ago the Louisiana legislature made the Archives Department of Louisiana State University the chief archival and historical agency of the state government. In West Virginia an anomalous situation has been created. With the Department of Archives and History at Charleston continuing in existence, the state legislature in 1934 gave permission to custodians of state and county archives to turn over their records to the Division of Documents of West Virginia University at Morgantown. In Oklahoma the State Historical Society is the archival and historical agency of the state. Florida appears to be the only southern state which has not, in some degree, followed the example set by Alabama in 1901.

The general pattern, then, of governmental organization for the preservation of the records of southern history has taken the form of a separate state agency, or a separate unit of a state agency, charged with the triple duty of taking custody of and preserving the noncurrent public records of the state, of collecting for preservation other records of the state's history, and of taking action otherwise to increase and diffuse knowledge of that history. This duty has been met by those agencies in widely varying degrees. Some few have placed themselves among the nation's leaders; some give promise soon of winning such a place; some lag far behind. If adequate support can be secured, all of them could do much more than has yet been done.

More recently than the states, the Federal government has given its attention to the preservation of the records of southern history. The Library of Congress, particularly through its Division of Manuscripts, has acquired many newspapers, other printed materials, personal papers, and transcripts or film copies from archives and other repositories abroad. The last are particularly valuable for the Colonial period of southern history. The National Archives is taking custody of great quantities of the records of the Federal government, among them much of outstanding value for the history of the South, and is making them conveniently available for consultation by students. Within the past few weeks, for example, such of the archives of the Confederate States of America as were in the possession of the Department of War, formerly stored in a garage in Washington, have been brought into the Archives Building.

The National Park Service of the Department of the Interior is preserving many historic sites in the South. The Public Works Administration has helped construct many buildings in the South in which records will be more safely and more conveniently housed than heretofore. Notable among these are buildings to be occupied by the Alabama Department of Archives and History in Montgomery and the North Carolina Historical Commission in Raleigh. The Works Progress Administration, as a part of its relief program, has spent millions of dollars on work which is of great importance for all persons who are interested in the history of the South. Its Survey of Federal Archives has inventoried practically all of the records of the Federal government now in the southern states and these inventories are being published in mimeograph form. Its Historic American Buildings Survey has made measured drawings and photographs of hundreds of the South's most historic buildings, and gathered information for a comprehensive history of architecture in the South. Most important of all, its Historical Records Survey is engaged upon an ambitious program which includes the inventorying of state, county, municipal, and church archives and institutional and private collections of manuscripts, the compilation of catalogs of early imprints, and the calendaring and indexing of documents, etc., in all the southern states. Much of the results of its work has been or will be published. Many local projects of the Works Progress Administration have rendered assistance of various kinds to those who have records of southern history in their custody.

In addition to what the state and Federal governments have done, much valuable work has been accomplished by nongovernmental agencies. In an earlier period local historical societies, often dominated by some one man or a small group of men, preserved records which otherwise would have been destroyed, or built up valuable collections only to have them destroyed. Individuals with the collector's instinct or with plans for the writing of local histories made their collections. Of recent years some universities have had marked success in developing collections of manuscripts, newspapers, pamphlets, books, etc., in the field of southern history. Notable among these are the University of Texas, the University of North Carolina, Duke University, Louisiana State University, the University of Virginia, and West Virginia University. Many other institutions have done similar work in their special fields of interest.

In spite of the fact that much has been done to preserve the records of the history of the South and that notable progress has been made in many respects in most recent years, there is much more that needs to be done if we would make available the records needed by the present generation for its study of the past and provide for future generations those records of our own which they will need when they come to study us in historical perspective. One of our major needs is that there be in each state a unit of the state government whose sole concern shall be the preservation of the official records in the state, the systematic collection and preservation of other records relating to the state's history, the making of them conveniently accessible for consultation, the furnishing of information from them, the execution of a carefully formulated plan of publication, and the dissemination otherwise of information regarding the state's history to its citizens and others. This historical commission or department of archives and history—its name is of no importance— should be professional in its administration and in its personnel. The director or secretary should be appointed for a long term of office on the basis of professional qualifications and not because of political affiliations or for sentimental reasons. It should normally be expected that he have a doctoral degree in history from a reputable university or the equivalent of such a degree, some training in or study of archival science, and that he also have those qualities of personality which are obviously necessary for the successful occupancy of such a position. Such an agency for the preservation of historical records might well be closely associated with the state university as is the case now in Louisiana, or with some other educational institution, when circumstances make such an arrangement desirable.

To such an agency, if its professional character can be assured, should be given greater authority than has yet been given to any of our existing agencies. It should have power to inspect all public records, state, county, and municipal, to prescribe regulations for their safekeeping, and to compel obedience to these regulations. It should have authority to transfer to its custody all noncurrent records which it deems worthy of preservation. It should be the agency for recommending to the legislative authorities which records should be destroyed, upon the request of the agency concerned, and no destruction without such action should be permitted. It should undertake systematically to collect for its state such records as have previously been referred to in this address as the records of southern history. It should classify, catalog, calendar, and otherwise facilitate the use of the voluminous records which it would accumulate. It should undertake a program of publication even more extensive than, for example, that at one time engaged in by the Mississippi Department of Archives and History or that consistently followed by the North Carolina Historical Commission.

Such an agency should of course be given adequate financial support, or, whatever the powers and duties vested in it by law, it will be as ineffectual in meeting present-day and future problems as some of our state agencies now are. It must have an adequate building, not only fire-proof and provided with modern devices for the preservation of records, but spacious enough to house the accumulations of valuable records which sometimes seem to be on the point of overwhelming us. It must have money for equipment, for publication, and for a professionally trained and sufficiently numerous staff. Too often our failures in the past have resulted in large part because of inadequate financial support. There is much wisdom in the comment of a former president of this Association, "Though poverty may not curb the imagination, it stifles action."

Above all else we need an awakened public interest in the problems of preserving the records of our history. The existence of the Southern Historical Association is both evidence of the existence of an interest in our history and a means of increasing that interest. We need in each state to have active societies with similar purposes, and in our smaller units of government local societies concerned with the history of those localities and the records thereof. What has been done in the past has been done in a hit-and-miss fashion. What records we have now are in considerable part the result of chance. What we should do now is to plan, under competent professional leadership, to preserve the records of our southern history in the future and to make use of them for an increasing knowledge of that history and thereby an increasingly comprehensive understanding of that particular part of the United States in which we live.

Chapter v

The Southerner
and the Laws

CHARLES S. SYDNOR

THE STUDENT of southern history constantly faces the fact that the South is not a political entity with boundaries clearly marked by treaty, constitution, or law.* From this circumstance flow two consequences: historians disagree about the metes and bounds of the South, and, what is of more importance, they are compelled to seek unifying principles of southern history in social, economic, and cultural fields rather than in governmental history. Therefore, historians have concerned themselves chiefly with unique southern characteristics and, to some extent, with the causes of these characteristics. Some of them believe that the distinctiveness of southern society can be traced to an inherited cultural pattern such as that of the English gentry. Others emphasize environment: high temperature, heavy rainfall, coast line, river systems, forests, and soil types. Yet others find the common denominator of the South in such characteristics as slavery, malaria, hookworm, staple crops, lynching, tenancy, states' rights advocacy, and mockingbirds. It is even true that some students believe that the unifying principle of the South is the prevalence of some intangible quality: its state of mind, way of life, attitude, loyalty, or viewpoint.[1] Into this twilight realm this essay ventures, for this is an attempt to set forth the southerner's attitude toward law, using that word in a broad sense to include several of the imperatives that control man and society.

But before going into this subject, one word of explanation and another of warning are in order. The explanation is that the southerner's attitude toward law is not being offered as the outstanding unifying principle of

*Presented in Lexington, Kentucky, November 3, 1939.

southern history; for it was but a secondary characteristic, a natural outgrowth and reflection of the social order of the region. The warning is that from the very nature of the subject this paper must deal with probabilities and trends rather than with absolute certainties. From some examples and a few indications the attempt will be made to arrive at the prevailing opinion of the dominant element in the Old South toward certain bodies of law. Opinion was not as unanimous as this paper may indicate because in brief space due consideration cannot be given to dissenting voices.

The southerner was aware of the authority of Federal law, especially the Constitution of the United States; of divine law as it is stated in the Bible; of those laws, most of which are made by the states, that regulate the dealings of man with man; and of the unwritten laws of society. His attitude toward each of these will be appraised, after which some comments will be ventured about the relationships between these attitudes.

The fact that the southerner chose to make comparatively few changes in the Constitution of the United States before adopting it as the Constitution of the Confederate States of America indicates his high regard for the older of these documents. Implicit in this decision and very clearly stated by many southern spokesmen is this distinction: the South liked the Constitution but it disliked the North's misuse and disregard of it. While it is true that the South was chiefly zealous for the defensive values of the Constitution, just as other sections have been when they have suffered from hostile legislation, the fact remains that for thirty years or so before 1861—years when the South was declining in its share of national population and wealth—it found that the Constitution was a very valuable asset. Naturally, its emphasis was upon states' rights and those parts of the Constitution that recognized the existence of slavery. During these same years the North sometimes found that the Constitution stood in its way as it tried to gain political power proportional to its growing population. Therefore, some northerners began to state that the Constitution was not the highest authority in American government; above it they placed other imperatives which were variously designated as the higher law, the laws of nature, the laws of God, the moral law, the spirit of the age, and the law of majority rule. Other and less radical northerners did not go so far as to deny the supremacy of the Constitution, but they nevertheless insisted that it had changed with changing times and that its words could no longer be taken in their original and literal meaning.

Not unnaturally, the South affirmed that the Constitution continued to be the supreme law of the land and that its words had not changed their meaning. Through repeated insistence upon the Constitution's supremacy in its original, literal meaning, the South came to regard itself as the special custodian and defender of this great legal document; its attitude toward the Constitution was one of great respect.[2]

In regard to the law of God, the South felt equally as well pleased with the orthodoxy of its own views. The barest outline of its reasoning was as follows: The Bible is the supreme revelation of God's law for man's guidance, and its validity is unchanged through the centuries; in the Bible are many passages recognizing the existence of slavery; therefore, slavery is sanctioned by the law of God. To such reasoning, antislavery theologians answered not with chapter and verse but with appeals to the broad teachings of Scripture: brotherly love, the Golden Rule, the equality of all men before God; and with nonbiblical ethical and social arguments. The South retorted that it was unorthodox to set up standards of conduct, no matter how plausible, contrary to the literal words of the Bible; it denied the propriety of the church committing itself to any program of social reform; and it added that northern reasoning about slavery was but part and parcel of northern religious anarchy evidenced by the rise of new cults, and the trend toward liberal theology, higher criticism, skepticism, and atheism.[3]

From the one Book defenders and opponents of slavery reached opposite conclusions, partly by antagonistic criteria of selection and partly by dissimilar principles of exegesis. The North usually appealed to the teachings of the New Testament, the South to verses of the Old. The North used what might be described as a liberal, modernistic interpretation; the South denied the existence of any authority in religious matters other than the Bible, and it insisted on word for word literalism. Although a very small part of the Bible was marshaled in the slavery controversy, the vehemence and volume of the dispute were so great that there seemed to be sectional differences in interpretating the entire Book. The South became convinced that it was adhering to the strict letter of religious law. Its attitude toward the Bible was like its attitude toward the Constitution; it claimed to respect the form of the law in both cases, and it charged the North with disregard for Christian as well as constitutional law.[4]

The apologists of the Old South seem to have exhausted their legal energies interpreting and defending the Constitution and the Bible, for they wrote very little about the southerner's attitude toward the body of common and statutory law that regulates man's daily relations with man. Because of this lack of a body of expressed opinion, other indices must be sought. An important indication of attitude is, of course, action; and, according to a number of witnesses, the southerner's life was made exciting by a high proportion of street fights, duels, harsh treatment of slaves, quickness to resent insults, and the common practice of carrying pistols and other weapons.[5] But it is unwise to accept all this evidence as unqualified proof of southern lawlessness. Some southerners have been known to give free reign to imagination when entertaining gullible strangers, and antisouthern abolitionists have shown equal and less innocent inventiveness in circulating atrocity stories concerning the land of slavery. Because of these streams of misinformation it is difficult to tell whether the southerner acted more or less lawlessly than other Americans.

Waiving any attempt to determine the southerner's attitude toward state law by the quantity of his illegal acts, there yet remain certain forces that must be reckoned with. In the first place, the South doubtless inherited its share of the frontier trait of personal law enforcement, which is sometimes called lawlessness. Some parts of it had been settled less than a generation when the Civil War began, while older settlements in pine barrens and mountain coves were in a sense retarded frontiers, relatively out of reach of sheriff and court. But in this respect the South was not unique. The frontier is supposed to have a lawless effect on all American society, and, generally speaking, the South at any given time was neither nearer to nor farther from the frontier than other parts of the United States. It is therefore difficult to suppose that the South had inherited more than its share of frontier lawlessness.

But what of those parts of the South where the frontier influence had faded into the relatively distant past, areas such as the Carolina low country, tidewater Virginia, the Kentucky bluegrass, and the lower Mississippi Valley, where age and conservatism and the accumulation of economic wealth and of political influence had created the way of life that has been accepted as most typical of the Old South? Were the legal attitudes of these plantation regions different from those of the commercial, industrial, and urban areas that symbolized northern progress? I think the answer must be affirmative because ruralness, slavery, the plantation system, and the existence of a strong unwritten code operated in the plantation areas of the Old South to restrict the power of ordinary law and to enlarge the area of life in which man acts without reference to legal guidance. This is to say that the segment of life that was controlled by law was reduced in these dominant regions of the Old South; it is not equivalent to saying that law, within its restricted zone, was held in disrespect. Nevertheless, one can readily understand how a citizen of another civilization could fall into the error of thinking that law was held in disrespect because its jurisdiction was not as large as he was accustomed to in his own community. But before generalizing it will be well to consider the influence of these forces on law and legal attitudes.

Ruralness was not considered the equivalent of backwardness by the southerner, who might have summed up his ideal of social progress in the phrase "from frontier to plantation." In the realm of ideas as well as in actuality, the acme of southern civilization was rural. It is generally accepted that the countryman is something of an individualist who shapes his actions according to local custom and his own notions of how he should behave rather than according to the dictates of law books. Like the frontiersman, he is physically remote from law-enforcing agencies. If it be true that ruralness lightens the weight of law, the South was subjected to this influence not only because of the high per cent of its agricultural population, but also because of the prominence of country-men in economic, social, and political life. Furthermore, the planters probably had less contact with commercial law than did the business men of the cities. The reading of extant plantation records and communi-cations between planters and factors makes one wonder whether any other business of equal size has been run with as few precise records and as little commercial and legal paper as was the southern plantation.

Slavery also affected legal customs and attitudes. Although attention is being directed in this paper to those years shortly before the Civil War, when the southern mind had long felt the influence of distinctive southern institutions, it is significant that the influence of slavery upon those who owned slaves was recognized very early. It was the opinion of eighteenth century observers that the introduction of slavery had made Virginians "haughty and jealous of their liberties, and so impatient of restraint that they could hardly bear the thought of being controlled by any superior power."[6] George Mason, one of the wisest sons of Old Virginia, declared in the Federal Constitutional Convention that "every master of slaves is born a petty tyrant."[7] According to Thomas Nelson Page, the Virginia gentleman was imbued with "a certain pride based on self-respect and consciousness of power."[8] Horace S. Fulkerson, who was thoroughly familiar with life in the lower Mississippi Valley, stated that the planters of that region were "arbitrary, self-willed, and dicta-torial," and that even from their equals "they could illy brook contra-dictions and opposition."[9] And Alexis de Tocqueville concluded that slavery "has modified the character and changed the habits of the natives of the South. . . . The citizen of the Southern States of the Union is in-vested with a sort of domestic dictatorship, from his earliest years; the first notion he acquires in life is that he is born to command."[10]

Slavery must have affected the planter's attitude toward law, for in a measure slavery put him above the law. On his own estate he was lawgiver, executive, and judge. In respect to the economic and social life of his slaves—work, food, clothing, housing, marriage, divorce, and religion—his word was final. He possessed the power normally exercised by the state in many kinds of cases, such as slander, assault and battery, larceny, and burglary. Law books gave him no guidance in settling important questions. But this silence of the law does not seem to have disturbed him, for even when it spoke clearly the slaveholder sometimes paid no heed. For example, if a slave stabbed a Negro belonging to another master, the neighboring planters might settle the difficulty without going to court.[11] This illustrates the fact that the slaveowner, while exercising the great power granted to him by the state, sometimes took yet more power. Occasionally the state even gave its blessing to such encroachments upon the state law. The South Carolina Court of Appeals once remarked, " 'A judicious freedom in the administration of our police laws for the lower order must always have respect for the confidence which the law reposes in the discretion of the master.' "[12] A disapproving southerner summed up the whole process by saying that slavery was " 'degrading the law by putting the authority of the master above it.' "[13] This was correct, for southern states left the slaveowner free to exercise some of the powers that usually belong to the state, and even where there was law the planter sometimes either paid it scant attention or interpreted it with marked liberality.

The fact that Negroes could not bear witness against white men[14] excluded a large number of cases from the courts of the South; in such instances reparation had to be sought, if sought at all, beyond the pale of law. As the critics of slavery pointed out, this rule compelled Negroes to suffer illegal treatment in silence.[15] Less often recalled is the fact that white men, both individually and as a racial order, suffered unredressed injuries because of this prohibition. For example, a tobacco planter might have a part of his crop stolen by the white boatman to whom it had been entrusted for transportation from Lynchburg to Richmond, and the boatman's Negro assistants might tell all that had happened; yet, the planter knew that it would be useless to enter suit because the Negroes could not testify in court against the white thief.[16] Similarly, when a Mississippi slave was dangerously wounded by a white man, his master could not get legal redress either for his slave's physical suffering or for his own economic loss unless he could secure some evidence other than the word of the wounded Negro.[17] If Negroes and white men joined in an insurrectionary plot, as they did in Louisiana in 1840, and if the conspirators were discovered and frightened into testifying against each other, the courts could sentence the slaves to death. In fact, at least three were executed. But because Negro testimony could not be admitted by the court, the white conspirators could not be convicted.[18]

These are three instances of the kinds of injuries that white men and white society could not redress through court action because the available testimony was not admitted to the courtroom. When it is remembered that one third of the South's population was thus incompetent, one may well suppose that a multitude of similar injuries created a constant urge toward the discovery of some means, which had to be extralegal, for securing substantial justice. Thus, the exclusion of Negro testimony, the rural pattern of life, the great authority of the planter, and, as will be noted presently, certain characteristics of the southern social order, and its code, all united to restrict the segment of life ruled by state law,[19] thereby creating within the South, even in the oldest and most cultivated parts of it, an attitude toward law that was much like that of the frontiersman. Geographical distance kept the full force of the law from touching the westerner; the social order diminished the force of law in the South. But the resulting attitudes toward law were too similar for easy distinction. For instance, was Andrew Jackson's mother speaking from a western or a southern pattern of thought when she gave her son the following advice: " 'Never tell a lie, nor take what is not your own, nor sue anybody for slander or assault and battery. *Always settle them cases yourself!*' "[20]

How did the southerner's attitude toward the laws of his state compare with his insistence upon a literal, close observance of the Constitution and the Bible? While he did not profess disrespect for state law, neither did he praise it. The planter simply went through life under the assumption that a relatively large number of his deeds had to be performed out past the margin of written law in what might be called a state of nature. To northern eyes this condition looked like an approach to anarchy and chaos; but planters thought their actions were no more lawless than the operations of a court of equity.[21] Although it might be debated whether the southerner's life was much better or worse than contemporary life in the most litigious parts of New England, it is more profitable at the moment to remark that the extralegal, though usually not illegal, areas of life in the South convinced many onlookers that here was a land where law was frequently broken and commonly held in contempt. It is not surprising that these observers were puzzled by the contrast between the southerner's reverence for the Constitution and the Bible and his apparent disdain for some of the laws of his state.

In those relatively large expanses of life that were not ruled by the written law the southerner did not live in a legal vacuum. Instead he found guidance, particularly in the field of personal relationships, in a fourth kind of law: his unwritten code. Some of the sources of this body of compulsive rules were ideas of social organization imported into Virginia and the Carolinas by colonists who were familiar with the pattern of life of the English gentry of the seventeenth and eighteenth centuries;[22] contacts with the military punctilio of French and British army officers, especially at the time of the American Revolution;[23] the remembrance of chivalric ballads;[24] the reading of romantic novels such as those of Sir Walter Scott;[25] and the tradition, which evolved in later years, that southern planters were descended from the aristocracy of Europe and should therefore live in the manner of their legendary ancestors.[26] In addition to these European heritages and influences, the social customs and mores of the Old South were affected by vestiges of the frontier practice of personal law enforcement and by certain characteristics of the planters. They were a dominant class, they were accustomed to the exercise of great authority, and some of them had the means to live like aristocrats. In parts of the Old South, more than anywhere else in the United States, countrymen had the wealth requisite for living on a high level of civilization.

A thorough understanding of the code of the Old South is difficult for several reasons. It has been much romanticized, especially by postbellum writers of fiction and memoirs, it varied somewhat from place to place, its tenets were not the same for all classes of society, it suffered infractions like other laws, and it was too complex to be learned except by a lifetime of living under its sway. It is possible that those who knew it best did not explain it because they thought it would survive longer if the uninitiated were left in their ignorance. When Thomas Nelson Page wrote: "To be a Virginia gentleman was the first duty; it embraced being a Christian and all the other virtues,"[27] he was suggesting the existence of knowledge rather than revealing it. An old family retainer once condemned a recently employed tutor with the remark: "Lord, what sort of a man is this master is got to teach his children! He don't even know how to get on a horse!" Now, although riding a horse was not in itself supremely important, it was an outward symbol of a way of life. The old Negro's remark was but a way of saying that this tutor was ignorant of other things that were exceedingly important. As one of the pupils later remarked more directly but no more informatively about this pedestrian teacher, he was "very ignorant of a thousand things we thought a gentleman ought to know."[28]

While each of the social groups in the Old South had customs and rules of conduct, the code became more complex and emphatic among the planters and their associates. Here was a relatively small group of men maintaining a superior position out of all proportion to their numerical power. They were not only claiming and holding a place of economic, social, and racial superiority above the millions of Negro slaves, but economic and to some extent social superiority above the poor whites, small farmers, artisans, and schoolteachers. Furthermore, they were exercising in national councils greater power than the population of the South warranted.

Each of these superior positions was held in the face of a constant threat by the subordinate forces. The planter class could have been destroyed by revolt of the slaves, by votes of the nonslaveholding southerners, or by the North. Nor were the planters blind to these dangers. The potential hostility held them together and required each member to defend the group and to conceal dissensions within it from envious and critical eyes. Self-interest as well as *noblesse oblige* required the planter to live in accordance with certain unwritten rules.[29]

Although it is impossible to state the code of the Old South with either fullness or precision, and although the code was imperfectly obeyed, perhaps some of its rules should be set forth because, being the ideals of a society, they indicate something of the nature of that society. Among the things that a gentleman of the Old South was expected to be, to understand, and to perform were these.[30] He must uphold the southern way of life by close observance of a complex body of rules of social and racial relationships. For example, even when performing acts of kindness to subordinates, familiarity must be shunned. Toward an equal a gentleman should be courteous. He professed no knowledge of how to behave toward superiors, for he denied the existence of any with the exception of the ladies. To these he must show perfect courtesy and always defer to their opinions. The gentleman's deference, however, was protected from too great strain because the ladies were expected to avoid expressing opinions on all subjects, such as politics, that lay in the realm of masculine jurisdiction.

Believing that southern life was well-nigh perfect, a southern gentleman was under no compulsion to change things. From this it followed that he had no public duty other than to keep society going in its accustomed way. Lacking the New Englander's zeal for improvement and reform, he could enjoy rest with a clear conscience. Thus it is that the southerner was the only American of his and possibly any generation to whom leisure was not a sin. He was interested in being rather than in becoming. He thought it was more important in the business world for a man to maintain poise than to sacrifice dignity for wealth. Increasing mortgages and other evidences of economic failure were no disgrace even when brought about by gross inattention to business. According to his code it was bad form to intrude business matters into social life as by boasting of hard work in pursuit of wealth or by discussing money and prices except of such quasipublic commodities as cotton, tobacco, and slaves. When his leisureliness and contentment with things-as-they-were were characterized as laziness, he countered by scorning the aimless bustle and hurry of urban life.[31] There was satire rather than kindly humor in his remark that New Englanders could not wear frock coats because they whisked around corners so fast the tails were snapped off.

The southern gentleman was expected to be truthful, an obligation that was not difficult of fulfillment by one who denied being accountable to superiors. The code required him to be brave, and skilled in managing horses and handling firearms. He must be willing to risk life itself in defense of his own good name or that of a member of his family.[32] As long as the Old South lived, duels were fought despite criticism of prominent southerners, abuse of the institution by adventurers, and a decline in dueling elsewhere in the United States.

The nondemocratic form of southern society was partly responsible for the survival of the duel, which is a phenomenon of aristocratic rather than democratic societies. Men may fight on the frontiers of Texas or California before law has arrived in full force. But these combats in the democratic society of the frontier are usually not conducted according to the code duello. In contrast, the duel is usually found in the upper classes of a complex society; it is found not in the broad base of the social pyramid but in the small apex—landed gentry, feudal barons, army officers—that towers above the cloud of laws that blanket and hold in place the lower orders. Therefore, gentlemen would challenge only gentlemen. To punish an insulting inferior, one used not a pistol or sword but a cane or a horsewhip.

In the practice of the duel certain cardinal ideas were implicit. First, a man's good name was more important than physical well-being, which is to say that in the South it was considered as brutal and uncivilized to call a man a liar as it was to bruise or cut his body. Secondly, questions of personal honor and integrity could not be decided by the judicial processes of democratic government; hence, slander, libel, and some other indignities could be better adjudicated with pistols in a quiet grove in the presence of only a few gentlemen than in the courtroom before a jury of small farmers, clerks, and mechanics. Furthermore, since the duel was restricted to gentlemen, a challenge carried along with its danger a certain recognition of social superiority and responsibility.

The fighting of duels and the imposition of other penalties sanctioned by the code was indeed looked upon as something of a social responsibility. A man fought because society demanded that certain issues be so adjudicated; and if one refused to obey this social demand, society would apply such complete ostracism that the offender would "never again be permitted to join gentlemen even in a fox hunt. He's utterly out of it."[33] Doubtless many a man decided that he must fight because he was conscious of this social pressure. The upper crust of society demanded the duel because it dared not submit all of its controversies to the adjudication of a democracy.[34]

This characteristic of the Old South, namely, that a man was conscious of belonging to and being a part of a thing larger than himself, has impressed such novelists as John Esten Cooke, Thomas Nelson Page, George Cary Eggleston, Joseph Hergesheimer, Stark Young, and Ellen Glasgow more than it has historians. It is natural that novelists should be sensitive to the organic nature of southern society because, as Henry Seidel Canby has written in an essay about Miss Glasgow: "The great subject for the novel since its beginning in the eighteenth century has been manners, and when the novels have been also great these manners have been no superficies of behavior, but a code, a habitual philosophy of living according to which men and women proceed."[35]

This sense of belonging to a definitely ordered society may have been the reason why southerners were the first Americans to make such use of the word "sociology."[36] But most of the citizens of the Old South instead of speculating about the nature of their society found their places within it and lived in harmony with its conventions. Naturally, those who enjoyed the favored places in society were most opposed to change. Their supreme patriotism was to their social order. Their highest law was the body of customs and rules that maintained this way of life. This was their code; this was the unwritten constitution of the Old South.

Most of the actions required of the southerner by his code were the host of undistinguished and innocuous deeds that make up the fabric of everyday life. But now and again the code required a man to requite a personal insult either by a duel or by some less ceremonious form of violence. This tendency to defend personal honor extralegally, and indeed illegally, seems to have been more prevalent in the South than in the North; it does not necessarily follow that notherners were more prone to take such questions into court. Although northerners declared that dueling was proof of southern lawlessness, southerners who approved this custom reasoned otherwise. Their statement of the case might be reconstructed as follows: in case of insult the code of honor required action; the state code enjoined submission. Here was a conflict of law. Therefore, the individual had to decide which body of law applied to the case, and if he decided in favor of the code of honor he was simply transferring the case from state jurisdiction to the jurisdiction of the unwritten code.

What then is the meaning of the southerner's legal attitudes? In the first place, they were reflections of important aspects of southern history. They might be described as rationalizations in legal terms of fundamental southern interests both national and local. The southerner's attitude toward the Constitution and the Bible was produced by his conflict with the North over slavery and kindred issues. His attitudes toward the written laws of the state and the unwritten code evolved out of southern domestic history. For instance, the occasional conflict between these two imperatives over questions of honor may be viewed as a product of the struggle of an aristocratic social order to maintain its position and power against the enlarging power of the democracy; a conflict of laws arose where the customs of the few clashed with the laws of the many.[37]

In the second place, the southerner's set of legal attitudes distinguished him to some extent from other Americans. The northerner, for example, living in a different social system and possessing dissimilar economic goals from those of the South, arranged the imperatives in a totally different order. To him a literal interpretation of the biblical sanctions of slavery and of the constitutional sanctions of slavery and of states' rights was undesirable; to him the meaning and the potency of the code were incomprehensible; but, on the other hand, he emphasized the sanctity of ordinary law because of its importance in the equalitarian democracy of the North.

In the third place, the southerner did not defend all forms of law with equal vigor nor did he place them all on the same level of importance. Neither did the northerner. But here the similarity ends; for in deciding which bodies of law deserved literal interpretation and strict application and which ought to be loosely interpreted and imperfectly enforced, North and South were in complete disagreement. Because men of both sections praised certain laws, all could consider themselves as law-abiding and therefore good men; but because they disagreed over the laws that ought to be given most respect, each thought the other was peopled with lawless and therefore bad men. To the northerner the southerner seemed to be dishonest, and the reverse was also true, because each was boasting of his respect for some laws while he was actually showing disrespect for other laws. Naturally, then, each concluded that it was futile to continue negotiations with a people who refused to respect legal obligations. By such means sectional differences in legal attitudes became something more than passive reflections of basic divergencies; these attitudes became active in increasing the antagonism between the sections.[38]

Examples of sectional differences in legal attitudes can be seen in a number of critical points in American history. For instance, when John C. Calhoun framed his powerful proslavery resolutions for presentation in the Senate in 1837, he was conscious of the fact that slavery could be and indeed was being judged by reference to several different authorities such as divine law, the moral law, and the Constitution. In his resolutions he therefore insisted that congressional legislation respecting slavery in the territories and in the District of Columbia should be framed with reference solely to the Constitution and that considerations of its alleged sinfulness or immorality should be excluded. The implications of this pronouncement could be discussed at much length, but such a discussion would be a digression from the point that is here of most significance. Calhoun was saying, in effect, that Federal legislation must be framed with reference to no more than one ultimate authority which was neither moral law nor divine law but the Constitution of the United States.[39]

One other illustration must suffice, and it will consist in a hurried review of the Brooks-Sumner affair. The first part of this sensational episode was a speech delivered in the Senate on May 19–20, 1856, by Charles Sumner, senator from Massachusetts, denouncing slaveowners in general and South Carolinians in particular. It was a studiously learned speech, replete with classical and historical allusions; at the same time it abounded in such coarse and opprobrious terms as harlot, mistress, rape, pirate, tyrant, falsifier, assassin, thug, swindler, and criminal. Much of the abuse was directed personally to Andrew Pickens Butler, senior senator from South Carolina, who was absent from the Senate while Sumner was making his attack. Certain aspects of this speech are significant. Sumner grossly and without provocation insulted Butler; in so doing he acted deliberately, for he had prepared his speech carefully with the purpose of making it "the most thorough philippic ever uttered in a legislative body";[40] finally, he was accusing slaveholders of being lawless.

The sequel to this tirade occurred two days later. Following an early adjournment, Sumner remained in the Senate chamber writing letters when Preston S. Brooks, a congressman from South Carolina, walked up to him and said: "Mr. Sumner, I have read your speech carefully, and with as much calmness as I could be expected to read such a speech. You have libeled my State, and slandered my relation, who is aged and absent, and I feel it to be my duty to punish you for it." Thereupon, with a cane, he struck Sumner over the head, and he continued with rapid, hard blows until the cane was broken and Sumner was bloody and insensible. This action of Brooks also deserves close scrutiny. Deliberation rather than quick anger is indicated by the fact that after hearing oral reports of Sumner's speech he took time to examine the printed record, he discussed the question with his friends, and he sought, though vainly, an encounter outside the Senate chamber. During the two days that were thus consumed he seems to have felt no uncertainty as to whether he should punish Sumner, nor is there an indication that he at any time considered challenging him to a duel. He felt that he ought not to call Sumner to account in the presence of ladies, and because some were present in the Senate gallery he waited until they departed before attacking Sumner. A question to which he gave some thought was whether he should use horsewhip, cowhide, or cane, all of which were weapons of dishonor. Citizens of Massachusetts, judging from their subsequent remarks, did not understand as thoroughly as did South Carolinians the delicate shades of meaning implicit in Brooks's decisions.[41]

Undoubtedly, the Brooks-Sumner affair was an expression of the angry passions of 1856 and a forerunner of yet more hatred in the years to come. But it was more than this, for the form in which anger is expressed often indicates much about the characteristics of the actor and about the mores of the society in which he lives. Brooks and Sumner were each viewed by their respective constituencies as worthy representatives: Sumner of the culture and learning of Massachusetts; Brooks of the chivalry of South Carolina. Following this encounter, the part that each had played was applauded by his people. The words "lawful" and "lawless" seemed to change their meaning as one crossed the boundary between North and South; for acts that the northerner branded as lawless were approved by South Carolinians, words that the southerner considered lawless met with no apparent disapproval in Massachusetts.

While peoples of all ages have faced the alternative of the ancient Hebrews: "Choose you this day whom ye will serve,"[42] this question presented itself on certain occasions to individual men in the Old South. At such times those who had never worn judicial robes had to decide which of the various imperatives they ought to obey, and at these moments of decision they often acted as if every man had been empowered to act as a court of last resort for determining certain types of questions. Perhaps, then, it was fitting that the southerner should have found the issue of 1861 stated in the form of legal alternatives.

The ordinances of secession placed the laws of state and of nation in such diametric opposition that no man could obey both. Facing this great conflict of laws each southerner assumed full power of judicial review and rendered his own decision as to which law he should obey.

Chapter VI

The Fundamental Cause
of the Civil War:
Egocentric Sectionalism

FRANK L. OWSLEY

IN THIS meeting of the Southern Historical Association great emphasis has been placed upon a re-examination of numerous phases of our history relating to the Civil War.* While several papers have dealt with certain forces which helped bring about the Civil War, none has attempted a general synthesis of causes. This synthesis has been the task assumed by the retiring president of the Association.

Before attempting to say what were the causes of the American Civil War, first let me say what were not the causes of this war. Perhaps the most beautiful, the most poetic, the most eloquent statement of what the Civil War was not fought for is Lincoln's Gettysburg Address. That address will live as long as Americans retain their love of free government and personal liberty; and yet in reassessing the causes of the Civil War, the address whose essence was that the war was being fought so "that government of the people, by the people and for the people shall not perish from the earth" is irrelevant. Indeed, this masterpiece of eloquence has little if any value as a statement of the basic principles underlying the war.

The Civil War was not a struggle on the part of the South to destroy free government and personal liberty nor on the part of the North to preserve them. Looked at from the present perspective of the world-wide attempt of the totalitarians to erase free governments and nations living under such governments from the face of the earth, the timeworn

*Presented in Charleston, South Carolina, November 8, 1940.

stereotype that the South was attempting the destruction of free government and the North was fighting to preserve it seems very unrealistic and downright silly. In the light of the present-day death struggle between freedom and the most brutal form of despotism, the Civil War, as far as the issue of free government was involved, was a sham battle. Indeed, both northern and southern people in 1861 were alike profoundly attached to the principles of free government. A systematic study of both northern and southern opinion as expressed in their newspapers, speeches, diaries, and private letters, gives irrefutable evidence in support of this assertion. Their ideology was democratic and identical. However, theoretical adherence to the democratic principles, as we know all too well in these days of plutocratic influences in our political life, is not sufficient evidence that democratic government exists. I believe that I shall not be challenged in the assertion that the economic structure of a section or a nation is the foundation upon which its political structure must rest. For this reason, therefore, it will be necessary to know what the economic foundations of these sections were. Was the economic structure of the North such as to support a political democracy in fact as well as in form? And was the economic structure of the South such as to permit the existence of free government? Time does not permit an extended treatment of this subject; it will be possible only to point out certain conclusions based upon recent research. By utilizing the county tax books and the unpublished census reports a group of us conducting a co-operative undertaking have been able to obtain a reasonably accurate and specific picture of wealth structure of the antebellum South, and to some extent that of the other sections. We have paid particular attention to the distribution of capital wealth and the ownership of the means of production. As has been generally known the Northwest was agricultural and its population predominantly small farmers, though a considerable minority were large farmers comparable with the southern planters. It seems that in 1860 about 80 per cent of the farmers in the Old Northwest were landowners. A fairly large fraction of the remaining farm population in that area were either squatters upon public lands or were the members of landowning families. Only a small per cent were renters. In those areas farther west the ownership of land was not as widespread because the farmers had not yet made good their titles to the lands that they had engrossed. Taken as a whole the people of the Northwest were economically self-sufficient. They could not be subjected to economic coercion and, hence, they were politically free. Their support of free government—as they understood it—was effective.

The northeastern section of the United States had already assumed its modern outlines of a capitalistic-industrial society where the means of production were either owned or controlled by relatively few. That is to say, New England and the middle states were fast becoming in essence a plutocracy whose political ideology was still strongly democratic; but the application of this democratic ideology was being seriously hampered by the economic dependence of the middle and lower classes upon those who owned the tools of production. The employee unprotected by government supervision or by strong labor organizations was subject in exercising his political rights to the undue influence of the employer.

To sum up: the economic structure of the Northwest was an adequate foundation for free government; but that of the East, though still supporting democratic ideals, was often too weak to sustain these ideals in actual government.

Turning to the South which was primarily agricultural we find the situation completely contradictory to what has usually been assumed. While the plutocracy of the East owned or controlled the means of production in industry and commerce, the so-called slave oligarchy of the South owned scarcely any of the land outside the black belt and only about 25 per cent of the land in the black belt. Actually, the basic means of production in the black belt and in the South as a whole was well distributed among all classes of the population. The overwhelming majority of southern families in 1860 owned their farms and livestock. About 90 per cent of the slaveholders and about 70 per cent of the nonslaveholders owned the land which they farmed. The bulk of slaveholders were small farmers and not oligarchs. While taken together they owned more slaves and more land than the big planters, taken individually the majority of slaveholders owned from one to four slaves and less than three hundred acres of land. The nonslaveholders, 70 per cent of whom, as we have noted, were landowners, were not far removed economically from the small slaveholders to whom we have just referred. While the majority of slaveholders owned from one to three hundred acres of land, 80 per cent of the landowning nonslaveholders owned from one to two hundred acres of land and 20 per cent owned from two hundred to a thousand. Let me repeat: the basic fact disclosed in an analysis of the economic structure of the South, based upon the unpublished census reports and tax books, is that the overwhelming majority of white families in the South, slaveholders and nonslaveholders, unlike the industrial population of the East, owned the means of production. In other words, the average southerner like the average westerner possessed economic independence; and the only kind of influence that could be exercised over his political franchise by the slave oligarchy was a strictly persuasive kind. The South, then, like the Northwest, not only held strongly to the democratic ideology but also had a sound economic foundation for a free government.

If the destruction of democratic government by the South and its preservation by the North were not the causes of the Civil War, what then were the causes? The surface answer to this question is that in 1861 the southern people desired and attempted to establish their independence and thereby to disrupt the old Union; and that the North took up arms to prevent the South from establishing this independence and to preserve the Union. Looking immediately behind this attempt of the South to establish a separate government, and of the North to prevent it, we discover a state of mind in both sections which explains their conduct. This state of mind may be summed up thus: by the spring of 1861 the southern people felt it both abhorrent and dangerous to continue to live under the same government with the people of the North. So profound was this feeling among the bulk of the southern population that they were prepared to fight a long and devastating war to accomplish a separation. On the other hand, the North was willing to fight a war to retain their reluctant fellow citizens under the same government with themselves.

The cause of that state of mind which we may well call war psychosis lay in the sectional character of the United States. In other words, the Civil War had one basic cause: sectionalism. But to conclude that sectionalism was the cause of the Civil War, and at the same time insist —as has usually been done—that the Civil War was the climax of an irrepressible conflict, is to seem to accept a pessimistic view of the future of the United States. For if the antebellum conflict was irrepressible and the Civil War unavoidable, we are faced with future irrepressible conflicts, future civil wars, and ultimate disintegration of the nation into its component sections. I say this because I do not see any way save some cosmic cataclysm by which sectionalism can be erased from the political, economic, racial, and cultural maps of the United States. Our national state was built, not upon the foundations of a homogeneous land and people, but upon geographical sections inhabited severally by provincial, self-conscious, self-righteous, aggressive, and ambitious populations of varying origins and diverse social and economic systems; and the passage of time and the cumulative effects of history have accentuated these sectional patterns.

Before accepting the possibility of future wars and national disintegration as inevitable because of the irrepressible conflict between permanent sections, let me hasten to say that there are two types of sectionalism: there is that egocentric, destructive sectionalism where conflict is always irrepressible; and there is that constructive sectionalism where good will prevails—two types as opposite from one another as good is opposite from evil, as the benign is from the malignant. It was the egocentric, the destructive, the evil, the malignant type of sectionalism that destroyed the Union in 1861, and that would do so again if it existed over a long period of time.

Before discussing that destructive sectionalism which caused the Civil War, some observations should be made of the constructive type, since, as I have suggested, the very nature of the American state makes one or the other type of sectionalism inevitable. The idea of either good or bad sectionalism as an enduring factor in American national life has received scant consideration by historians as a rule, either because they, who have usually been of the North, have desired to justify the conduct of their section on occasion as being the manifestation of nationalism when in truth it was sectionalism writ large; or because, and more important, they have apparently been unable to reconcile sectionalism with nationalism.

Since sectionalism from the very nature of our country must remain a permanent and basic factor in our national life, we should look it in the face and discriminate between the good and the bad features. Above all else, we should recognize the fact that sectionalism when properly dealt with, far from being irreconcilable with nationalism, is its strongest support. It is only the malignant, destructive type that conflicts with nationalism or loyalty to the the national state or empire. Great Britain once failed to make this distinction and to grasp the fact that the American colonials could be good Americans and good Britishers at the same time, and the result was the loss of the American colonies. After the lesson learned from the American Revolution, the British mind grasped the fact that good Canadians or good Australians are all the better Britishers because of their provincial or—may I say?—sectional loyalty. Provincialism, dominionism, and, in the case of the United States, sectionalism, far from excluding nationalism, when properly recognized and not constantly frowned upon, and the interests of sections ignored and their ambitions frustrated, are powerful supports of nationalism. Such provincialism or sectionalism becomes a national asset. It is a brake upon political centralization and possible despotism. It has proven and will prove to be, if properly directed, a powerful force in preserving free institutions. It gives color, variety, and vitality to all segments of the national state. Because of this vitality in all its parts, the United States, unlike France whose lifeblood seems to flow entirely through Paris, would prove a difficult country to subjugate by a foreign enemy, and its government and society more difficult, if not impossible, to overthrow by violent revolution. It is because Great Britain has, as the result of her lesson learned from the American Revolution, fostered a good sectionalism within her empire, that she has baffled the orderly mind of the Germans and defied conquest. By loosening the ties that bind the component parts of this straggling union of colonies and dominions, Great Britain has made these bonds all the stronger. She and her commonwealth of nations thus live in all their parts. Tragically, the American people failed to learn adequately the very lesson that they so thoroughly taught Great Britain: that local differences and attachments were natural, desirable, and formed the very rootbed of patriotism; indeed, that such differences, when given decent recognition, greatly strengthened nationalism and the national state. It was this failure to recognize or respect local differences and interests, in other words, the failure to recognize sectionalism as a fundamental fact of American life, that contributed most to the development of that kind of sectionalism which destroyed national unity and divided the nation.

There were three basic manifestations of that egocentric sectionalism which disrupted the Union in 1861. First, was the habit of the dominant section—that is, the section which had the larger share in the control of the Federal government—of considering itself the nation, its people the American people, its interests the national interests; in other words, the habit of considering itself the sole possessor of nationalism, when, indeed, it was thinking strictly in terms of one section; and conversely the habit of the dominant section of regarding the minority group as factional, its interests and institutions and way of life as un-American, unworthy of friendly consideration, and even the object of attack.

The second manifestation of this egocentric sectionalism that led to the Civil War was the perennial attempt of a section to gain or maintain its political ascendency over the Federal government by destroying the sectional balance of power which, both New England and the South maintained, had been established by the three-fifths ratio clause in the Federal Constitution.

The third and most dangerous phase of this sectionalism, perhaps the *sine qua non* of the Civil War, was the failure to observe what in international law is termed the comity of nations, and what we may by analogy designate as the comity of sections. That is, the people in one section failed in their language and conduct to respect the dignity and self-respect of the people in the other section. These three manifestations of sectionalism were so closely related that at times they can be segregated only in theory and for the sake of logical discussion. Indeed, as I have suggested, all were manifestations of that egocentric sectionalism that caused a section to regard itself as the nation.

Let me call to your mind some familiar facts of American history that illustrate each of these phases of sectionalism. During the first twelve years of the government under the Federal Constitution, the old commercial-financial aristocracy of New England, with the aid of the same classes of people scattered throughout the urban centers of the seaboard, controlled the national government through the instrumentality of the Federalist party. An analysis of the chief measures of the Federalist regime and of the mental processes behind their enactments—as disclosed in speeches and letters and newspaper editorials —reveals the dominant section, New England, with its compact, homogeneous population, its provincial outlook, thinking, talking, and acting as if it were the United States; its way of life, its economic system, and its people the only truly American; while the remainder of the country, the people, and their interests and ways of life were alien and un-American. Most of the laws enacted during the control of the New England Federalists were considered by the South and much of the middle states as being for the sole benefit of the commercial and banking interests of the East, and as injurious, even ruinous, to the agricultural sections. In order to give constitutional sanction to these centralizing, sectional laws, the Federalist party under the brilliant leadership of Alexander Hamilton evolved the doctrine of implied powers, which seemed to the agricultural sections, now under the leadership of Thomas Jefferson, to be pulling the foundations from under constitutional government. This sectional and centralizing policy of the New England-dominated Federalist party culminated in the Alien and Sedition Laws which were met by the Virginia and Kentucky Resolutions. These resolutions may be regarded as a campaign document to be used in ousting the Federalists and New England from power. They were also a threat of the minority section to withdraw from the Union should Federalist New England continue in power and continue its policy of ignoring the agricultural sections of the country or of running roughshod over their interests.

The overthrow of New England's control of the national government by the Jeffersonian party in 1800 resulted in a twenty-four-year regime of the Virginia dynasty, during fifteen years of which—that is, until after the War of 1812—the government was distinctly dominated by the South and Southwest. If Hamilton had been positive that the welfare of the nation depended upon reinforcing and maintaining by special government favor the capitalistic system of the East, Jefferson was more positive that democratic and constitutional government and the welfare of the American people depended upon maintaining the supremacy in government and society of a landowning farmer-people whose center of gravity was in the South and middle states. To Jefferson, commerce, finance, and industry were only necessary evils to be maintained purely as conveniences and handmaidens of agriculture. Such doctrinaire conception of government and society boded ill for New England; and the period from 1801 until the end of the War of 1812 was filled with laws, decrees, and executive acts that seemed to threaten the economic and social existence of that section. One measure in particular seemed to be destined to end forever in favor of the South the sectional balance of power, namely, the purchase of Louisiana. During all this time New England's standing committee on secession, the Essex Junto, was maneuvering to bring about the withdrawal of New England from the Federal Union; nor is there any sufficient reason to suppose that it would not have eventually succeeded in the disruption of the Union had not the ending of the war with Great Britain brought a termination of the policies that seemed so detrimental to the social and economic interests of the East; and had not the outburst of genuine nationalism at the victorious ending of the war actually resulted in the adoption of measures distinctly favorable to New England. The point that I wish to emphasize is that the rise to power of the South and middle states was marked by the same egocentric sectionalism as characterized the dominance of Federalist New England: the agricultural sections thought of themselves as the United States, thought of the American farmers as the only simon-pure Americans, and looked upon the interests of the agricultural population as the national interests.

It is not the ambition of this paper to attempt a summary of the antebellum history of the United States; but simply to use the twelve-year sectional regime of the Federalists and about the same length of rule by the Jeffersonian party to illustrate that tendency of the dominant section to consider itself the United States and its people the American people, and by the same token ignore or treat with contempt the peculiar needs of the minority sections.

The second manifestation of that egocentric sectionalism which led to the American Civil War was, as you will recall, the attempt of one section to gain a permanent ascendency by destroying the sectional balance of power or permanently undermining the prestige of the other section. Let me pause for a moment, in discussing the overthrow of the balance of power, and review for you very briefly just how and why there had been an approximate balance of power established between the slaveholding and nonslaveholding states during the constitutional convention. The delegates to the convention, from both the northern and southern sections of the country, were unanimously in favor of a constitution that would establish a much stronger and more effective government than that which had so signally broken down under the Articles of Confederation. There was a fundamental difference, however, as to what specific powers should be granted to this new government. New England and the capitalistic segments of the middle states were above all else determined that the new government should be able to control foreign and interstate commerce and to make commercial treaties that could be enforced. The agricultural sections of the country looked with considerable disfavor upon such a grant of powers. The South was so much opposed that it quietly passed out the word that it would never enter a Union where commerce was so thoroughly controlled by the national government unless it were assured a position of approximate political equality in that government. Otherwise, the power over commerce would be used by the North, dominated by the East, for its sole benefit and to the detriment of agriculture and the South.

Finally, the balance of power was worked out by the technique of counting three-fifths of the slaves in apportioning representation in Congress and in the electoral college. This was called the three-fifths compromise between the North, which wanted to count all the slaves in apportioning direct taxes and none in apportioning representatives, and the South, which wanted to count all the slaves in making up representation and none in making up taxation. But an examination of the speeches and correspondence of the delegates indicates that it was also, and more important, a means of giving the South approximate equality in the Federal government in return for granting New England's profound desire to have the Federal government control interstate and international commerce.

That the sectional balance of power should be obtained by the process of counting three-fifths of the slaves in determining representation was a natural but unfortunate arrangement. It was natural inasmuch as the southerner regarded his slave as a human being and as part of the population; it was unfortunate in that it quickly identified the political influence of the South with the institution of slavery, and in doing so it went far toward engendering or increasing hostility in New England and finally in the whole North toward both slavery and the South.

As long as New England was able to dominate the Federal government there was no important opposition to the theoretical balance of power obtained by the three-fifths ratio; but when New England lost her status with the collapse of the Federalist party her leaders immediately seized upon the three-fifths ratio as the explanation. During the period that ended with the Hartford convention and the treaty of peace the New England leaders were unceasing in their attack upon "slave representation," as they called it. At the Hartford convention it formed the leading grievance. The convention demanded an unconditional repeal.

During this same time Jefferson purchased the Louisiana territory, not for the purpose of destroying the sectional balance of power, but complacent in the belief that it would do so. We thus behold, during the earlier Jeffersonian period, the spectacle of the agricultural South and the commercial East tampering with the sectional balance of power. Of course, permanent balance of power was impossible in a rapidly expanding country, and both sections must have realized that eventually the forces of nature would tip the balance in favor of one section or the other or in favor of a section not yet born. Such eventualities were regarded as remote and were not permitted to disturb the peace of mind. It was the overthrow of the sectional balance by artificial, political methods which caused uneasiness and wrath, for it indicated intersectional ill will or gross selfishness.

The Missouri controversy, 1819–20, marked the decline of the agitation by the Northeast to repeal the three-fifths ratio clause as a means of weakening the political power of the South and inaugurated the second and final phase of the struggle of the North to destroy by artificial methods the sectional balance of power. This second phase was to prevent the formation and admission into the Union of any more slave states, which meant, from the political and social point of view, the exclusion of southern states. While the demand for exclusion was based partly upon what we may call moral reasons, Rufus King and the other northern leaders in this debate were quite frank in asserting that the Missouri debate was a struggle between the slave and free states for political power.

The two phases of that sectionalism which led to the Civil War, while causing a slow accumulation of sectional grievances, were not marked during the thirty years prior to the Missouri debates by excessive ill will or serious disregard for the comity of sections. Indeed, up until the time of the Missouri debates, despite the rivalry of sections which almost disrupted the Union, there was maintained a certain urbanity and self-restraint on the part of the leaders of the rival sections; for as long as the founding fathers lived and exercised influence over public affairs, there seems to have been a common realization—indeed, a common recollection—that the nation had been founded upon the principle of mutual tolerance of sectional differences and mutual concessions; that the nation had been constructed upon the respect of each section for the institutions, opinions, and ways of life of the other sections. But the years laid the founding fathers low and their places were taken by a new and impatient generation who had no such understanding of the essence of national unity. The result was that urbanity, self-restraint, and courtesy—the ordinary amenities of civilized intercourse—were cast aside; and in their gracious place were substituted the crude, discourteous, and insulting language and conduct in intersectional relations now so familiar in the relations between the totalitarian nations and the so-called democracies. It was the Missouri debates in which intersectional comity was first violated; and it was the political leaders of the East, particularly the New Englanders and those of New England origin, who did it when they denounced in unmeasured terms slavery, the slaveholder, and southern society in general. It is noteworthy that the southern leaders, with the exception of one or two, including John Randolph, ignored this first violent, denunciatory, insulting language of the northerners during and immediately after the Missouri controversy; ignored them at least in that no reply in kind was made with the possible exception of two or three, including John Randolph, who demanded that the South withdraw from the Union before it was too late. The private correspondence of the southerners, however, reveals them as resentful and apprehensive of future bad relations with the North.

Ten years after the Missouri Compromise debates, the moral and intellectual leaders of the North, and notably those of New England origin, took up the language of abuse and vilification which the political leaders of that section had first employed in the Missouri debates. Quickly the political leaders resumed the tone of the Missouri controversy: and thus was launched the so-called antislavery crusade, but what in fact was a crusade against the southern people. For over three decades this attack upon slavery and the entire structure of southern society down to the custom of eating corn bread and turnip greens grew in volume and in violence. (A discussion of the motives behind this crusade would lead us far afield and into bitterly controversial questions. It does seem clear, however, that political and economic considerations were thoroughly mingled with the moral and religious objection to slavery.) One has to seek in the unrestrained and furious invective of the present totalitarians to find a near parallel to the language that the abolitionists and their political fellow travelers used in denouncing the South and its way of life. Indeed, as far as I have been able to ascertain, neither Dr. Goebbels nor Virginio Gayda nor Stalin's propaganda agents have as yet been able to plumb the depths of vulgarity and obscenity reached and maintained by George Bourne, Stephen Foster, Wendell Phillips, Charles Sumner, and other abolitionists of note. Let me use a few of these—most of them are too indecent to quote. Phillips characterized the South as "one great brothel, where half a million women are flogged to prostitution." Bourne went Phillips one better and estimated that there were a million slave women in the South who constituted "one vast harem where men-stealers may prowl, corrupt and destroy." However, Bourne was not satisfied with implicating the entire white male population of the South in the charge of miscegenation; he gave what he claimed were revolting examples of the same practice among the young white women of the South and insinuated that such practices were universal. Foster and Bourne both attacked the morality of the southern ministry. Bourne said that the pulpits of the South were often filled with "man stealing, girl selling, pimping and slave manufacturing preachers," and that the churches were "synagogues of Satan." It would be far better, he insisted, "to transfer the inmate from the state prison, and the pander from the brothel to the pulpit" than permit a southern minister "to teach us righteousness and purity" in a northern church. Foster in a book significantly entitled the *Brotherhood of Thieves* charged that the Methodist church was "more corrupt than any house of ill fame in New York," arguing that the fifty thousand adult female slaves who were members of that church "were inevitably doomed to lives of prostitution" under the penalty of being scourged to death. Foster, Bourne, Phillips, William Lloyd Garrison, Theodore Parker, indeed, most of the abolitionists put forward such attacks upon southern morality. No one was spared in this charge. All crimes were laid at the door of these people: they were kidnappers, manstealers, pimps, robbers, assassins, freebooters, much more "despicable than the common horse thief." Neither time nor good taste permits any real analysis of this torrent of coarse abuse; but let it be said again that nothing equal to it has been encountered in the language of insult used between the nations today— even those at war with one another.

This crusade against the South has often been brushed aside as the work of a few unbalanced fanatics. Such is not the case at all. The genuine abolitionists were few in number in the beginning; but just as radicalism today has touched so many of the intellectuals of the East, so did abolitionism touch the intellectuals of the East and of the North generally. So did it touch the moral and political leaders. The effects upon the minds of those millions who did not consider themselves abolitionists were profound. In time the average northerner accepted in whole or in part the abolitionist picture of southern people: they became monsters and their children were not children but young monsters. Such a state of mind is fertile soil for war. The effect upon the minds of the southern people was far more profound, since they were recipients of this niagara of insults and threats. To them the northern people were a combination of mad fanatics and cold-blooded political adventurers. As years passed slow and consuming fury took hold of the southern people; and this fury was combined with a deadly fear which John Brown's raid confirmed: a fear that most of the northern people not only hated the southern people but would willingly see them exterminated. This fear was further confirmed when such a kindly philosopher as Ralph Waldo Emerson approved of the incendiary, John Brown, by likening him to Jesus.

The political, intellectual, and moral leaders of the South did not remain silent under the abuse of the crusaders and the fellow travelers and well-wishers, but replied in a manner that added fuel to the roaring flames which were fast consuming the last vestiges of national unity. The language of insult which the so-called fire-eaters employed, however, was not usually coarse or obscene in comparison with the abolitionists'; it was urbane and restrained to a degree—but insulting. Thus in language of abuse and insult was jettisoned the comity of sections: And let me repeat that peace between sections as between nations is placed in jeopardy when one nation or one section fails to respect the self-respect of the people of another section or nation.

Chapter VII

The Colonial Status
of the South

B. B. KENDRICK

IF IT IS true that the South is "the Nation's No. 1 economic problem," the fundamental historical explanation of that condition is to be found in the fact that for more than three centuries this region, in greater or lesser degree, has occupied the status of a colony.[1] Generally colonials produce raw materials which they exchange on unfavorable terms with citizens of the imperial power for manufactured goods.* As a result they fall increasingly into debt to those with whom they trade. Meanwhile, the outside creditors often invest some, or all, of their balances in the colonial area. These investments in the old days were mostly in agricultural real estate, enterprises for trapping and fur trading, and companies for the exploitation of timber and mineral wealth. Outsiders also generally owned the means of transportation and collected the freight on incoming and outgoing traffic. In the past seventy-five years, outside investments, while continuing in some of the older forms, have gone into internal transportation and communication companies, urban real estate and mortgages thereon, financial organizations and—perhaps of greatest importance today—into manufacturing. To this general pattern the South has almost perfectly conformed. At the present time the productive property of this region is largely owned by persons living outside its bounds. The fact that the owners are citizens of the same sovereign nation as are the people of the South, has, in some manner, obscured the fact of the region's colonial status.

The purposes underlying this interpretative essay are: first, to suggest that the colonial status of the South might have been ended permanently

*Presented in Atlanta, Georgia, November 7, 1941.

90

by the American Revolution if, after that event, it had become an independent sovereignty instead of uniting with the Northeast in the United States of America under the Constitution of 1787; second, that having failed to take advantage of the opportunity offered by the so-called "Critical Period," it thereafter became too late to remedy the situation either by internal compromises or by secession; and third, to suggest that at present finance capitalism and imperialism hold the region in so firm a grip that no escape from the colonial status appears possible short of some catastrophic collapse of the whole imperialistic system.

Even as early as 1600, the rising middle classes in Great Britain were aware that it was a good deal more profitable to engage in manufacturing, shipping, and buying and selling than it was to produce raw materials. This awareness explains why persons of the middle class should have concerned themselves with the establishment of an American colonial empire. In the colonies the "superfluous" populations of England and other western European countries could be put to work producing raw materials which were sold at a low price to merchants, transported for a good profit by shipowners, fabricated with considerable gain to manufacturers, and resold at home, abroad, and to the colonists at a dear price, again by the merchants. It would be unfair to imagine for a moment that the gentlemen adventurers who established the London Company to carry into practical effect these ideas were in any sense parasitical. As a matter of fact, without their initiative, enterprise, and willingness to take a gambler's chance, the colonization of America would have been long delayed. History records that these first adventurers actually lost most of the money they advanced. But in the long run English merchants as a class did gain not only from the Virginia colony but also from the four other plantations which by 1733 dotted the Atlantic coast from the Chesapeake Bay to the St. Mary's River.

Between 1607 and 1776, there elapsed 169 years—a period slightly longer than that since 1776. During these five or six generations, there evolved in the South some colonists who became owners of broad acres and many slaves. But these southern landowners who grew tobacco or rice for Old World markets, and in addition shipped abroad timber, naval stores, and a variety of other raw materials, were always aware that they were netting but little beyond a fair living from their investments and their entrepreneurial efforts. Year by year their debts increased until on the eve of the Revolution, Thomas Jefferson could say truthfully of himself and his neighbors that they were merely "a species of property, annexed to certain mercantile houses in London." And later Oliver Wolcott could say: "It is a firmly established opinion of men well versed in the history of our revolution, that the Whiggism of Virginia was chiefly owing to the debts of the planters." Over a century later, the historical researches of Arthur Meier Schlesinger and other scholars largely corroborated the truth of Jefferson's and Wolcott's statements.

One of the first sovereign acts of the new states was the confiscation of debts to British merchants and the expropriation of the property of British subjects, including that of native Tories. This exercise of the power to confiscate, be it noted, was one method employed by the colonial planters and merchants to escape from their colonialism. In New England and the Middle States the escape was permanent. Moreover, by gaining control of the commercial and financial policies of the new general government the merchants, manufacturers, shipowners, and money-lenders of those states were eventually able to replace the similar groups in England in the exploitation of producers of raw materials and agricultural products not only in their own area but also in the South. Therefore, since the southerners were destined for at least another century to continue as almost entirely agricultural producers and as purchasers of fabricated articles, it can be argued that it would have been better for the region to have relied principally upon Old England instead of upon New England as a source of supply of manufactured goods. For a century at least, Old England could have sold the South better goods for less money than New England was able to do. The terms of trade would have been unfavorable in either case, but it is more than probable that they would have been somewhat less so had the southern states remained economic dependencies of Great Britain.

From this it does not follow that the revolt of the South against England was not entirely justifiable on other grounds, for it was both reasonable and just for the members of the southern elite to desire for themselves honorable positions in social and political life. This understandable and natural ambition was an even more dynamic factor than debts in transforming such fundamental conservatives as the Habershams, the Pinckneys, the Johnsons, the Washingtons, and the Carrolls into revolutionists. Moreover, it was right, that, in consultation with their constituents, they should wish to formulate and direct their own domestic and foreign policies without regard to British Tory interests and opinions. Since a war was necessary for them to attain their objectives they were wise to ally themselves with their neighbors to the north and with France in order to assure the winning of that war.

But their northern neighbors and the French monarchy were actuated by a different set of motives from their own. With the latter, they entered into a military alliance which the French hoped and expected would eventuate in their becoming dependencies of France instead of England, when once the war was over. In this expectation the Gallic ally, as is well known, was disappointed. With the North, the South made a verbal compact, later formalized in the Articles of Confederation, which rendered mutual assistance possible without calling into question the sovereignty of the states. When commercial, financial, and speculative interests found this loose federation too weak to serve their purposes and began moving for a stronger central government, the southerners should have been as wary of them as they had been of the British and French.

The foregoing statement brings up the delicate question of "historical relativity." "Historical relativity" places the historian dealing with the actions of men of a past epoch under obligation to do so not in the light of his own time but in that of the era with which he is concerning himself. Some thirty years ago, Charles A. Beard in his *An Economic Interpretation of the Constitution* and his subsequent *Economic Origins of Jeffersonian Democracy* proved to the satisfaction of most open-minded students that, in large measure, the Constitution was the handiwork of a revolutionary minority bent upon safeguarding and promoting the interests of commercial, manufacturing, and financial groups. Such groups were located almost entirely in the North, but they received the support and temporary alliance of southern plantation owners and speculators in western lands.

The keen political instinct of small farmers in general, and of the piedmont South in particular, warned them that the newly proposed Federal government would not be to their benefit. In North Carolina the small farmers were able to prevent ratification on the first test, while in Virginia they might have been successful in doing so had not some of their delegates, when subjected to pressure in the convention, apparently regarded their election promises as mere "campaign oratory." Even in South Carolina and Maryland their opposition was well known and articulate. In Georgia, where a temporarily exposed position made fear a predominant emotion, there seems to have been little opposition to the new and stronger union; but Georgia counted for but little at that time, and in the end would have followed the lead of her four more northerly neighbors had she received such a lead.

According to Beard, some of the plantation owners stood for alliance with other propertied groups because they were suspicious of the radical tendencies of their own westerners. In the light of their own time and the experiences they had had with the British merchants, it seems reasonable to assume that they should have feared the western radicals less and the northern businessmen more, since these latter were little different from similar groups in England and Scotland. Indeed, some few southern leaders did just that. For instance, John Mason and Patrick

Henry in Virginia, and Willie Jones and William Lenoir in North Carolina opposed ratification. But the influence of men like Washington and
Madison outweighed these latter.[2] The influence of such men must have
been out of all proportion to their numbers, and while it is to their credit
that they were able to take a large view of the situation, it was not in
the long run advantageous to themselves, their class, or their section
that they did so. Doubtless, some of them hoped and expected that the
South would become relatively as much a commercial, industrial, and
financial section as the North.[3]

Were there good grounds for such hope? Had they been able to concentrate on just two facts, it seems that they should have answered this
question in the negative. The first of these facts was the slave system,
which by that time was firmly fixed on the South, despite the opinion of
some historians who believe that only the evolution of cotton culture on
a grand scale made the continuation of the slave system inevitable.
Actually the southerners were habituated to the institution and would
have been loath to part with it even had they been convinced that it was
financially unprofitable. This attitude can be accounted for partly by the
fact that the question was more social than economic at almost all times,
as the late Ulrich B. Phillips perhaps overemphasized. Since a good part
of southern capital had to go into the ownership of labor, it could hardly
have been expected that there would be much left over for commercial,
manufacturing, and financial enterprises.

The second fact is that, other things being equal, men follow the
line of least resistance. Even in the 1780's everyone knew that the South
had an almost limitless hinterland adaptable to the slave-plantation
system, and that such capital as might be accumulated would necessarily
go into the exploitation of this hinterland. The historical accident that
the land claims of wealthy Virginians were mostly north of the Ohio,
rather than south of it, may have been determining, but of that no one
can be sure.

By way of summary it may be said that indeed the decade of the
1780's was a "Critical Period." But for the South it was "critical" in a
sense exactly opposite to that in which the phrase was employed by
John Fiske a century later. Fiske as a philosophical representative of
and spokesman for industrial and commercial interests saw that what
did in fact take place very well *might not* have done so, and such an
eventuality would have been "bad" for the system for which he was an
intellectual spokesman. To the South the period was "critical" because
what did happen was "bad," while the establishment of a separate
southern confederacy at that time would have been "good."[4]

Had the Constitution of 1787–89 not been ratified by the southern states it is almost a certainty that the eight states to the north of Maryland, and perhaps Maryland too, eventually would have provided themselves with *a* constitution substantially identical with *the* Constitution we know. Indeed, that very Constitution might well have gone into effect, for by its own terms it provided that it would become operative when ratified by nine states. Had Virginia steadfastly refused to ratify, it can readily be assumed that in a relatively short time she would have been joined by the two Carolinas and Georgia in establishing a southern confederacy. We may be sure that such a confederacy would have been aggressively expansionist and would have obtained Florida, Louisiana, Texas, and California in an even shorter time than they were actually secured by the United States. Be it remembered that it was the South which furnished the driving force for making these acquisitions when the Northeast was holding back. The southern confederacy would have provided by advantageous trade treaties for the sale of its agricultural and other raw materials in whatever markets seemed most desirable. That cotton, tobacco, and rice would have gone to northern markets in payment for fabricated materials is certain, but such trade would have been on much more favorable terms than was actually the case. The bulk of southern commerce, however, would have been with Great Britain and the countries of northwest Europe, for the reason that for a long time, at least, these countries manufactured better and cheaper consumers' goods than did the North. Moreover, there would have been few if any tariff duties to pay on imports, with the result that the differential between prices paid and prices received would not have been nearly so great as it actually was. In short, a separate confederate government would have harmonized much better with the economic and social life of the region than did that of the United States. And, *pari passu,* it can with almost equal certainty be maintained that the government of the United States, with the South out of it, would have harmonized with greater precision with the life of the northern region. Finally, the relations between North and South would have been much more peaceful and mutually respectful had each been an independent sovereignty from the start. This can be said if for no other reason than that it is hard to conceive of such relations being *worse* than they actually were during the long years lying between the enunciation and adoption of Hamilton's financial policies in 1789–91 and the withdrawal of Federal troops from Louisiana and South Carolina in 1877. In fact, it is reasonable to suppose that there would have been no greater ill feeling and squabbling between the two countries than actually existed between the United States and Canada. The Potomac-Ohio line formed a fairly natural boundary on this side of the Mississippi, while the western boundary probably could have been fixed as well by treaty as was that between Canada and the United States in 1846.[5]

If we think of the adoption of the Constitution as a marriage between the two sections, we may consider the Revolution as a period of friendship formed for the duration of a common danger, while to the Confederation period we may assign the status of a formal engagement. Just as it is usually much less tragic to break an engagement than to dissolve a marriage, so likewise it would have been better for the South never to have entered into a union with the North than later to have sought a dissolution. Perhaps the same excuse may be made for her action as is sometimes made for a young bride—namely, that she was not aware of the seriousness of the step she was taking. Certainly if she had married in haste, there was ample leisure for repentance. And repentance began immediately.

With this remark we turn now to consider the second purpose of this paper, which is an examination of the question: Was a compromise of the interests of the two sections possible under the Constitution, and if not, was subsequent separation feasible? That the South was yoked in an unequal union became apparent with the adoption of the Hamiltonian financial schemes, aimed as they were at enriching and strengthening the commercial, industrial, and, above all, the financial interests which were concentrated in the larger cities of New England and the Middle States. It is true that Hamilton rationalized that these measures would be beneficial to small property and agricultural interests as well, but just here began that disingenuous sophistry which to this day has characterized spokesmen for business interests and which more straightforward and forthright persons have found so difficult to parry.[6] Of almost equal importance in aggrandizing commercial and financial interests at the expense of agricultural interests in general and of the South in particular, was the pro-British foreign policy of the Federalists. Already the moneyed men of the northern cities were linking their destinies with those of similar groups in England, who, since the days of the Glorious Revolution, had largely controlled the financial and foreign policies of the motherland. With these policies the Federalists pursued one which recently we have called "parallel action." Name this reason or instinct, it was sound. Equally sound was the pro-French attitude of most southerners, for the French Revolution had proclaimed undying hatred of monopoly of all sorts and everlasting devotion to "security, liberty, property, and resistance to oppression." And for "property" we may read "small, tangible, real and personal property"—that is, the sort to which the South was devoted. In other words, both sides seem to have recognized their friends and enemies when they saw them.

To the leadership of the Republicans now came Jefferson, seconded by Madison, Monroe, and lesser leaders. If we return for a moment to our engagement, marriage, and divorce figure, we may with propriety lay down the further elaboration of it by saying that if there is to be a divorce at all, it is better for it to come soon—preferably before there are any children (in this case, new states) to complicate matters. Jefferson had the choice of two policies. Either he could undertake to rally agrarian and small-property classes in the North to unite with his southern constituents to capture the central government and undo the Federalist policies, or he could disregard any potential allies in the North and endeavor to commit the South to separation. Indeed, Jefferson could and perhaps did regard these procedures not merely as alternatives but as sequentials. That is to say, if the former should fail, he could fall back on the latter. There is no doubt that his personal preference was for the former, but that he was willing to resort to secession the Kentucky Resolutions of 1799 seem to attest. It is extremely doubtful, however, whether Jefferson would have led a southern secession movement had he and his party failed of victory in 1800. Hamilton's estimate of Jefferson—that he was a man bold in theory but timid in action—is probably correct. And this estimate of Jefferson is even more true of his closest associate and successor, Madison. The compromising character of the administrations of both men as well as that of the third member of the triumvirate, Monroe, is further proof that the Virginia hegemony was Girondin in character and not Jacobin, as some Federalist contemporaries professed to believe.

Not only did Jefferson and his successors fail to undo most of the special privileges that the Federalists had bestowed upon the business interests, but before Madison's second administration was over the protective tariff principle had been firmly established, and the Second Bank of the United States, much stronger and more monopolistic than the first, had been chartered. This weak leadership, after having made a great show of kicking special privilege out the parlor door, was responsible for allowing it to sneak back through the kitchen door. So far had this process gone that in 1824 the John Quincy Adams-Henry Clay coalition gained possession of the government in the name of National Republicanism! For this denouement, in addition to the timid character of the Virginia leadership, two other factors were responsible: (1) Most of the younger Federalists, despairing of rejuvenating their party after its unheroic conduct in the War of 1812, went over to the Republicans carrying with them their Federalist principles. (2) Many of Jefferson's northern lieutenants were beginning to embrace such principles in response to the improving economic and social status of themselves and some of their constituents. The two groups quickly fused and formed a veritable "fifth column" within the Republican body.[7] From this point of vantage they were able to "bore from within" as the modern Communist phrase has it, and to play the ancient Roman game of *divide et impera*. For this game the abolitionists furnished bats, balls, and gloves, while good diamonds were found in the Louisiana Purchase and later in the Mexican Cession.

So much has been said about the antislavery movement—its origins, motives, and progress—that it would be supererogation to attempt here any original contribution to the discussion. For the purposes of this paper, however, it is necessary to make two or three observations on the subject. The antislavery movement sprang from two sources. In the first place, it was a handy and, in most cases, a relatively inexpensive method for members of a conscientious nonslaveholding middle class to pay their debts to God. Long before 1800 Quakers and similar sects had begun so to employ it. It was none other than the very moral John Stuart Mill who first made the observation that morality is primarily a middle-class virtue. The poor, said Mill, *cannot* afford to be moral whereas the rich *can* afford *not* to be. Like every other aphorism of general significance this one has plenty of exceptions in its specific application. The general truth of Mill's statement, however, is reasonably apparent. Members of antislavery societies were drawn almost exclusively from groups who, economically, were small property owners and who, religiously, stemmed from seventeenth century English Puritanism—itself a middle-class movement.

In the second place, slavery collided head on with the eighteenth-century dogma, so eloquently incorporated into our Declaration of Independence in the ringing phrases: "that all men are created equal, that they are endowed by their Creator with certain unalienable Rights, that among these are Life, Liberty and the pursuit of Happiness." This egalitarianism was taken seriously everywhere by small property owners, but in the South it was applied in fact, even from the first, only to whites, and also in theory after the formulation and general acceptance of the proslavery argument. In the North, on the other hand, where the social problem of the Negro was either nonexistent or not acute, egalitarianism had no need to draw the color line. Indeed, the devotees of the dogma in that section came eventually to assert that the genuine article could be distinguished from the spurious by subjecting it to what we may call the color test. So far did this conceit go that even the author of the immortal Declaration himself came to be suspected and, by the extremists, openly accused, of blackhearted hypocrisy. Even before his death it was already apparent to the more discerning, including perhaps

Jefferson himself, that a wedge in the shape of the slavery controversy was being driven between his followers in the North and those in the South. The point here is that while financial and industrial capitalists and their political henchmen did not forge the wedge, when they saw it already entering the body of the Jeffersonians, they did not neglect to give it some mighty mauling. *Divide et impera.*

In cleaving the body of Jeffersonianism the financial and industrial groups did not intend to rive the body of the Union. So much "aid short of war" had they given to the abolitionists, however, that by 1860 the latter were able to drive the wedge home and split asunder not only the body of Jeffersonianism but also that of the Union itself. And so had ended in failure the effort begun by Jefferson and continued by other apostles of small property to create and maintain on a national scale a party which could and would hold in check the overgrown pretensions and overweening ambitions of the party of special privilege. That is to say, it had proved impossible to prevent industry and finance from becoming the mistresses instead of remaining, as the Jeffersonians desired, the handmaidens of agriculture and commerce.

During few if any of the first seventy years of the Federal Republic were the terms of trade between the South and the industrial and financial centers of the North in favor of the former. The colonialization of the South was proceeding slowly but surely. During the first fifty of these years it was mainly in the older sections of the South that the pinch was felt acutely. During these years, indeed, it was the existence of a vast southern hinterland into which the more hard-pressed citizens of the older South could escape that prevented such near-crises as the Nullification and Wilmot Proviso controversies from becoming real crises. In the last twenty years of the period the pinch tended to become widespread throughout the region. It was during this time that southern leaders came to adopt two policies as sequentials: (1) further extension of the southern hinterland; and in case of the failure of this policy to fall back on (2) secession and an independent southern confederacy which they believed could prevent the bankruptcy which stared many of their constituents in the face. Add to this the obloquy and contumely in which southerners were held by many of the "best" people of the North, and there remains no wonder that the stroke for southern independence was finally made.[8]

It was the British historian and publicist Lord Acton who once undertook to compress the nature of the American Civil War into an aphorism. "Secession," ran the noble saw, "was an aristocratic rebellion against a democratic government." Except for the fact that a relatively few large plantation owners gave tone to and, in some degree, controlled social and political life in the South, and hence lent color to the aristocratic picture, the almost exact opposite of the Acton dictum is the truth. There is no need to labor this point, but it is pertinent to stress the fact that democracy, as a social and political system, arose with and flourished upon that sort of capitalism where private property was widely distributed, individually owned, and personally managed.[9] This was the character of the southern economic system previous to 1860. Even the so-called "poor whites" were seldom tenants. Manufactories, commercial enterprises, and financial institutions conformed to the pattern as well as did farms and plantations. Absentee ownership in any of these sorts of business was the exception rather than the rule. But as has been already emphasized, the South, even when its influence in Washington was considerable, was never able to control the terms of its domestic and foreign trade nor the money system in which trade was carried on. Consequently a new colonialism was taking place. But unity in the South, although greater in 1860 than ever before, was still far from complete. This lack of unity was the most important single factor contributing to the ultimate defeat of the South.

> There is a tide in the affairs of men,
> Which, taken at the flood, leads on to fortune;
> Omitted, all the voyage of their life
> Is bound in shallows and in miseries.

The flood tide of 1787 was omitted; and the voyage which before the Civil War was "bound in shallows and in miseries," has since that event continued to be so bound.

For a decade or more after the Civil War the North undertook to rule the "conquered provinces" of the South by means of northern adventurers and southern "loyalists" whose political power rested upon universal Negro suffrage. Such rule needed to be buttressed constantly by Federal military force, for the "political potential" of Carpetbaggers, Scalawags, and Negroes was not equal to that of the former Confederates even in their pitifully weakened postwar condition. Such immature, brutally direct, and crassly inept imperialism, however camouflaged by such propaganda terms as "equality," "democracy," and "loyalty," sooner or later was bound to antagonize a sufficient number of nonimperialist elements in the North as to spell its doom. And so it happened in 1877. The significance of the great compromise of that year turned out to be this: No longer would the northern imperialists undertake to rule the South by their own henchmen; on their part, the native southern elite would guarantee the protection of northern imperialist interests in the region.

This more mature policy worked exceedingly well. During the following half-century, ownership of transportation, communication, financial, manufacturing, mining, and finally distributing corporations came to be largely held in the great cities of the Northeast, especially New York. Northern corporations and individuals owned most of the certificates of public indebtedness issued by the states, counties, and municipalities of the South. Likewise mortgages on southern agricultural and urban property were largely held in the North. The profits on the insurance business done in the South were channeled off to New England and New York. While the total number of businessmen in the South was ever increasing, the proportion who were independent owners of small businesses was constantly decreasing. In short, southern businessmen were becoming mere agents and factors for northern principals. In the last quarter-century the process has been accelerated. The World War, the era of "Coolidge Prosperity," the depression of the 1930's—each in its own way was a contributory factor. Today the subordination of all ordinary production to "defense" production, concentrated as it is in a few score great corporations, threatens the final ruin of such small businesses as still remain.

With the major part of income derived from profits, dividends, interest, and rent being siphoned out of the region to dwellers in the metropolises of the Northeast, the southern people were left to live mainly on wages, salaries, commissions, and other forms of income of similar nature. From studies made by Clarence Heer and others we know that these types of income were low in the South, relative to similar sorts of income outside this region. Necessarily this was so, not only because of the drain occasioned by payment of "invisible" items, but also because the South continued to be primarily a producer of raw materials and the coarser types of manufactured goods. This meant that the prices for which agricultural commodities were sold were much lower than prices paid for fabricated articles. In short, the southern people were obliged to work relatively more and more for less and less.

By the mid-1920's the second cycle of southern colonialism had made full revolution. The articulate political people of the South were the businessmen. To them the press and professions were largely subservient. In maintaining their ascendancy they were greatly aided by all sorts of national associations of businessmen, such as chambers of commerce, so-called service clubs, and the like. The policies promulgated by such organizations emanated largely, if not entirely, from the great centers of finance capitalism and imperialism. The burden of their propaganda was that the interests of all businessmen were parallel to, if not identical with, those of the financiers. On a national scale the magazines, the movies, and finally the radio carried the propaganda of the vested interests into almost every nook and cranny of the land. In the Northeast and especially in the West there was considerable organized opposition to the avalanche, but in the South there was almost none. Hence we are confronted with a paradox more amazing and ironical than any ever conjured by the imagination of Gilbert and Sullivan. The people of the South, who all their lives had suffered deprivation, want, and humiliation from an out-side finance imperialism, followed with hardly a murmur of protest leaders who, if indirectly, were nonetheless in effect agents and attorneys of the imperialists. Even our "Good Neighbors" and "Sister Democracies" to the south of us have never taken their medicine in so prone a position. Here from Virginia to Texas, the Glasses and the Garners strove to "out-Mellon" Mellon. Never before in the history of this country had a single group so fully dominated public policy as did the finance capitalists during the "Golden Twenties." And nowhere was their dominance more complete than in their southern "colony."

That their direct rule was at least temporarily halted in the 1930's was not due to the activities of a well-organized opposition, but to the confusion into which the financiers were thrown by the utter failure of their own most cherished principles to work satisfactorily even for themselves. As a result, the election of 1932 brought into control of the Federal government a more strangely assorted group of men than Washington had seen since its establishment as the nation's capital. Under the spreading New Deal tent were gathered, from left to right, Communists, State Socialists, other varieties of Marxists, delegates from the camps of both radical and conservative labor, old-fashioned Democrats speaking for agriculture and small business, many kinds of reformers, representatives of the political "rings" of the great northern cities, and even a few "money-changers" whom Mr. Roosevelt had pledged himself to "scourge from the temple"—into the treasury, as it eventually turned out. To these multicolored groups the southern Democrats were added by the exigencies of party politics.

Obviously among men of so many "principles" the only one which in the long run could serve as a cohesive force was the "principle" of continuity in office. For nearly five years political power was maintained by promoting the three R's of Recovery, Relief, and Reform with that age-old mechanism of governments for escaping from domestic difficulties —a vigorous foreign policy, lurking more or less consciously in the minds of some New Dealers in case the three R's should fail them. Toward the recovery and relief measures, practical politics, and doubtless in many instances personal conviction, demanded that the southern politicians assume a friendly attitude. On the other hand, many of them either openly opposed or secretly undertook to sabotage the reform bills.

This concluding excursus into contemporary history, however, is taken not to discuss New Deal domestic policy in relation to the South but in order to raise the question whether it has effected any fundamental change in the colonial status of the South by indicating the attitude of southern politicians toward the recent imperialist foreign policy of the New Deal.

When the "recession" of 1937 and the failure of the Court "packing" bill in the same year made it apparent to the "inner circle" of New Dealers that their days of rule were numbered if they continued to confine their attention to domestic issues, they began to seek new means of attracting support. In this quest, events, and more important, *the popularly accepted interpretation of events,* played into their hands. By 1937 the regime of the Nazis in Germany, generally detested in this country from its beginning, had become so aggressive as to be a matter of grave concern to several social and economic groups in America. Among these were the national and international finance capitalists and imperialists; the Anglophiles who included in their number most of the "best" people; except for some of the Irish, Italians, and "Aryan" Germans, immigrants and their offspring who still had a strong emotional and cultural tie with their European kinsmen; most "liberal" journalists, publicists, and social scientists; moralists, who could see "sin" written all over the countenances of the leading Nazis; and except during the period of the Hitler-Stalin pact, Communists and their numerous "fellow travelers."

The signal that the foreign policies of American Continentalism and Pan-Americanism, to which the New Deal administration had previously adhered, were to be superseded by a policy of death to Japanese and German dictatorships, to be made effective ultimately by means of an Anglo-American alliance, was sounded by the President's Chicago "quarantine" speech in October, 1937. By what devious roads the New Deal band wagon traveled from Chautauqua to Chicago to London and finally to Moscow need not detain us. It is important to note, however, that at various points along that road all those groups just enumerated—many of them formerly wayside scoffers—climbed aboard. It is also significant that they took with them most of the powerful propaganda agencies sorely needed to convert the American people to the view that national defense, with which no one could quarrel, was identical with intervention. Some of the groups were content to let the New Deal do the driving, but the imperialists and the Communists each hoped and expected to sit in the driver's seat before the journey's end.[10]

Of chief interest to us, however, is the fact that it was our own region which furnished the greatest amount of the political power necessary for the achievement of the revolution in New Deal foreign policy. This is clearly revealed by the vote in Congress on the crucial first Lend-Lease bill passed in the spring of 1941. For purposes of analysis, the country may be divided roughly into three sections: (1) The Northeast, consisting of the six New England states and the five Middle Atlantic states; (2) the South, consisting of the eleven ex-Confederate states, West Virginia, Kentucky, and Oklahoma; and (3) the West, consisting of the other twenty-three states. The vote on the bill by houses and sections follows.

SENATE

Section	For	Against	Absent or Not Voting
Northeast	16	6	0
South	25	1	2
West	20	25	1
Totals	61	32	3

HOUSE

Northeast	81	46	2
South	119	5	1
West	61	119	1
Totals	261	170	4

Had the southerners voted on the bill in the same proportion as the westerners, it would have barely passed in the Senate and would have been defeated in the House by a substantial majority. Likewise, most other interventionist bills have become laws because of overwhelming southern support. Why this southern belligerency? This question raises many others, which are not answerable at this time, but at least two may be presented now for future consideration. They are: (1) Is it not conceivable that the huge southern majority for Lend-Lease and other interventionist measures indicates that the finance capitalists and imperialists who receive so much of the South's social income exercise an even greater political power in their "colony" than they do in their own bailiwicks? (2) Does it not appear from even a casual acquaintance with the propaganda of the American imperialists that they believe they must survive or perish with their confreres who direct the destinies of the British Empire? Lack of perspective and adequate information as well as a decent regard for the proprieties and the claims of patriotism demand that answers to these two questions be postponed until a time more calm and propitious to the researches of the objective historian.

Meanwhile, it may not be out of order to remember that it was long ago said, "Whom the gods would destroy they first make mad." We do not know with whom the military victory will ultimately rest or who will be in the driver's seat when it is won, lost, or drawn. But it has been suggested, and not without some reason, too, that no matter what the outcome, finance capitalism and imperialism are doomed. If this prove true, then the objective historian in that more propitious time may well record with Socratic irony that those southerners who sought to serve an opposite purpose, did in fact all unwittingly unloose the chains which bound the South to an ancient and enervating colonialism.

Chapter VIII

One Hundred Years
of Reconstruction of the South

A. B. MOORE

THE SOUTH has long been, and to some extent still is, in the throes of being reconstructed by forces operating from outside the region.* Ramifications of this reconstruction process account in large degree for certain conditions in the South today and for its place in the nation. They explain how the South has acquired a colonial status, not only in the economic system but also in the psychology, sentiment, culture, and politics of the nation.

While this address is concerned primarily with the reconstruction of the South after the Civil War, it takes cognizance of the fact that the reconstruction of the South by the North has been going on more than one hundred years. Prior to the Civil War it took the form of a savage attack upon slavery and southern society, although it had other connotations. The Northeast with its western extensions, possessed of what one writer has called "egocentric sectionalism" (that is, the conviction that it was not a section but the whole United States and that, therefore, its pattern of life must prevail throughout the country), undertook after 1830 to reconstruct the South into conformity and into a subordinate position. With furious denunciations and menacing gestures and actions, it drove the South into secession and war, destroyed its power, and reconstructed it with a vengeance and violence remarkable in the history of human conflict. This is not to give the South a clear bill of health, but whatever the rights and wrongs of the controversy, the Civil War, broadly speaking, was the tragic drama of a movement to reconstruct the South.

We have formed the habit of examining the phenomena of the re-

*This paper was prepared for presentation as the 1942 presidential address, but its delivery was prevented by cancellation of the meeting.

construction of the South after the Civil War—that is, the period
1865–77—in a very objective, almost casual, way and with little regard
to their essence and their significance in southern and national history.
While avoiding the emotional approach one should not forget that it
was, after all, a settlement imposed by the victors in war and should
be studied in all its effects, immediate and far reaching, on its victims.
An investigation of the effects on the victors themselves would also be
an interesting adventure. It is a chapter in the history of the punishment
of the defeated in war. The observations of a competent historian from
another country, coming upon the subject for the first time, taking nothing
for granted, and making a critical analysis of its severity compared with
the punishment of losers in wars in general, would make interesting
reading.

The war set the stage for a complete reconstruction of the South.
Furious hatred, politics, economic considerations, and a curious conviction that God had joined a righteous North to use it as an instrument
for the purging of the wicked South, gave a keen edge to the old reconstruction urge. The victories of bullets and bayonets were followed
by the equally victorious attack of tongues and pens. Ministers mounted
their pulpits on Easter Sunday, the day following President Lincoln's
tragic death, and assured their sad auditors that God's will had been
done, that the President had been removed because his heart was too
merciful to punish the South as God required. An eminent New York
divine assured his audience that the vice-regent of Christ, the new
president, Andrew Johnson, was mandated from on high "to hew the
rebels in pieces before the Lord. . . . So let us say," with becoming piety
and sweet submissiveness he enjoined, "God's will be done."[1] Whether
the ministers thought, after they discovered that Johnson was opposed
to a reign of terror, that the Lord had made a mistake is not a matter of
record. As Professor Paul H. Buck has said, "It was in the churches
that one found the utmost intolerance, bitterness, and unforgiveness during the sad months that followed Appomattox."[2] Henry Ward Beecher,
one of the more moderate northern preachers, thought the South was
"rotten. . . . No timber," said he, "grown in its cursed soil is fit for the
ribs of our ship of state or for our household homes." The newspapers
spread abroad the preachers' gospel of righteous vindictiveness and expounded further the idea that drastic punishment of the South was
essential for the security of the Union.

Many unfriendly writers invaded the South, found what they wanted,
and wrote books, articles, and editorials that strengthened the conviction
that the South must be torn to pieces and made anew. Books, journals,
and newspapers stimulated the impulse to be vigilant and stern, to repress

and purge. A juggernaut of propaganda, stemming from the various sources of public instruction, prepared the way for the crucifixion of the South. The South of slavery and treason, of continuous outrages against the Negroes and northerners, of haughty spirit and stubborn conviction, and of superiority complex, must be humbled and made respectable or be annihilated, so that it could never become again a strong factor in national politics.

The South did little or nothing to neutralize Radical northern propaganda. To be sure, a few journalists, like A. T. Bledsoe, complained about "the cunningly devised fables, and the vile calumnies, with which a partisan press and a Puritanical pulpit have flooded the North,"[3] but their vituperative responses to vituperative attacks did more harm than good. There was, in the very nature of things, little that the South could do to disabuse the Radical northern mind that was disposed to believe evil of it. There was simply no escape for southerners from an awful scourge. Even more courage and fortitude than they had displayed on the battlefield would be required to endure what was in store for them.

As much as Reconstruction has been studied in this country it should not at this late hour be necessary to point out its severity, its permanent effects upon the South, and its influence upon various aspects of our national history. Yet few have examined critically the harshness of it and its persistent and manifold effects. While crucifying the South the dominant Radical group of the North, thanks to the blindness of hatred, believed it was being lenient. Because no lives were taken—there are some things more agonizing than death—for the "crimes of treason and rebellion," the North has prided itself on its magnanimity; and its historians have been strangely oblivious of property confiscations and mental tortures. It seemed to the late James Ford Rhodes "the mildest punishment ever inflicted after an unsuccessful Civil War." But this was no ordinary civil war, if, indeed, it should be classed as a civil war. The thesis of leniency has oddly persisted. When the Germans protested to high heaven against the severity of the Versailles Treaty they had sympathizers in this country who compared the generosity of the North in its treatment of the South with the harshness of the Versailles Treaty. But the late Professor Carl Russell Fish of the University of Wisconsin, in his article on "The German Indemnity and the South," discredited the theory of generosity on the part of the North. He showed that the South was punished more than Germany, though he touched upon only a few phases of the South's burdens.[4]

Professor Buck in his delightful and highly informative book, *The Road to Reunion,* recognized Reconstruction as "disorder worse than war and oppression unequalled in American annals," but made a serious error when he stated that "virtually no property" was confiscated.[5] He overlooked the confiscation of large quantities of cotton—estimated in the minority report of the Ku Klux Klan Committee at two million bales—then selling for a very high price and most of which belonged to private citizens. The abolition of slavery wiped out about two billion dollars of capital and reduced the value of real estate by at least that amount. This was confiscation of property and the repudiation of Confederate currency, the Confederate bonded debt, and the war debts of the states, all amounting to no less than three billion dollars, was confiscation of property rights. As inevitable as much of this was, it represented a frightful confiscation of property.

The freeing of the slaves not only cost the South two billion dollars but it also forced upon that section an economic and social revolution. It subverted a mode of life almost as old as the South itself. The repudiation of its debts impoverished the South and destroyed its financial relationships. While the South lost its debts, it had to pay its full share of the northern debts which amounted to about four-fifths of the total northern war expenses. The money for this debt was spent in the North for its upbuilding. It paid also its share of the $20,000,000 returned by the Federal treasury to the northern states for direct taxes collected from them during the war and of extravagant pensions to Union soldiers. Professor James L. Sellers estimates that the South paid in these ways an indemnity of at least a billion dollars to the North.[6]

The South accepted the results of the war—the doom of slavery and the doctrine of secession—as inevitable, and its leaders sought to restore their respective states as speedily as possible to their normal position in the Union. But despite its acceptance in good faith of the declared aims of the North, the South was forced through the gauntlet of two plans of Reconstruction. The people conformed in good faith to the requirements of President Johnson's plan, but Congress repudiated this plan and forced the South to begin *de novo* the process of Reconstruction. Pending its restoration, the South was put under the heel of military authority, although there was no problem that exceeded the power of civil authority to handle. Objectively viewed, it is a singular fact that it took three years to restore the South to the Union. It is little short of amazing that for a dozen years after the war Federal troops were stationed in the South among an orderly people who had played a leading role in the building and guidance of the nation since colonial times, and who now sought nothing so much as peace and surcease from strife. For much of the period government was a hodgepodge of activities by the civil authorities, the army, and the Freedmen's Bureau, with the President of the United States working through any or all of these agencies.

Most of the serious problems of government were precipitated by outside influences and conspiracies.

The political enfranchisement of four million Negroes, from whose necks the yoke of slavery had just been lifted, is the most startling fact about Reconstruction, and a fact of tremendous impact in southern history. There is nothing in the history of democracy comparable to it. To give the Negroes the ballot and office—ranging from constable to governor—and the right to sit in state legislatures and in Congress, while depriving their former masters of their political rights and the South of its trained leadership, is one of the most astounding facts in the history of reconstruction after war. It was a stroke of fanatical vengeance and design. The basic purpose of this sort of political reconstruction was to vouchsafe for the North—while chastising the South—the future control of the nation through the Republican party. The South was never again to be allowed to regain the economic and political position which it had occupied in the nation prior to 1860.

Negro voting laid the basis for the Carpetbag regime. For eight years Radical northern leaders, backed by the Washington authorities and the army and aided by some native whites, pillaged and plundered and finished wrecking the South. Northern teachers who invaded the South to reconstruct its educational and social system, and northern preachers who came down to restore the unity of the churches by a reconstruction formula that required southerners to bend the knee and confess their sins helped the politicians, the Freedmen's Bureau, and the Loyal League to undermine the Negroes' confidence in their white neighbors. The reconstruction policy of the churches did its part in stirring up both racial and sectional enmities. The *Nation* remarked in 1879: "Churches are doing their full share in causing permanent division."[7] Reconstruction affected the religious life of the country for fifty years and more after the Radicals were overthrown. The character of the Carpetbag-Scalawag-Negro governments was well stated by the New York *Herald* which said the South is "to be governed by blacks spurred on by worse than blacks. . . . This is the most abominable phase barbarism has assumed since the dawn of civilization. . . . It is not right to make slaves of white men even though they have been former masters of blacks. This is but a change in a system of bondage that is rendered the more odious and intolerable because it has been inaugurated in an enlightened instead of a dark and uncivilized age."[8]

It would be safe to say that the people of the North never understood how the South suffered during the Radical regime. The Radicals who controlled most of the organs of public opinion were in no attitude of mind to listen to southern complaints, and most people were too busy with the pursuit of alluring business opportunities that unfolded before them to think much of what was going on down South. In some respects conditions in the South at the end of the Radical regime remind one of the plight of the Germans at the end of the Thirty Years War.

The South staggered out of the Reconstruction, which ended *officially* in 1877, embittered, impoverished, encumbered with debt, and discredited by Radical propaganda. It had won after many frightful years the right to govern itself again, but there were still white men who could not vote and for many years there was danger of the federal regulation of elections and a resurgence of Negro power in politics.

The tax load had been devastating. The lands of thousands upon thousands had been sold for taxes. Huge state and local debts, much of which was fraudulent, had been piled up. So many bonds, legal and illegal, had been sold that public credit was destroyed. The people stood, like the servant of Holy Writ, ten thousand talents in debt with not one farthing to pay. They had to solve the paradoxical problem of scaling down public debts—a bewildering compound of the legal and illegal and far too large to be borne—while restoring public credit. Northern hands had imposed the debts and nothern hands held the repudiated bonds. Repudiation became another source of misunderstanding between the sections and another basis for charges of "southern outrages."

Reconstruction profoundly and permanently affected the political life of the South. It gave the South the one party system. The white people rallied around the Democratic party standards to overthrow the Radical regime, and their continued cooperation was necessary to prevent the Negroes from acquiring again the balance of power in politics. The terrible record of the Republican party during the Radical regime was an insuperable obstacle to its future success in the South. Hostility toward this party promoted devotion to the Democratic party. The complete domination of the latter party not only invested southern politics with the disadvantages of the one party system, but proved to be costly to the South in national politics. The Democratic party has been out of power most of the time in national politics and the Republican party naturally has not felt under obligation to do much for the South when it has had control of the national government. Even when the Democratic party has been in power the South has not had its share of patronage and appropriations, or of consideration in the formulation of national policies. The inequitable distribution of federal relief funds between the states since 1930 is an illustration in point. Political expediency has been the controlling consideration and not gratitude for party loyalty, which calls to mind an old Virginian's definition of political gratitude. Political gratitude, he said, is a lively appreciation of favors yet to be received.

Radical Reconstruction corrupted southern politics, and the prejudice aroused against Negro participation in politics led ultimately to the disfranchisement of most of the Negroes. Political habits formed in counteracting Carpetbag machinations and the presence of Negro voters continued to influence politics. Fraudulent methods were employed to control the Negro votes, and when factions appeared among the whites they employed against each other the chicanery and frauds which they had used against the Radicals.

Reconstruction contributed to the proscription of the South in national politics and to provincialism in southern politics. Southerners so feared a recrudescence of Reconstruction in some form or other that for a gerenation they generally shrank from active participation in national affairs. Their attitude, generally speaking, was that if the North would leave them alone it could direct national affairs. This begat provincialism and made the continued proscription of the South easier. Such a situation was not good for either the South or the North.

Race friction and prejudice were engendered by Reconstruction, which was an unfortunate thing for both races and especially for the Negroes. It caused greater discriminations against the Negroes in politics and education and in other ways. The Negroes had been so pampered and led as to arouse false notions and hopes among them and to make them for many years lame factors in the rebuilding of the South. The Negro after Reconstruction, and in large degree because of it, continued and continues to be a source of division between the North and South. The North either could not or would not understand the necessity of race segregation, and the idea that the Negro must have a definite place in the scheme of life was obnoxious. Disfranchisement of the Negro, occasional race riots, and the sporadic mobbing of Negroes accused of heinous crimes gave rise to continued charges of "southern outrages." Criticisms from the North, generally based upon a lack of understanding of the problem, seemed more a matter of censure than of true interest in the Negro. Thus, those who expected to see sectional strife over the status of the Negro disappear with the emancipation of the slaves were disillusioned.

The Negro has been the cause of more misunderstanding and conflict between the sections than all things else. The North freed the Negro from slavery, but by repressing and exploiting the South it has contributed much to conditions that have deprived him of some of the opportunities that a free man should have. If southern whites have suffered the pangs and restraints of poverty, the lot of the Negro has inevitably been worse. The shackles upon the Negro's economic and cultural advancement have been formidable and deadening in their effects. Their inescapable lack of educational opportunities has been epitomized by the saying that the South has had the impossible task of educating two races out of the poverty of one.

In some respects the South has not pursued an enlightened policy toward the Negro. In ways it has exploited him. In the struggle for existence the Negro too often has been overlooked. Prejudice, too, resulting to a large extent from Reconstruction experiences, has done its part. Southerners, determined that the political control of Negroes back in the old Reconstruction days shall not be repeated, and probably too apprehensive about the breaking down of social barriers between the two races, have been conservative and slow to see adjustments that need to be made and can be made for the good of both races. Northerners with little information, but sure of their superior understanding, have scolded and denounced after the fashion of the old abolitionists. They have protested and cast sweeping aspersions without making constructive suggestions or troubling themselves to procure information upon which such suggestions could be based. Occasional violence against Negroes by ignorant mobs and discriminations against the Negroes in the enforcement of laws have evoked brutal and indiscriminating attacks from the northern press that remind one of journalism in the old Reconstruction days. Needless to say, such criticisms have contributed nothing to the southern Negro's welfare or to national unity.

The growing political power of the Negro in the North is adding to the Negro problem in the South. Many northern politicians, in order to gain the political support of the northern Negroes, and, eventually, those of the South, are now supporting radical Negro leaders in their demand for a sweeping change in the status of the Negro in the South. But efforts to subvert the social system of the South will lead to more friction between the North and South and to bitter racial antagonisms.

The impoverishment of the people by Reconstruction and the heavy debt load imposed by it were most serious impediments to progress. They hindered economic advancement and educational achievement. Vast hordes of children grew to maturity unable even to read and write. It is impossible to measure the cost to the South of illiteracy alone resulting from the war and Reconstruction. Conditions brought about by Reconstruction also caused a tremendous loss of manpower. They caused a large exodus of the white people of the South to divers parts and made the Negroes unfit to apply their productive powers. The loss of

whites is well illustrated by Professor Walter L. Fleming's statement
that Alabama lost more manpower in Reconstruction than it lost in
the war.

The poverty attending Reconstruction laid the basis for the crop-lien
system and promoted sharecropping, and these more than all things
else have hindered rural progress. Hundreds of thousands of both the
landless and the landed had nothing with which to start life over and
the only source of credit was cotton. Merchants, with the assistance of
eastern creditors, advanced supplies to farmers upon condition that
they would produce cotton in sufficient quantity to cover the advances
made to them. The merchant charged whatever prices he chose and
protected himself by taking a lien upon the cotton produced. Under the
system the great mass of farmers became essentially serfs. To throw off
the shackles required more resources than most of them possessed.

Even at present a majority of southern tenant farmers depend for
credit on their landlords or on the "furnish merchants" for their supplies. The landlord, moreover, who stakes all on cotton or tobacco is a
bad credit risk. For this reason he pays interest rates as high as 20
per cent, and naturally his tenants pay more. It has been estimated that
those who depend on the merchant for supplies pay as much as 30
per cent interest even on food and feed supplies. Credit unions and the
Farm Security and Farm Credit Administrations have helped many of
the farmers, but farm credit facilities are still sadly lacking in the South.
Louis XIV's remark that "credit supports agriculture, as the rope supports the hanged" has been abundantly verified in the South.

Thus, Reconstruction made a large contribution to the development
of a slum-folk class in the rural South. The sharecropper–crop-lien farm
economy of the South has produced a human erosion system more
costly than soil erosion. In fact the two have gone hand in hand. These
things always come to mind when in this day of national championships
the South is referred to as the nation's "Economic Problem No. 1."

Reconstruction and its aftermath prevented the flow of population
and money into the South. The 37,000,000 increase in population between 1870 and 1900 was largely in the North. The South's increase,
except in Florida and Texas, was principally native and, as has been
observed, it lost part of this increment. Northerners who moved and
the millions of Europeans who came in either flocked to the industrial
centers of the North or settled down on expansive fertile lands between
Ohio and Kansas made available by the Homestead Act. Most of the
nation's capital and credit resources were put into railroad building and
industrial and business pursuits north of the Mason and Dixon line.
By 1890 the railroad pattern was laid and most of the roads had been

built to feed the North. In every phrase of economic activity the South was a bad risk compared with the North. Not the least of the things that kept men and money out of the South were its debt load and the stigma of debt repudiation. Northern newspapers and journals lambasted the South for the sin of repudiation and warned investors and emigrants to shun the South. In addition to other risks, they would find, the *Nation* said, that in the South the "sense of good faith is benumbed, if not dead," and if they had anything to do with the South they would make themselves a part "of a community of swindlers." Even Henry Clews, who had conspired with the Carpetbag racketeers to sell shoddy Reconstruction bonds to gullible buyers in the North and Europe, railed out against the spectacle of "southern robbery." The notion of southern depravity was long-lived.

Between 1865 and 1900 a new republic of tremendous wealth and productive power was forged, and concurrently there was a great educational development and a general advance in culture throughout the North. The South was a mere appendage to the new nation advancing through these epochal transformations. Reconstruction had assigned it a colonial status in all its relations with the North. J. M. Cross of New York City, for example, wrote to John Letcher of Virginia on March 8, 1867, that "northern civilization must go all the way over the South, which is only a question of time." Some of those who had wanted to make the northern way of life the national way lived to see their wish a *fait accompli*. The patterns of national life were forming and henceforth were to be formed in the North and national unity was to be achieved by the conformity of the South to these patterns. Northerners have made little or no distinction between the North and the nation. The idea has become deeply imbedded throughout the country. For example, Professor Buck unconsciously expresses this attitude when he says, "The small farm worked in countless ways to bring Southern life into closer harmony with the major trends in national life"[9]—that is, northern life. The same idea is carried in one of the chapter titles—"Nationalization of the South"—in Professor William B. Hesseltine's recent *History of the South*. When the South has failed to conform it has been stigmatized as backward, provincial, and sectional.

By 1900 the Old South was largely a thing of memory. Yearning for some of the good things of life, impulsive young men rejected antebellum traditions as inadequate to the needs of the new South which must be built. They sneered at "mummies," "mossbacks," and "Bourbons" who cherished the Old South. Others, just as avid about the future of business and industry, hoped to bring over into the New South of their dreams the best of the old and thus merge "two distinct civilizations" into a compound that some good day would surpass anything the North could show. They would leaven the lump of crass materialism with the leaven of graceful living. But to the older generation it seemed that those who were breaking loose from old moorings were bending "the knee to expediency" with little or no regard for principle.

By scraping together small savings the would-be industrialists proved the mineral wealth of the South and laid the foundations of mineral industries and of tobacco and cotton milling. Northern capitalists were given an urgent invitation to come down and exploit the bonanza of physical and human resources. Labor was docile and cheap and helpless. The shearing would be easy. Northern capital began to trickle down and ultimately it came in larger quantities after businessmen had plucked the tall grass of opportunity in other parts of the country. A union was formed between northern and southern men in the field of business that took the place of the former union in politics of the Carpetbaggers and Scalawags. The business Carpetbaggers were received with bands and banquets and eloquent addresses of welcome. They found men ready to serve them as overseers, legal retainers, and lobbyists. If, as one writer has said, "the worst carpetbagger stayed at home," perhaps some of their representatives in the South have been among the worst Scalawags.

The urge became strong to acquire the attributes of the bounding North. Southerners lost faith in their own standards. To achieve high rating in the South, men must first win recognition in the North. Budding and bulging towns sought to become like the cities of the North with their smokestacks, skyscrapers, parks, and boulevards. The imitation of Yankee ways became the vogue. The inferiority complex of southerners since Reconstruction, and to a great extent because of Reconstruction, is a cruel and potent fact in the history of the South. Not a few regretted that the grandeur of old southern life was being sacrificed, but more, in the spirit of Scarlett O'Hara of *Gone with the Wind* fame, resolved that they would not longer deny themselves. Come what might, they would accumulate for themselves and make the South great by the northern formula. Some of the ablest and most ambitious could not wait for the New South to arrive; they pulled up stakes and moved North to be as near as possible to the springs of wealth and power. Thus an "all-out" reconstruction of southern life was under way. The North was the nation and the South strove hopefully for a while to become a potent part of it.

But the prophets of a new day and of a new and better way for the South were extravagant. They did not see that the South was not free to integrate itself, with a chance to use all its natural advantages, into the national economic system. They thought only of nature's lavish gifts to the South in raw materials and natural resources. Southerners had but to resolve and plan and work to achieve a prosperity that would make the old plantation economy seem flabby by comparison and ultimately give the South primacy among the sections of the country. But they were victims of teasing illusions. They did not understand that its new economy would be a catch-as-catch-can economy. They did not know—though more perspicacity might well have raised questions—that the powerful and entrenched interests of the North would give the South about the same place in the national economic system that the Negro occupied in the South. In their wishful thinking they overlooked the privilege cornucopia that pended over the North and was certain to hold the South in economic bondage.

Special privileges at the hands of the national government have conferred blessings and billions on the North at the expense of other sections. Tariffs have protected it on coast and frontier, and freight rate discriminations have shielded it from the competition of southern manufacturers.

Tariff alone has added billions of dollars to northern coffers at the expense of the South and West. One shrewd New Englander remarked that the tariff of 1828 would "keep the South and West in debt to New England the next hundred years." Evidently he understood the significance of protection for industry, but he did not foresee the enormous tribute that even higher tariffs of more recent times would extract from the other sections for the North. High tariffs have not only taken a heavy money toll from the South for northern industries, but by curtailing imports they have hindered the sale of southern cotton, tobacco, and other farm products in foreign markets. Trade restraints have hurt the farm-staple producing South more than any other region of the country.

Pensions for war veterans between 1862 and 1936 turned loose nearly seven billion dollars more in the North, while the South and West received together only about one billion dollars of pension money. Southerners helped to pay Civil War pensions to all those who had helped, or said they had helped, to save the Union; but in the very nature of things few southerners could qualify for this particular government subsidy. Union veterans were also allowed to count the time of their service toward the five-year period required for "proving up" on a homestead. War pensions not only released a vast deal of purchasing power in the North, but they helped small manufacturing establishments to make a start. One historian has remarked that there were "pensions in the industrial woodpiles of the North in the period between 1865 and 1890."[10]

The patent subsidy has been another source of great wealth to the North. It has been estimated that at least 90 per cent of "the effective money-producing patents are owned in the North." Professor Walter P. Webb has shrewdly remarked that "the government has conferred upon the North a subsidy for business, an annual bonus for patriotism, and a monopoly for ingenuity."[11] The privilege triumvirate of tariff, pensions, and patents—all gifts by a northern controlled government —have added enormous wealth and power to the North at the expense of the South and West. The loss of political power by the South, resulting from the Civil War and Reconstruction, has made possible this momentous fact in intersectional relations. While the South in many ways has suffered most, the political and economic hegemony of the North has also been very costly to the West.

The scarcity of capital and credit resources has forced the South to look to the North to finance practically all of its large industries and many of its small ones. The result of this is not far to seek. The institutions that supply capital for southern industries have been first concerned with protecting their larger investments in northern railroads and industries. They have used their power to preserve the established economic relations between the North and South.

There have been many other differentials against the South which can be traced back to Reconstruction. One of the most serious impediments to the development of southern industry has been freight-rate discriminations against the South. Instead of a unified national freight-rate structure we have five regional freight-rate structures that have grown up in a topsy-turvy manner. The region east of the Mississippi and north of the Ohio and Potomac rivers has had the advantages of relatively low freight rates on manufactured and processed articles. In freight-rate literature this area is designated as "Official Territory," and in all other respects it is the hub of the United States.

First-class freight rates from Southern to Official Territory are considerably higher—much higher in some cases—mile for mile, than intraterritorial rates of the Official Territory. It has been estimated that the southern manufacturer shipping goods into this area is at a relative disadvantage of about 39 per cent in freight charges. On the other hand, a shipper in Official Territory can move his goods down into Southern Territory at a cheaper rate than that paid by southerners for shipping similar goods wholly within their own territory. Thus, while freight-rate differentials largely close to southern manufacturers and processors the markets of the greatest consuming territory of the country (about 51 per cent of the total population resides in the Official Territory region) they open southern markets to northern producers. In other words, they give northern manufacturers the advantages of a protective tariff against southern-made goods and deprive southern manufacturers to a great extent of their natural advantages of assembly and production costs in their own markets. Manufactured products and processed goods, and some raw materials, can be shipped from eastern Canada into Official Territory at a lower rate than that "available to shippers in Southern, Southwestern, and Western Trunkline Territories."[12] The Pittsburgh Plus system, superseded since 1924 by the multiple basing point system, has been a serious obstacle to the southern steel industry.

Another differential against the development of the South has been the superior opportunities in the North for capable and ambitious young men. Of the southern-born men listed in the 1932–33 edition of *Who's Who in America,* 37.1 per cent were at that time located in other sections. Thus the South has lost much of its finest business and professional talent. In recent years many able and finely trained young men have located in' the South, but the inflow of northerners has been small compared with the South's contribution of manpower to the North.

As a result of these special privileges and differentials in favor of the North, most of which have been the fruits of Civil War and Reconstruction, it is probable that the South is relatively worse off today than it was forty years ago. The North owns approximately 90 per cent of the country's wealth and probably 95 per cent of its money. Only nine of the two hundred largest corporations in the country are located in the South, and probably not more than 5 per cent of their stock is owned in the South. The public utilities in the South, the major railroad systems, the great electric company holding systems, insurance, the distribution of natural gas, oil, and gasoline, and the manufacturing industries are largely owned and controlled by outside interests. Much of its mineral wealth is shipped away in raw or semi-finished form and the higher wages paid for the conversion of this natural wealth into finished product are not available to southern wage earners. Likewise the large profits from the manufacture of such materials go to northern business concerns. When a southerner buys the finished product he pays for all the wasteful cross-hauling involved in the system, as the cycle of zinc from the southern mine to the southern home well illustrates. The ore and the finished product "are separated by a long northern detour, because absentee ownership and discriminatory freight rates make it cheaper to ship raw materials north for processing than to manufacture them at home."[13]

The present war will not alter appreciably the relative wealth of the two sections. It has contributed new industries to the South, but most of the large government contracts have been let to northern corporations. This has resulted from northern control of the government and because of the vastly superior production facilities of the North. The nation at war must use its resources wherever they may be. This is another example of the North succeeding because of previous advantages gained. "For whosoever hath to him shall be given, and he shall have more abundance...." Northern manufacturers and builders have followed war industries into the South and with their superior resources have snatched opportunities out of the hands of southern producers and builders.

The North also dominates the publishing business and other agencies of public instruction. This not only constitutes another differential against the South in the matter of accumulating wealth, but of more importance is the fact that it gives the North a tremendous advantage in the shaping of public opinion. Most of the books we buy and the national magazines and newspapers we read are published in the North, especially the Northeast. The news-gathering agencies and the national radio systems are centered there. Worse still, many of the large dailies of the South are owned by northern men and the syndicated columns of southern newspapers are written by northern columnists. The radio commentators on the national radio systems live in the North. The fact that some of the columnists and commentators are southern born does not alter the situation appreciably. Naturally they tend to "slant" their presentations to the northern public that supports them. Southern radios and southern newspapers carry the northern voice. Men who have little or no knowledge or sympathetic understanding of the South are attempting to interpret the South and to instruct it on national questions from the northern viewpoint. Even southern speech is being "reconstructed" by them. The situation "does not tend, as some think," says Peter Molyneaux, "to curb local provincialism. On the contrary, it tends to make Eastern provincialism national."

The manufacturers and distributors of the North and various adjunct agencies are bleeding the South white. The same thing may be said of a very large part of southern industries, owned, as has been observed, in the North and operated by local overseers. To a great extent the region is controlled by the absentee owners through their overseers and retainer agents. These agents are the symbols of success in the South and the paragons of social life. Their mansions stand on a thousand hills. It is good to wine and dine with these genial, if patronizing, viceroys. The absentee overlords retain the best legal talent to help them with their battles in the courts and the legislatures. Other types of influential persons, good public relations men and lobbyists, are also retained. Some of their retainers are always members of the legislatures. By selling some stock locally they raise up other friends and defenders.

Small wonder, then, that the corporations have exercised a large influence over law-making in the southern states. Too often they have been able to defeat measures objectionable to them—especially tax measures—and to promote those favorable to them. Too often they have not been willing to pay their fair part of the cost of public services or a fair wage to their employees. Such industries are of questionable value to a community. The South has advertised its cheap labor, and industrialists from the North have tried to keep it so. There are other differentials against the South, already noted, that have also been a factor in the lower wage scales of southern industry.

The absentee masters of southern industry and the chain store magnates are interested in profits and not in the welfare of the South. This is natural, but it illustrates a fundamental weakness in an industrial system based on outside capital. It would seem that those who gather their wealth from the South might reasonably be expected to give some of their educational benefactions to higher education in the South. But their gifts have generally gone to northern institutions that are already rich compared with those in the South. Their contributions to cultural development, whether in the form of gifts or taxes, go largely to the North.

The North has not only held the South in colonial bondage, but it has been very critical of the South, even for conditions that inhere in such an economic status. This has led Jonathan Daniels to say that after the Romans destroyed Carthage "Cato did not ride through Carthage on the train and blame its condition on the Carthaginians." It is doubtful if the British ever had a more superior and intolerant attitude toward the American colonists. The "southern outrages" complex, fomented by Radical politicians in the old Reconstruction days, has persisted. Incidents that have escaped editorial eyes if they happened in the North have been denounced as outrages if they occurred in the South. A public lynching in a well-known western state a few years ago did not evoke nearly as much condemnation as does the lynching of a Negro by a clandestine mob in the South. The people of the North are not denounced as being crude and barbarous because of the persistent activities of murderous bands of racketeers in large northern cities.

Strange notions have developed about the South. It is taken for granted that southerners are a slow and lazy people. The Abolitionists and Radical Reconstructionists conveyed the impression—and fiction has augmented it—that plantation whites lived in idleness and ease while black hands did labor and chores for them. The white women of the South are still thought to be lazy, pampered, helpless, spoiled creatures. All this comes out in fiction, shows, movies, and in street corner and parlor conversations. A conventional southerner has evolved. He is tall, lanky, lazy, slow—except with the trigger finger—speaks with a drawl, says "you all" even to one person, and possesses a sort of insolent dignity.

The South is regarded as a backward, ignorant, hot-tempered, and violent section, especially in its dealing with Negroes. Extravagant fictional treatments of the extremes of southern life are quite generally accepted as accurate cross-section views of the South. In one of the most violent scenes of "Tobacco Road," as played in a New York theater, an intelligent looking woman remarked to her companion: "That's just like the South." Asked what part of the South she was from, she squirmed in her seat and soon left the theater. *Mud on the Stars,* a lurid and patently preposterous story about life in Alabama, was well received by New York critics. One reviewer said that it is from such men as the author of this filthy story, who incidentally is a self-confessed rake, that we must look for information about the real South. When *Stars Fell on Alabama,* a grotesque portrayal of life in Alabama, appeared, it was widely acclaimed in the North, but when the same author wrote a similar book—*Genesee Fever*—about a certain community in New York State, the reviewers and commentators of New York were quick to point out that it represented a purely local and extreme situation in the state, and that it contained extravagant overtones and distortions for the purpose of literary effect.

The South has been called the Prohibition Belt, the Bible Belt (meaning a place with a fanatical zeal for fundamentalism to be expected of an ignorant and superstitious people), the Hot Biscuit Belt, the Sahara of the Bozart, and any other smart appellations that may have occurred to its sharp-shooting critics. Southerners are not inclined to apologize for their religion or their hot biscuits, but they realize that an effort has been made to slur their spirituality and their diet. Paradoxically, the South has been publicized for both its prohibition proclivities and its exquisite mint juleps and raw, hair-raising corn liquor. In this situation there should be a warning to all critics of the South. It is not a simple, uniform whole in any sense. Its life is quite as variegated and contradictory as human life and society elsewhere.

Southern politics has been the subject of trenchant criticism by Republican newspapermen and journalists of the North. The "solid South" has been held up to ridicule and scorn, though many northern states until very recently have just as regularly supported the Republican ticket in national elections—some in state elections—as has the South the Democratic ticket. Southerners are supposed to have a preference for demagogues and to enjoy political ranting. They have not had, however, a monopoly of ranting in politics, though they have had much to rant about. For the past fifty years the South has had more than its share of demagogues of a kind. And there are several kinds of demagogues. The South's demagogues have frequently been the "rabble-rousing" kind. It may well be doubted, however, whether this type of demagogue has done more harm than the refined, suave, cunning, respectable kind who has been a tool of entrenched privilege and greed. Poverty and oppression have made the masses in the South susceptible to demagogic appeals. It has taken betimes a little of what Mrs. Mary E. Lease of Populist days called hell-raising to dislodge the Bourbons who generally have represented their own class interests and the interests of business (the "new mastery"). From this irresponsible coalition the people have turned occasionally for relief to the so-called demagogues. It may be that some day the impartial student of southern history will give some of the demagogues a large place in the progress of the South.

The South has adhered to the Democratic party in national politics to its own hurt. Just now, however, a rebellion is developing against the New Deal leadership of the party. There are northern Democratic leaders today who are as indifferent to the South as were many of them in the days when Calhoun and Yancey spoke dire warnings. Indeed, they are apparently about as little interested in the South's welfare as were the Radical Republicans of Reconstruction times. They would for Negro votes, if for no other reason, reconstruct the social order of the South. Governor Frank M. Dixon of Alabama, in a recent address before the Southern Society of New York, warned the Democrats of the North that the South puts its social system above loyalty to the party. If New Deal Democrats in the North help the South to overcome the habit of unswerving fidelity to the Democratic party they will unwittingly make a fine contribution to the South's well-being.

The South's poverty and shortcomings have been so constantly exposed to public view by pen, pictures, and theatricals that it has become as sensitive as a child whose faults are discussed with neighbors in its presence. It has been surveyed by the specialists—educational, social, political, and economic—until it feels like a patient in a charity hospital who is probed and discussed daily by the hospital staff in the presence of curious visiting doctors and interns. No section of the country has been discussed nearly so much as the South. It has been easy copy for the journalists, a fertile field for the social scientists, and positively alluring to the fictionists. Whatever one's emotional reaction to the South, its appeal has been irresistible. It has been a veritable Thebes, but fortunately it has not killed all those who failed to explain its riddles. Since the days of Frederick Law Olmsted legions of unfriendly writers have swooped down out of the North, investigated for a few weeks, maybe only days, found what they expected and wanted and then entertained their reading public back home with racy accounts that perverted perspective.

A throng of literary Scalawags has sprung up in the South and has outdone most of the literary Carpetbaggers in slandering the South and distorting true perspective. The object has been to write something that the northern press would publish and to win recognition as writers —bold, fearless, and *realistic* critics of their own South. Actually, what most of them have written is worthless—worse than worthless—as a means of understanding the South. They have known that there is a market in the North for the sort of stuff they have written about the South, much of it lecherous and filthy, and they have exploited the market. For a mess of lucre and laudation they have been willing to bring disrepute upon the South that nurtured them. These Scalawags compare sadly with most of the Scalawags of the old Reconstruction days.

The manifold needs of the South to achieve parity of opportunity with the North and a position of equality in the nation should be a matter of concern not only to the South, but also to the entire nation. The treatment that the South has had since 1865—much of it the result of indifference and unconscious prejudice and avarice, rather than of malice aforethought—is extraordinary in a country that makes any pretense to true nationality and to democracy.

The South of today, the product of forces set out in this paper, gives the nation an economic and political unbalance. With its immense wealth of capital resources and its manifold economic problems and potentialities, what it can give to the nation and what it could consume, were it generally prosperous, are things of prime concern to the whole nation. It does not need alms; it cannot subsist on the crumbs that fall from the sumptuous northern business table which it has helped to provide. It does not need reconstruction to conform to any particular mold; it does not need the nostrums of professional social uplifters who know nothing of southern traditions and mores and who have what Roscoe Conkling called the "man-milliner" complex. It is tired of Carpetbaggers and Scalawags in politics, education, up-lift work, and literature. It will not want to give up its individuality and become a part of a monotonous whole. It will not be willing to barter its birthright for a mess of pottage. It may, as Jonathan Daniels has said, even "prefer a sloppy South to a South planned in perfection by outlanders." What it needs is to be given parity of opportunity and to be treated as a full-fledged part of the nation. It must be emancipated from a labyrinth of adverse and deadening differentials. Another abolition movement is needed, this time to free both Negroes and whites in the South from the yoke of economic oppression.

The welfare of the 37,000,000 people of the South is a matter of great national importance. The white people are in the main descended from old American stock and are steeped in American traditions. In this important sense the South is the most American part of America. About 97.6 per cent (71 per cent white) of the people are native born. Their present lot, by and large, contrasts sadly with the dreams of their forbears who helped to launch the nation on the wings of hope and high promise. The very poor whites, underfed, underprivileged, without incentive, and inured if not reconciled to a wretched existence, have seemed to many critics a worthless lot. But they are not, as many have supposed, biologically degenerate. Nor is the Negro a hopeless creature. Wherever the poor whites of the South have had a chance they have shown themselves to be capable of doing the highest type of work. These whites and the blacks can profit by training; they may continue to be a liability or they may contribute something to the nation's progress.

The South is the chief population replenishing area of the United States. "It is the land of children." Many of these children do not have a decent chance in life. Adequate food, clothing, health protection, and training for them are essential to the successful functioning of our democracy. With only one-sixth of the nation's school revenues, the South must educate one-third of the nation's children. The task is even worse than these facts indicate, because the South maintains separate schools for its white and colored children. Southerners are not indifferent to their educational problems. The southern states devote a larger share of their tax income to schools than do some of the northern states, and their taxes in proportion to the ability of the people to pay are relatively higher.

In the language of the National Emergency Council: "The South, in fact, has been caught in a vise that has kept it from moving along with the main stream of American economic life.... Penalized for being rural, and handicapped in its efforts to industrialize, the economic life of the southern people does not provide an adequate market for its own industries nor an attractive market for those of the rest of the country."

The national government has been little influenced by southern con-

ditions, interests, and viewpoints, in either its legislative or its administrative policies. Many examples could be given. Recent labor policies
well illustrate. Southern conditions were of little consequence when
Congress was legislating on the labor question. When John L. Lewis,
with the approval of President Roosevelt, forced southern coal operators, regardless of the extra cost of mining coal in the South, to pay
the same wage that northern miners were receiving, David Lawrence,
the national columnist said: "The worst economic blow the South has
received since the War Between the States has just been administered
by the Roosevelt administration." It is a significant fact that although
southern coal operators were made to pay the northern wage (a situation favorable to the northern operators, whether so intended), the
WPA has paid a 17 per cent higher wage to northern workers than to
southern workers. Incidentally, this is an example of a differential against
the South set up by the deliberate action of a national administration.

In this narrative of the South's plight it should be stated that southerners have not always made the best of their opportunities. They have
not always been enterprising and resourceful. They have too often ex-
cused themselves for not doing more because of abject poverty visited
upon them by the Civil War and Reconstruction. They have too long
lived in an atmosphere of despair, although there has been much to
depress their spirits. They have suffered from the habit of acquiescing
in a do-without economy. They have been the victims of both their own
inferiority complex and the superiority complex of the North. Northerners have assumed their superiority because of their superior achievements in material things, and because wealth and cultural facilities are
centered in their section. They have not made a critical self-analysis to
see how it has all come about and what the South has contributed.
They have not been timid about asserting their superiority or pushing
themselves into positions of leadership. When large technical and business engineering projects are sponsored in the South by corporations or
the federal government northern men generally are employed, although
southern men just as well fitted may be available. Southerners have
lacked boldness and aggressiveness. They have given outside capital
more advantages than were necessary to procure it.

There are optimists in the South who believe that the South, the
stone rejected by the builders since 1865, is destined to become the
"head of the corner" of the national edifice. This is a dream. To be
sure, there are some encouraging signs. There are dozens of things that
tend to promote understanding and good will among the sections, and
to produce a disposition to deal fairly with each other and to think on
the national scale. Just now a very potent cementing influence is the

fact that men and women from all sections are offering their all for the defense of a common heritage. The South is awakening. It is acquiring a much-needed faith in itself and is beginning to rebel against the do-without economy. It is doing considerable introspection. Its scholars and business men are planning. As opportunities multiply, fewer of its talented youth will go North. Research has made available the materials needed for a planned economy for the region and for pooling its resources for an "all-out" attack upon its problems. There are growing signs, too, that the South may in the not-too-distant future place its own interests above party loyalty, that it will not submit to continued discriminations even at the hands of the Democratic party. It is learning, if slowly, that it it not necessary to pamper capital in order to attract it. All this augurs well. The South's destiny is in many respects in its own hands. There is some hope if it will commit itself to intelligent and courageous leadership.

The task, however, of rejuvenating the South and lifting it to a place of dignity and equality in the nation is herculean. It cannot be done wholly by the South. There will have to be a change of attitude and a change of perspective on the part of the North. Northern interests will have to give up those advantages and privileges on which they have battened. But discriminations against the South are deeply imbedded in the economic system of the nation. To give the South a chance by obliterating these discriminations would be shocking to the North that has grown rich on advantage. It would extract many eyeteeth and precipitate serious problems of adjustment. The North will oppose this with all its might, and it has the might and votes to protect itself. The argument that the North and the entire nation would gain much from a prosperous South, not to mention the matter of justice to the South as a part of the nation, will probably not suffice, for men do not readily give up immediate advantages for opportunities that may evolve in the distant future.

What can be done about outside ownership of most of the great capital resources and large industries of the South? How are more than half of the farmers, who own no land, to procure lands now in the hands of northern insurance companies and other corporations, or in the bloated estates of wealthy individuals? What is to be done about the large and growing ownership of the distribution business in the South by northern corporations?

Ninety-three years ago John C. Calhoun died while leading the South in a bitter fight for its rights. When told by Robert Barnwell Rhett that the South needed him more than ever before in Washington, he remarked, with tears in his eyes: "There, indeed, is my only regret at going,—the South,—the poor South." The South's position in the nation today is in some important respects worse than it was in 1850. Were Calhoun living he could still say with the same solicitude, "The South, the poor South."

Chapter IX

Three Centuries of
Southern Records, 1607-1907

J. G. DE ROULHAC HAMILTON

Time and Accident are committing daily havoc on the originals deposited in our public offices.* The late war has undone the work of centuries in this business. The lost cannot be recovered, but let us save what remains."[1] So wrote Thomas Jefferson in 1791; and in 1809, William Hening, in his introduction to the *Statutes at Large ... of Virginia,* supplemented the statement of the man to whom he gave chief credit for making the work possible: "But it is a melancholy truth, that though we have existed as a nation but little more than two hundred years, our public offices are destitute of official documents."[2]

Those of us who have to do with historical documents find ourselves in better case than Hening, but there are few, if any, who do not possess a sympathetic and full understanding of the situation and of how he and Jefferson felt about it. Most of us sometimes, and many frequently, have discovered that many places where we might properly expect to find historical documents gathered and preserved were similarly destitute of those we sought.

The historians of the older days knew little of the sense of frustration, the disappointment, and the acute distress which is part of the common lot of the modern members of the craft. What tradition lacked of a complete story, imagination could always supply. And while reliance upon records crept in, it crept very slowly through a great many years. Nor were there many historians; and so was lacking the steady, if oftentimes fruitless, pressure which to our credit we moderns seek to apply to those in whose hands is the power to compel the keeping and the preservation of records.[3]

*This paper was prepared for presentation as the 1943 presidential address, but its delivery was prevented by cancellation of the meeting.

It is a familiar fact that men began to make records at a very early period and have continued to do so ever since. Why, it may be asked, has so small a part of such records survived?

When we apply the question to the South, we must not overlook the fact that American colonization took place in modern times, and that it was carried on by people from lands long civilized, with highly developed governments, where records, public and private, had been kept for centuries. It might have been supposed that from the beginning adequate records would be kept, in conformity with the law and the practice at home. Said Hening: "The colony of Virginia having been planted long after the revival of letters in Europe, as well as the general introduction of the use of the press, it might have been expected that everything relating to our early history would have been reserved," and then wrote the lament which serves as an introduction to this paper.

But there was, of course, a period in the beginning of practically every one of the colonies when few records, public or private, were made. The reasons for this seem fairly clear. In most cases the early settlers were not of a type to be interested in records, even when capable of making them. In a new country, far distant from the home land, confronted by the primeval forests and swamps, by wild beasts, by savages, by famine, and by disease, the settlers were fully aware that a continued existence of the settlement was highly problematical, not to say doubtful in the extreme. Why keep records, they would have asked if, indeed, they had ever thought of it.

Further, in such periods of a community's life, its people are too busy, too concerned with the existing realities of life—indeed with its very preservation—to think about records. Only when there is reasonable probability of a future for the community, when it is envisioned as the home of their children and of their children's children through many coming generations, does the matter of keeping records assume any importance, even to the thinking portion of the population. Otherwise we might, for example, have records which, free from the taint or even suspicion of fraud, would show the fate of Raleigh's lost colony, of Ananias and Eleanor Dare, and the little girl, whose primacy among Americans of English blood possibly carried with it early destruction. As it is, the three letters, C R O "curiously carved" upon a tree, and graven on a post, "in fair capital letters" C R O A T O A N, furnish us food for imagination and little else.

I will agree, of course, that what happened to Virginia Dare exerted no influence upon the course of American history, but I venture, nevertheless, to maintain that a body of historical documents destitute of all such questions, of human feelings and behavior, of romance, if you will, of all those things that stimulate the imagination and humanize the past, would be a dreary expanse of documentary evidence.

A further question arises. Why, when once records were kept, were they not saved as they were in England? This inquiry, also, seems simple to answer. Even after the future security of the colony was assured, a stable government established, and records kept, there was, for a time at least—and usually a long time—no settled abode of the government where repositories for the preservation and care of records could be built. In such a period records followed officers—or, worse still, failed to follow—and at best were not more secure than Abraham Lincoln's law papers were in his old plug hat. There could not fail to be constant and heavy loss in such a period. Officials died and their families scattered and lost official papers, not, it must be supposed, with any special purpose or desire to do so, but from ignorance, carelessness, or procrastination. In the steady flux of American population, most of those retained by private individuals were destroyed in the course of time, but some emigrated with their holders to distant states where even today they probably survive. I, personally, have known of three North Carolina county court records of the colonial period in private hands in other states, and in none of these cases was there, apparently, the slightest recognition of the state's title to them. Even when the colonial government had "settled down" and public buildings were erected, there was nowhere adequate protection against fire, water, vermin, insects, and even the citizenry.

And finally there was no conception anywhere of the real relation between records and history. Records were kept for strictly utilitarian reasons and in a fairly short period of time most of them seemed completely obsolete, and consequently, in the minds of most people, entirely worthless. Even among the educated there was little realization of their importance to future generations. In this connection, it must be remembered that the idea that historical writings must be fully documented to be held authentic is a relatively modern development.

When destruction seemed almost the rule with public archives, it is not difficult to determine what happened to personal papers. Of course in the early period of all the colonies there was no great amount of such material, and at no time could there have been the possibility of accumulations which by modern standards would be called large. The whole way of life made this particularly true of the South. A sparse population, widely scattered, with the most limited means of communication, with few towns and most of those small, is not given to correspondence; and the keeping of diaries and other personal records must have been very exceptional. As time went on, some people, of course—but only a minority—carried on considerable correspondence and made personal records of various kinds, but the mortality of such accumulations was tremendous. When the owner moved, as most owners did sooner or later, not only in the colonial period but all through our history, the papers were apt to be left behind, or destroyed, or lost on the way. If the owner did not move, sooner or later his house burned, or, in the rare exceptions to this rule, rats, mice, and moths were apt to get in their devilish work. The real wonder is that any at all survived.

The original southern colonies all attempted by legislation to protect their public records. Virginia, like the other colonies, was chiefly interested in proceedings in the courts, and the first mention of records in the laws of Virginia was in Act I of the Grand Assembly of 1645, which provided for records of all court cases being kept by the clerks.[4] The preamble of an act passed in 1674, "concerning the regulating the Secretary's Office," contained the following explanation: "It appears that there hath beene a greate neglect in keeping the records in this country."[5] This statement brought from Hening this sharp comment: "Perhaps in no civilized country whatever, were the records so badly arranged and kept as in the former Secretary's office of Virginia."

In November, 1713, an act was passed providing for the registration with the minister of the parish of births, christenings, and burials. A statement in the preamble recites that a similar law of 1662 "hath for a long time been disused."[6] An act of December, 1787, for the protection of the county court records indicates that there must have been constant loss of them, as does the act of November, 1789, which made embezzlement of records a felony.[7] But nowhere have I been able to discover any law which made provision for proper housing and care of records.

In 1715 the governor of Maryland, reporting the loss of some records and injury to others, recommended, and the legislature passed, a law penalizing such action.[8] At the next session a committee appointed to investigate the condition of the records reported that in the move from St. Mary's to Annapolis some had been lost and a greater part of the rest were "much worn and damnified." A stronger act was then passed and was in force throughout the remainder of the colonial period.[9]

In North Carolina, as Stephen B. Weeks points out, the Fundamental Constitutions of Locke made the first provision for records, introducing to the English speaking world the formal recording of deeds of sale. They also specified that "the time of one's age that is born in Carolina, shall be reckoned from the day that his birth is entered in the registry and not before"; and that no marriage shall be lawful till it had been registered, "with the names of the father and mother of each party."[10] Penalties for failure to report births and deaths were also provided.

The *Revisal* of 1715 provided that in every precinct where there was no clerk of the church, the registrar of the precinct should record all births, marriages, and deaths.[11] Although the statute remained in force until the revolution, there is little evidence to show that it was widely obeyed.[12] Governor William Tryon in 1767 thus stated the case:

There is no regular register of births, burials, or marriages kept in any county in the province, although prescribed by some of our acts of assembly and a fee established for it. The reason for this neglect is chiefly owing to the extensive residence of most of the parishioners from the parish clerks or readers in their respective parishes or counties, many of which are from forty to fifty miles square and upwards, besides most families having a private burying place on their plantations.[13]

In 1738 an act was passed appropriating £2000 for the erection of "a sufficient gaol and office place for the safe keeping the records of the General Court,"[14] but apparently none was ever built. As a matter of fact, two years later the records were at the home of the secretary on the Cape Fear where they were in danger of being lost, altered, erased, or scattered, "to the great prejudice of the inhabitants."[15] In the same year Governor Gabriel Johnston complained that "the papers and records of the several offices are so dispersed that I am frequently obliged to send from one end of the province to another for them."[16] The secretary, as a matter of fact, kept an office in Brunswick, another in Edenton, a third in New Bern, and a fourth in Edgecombe County.[17]

Seven years later Governor Johnston mentioned, as a chief reason for establishing a capital and erecting public buildings, the urgent need for the preservation of the records in one place. The assembly agreed, promised consideration of the matter, mentioned the scarcity of funds, and did nothing.[18] Nor did the condition of the records improve. Matthew Rowan, acting governor in 1753, wrote the Board of Trade: "The public papers have come through so many hands of late that I am the less surprised at so few of them being delivered to me; but I shall cause strict search to be made and the Papers of the late Governor and President by their executors for such as remain."[19]

The next year Governor Arthur Dobbs said that "for want of proper places to keep the Offices in and to preserve records upon account of the changeable state of this Province," whenever officers "died, all papers die with them, for the Successors say they have got no papers, or, if any, those very insignificant, from their Predecessors."[20] Six years later he ordered all the records taken to Wilmington. The assembly objected strongly,[21] but in 1768 its clerk reported "that for want of a proper place for depositing and safe keeping" its own papers and journal books, several were "in part eaten by rats and mice and some totally destroyed."[22] Finally in 1771 the records were lodged in the Governor's Palace, where they stayed until they were removed to Raleigh.

After 1771 the only important legislation respecting records enacted for many years was the resolution of 1787, directing outgoing governors and the two houses of the general assembly to deposit all the documents in their possession with the secretary of state.[23]

The provisions of the Fundamental Constitutions applied, of course, to South Carolina as well as to North Carolina, and because of the strength of the Anglican Church, which made the parish system quite effective, they were put into operation far more fully. The existence of Charleston, too, made for better keeping and preservation of records. Keeping records, however, did not always mean their preservation. It was "very discouraging," as an official wrote the Lords Proprietors in the seventeenth century after a violent hurricane, "to a public officer to find his records floating about in three feet of water in his office." And through the years many records in Charleston, both public and private, floated in water—or else could be recorded as *spurlos versenkt*. But it was not for lack of early recognition of the importance of keeping records.

In 1694 the general assembly passed "an act for the better and more certain keeping and preserving of old registers and Publique Writings of this part of the Province."[24] The act of 1706 "for the Establishment of Religious Worship in this Province, according to the Church of England," after providing for the establishment of a vestry in every parish, made provision also "for the keeping a fair register of all such vestry's proceedings, and for registering of all births, christenings, marriages, and burials in each respective parish."[25] As Alexander S. Salley points out, "The vestry of a parish not only managed the affairs of the church, but attended to the business of the parish, such as building and repairing roads, bridges, and ferries; caring for the poor and providing schooling for the children of those who were too poor to pay tuition."

Three acts closed the colony's legislation on the subject of records. They were: an "Act for Preventing the embezzellment of the Public Records of this Settlement and for obtaining the Same out of the Hands of such persons as now have the custody thereof,"[26] passed in February, 1719/20; the appointment of a committee in 1736 to consider "the State of the Public Records of the Province ... and of a proper means to preserve the Records in a better manner than has been heretofore usually done"; and an act of the same year, putting into effect an English statute, making it a felony to "falsely make, forge, counterfeit, alter, change, deface, or eraze" any record of the province.[27]

In the years following the establishment of seats of government, central and local, in the colonies, the progress of destruction, while checked, was never stopped. State house and courthouse fires were numerous. Changes in the location of capitals and county seats occurred frequently. In Maryland, the first recorded loss of records occurred in Ingle's Rebellion, when nearly all the early ones were destroyed. St. Mary's was the capital of the province until 1695 when it was moved to Annapolis, with a considerable loss of records. Nine years later the state house burned with even greater loss.

Numerous Virginia records narrowly escaped destruction in Bacon's Rebellion, only to be otherwise lost. Fire at Jamestown in 1698, at Williamsburg in 1705 and again in 1746 when the capitol was burned, in Richmond during the Revolution, particularly in Arnold's raid, again at William and Mary in 1859, and in Richmond in 1865 when the general court building was burned by Federal troops, made a wreck of Virginia archives. Much, too, was destroyed during the intervals between fires through lack of care in storage.[28]

North Carolina, having steadily lost records in the colonial period, as already described, lost heavily when the capitol was burned in 1831. Federal occupation of the capitol in 1865 was almost as destructive.

South Carolina suffered losses of records in the fire of 1698 and when the state house in Charleston burned in 1778, as well as in the British invasion of 1780–81. So long as the capital remained at Charleston the records were exposed to constant danger also from tempest and flood. Later on, in the fire of 1842 there was loss, as there was when Sherman's army reached Columbia; but South Carolina's losses were lighter than those of either Virginia or North Carolina. This was partly the result of better arrangements, from the beginning, for preserving records, and partly because of prompt measures to secure duplicate records whenever possible in case of destruction.[29]

Georgia records, in addition to the perils of fire, flood, vermin, and official carelessness common to all the states, encountered those of frequent travel. During the Revolution they were taken from Savannah to Charleston, then to New Bern, and thence to Maryland, and at last to Augusta, remaining there until 1799 when they were carried to Louisville. They tarried there until 1807, when they were moved to Milledgeville, to remain there—such as survived—for sixty years, and then to come to rest, finally let us hope, in Atlanta in 1868. Anyone who has ever gone through the horrifying experience of moving—or who has watched others move—from houses long occupied will not need to be told what those moves cost in terms of destruction. And in addition, the archives lay in the path of Sherman's army in 1864 with the usual result of such proximity. The capitol was occupied and sacked, and it is little short of a miracle that any were left to be moved to Atlanta. Sufficient to say that "nearly all of the papers relating to the twenty years of the government of the Trustees which had ever been in Georgia, and many of those relating to the rule of the Royal Governors, were lost or entirely destroyed."[30]

Nor is this the whole of the sad story. The state through all these years had shown little interest in the preservation of its records, but during one period there were signs of an historical awakening. In 1824 the legislature appropriated a small sum of money to be paid to Joseph Valence Bevan, a collector of Georgia material, for the purpose of collecting and publishing all the historical papers in the capitol. Bevan began his work with enthusiasm, visited England in connection with it, and then died. In 1837 the legislature authorized the appointment of an agent to secure copies in Great Britain of the records relating to Georgia, and Charles Wallace Howard was appointed. He spent two years in England, and at an expense of about $7,000 brought back twenty-two large volumes of transcripts of great historical significance. These were used by Stevens, White, and Jones, and doubtless would have been used by many later investigators, but for the fact that, lent by the secretary of state to Henry A. Scomp, of Oxford, then writing a work entitled *King Alcohol in the Realm of King Cotton,* they were destroyed by fire in his house.[31]

To Florida belongs the distinction of never losing a capitol and of paying much less attention to her records than any southern state. Records were poorly kept and quite as poorly preserved. The coal bin and the garret alike were repositories of many that were made.[32]

Alabama records, like those of Georgia, were peripatetic. The first capital was St. Stephens. Then Huntsville served temporarily until suitable buildings could be erected at Cahaba. In 1826, six years after they were moved to Cahaba, they were carried to Tuscaloosa where they remained until 1846, when they made their supposedly last trek. Packed in 113 boxes, they rode to the new capitol at Montgomery, where most of them were burned three years later when the building was destroyed. Again, in 1865, when the records were moved from Montgomery in advance of Wilson's raid and carried to Eufaula, and some even to Augusta, there was heavy loss on each step of the trip.[33]

Mississippi records have fared better, though they, too, moved frequently. During the Civil War, part of the records were moved to Meridian, then to Enterprise, Columbus, and Macon, then to the penitentiary in Jackson, and finally back to the capitol. In 1863 Federal troops occupied the capitol and much of what had been left was destroyed. On the whole the state is fortunate in what has survived.[34]

Louisiana had eleven changes of capital between 1722 and the close of the period under consideration.[35] She has had only one capitol fire, but a disastrous one—when Federal troops occupied Baton Rouge in 1862. The destruction of the capitol was accompanied by the loss of most of the state records and those of the Louisiana Historical Society. Through the assistance of Lyman C. Draper, a considerable portion of the unburned archives owned by the Historical Society were later recovered from the widow of a Federal officer. Returned to Baton Rouge, they were speedily forgotten; but when Tulane University was founded they were sent there, stored in an attic and again forgotten, until they were rescued and brought to light by Colonel William Preston Johnston.[36]

The archives of Texas suffered the usual losses prior to the Civil War, the most serious one occurring when the office of the adjutant general burned in 1855 with irreplaceable records of the early days of Texas and those of the army and navy of the Republic. In 1881 the capitol burned, but very few records were lost.[37]

Arkansas archives have suffered, in the words of one closely familiar with their history, from "carelessness, the fortunes of war, and the lack of store room." On the Federal capture of Little Rock in 1863, the capital was moved to Washington and some of the archives were moved there by wagon. It was reported that when paper became scarce some of the record books were used in making cartridges. Some not thus used probably were never returned to Little Rock. By the opening of the twentieth century some of the offices had become so crowded that, in desperation, officials dumped out some of the archives and sold them to a dealer to be shipped to a paper mill.[38]

Tennessee records suffered heavily through the movement of the capital. This moving, combined with carelessness, ignorance, and indifference, contributed to the destruction. The state house never burned, but the archives, many of them, moved from pillar to post, packed into the basement of the building, "piled in masses on the stone floors among old paint barrels, ashes, trash of every description, dirt, and grime," grew wet, rotted, and many were burned because the janitor thought them "nasty" and they "smelled bad."[39] Many were sold as waste paper. Hunters for stamps and autographs wrought their wicked will among them. Altogether it is the saddest story among the fourteen I am endeavoring to tell.[40]

Kentucky has been one of the unlucky states as regards fire. Her capitol burned in 1813 and in 1824; the secretary's office in 1865; and during the Goebel-Taylor struggle, when troops occupied the capitol, they made beds of archival manuscripts and lighted pipes with them, not even pausing to economize by making allumettes.[41]

And, to complete the dreary record, Missouri lost her capitol by fire in 1837, losing her most valuable archives, and repeated the performance in 1911.

The story is as bad, perhaps worse, with respect to local records. Every state has had many and disastrous courthouse fires. The figures are not obtainable, but the facts are well known. For example, North Carolina has had fifty-four courthouse fires; Arkansas, thirty-five; South Carolina, after considerable loss by accidental fires, was to have, during the Civil War, a major calamity when several of the Low Country counties moved their records to Columbia for safety. Virginia counties have suffered terribly. From various causes—fire, water, enemy invasion, and domestic carelessness—the early records of eight counties have been completely destroyed; those of fourteen have been partially destroyed; and still others have suffered heavily. Louisiana has had many courthouse fires, and the records in very few parishes go back as far as fifty years.

Fire and war account for much of the loss of county records, but the utter carelessness of their legal custodians must be regarded as more responsible. That carelessness has been almost incredible. Nor is it entirely a matter of the distant past. I myself have seen in several states records historically valuable beyond calculation rotting in the basements and being eaten by rats in the attics of courthouses. I once rescued eight volumes of colonial county court records from a mass of papers already destined to destruction by county officials. Another time I received a message from a county official in a state not my own, that if I would notify him in advance and come with two trucks he would fill them with pre-Civil War records. It is scarcely necessary, I hope, to say that the invitation was not accepted.

Perhaps the most startling example of official carelessness is the case where the chief of the fire department in a southern capital ordered the burning of a very large accumulation of boxes and bundles of papers on the floor of a basement room of the capitol. They proved to be personal manuscript material, sent in over a number of years to the state department having charge of manuscripts. These cases are undocumented for obvious reasons, but they are facts. They form part of a vast amount of confidential, "hush-hush" information of which I have been made the repository during years of manuscript hunting.

Such in brief is the story of public records. Let us examine briefly the story of private and personal ones, as well—those human documents which, not less important than public archives, are far more living and fascinating than archival material can ever be, and which serve to clothe the skeletons of public records with flesh and blood, as it were, and to breathe into their nostrils the breath of life.

The same seemingly relentless fate that has overtaken much of southern archival material has pursued personal records of every kind, and with even greater success. It could not be otherwise. The repositories for public archives were inadequate; there were none for private papers other than individual homes. Public buildings burned frequently; private dwellings practically always.[42] Invading armies, whether in the heat of battle or in the calmer and more dangerous throes of hate, were much more likely to destroy residences than capitols and courthouses. While public officers were usually incompetently and ignorantly careless of records, some realized their importance; but nobody was responsible for private papers and, except in the case of those of outstandingly great men, no one thought them of any importance. Even when cared for as part of the *lares* and *penates* of a home and family, eventually a godless generation would let them be destroyed.

For an example, take the case of the papers of Colonel Theodorick Bland, a distinguished Virginian of the Revolutionary period. Colonel Bland died in 1790, leaving no children. His widow, twice remarried, died in France, and the home and his papers became the property of the nephew of her second husband, who took no interest in them or care of them. In consequence, he had "fulminated upon his head certain inverted blessings" by John Randolph, who sought vainly to get the papers for preservation.

The Cawson's house, in which the manuscripts were stored, burned down. "An apartment to which they were afterward removed, from age actually rotted down underneath them. At another period the papers . . . were deposited in the mouldy damps of a cellar, tossed in a heap together pell-mell. The next translation they underwent was to a carriage-house or barn." The first intimation of their continued existence came through the finding by the owner of a neighboring place of a letter of George Washington on the bottom of a bucket of eggs.[43]

About 1833 Charles Campbell, happening to hear of the existence of some papers of Colonel Bland at Cawson's, met the lady of the house, who, when he inquired about them, "very obligingly reached down a bundle of letters of divers revolutionary worthies, from the interstices of the eaves of the porch, where they were nicely pigeon-holed." A Negro boy then led him to "a small, new-built out-house in one corner of the yard, wherein, on opening the door, was found a capacious wooden chest, full to the brim of manuscripts. . . . One of the first my eye lit on was a letter, on an ample sheet, from George Washington, dated at Cambridge,

Mass. The manuscripts were (many of them) mouse-nibbled, rat-eaten, stained, torn and faded; and they certainly breathed anything but 'Sabean odors from the spicy shore of Araby the blest.' " How familiar it all sounds!

Campbell, in spite of "a wish to revisit the place," shortly afterward left Virginia with the wish ungratified, and remained away for several years. From Alabama he wrote the secretary of the Virginia Historical Society and Edmund Ruffin about them. Ruffin obtained a basket of the papers, but examined them only briefly and kept them until Campbell's return. After some arrangement of them, and after a plan to publish them had failed, Campbell, too, put them aside. "The old papers were now consigned to the drawers of an antiquated bureau, up three flights of stairs, and there allowed to repose." Later, Campbell found some more at Cawson's. From these came the well-known Bland papers, very valuable historically, but only a fragment of those which Colonel Bland left behind him.

Private papers, too, were beset by dangers unknown to archives. To begin with, social history, which relies so heavily on ordinary letters, is essentially a comparatively modern development. To a majority of southerners of an older day the thought of personal family letters being in a library, exposed to the eyes of outsiders, was a horrible one; nor is that point of view unknown in these more enlightened days. As a matter of fact and of personal reminiscence, I can recall a number of occasions when I suspect that only the obligations of hospitality were all that prevented the dogs from being loosed on me! Dr. William P. Palmer, in the introduction to his *Calendar of Virginia State Papers,* indicates that he had experienced similar difficulty. "It cannot be amiss to refer to the persistence with which private individuals retain in their possession valuables, which, with mistaken pride, they keep constantly exposed to the common accidents of life. This has been a fruitful cause of loss."[44]

Perhaps worse than any other single scourge has been the mistress of the house, obsessed with a horror of "trash" and bent upon its destruction. Candor compels the admission, however, that frequently she has been aided and abetted by members of the other sex, who, if for no other reason than that difference, ought to have known better. And, finally, there was the cause, referred to by Moses Coit Tyler in 1886 as common to the whole country,

... that the private papers left by men in public life, which would in after time become of confidential, delicate, and priceless value in the study of events touched by these men's careers, should be negligently kept by their descendants or heirs, or as negligently dispersed, or left to destruction through the assaults of accident. American society is composed of more movable elements than was the case even in the Colonial time. We have few examples of families maintained through several generations in the same houses; our homes are of combustible material; and our habits are those of recklessness as to fires. The result of our present social conditions is that the kinds of historical documents now referred to, if retained in private custody, are peculiarly liable to neglect, and even to destruction.[45]

In the South, a rural region, sparsely settled, this danger was certainly intensified.

The result of it all is known to everyone who has ever attempted to carry on investigation in southern history. Because of it, innumerable interesting and important southern characters in American history are virtually unknown as persons; they are merely names. Many are not even names. What Milton, in the *Areopagitica,* said of the destruction of a book applies with greater force to the destruction of those documents which reveal the thoughts, aspirations, and plans of human beings as they lived their lives rather than wrote books.[46] William Palmer, much later, evidently so thought: "The loss of a single manuscript is often a sort of literary homicide; it is the utter and irremediable destruction of an author."[47]

When we call a roll of men distinguished in the life of the South, we find that only a few have correspondence and other papers surviving. For every one whose personal papers have been preserved, dozens can be counted whose papers cannot be found. It is understandable for characters of the Colonial and Revolutionary periods, and of some, even many, of later periods; but it is none the less regrettable. We have had so much to say of our pride in and our devotion to the memory of the Confederacy that it is a somewhat startling fact there remain today papers of only a handful of the men to whom the South turned in the fateful days of 1860–61, during the years of war, and in those later years, even harder in many respects, that we know as Reconstruction. The hundreds of men who constituted the secession conventions, the Confederate cabinet, Congress, and judiciary; the generals; and the members of the constitutional conventions (so-called) which followed the war, all together have left behind only a pitiful fragment of the important papers they must have owned. Some unreconstructed denizen of the region north of the Mason and Dixon line might be pardoned for believing that this is a part of a just retribution for their sins!

Harsh years of poverty and of readjustment following the war account in part for this situation, but the lack of care by their families in later years accounts for much more. The papers belonged to them legally, it is true, but I think all historians will agree with me in denying their moral right to destroy such vital records as those we know they did destroy.

And on the foundation of our knowledge we can safely erect an even vaster edifice of imagination or suspicion. Why, for example, should the papers of one of the two Confederate admirals have been fed to the fire over two whole winters, and those of the other left in a garret after the house was sold? Why should the papers of two of the most distinguished southern naval officers, one of the United States and the other of the Confederate navy, have been deliberately burned by the nephew of one who was also the son of the other? Was the consignment to the flames of a diary kept by the New England wife of an important member of the Confederate administration in Richmond—a superbly critical and clever picture of the Confederate government and capital—justifiable otherwise than in legality? We have to regard the burning of a house or its destruction by flood as one of the changes and chances of this mortal life, and I suppose we must include such quasi "acts of God" as the destruction of records by rats and mice; but we can be pardoned for any judgment we may form of those who store in cellar, barn, or corncrib—or, worse still, burn—the papers of ancestors, whether distinguished or undistinguished, for all have value equally in the sight of God and the historian.

I could multiply these cases indefinitely, but why? All southern historians probably have—or should have—their own list of offenders ready should some day the southern historical world decide to get revenge for all these crimes and injuries by setting up its own Hall of Infamy. Hening bitterly reproached the "myrmidons" of George III, who "with more than the savage barbarity of the Goths and Vandals committed to the flames" Virginia records. Dean William R. Inge was more just in his observation: "Ancient civilization fell by the invasion of barbarians. We breed our own." And so every one who knows the whole story will realize that our own people have destroyed a large part of what we may call our own Alexandrine Library.

Perhaps it is sound philosophy to realize that while ignorance of law is not a valid excuse for its violation, it can be so regarded in other fields than law. Perhaps we should agree with the statement of Worthington C. Ford that "Until recently we have done our best to destroy what we have, and shall be profoundly grateful that even a part remains." But all who profess to have a special interest in the history of the South will share the guilt of any destruction that may hereafter occur if they lose an opportunity to inform the manuscript-holding population of its duty in the premises. But in the light of experience, some of it acquired since I began to plan this paper, I can confidently prophesy that however gifted many may be as teachers they will fail hopelessly in the effort. The best we can hope for, as is the case in much of human attempts at instruction, is far from our ideal.

It must of course be remembered that not all of the destruction and other loss of southern documents can be attributed to natives or residents of the South. Dwellings in countless numbers were burned by Federal troops, and others were completely ransacked. As has already been mentioned, the papers in the various state houses that were occupied by Federal troops were stolen or destroyed in huge quantities. Innumerable courthouses suffered similarly. No year passes that some of the stolen papers do not turn up at auction sales or elsewhere. Benson J. Lossing gathered from returned soldiers a mass of such material, part of which was claimed after his death by the state of Virginia. They were finally withdrawn from sale, and, according to the latest evidence I have on the subject, are still held for some future final settlement.

The document of this sort that attracted the widest attention was the will of Martha Washington. A Federal colonel, whose headquarters were in the Fairfax County courthouse, found his men feeding county records to a stove; and on finding the will among the papers which remained, took possession of it. After his death his daughter sold it to the elder J. P. Morgan. In 1908, the board of county supervisors, having learned of its whereabouts, twice requested its return, but received no reply. After the death of Morgan a local chapter of the Daughters of the American Revolution, in a letter endorsed by the county clerk, requested its return, but J. P. Morgan, Jr., who had inherited it, declined to return it. A bill was then passed by the legislature instructing the governor to make a formal demand for its return, and the attorney general was authorized, in the event of a refusal, to bring suit in the Supreme Court of the United States for its recovery.

An informal request was made by Governor Henry C. Stuart, and Morgan again refused, declaring that the document would not be safe from fire in Fairfax. He offered, however, to give it to Mount Vernon if the will of George Washington should also be given; and as an alternative he made a similar proposal with respect to the Library of Congress. A personal interview between Governor Stuart and Morgan brought no agreement, and the formal demand of the state was then made. When no answer was received, suit was entered. Before the date when his answer to the complaint was due, Morgan sent a letter by Fairfax Harrison to the president of the Court of Appeals, stating that "eminent counsel" had assured him that the title of his father's estate to the will was "perfect and unassailable," but that rather than have the case tried he would return the will. The will was delivered with the letter, and finally was once more at home in Fairfax.[48]

I have thus far dealt with a gloomy matter—destruction. Are there no cheering aspects of my subject? There are several such aspects, even

in the period to which I have limited this discussion, as well as many
in the years immediately following. In outline they are known to many
of you and I shall deal with them only briefly.

Movements in the southern states looking to the preservation of records and making them available have taken several forms and have been
directed toward both state and semipublic activity. In point of time,
priority must be given to the latter type. In 1791 Massachusetts, the
birthplace of so many fine movements—whatever we may, hereditarily
or otherwise, think of some of them—and of so much forward-looking
legislation, led the way toward one method by the establishment of the
first, and in most respects the most successful, state historical society.
In the Introductory Address of the Society are two striking sentences
which should be read at every meeting of every historical society—general, state, or local—in the South: "Among the singular advantages
which are enjoyed by the people of the United States none is more
conspicuous than the facility of tracing the origins and progress of our
plantations.... With such advantages in our hands, we are wholly in-
excusable if we neglect to preserve authentic monuments of every memorable occurrence." And for good measure the following extract from a
letter of Jeremy Belknap to Ebenezer Hazard, about the same time,
concerning the Society, might be added: "We intend to be an active, not
a passive literary body; not to lie waiting, like a bed of oysters, for the
tide of communication to flow in upon us, but to seek and find, to
preserve and communicate literary intelligence, especially in the historical way."

Seven other northern states had also established such societies before
any southern state followed the good example. The Virginia Historical
Society was founded in 1831 and chartered three years later. It has led
an active, honorable, and useful career since that time. The Historical
Society of North Carolina was incorporated in 1833, but did not actually
come into being until 1844, by which time Louisiana, Georgia, Kentucky,
and Maryland had organized societies. Tennessee followed in 1849,
Alabama in 1850, South Carolina in 1855, Florida in 1856, and Mississippi in 1858. After the Civil War, Missouri in 1866, Texas in 1897, and
Arkansas in 1903, made the roll complete. But in actual fact some died
a-borning and others later, and through many years there were numerous
reorganizations and foundings of new societies to take their places. Only
the Maryland, Virginia, South Carolina, Georgia, Texas, and Missouri
societies lived on without resuscitation or replacement. Throughout the
earlier period of their existence, the southern societies in most cases
neglected their most fundamental function, namely, collecting source
material and making it available to writers. They were also notably, not

to say criminally, careless with such material as they gathered, and a considerable portion was lost.

In no southern state have local societies in any number flourished, though innumerable ones have been founded only quickly to die. Where they gathered manuscripts and other historical material, it was usually lost. Encouraging exceptions have been the Filson Club of Louisville, founded in 1884, and the Wachovia Historical Society of Salem, North Carolina.

Two notable contributions to the preservation of southern historical material deserve special attention. The first of these began in 1869, when a group of southern men, nearly all of whom had been conspicuous for service in the Confederacy, met in New Orleans and organized the Southern Historical Society, with General Jubal A. Early as president. The New Orleans organization was designed to be the parent of branches in all the southern states, but the plan did not work well, and in January, 1873, at Montgomery White Sulphur Springs, Virginia, a reorganization took place by which the home of the Society was moved to Richmond. In 1876 the publication of the *Southern Historical Society Papers* was commenced and, with several brief intervals, it has continued to the present. Through its forty-nine volumes a tremendous amount of source material in the form of records and reminiscences, as well as many secondary studies, has been preserved and made available. Its primary success was largely due to the passionate enthusiasm and devoted labors of Dr. J. William Jones, who served as secretary until 1886. His work was later carried on by Robert A. Brock, James Power Smith, and Harrison J. Eckenrode; and the president and moving spirit today is Douglas Southall Freeman.

The second came as a result of the discussions and conferences of a group of historically minded men in Washington, among whom may be mentioned General Marcus J. Wright, Thomas Nelson Page, Thomas M. Owen, Stephen B. Weeks, J. L. M. Curry, and Colyer Meriwether. A call for a meeting in Washington to organize a southern historical society, signed by ninety-five well-known men interested in history, was widely disseminated. On April 24, 1896, the meeting was held and the Southern History Association was formally organized, with William L. Wilson as president and Colyer Meriwether as secretary. It struggled for eleven years against all the obstacles which confront such organizations, chief among them, of course, being lack of popular interest and of adequate support. Largely through the untiring labor and interest of Colyer Meriwether, aided greatly by Stephen B. Weeks and General Marcus J. Wright, eleven annual volumes of its *Publications* and one extra volume were printed. They contained much valuable source material, many significant articles, and a wealth of reviews and notes which cover adequately the course of historical work in the South until 1907, when they ceased. The Association, miraculously solvent, suspended at the same time.

The part played by collectors in connection with southern records has been both good and bad. The autograph collector, as such, has been, historically speaking, not only an unmitigated nuisance, but a positive menace as well. No other agency has been so responsible for the deliberate dispersal of manuscript collections, to say nothing of the destruction incident to their work. But there are other types of collectors, whose work has been highly beneficial. At the sale of the library of the Earl of Southampton, who had been president of the London Company, William Byrd purchased three large folio manuscript volumes which contained the minutes of the Company and a summary of the legislature and judicial acts of the colony of Virginia. Jefferson saved many invaluable Virginia records. Lyman Draper's collection is known to every student of American history, with its records of Virginia, North Carolina, South Carolina, Georgia, Tennessee, and Kentucky. A large part of its contents would undoubtedly have been lost or destroyed but for his work. Louise Kellogg imaginatively describes Draper's collecting career as follows:

Everywhere he was received with great cordiality; his mission was approved, his aims commended. In the isolated farmsteads of the Old Southwest his coming was an event. Earnest and enthusiastic himself, he inspired confidence in his hosts; they accepted his own estimate of his mission and saw in him the chosen vessel ordained to present the lives of the pioneers to the world. To them he was in fact the savior of pioneer history, the inspired prophet who should cause to rise again the dry bones from the valley of the past.

Every possible effort was made to assist him in his chosen work. Not only were memories ransacked, but from their hiding-places old letters and documents were brought forth and pressed into his hands. No thought arose as to either loan or gift. Here was the rescuer of their forefathers' fame; here was the apostle of the historic record. Everything must be put at his disposal to make his work authentic. The half-forgotten, neglected papers would most of them soon have perished had not this knight errant of historic adventure passed by that way. The donors felt themselves privileged to cooperate with one whom they recognized as a scholar, who was to make the names they bore glorious before the world.[49]

A somewhat more realistic discussion of the collector, however, is the following comment by Worthington C. Ford:

I have a high admiration for the old-time collector, while thankful that the breed has died out. He took anything without perplexing his mind with questions of right or fitness. He thought nothing of borrowing from private and State offices, and training his memory to forget the fact of borrowing. His zeal was fed by his acquisitions, and while he started a church member in good standing he ended with a system of bookkeeping which gave a balance only in his favor. According to his lights he was correct in his position, for he sought to counteract the neglect of others, and in default of any other recognized custodian, he constituted himself master of the rolls. No doubt much has thus been saved which would otherwise have been lost, and for this he should have full credit. But much was also lost through his ignorance, lost actually and geographically, for what he got so cheaply he scattered with lavish hand and never appreciated the advantage of keeping great collections intact. A single autograph desired led him to break a series of letters, and never could the series be made good. His actions, entirely well intentioned, were unmoral, and rarely did he rise to so high a plane as to merit our gratitude unmixed with real regret that he should have been permitted to have his way.

In his blind and unmoral methods he represented the beginnings of the modern idea of preserving records; his methods, however, are directly opposed to this modern idea of preservation—truly a modern idea in this country, for it has come into application within the last 30 years. There is not in existence a private collection of size which does not contain documents easily recognized as public documents, drawn in some manner from some public source. No auction sale of autographs is held without a good sprinkling of state papers which have evidently strayed, and improperly, from their proper place of deposit. The romance of collecting is full of unexpected finds, but the romance of collecting is more than equaled in vivid interest by the sordid phase of obtaining by underhand methods what is desired.[50]

In a discussion of manuscript collectors, I cannot fail to take note of another type of collector in the recent past of the South, and recite the names of some of the notable pioneers in collecting for the cause of history—Saunders, Browne, Stanard, Tyler, Bruce, Owen, Connor, Salley, Rowland, Swem, Candler, Winkler, and Robinson. Their states, the South, and the nation are permanently richer for their work.

The southern states as well as the others were slow in waking to the importance of preserving records of the past and slower still in conceiving of the task as a duty and a responsibility of the state. Consequently, public record legislation, beyond routine provisions for keeping records, was long in coming. In nearly every case when action was taken, it was the result of the influence and efforts of a small group of public-spirited and historically minded men whose ceaseless appeals and powerful arguments finally prevailed over the indifference or, at best, listless inaction of politicians. Hening foresaw this in 1809 and wrote: "It is to the pious care of individuals only that posterity will be indebted for those lasting monuments."[51] As we shall see, this continued to be the case throughout all the period under discussion.

A more successful movement was a somewhat later one to induce the states to take action with respect to archives. A large part of the important records of the original states, as well as of most of the later ones, are in Europe, and gradually efforts were made to procure copies of such records. New York led the way, when in 1814 the Historical Society called upon the state to save its records. As a result, agents were sent to England, Holland, and France, for copies of all records relating to the colony, and presently publication of the *Documentary History of New York* was commenced.

North Carolina was the first southern state to take similar action. Its legislature, in the session of 1826–27, passed a resolution requesting the governor to make application to the British government for permission to procure for the state copies of all papers and documents in the office of the Board of Trade and Plantations that related to the Colonial history of the state. The only immediate result was that the desired permission was obtained and an *Index to Colonial Documents Relative to North Carolina* was prepared. In 1831 the legislature grew excited about the discussion of a supposed Mecklenburg Declaration of Independence, and appointed a committee to investigate the subject with provision for printing their report. It also provided for printing the journal of the provincial congress of 1776 and some other Revolutionary material. The burning of the capitol later in the year tended to discourage the historical movement for some years.

In 1843 the *Index* was printed by the state, and in the following year Governor John M. Morehead recommended that an agent be sent to London to copy the papers. The suggestion was not followed, but important legislation looking to the preservation of valuable records in the state was enacted. The establishment of the Historical Society, David L. Swain's statement of its purposes,[52] and its success in securing valuable historical records, enabled Governor William A. Graham to make so strong a report to the legislature of 1846–47 that it passed a resolution giving him very extended authority in the matter of publication of historical material. Nothing was published, but the succeeding legislature authorized the governor to expend a thousand dollars in procuring copies of the North Carolina records in England. Swain was appointed agent, and succeeding legislatures authorized an extensive program of printing, together with the expenditure of sufficient funds to send the agent to England and to have all the North Carolina records copied.

Work was actually begun when the Civil War intervened. The problems of war and later of Reconstruction were demanding and prevented the giving of much attention to records of the past. But the people emerged from the struggles of the period with a new vision and an enlarged conception of the meaning of history, and the task of those who sought to care for the past was never again so difficult. Through the efforts of

Colonel William L. Saunders and Governor Thomas J. Jarvis the legislature of 1881 was induced to pass a bill authorizing the publication of a body of Colonial and Revolutionary records which had recently been found. The legislature of 1883 authorized the collection and inclusion of material not in the possession of the state, and Colonel Saunders was thus able to secure the services of W. Noel Sainsbury of the British Public Record Office and to obtain a mass of valuable records.[53]

The result was the compilation and publication of the *Colonial Records*. Into them, Colonel Saunders as editor, who had for his monumental task no other equipment than a fine mind, capacity for unremitting toil, and unbounded love for his state, and who was so crippled by rheumatism and wounds that most of his time was spent either in bed or in a wheel chair, suffering intense pain almost all the time, put eleven years of his life, and died as the task was completed. The work then stopped for a time, but Judge Walter Clark succeeded to the editorship and through his industry, interest, and ability the sixteen volumes of *State Records* were added.[54]

In Virginia, Angus McDonald, acting under authority of the legislature, brought copies of important documents from England as early as 1859. The Civil War followed almost immediately, and for a good many years thereafter the state did nothing further toward the acquisition of copies of its early records or the preservation of those records it had. In a limited way the Historical Society continued its work, but in the 1870's the state library began to procure transcripts from the Public Record Office. These were supplemented by the purchase of various collections of Virginia records. In 1892 the legislature appropriated five thousand dollars to be expended in copying the county records previous to 1700, and under this act forty-one large volumes containing copies of records of eleven ancient counties were prepared.[55] Later, an elaborate program of publication was undertaken by the state library, but the greater part of that work was done later than the period of this study.

The legislature of Maryland took a highly important step in 1882. The records of the state had been reported on at intervals from 1722, and in 1835 the Ridgely report had described them as stored in "disused offices, cupboards, underneath the staircases, . . . the lofts, the cellars, and even the stairway to the dome." It told of finding "the remains of two large sea-chests and one box which had contained records and files of papers which were in a state of total ruin."[56] Their condition had not been greatly improved since. In 1847 the state had made the Historical Society custodian of a considerable body of records, and by the act of 1882 it was made the custodian of all records of Maryland prior to 1783, and the necessary appropriation for publication was provided.

Much had already been lost other than by fire. "Many early Maryland documents seem to have disappeared in connection with the researches of Scharf, the historian of the State. The notable collections of Peter Force and Joseph [Jared?] Sparks appear, however, to have been enriched in the same way."[57] In addition to the manuscript material thus secured, the Society during the next few years obtained transcripts from the Public Record Office of all the Maryland papers down to 1668, and a volume containing copies of the laws from 1649 to 1676. It also recovered some important records that had been sold for waste paper, and the Council Journals of 1692–93, which had been given to the Mercantile Library Association. It then began the publication of the *Archives of Maryland,* which has continued ever since.

The evil fate of Georgia's copies of its records has already been mentioned. From 1837 almost to the very end of the century "the State, as such, gave little further heed to this problem. . . . During this long period of three-quarters of a century, not a single legislative act was passed looking to the preservation of the records; and in this same time not only were the records of the immediate past not being properly safeguarded and preserved, but the priceless papers of an earlier day were being rapidly lost, destroyed, or allowed to deteriorate." Nobody was charged with their preservation, and priceless documents were stored in basements to rot or to be used for lighting fires.[58] The only redeeming feature in the historical situation of the state was the Georgia Historical Society. With limited means, with a small membership, in a state which lacked any interest in history, but fortunately in an historic community, justly proud of its past, it kept the torch alight.

In 1885 provision was made by law for the compilation of a roster of Georgia troops in the Civil War, but not until the very end of the century was any forward step taken. Then under the leadership of Governor Allen D. Candler, who, as secretary of state, had discovered the condition of the records and had become keenly anxious for their salvation, something was accomplished. His urgent recommendations to the legislature bore fruit. The office of compiler of state records was created and Candler upon leaving the governorship was appointed to it, charged with the editing and publication of the state's Colonial, Revolutionary, and Confederate records.[59]

As has been seen, South Carolina, as judged by her legislation, throughout the Colonial period was forward-looking as well as backward-looking with respect to records. She continued to be so during the period of statehood. In 1800 provision was made for indexing records and, in the following year, for procuring suitable cases in which to keep them. In 1804 an act was passed to compel all persons having papers of the recently abolished county courts to turn them in to the district courts of ordinary. A few years later nearly $15,000 was paid for copying of old records in order to save them, and through the years up to the Civil War considerable sums were expended for filing cases, arranging, and indexing. During this period the state bore part of the expense of publishing John Drayton's *Memoirs of the American Revolution* (2 vols.; Charleston, 1821), Bartholomew R. Carroll's *Historical Collections of South Carolina* (2 vols.; New York, 1836), Robert W. Gibbes's *Documentary History of the American Revolution* (3 vols.; New York, 1853–57), and the first three volumes of the *Collections* of the South Carolina Historical Society. In the case of Gibbes, the bread cast upon the waters returned with generous increase, for he gave the state the original documents which he had spent many years in collecting.

In 1849 the legislature authorized the appointment of an agent for "the collecting, arranging, and indexing of the records which relate to the Colonial and Revolutionary history of South Carolina," and as a result, many papers were found in the various offices and progress was made in arranging them. Interestingly enough, a movement begun in 1850 to construct a fire-proof building for the preservation of records led to the construction of a new state house. A committee appointed to make plans reported in 1851:

> The Legislature will remember that at the last session it was agreed that the sales of lots in the town of Columbia, shall be placed at the disposal of the Committee, for the purpose of erecting the basement story of a fireproof building, for the deposit of the Records of the State.
> The Committee, after great deliberation, have determined to erect the said building as a part of a plan which might be used as a State House.

The general assembly approved the plan and authorized the construction of the building, which was so impressive, though incomplete, that Sherman spared it and invaluable records were thus saved.[60]

Even during the Civil War South Carolina enacted legislation providing for preservation of the records of the Palmetto Regiment in Mexico, and passed the first of a long series of acts designed to secure for the state complete records of its part in the war which was then raging. And in 1894 the Historical Commission of the State of South Carolina was created, "to procure such documents or transcripts of documents and such other material relating to the history of South Carolina as they may deem necessary or important." By it forty large manuscript volumes of transcript of South Carolina documents were procured from the British Public Record Office, most of which are still unpublished.

When we consider how cursed Charleston and the Low Country have been by invading armies and by earthquake, tempest, flood, and fire, it is little short of miraculous that so large a proportion of their records have been preserved.

The preservation and care of Texas records have been the joint work of the state and the University of Texas, most of their activity having occurred later than the time covered here. The state's part of the work has been done largely through the state library. In 1898 the University of Texas acquired the Bexar Archives in 300,000 folios, to which it has added 70,000 transcripts. Thousands of documents in the United States and abroad have also since been copied by photostat or microfilm, and the acquisition of the Genaro Garcia Collection, also in later years, should not be overlooked.[61]

Mississippi, likewise in the later period, secured twenty-two volumes of transcripts from England, thirty-two from France, and nine from Spain.[62] Very few of these have been published.

Although provision was made in the Louisiana Purchase for the transfer of the French and Spanish archives of the territory, it was discovered later that when the Spanish regime came to an end the records were looted and the larger part of those of the Spanish period taken to Havana and Pensacola. Those at Pensacola were later destroyed by fire, and that or some similar fate probably overtook those at Havana. Many of the French records also disappeared. When François Xavier Martin was preparing to write his *History of Louisiana,* he found in Paris and used extensively the "Archives de la Marine," which contained all the most important records concerning the discovery and colonization of Louisiana. As Grace King says: "It is to him, writing in full comprehension of the history of the state, that we are indebted today for all that we possess of the archives of Louisiana."

Judge Charles E. A. Gayarré was probably chiefly instrumental in inducing the legislature in 1847 to appropriate $2,000 to procure documents from Spain. The agent employed, Pascual de Gayangos, went to Seville and Madrid, and after great difficulty secured a thousand pages of manuscript in two quarto volumes, prepared by Felix Magne of New Orleans, then residing in Paris. Gayarré was also largely responsible for the temporary revival of the comatose Historical Society, and actively associated with him in this interest were Benjamin F. French, who compiled the well-known *Historical Collections of Louisiana,* and Edmond Forstall. Gayarré, secretary of state at the time, was working to procure copies of the Louisiana archives in Spain when he ceased to hold office, but he personally obtained documents for his *Spanish Domination.* Forstall and John Perkins, commissioned by the Historical Society to make investigations in France, arranged with Pierre Margry for transcripts of all the Louisiana records in the "Archives de la Marine."[63]

Just before and after the end of the nineteenth century, nearly every one of the southern states had become sufficiently historically minded to make the most important step yet taken for the future organized care of their records—both public archives and personal manuscripts. This was the establishment, with more or less adequate support, of departments of archives and history, or historical commissions, acting through directors or secretaries. In this new venture, Alabama led the way in 1901 under the guidance of Thomas M. Owen. Mississippi followed the next year, and Georgia took a definite step in the same direction. North Carolina in 1903, South Carolina in 1905, Virginia in 1906, Texas and Arkansas in 1909, Maryland in 1935, and Florida in 1941, complete the list. Missouri put its archival responsibilities in the hands of the State Historical Society, and Kentucky has taken a short step in the same direction. In Louisiana the Historical Society, thanks largely to the inspiration of the late Henry P. Dart, has been increasingly active, and the University has established a vigorous department of archives with state sanction and support. In 1900 the Public Archives Commission said that "The Southern States have done relatively much less than the others in this direction." Thirteen years later Worthington C. Ford was able to say: "Yet in spite of this drawback the history of the South and of Southern men is taking a form which promises good results, and every one of the original Southern States is doing more to make what it has available for history than is my own State of Massachusetts."[64]

It is not within the province of this paper to discuss the developments of the past thirty-five years, but it is not amiss to say that they have done much to put a better taste in the historical mouth. There has been much education of the southern people with respect to the value of records. Great masses of them have been saved and made available to historical investigators. State agencies, universities, and historical societies cooperate in the patriotic task of perpetuating the story of our past.

Yes, we have come far on the road to reform, but we can travel faster and farther. It is not enough merely to provide the safe homes for manuscript material and gather it in when found. We must continue to educate the people of the South until they realize the value of documentary material. Nearly half a century ago William P. Trent, in an address at Vanderbilt University, humorously related a southern happening. It would be gratifying to think that it was characteristic only of a bygone period. Not so; it can be matched again and again in the recent past. It was then, and is only to a lesser degree today, in accord with what used to be called "good Southern tradition." The story follows:

A certain Georgia lawyer, whose name is not given, wrote an account of some stirring scenes in his State's early history. He died before his monograph was published. Two brother lawyers of high standing were appointed his executors. They approached the delicate task of apportioning the estate among the several heirs and things went on swimmingly for a time, until they came to the testator's manuscript. Here a difficulty arose. It could not be divided. To publish it would be an unheard of extravagance. It could not be left to become a bone of contention among the heirs. What then did these erudite lawyers, men who could have defended with great zeal and eloquence the institution of slavery or the practice of duelling, do with this manuscript? They burned it.[65]

May it be the happy fortune of the Southern Historical Association speedily to make such happenings matters merely of tradition and no longer of practice.

Chapter x

A Half-Century
of Southern Historical Scholarship

WENDELL H. STEPHENSON

BEFORE entering definitely upon my subject I wish to congratulate Vanderbilt University directly, and the Southern people indirectly, upon the establishment and successful career of the society to which I am to speak tonight.* I have long held not only that Southern history ought to be more carefully studied and the materials for it gathered together, but that our universities are the proper places of all others for such study and for the gathering of such materials."

In these words William P. Trent, professor of English and history at the University of the South, began an address before the Vanderbilt Southern History Society a half-century ago. Enlightened scholar and prescient penman, he observed that Vanderbilt's central location enhanced her opportunity to become a hub of historical activity, alluded to the modern scientific attitude toward history, encouraged avoidance of partisanship and sentimentalism in writing the history of the South, deplored the unliterary character of monographic studies, and pleaded for "a poet's imagination and a philosopher's intuition" in establishing values and relationships. He pointed to the necessity for assembling collections of letters, plantation account books, southern newspapers and periodicals, Indian relics, the writings of southern authors, and the imprints of southern presses. Prophetically, he spoke of publishing monographs "in a magazine of Southern history."[1]

If Trent had been active in the historical guild a decade ago, he would have witnessed the materialization of a cherished desideratum; if he could inventory advancement from the perspective of 1944, his hope-

*Presented in Nashville, Tennessee, November 3, 1944.

fulness of fifty years ago would give place to genuine optimism. The transformation that has been wrought in southern historiography is a significant theme in the development of a New South.

This annual meeting marks the tenth anniversary of the Southern Historical Association and the *Journal of Southern History*. In the decade that has elapsed since a score of historians assembled in Atlanta to found the Association and its magazine, southern historical scholarship has broadened and deepened; historians of the South have become conscious of their unity and strength; accessible annual meetings have promoted professional improvement; new state historical magazines have appeared and old ones have been revived; the assembling of records in archives and libraries has been accelerated; college and university courses in southern history have increased rapidly; research and writing have been stimulated by the publication of a reputable review; and a cooperative history of the region has been projected. In short, historical scholarship has advanced appreciably beyond the frontier of 1934.

It must not be supposed, however, that southern historiography was a voice crying in the wilderness or that a new era dawned abruptly with the founding of the Association and the launching of a scholarly magazine. Pioneers had been laboring for a generation to promote impartial, objective investigation of the South's history. Their efforts were coeval with the development of systematic, scientific procedure so closely related to the origins of the American Historical Association exactly a half-century before our own society came into existence. The closing years of the nineteenth century witnessed the birth of a new departure; its application to the history of the South paralleled its influence on the writing of other American history. A new approach and a new method became the order of the day regardless of period or section.

From the vantage point of the 1940's, it is clear that southern historical scholarship received its initial impetus at the Johns Hopkins University under the leadership of that aggressive scholar, Herbert B. Adams. His interest in the South was incidental to his major emphasis, institutional history; but he published some significant monographs in that field, notably the *College of Willam and Mary* (1887) and *Thomas Jefferson and the University of Virginia* (1888); trained a score or more of young southerners in historical methodology; provided a medium of publication through the establishment of the Johns Hopkins University *Studies in Historical and Political Science;* and exerted a wholesome and constructive influence upon an incipient scholarship in the southern region. Courses in the history of the South were first offered at the Hopkins in the 1890's, and in the same decade a beginning was made in assembling a southern collection in the University library. Adams' reputation for objectivity, a conviction that Baltimore was a southern city, and special scholarships available to residents of Maryland, Virginia, and North Carolina were factors that attracted competent graduates of southern colleges to the Hopkins for advanced work.

There was nothing in Adams' nativity or education to foretell a debt of gratitude the South eventually owed him. A native of Massachusetts, he grew up in an atmosphere of Puritanism, attended Phillips Exeter Academy and Amherst College, and took the doctorate at Heidelberg University in 1876. Scientifically trained in politics, history, philosophy, and literature by the able German scholars, Heinrich von Treitschke, Johann C. Bluntschli, Wilhelm Ihne, and Kuno Fischer, he returned to the United States to accept a post-doctoral fellowship at the new Johns Hopkins University. For the next quarter-century he occupied a pivotal position in the development of historical scholarship in the United States. "If I were to sum up my impression of Dr. Adams," Woodrow Wilson recalled, "I should call him a great Captain of Industry, a captain in the field of systematic and organized scholarship." Neither a profound lecturer nor a brilliant writer, Adams discovered "talent where others did not see it," inspired students with enthusiasm for the study and writing of history and politics, and stressed "more fields to be cultivated and more reputations to be made."[2]

The nucleus of the Adams system was the "Seminary in History and Politics," embracing four or five teachers and twenty-five to fifty graduate students. Physical surroundings were conducive to an atmosphere of scholarship: tables were covered with historical, political, and economic journals; cases contained books and manuscripts of Bluntschli, Edouard Laboulaye, and Francis Lieber; cases and walls were lined with busts and pictures of statesmen and historians; and a special shelf was reserved for publications of former students.[3]

As graduate students from the South increased, a southern history room was provided to house a collection of materials on the history and literature of the region. The year 1891 witnessed the acquisition of two invaluable collections. Books and pamphlets relating to slavery, assembled by James G. Birney and his son, General William Birney, were presented to the University. Probably as a result of the Birney donation, Colonel J. Thomas Scharf of Baltimore gave to the Hopkins library his collection of pamphlets, manuscripts, autographs, and books. "I have long noted with regret," the donor wrote, "how imperfectly the history, general and local, of the Southern States has been written, and the fact that this imperfection has been largely due to the absence or inaccessibility of material. . . . It is my hope that the Johns Hopkins University, founded by a Southern man in a Southern city, may see the way to do for the South what the Northern Universities have done for the North."[4] Unfortunately, the original zeal for building up a great collection at the Hopkins did not long endure, and after the lapse of a decade or two, other southern universities continued this pioneering work so auspiciously begun in Baltimore.

Special lectures on topics in the history of the South were both cause and result of expanding interest in that field. In the last decade of the century, Adams invited J. Franklin Jameson to lecture on the political and constitutional history of the southern states, David F. Houston on the nullification movement, and John S. Bassett on the Negro.[5] In 1896 James C. Ballagh, instructor in the department, inaugurated a course in southern history. Lectures, based upon original research, discussed land and labor, the tariff, internal improvements, westward expansion, agricuture, commerce, and manufactures. Students were sent to the sources for research on topics in Virginia, Carolina, and Alabama history.[6] Here again, a policy that contributed to the development of southern historical scholarship was ultimately abandoned at the Hopkins, but other schools carried it forward. By 1913 six colleges and universities were offering courses in the history of the South; the number had increased to thirty or forty by the 1920's, and to nearly a hundred by 1940.

One other aspect of the Hopkins influence on the South remains for discussion. With few exceptions, Adams-trained men were productive scholars. Quantitatively, their record of achievement was exceptional. By 1901 southern Hopkins men, students and faculty, had published over seven hundred books, monographs, and articles, 42 per cent of which dealt with the South; and men from other sections had produced an additional fifty-one articles. Some of the monographs were printed in the University *Studies,* with the number on the South during the preceding six years equaling the total for the first twelve. "Such a record is one to be honored in any field of research," a Dunning student wrote, "especially in one so important and long neglected."[7] Qualitatively, many of the early numbers seem more like unpublishable term reports than serious contributions to knowledge. It is questionable whether some of the doctoral dissertations published in the *Studies* in Adams' day would now be acceptable as masters' theses.

If one were to call the roll of southerners trained in history, economics, and politics at the Hopkins, the sheer weight of names would reveal the University's influence on the southern region. Most of them found academic or editorial positions in the South, and some attained enviable reputations as teachers of local or southern history, as founders of historical societies, and as productive scholars in the southern field. The careers of a few indicate how the spirit and atmosphere of the Hopkins were carried to southern colleges and universities.

The varied activities of Bassett at Trinity College yielded tangible results.[8] He became at once a productive scholar; he assembled books, pamphlets, newspapers, and manuscripts in the Trinity College Library; and he founded the *Historical Papers of the Trinity College Historical Society* and the *South Atlantic Quarterly*. Bassett's letters to his mentor,[9] unlike those of other Hopkins men, reveal a dynamic interest in cultural, political, and social problems of his state and the southern region. His professional zeal was not limited to history, for he also sought to promote literary criticism and academic freedom.

Then, as now, institutions of higher learning expected professors to teach, and Trinity College was no exception to the rule. Bassett offered a wide variety of courses, some of them far afield from history. In 1897 he introduced two courses in North Carolina history, one for seniors and one for graduates, but both demanded research in original materials. Two years later he offered the "Secession Movement in America," designed to examine antebellum and postwar political life and to study impartially the military history of the Civil War. Not until 1907, after William K. Boyd succeeded Bassett, was a course in "Southern History" offered by the department, but it was in no sense a survey of the subject as it is conceived today.[10]

Through the medium of the Trinity College Historical Society, Bassett assembled materials on North Carolina and the South and promoted the writing of southern history. "I am trying to put a new spirit into the historical work of the South," he wrote Adams after addressing the Society in 1897.[11] The trained historian must replace the Confederate brigadier; memoirs and anecdotes and "flimsy evidences" must give way to "history systematically and comprehensively" written. But scientifically trained historians could not record and interpret the South's past without source materials. To particularize, they needed account books, diaries, letters, minutes of assemblies, newspaper files, pamphlets, and historical objects. Original materials would profit little, however, as long as "devotion to truth" were lacking. Accuracy demanded that evidence on both sides of controversial issues be admitted, but when any southerner dared to depart from the traditional view, "he has been denounced as a traitor and a mercenary defiler of his birthplace." The Society could revolutionize the writing of history in the South. "Let us conduct ourselves," Bassett urged, "that the world may know that there is in the South at least one spot in which our history may be presented in all its claims, and where it may receive a respectful and unimpassioned hearing."[12] It is doubtful if the scientific concept of history, the need for trained historians, and the obligation to preserve historical materials were better stated in the closing years of last century than by the thirty-year-old Bassett. The conservatism of southern society at the turn of the century made his liberal and provocative preachments little less than revolutionary.

It was Bassett's ambition to provide a medium of publication for the Trinity College Historical Society. His dream materialized in 1897 with the launching of the *Historical Papers;* but, useful as this publication was, it did not serve every purpose that he had in mind. He was tremendously interested in the race question as a social problem; he was dissatisfied with the political situation in North Carolina; and he desired to promote toleration and critical, independent thinking. In the past, southern provincialism had fostered antiquated subject matter and "destroyed that literary atmosphere which writers find essential to creative work"; shallow learning in southern colleges and universities could not provide "the culture which must underlie literary production."[13] To stimulate and vitalize literary and historical activity, the *South Atlantic Quarterly* was founded in 1902. It was not primarily a magazine of southern history, though there were articles on the South by the editor and by Ballagh, William E. Dodd, Walter L. Fleming, Ulrich B. Phillips, J. G. de Roulhac Hamilton, and Holland Thompson —a galaxy of young southerners who soon attained recognition as chroniclers of the South's history.

Bassett's war on politicians and churchmen, prejudice and provincialism, eventually aroused a storm of protest. His article on "Stirring Up the Fires of Race Antipathy"[14] raised a clamor for his dismissal, but his resignation was declined. He retired as editor of the *Quarterly* in 1905 "because of an accumulation of other labors," and a year later accepted a call to Smith College. For twelve years he had toiled in the South to plant the seeds of historical scholarship. The academic hospitaility of New England did not lessen his interest in the homeland. Years later he could write in the preface of his *Southern Plantation Overseer,* "After residing nearly two decades in New England, always a hospitable home for a student, he has found a special joy in getting back into the history of Southern conditions."[15]

With the publication of *The Federalist System* in 1906, Bassett attained national recognition; theretofore he had exploited his own state's history.[16] In concentrating upon local materials in his formative years, he was following sound principle; but perhaps a major factor in determining his interest was the publication of *The Colonial Records of*

North Carolina (1886–90). Nearly 80 per cent of the citations in his *Constitutional Beginnings of North Carolina* (1894) were to that monumental work; *The Regulators of North Carolina* (1895), the best of his North Carolina monographs, depended upon it in equal amount; and more than half of the material in his *Slavery and Servitude in the Colony of North Carolina* (1896) was drawn from it. In both colonial and state studies, North Carolina laws, codes, and court reports were used to good advantage. Newspapers were employed on occasion, particularly in *Anti-Slavery Leaders in North Carolina* (1898) and in *Slavery in the State of North Carolina* (1899). There is a sprinkling of manuscript citations, mainly to unpublished laws and records of religious groups.

Judged by present standards, Bassett's studies, like those of most of his contemporaries, were based upon meager sources. As a result, many of them were narrowly conceived, embracing a monotonous recital of constitutional and legal provisions. In his slavery monographs, tobacco production and plantations are alluded to in the most general terms; rice is mentioned incidentally. A section on social life in one of them has little to do with that subject. Not until Phillips began to exploit agricultural periodicals and plantation diaries, journals, and account books a decade later did studies of the subject acquire a social and economic flavor. Bassett himself, in later years, used journals and letters with pregnant effect.

As would be expected of a disciple of the new scientific group of historians, Bassett assembled facts on both sides of controversial questions, weighed the evidence carefully, and exercised a degree of detachment. After doing so, he did not hesitate to state his conclusions boldly. Whether writing letters to Adams or historical monographs, he did not avoid a frank expression of his sympathies on issues past and present. They lay with the Regulators, with slaves, and with free Negroes.

From Bassett and Trinity College the scene shifts to the transmontane University of the South where another pioneer in southern history, William P. Trent, labored for the last thirteen years of the nineteenth century. Like Bassett, he was a graduate student at the Hopkins, and like most students who passed through Adams' seminar, he was inspired to engage in productive work. Before leaving Sewanee in 1900 for a professorship at Columbia University, he had published *English Culture in Virginia* (1889), *William Gilmore Simms* (1892), *Southern Statesmen of the Old Régime* (1897), and *Robert E. Lee* (1899). He had also written a number of articles on historical subjects, some of which possessed substantial merit. As founder and editor of the *Sewanee Review,* he antedated Bassett by a decade in promoting unbiased thinking and literary activity through the medium of a quarterly magazine. He was a southern liberal, unbound by traditional concepts, and willing to pioneer despite criticism of conservatives. He paid his respects to the narrow, intolerant, and provincial atmosphere at Sewanee; as for the South, "Shallow thinking on political matters, provincialism of taste & sentiments—ignorance & vanity are the dominant characteristics of our people." After teaching a decade at the University of the South, he concluded that it would take a generation to set southerners aright.[17]

Trent's first significant work was a biography of Simms. Handicapped by a heavy teaching load and by lack of material in his "mountain fastness," research materialized slowly. While it cannot be said that he exhausted all the sources, he examined a great mass of printed and manuscript materials, traveling to Charleston, Richmond, Washington, and Baltimore to assemble notes and interview relatives and friends of his subject. He searched magazines of Simms's generation, he read "dreary" American novels of the antebellum period, and he studied the southern background. To meet the publisher's deadline, he composed the first draft of 850 manuscript pages in seven weeks while teaching fifteen hours work; a revision which deleted 150 pages consumed a fortnight. This accelerated program left him "nearly dead," and he reflected over his experience "with a kind of shuddering wonder."[18]

The Simms study was published a half-century ago, but it has not yet been superseded. Evaluating it on the basis of standards of that day, it was a superior work whether judged as biography, history, or literature. Trent's appraisal of Simms's creative and editorial work is critical and fairly trustworthy, but his general theory of literary development and his treatment of politics in the old South met vitriolic condemnation from southern reviewers. Anticipating criticism, he nevertheless studied thoroughly the environment in which literature was produced in the Old South. Slavery, according to Trent, was not only responsible for the "Lost Cause"; creative writing could not flourish in such an environment, and the low estate of contributions to the *Southern Literary Messenger* and the *Southern Quarterly Review* was traceable directly to the South's peculiar institution.[19] Trent and other critical, liberal southerners of the period exaggerated the evil influences of slavery. Dissatisfied with the uncritical writing of the past, they sought an objective approach to the study of southern history and literature. In their zeal for the new order, some of them went too far in repudiating institutions of the Old South and in condemning the philosophy of their antebellum ancestors. Unlike Bassett, whose literary interests were always secondary to his historical efforts, Trent was making the transition from historian to littérateur in the 1890's. In doing so, he became less objective and more imaginative. Never again did he delve into the sources with that thoroughness that characterized his biography of Simms. He was satisfied thereafter to write history mainly from secondary accounts, supplemented by casual examination of limited source materials.

In 1896 Trent was invited to deliver at the University of Wisconsin a series of lectures on prominent antebellum southerners. It was his purpose to depict the old régime through some of the able men of the middle period. His appraisal of George Washington was uncritical—almost eulogistic. In treating Thomas Jefferson's career he regained his historical composure and discovered some very human weaknesses as well as many praiseworthy qualities. John Randolph provided plenty of opportunity to exercise critical ingenuity; he was downright angry with John C. Calhoun. Inclusion of Alexander H. Stephens and Robert Toombs gave occasion to observe that "the Georgian is the Southerner who comes nearest of all the inhabitants of his section to being a normal American." Jefferson Davis was not "a thoroughly great man," though Trent credited him with ability, versatility, gallantry as a soldier, "pure intentions," and gentlemanly qualities. He was a statesman who failed "not so much through his lack of ability to govern, as through the inherent weakness of the cause he represented." Here again, Trent was blaming southerners' ills upon slavery. The institution was responsible for poor roads, oldfield schools, paucity of cities, and lack of immigrants. Slavery "stamped its evil mark on everything . . . [the southerner] wrote or said or did." Most of these charges laid at slavery's door were either overstated or entirely wrong, but the soundness of the following statement, which might easily be attributed to a scholar of the 1940's will not be questioned. "The more fiercely the abolitionist leaders inveighed against slavery the more vehemently the pro-slavery advocates asserted their own virtue and the baseness of their enemies. The Northerner began to think all Southerners slave-drivers; the Southerner began to think all Northerners either fanatics or cowardly shopkeepers." [20] In his *Robert E. Lee,* Trent emphasized the "logic of passion" as a determinant,[21] though he did not speak of "symbols."

Two factors prompted Trent in establishing the *Sewanee Review:* the zeal of Hopkins students to publish and to promote media of publication, and his study of antebellum southern magazines which indicated a present need for a critical quarterly in the South. The *Review* emphasized literature and literary criticism more than the *South Atlantic Quarterly,* but it also devoted attention to education, philosophy, theology, fine arts, contemporary questions, biography, and history. With such contributors as Bassett, Phillips, Fleming, Hamilton, David D. Wallace, Colyer Meriwether, St. George L. Sioussat, Philip A. Bruce, and Thomas J. Wertenbaker, some authentic southern history found its way into the *Sewanee Review*.

More than a decade before the end of last century, George Petrie began his labors at Alabama Polytechnic Institute that were to continue beyond a half-century. Trained in the Adams seminar at the Hopkins, he wrote a dissertation on *Church and State in Early Maryland* (1892), and returned to Auburn to teach history and Latin. His philosophy and methodology are worth transcribing. "In this department," he wrote, "the aim is not so much to memorize facts as to understand them. . . . The students are taught to investigate the growth of ideas and institutions, the rise and progress of great historical movements, and the reciprocal influences of men and circumstances. Frequent use is made of diagrams, photographs, charts and maps. . . . Instruction is given by textbooks, lectures and class discussion, but a constant effort is made to stimulate to wider reading and research in the library."[22]

There is tangible evidence that Petrie was successful in his efforts to inspire students to "wider reading and research." As an example, Fleming had read more than one hundred and fifty volumes of history and biography before leaving Auburn in 1900. These treated many countries and all periods; thirty-seven of them dealt with the South and southern leaders. He had also produced a meritorious paper on Buford's expedition to Kansas. Fleming was, as Petrie put it, "one of our crack men."[23]

The word *seminar* had little to recommend it at an agricultural and mechanical college, so all work in history for juniors, seniors, and graduates was "conducted by the laboratory method" to elevate the subject to the level of a science in a school that emphasized technology. "Emphasis is laid," Petrie said, "on the importance of securing proper material for investigation and every incentive is given to the collection and use of new documents, papers and letters illustrative of Southern, and especially Alabama history." In the freshman program, the study of Alabama history was placed on a parity with United States and English history. A junior-senior course in American history included lectures on such southerners as John Randolph, William L. Yancey, Stephens, Toombs, and Davis.[24]

Petrie published a few studies and devoted years to the assembling of material for a biography of Yancey, but his great contribution lay in inspiring young men with a genuine love for the history of the South. Such were Fleming, Albert B. Moore, Frank L. Owsley, Herman C.

Nixon, William O. Scroggs, Dallas T. Herndon, Alfred W. Reynolds, Watson Davis, John B. Clark, Charles S. Davis, and a dozen others whose accomplishments have been creditable.[25]

The historical renaissance that appeared in Mississippi in the 1890's was inseparably associated with the pioneering activities of Franklin L. Riley.[26] Graduating from the Hopkins in 1896, he served a year as president of Hillman College and then accepted a call to the new chair of history and rhetoric at the University of Mississippi. As was to be expected, Riley brought with him a zeal for scholarly productivity, a penchant for organized historical activity, and a determination to inaugurate a medium of publication. In addition to his dissertation, he had already published a half-dozen articles, one of them on the "Study of History in Southern Colleges." He was the moving spirit behind the revival of the Mississippi Historical Society in 1898 and the launching of its *Publications* which he edited until 1914. He also edited the volume, *A Political History of the South* (1909), in *The South in the Building of the Nation*. To these two publications, and others, he contributed sundry monographs.

After a triennium at the University, rhetoric was removed from Riley's department, and thereafter his teaching was concentrated in the field of history. In 1908 he inaugurated a course on the political history of the South, one of the earliest in that field. Meanwhile, in 1898, the University Historical Society was organized to promote research, with a room in the library to house its archives, embracing manuscripts, newspaper files, and museum pieces. The Society met monthly to hear papers on the history of the state. A seminar replaced it in 1906, and members prepared studies on the Reconstruction period of sundry Mississippi counties, a few of which were printed in the Mississippi Historical Society *Publications*.[27]

At the turn of the century young William K. Boyd faced a perplexing problem. He had taken the bachelor's and master's degrees at Trinity College under Bassett's tutelage and had acquired teaching experience as assistant in history at Trinity and as master in history at Trinity Park High School. One thing he yet lacked—the doctorate. With few exceptions young southerners of that era had two choices if interested in the history of their region. They could cast their lot with Johns Hopkins where the maestro, Herbert B. Adams, had been attracting southern men for a decade or so; or they could cross Mason and Dixon's Line to study with the magister at Columbia University, William A. Dunning, whose reputation as an impartial authority on the Civil War and Reconstruction periods was well established. Boyd's decision was not an easy one. His mentor at Trinity College urged the Hopkins;

in fact, Bassett wrote Adams several times extolling his protégé's virtues and appraising his study of Governor William W. Holden as "the best thing ever done in N. C. Reconstruction times." But, he added, "Dunning is so pleased with it that inducements are held out to him to go to Columbia." The "inducements" were apparently sufficient, for Boyd chose Columbia, but with mental reservations as to the correctness of his decision. Finding "a lack of personal touch" there, he thought of transferring to the Hopkins the following year if an able successor to Adams were appointed.[28] He continued at Columbia.

Adams and Dunning left such an impress upon their students that bonds of personal friendship and intellectual interest promoted a recognizable unity. Adams founded the Hopkins "colonial system," for each institution in which a Hopkins man was placed became a colony of the parent university. Dunning's students esteemed their " 'Old Chief,' whose shining personality, keen intellect, warm personal interest, and painstaking guidance placed them under obligations too great ever to be fully discharged, and bound them to him by ties of warm affection."[29] What was the background of the man whose magnetic qualities attracted to Columbia such southern scholars as Boyd, Fleming, Phillips, Hamilton, Milledge L. Bonham, James W. Garner, Benjamin B. Kendrick, Charles W. Ramsdell, Thomas S. Staples, David Y. Thomas, and C. Mildred Thompson?

It is impossible to find in Dunning's geographical and intellectual heritage factors that foreshadowed an important role in advancing southern historical scholarship.[30] Born in New Jersey four years before the Civil War began, his formal education was eastern, except for study at the University of Berlin with Treitschke. A freshman-sophomore altercation led to suspension from Dartmouth and removal to Columbia where he took the bachelor's, master's, and doctor's degrees, the last in 1885. His dissertation, *The Constitution of the United States in Civil War and Reconstruction, 1860–1867* (1885), revealed independence of thought and maturity in judgment; his *Essays on the Civil War and Reconstruction* (1898) demonstrated historical detachment in the treatment of controversial problems. Invited to contribute the volume on postwar years to the *American Nation* series, he published in 1907 *Reconstruction, Political and Economic, 1865–1877,* a judicious analysis of a period that witnessed a pronounced transformation in American life. A pioneer in scientific research, a precisionist in literary craftsmanship, and a genius in the art of teaching, Dunning exerted tremendous influence on southern students who enrolled in his courses on Civil War and Reconstruction.

In appraising the Reconstruction monographs of Dunning's students, it should be noted that they were based upon a wide assortment of sources, many of them used for the first time. Never before had so great a bulk of material been sifted and woven into the fabric of Reconstruction history of the southern commonwealths. The assembling of pertinent data is a permanent legacy. In the arrangement and interpretation of data, they made an honest effort to divest their minds of sectional bias, and to understand the interrelationships of conservative whites, southern unionists, northern immigrants, and freedmen. A sympathetic inclination toward the first group appeared as they marshalled evidence to show the ill effects of a radical program on southern society and economy. Sympathies in this direction were not entirely counterbalanced by parading praiseworthy qualities in representatives of other groups. Their approach represented a new departure, for much of the history of the period had been observed through the specatcles of Radicals, with little understanding of Conservative reaction to emancipation, the Lost Cause, and the Congressional policy applied to the South. If the historical pendulum swung too far to the right in the hands of Dunning revisionists, the new statement was certainly nearer gravitational equilibrium than it had been before.

The first significant monograph on state Reconstruction that emanated from Dunning's seminar was Garner's *Reconstruction in Mississippi* (1901). He declared that animosities and passions aroused during the period had been sufficiently dissipated to permit an unprejudiced study, but that the history of the era "ought to be written by a Southerner, for it is the Southerners who best understand the problems which the reconstructionists undertook to solve and the conditions under which the solution was worked out." He hastened to explain that this did not mean a presentation "from the Southern 'point of view' or from any other 'point of view.' " It was the historian's function, he thought, "to *relate* and not to *judge*," and he therefore "left the reader to form his own conclusions."[31] While the emphasis was on political, legal, and constitutional history, he devoted chapters to economic aspects, to education, and to the functions of the Freedmen's Bureau.

Studies by Hamilton, Ramsdell, Davis, Staples, and Edwin C. Woolley[32] likewise stressed political and constitutional themes; but Fleming and Miss Thompson[33] elected to go beyond these standard aspects of history. Writing forty years ago when social and economic history received meager attention, Fleming devoted 40 per cent of his *Civil War and Reconstruction in Alabama* (1905) to social, industrial, educational, and religious history. It was an innovation to include such subjects as farm life during the war, clothes and fashions, makeshifts and substitutes, and drugs and medicines. Miss Thompson, in her *Recon-*

struction in Georgia (1915), carried the same emphasis further, devoting fully two-thirds of her book to society, labor, agriculture, industry, banking, transportation, education, and religion.

While all of these monographs stressed Reconstruction in the South, there was a constant awareness of the states' relationship to the national picture, though it was subordinated to the local scene. As Ramsdell put it, he had kept "the national point of view . . . in a corner of his mind," and had "often found it a valuable corrective."[34] Students were thus reversing Dunning's emphasis; he viewed "the period as a step in the progress of the American nation" and underscored the record "of the victorious section."[35] Into the national design he fitted the southern problem, drawing upon the researches of Garner, Fleming, and Hamilton for his *Reconstruction, Political and Economic.* One cannot escape the conclusion that the master had confidence in the neophyte, and thus that influence operated in two directions. It was a wholesome, constructive relationship.

Some of the weaknesses of the Reconstruction monographs may be accounted for by the fact that they are doctoral dissertations, the first extensive pieces of research engaged in by the writers. If some of them are narrowly conceived and limited in scope, they are not unlike most monographic studies, then or now, in this premise. One could hardly expect that graduate students would say the final word on a controversial period. That some lacked definitiveness does not seriously reflect on the authors; as doctoral dissertations they possess much merit whether judged by standards prevalent in the first and second decades of the twentieth century, or in the third and fourth. They represent a distinct advancement in historical scholarship, and anyone essaying to do the task again must necessarily utilize them as a point of departure. Admittedly there are gaps to be filled, especially in social and economic themes; refinements in judgement are in order; a reconsideration of the Negro's places in the economic and social picture is necessary; and a measure of credit is yet to be assigned to the Radical régimes for constructive provisions they placed in constitutional and legislative enactments.[36] A careful reading of the Dunning studies will reveal that many of these things are sensed if not completely understood.[37]

The Reconstruction dissertations prepared at Columbia after 1900 are superior to theses written on southern subjects under Adams' direction. For the most part, they were more ambitious pieces of work, and they utilized a wider variety and a greater mass of source materials. Adams and his students had charted a course; one would normally expect improvement in those who followed. It is doubtful if members of the Dunning group surpassed Adams' students in the application of cold objectivity to research and writing.

Adams and Dunning were not historians of the South. They were eastern men, educated in the East and in Germany. The excellence of the graduate schools with which they were associated, together with their own reputations for impartiality, attracted students from the South to their seminars; these in turn wrote dissertations on southern topics, and many of them returned to southern colleges and universities to teach and write the history of their section, to establish historical societies, and to build up collections of southern material. The contribution of the two pioneers was indirect, but it was nonetheless significant in the origins of southern historical scholarship.

The turn of the century ushered into the historical guild two young southerners—Dodd and Phillips—who were destined to play important roles in promoting scholarly treatment of their region's history. Their dominating influence during the next generation brought the South well on the road to historical maturity. Their careers present interesting parallels, but in many respects their methods and interests stood in sharp contrast. Both received their bachelor's and master's degrees at southern institutions; both taught in southern schools before receiving calls to professorships in northern universities; both made their major contributions to the antebellum period of southern history; both projected a multiple-volume history of the South; both died before completing it. Dodd, like Adams, took his doctorate at a German university; Phillips, like Dunning, received his degree at Columbia. Dodd held primacy as a writer of biography, especially interpretative portraiture; Phillips preferred social and economic history, particularly plantation economy. Dodd was given to generalization, to painting composites; Phillips particularized, hesitated to state conclusions. Dodd excelled as a stimulating lecturer; Phillips was at his best in the seminar room. Dodd's writings brought political preferment and a sojourn in Nazi Germany; Phillips' productive work won for him an Albert Kahn Fellowship and a trip to darkest Africa.

Innumerable conditioning factors united in the development of Phillips as the historian of the South, among them his Georgia background, the opportunity to study with Dunning, and intimate contact with Frederick J. Turner.[38] His native state provided the subject and much of the material for his dissertation, *Georgia and State Rights* (1902), an antebellum political history with emphasis on Federal relations. From Dunning he learned much of historical method and meticulous writing, but it was Turner who supplied the approach and the key to the problem. Called to an instructorship at Wisconsin following the awarding of the doctorate, he had further opportunity for association with Turner. Whether at Wisconsin, Tulane, Michigan, or Yale, Phillips offered instruction in southern history—usually a lecture course on the antebellum South, designed for upperclassmen and graduates, and a seminar for graduate students.

Perhaps Phillips' most enduring contribution was the exploitation of new sources. He was not the first southern historian to realize the value of plantation records, but his priority in utilizing them effectively will not be denied. They were a primary source for many of his contributions to historical magazines, he drew upon them heavily in writing *American Negro Slavery* (1918) and *Life and Labor in the Old South* (1929), and he assembled pertinent illustrative material in *Plantation and Frontier* (1910) and in *Florida Plantation Records* (1927). After he demonstrated their utility as a source, a younger generation of historians explored an ever-widening mass of plantation data to fill in details of a picture for which Phillips had provided an authentic mosaic.

Occasionally Phillips turned his hand to political subjects, as in his essays on the South Carolina Federalists and the southern Whigs, his biography of Robert Toombs, and the correspondence of Toombs, Stephens, and Cobb. His greatest achievement in this field was a series of lectures delivered at Northwestern University in 1932 and published posthumously as *The Course of the South to Secession* (1939). The essays in this fragment, designed as part of a companion volume to his *Life and Labor in the Old South,* reveal ability in analyzing and interpreting political trends and movements that led to a stroke for independence. Stylistically and organically they are as unorthodox as his other later works, but in this unorthodoxy lay the originality that made his writing dynamic and virile.

In method, Phillips preferred particularization to generalization; the more research he did, he often commented, the less willing he was to generalize. He wrote of planters and their plantations with specific identification. The names of individual overseers and slaves easily found lodgment in his writings. He permitted himself few composites, though those he did employ are estimable. For the most part he was content to narrate and analyze, arranging illustrative material so cogently that the reader could hardly mistake an implied conclusion.

Phillips' great work, *Life and Labor in the Old South,* disappointed many scholars who expected a synthesis of southern history. His dominant interest remained unchanged—the economic and social history of the antebellum plantation régime. Manufacturing, lumbering, mining, education, urban life, the common man—received scant attention or were completely ignored. His emphasis was by design, not because he depreciated other themes. Phillips encouraged his seminar students to investigate topics of their own choosing, even though they were far afield from his own major interest. But the student who thought his report might escape the critical eye of the master soon discovered that Phillips was acquainted with the sources. To the neophyte his knowledge seemed broad indeed; and the mature scholar found a lively interest in any aspect of southern or sectional scope. His own writings touched lightly on the abolition crusade; he was not unfamiliar with the subject, but contented himself with encouraging others to explore it meticulously.

As a writer, Phillips' evolution from the monographer of early years to the literary craftsman of maturity indicates a remarkable transformation. Seminar students recall his dictum, "The writer must take pains to save the reader pains." He was gifted at compressing phrases into words, paragraphs into sentences. He redrafted much of his own writing ten or twelve times to delete superfluous words and phrases. In the polishing process he labored to find the word with the delicate shade of meaning to convey an exact idea. He used quoted matter copiously and effectively, and with a minimum of intrusion.

In William E. Dodd the South found a teacher and chronicler whose talents served the cause of historical scholarship in superior fashion. Born in North Carolina in 1869, he received the bachelor's and master's degrees at Virginia Polytechnic Institute. He took the doctorate at the University of Leipzig in 1900, presenting as a dissertation a study of *Jefferson's Rückkehr zur Politik*. Returning to the United States, he sought an academic location and opportunity to write a biography of Nathaniel Macon. The summer of 1900 yielded research on the North Carolinian in the Library of Congress and correspondence with Adams relative to a post-doctoral fellowship at the Hopkins or a position as teacher of modern languages in one of the Baltimore boys' schools. Either alternative would enable him to take courses in institutional history with Adams and permit work on the Macon biography.[39] Before the end of the summer, Dodd was elected professor of history and economics at Randolph-Macon College.

Pioneering activities began immediately. The Randolph-Macon Historical Society was established, with its objectives the study of American history and the assembling of Virginia documents; and the *Branch Historical Papers* were inaugurated, published by the Society with funds from a Richmond patron, John P. Branch. The *Papers* would "stimulate and encourage the study and writing of history" and provide the editor with a medium for publishing Virginia sources. An early evidence of Dodd's interest in biography appeared in his decision to limit articles to sketches of Virginians, a dozen of which appeared under his editorship. These were contributed mainly by Randolph-Macon students, divided about equally between seniors and graduates. To encourage competition, the Bennett History Medal was awarded annually to the student who prepared the best essay, and it was usually assigned first position in the publication.[40] With a minimum of editorial effort, Dodd contributed to the *Papers* letters of Leven Powell, Thomas Ritchie, Spencer Roane, Nathaniel Macon, and John Taylor of Caroline.[41] As further evidence of an interest in local and southern history, he offered courses on Virginia and the Confederacy.[42]

Dodd's great opportunity came in 1908 with a call to a professorship in American history at the University of Chicago. For the next quarter-century he taught southern history to an increasing number of graduate students, and, with frequent southern research excursions to supplement Chicago library holdings, delved into the South's past to produce a notable array of books and monographs.

No systematic courses on the history of the South were offered at Chicago before Dodd's appointment to the faculty, but some that touched upon the field were given by Jameson and Edwin E. Sparks.[43] Dodd's own offerings were diverse, whether in lecture courses or in seminars. Beginning with a survey of the political, social, and economic history of the South from 1607 to the present, he frequently taught some segment thereof or concentrated on the lower South. Occasionally he lectured on civilization of the antebellum South, the South and the Civil War, the social and economic bearings of the war, and Reconstruction history. His seminars showed even greater diversity of title, with a score or more of subjects receiving catalogue recognition.[44] Any recital of listings should be qualified by the observation, first, that variation in title did not necessarily mean a proportionate change in subject matter; and second, that seminar students were not required to choose topics which fell within the limits of the description. It is more important to understand that Dodd was a stimulating lecturer, that he proceeded informally, and that, because of an intense interest in the human equation, he often used a personal approach and talked about people. In seminars, as in the direction of dissertations, independent work was encouraged by a minimum of direct instruction and a maximum of student initiative. Important as were Dodd's writings, perhaps his greatest contribution to southern historical scholarship was his inspirational teaching which set the sails of a number of able scholars in the direction of the South and its history. However that may be, his productive work constitutes a substantial contribution to the literature of southern history.

"Democracy is the only thing worth fighting for in this world." This opinion Dodd expressed to a southern colleague in 1915 when a group of reformers, some of them southerners, undertook to rid the American Historical Association of alleged "ring" rule. "My sympathies are all with the mass of the membership," he said, but he "would not move an inch to swap cliques," especially when "democracy is the last thing in the world that the leader of the present fight desires." [45]

With Dodd, democracy was an obsession. The democratic tradition in American life permeated much of his writing. Recall the names of statesmen who absorbed his research and editorial interests—Thomas Jefferson, Spencer Roane, Thomas Ritchie, John Taylor, Nathaniel Macon, Jefferson Davis, John C. Calhoun, Abraham Lincoln, Woodrow Wilson. Recall also his volume on *The Old South,* which he subtitled *Struggles for Democracy* (1937). This first of a contemplated four-volume study emphasizes, in interpretative fashion, self-government, freedom of religion, free trade, and free homesteads. It is questionable whether there was as much democracy in the seventeenth-century South as Dodd indicates, or whether warring contemporaries recognized the democratic issue as squarely as he would have us believe. Occasionally he abandoned his chief concern, as in his *Cotton Kingdom* (1919), a readable synthesis of the last two antebellum decades; and once he considered a biographical study of the American system exponent. "Of recent months," he wrote in 1916, "I have been re-studying Henry Clay from the Durrett materials here and what new light I am getting on him! I am tempted to stop all and write a life of him, but one cannot do everything. But Clay was a great one from 1817 to 1825." [46]

In his biographical efforts, as in other studies, Dodd did not disassociate politics and economics. American history must be written, he thought, "not with a view to economic determinism ... but with full appreciation of economic factors. By appreciation I mean actual use of these factors in the warp and woof of written history." [47] He declared in his *Woodrow Wilson and His Work* that industrial development since the Civil War was as dangerous to American life as the slave régime of the Old South had been. [48] Several years earlier, in his *Jefferson Davis* (1907), he overstated this thesis and immediately apologized to a reviewer: "Indeed I do not remember to have said the ills of our industrialism are 'worse' than those of slavery. I ought to have said as bad as those of slavery—that is my opinion." [49]

The uniqueness of Dodd's writings lies partly in his racy, rollicking style which carries the reader along with gusto, unless he pause to turn grammarian and attempt to analyze sentences that fill half a page or more. Between capital and period one frequently meets the whole gamut of punctuation known to composition—comma, colon, semicolon, and dash—only to find an exclamation point where the period ordinarily performs its proper function. Witness the opening sentence in his *Lincoln or Lee:* "When Andrew Jackson, the happy warrior trim, correct, both feet out of the grave, well dressed and well mounted, bade farewell to Washington that memorable March day, 1837, the next great President of the United States was in the making, far off on the prairies of Illinois: Abraham, son of poor Nancy Hanks and trifling Thomas Lincoln, who had hired the boy to hard-fisted farmers on Pigeon Creek, Indiana, for twenty-five cents a day and put the proceeds into his own dirty pockets; Abraham Lincoln, six feet four, awkward, loose-jointed, and uneasy—used to the ills of a life that promised little but ill; meditative, restless, now and then called 'the mad Lincoln,' a young lawyer, twenty-eight years old, a member of the legislature of Illinois, and engaged, with his hustling, calculating little friend Stephen A. Douglas, twenty-four years old, in a piece of the most foolish legislation that was ever enacted."[50] Thus, in a single sentence of 152 words, punctuated by 26 commas, 2 semicolons, a colon, a dash, and a period, the writer presents a personal and descriptive characterization of the first Democratic president, introduces Lincoln's immediate ancestors and comments on his father's financial policy, describes and psycho-analyzes the prairie lawyer-politician, alludes to a cooperative effort of the Illinois political rivals, and indirectly passes judgment on all presidents from Martin Van Buren to James Buchanan. In form, many of Dodd's sentences resemble the "loose-jointed" Lincoln; in substance, they remind one of the superior resources of the victorious North. They provide the reader with opportunity to develop memory, and blest be he who can recall the opening idea before the sentence is closed. But as a stylist, Dodd was an extremist, for later in the same book he wrote a one-word sentence, "Hardly [period],"[51] which is hardly a sentence.

In discussing the contributions of Adams, Dunning, Dodd, and Phillips, the expression "school of historical thought" has been consciously avoided. Too often it is applied undeservedly to a group of students in relation to their preceptor. The connotation is not always acclamatory, for there is an implication of subservient conformity. If carried to the *n*th degree, formulistic writing prevails and a stereotype obtains, with a consequent loss of independent thinking and valid conclusion. If, on the other hand, the expression involves only a kindred interest, a common approach, and the application of legitimate methodology in establishing historical verities, the end result may satisfy the scholarly concept. The test lies in the freedom of the mind to follow the whole truth even though it may modify or even disprove a stated thesis.

If there be validity in this analysis, it is difficult to conclude that any of these pioneers, with the possible exception of Dunning, established a school of thought. There is clearer indication of a pattern in the dissertations he directed, but even they have striking differences as well as similarities. With little evidence of special themes or theses transferred to later generations of scholars, it seems proper to conclude that independence of thought and judgment has characterized much of the research and writing in the field of southern history. The hundreds of scientifically trained historians who have chronicled the South's past during the last half-century have, with few exceptions, employed their talents in investigating narrow segments, in time and space, or in tracing the growth of particular institutions and concepts through longer periods of time. Most of the writing has been monographic in character, with adequate syntheses awaiting future effort.

The historical activities of men who did not have classroom contact with great scholars have also been significant in promoting historical scholarship in the South. One must credit Herbert E. Bolton and his students with contributing toward an understanding of the non-English periphery of the South, but it should also be recalled that Peter J. Hamilton produced some meritorious studies of the same region. Thomas M. Owen was the real pioneer in effective, organized historical activity, yet he was without benefit of training such as Riley received. The young Alabama lawyer was the motive force that vitalized the Alabama Historical Society, provided for a History Commission, and established a Department of Archives and History. The comprehensive survey of his state's historical records and resources and the department he created and directed for a score of years served as models for other states and became monuments to his industry and organizing genius.[52] The commanding historical stature of men like Philip A. Bruce, pioneer in the use of court records as a source of information, should not be ignored. His trilogy on the economic, social, and institutional history of Virginia in the seventeenth century still remains a standard reference after the lapse of a generation. It does not detract from his reputation to know that, while his *Economic History of Virginia* (1895) was in press, he felt the need of scientific training and sought financial aid to permit study for the doctorate at the Hopkins.[53] Nor does the revised and more adequate concept of the Old Dominion's colonial history by Thomas J. Wertenbaker invalidate the fundamental contribution that Bruce made.

This study has been primarily concerned with the pioneering activities of two generations of historical scholars whose work spanned the half-century prior to the Association's inception. The intellectual grandchildren and great-grandchildren of the first generation were active participants in establishing the society and in promoting its usefulness during the past decade. It remains to be said that their work and the contributions of scholars with other lineage, indeed some without historiographical ancestry, form an important chapter in southern historical scholarship.

Chapter XI

Democracy in the Old South

FLETCHER M. GREEN

THE AMERICAN dream of democracy and equality, based upon the philosophy of natural rights and popular sovereignty, found full, free, and adequate expression in such Revolutionary documents as the Declaration of Independence and the bills of rights of the state constitutions.* "We hold these truths to be self-evident, that all men are created equal, that they are endowed by their Creator with certain unalienable Rights, that among these are Life, Liberty and the pursuit of Happiness." "All power is vested in, and consequently derived from, the people; . . . magistrates are their trustees and servants, and at all times amenable to them." "No man, or set of men, are entitled to exclusive or separate emoluments or privileges from the community but in consideration of publick services." These and similar expressions of democratic equalitarianism were familiar to the people in all the states of the American Union.

The mere declaration of these ideals did not insure their acceptance and enforcement; a vigorous and continuous defense of liberty is essential if it is to be preserved. Thomas Jefferson, spokesman for democracy, early observed that men were by their constitutions naturally divided into two classes: (1) those who fear and distrust the people and seek to draw all power into their own hands; and (2) those who have confidence in the people and consider the people the safest depository of public happiness and general well being. These two classes he called aristocrats and democrats. From the very beginning of American independence these two groups began a contest for control of the governments. This contest between the forces of aristocracy and democracy was one of the most important issues in the political development of the American nation during the first half-century of its existence. In the northern states it was

*This paper was prepared for presentation as the 1945 presidential address, but its delivery was prevented by cancellation of the meeting.

177

fought between the commercial-financial aristocracy and the working men, in the southern states between the aristocratic slaveholding planters and the yeoman farmers.

The first state constitutions were framed in an atmosphere of equality and the recognition of human rights, without hint of race or class distinctions, but they established property and freehold qualifications for voting and office-holding, and a system of representation, that gave control of the state governments to the wealthy, conservative, aristocratic classes. The power and influence of the aristocracy were further enhanced by the victory of the conservative group that established the Federal Constitution. The Jeffersonian democrats, accepting, in theory at least, the doctrines of natural rights, popular sovereignty, government by compact and contract, and the perfectability of mankind, began a militant assault upon the strongholds of aristocracy. They demanded and obtained a bill of rights to the Federal Constitution, and an extended suffrage and a greater equality of representation in the state governments. Under their attacks the powers of aristocracy were gradually whittled away. Finally, with the accession of Andrew Jackson to the presidency in 1829, it seemed that democracy would certainly triumph. Most American people agreed with Alexis de Tocqueville that the democratic revolution was an irresistible one, and that to attempt to check it "would be to resist the will of God."[1]

As democratic reform moved into high gear under Jackson its forces were divided by the emergence of the bitter sectional controversy over slavery. The northern abolitionists saw in the institution of slavery the absolute negation of liberty and equality and they began to weigh and to find wanting almost every feature of southern society. In particular they condemned the southern state governments, declaring that in them political democracy was being overthrown by a slaveholding aristocracy. This change, said they, was the result not of caprice or political accident but of deliberate design on the part of the aristocracy; and it was succeeding because *"the non-slave-holding people of the South lacked the enterprise, intelligence and daring to demand and extract their democratic rights."*[2] In other words, they held that the masses of free whites were incapable of understanding or maintaining their rights, and that the planter aristocracy was bitterly hostile to free institutions and the democratic theory of government universally.

By the time the sectional controversy reached the breaking point, the abolitionists had decided that the slaveholders had become a "DOMINANT CLASS, having positive control of the ... political power of those States ... the system of slavery concentrating, as it does all political influence in a few men who are virtually absolute in their respective States."[3]

Contrasting the two sections, Richard Hildreth, the historian, declared: "The Northern States of the Union are unquestionable Democracies, and every day they are verging nearer and nearer towards the simple idea and theoretic perfection of that form of government. The Southern States of the Union, though certain democratic principles are to be found in their constitutions and their laws, are in no modern sense of the word entitled to the appellation of Democracies: They are Aristocracies; and aristocracies of the sternest and most odious kind."[4]

This interpretation of southern society and government was based upon moral hatred of Negro slavery, rather than a true knowledge of southern state governments or a philosophical or realistic understanding of democracy. Its appeal to the excited and hostile North was so powerful that most people accepted it as unquestionably accurate; and the general historians of the United States incorporated it into their writings. For instance, James Ford Rhodes says in his *History of the United States from the Compromise of 1850* that the "slaveholders, and the members of that society which clustered round them, took the offices. . . . The political system of the South was an oligarchy under the republican form." And Lord Acton, the British historian and publicist, wrote that "secession was an aristocratic rebellion against a democratic government."[5]

The abolitionist promoters of the theory of the aristocratic nature of southern governments never attempted to define just what they meant by either aristocracy or democracy. Indeed democracy has always been difficult of definition. It is a relative term, and has had various meanings among different peoples and for the same people at different stages of their political development. In this paper it will be used in its general sense as a form of government in which the sovereign power is held by the people and exercised through a system of representation in which the representatives are chosen by a fairly large electorate. The electorate has not been a fixed one in the United States. In the early days of the American republic the suffrage was bestowed upon adult male property owners; in the second quarter of the nineteenth century it was extended to all adult white males; during Reconstruction the Negro was given the ballot; and in 1920 women were permitted to vote in all elections. Recently, Georgia has given the ballot to youths eighteen years of age. No one would say that the state governments were undemocratic in 1850 simply because women did not vote; but they were *more* democratic in 1920 because women did vote. The same may be said in regard to Negro suffrage. Furthermore, up to the Civil War the emphasis on democracy was placed on *political* equality; since that time greater emphasis has been placed on social and economic equality. Modern thought presupposes that institutions, in order to be understood, must be seen in relation to the conditions of time, place, and thought in which they appear. It is difficult to look at democracy in this way, for one is prone to judge democracy of the past by the criteria of today. Yet the degree of democracy prevailing under the constitutions and governments of the Old South must be judged by the democracy of that era, not of the present. George Sidney Camp was but speaking for his generation when he wrote in 1840 that democracy "is not of an agrarian character or spirit. Its immediate object is an equal division of political rights, not of property. . . . But republicanism does aim a death blow at all those laws and usages the object of which is . . . to give it a particular and exclusive direction as a means of political power."[6]

As noted above, the Revolutionary state constitutions utilized to a large degree the framework of colonial governments and constitutional practices of the colonial period which had recognized and established a governing class of the wealthy aristocracy. Only eight of the thirteen states made any change in suffrage requirements, and these changes did not abolish the principle that only property holders should vote—they merely reduced the amount of property required. Property and freehold qualifications for voting and office-holding meant that the governing class in the southern states was in large measure a planter aristocracy. The system of representation also favored the planter group of the eastern section. Though democratic in form, these constitutions were certainly not democratic in fact. They did, however, lay the basis for the expansion of popular control, the chief element in a political democracy, to the majority of the people.

Hardly had the landed aristocracy established themselves in power when demands for revision and readjustment were heard in each of the states. Among the specific reforms called for were the disestablishment of the church and the abolition of religious qualifications for office-holding; the abolition of the laws of entail and primogeniture; the broadening of the suffrage; the equalization of representation; and the reduction of property qualifications for office-holding. All looked toward the curbing of the powers of the landed aristocracy. Piecemeal amendment and revision of the constitutions partially satisfied these demands.

In South Carolina the dissenting Presbyterians and Congregationalists, led by William Tennent, a Presbyterian minister, and Christopher Gadsden, prepared a memorial which was signed by thousands of people and presented a petition to the legislature in 1777 asking "free and equal privileges, both religious and civil" for all Protestants. Another group of reformers joined forces with the dissenters and demanded an elective upper house of the legislature rather than the appointive council. These changes were too democratic for the conservative and aristocratic element; but when the next elections showed a majority of the people favorable to the reform, and after the popular party had blocked an appropriation bill, the conservatives yielded. Even then Edward Rutledge and Arthur Middleton resigned the governorship rather than approve the changes. Maryland, too, modified her constitution in favor of Quakers, Mennonites, and other minor religious groups. Jefferson, Madison, and Richard Henry Lee succeeded in securing the disestablishment of the Episcopal church in Virginia by legislative enactment.

South Carolina amended her constitution and joined Georgia and North Carolina in prohibiting entails and primogeniture. While no change was made in the Virginia constitution, the democratic element led by Jefferson forced measures through the legislature in 1786 abolishing entails and primogeniture. Jefferson believed that this legislation formed part of a system by which "every fibre would be eradicated of ancient or future aristocracy and a foundation laid for a government truly republican." The Virginia aristocracy never forgave him for this action.

The aristocracy made some slight concessions to the democrats in regard to suffrage and representation. South Carolina reduced the property requirements for voting from one hundred to fifty acres of land, and Georgia reduced it from ten pounds to the payment of all taxes levied by the state. Both states reduced considerably the property qualifications for office-holding. And the up-country counties, inhabited largely by small farmers, were given a more nearly equal share of representation in the state legislatures. All efforts at change in these particulars failed in Maryland, Virginia, and North Carolina. In spite of the concessions granted, the conservative aristocracy was still in control of all five of the original southern states at the close of the eighteenth century.

The constitutions of the two new southern states added to the Union during this period of readjustment, Kentucky and Tennessee, show some influence of the frontier ideals of democracy. Kentucky gave the suffrage to all free adult male citizens in 1792, but limited it to free white males in 1799. Representation was apportioned to free adult male inhabitants in 1792, and to qualified electors in 1799. No property or religious qualifications for office were prescribed, and the governor, after 1799, was to be elected by popular vote rather than indirectly by an electoral college as in 1792. Tennessee showed somewhat more aristocratic leanings in her constitution of 1796. Suffrage was limited to freemen possessed of a freehold; legislators and the governor were required to possess freeholds of two hundred and five hundred acres of land, respectively; representation was apportioned to the counties according to taxable inhabitants; and no person who denied the existence of God was eligible for any civil office. Though somewhat more democratic than the seaboard states, Tennessee nevertheless belongs with the group of older states controlled by the landed aristocracy. It should be pointed out, however, that in all these states there was much cheap land to be had; hence, it was no great burden to qualify for voting in any of these states.

The political revolution of 1800 which brought Jefferson and his party to power in most of the southern states, as well as in the Federal government, led to the demand that the principles of the bills of rights be translated into realistic democracy rather than to stand as mere glittering generalities. In every state, democratic leaders condemned the discrimination made between those who had property and those who had none. They declared that where property had representation the people could not be free; and they were able to show that under the existing system of representation a minority of wealthy men of the east had absolute control of the state governments. They appealed to the philosophy of natural rights and demanded equality of political rights and privileges. This movement came largely from the small farmer or yeoman class concentrated in the newer counties of the up-country or the western parts of the states; hence it took on something of the nature of an intra-state sectional fight. It naturally involved social and economic issues as well as political rights.

The rapid settlement of the piedmont and mountain region of these states in the first quarter of the nineteenth century gave to the up-country a majority of the white population. These small farmers had somewhat different interests from the low-country planters. They desired internal improvements—roads, canals, and railroads—at state expense, in order that they might have an economic outlet for their farm produce, cattle, and domestic manufactures. A supporter of reform predicted that if the westerners were given their way roads and canals would be built, domestic manufactures would increase, wealth would multiply, and that the "Old Families . . . imbecile and incorrigible," would be replaced by a "happy, bold and intelligent middle class."[7] But the legislatures were controlled by the planter aristocracy of the east, who feared heavier taxation if the western farmers were given equal representation and resisted all change.

The yeoman farmers were joined by a small class of industrial laborers of the eastern cities. These people were smarting under the provisions of the constitutions that required a freehold for voting just as the yeoman farmers were smarting under the unequal system of representation. The laborers demanded manhood suffrage. The aristocratic planters feared to grant their demands lest the laborers join the small farmers in taxing the wealth of the east.

The democratic reformers demanded conventions fresh from the people with power to rewrite completely the constitutions. But since most of the constitutions left it to the legislature or made no provision for calling a constituent assembly, and since the aristocracy with their control over the legislatures could prevent a call through that body, the democrats were blocked at the very threshold of reform. The aristocratic minority fought doggedly to maintain its favored position, contesting every move of the democrats, and yielding only in the face of an open revolt. In Maryland they permitted a series of amendments between 1805 and 1810 that brought reorganization of the judicial system so as to bring justice closer to the people and make the courts more expeditious and less expensive. Property qualifications for officers were swept away; the suffrage was extended to adult white males, the written ballot was required, and the plural vote was abolished; and some minor officials were made elective. In South Carolina representation was reapportioned in the house on the basis of white inhabitants and taxes combined. By this method the large slaveholding districts and parishes lost some of their representatives as allotted under the earlier constitutions. Suffrage was extended to include all white adult males who had resided in the state two years and were possessed of a freehold of fifty acres or a town lot, or who, if possessed of neither, had lived six months in the election district. This in reality meant white manhood suffrage. A series of amendments in Georgia between 1808 and 1824 made all officers from constable to governor, including judges of all the courts, elective by popular vote. These changes looked toward a greater participation in governmental affairs by the people and made the governments more responsive to the public will; but, except in South Carolina, they did not appease the democratic reform spirit. The conservatives had prevented any change in North Carolina and Virginia.

Four new southern states, Louisiana, Mississippi, Alabama, and Missouri, were admitted to the Union during these years. Louisiana, admitted in 1812, fell to the control of the landed aristocracy. Only free white males were permitted to vote, and they were required to pay a state tax before qualifying. Members of the legislature and the governor were required to possess freeholds ranging in value from five hundred to five thousand dollars. Representation was apportioned according to qualified voters, or property holders. The governor and other officers were chosen by popular vote. Mississippi, too, was controlled by property holders. All officers were elected by popular vote; voting was limited to free white males who were enrolled in the militia or paid a tax; representation was based on white population; but members of the legislature and the governor were required to possess land ranging from fifty to six hundred acres, or real estate ranging in value from five hundred to two thousand dollars. Alabama greatly broadened the base of political power. Suffrage was granted to all adult white male citizens; no property qualifications were required for state officials who were elected by popular vote; and representation was according to white inhabitants. Both Mississippi and Alabama declared that freemen only were possessed of equal rights. Missouri required no property qualifications for voting or office-holding, though members of the legislature must pay taxes. Only whites could vote, and representation was based on free white male inhabitants.

Thwarted by the aristocratic minority in calling legitimate conventions, the democratic majority in the old states now threatened to take the matter in their own hands and call extralegal conventions. Mass meetings were held in Georgia, North Carolina, Virginia, and Maryland; polls were conducted in various counties, all of which voted overwhelmingly for calling conventions; grand jury presentments called attention to the need for reform and recommended direct action if the legislatures failed to act; the voters in many counties instructed their representatives in the legislature to support a bill calling a constitutional convention; and hundreds of petitions went to the legislatures demanding relief. Typical of the sentiment for calling extralegal conventions is the statement of a North Carolinian that if the legislature failed "to comply with the wishes of a great majority of the State," then "a convention will be assembled in the west, and the constitution amended without the concurrence of the east; and this being the act of a majority, and the legal act, will consequently be obligatory on the whole State. The constitution *will be amended*."[8]

A state-wide reform convention assembled at Milledgeville, Georgia, on May 10, 1832, and issued a call for an election of delegates to a convention to meet at the capital in February, 1833, to alter, revise, or amend the constitution, or write a new one. It issued an address to the people in which it declared "that the people have an undoubted right, in their sovereign capacity, to alter or change their form of government, whenever in their opinion it becomes too obnoxious or oppressive to be borne. That crisis . . . has arrived, when the people should assert their rights, and boldly and fearlessly maintain them."[9] The legislature now capitulated and called a convention to meet at the same time and place as that called extralegally. Comparable action took place in Maryland in 1836, but the legislature passed a series of amendments similar to those proposed by the reform convention and forestalled extralegal action. In like manner the legislatures of Virginia and North Carolina capitulated to the reform party, and submitted the question of a "Convention or No Convention" to the voters. In both states the call was adopted by large majorities. Mississippi and Tennessee, too, at the demand of the people, called conventions to revise their constitutions. This was one of the most signal victories for majority or popular rule in American history. In these states the people without political voice had, by threat of appeal to numerical majority action, forced the landed aristocracy who possessed the legitimate and constitutional political power to submit the fundamental law to the scrutiny and revision of delegates elected from the people for that purpose alone.

Democracy had won a victory over aristocracy. The people had compelled the wealthy planter class in control of the legislatures to call conventions to revise the fundamental law of the states. Majority rule had exerted its power and justified its right. One democratic spokesman declared that the freemen had united their forces "to break to pieces the trammels of aristocracy, and show to the enemies of republican equality that the sons of freemen will still be free."[10]

John C. Calhoun, Abel P. Upshur,[11] and other aristocratic leaders of the South openly denied the Jeffersonian ideal of equality of all men and bitterly condemned majority rule as the tyranny of king numbers; and they had their supporters in the North among such men as James Kent, Joseph Story, and Orestes A. Brownson.[12] The less famous and little-known leaders of democracy just as boldly proclaimed the doctrine of political equality. The views of the former have been given much attention by the historian; those of the latter have been generally ignored. The significant thing about the controversy, however, is that the views of the latter prevailed. The bills of rights remained unchanged and the majority forced the aristocracy to grant all white men an equal voice in the state governments. Charles James Faulkner, spokesman for the Virginia democracy in 1850, said that nothing short of a radical and fundamental change in the structure of the state constitution "could satisfy the progressive aspirations of a people who felt that their energies were held in subjugation by artificial restraints of republican freedom and equality." And, after the Virginia convention of 1850 had adjourned, he declared: "Its results was one of the proudest triumphs of popular government which the records of history attest. A revolution as decided in its results as any of those which for the last century have deluged the monarchies of Europe with blood, passed off under the influence of the acknowledged principles of popular supremacy as quietly and tranquilly as the most ordinary county election."[13]

The reform movement begun about 1800 now bore fruit in numerous constitutional conventions,[14] and these conventions rewrote the state constitutions in line with the ideals of Jacksonian democracy. Many writers have attributed the democratic reforms of the 1830's to the influence of the western frontier. A study of the movement in the southern states gives an emphatic denial to this assumption. The people of the southern states were cognizant of what was going on in the West, but the demands for reform grew out of local conditions and would have arisen had there been no "New West" beyond the Appalachians. In fact, it would be more nearly accurate to say that many of the ideas and motives of Jacksonian democracy were southern in origin.

To what extent was aristocracy weakened and democracy strengthened by the work of the conventions of the 1830's? In the first place, property qualifications for voting were abolished in all southern states except Virginia and North Carolina, and with Louisiana still requiring the payment of taxes.[15] The last of the religious restrictions were also abolished. In a similar manner property qualifications for office-holding were wiped out except for South Carolina and Louisiana, and age and residence requirements were reduced. A large number of officers heretofore selected by the legislature or appointed by the governor were now elected by popular vote. These included civil and militia officers, justices of the peace, superior court judges, and governors in all the states except Virginia and South Carolina. Rotation in office was generally applied through short terms and restricted re-eligibility. Progress was also made in the equalization of representation. There was no uniformity in the states, however. Some used white population, some qualified voters, some federal population returns, and some a combination of population and taxation. Those states that had heretofore granted special borough representation abolished it.

In still another way these changes broadened the base of democracy. For the first time the people had been consulted as to the revision and amendment of their constitutions. The conventions were called directly or indirectly by action of the people. The revised constitutions were in turn submitted back to them for ratification or rejection. In at least one state the people twice rejected the changes and forced the desired reforms through by legislative amendments. And the new constitutions provided for future amendment and revision.

In one matter there was a definite reactionary movement. This was the issue of free Negro suffrage. Virginia and North Carolina joined Maryland and Kentucky in taking from the free Negro the ballot he had heretofore possessed. In like manner all new states of the period, North as well as South, denied suffrage to free Negroes. The action of the old southern states was paralleled by that of the northern states. Delaware, Connecticut, New Jersey, and Pennsylvania took the ballot from the Negro. And New York in 1821 limited Negro suffrage by requiring that he possess a freehold valued at two hundred and fifty dollars over and above all indebtedness. Hence only five of the northern states granted equal suffrage to Negroes. Whether or not Jefferson, Mason, and other Revolutionary proponents of natural rights philosophy intended to include Negroes in the statement that "all men are created equal and endowed with certain unalienable rights" is a debatable question;[16] but in actual practice the American people had decided by their constitutional provisions that Negroes were not included in the *political people*. From the very day of the Declaration of Independence the race problem had caused the American people to make an exception to the doctrine that "all men are created equal." But the partial exclusion of the Negro from the promises of democracy did not impair the faith of the whites in those promises.

The influence of the democratic reforms of the Jacksonian period were far-reaching. Evidence of this is to be seen in many phases of southern life—social, intellectual, economic, and political. But the people were not satisfied with their partial victory, and the signs of progress only made them more determined to complete the democratization of their state governments. Their increased political power made the task of securing additional amendments and revision of their constitutions easier than had been that of calling the conventions of the 1830's. In the first case, they had threatened extralegal action; in the second, they simply used the powers already possessed to put through additional reforms. This time they determined to take from the aristocratic class its last remnants of special political privileges. Important amendments in Georgia, Missouri, and North Carolina, and revision by convention in Louisiana, Kentucky, Maryland, and Virginia,[17] brought those states in line with the most democratic ones. Virginia in 1851 was the last state to provide for popular election of governor; and North Carolina in 1856 abolished the fifty-acre freehold required to vote for members of the state senate. The three new states, Arkansas, Florida, and Texas, all established complete equality of the whites in political affairs, and made all officials elective by popular vote. *The United States Magazine and Democratic Review,* analyzing the progress of constitutional reform in the nation, declared that the constitution of Louisiana showed "more political insight, and a more absolute reliance upon the principle upon which popular governments are based, than appears in the fundamental law of any other state in the Union." But the Missouri constitution "affords more efficient guarantees to individual rights, and leaves fewer opportunities for political corruption and for intercepting the fair expression of the wishes of the people" than that of any other state.

These changes left South Carolina the one remaining stronghold of the landed aristocracy in the South. While she had granted manhood suffrage in 1810, she continued to require her governor to possess a freehold until after the Civil War; the governor and presidential electors were chosen by the legislature; and representation was apportioned on a combination of white population and taxation. But among the northern states, Massachusetts continued to apportion representation in her senate on property until 1853; and Rhode Island continued to require voters and office-holders to possess real estate valued at one hundred and thirty-four dollars over and above all incumbrances, or with a rental value of seven dollars, until 1888.

The establishment of white manhood suffrage, the abolition of property qualifications for office-holders, the election of all officers by popular vote, and the apportionment of representation on population rather than wealth, with periodic reapportionment, dealt a death blow to the political power of the landed, slaveholding aristocracy of the Old South. No longer could the members of that class dictate to the great majority of free white men. The aristocracy still had influence, as the wealthy merchant and industrialist of the northern states had influence, and as men of property in all times and places have influence, but they did not possess that influence because of special political privileges. Some southern planters possessed baronial wealth but this wealth no longer gave them political control. They constituted a social not a political aristocracy. "Such an aristocracy, although it may confer personal independence, cannot create political authority."[18]

If the landed aristocrat wished to sit in the seat of power and administer the affairs of state he must seek the support of the voter, his master. He must recognize every voter, however poor, as his political equal. And in the political hustings landlord and squatter, wealthy planter and poor white, did mingle as equals.[19]

The political revolution also meant that large numbers of the small farmer and yeoman classes began to enter politics, and win seats in legislature, Congress, and the governor's office. The first governor chosen by popular vote in Virginia, in 1851, was Joseph Johnson, whose childhood had been spent in abject poverty without the opportunity for formal schooling. Despite these handicaps he had served in the legislature and Congress, beating some of the wealthiest men of his district.[20] Indeed six of the eight men who served Virginia as governor in the years just prior to the Civil War came from the plain people; two began life as farm hands, one as a tailor, one as a mill hand, and another as a mail contractor. Henry County, Virginia, had the second highest percentage of large slaveholders in the state, yet only two justices of the peace, chosen between 1853 and 1858, possessed as many as ten slaves, while seven owned none and five owned only two each.[21]

Few studies of southern leadership have been made, but preliminary investigations suggest that a majority of the political leaders of the Old South between 1830 and 1860 came from the plain people rather than from the large planter class. Many such men received aid from wealthy planters to secure their education, as did George McDuffie and Alexander H. Stephens. The literary societies at the University of North Carolina paid all expenses of one "penniless student" each year. Several of these students rose to high rank in the state, one becoming a United States senator.[22] Dozens of the men who rank at the very top in political leadership began as poor boys and became planters and men of wealth by their own efforts. Let one of these men tell his own story. "When I was a boy—a very little boy—an honest but poor man settled (squatted is a better word) in a country where I yet reside. . . . Day by day he might have been seen following his plough, while his two sons plied the hoe. . . . The younger [of the sons] studies law and . . . was drawn into politics. He was elected to the State Legislature, to Congress, Judge of the Circuit Court, Governor of his State, to Congress again and again, but he never forgot that he was a squatter's son. He stands before you today."[23] Like Albert Gallatin Brown, many of the leaders of the Old South grew up on the frontier where free men could not and did not recognize any political superior. In fact much of the South was only one generation removed from frontier society in 1860. Aristocracy takes more time to establish itself than one generation.

One test of the effectiveness of democracy is the exercise of the suffrage by those qualified to vote. The southern states met this test to about the same degree that the northern states did. There was considerable variation from state to state in both the North and the South, but the percentage of votes cast, according to the voting population, in the southern states exceeded that of the North as often, and to about the same degree, as it failed to reach it. For instance, in the presidential election of 1828, Georgia with a white population of 296,806 cast 18,790 votes, and Connecticut with a white population of 289,603 cast 18,277 votes; Alabama, however, with a white population of 190,406 cast 19,076 votes. Thus the vote of Georgia and Connecticut was 6.3 per cent of the voting people, but that of Alabama was 10.1 per cent. In the same election, Massachusetts with 603,351 free people cast 35,855 votes; Virginia with 694,300 whites cast 38,853 votes; but Tennessee with only 535,746 whites cast 46,330 votes. The percentages of these states were 5.9, 5.5, and 8.2, respectively. In the presidential election of 1860, Georgia with a white population of 595,088 cast 106,365 votes; Connecticut with 406,147 white people cast 77,146 votes; and Alabama with 529,121 whites cast 90,307 votes. The percentages for the three states were 18.0, 16.7, and 17.0, respectively. In this election, Massachusetts had 1,231,066 free people and cast 169,175 votes; Virginia had 1,105,-453 whites and cast 167,223 votes; and Tennessee with 834,082 whites cast 145,333 votes. The percentages were 13.7, 15.1, and 17.4, respectively. A comparison of all the southern with all the northern states shows a white population of 7,614,018 casting 1,260,509 votes and 18,736,849 people casting 3,369,134 votes, or a percentage of 16.6 for the South and 17.9 for the North. The western states gave the North the advantage in the over-all comparison. But if one uses adult white male population, which is more accurate for voting percentages, then the South had a percentage of 69.5 and the North of 69.7.[24]

The vote of the southern states was almost equally divided between the Whig and the Democratic parties in the presidential elections from 1836 to 1852 inclusive. In the five elections the total popular vote of the Whig candidates was 1,745,884, that of the Democratic candidates was 1,760,452, or a majority for the Democrats of only 14,568. The Whigs had a majority in three elections, but in 1836 it was only 1,862 votes and its biggest majority was in 1840 with 52,851. The Democratic majority in 1844 was only 23,766, and in 1852, when the Whigs were weakened by the compromise issue, it was 79,690. There was a total of twenty-seven states in the Whig column and thirty-seven in the Democratic column for the five elections, but except for the election of 1852 there was no overwhelming majority for either party; and in 1848 the parties divided the states equally. Such an equal division of party strength prevented any one group from dominating the political situation in the South. The states were shifting back and forth between the two parties so rapidly that no one could hope to retain power long enough to consolidate party, much less planter-class, control. This situation also enabled the southern states to exert popular control over the United States senators who were elected by the state legislatures. With party changes in the states the senators were often instructed by the legislature how to vote on major issues in Congress. While the purpose of instruction was partisan it nevertheless resulted in the senators being made responsible to the majority will as expressed in state elections, for many senators voted according to instructions and others resigned rather than do so.

With the coming of manhood suffrage came the demand for popular education so that the voter might cast a more intelligent ballot. It was recognized that democracy and republicanism could work effectively only with an educated electorate. Since "the chief object of constitutions and laws" is "to render its citizens secure in their lives, liberty and prosperity," the importance of "a good education to each individual, to every community, and to the State, cannot be too highly valued," declared a report of the Louisiana constitutional convention of 1844.[25] Popular education, wrote James M. Garnett of Virginia, "is of most importance in all governments. But it is indispensible in ours where all political power emanates immediately from the people, who must be themselves both intelligent and virtuous, or it will rarely happen that their public functionaries will be any better than themselves."[26] Even the aristocratic element recognized the principle that they must now educate their masters, although many did not wish to support education by taxation. One of them declared "that in adopting universal suffrage, we took necessarily the consequences that would flow from it were any portion of the people ignorant and debased. . . . Without you enlighten the sources of political power, we shall have no government. . . . You have adopted the principle of universal suffrage, but the basis is public education."[27]

Recognizing the need every southern state, with the exception of South Carolina where a system of poor schools existed, provided for the establishment of a public school system of education before 1860. North Carolina led off in 1839; the question had first been submitted to popular vote and carried by a large majority. In some states, Louisiana for instance, the constitution required the legislature to provide a state system and to support it by taxation. All the states except Virginia and South Carolina provided for a state superintendent of public instruction; in most states the superintendent was elected by popular vote. The systems of public education in the southern states, in provisions for administration, support, and general results, compared favorably with those in the northern states in 1860.[28]

In like manner, popular control of southern state governments brought measures designed to minister to the economic wants of the people. In fact some leaders of democratic reform boldly proclaimed that this was one of the major purposes of government.[29] Boards of public works, popularly elected, were created to supervise internal improvements and to further the economic progress of the states. They were interested also in the public utilization of the natural resources of the states. Imprisonment for debt was prohibited; banks were brought under state control; provision was made for chartering corporations; monopolies were prohibited; and provisions were made for uniform and equal taxation of property according to value. All these measures were included in the state constitutions. The states, too, safeguarded the rights and interests of the unfortunate classes. State asylums for the insane and schools for the deaf, the dumb, and the blind were established at state expense.

The history of the southern state constitutions and governments from 1776 to 1860 reveals a progressive expansion in the application of the doctrine of political equality. By 1860 the aristocratic planter class had been shorn of its special privileges and political power. It still gave tone and color to political life but it no longer dominated and controlled the political order. On the other hand, the great mass of the whites had been given more and more authority, and majority rule had been definitely established. The interpretation of the southern states as "political aristocracies of the sternest and most odious kind" had no basis in fact. With the exceptions already noted the southern state governments were as democratic in 1860 as their northern sister states. They had not attained the ideal goal of absolute equality, but in spirit and administration as well as in form they had progressively become more and more concerned with the rights and interest of the people.

Chapter XII

Reconciliation Between the North and the South

ELLA LONN

ON MARTHA'S VINEYARD in abolitionist Massachusetts stands a memorial to "The Brave Soldiers of the Civil War," one side dedicated to the soldiers of the Union army and the opposite side to the soldiers of the Confederate army, the tribute of a New England woman to the heroic devotion of the American fighting man.* A different motive from that which prompted the erection of this memorial has permitted or even assisted in the erection of two or three memorials in the North by ex-Confederates. The spirit actuating the tribute at Martha's Vineyard epitomizes the spirit to which we are dedicating an hour tonight—understanding and generosity, but a generosity which can tolerate nothing but the truth on and for both sides.

This paper, it must be stated at the outset, represents no desire to retrace the ground which Professor Paul H. Buck has covered so admirably in *The Road to Reunion*. Rather is it an effort to carry on the golden thread of reconciliation from where he drops it about 1900 and to try to interpret the significance of what in less than a century approaches a complete reconciliation.

It is probably worthwhile to recapitulate the main steps in this progress toward reconciliation in order to see where the country stood in 1900. The account for the purposes of this address must be modified and simplified—possibly oversimplified. Let me enumerate important steps occurring in less than thirty-five years. Complete amnesty and pardon to Confederates was granted by President Johnson at the close of 1868. Disability to hold state or Federal office was removed by the Amnesty

*Presented in Birmingham, Alabama, November 1, 1946.

Act of 1872, leaving about three hundred men disqualified. The Liberal Republican movement of 1872, though it failed politically, espoused a more generous policy toward the South. Restoration of home rule to the southern states became a reality by withdrawal of Federal troops in 1877. There occurred formal exchanges of visits to celebrations and expositions, in the South as well as in the North, especially the centennial celebrations of 1875–81, cleverly designed to recall all sections of the country to the ideal of a common nationality. The wise gift and wise administration of the Peabody Educational Fund was a distinct help. The rebuilding and extension of the railroads in the South helped absorb the old Confederacy into a better economic unity with the rest of the country. The economic advance of industries and the growth of cities produced the economic awakening which has been christened the New South.[1]

Almost a half-century has passed since the end of the period covered by Professor Buck's study. In over four decades what might be termed military, economic, and social amalgamations present no new features. There has been no change of direction, only further development of trends already present and acceleration in the rate of nationalization. Inevitably the South has drawn closer to the North: there are fewer differences between the sections, and the whole nation has been knit into a closer unity, economically, socially, and culturally. It has become more compact.

Military amalgamation was begun in 1898 by the Spanish-American War. In that conflict loyalty to the reunited nation was completely demonstrated. Confederate veterans had frequently asserted that in the event of another war former wearers of the gray would rally as promptly to the Stars and Stripes as they had to the Stars and Bars. Ample justification of the claim was afforded when the news of the sinking of the *Maine* rang through the land. The national government, on the other hand, proved its complete trust in former "rebels" by appointing "Joe" Wheeler and Fitzhugh Lee to two of the four major-generalships.[2]

The two wars of the twentieth century had little to contribute toward unification except in the almost infinitely larger numbers of men in the armed forces who brought home to all sections of the country the feeling of identity with the nation, and except in the application of the draft in the once subjugated territory without the slightest expression of resistance. The fact that there had ever been a crucial difference between the sections might easily have been forgotten except for a veiled editorial in the New York *Herald-Tribune* recalling the Civil War.[3]

More potent than the two wars as an integrating influence, because more constant, was the growth of industrialism. Land is local but capital is cosmopolitan. The Yankee farmer and the Georgia planter in pre-Civil War days were strongly contrasted types, but the factory operative of Lowell, Massachusetts, could not differ greatly from his fellow mill-worker in Atlanta. By the turn of the century the development of the coal and iron industries, of lumbering, and particularly of cotton mills—all embraced under the convenient phrase, New South—was well under way. Most southerners had forgotten as they saw large tonnage of pig iron pass out of Birmingham to the North and West that up to 1871 the site of this giant of industry had been a small cotton town. Textiles, it will readily be recalled, had not long after the Civil War established themselves firmly in South Carolina and were then mainly financed by southern money painfully collected. Already in 1889 the first migration of an entire cotton mill from New England to South Carolina had taken place; within the last decade of the nineteenth century the owners of this factory built mills which added two million spindles to this southern industry.[4]

Indeed, the economic development of the South as a whole in the last half-century has proved even more rapid than that of most parts of the North. Cotton spinning shifted increasingly to the region of cotton planting. The increasing use of water power in manufactures constituted a major explanation of industrial expansion in the southern highlands. The use of electricity was greatly extended. Alabama, Tennessee, and North Carolina show in a high degree the effects of the new industrial revolution. North Carolina above the rest presents the outstanding example of rapid economic progress. Overshadowed by her neighbors in the days of the great plantations, this state, when touched by the industrial revolution of the South early in this century, sprang into life as by a renaissance, though the development there did not attain great impetus until after World War I. The example of efficient organization and operation set by the big combinations helped the small factories to systematize their practices.[5] Somewhat later the discovery of the oil wells of Oklahoma and Texas brought a new influx of wealth to that section. In the South the growth of large cities still further eliminated provincialism.[6] Industry gave the South a wide identity of outlook with the North on many subjects and an adjustment to healthful competitive forces.

The rapidly growing labor movement was certain to make its effort to unionize southern workers. Though the Knights of Labor had entered Alabama and Kentucky as early as 1879, and though the American Federation of Labor had built up a membership of a million and a half by 1903, after the First World War unionism as a positive force ceased to be of any importance in four major industries. In 1930 the federation climaxed all earlier attempts with a supreme effort at organization in the South but in the deepening economic depression this brought small reward to the organizers and financial loss to the national organization. Unionization of textile workers, though that industry invited the first attempts, came on slowly for fairly obvious reasons, chief among which were the company unions with their elaborate welfare programs, the heavy union dues in contrast with the poverty and, up to 1920, illiteracy of the workers, and the reluctance of white operatives to admit Negroes. Even the organization developed in recent years since the passage of highly favorable federal legislation remains still to be tested as to stability. The larger results seem to have been garnered by the American Federation of Labor in the tobacco industry, coal-mining, pulp and paper, printing, and the shipbuilding trades; the Congress of Industrial Organizations controls the unions in the iron and steel industry in Birmingham, the iron ore mines, and the larger number of the textile mills. No appraisal of the effectiveness of the campaign to sweep the South just launched by the C.I.O. is yet possible. The fact, however, that the textile workers are still largely unorganized, as is the lumber industry, shows that labor conditions in this region have not been assimilated to those in the North and are complicated by the presence of large numbers of Negroes.[7]

Despite the fact that writers have repeatedly declared that cotton has been dethroned, the facts remain that the South is still predominantly agricultural and that cotton provides a large part of the southern farmer's income. Although the amount of cotton production decreased by one-third from 1920 to 1945, about one-half of the southern farms were growing cotton in 1939. The tenancy and share-cropping system by which the planter of the immediate postwar era solved his problem still remains the agricultural method in the cotton states. Furthermore, the one-crop system persisted in the cotton belt until the combined effort of the boll weevil and the British blockade of German ports in the early stages of World War I, temporarily reducing cotton exports, forced the cotton grower to diversify his crops.

The South has had its part in the so-called "Revolt of the Farmer." This is the expression by which we designate the pooling of their strength by the farmers. The movement concerns this study because it involves the coalescence of the western and southern farmers. As early as the 1870's the farmers, realizing their failure to reap benefits in any degree comparable to those of business men, became increasingly restive. As prices for farm produce fell, their fixed prices fell, while mortgages and tenancy steadily increased. When wheat averaged seventy-three cents a bushel from 1883 to 1889 and cotton fell to fifteen cents a pound in 1873, and even lower, to eight cents a pound a decade later, the growers of both crops grew perplexed and angry. The resentment of the prairie farmer at the abuses by the middleman almost equaled his bitterness against the discriminatory rates of the railroads. Neither cotton grower nor wheat farmer understood the economic causes of his difficulties—the competition with Russian and Australian wheat and the competition with Egyptian and Indian cotton; nor did either grasp the evils of overproduction. As a result of these harsh conditions, constant farm revolts, in which farmers broke with their old parties, characterized the entire period from 1883 to 1933. First came the Grange movement of 1873-78; at its height there were ten thousand local granges in the South.[8] This was followed by the more radical Farmers' Alliance, which had its inception in the Southwest. Then came the move for cheap money or the Greenback movement; a third party movement, Populism, in the early 1890's; Bryan's solution in free silver and emancipation from the "Cross of Gold"; the Progressive Republicanism of the Theodore Roosevelt era; the Non-Partisan League of World War I; the Farmer-Labor party of the early 1920's; and the LaFollette Progressivism of 1924. In these periodic outbursts of anger the South has not, with the exception possibly of Benjamin R. Tillman, produced prominent leaders but has furnished followers for the aggressive western insurgents. The farmer of the South is no more a Socialist than his brother of the western prairie, for both are men of individualistic tradition, but they clamor insistently for the power of the state and nation to be used to relieve their hard times. Their remedy differs with the emergency, and their means of pressure varies—economic union, cooperatives, or a third party.[9] In 1926 the South for the first time joined the West in agitating for an effective farm-relief program, an agitation which became so insistent as the depression of 1929 drove home the plight of the farmers that it, together with other radical departures, eventuated in the New Deal. Undoubtedly, the average farm in the cotton states is too small to provide a proper level of living for the people working it. Perhaps enough has been said to account for the participation of the cotton growers in the farm revolts when it is recorded that 15 per cent of all cotton farmers produce one bale or less, and that in 1944 the per capita farm income in ten cotton states, according to government data, was $419.[10] These movements not only developed class-consciousness but drew certain classes of the South closer to certain classes of the North than they had ever been before.

Social, as well as industrial, amalgamation has served to accelerate the blending of the people of the two sections. The geographical isolation of the South is now a matter of history. A prime factor has undoubtedly been the unprecedented mobility of the people. The trickle of tourists who in 1900 sought relief in Florida from the northern winter has become a flood of vacationists and winter golfers who pour over the entire peninsula. The hotels and chambers of commerce are preparing for a million visitors this season. Many who have in the last forty-odd years become permanent or winter residents of the South, especially of Florida, have made investments in the citrus or nut groves, the packing houses, or trucking business. They have so completely altered the character of the population in many parts that the visitor almost feels that he is back home among his neighbors of Minnesota, or Indiana, or Iowa.

The migration southward is partially compensated for by the movement northward of southern laborers, especially colored workers, seeking to relieve economic pressures. During the decade of the 1920's the number of migrants leaving the South exceeded the number entering by an average of 130,000 annually; during the recent war it reached the unprecedented level of 300,000, a response to the demand for labor created by war contracts placed largely in the North and West. Fully two-thirds of these recent migrants were whites, largely from the piedmont and mountain sections of the South, a fact which made for a greater degree of mingling with the native population of the North than is possible for Negroes.

However, the migration of Negroes northward, which has been occurring in increasing numbers since 1910—over a million from 1915 to 1928—has transferred to the North some of the problems which had seemed peculiar to the South. Race riots, some on a scale as large as any farther south, manifesting themselves as far north as Chicago, Omaha, and the factory towns in Pennsylvania; lynching at the very time when it was showing signs of declining in the South; a Harlem with a colored population of 170,000 within New York City; and one additional problem, which the South had largely eliminated—the colored vote—have transformed the race problem into a problem of the entire nation. Meanwhile the sturdy growth of manufacturing has given the South an entirely new social and economic class, composed of the mill operatives, the miners, and the foundrymen, drawn largely from the piedmont; it has afforded a miserable rural population a taste of a wider town life and helped to efface the worst phase of poverty. It is not too much to say that the seven hundred thousand Negro farmers scratching a living from some thirty million acres were gradually improving their condition between the wars; and even more so in World War II as the demand for food encouraged the raising of poultry, hogs, cattle, and garden produce.[11]

In the realm of education the national associations, like the American Historical Association, the Modern Language Association, and the American Association for the Advancement of Science, bringing in ever more members from all sections, reduce the likelihood of provincialism and sectionalism in scholarship. Especially was the merging of the Association of Collegiate Alumnae, founded in 1882, with the Southern Association of College Women, which had its birth in 1902, to form the American Association of University Women an event of real significance. The women who were privileged to be present in 1921 when the Southern Association marched into the hall where the larger group was waiting will not readily forget the thrilling scene as a symbol of the complete union of the South and North in a vision for American womanhood with the same emphasis on freedom, opportunity, and high educational standards.[12] The movement of students from the North to southern universities is another factor which must help to forward understanding.

To the scholar surveying the period from 1900 to 1946, there appear really only three areas within which the sections remained still unreconciled: the religious area, with divisions dating back to the decade of the forties of the last century; the political alignment which shows one party completely dominant throughout one section; and a certain area of sentiment, if I may so term it, where prejudice and lack of information cloud clear understanding.

Because of exceptionally favorable conditions the two branches of the Episcopal church, which had separated only after the actual outbreak of the war, merged almost immediately at its close. These conditions were the short period of separation, the total absence of recrimination and bitterness, owing to the rigid exclusion of political subjects from Episcopal ecclesiastical assemblies, and the circumstance that the presiding bishop of the northern church in 1865, though a native of Vermont, had defended slavery as a divine institution. Already at the General Convention of 1865 reunion became a certainty and was consummated by May, 1866.[13]

In the branches of the Methodist church, North and South, acerbity of expression had been unrestrained and radical sentiment had forced resolutions approving the policy of Congress through various Methodist conferences. Thus the controversy had been kept alive through the whole critical Reconstruction period, with the sad result that the two branches could not effect reunion as long as men lived who recalled the charges of heresy and blasphemy. And so it was not until almost a hundred years after the separation that the three branches, including the Methodist Protestant church, which had broken away in 1824 in opposition to a close adherence to the form of the Anglican church, were able to unite in a single organization of eight million members. Though favorable votes began to be recorded in May, 1936, it was only in 1939 that the long fight for reunion came to a favorable, though not unanimous, conclusion. Concessions were made to southern sentiment by excluding Negro annual conferences from the five geographical jurisdictional conferences created to conserve sectional interests, but including them in the central jurisdiction.[14]

Though the northern and southern branches of the Presbyterian church have created committees from time to time, beginning shortly after the Civil War, for more fraternal relations, and though the northern church in 1917 urged organic union, reunion has not as yet been achieved. It should, however, be stated that inability to bring the two churches together turns upon two small points which bear no relation to any hostility surviving from war antagonisms. The move toward union has been prompted less by the thought of conciliation between two sectional churches than the conviction that outward unity of organization is at the present time the great need and goal of Protestantism. Likewise, the failure to heal the cleavage in the Baptist church bears no relation to the issues which brought about separation in 1845, for the dissensions within that church have dealt with autonomy of the local churches. However, the Northern Baptists probably do not forget that there are four million members of their denominational persuasion in the South.

The one conscpicuous area of conviction in which no progress toward fusion between the sections has been made and which sets the South apart is the realm of politics—the Solid South. Only once, in the election of 1928, has the Republican party been able to break the southern phalanx; then five traditionally Democratic states of the old Confederacy broke away to vote for a Republican candidate. A complex psychology explains the unprecedented phenomenon: religious prejudice, the prohibition issue, and class-consciousness expressing itself in the feeling of the unavailability of a son of Eastside New York for the highest office in the gift of the nation.

All thoughtful citizens will agree that this geographical cleavage is utterly unhealthy and prevents sound, wholesome action on many existing problems. The times call for an entirely new alignment. We are not now threshing the old straw of the right to secession or slavery or the problems of Reconstruction. In 1900, the terminal date of Professor Buck's study, this was true; it is just as true in 1946. The problems of our nation today are social and economic. The common man is determined to be heard and, whether we like it or not, the issue is clearly free enterprise or a more or less planned economy. It is partly concerned with balancing production with needs, for the western wheat grower and the southern cotton grower seem unable to strike that balance for themselves. Into the complex also enters the element of class struggle with hot debate as to the rights and abuses of labor and the social security of all classes. Moreover, beclouding the issues is a small minority which seeks to obtrude alien ideas. Meanwhile both major parties cling to old labels without relevance to modern issues, even though the parties themselves are fossilized alignments. For years politicians divorced the two sections from political reconciliation instead of promoting it by fostering alignment according to convictions on existing problems. Because each party is now divided within itself into radicals and conservatives, the crying need is to resolve this old political legacy from the war and Reconstruction into new party alignment according to existing issues.

Thirdly, there is the area I have called sentiment, where prejudice and lack of adequate information hold sway. Here, I confess, I am asking you, my historical colleagues, to become conscious of the wider audience outside, persons who have not, as we have, studied the source materials. I am thinking of the Confederate veteran who not too long ago resented so bitterly my documented evidence of desertion in the Confederate army; I am thinking of a young scholar whom I met at the archives of one of the southern states, who told me that, if he had not read them with his own eyes, he would never have believed the tales of dissension among the Confederate leaders; I am thinking of the comment of a number of the publishing staff which brought out *Foreigners in the Confederacy*: "That book can't sell and it should not."

It is just here that this association and organizations like ours can render a great service in combating lack of information and misinformation. We can remove the last vestiges of prejudice and obstacles to reconciliation, first, as research scholars in searching out the truth, and secondly, as teachers in spreading the gospel of the truth we have learned. The search for the truth is steadily uncovering new facts which often require revision of old conceptions. This revision is of the utmost importance, not only to historians, but also to society.

I shall accordingly proceed to bring forward first some facts of which I do not believe southern society as a whole is too cognizant, and then other facts which I believe need to be impressed on northern society.

Undoubtedly, many southern students, even children in the grades, have conceived a contemptuous idea of Union soldiers and Union officials directing the war effort, unable with superior numbers and resources to defeat the Confederacy in less than four years. Few laymen have any adequate conception of the difficulties which beset the Lincoln administration. They were so manifold and overwhelming that Wood Gray required a sizable volume to discuss them. For instance, for years I had read of Copperheadism, but it was only while working with a foreign language newspaper at Decorah, Iowa, that the seriousness of this disloyalty came home to me with full force. Upon report of a display of Copperheadism at the town of Ossian, not far distant, a group of four hundred loyal citizens, assembled from Decorah, Castalia, and other nearby places, marched to the neighboring town and burned a shop over which a large body of secessionists had dared to raise a Confederate flag. The existence of Knights of the Golden Circle in the northeastern corner of Iowa close to the Minnesota border seemed incredible to me. Of course, I knew of disloyalty in southern Ohio, Indiana, and Ilinois, and even near Keokuk in Iowa, but not a few miles from the Canadian border![15] But it was even more startling to learn of the existence of chapters of the Golden Circle in Massachusetts, Connecticut, New York, New Jersey, and Pennsylvania. These beset the government from the beginning almost to the end of the war.

Added to unpreparedness and stunned amazement when it appeared that the long threat of secession was actually to be put into effect, was the disheartening loss of fortified positions in the South. There was much division of opinion within the Union camp: opposition from many Democrats, after the first burst of patriotism had subsided; the hostility of a considerable number of newspapers which remained irreconcilable, some defending at first the right of secession, and then clamoring incessantly for compromise. Then came the defeatists, who insisted that suppression of the Confederacy was impossible; that even in the unlikely event of success by force, there would remain the necessity of holding a rebellious people, ten million of them, in perpetual subjection. As history offered no precedent for forcible suppression of separation on such a vast scale, many of both parties counseled acquiescence in secession. Against this background of dissension and repeated defeats on the battlefield the Union government had to hold a wearied people through long years to the task of completing the job.[16] I have said repeatedly that it was a miracle that the Confederacy with its lack of resources could hold out for four years; now I state my conviction that it was a miracle that the Union, against such obstacles as I have merely suggested, could win through to victory.

Another misconception which may still linger in the mind of the southern layman is that of "foreign mercenaries" in the Union army. It was repeatedly asserted that the Federal army consisted mainly of foreign soldiers, and the Confederates seemed firmly convinced that except for the host of "mercenaries" the outcome of the war would have been quite different. The Richmond *Examiner,* for instance, believed that the Negroes would be "but little inferior to the riff-raff of Germany and Ireland, which enters so largely into the composition of the Northern army."[17] Certainly the Confederate literature of the time betrays not the slightest conception of the real motives actuating the vast majority of the foreign-born soldiers enlisting for Uncle Sam. It should not be forgotten that the population of the North embraced a large number of Europeans, who by naturalization had acquired the rights of citizenship and also its obligations. Bounties were certainly used to stimulate enlistments, but in the complex of motives actuating the foreign-born, gratitude, patriotism, and devotion to the cause for which they were fighting are abundantly proved.

It is a pity that every American cannot read a letter to his wife written by Colonel Hans Mattson. He was a Swede who led to the battlefield a company of his countrymen from Red Wing, Minnesota. In this long letter he sets forth in honorable, manly terms the motives which actuated him in enlisting. Similar in unaffected patriotism are the letters of Colonel Hans Christian Heg, who organized and led the "Scandinavian Regiment" of Wisconsin.[18] Again and again foreign leaders of many nationalities told their readers that only a tremendous effort could save the Union and that all those benefiting from its liberality must prove their gratitude. This devotion was beautifully phrased by a German speaking for his fellow-countrymen at a dedication ceremony at Gettysburg some years later: "We love this land; it is the land of our children and our children's children. We may differ politically [many Germans had been Democrats] but in the love of our country and its institutions, we are one. . . . Henceforth your country is our country, your people our people, your destiny our destiny, your flag our flag, and your God our God."[19]

If the hearer were asked to identify the writer of the following letter, he would doubtless insist that he was a grandson of some New England Revolutionary hero: "Let our countrymen remember that this war is waged for our children and grandchildren; just as our forefathers fought in the Revolution against England to secure us freedom . . . so it is our holy duty now to take up arms to preserve this splendid gift for our descendants." It was, however, a Norwegian who had thus completely identified himself with the Union and its cause. "And therefore forward Scandinavians!" he exhorted his countrymen. "Let us show our fellow citizens of other nationalities, that when it concerns fighting for a holy cause, the Scandinavians are just as patriotic as any other class of naturalized citizens."[20] Furthermore, it was a Swiss who wrote, "It is beautiful to fight for an idea that is to bring freedom to all men."[21]

The military service of the foreign-born, officers and privates alike, was significant; generously should the Union acknowledge it. But for any adequate conception of the service of the foreigners and foreign-born the researcher must turn to Wilhelm Kaufmann's *Die Deutschen im Amerikanischen Bürgerkriege,* to Regis de Trobriand's *Quatre Ans de Campagnes à l'Armée du Potomac,* to Miecislaus Haiman's work for the Poles, to Edmund Vasvary and to the manuscript by General Julius Stahel for the Hungarians, and to Rudolf Aschmann's *Drei Jahre in der Potomac-Armee* for the service and sufferings of the Swiss.

Bob Wheat's Confederate Irishmen of Louisiana handed down to posterity the finest tribute paid to General Thomas Meagher's "Irish Brigade" of the Union army at Fredericksburg when they saw them advancing with their usual intrepidity against Marye's Heights. "My God," cried the Confederate Irishmen, "here come Meagher's men! What a pity!" The fact that German-American citizens saved Missouri to the Union is undeniable. It was a Swedish knight errant, Colonel Vegesack, who held the Germans of the Twentieth New York Regiment steady at Antietam. General August Willich and his Germans of the Thirty-second Indiana distinguished themselves on a dozen fields from Shiloh to Missionary Ridge. It was Hubert Dilger's German battery whose presence on the battlefield always gave the infantry assurance.[22]

Honesty and accuracy require, however, that the real proportion of foreign and native-born fighting for the Union on the battlefields should be pointed out. Thomas Speed, Benjamin A. Gould, and Wilhelm Kaufmann have made this investigation. The proportion of American-born was far larger than the average Confederate soldier seemed to believe. Let it be remembered that the foreign-born constituted only from one-fourth to one-third, which means that at the lowest estimate at least two-thirds of the army were drawn from native sons. Another fact is deeply significant. Both North and South should fully grasp the fact of the relative equality of the forces actually engaged in many of the conflicts. Francis Marshal Pierce has computed that on account of the heavy Federal detachments needed both to protect the rear against treason at home and for frontier duty, the forces actually engaged in fifty important battles were *at the point of contact,* almost equal. Rarely, he declared, did Federal superiority of numbers more than offset the physical advantages of the Confederates. The North could not fully avail itself of its superior manpower and resources, because a war too remote from home for the northern citizen to feel vitally his did not fuse the people into a common cause.[23]

On the other hand there are many aspects of which northerners should be more acutely aware. Northerners have been reminded time without end that in the beginning both New England and Old England participated in the slave trade. What needs to be grasped is that the situation in 1861 was complex; that it called for infinite patience on both sides, but instead of that tempers were allowed to become inflamed at the intransigence of the other side. Southerner raged at the rabid abolitionist; New Englander at the southern fire-eater. Given time, the uneconomic aspects of slavery, already glimpsed by some economists of the South, must have been discerned by many, especially by those most concerned, the planters. What if this education had taken until the close of the century? Forty years might not have been too big a price to pay for the avoidance of war.

Slavery is today comprehended as a mutual bondage, fettering both master and slave. New England might well remember that among the first abolitionists were two southerners, named George Washington and Thomas Jefferson. The average psychology associated in the mind of the northern layman with the word slavery is that of endless beating of slaves, as the result of too realistic portrayals of *Uncle Tom's Cabin* in northern provincial theaters. Of course, we all know that there were instances of harsh, even brutal, treatment of slaves, but I wonder if all northerners realize the beautiful relation between the races to be found in the antebellum South. Indeed, I confess that it was only in my graduate work that I glimpsed from a war diary the relationship which could and often did exist. Many of you will recognize the incident I am going to use to illustrate the relationship possible between the races as coming from Mary Gay's *Life in Dixie during the War.* You will remember that she had taken the slave boy Toby with her on an errand to Atlanta, that when she found the rail connection to her home at Decatur cut by a raid, she coaxed and urged the sick boy to make the six-mile walk to their home. After their arrival home, he became seriously ill. As he lay dying, her avowal to him is a classic of Christian humility and interracial uprightness: "I have not always been just to you. I have often accused you of doing things that I afterwards found you did not do, and then I was not good enough to acknowledge that I had done wrong. And when you did wrong, I was not forgiving enough; and more than once I punished you for little sins, when, I with all the light before me, was committing greater ones every day, and going unpunished save by a guilty conscience. And now, my boy, I ask you to forgive me."[24]

Despite all the endless volumes that have been written on secession, the northern lay mind sometimes fails to realize that to the southerner the right of a state to withdraw from the Union was the very soul of freedom. The parallel which the southerner readily drew between 1861 and 1776 either escapes the northerner or leaves him cold. And yet that was the crux of the entire movement that nerved men and women alike to make the supreme sacrifices to the bitter end—the feeling that they were fighting for their freedom from an oppressive relationship.

Still another conception difficult for the northern mind to sympathize with is what he terms, "clinging to a lost cause." Perhaps a recasting of phraseology would help, "clinging to *the* lost cause." The hostility voiced in the North at the time to Lee's appointment to the presidency of Washington College must have been grounded in some such feeling, an antipathy to the idea of young men being tutored in a mistaken devotion to the lost cause. Time ameliorates much. Now in 1946, the same section that could object to a defeated general becoming head of an educational institution receives with approbation the proposal to raise ten million dollars to convert Jefferson Davis' home, *Beauvoir,* into an historic shrine. Burial of the dead past seemed to many northerners more appropriate than erection of monuments in every city or hamlet, organization of memorial societies, and the preservation of the Confederate flag, but it was because people lacked imagination to see that it was like the yearning of a mother's heart over her lost child. She does not expect his resurrection but her love cannot on that account die.

Another lack of understanding on the part of northerners may perhaps be mentioned. It is the northern reaction to the feeling which southerners call "feeling apart." I recall distinctly my shock when I heard a southern friend tell me that this feeling is one reason for the persistence of the Solid South. Today I understand and so feel no sense of shock. The South is a unity within a unity. It still differs collectively from other parts of the nation in certain important particulars. It is still set apart by the large number of Negroes, the relative paucity of European immigrants, its agricultural economy, the closeness and far-reaching extent of the tie of kinship, and, despite the New Deal, its general conservatism. Probably greatest of all is its determination to remain a white man's country. The nation would be artistically and culturally the poorer if the South were to be entirely merged in the whole. Any one who has visited the South would not willingly lose the flavor of the French quarter of New Orleans, the sleepy charm of Savannah, nor the atmosphere all their own of a host of other places. The intelligent northerner is glad to understand and preserve the sectional South which is still everlastingly part of the larger whole.

In conclusion a few philosophical reflections on the subject of reconciliation will be in order. That there should have been a period, a generation, of bitterness was inevitable. It was not in human nature for a section which had dominated the national scene so long to yield its position easily and without resentment to sink into poverty and insignificance.

That so large a measure of reconciliation was achieved by the end of the nineteenth century—in less than forty years—was remarkable. That men who had fought each other even with ferocity could mingle as brothers-in-arms in mutual respect a scant quarter of a century later on the battlefield which marked a decisive defeat of one of the combatants is little short of a miracle. Naturally, the scholar seeks explanation for such a remarkable phenomenon. Fundamentally we were one people. There were no barriers of language such as exist when two different nations engage in combat. Further, both sections were dominated by the same Anglo-Saxon traditions, both had the same English background and developed through the same pioneer experience—in a word, they had a common heritage. Furthermore, despite the large admixture of foreign blood, the northern states represented no great deviation from American ideals, for the various nationality elements had been absorbed and proved themselves, when the testing time came, loyal Americans. That the South had foreign strains, though only a small percentage of the whole and not highly regarded by the native southerners, was an advantage, for she must have perceived that, aside from the Germans in Texas, they were an asset in the war. This fact of absorption of foreign strains partly explains why bitterness did not long linger, in contrast with the situation in Europe where it has poisoned for centuries the relations of Germany and France, and of Germany and Italy, making those peoples irreconcilable. This heritage is what has made possible mutual respect and mutual pride in the Confederate soldier fighting against hard odds; and, on the other hand, mutual pride in the Union soldier fighting on doggedly in the face of repeated defeats. The native of the South could respect a good antagonist whether Celtic Irishman or tough Teuton, once he had felt his metal on the field of battle. This same spirit in turn made possible the present northern pride and delight in a South returning loyally into the Union in a spirit of good sportsmanship and rising like a Phoenix from its ashes.

In the second place, both sections were devoted to the same system of government. We know that there was much Union sentiment in many parts of the South in 1861, sufficient to be articulate in some of the secession conventions. The respect for the Constitution of the

United States as an instrument of government was so great that it was accepted as the constitution for the Confederacy with almost insignificant changes.

A point of peculiar significance is that no ideologies were involved. A difference in ideology would cleave far deeper than a mere difference in system of government unless that government were exalted, as has happened in three recent ideologies, into what might be termed a creed. The separation came over the right of secession and was settled by the sword. The Confederate put forth his supreme effort, but, like a good Anglo-Saxon, and one of the proudest of his breed, he accepted the conclusion. Indeed, the issue may even be viewed as one of local autonomy, for the southerners feared interference with their peculiar problem. With the Negro freed, the issue remained during the long struggle over Reconstruction a question of local autonomy, which, despite the outcome of the war, was resolved in 1877 in favor of the South. She remained mistress of her destiny so far as the status of the freedman was concerned. No ideology such as brought irreconcilable differences over religious questions in most countries of Europe in the sixteenth century was manifest in this American situation; and no economic ideology such as is dividing the world in the twentieth century into two camps. It was the irrepressible conflict but not the irreconcilable conflict.

The almost miraculous promptness with which reconciliation came was also partly due to men of good will on both sides. To them America owes a great debt of gratitude. Carl Schurz and Horace Greeley, the latter among the bitterest of the bitter during the war, and all the Liberal Republicans, made the first contribution and spoke the language of harmony. Even though the movement failed, to have this group secede from the Republicans to stress moderation toward the ex-Confederates was a progressive step toward reconciliation. Greeley put a warmth, a pure sincerity, and unselfish devotion into his plea for peace that the South fully recognized. Lucius Q. C. Lamar, the bitter irreconcilable of early Reconstruction, changed completely when he was relieved of disability and allowed to take his seat in Congress in 1874. He made his supreme contribution to conciliation when he delivered in the Senate the memorial address for the Massachusetts senator, Charles Sumner. As Buck says, "If words could reconcile, it would have made the sections one."[25] A second Confederate of good will was General Benjamin H. Hill, who could say during Reconstruction, "My Constitution is my only client and its preservation is the only fee I ask."

Another and younger group of writers, growing up during the war and Reconstruction, were powerful exponents of reconciliation—Woodrow Wilson, Walter Hines Page, Henry W. Grady, and Henry Watterson, each in his own way helping to revise the judgment of southern history and interpreting the South to the North. Joel Chandler Harris gave all America an American, if southern, character in Uncle Remus. In turn the editors of the leading northern magazines in sending men to prepare first-hand articles on the South reciprocated by a consistent policy of conciliation.

The spirit of the foremost leaders of the era of conflict wielded after death, one might even say, a greater influence for conciliation than in life. Jefferson Davis, unfortunately, was not a man to arouse a strong, popular affection; even in my childhood the name of the president of the Confederacy was still inseparably associated with the sour apple tree. But slowly the North came to respect his intellectual honesty. It was not until my mature years, when I met a woman who as the intimate friend of Winnie Davis had had free entrée to the Davis home, that I glimpsed the lonely man, slaving to fulfill the task to which he had dedicated himself, the justification of secession. Comparatively few northerners seem to grasp the fact that the conclusion to which he comes in his *Rise and Fall of the Confederate Government* is that secession was as a right impracticable. More than that it would have been impossible for a Davis to concede. The North might recall that in 1875 he accepted the olive-branch, an invitation to deliver two addresses, one in Indiana and one in Illinois, defined by the terms of the contract as seeking "the promotion of sectional peace." But the North could not yet reconcile itself to the "arch traitor."

The North could, after not too long an interval, take Lee to its bosom. He did not, like some Confederate leaders, shake from his feet the hateful dust of America and seek voluntary exile in Mexico or Brazil, but urged his soldiers to return home to rebuild the devastated homes and country. His injunction, "Make your children Americans," came to be valued at its true worth as genuine, exalted patriotism.

Grant's plea in his presidential campaign of 1868, "Let us have peace," proved futile. The South might do well to remember all the magnanimity of Appomattox which research has unearthed. This was Grant's real glory. To spare Lee the humiliation of personally discussing the terms of surrender, Grant suggested that he send one of his officers. But Lee was not the kind to evade a difficult task and appeared in person. Again compassionate, the victorious general in the interview permitted the defeated general to raise the issue. At its conclusion Grant stated in reply to Lee's frank avowal of the condition of his army that he would send twenty-five thousand rations for the Confederate soldiers, an act which Lee found "a great relief." Grant's spirit extended to his army and found beautiful expression in the act of General Chamberlain in ordering his line to present arms to the brave foe. General Gordon, who was at the head of the men so honored, wheeled his horse to acknowledge the unexpected and touching salute. We are all proud that a fratricidal war could end in so beautiful an act of chivalry.[26]

While the South, we are told by a southern writer, never took Lincoln to its heart as the North did Lee,[27] some of the Confederates saw clearly at the time that in Lincoln's death the South lost its best friend. Certainly, if the North could relive the Reconstruction period, it would follow his tolerance and generosity rather than the harshness, bitter intolerance, and injudicious haste of the Radicals. Rather than dwell upon Lincoln's magnanimity, however, I would stress here the soundness of his thinking, to which the South today subscribes: to have permitted secession or to have granted concessions in the face of secession would have been to dissolve the binding power of the Union. Rooted deep in the American mind had always been the conviction that the cause of republican government or free democracy— use either word—stood or fell with the preservation of the Union. This nation had been the great experiment in democracy and the world would have been vastly poorer if it had been allowed to fall.

The picture I wish to leave with you in closing is that of the large entrance room at Robert E. Lee Hall in the North Carolina mountains as a crystallization of the reconciliation between the two sections of the once divided Union: at one end of the hall hangs a portrait of Lee, at the other end a portrait of Lincoln, a fitting sequel to the monument which stands on Martha's Vineyard.

Chapter XIII

The Country Newspaper:
A Factor in Southern Opinion, 1865-1930

THOMAS D. CLARK

THE COUNTRY paper was an important institution in the New South.* It flourished on a well-established antebellum tradition of journalism. Surviving the Civil War there were 182 tattered weeklies which owned enough type and paper to continue publication. By 1868 there were 499, in 1885 there were 1,827, and by 1929 the number had increased to 2,201 papers.[1]

No major collection of southern country papers is available in a single depository. The tendency has been for special libraries, such as those of the historical societies and commissions, to collect only those journals published in their states. Libraries which have acquired files covering larger areas have only miscellaneous numbers or brief single runs. In the eyes of the historian few or no local publishers have rivaled the more spectacular daily editors for journalistic laurels, and few country papers have attracted major attention beyond the borders of their counties. By the same token few scholars have sought the files of these journals as sources of information pertaining to the New South. Because of their highly circumscribed geographical scope, a broad and tedious sampling is necessary to establish a trend of influence and thought and to recognize their important bearing on opinion. Yet scholars in many areas of southern history have failed, at serious loss to their readers, to investigate this major source of local history. Students of such important subjects as race, economics, politics, the southern mind, folkways, industry, agriculture, transportation, and the process of reunion have practically ignored the existence of the country press. One

*Presented in Savannah, Georgia, November 14, 1947.

serious journalistic scholar has drawn a highly unfavorable conclusion about the southern weekly paper. Apparently his researches extended no further than a bundle of contemporary papers which he collected for writing his essay.[2] It might be said by a cynical historian that country newspapers were only vehicles for patent medicine advertising and puerile country social correspondence. Such a judgment, however, would be uninformed. To understand the place of the weekly paper in post-Civil War southern history requires far more extensive investigation than a casual physical one by a hypercritical perfectionist.

Daily papers have adhered to some degree of editorial and news formality. Often personal opinion has been glossed over with the trappings of synthetic objectivity. This has not been true of the weeklies. A vast majority of their readers have known the editors and generally have regarded them as stable and well informed. Country people have trusted their judgment and accepted their editorial slanting of news stories as a matter of course. The basic influences which the country papers have exerted on local opinion have been one part formal editorializing and two parts personal. Because editors were close to their readers another fact is significant: the editors have shared the people's prejudices and respected their mores.

It was said frequently in obituaries of editors that their outstanding capability lay in the field of knowing what not to print. For this reason it is imperative that any comment on the southern country paper as a factor in regional opinion recognize clearly this negative and unprinted element. At the same time the positive aspects were many. In no printed source in southern history is there a better and more contiguous reflection of the common man's thinking and changing opinion than in the country journal. Its fields of news and editorial comment were as broad as life itself. Its specific treatment of issues was often tempered by foreknowledge of its effect upon the local readers, and definitely there is a reflection of reader response in the solution of local problems. A consideration of this factor in public opinion is necessary, because essentially the history of the New South is one of numerous open issues directly affecting the lives of the people. At the same time a decisive force in the solution of southern problems was the thought and action of the common man.

Editing a country paper was one of the more desirable professional callings of the New South. It promised much prestige and guaranteed the conscientious journalist a commanding position of community influence. Public subsidies for being the county organ were reasonably inviting, and little capital was needed to begin operation. Mechanically, country printing from 1865 to 1900 was in virtually the same primitive state as in the age of the Bradfords and Benjamin Franklin. Few improvements of a fundamental nature were made in the operation of country print shops. Deep toe holes were still being worn in shop floors by strong men pulling the levers of old-fashioned Washington and Franklin hand presses, and it was still necessary to slave away before type cases setting news copy by hand. The only other equipment needed, aside from type cases and a hand press, was a composing stone, a pair of simple iron chases, and a foot-treadle job press.

The Civil War had introduced one significant innovation. Readyprint and boiler-plate matter were made available in large quantities. Ingenious printers in Illinois and Wisconsin introduced the patent "insides" or "outsides" by 1864, and by August, 1865, the A. N. Kellog Newspaper Company of Chicago was distributing "ready print" on a rather extensive scale.[3] This service soon reached the South, and reduced by half the work and equipment necessary to publish a paper. Readyprint houses, such as the Western Newspaper Union, had distribution centers throughout the region, and many country papers were founded with nothing more than a green but ambitious editor, a handful of type, and a bundle of readyprint pages to mark their beginning.

Southern weekly journals expanded in number like cells in a living body. In the beginning a single weekly often served several counties, but within a remarkably short time every county seat and major town had its own paper, and the publishing field narrowed down to specific political localities.[4] Prior to the war the flavor and policy of the country paper was almost purely political, but the weekly of the New South entered a much broader field. Alert editors now gave more attention to local and personal news, extended the influence of the daily journal, and discussed community economics, morals, welfare, and racial problems.

To measure definitely the influence of the postwar weekly paper on so broad a subject matter scale is extremely difficult. It must be said at the outset that it is not always possible to determine whether editorials and slanted news stories were original in thought and purpose, or merely reflected a popular trend of local opinion. Editorials, which were frequently sporadic, were usually brief, pungent, and specific. Many editors were little more than paragraphers, but some of them were most effective in transmitting a forceful point of view in remarkably few words. Editorializing was not always confined to the first two or three columns of the left-hand inside page. Reports of crime, important news, and observations on community affairs were often tinctured with editorial prejudgments and opinions. The use of the libel suit as a personal protective device seems to have been unknown in most southern counties.

Many a prisoner went before a court with a thumping editorial condemnation already against him. Candidates standing for election were sometimes passed upon by editors in phrases less than adulatory. Bold editors recognized no limitations in expressing strong personal views. One courageous old Kentuckian informed discontented readers that it was not necessary for them to beset his reporters with their complaints. If they had courage, let them consult the source of authority for what appeared in the paper and he would give them satisfaction in any form they wished. He interpreted freedom of the press to mean complete freedom to sit in the seat of the community scorner and say what he pleased.[5]

In assessing the opinion-forming aspects of southern country journalism it is imperative that the historian bear in mind the fact that editors often approached obliquely the solution of problems. Crime could not be reduced until law enforcement was improved. General social changes could not be effected until means of transportation and education were advanced. There was an intimate relationship between many of a community's social needs, and the solution of them depended upon a precise approach to all problems. Editors and general storekeepers were among the few people who have understood the subtleties of the southern agrarian mind. What to an objective reader is a mild and practically meaningless editorial paragraph might actually have been controversial enough to touch off a community feud. There is no method by which the temperamental brooding over the implication of the printed word can be measured. Yet this has been a significant by-product of country journalism.

A less militant but no less important factor than the expression of frank personal opinion in assessing the influence of a local paper is that of the degree of consistency in which editors followed up their editorial admonitions. The student of opinion must realize that few editors were intellectually capable or had the time and reportorial force to push many issues to a satisfactory conclusion. They had to be content to strike one or two deft blows for most causes and step aside.

Some public needs, however, were discussed with consistency, and eventually underwent some kind of readjustment. The alertness of a country journal depended directly upon the willingness of its editor to do the necessary reading and thinking to keep himself informed on changing conditions elsewhere. Likewise, the editor's willingness to disturb the provincial *status quo* governed the social effectiveness of a paper. Many publishers were satisfied to allow their journals to be tiny arteries feeding readers the editorial opinions of the better daily papers. Henry Watterson, Henry W. Grady, Francis W. Dawson, Josephus

Daniels, C. P. J. Mooney, and others influenced directly rural southerners who never saw their dailies. Henry Watterson alone exerted a
powerful influence on attitudes toward southern problems, and his
editorials reached far beyond the immediate territory of his *Courier-
Journal.* The writings of Bill Arp, Joel Chandler Harris, and Henry
W. Grady were read in areas where the Atlanta *Constitution* was all
but unknown. So it was with the Charleston *News and Courier,* the
Montgomery *Advertiser,* the Memphis *Commercial Appeal,* the Charlotte *Observer,* and the Augusta *Chronicle.*[6]

Country papers gave those patron saints of the New South, Grady,
Dawson, Curry, Watterson, and Edmonds, a wide reading public. Liberal news space was devoted to excerpts from the *Manufacturer's
Record.* In many areas of the South there was something of religious
fervor in the numerous editorials on immigration and on exploitation
of land, timber, and mineral resources. Since 1867 country editors
have told their readers that they were living in a land of golden opportunity. Their section, they have always said, needed only population,
capital, industry, and mechanical knowledge to make it wealthy. As
early as 1871, so partisan a paper as the Forest (Mississippi) *Register*
sanely analyzed southern conditions and needs. Looking about him,
Editor J. H. Blackwell detected the failures of his country. Grain growing was limited; lands were either going back to the pines or were
being robbed of fertility by erosion; fences were falling apart; and
there were no sheep and few cattle. Aggressive action was imperative.
Southern land had to be made attractive, and southerners must give
up the one-crop system and acknowledge that the day of the big plantation was gone. The South had to pasture livestock all year, manufacture its cotton at home, and profitably employ its labor. Material
progress in the South would relieve political tension, said the Forest
editor. A progressive South with diversified farming would tend to
scatter the Negro population and thereby destroy its political influence,
whereas the plantation tended to concentrate it. As long as the South
was a cotton plantation it would remain a colony of the North and
England.[7]

Many Yankees appeared to see much economic hope in the South.
In the spring of 1885 Henry Ward Beecher traveled below the Potomac
and published one of his few favorable comments about the region.
To him it was a land of promise, and "reminds me," he wrote, "of a
budding spring, intellectually, morally, spiritually; spring has broken
up the winter that so long reigned in the South. Everyone seems young
and full of energy."[8] This eloquent outburst by the famous Brooklyn
preacher was aimed at giving the cause of immigration to the South

a boost. Cheap, industrious white labor was regarded as a primary need by the country editor as well.

Outstanding among the early editorial responsibilities was that of keeping the southern population itself at home, and attracting northern and European immigrants to help develop native resources. This was a two-fisted job. Most editors appeared to prefer northerners to European settlers. It was a remarkable fact that editorial attitudes toward northerners varied with individual viewpoints. If the outsider came as a settler or as an investor, the southern press welcomed him. Even a Vicksburg editor said that he could forgive the Yankee capitalist if he proved generous in lending his money.[9] The Greensboro (Georgia) *Herald* expressed seemingly a universal sentiment. Land should be sold cheap; northerners were more desirable than foreigners because they would compete successfully with the Negro, and their racial attitudes might resemble those of southerners. It was an established fact that they had both capital and factories, and doubtless they would bring them South.[10] There lies buried in weekly paper files an eloquent chapter on the South's arduous efforts to increase its population. Editors reasoned that the more people there were, the more stable the communities would become, and opportunities to exploit natural resources would be much brighter. Contrary to some popular belief, publishers did not hold out promises of abundant cheap labor in all areas of the South. They hoped factories would attract the necessary population to supplement the southern supply.

In 1881 Sidney Lewis of the Sparta (Georgia) *Ishmaelite* was challenged to give one reason why he favored immigration, and he answered with many. Among them were increased political power of the southern states, added wealth, brains, and muscle, numerous factories, the ascendency of the white race, increased land values, settlement of barren territory, increased per capita tax income, and a cessation of the stream of southerners moving westward.[11]

In the last of these suggestions the *Ishmaelite* singled out a major point of editorial contention. From 1865 to 1890 southerners were captivated with the idea of going to Texas and the West. To discourage this disturbing trend, local papers often pictured Texas as a most unpromising place. It was Godless, hot, hard on women, children died young, and men perished from strenuous labor and ill health. Returning families were interviewed and their stories of heartbreak and failure publicized in combination news-editorials. On the other hand the weekly publishers were forced to give an unwilling impetus to the Texas exodus. Hundreds of open letters were written to the papers, and many of them described a land far too rosy for editorial pleasure.[12]

While the white man migrated westward, the Negro went to the delta South, the West, and the North. "Exoduster" stories appeared weekly during four periods of postwar southern history. The 1870's, early 1880's, late 1890's and early 1900's, and the years of the First World War saw a general restlessness among the Negro population. Labor agents were active, and editors regarded them with mixed emotions. They wanted to retain a sufficient quantity of cheap labor, but they were not always positive that they wanted the Negro to remain in the South. In areas where the Negro population was large and the land approached exhaustion of fertility, they bid the exodusters godspeed until their loss threatened the local farm labor supply, and then they bitterly opposed the agents. At the turn of the century Negroes departed from the older cotton belts of Georgia, North Carolina, and South Carolina for the bottom lands of Mississippi and Arkansas. This provoked an editorial crusade which helped to halt the movement. That the local papers influenced public opinion on the subject of immigration appears obvious. They conditioned their readers' provincial minds to accept northern immigrants and at the same time they kept them alert to possible loss by the outward migration of Negroes.[13]

The year 1880 saw the development of a new economic vision in much of the southern press. Papers everywhere publicized the Atlanta Cotton Exposition of 1881.[14] Their editors regarded this venture as the dawn of a prosperous era in the South. One paper said it was the first step in silencing the spindles of the North. "Of all civilizations of the nineteenth century," wrote this editor, "the old South was the only one that would have paid more than $2,000,000 to the hated North to spin its cotton, cost of a thousand miles of transportation, the cost of baling, [and] injury to the fibre by pressing and separating for the spindles."[15] Too, this unfavorable balance of industry increased the income of northern labor, while southerners went unemployed. This situation was to be changed. "The Atlanta Exposition," said the Marietta *Journal,* "was merely a huge blackboard on which is presented to the whole South the plain lesson that $300,000,000 worth of cotton, produced this year, will be worth $300,000,000 more when the ample and iceless waters of the South shall be employed to whirl the merry spindles at home."[16] Grady, Kimball, and Dawson were well on their way to becoming heroes. Grady and Dawson, especially, spread their New South gospel through the intricate channels of the exchanges. Like Sam Jones, the barnstorming evangelist, they had a South-wide tabernacle, the country editors were their deacons, and the weekly papers their amplifiers. Full columns were used in spreading the doctrine of industry. Editorials were lifted bodily from the *Constitution* and the *News and Courier* for republication. Thus the movement for industrialization in at least three cotton states was not a matter of accident. Editorial fervor in parts of the Carolinas and Georgia made it appear downright sinful to be without a textile mill.

Rural editors everywhere were captivated by the promise of a New South. Industrialization sounded wonderful to them, even if they could not always interpret its meaning. When northern papers praised the South or commented on its rich potentialities, the weeklies used their articles as exchanges. Sometimes they were published simultaneously in readyprint pages. When Henry Grady delivered his famous address at the New England Club dinner, weeklies for January, 1887, carried its complete text.[17] This required many hours to set it in type, but its spirit was in keeping with the hopes and aspiration of much of the southern press.

When Grady and Dawson died in early life, many country editors gave them as much space as they did Robert E. Lee, Jefferson Davis, James A. Garfield, and "Little Aleck" Stephens. Their passing was as that of prophets, because they had set the progressive theme for a large portion of the editorial fraternity. They had scaled the heights of the journalistic Pisgah and had seen over into the rich industrial land of Gilead and Dan, but the end came for them while they were still on the plain and while their people still labored as colonials in a single-crop Moab. With the deaths of the industrial prophets much of the future of the South rested with the captains of the weekly papers, and with an occasional city editor to point the way. Their duty was that of leading the southern people into the land of a productive Canaan and Lebanon, where their rivers of Jordan would supply iceless and abundant currents to turn cotton mills twelve months a year. The 1880's, 1890's, and the first decade of this century saw many spies of southern industrialization go forth to search out the land of Providence, Pawtucket, and Fall River, and to entrust themselves to the favors of whoring capitalistic Rahabs in the brothels of the Yankee Jerichoes of Baltimore, New York, and Boston.

The old ways of the southern agrarian Israel, however, were set in opposition to those of the new. Editorial Joshuas stormed the ramparts of the one-crop citadels from the time of Appomattox to the advent of the New Deal. A central theme of local journalism may well be considered its persistent attack upon the South's agricultural system. Perhaps not a single file of a country paper is without its statistical recitations of the failures of the traditional system of planting. Essentially these papers were agricultural journals, and any improvements in southern farming promised greater opportunity for the press. Annually, synopses of what it cost the South to adhere to the standards of the single crop were published. In 1882 the Toccoa (Georgia) *News,* in a characteristic story, said that while the western grain and meat bill was $200,000,000, the value of cotton was only $300,000,000. The cost, thought the editor, was even greater than the tangible monetary value. The southern system made poor consumers, discouraged intelligent fore-thought, encouraged idleness, and prevented diversified farming.[18] In the editorial mind diversified farming was the solution of southern agrarian economy. Rotation of crops, living at home, and improved breeding of livestock became a doleful journalistic dirge. Editors believed they had one dependable answer in their steadfast plea for crop rotation. Their region, however, cried out for agricultural reforms of all kinds; but before they could be accomplished, the vicious lien laws needed to be removed from the statute books and markets for perishable products developed. Though the weeklies were astute in pointing out the funda-mental failures of the South, their editors lacked mature experience and foresight to understand the complex need for adequate marketing facili-ties. Here was the weak spot in their armor, and one which brought them into conflict with their agrarian readers. This was perhaps the chief reason why they could not effect material change in agricultural opinion until the last two decades.

Throughout the South the weekly press was vigorous in opposing the lien laws. Again the editors were accurate in analyzing and exposing to public view failures of this method of financing agricultural produc-tion. They marshaled an overwhelming volume of incriminating evidence against it, but not until fundamental changes were made in rural mar-keting and financing did they achieve their objective. From the beginning this journalistic contention was sound, but no one could suggest a certain solution for the South's credit needs. But the influence of the rural press on this important aspect of southern economic life is not to be measured in terms of positive accomplishments. The press was able to bring about a total awareness that eventually the prevailing system of southern farm-ing would become bankrupt.

If the weekly press failed to destroy the lien laws, there was an area in southern agriculture where it had a forthright bearing on farm opinion. It would have been difficult, if not impossible in some states, to establish experiment stations and have them function as effectively as they did without the cooperation of the country papers. By means of news stories, farming hints, scientific analyses, and vigorous editorials the rigid southern agrarian mind was converted from outright antagonism to reluctant cooperation within the first two decades of experimental work. In Mississippi, for instance, a press defense of the Agricultural and Mechanical College and its experiment station made a definite impression upon popular opinion. Such was the case too in South Carolina in connection with Clemson College. By subtle news stories telling of people growing their own supplies, and of large yields of produce per acre, rural leaders were converted to change. Before the advent of the Hatch Act and Dr. Seaman A. Knapp, editors knew that the most effective way to induce southern farmers to try new farming methods was to give them practical and comparative solutions of their problems. When they read that their neighbors were succeeding with new methods they were much more willing to try improvements themselves. Seaman A. Knapp was one of the first men in the South to succeed in effecting change by the precept method. Much of his success lay in the favorable publicity which the country papers gave his projects, especially in advertising boys and girls club work.

New ideas for livestock and plant breeding and improved mechanical methods were accepted hesitantly. Much publicity was given projects to accomplish the breaking down of old and unprofitable farm practices. Boys and girls clubs and demonstration groups functioned more efficiently because of the interest of local papers. Two specific instances of opinion-forming service will suffice as illustrations. At the turn of the present century two major calamities threatened southern farmers of the Gulf coastal cotton-planting areas. Both the boll weevil and the Texas tick promised ruin. The course and progression of the boll weevil in Texas was widely publicized, and the yearly expansion of devastation was charted. Vigorous efforts were made to prepare cotton farmers for its eventual appearance elsewhere, and considerable headway was made in this undertaking. For once in their long fight editors could preach crop rotation and diversification with reasonable effectiveness. The approach of the weevil to many parts of the South found farmers well warned and partially conditioned for economic changes which faced them. Too, methods of combating this insect infestation were made known through scores of publicity releases from county agents, the experimental stations, and the United States Department of Agriculture. As for the Texas tick, after July 1, 1906, when federal quarantine laws became effective, the issue of dipping cattle in certain specified areas became bitter. The press explained generously the necessity for such action, and strongly advocated the eradication of this parasite in order to develop the cattle industry. There was much popular resistance, and editors were quick to condemn the ancient Whitecapping practice of blasting dipping vats and to give ignorant and superstitious resisters common-sense reasons why they should obey the law.

Closely allied with the dipping-vat law was the older contention of the open and closed range. In many areas the New South was raw frontier country, and this fact must be recognized in order to comprehend some of the problems which confronted the press. No public question better illustrated this condition than the status of the cattle range. Beginning in the late 1860's this dispute was publicized at great length in almost every country paper in the South. Progressing like a slow-moving hurricane, this issue swept across the region from county to county. Apparently no other public topic has ever been more adequately discussed in the local papers than was this one. Thousands of "open letters" were printed. Proponents of the closed range produced innumerable sound reasons for their stand, and the opposition resisted with astounding demagoguery. The poor widow, the tenant farmer, the town laborer, the Bill of Rights, and the Bible were all used as opposing arguments. To require cattle owners to build fences around their pastures and confine their livestock within a given plot of land was an invasion of individual privileges. It mattered not to opponents that the old system of fences was rapidly exhausting both timber and labor resources, nor that the South could not hope to improve breeds of livestock with scrub bulls and boars enjoying their inalienable rights.[19] Despite the furor of blatant demagogues, the more populous areas of the South adopted the closed range, and clearly the country papers were decisive factors in the elections.

In other fields editors fought back the frontier and prodded their people into making progress. A campaign for railroads and highways went on for seventy years. The story of the location and building of southern railroads involved a tremendous amount of agitation by the press. Editors left no doubt in their readers' minds that railroads were both expensive and necessary. To them it was the differential between being able to reach out to the world by means of fairly efficient transportation and lingering in the backwoods hemmed in by a large land mass and impassable dirt roads.

It was in the campaign for improved highways that editors actually exerted some of their greatest influence. They were collectively powerful in agitating for railroads, but often the bigger problem of finances was beyond their capacity to solve. Highways, however, could be as local as a farm community-to-town connection. Almost from the end of the Civil War, weekly newspapers reflected either a total lack of roads in many directions from their towns or the seasonable impassability of those in existence. Grand jury presentments most often drew fire. The aimless and disorganized plan of common work by which all able-bodied men from 17 to 56 years were required to labor for given periods each year on the roads was severely criticised.[20] Overseers were upbraided for their laxity in getting their work done. Two specific movements were promoted by progressive editors to improve the highways. Their first undertaking was that of making taxpayers see that it was wiser to abolish the indifferent overseer and the shirking citizen and to pay for having the roads worked. Private contractors could do the job much more efficiently, and they could be made directly responsible to county officials. This first plan was hardly before the people in concrete form before a larger one was ready for discussion. After 1895 the so-called good roads movement was under way across the South from Richmond to Houston. Progressive editors campaigned constantly for the building of arterial highways. Meetings of good roads committees were publicized. News stories of the accomplishments of other southern communities filled the papers, and columns of editorial prodding kept the movement alive. Obviously a combination of circumstances ultimately aided in developing the southern roads, but none was more effective than the agitation of the weekly papers. They could claim a lion's share of credit for driving the trifling overseer and his irresponsible common laborers back to their picayunish affairs, and of introducing the private contractor and the more comprehensive system of courthouse-to-courthouse roads which now connect southern counties.

In the broader field of social life the southern weekly editor was faced with problems which were seldom so well defined as those pertaining to politics and regional economics. He had to recognize the place of folk culture, and to utilize it so far as he could in making his paper both popular and useful. Again the social historian has failed to uncover with full understanding this meaningful vein of southern life. A stern evangelical religion paying obeisance to an intensely personal God created a social complexity which required an intimate editorial understanding to prevent constant conflict. This condition of the rural southern mind made the shaping of public opinion in the social sense a slow and tedious process. The border line between intelligent understanding and superstitious resistance was a thin one, and it made editorializing and news reporting on such subjects as religion, modern medical care, veterinary science, scientific agriculture, home improvements, and dietary habits a highly circumscribed undertaking. Again the newspapers for the first fifty years after the Civil War were more reflective of folk habits than of a changing public opinion. Informed and intelligent publishers early recognized this factor as a block to rapid southern development. It was perhaps impossible for them to convert the popular mind to an acceptance of social advances except through the channel of public education.

Public education itself was a confused issue. It involved many sacrifices and perplexities, among them taxes, appropriations from state legislatures, the loss of child labor, the procurement of adequately trained teachers, the eternal race question, and an enormous amount of moral support. Yet education, to even the most reactionary publisher, was a prime necessity. Looked at from a selfish point of view, there was little to be gained from publishing a newspaper in a county where a large percentage of the population was illiterate. When the 1880 census report was made public, the Pulaski (Tennessee) *Citizen* was disturbed to find that its state ranked thirty-seventh in literacy, and that the rate of illiteracy was 27.7 per cent. The editor said that frequently a good-looking, stalwart man stepped into his office, and when solicited for a subscription replied, "I can't read and none of my people can't, and I ain't got any use fer er paper."[21]

The country journalists were thoroughly cognizant of the fact that a community took advantage of its opportunities in the same ratio as its people were educated. "If you make a tour of Georgia," wrote the editor of the Elberton (Georgia) *New South,* "you will find many pleasant little towns where it is delightful to live by reason of the quiet and seclusion which seems to pervade them." But if the same traveler viewed the academy, he would have seen paneless windows, dingy walls, rough pine desks, and premises grown wild. This condition prevailed not because of a lack of children, nor because they were less eager for learning.[22] There were some Georgians, perhaps, who like a Florida backwoodsman, were afraid to send their children to school because they might become lawyers, but they were indeed few.[23] The *New South* refuted in a flat statement the ancient southern plea of poverty. It was not necessarily a monetary poverty which held the South back, but a poverty of energy, imagination, and desire to see the South advance.[24] A plea of a lack of money and a promise of economy were the springboards used by demogogues to get elected to office, said F. B. Shipp of the Greensboro (Georgia) *Herald.* It was all right to talk retrenchment in 1900, but $6.00 per capita for Georgia school children was not economy. "Ride into office on retrenchment, but let not lack of education of Georgia's 500,000 children be another Galveston flood of ignorance."[25] Earlier, a bill was introduced in the North Carolina legislature to divert liquor taxes from the school fund to veterans' pensions. Immediately the Fayetteville *Observer* responded: "If the Democratic Party adopted such a policy it would boomerang. Surely soldiers would rather educate their children than have a little tobacco money. If the party is earnest about pensions let them dig them up. *But the School Fund Must not be Touched.*"[26]

Much space was given to the affairs of the Peabody Fund. Just as Grady, Dawson, and Edmonds spoke for industrialization, Barnas Sears and J. L. M. Curry were spokesmen for education. In the 1880's the extended debate on the Blair Bill was given much publicity, and the opinions of Senators John T. Morgan and Matthew C. Butler were much in the news. At first many country editors regarded the Blair Bill as a godsend to the South, but as the race issue and the tariff were confused with it, opposition developed. N. G. Grist of the Yorkville (South Carolina) *Enquirer,* thought Senator Butler was guilty of turning southern opinion back to the flesh pots of earlier days. He failed to see the Negro as a free man. Absence of public opinion against the Blair Bill had shamed most of its opponents into silence—now they could stand under the protective shelter of a prominent name, and were once again aggressive. Grist said the northern Republicans had little enthusiasm for the bill, and southern Democrats cared little for public welfare in the face of partisanship.[27] When Congress adjourned in 1887 without enacting the famous education bill, the Winnsboro (South Carolina) *News and Herald* lamented: "We need more money and more and better schools about as much as we need anything else in this country. The Blair Bill will some day become a law, and the sooner the better."[28] The Blair Bill did not become law, and it is doubtful that the southern country press much affected its fate, but there is reflected in its files the sort of whispering campaign which has injured many public movements of this sort.

From 1890 to date the weekly paper has been important in developing a sane desire for improved schools and plants, better teachers, adequate tax programs, compulsory attendance, consolidation, and improved administration. Better roads and better schools were twin issues, and in writing of both editors were able to arouse the Rip Van Winkles of southern apathy, self-satisfaction, illiterate indifference, and selfishness to the extent of developing a public school system reasonably free of the handicapping defeatism of the last half of the nineteenth century. Crusading for schools often took the subtle form of news stories of social activities of school communities and of academic and athletic contests. In fact, in recent years the historian gets the impression from the country paper that popular opinion has come to favor the maintenance of schools as basic to an adequate athletic program.

Local editors were able to publicize certain other aspects of state management of social responsibilities. There were many instances where revision of public practices depended upon the attitudes of large blocks of citizens. Alongside education and the good roads movements, one-crop farming, lien laws, and the open range, was the complex question of employing convicts in productive labor. Just as in the case of road maintenance, the states lacked penitentiaries because of inadequate planning and taxes, and were forced to shift their responsibilities to private hands. For the private lessor, here was a certain source of cheap labor from which he could expect considerable gain. He could even use convicts to break up threatened strikes and maintain wages at a low level. As Colonel Albert S. Colyar, general counsel for the Tennessee Coal and Iron Company, said: "For some years after we began the convict labor system we found that we were right in calculating that free laborers would be loath to enter upon strikes when they saw that the company was amply provided with convict labor. I don't mind saying that for years the company found this an effective club to be held over the heads of free laborers." [29]

The convict camp was pictured as a place of horror in the public press. Accounts of filthy living quarters, brutality, murder, and fraud were numerous. Letters from private citizens provoked investigations, and reports of these inquiries appeared in the papers to awaken an apathetic people. Convicts were moved from place to place on trains and through towns, and countless news stories revealed their miserable conditions. After 1870, until penitentiaries were built, scarcely a year passed without the publication of horror stories which rivaled those of medieval France and England. In 1882 the Troy (Alabama) *Messenger* said: "We might just as well have watched a Chinese praying machine," as to wait for the Montgomery *Advertiser* to blast the Alabama system of convict leases. "Colonel John Bankhead has inspected the prisoners and found their shirts sticking to their bruised backs."[30]

William D. Jelks's Eufaula *Times and News* said that the story of cruelty to convicts at the Comer and McCurdy mines in 1898 had few parallels. "Let free-born Alabamians shudder," wrote the future governor-editor. The people would be shocked to know what cruelty was practiced in the mining camps. When everybody else was drunk or wrapped up in George Washington and the American flag, convicts were being flogged to death on the Fourth of July.[31] Throughout Mississippi weekly papers published the Hinds County Grand Jury report which said that state prisoners bore marks of inhuman treatment. Backs were gashed with the whip, feet and hands were frost-bitten, and the stamp of manhood was blotted from their faces.[32] Editors accused the southern states of accepting blood money for their bestial practice of selling human souls to grasping contractors.

In Georgia the Ellaville *Schley County News* said, in 1897: "It [the convict lease system] has been a blot upon the civilization of Georgia which is one of the last states to change to a more humane system. The administration of no particular governor in which the cruelties of the infamous system have come to light is to be blamed. The leasing of the prisoners has been a pernicious evil from the beginning. Southern newspaper men, from pride in their native land, in many cases suppressed the details of brutal treatment of convicts, because it would be a disgrace to humanity. If all the cases of inhumanity to convicts under the penitentiary lease system were written they would tell of a hell on earth."[33]

Many of the stories of brutality were told in editorials and open letters. Without question the country papers influenced public opinion all over the South on this issue. They carried tales of inhumanity to the place of origin of the convict, and his family became acutely aware of the inhumanity inflicted upon their erring son. In Kentucky, Governor Luke P. Blackburn, a heroic old figure of rather uncertain administrative morals, was caught in a gross misrepresentation to the local press. The DuPont mining interest of Louisville attempted to secure a monopoly on the western Kentucky coal mines. To do this it needed cheap labor and connived with Governor Blackburn to lease the state convicts. When one contingent reached the western mines a group of country editors visited the Governor and asked that he recall them to the penitentiary, and that no other prisoners be leased. This he agreed to do, but when the publishers were ready to board their train they discovered that convicts were still being shipped away from the penitentiary for Central City. The Governor was confronted with his own deception and was forced to unload the train of its human slaves and to bring the original shipment home. It was due directly to the influence of the press that Kentucky escaped this chapter of social horror.[34]

Convict leasing was just a part of southern criminal history. It was only one of the results of lax law enforcement and personal defiance of the rules of society. Everywhere southerners seemed to delight in loading themselves down with pistols and other instruments of destruction. Endless accounts of crime tell of the fatal work of the gun and the knife. A man's sense of honor appears to have been just as impulsive as his trigger finger. Between 1870 and 1915 the code of the hip pocket was more demanding than ever in the South's history. Men shot one another because of the passing of the lie, or because of imagined slights to their womenfolk, dogs, saddle horses, or kinfolks. Nervous young men even shot holes in their shoulders while posing, Buffalo Bill style, in country picture galleries.[35] Occasionally they accidentally shot their best girls while showing off their Smith and Wesson badges of manhood. At least two state legislatures, Georgia and Kentucky, enacted laws making it a misdemeanor to point pistols at human beings.[36] The Kentucky legislators approaching this subject, so near and dear to their constituents, provided that it was a misdemeanor only to point loaded guns at persons.

The editor of the Gibson (Georgia) *Enterprise* said carrying a pistol did not necessarily make a boy a man. "God made us and he made us right, if he had needed a revolver attached to us he surely would have done that." Editor McGahee also believed that the fashionable young man "didn't need a gun to make us [*sic*] pretty or respectable any more than a Hottentot needs a ring in his nose to make him kissable. . . . A man who carries a concealed weapon must either be a great coward, or else he has the mark of Cain on his conscience, 'Everyone that sees me shall kill me' and make preparation to defend himself."[37]

For fifty years public gatherings in the South were accompanied by fear of disturbances caused by drunken pistol "toters." A famous story, which was published countless times, was that of a Judge Lester who ordered a North Georgia courthouse locked, and then pretended he had seen a man with a pistol, and intended to indict him unless his pistol and a dollar were delivered to the court. A lawyer deposited a pearl-handled beauty and a dollar bill, but the judge said he was not the man he had seen. Before this farce was ended twenty-one dollar bills and twenty-one pieces of southern masculine adornment lay on Judge Lester's table.[38] So prevalent was the use of the pistol in Mississippi that J. Lem Seawright of the *Choctaw Plaindealer* said the greeting "Good evening, Sir!" was answered by "That's what I say, but don't shoot!"[39]

State legislatures dealt timidly with the task of emptying constituents' pistol pockets. In 1902, the South Carolina assembly passed an act making it unlawful for an individual to carry a pistol weighing less than three pounds and with a barrel measuring less than twenty inches.[40] This drew loud editorial guffaws from all over the South. The Newberry (South Carolina) *Observer* adequately appraised the situation when it said: "The fellow that totes the ordinary pistol does not seem in a hurry to dispose of it and get one that conforms to the new law of twenty inches long and three pounds in weight. Why should he? The old law has been a farce on the statute books; the new one will be equally moreso. A few Negroes will be caught up with; but that will be all."[41]

Editors crusaded continuously against the pistol, but back of their crusading they knew there were many other reasons for the prevalence of violence. Frontier conditions, antiquated forms of county government, fixed juries, lawyers who were shrewd at circumventing the law rather than seeking justice, spineless partisan judges, illiterate justices of the peace, and politically minded governors who granted pardons promiscuously because they thought more of results at the ballot box than well-ordered state social systems—all of these were effective barriers athwart the paths of conscientious editors. They could criticize juries and judges and upbraid an apathetic citizenry for its shortcomings, but in some sections of the South it was extremely difficult to correct social failures.

Crimes of every sort filled the news columns. Stories of murder, rape, robbery, arson, assault and battery, thievery, and malfeasance in office were as commonplace as notices of camp meetings and barbecues. These accounts were published both because of news value and because editors wished to awaken readers to a need for social reform. Country editors had to handle criminal news carefully. Unlike city editors, they were too close to the scene of many crimes to be entirely objective. There was always danger of an editor becoming personally involved with friends and members of a criminal's family in cases where he was sufficiently critical to influence the court decision.

In two instances the press was partially successful in making some headway toward correction of social evils. First it was eventually able to aid in driving hangings behind walls and to break up the horrible Roman holidays in the South where condemned men orated to drunken and curious thousands upon the last-minute salvation of their souls. Some editors said that conditions had reached the point where it seemed the easiest way to enter heaven was to be hanged for murder. A second effective influence was in facilitating reduction of lynchings. There was definitely mixed editorial feeling on this subject. Some editors condemned lynching as a barbaric miscarriage of justice, while others pretended it to be certain punishment for capital crimes so long as courts and lawyers permitted delay, flimsy jailhouses invited jail breaks, and conscienceless governors granted pardons as freely as they did invitations to state receptions. Definitely the country editor cannot claim sole credit for reducing lynchings within the last fifty years from hundreds yearly to less than ten, but their attitude was extremely important in conditioning a frontier southern mind to allow the law to take its course.[42]

Almost without exception the question of criminality and social justice involved the complicated race issue. Too long, scholarly studies have fed upon the daily papers, official documents, social surveys, and one another as sources of information on the South's racial attitudes. Every country paper published since the Civil War has liberally covered the subject of the Negro. Yet it is safe to assert that too few scholarly works have included any appreciable mention of country newspapers in their bibliographies. It is impossible for erudite students to explain their failure to exploit this source with the excuse that they would find nothing new. Many of the basic racial attitudes are revealed in the country newspaper in their most elemental forms. Not only did editors give generous coverage to the Negro in general, but likewise to white reactions.[43]

At least three standard points of view have been kept alive by the southern weekly press. The Negro was good so long as he behaved like a "good old southern darkey"; he was questionable when he behaved like a free man; and southerners had an inborn and intimate understanding of the Negro. As late as 1902 the editor of the Linden (Alabama) *Reporter* wrote that "the old slave Negro is fast crossing to, or are [*sic*] near, the shady side of life, and the young ones are coming on. The later is [*sic*] unreliable and arrogant and rotten, politically. He became a subject of barter and the time for restricting his political rights had come and he was disfranchised. He will be better off and the country will profit by the act."[44]

Editors generally believed that the Negro should be denied the right to vote until by education and extensive experience he could do so intelligently and show that he was free of outside exploitative influences. The Negro, in a significant segment of editorial opinion, was believed to have natural and primitive tendencies which only hard labor would subdue. As the ubiquitous Larry T. Gantt of the Oglethorpe (Georgia) *Echo* said: "The nigger couldn't grow corn, cotton's his fort. Believe Lord made niggers and mule in same mould. One ain't worth a cent without the other. Nigger puts up his cabin in a hot field as far from water as possible. Sunflowers furnish all the shade he gets. He'll eat anything from a highland terrapin to a polecat. Is fond of company and will return every visit, [especially] when neighbors get a new side of bacon. He is religious when it does not interfere with his passions and desires. He is timid but not cowardly, and can be mentally improved but is not original." He wound up this estimate by saying that he could not help liking the old-time Negro, but he thought the young ones, especially the mulattoes, mean.[45]

Perhaps a major portion of the press believed at times that the Negro was fit only to do manual labor. So long as he remained in the field he was a worthy asset to the South, but contrary to their contention that he needed education to vote, if he sought an education he became potentially dangerous. He either sought to exploit his fellows or to get "biggety" with the white man. There was a marked tendency on the part of editors to exhibit the same provincial shortsightedness toward the race issue as obscured the vision of their readers. Too often they were apt to take a specific local incident and give it a broad general application.

Since the time when the South began to reckon with the problem of the free Negro, the press has not been certain what it wanted to do with him. At times it hoped the Negro would find his way back to Africa, or would at least go to the North. But editors have reneged every time there has been a threat of such a thing happening. The various movements of Negroes out of the South have always incurred the eventual wrath of the press at that point where the agricultural labor supply was being threatened with exhaustion. In the same vein editors were never quite certain which they preferred, the Negro as a small landholder and independent farmer or as a tenant. As stable and somewhat educated farmers, they were desirable neighbors. There was no danger of racial friction and uprisings. Continuously the popular mind in many parts of the South was in constant fear of race conflicts, and the papers did much to publicize this state of tension and animosity—possibly with the hope of reducing it by revealing prevailing conditions to the light of common knowledge.[46]

Southern editors were not undecided on one fundamental point, and that was the desirability of white political supremacy. Almost every public issue of consequence involved this point. Driving the Negro out of politics was a major undertaking. Characteristic of this attitude of the weekly press, an Alabama editor said, in favoring a white Democratic primary: "The day of the long-legged, lantern-jawed, slab-sided, pigeon toed, jangle-kneed, box-ankled, turkey-trotten [sic] unforgotten political polawog is gone. The day of white supremacy dawneth and the black clouds of Ethiopia are receding from the American horizon. We have not had white supremacy in Alabama since the darkey was invested with the elective franchise. It is true we have had white officers, and sometimes, through political intrigue and the counting of 'dead niggers and dogs' they were honored with the toga of official preferment. We are now and always have been willing to bow to the behest of Caucasian rule."[47]

In October, 1901, weekly papers in Alabama carried news stories and editorials on the new state constitution. Sixteen reasons were published as to why it should be ratified. Reasons *eleven* and *fifteen* explained that the Negro was denied the right to vote. "Reason Fifteen" was clear-cut: "THE WHITE MAN WILL RULE FOR ALL TIMES IN ALABAMA."[48]

While Alabama papers were shouting sixteen reasons for ratifying a new constitution, and printing in capital letters those relating to the disfranchisement of the Negro, the southern press generally was going mad over Booker T. Washington's famous luncheon at the White House with Theodore Roosevelt. Seldom in the history of American journalism has a single minor incident set off so wild a public tirade. If all the editorial energy expended in fighting back at Teddy and Booker had been exerted in behalf of southern public education, the school system would have advanced at least a half a decade. This simple gesture of racial harmony on the part of the President of the United States exploded into one of the most violent social bombshells this side of Reconstruction.

From Bill Arp to the most insignificant little "patent sides" editor there was intense bitterness which did irreparable harm to race relations for the decade 1900–10. Closely related to this affair in the public mind was the uproar over the famous Bassett affair in North Carolina, and the Sledd incident in Georgia. Fortunately, four decades have somewhat absorbed the bitterness of the turn of the century. Although a majority of southern editors still guard white supremacy, they no longer refer in news articles to Negroes as "goat-scented sons of Ham," "contrabands of freedom," or "flat-nosed, thick-lipped and long-heeled fiends." Many weekly papers now contain columns of Negro farm and church news and seek Negro subscribers.[49]

Editors began their battle for white supremacy the moment the federal civil policies were discernible after 1867. Politics has ever been a leavening factor in southern journalism. In a vast majority of their policy statements new editors have declared that they expected to be "strictly Democratic."[50] Over the years the country paper's political influence has followed a rather consistent policy so far as party and white supremacy have been concerned. Third-party movements have caused a majority of the weeklies to rally around old and conventional political standards. In many instances Populist papers were established to combat the conservatism of the older journals.

A self-estimate of the power of the country paper in downing third partyism was published by the Senatobia *North Mississippi Democrat*. "It would be difficult," said the *Democrat,* "to exaggerate the influence of the country papers of Mississippi in the overthrow of the enemies of the Democratic Party. The press almost solidly fought the heresies of the third party from the hour the war cry was shouted. The country papers are near to the people, familiar with their wants and needs, and can always be depended upon to espouse the cause of right and justice. Not enough credit is accorded the weekly papers in the distribution of the honors of the victory. They are the most potent factors in the material development of the country outside of their political influence." This opinion was endorsed by the Jackson *Clarion,* which thought that the election of 1892 had proved signally that the weekly newspapers were devoted to the welfare of the state. "In many instances it would have been to the temporary material interest of county papers to have been luke-warm or non-committal. But almost without exception, they have been true and emphatic in assailing the specious fallacies which have sought political sway in the state. The Democrat is right. The chief agency in downing 'Third Partyism' has been the weekly press."[51]

The Populist era was at most a brief interlude in country paper history. Editors were to exert their greatest opinion-forming influence in their factional support inside the Democratic party. In earlier years, the major portion of the papers were conservative to the extent of wearing a pronounced Bourbon complexion. During this century, however, weekly papers have adopted political coloring according to the economic background of their localities. Poor hill-country and piney-woods papers in Mississippi have shown a tendency to support Vardaman and Bilbo, while prairie and delta papers have been more conservative. In South Carolina, Georgia, and Alabama apparently similar divisions of opinion have followed lines of economic and geographic influences.

Political influence of the country papers over a period of eighty years of post-Civil War southern journalism is to be measured in the rigidity of the one-party system. Locally there can be little doubt that editors have exerted strong personal influences over popular opinion by favoring certain candidates and contributing generously of editorial and news space to publicizing their campaigns. In nonpersonal campaigns editors have had a major hand in forming popular opinion. Especially has this been true in instances involving changes of city and town charters, revision and amendment of state constitutions, the floating of bond issues, and the advocacy of public legislation. Voters early learned to depend on editors for information where technical issues were involved. So effective have they been in this field of interpreting questions for their readers that local editorial support is a highly desirable thing when approaching a southern electorate with a fundamental proposal. Again the publishers' influence in instances of this kind has been one part editorializing and two parts personal appeal.

Politicians early discovered that the editorial chair was a good springboard for launching a political career. Among those putting this lesson to practical use were James K. Vardaman, William D. Jelks, Robert L. Taylor, Urey Woodson, S. A. Jonas, and many others. Politicians generally have found country papers exceedingly valuable supporters. Theodore G. Bilbo, Huey Long, Lee O'Daniel, and Eugene Talmadge discovered that weekly papers were excellent mediums in which to communicate with their constituents. Many southern politicians have often utilized the services of "bought" policy papers which spoke for them in the heat of political battle.

No field of public endeavor in the small town and rural South has been devoid of the country press influence. Editors have never felt that they were restricted to special subjects in their writings. Their own personal courage and imaginations have been the only limiting factors. Wherever editing a country journal has been accepted as a profession by an editor who conscientiously wished to render public service, it has yielded rich dividends of community respect and esteem. Many editors reached the pinnacle of local journalism and became a balance wheel in the civic functioning of their communities. Where eighth-grade printers have risen to editorships because of the death or retirement of professional publishers, or have established weekly papers as adjuncts to job-printing plants, the tendency has been to focus attention on the financial returns from the printing business and to neglect the paper's community responsibility. Too, rapid means of transportation and communication have robbed the conventional local journals of much of their news and feature values. Journalism graduates have often attempted to make metropolitan papers out of old-line weeklies with the result that they ceased to be valid weeklies and become vapid imitations of city dailies. But whatever the plight of many country papers today, historically the southern country press undoubtedly influenced public opinion and ably reflected the efforts of the South to overcome the stifling effects of its poverty and the drawbacks of a frontier country, to establish industries, to diversify its crops, to enclose its convicts in organized penitentiaries, to close its ranges, to maintain a modern system of universal education, and to recognize the sanity of modern medical care.

Chapter XIV

The Old South to the New

ROBERT S. COTTERILL

THE TERM "New South," if not coined by Henry W. Grady, at least first put into circulation by him, had reference originally only to the cotton manufacturing development of the 1880's.* To contemporary observers the name was justified since it seemed evident to them that the South was at that time altering the pattern of its economic life, turning its back on its own history, and entering upon new roads to economic salvation. In the course of years the meaning of the term was broadened to include all phases of southern life since 1865. But the very name "New" South implies an "Old" South, and this latter term now became attached to the period prior to that conflict which southern people, stubbornly and ungrammatically, insist on calling the War Between the States. Inherent in the two terms is the concept not merely of a difference in time but of a change in civilization.

This concept of discontinuity between the Old South and the New has been strengthened in two ways. One of these is the glorification of the War Between the States and the emphasizing of the ruin and devastation it brought to the South. Denied the pride of victory, the southern people developed a pride of suffering. And the thought was an inevitable one that in a tragedy so terrible and a ruin so complete no previous pattern of life could possibly have survived. Therefore, the Old South must have died. The other way in which the idea of discontinuity has been increased is by the growth of a legend of the Old South as a land of plantations, slaveowners, aristocracy, and agricultural philosophy. White people, according to the legend, disdained manual labor and refrained from any debilitating practice of it. All work was done by Negro slaves, apparently in intervals between singing the praises of their Old

*Presented in Jackson, Mississippi, November 5, 1948.

Kentucky Home and making metrical demands to be carried back to Old Virginny. What few common people there were in the Old South were serfs subsisting on the economic crumbs which fell from the gentry's table. Such was the Old South of legend, and since the people of the New, looking around them, saw nothing even remotely resembling it, they reasoned, quite logically, that it must have died—as the genealogists so deftly put it, OSP.

These, then, are the three concepts inherent in the terms "Old South" and "New South"—a legendary "Old South" that has no present counterpart, a "New South" with a pattern of life unrelated to the Old, and between them a war so devastating that it destroyed the old order making it necessary to start all things anew.

The first of these ideas may be dismissed without argument. If the Old South of legend be no longer present, it is not because it died but because it never existed. It is a figment of imagination, originating in the ignorance, or malice, of northern abolitionists and adopted by southerners suffering from nostalgia. It was at once a distortion and an idealization, and in neither capacity could it transmit any part of itself to later times.

But the cotton manufacturing development of the 1880's which first gave rise to the name "New South" was no hallucination. The only question about it is not whether it existed but whether it was *new*. Certainly the people of that time called it "new," and its coming was accompanied by such a rash of publicity as had not broken out on the southern body politic since the railroad building of the 1840's. Editors, orators, ministers, poets, novelists, and businessmen hymned its praises, and canny politicians hastened to cast their political bread on its waters. They proclaimed that a New South was being born. There were some people then (and there have been more since) who viewed the development of manufacturing as a surrender of southern ideals and the adoption of a low, Yankee culture. But most commentators have considered it as a beneficent dispensation which had been denied to the Old South because of the enervating effects of slavery. The most noted of these has declared in one of his books: "In the face of a freed negro population, the idea of work first seriously presented itself to the Southern white mind."[1] But since the fifteen years that had elapsed between the adoption of the Thirteenth Amendment and the supposed beginning of the manufacturing movement seemed a bit longer than should have been necessary for such a powerful regenerative force as emancipation to get into mass production, supplementary explanations had to be given. These ranged all the way from the resumption of specie payment to the psychological shock of James A. Garfield's election. They ascribed the beginning of the manufacturing movement to the poverty of the 1870's and to the prosperity of the 1880's, to jubilation over the collapse of carpetbaggery and to despair caused by war and reconstruction, to exultation over the preservation of southern ideals and to repentance for ever having had any. But although the writers differed on the origin of the phenomenon, they all agreed on the nature of it. They all agreed that it was new: it was a revolution, unrelated to the past, barren of ancestry, destitute of inheritance.

But the student of history is insistent on sequence and consequence; he demands continuity and cause. He is uncontent to find an explanation of mundane affairs in the doctrine of virgin birth. Every historical event, he considers, must have a family tree as an accessory before the fact.

The difficulty writers have experienced in explaining the origin of the "Industrial Revolution" in the South may be primarily owing to the fact that there was no Industrial Revolution to explain. The so-called revolution was, in fact, not a revolution but an *evolution* from the Old South to the New. If in the Old South manufacturing was only a handmaiden to agriculture, it was not because of agricultural philosophy but of agricultural profits. By 1860 the South had 188 cotton mills, the yearly output of which was valued at $14,000,000. If it be true that it was in the face of a freed Negro population that "the idea of work first seriously presented itself to the Southern white mind," it is pleasant to reflect that all this was done without effort. The recipe seems to have been lost. Certainly the growth of manufacturing in the Old South was sufficient to excite the apprehension of northern mill-owners, apparently unaware of the fact that manufacturing was impossible in a slavery regime. And if it were not uncharitable, one might suspect that the patriotic fervor of General William T. Sherman in destroying southern cotton mills was not unadulterated by a desire to eliminate competition. But Sherman, unlike Kilroy, was here only once and some two-thirds of the southern mills escaped his evangelical efforts. It is only reasonable to suppose that the war stimulated southern interest in manufacturing. But when southern people after the war engaged in manufacturing it was neither because of prosperity during the war nor of poverty after it. It was because cotton manufacturing was one of the recognized and accepted ways of making a living. They did not *begin* manufacturing after the war: they *resumed* it; they were actuated not by novelty, but by tradition. By 1870 the losses of war were almost fully recovered: then came the seven lean years of the early 1870's, the recovery late in the decade, and then the well-trumpeted development of the 1880's. But the South in the 1880's did not become suddenly *industrial*; it only became suddenly *articulate*. The beginning was not in *manufacturing,* but in *publicity.*

The industrial inheritance of the New South from the Old was not confined to cotton manufacturing. The derivation of the Durham cigarette from Russia and of the Tampa cigar from Cuba cannot alter the fact that the paternity of southern tobacco manufacturing lies in the Old South. In the antebellum period it was the output of plug tobacco from southern factories that lifted expectoration in the United States to a position among the fine arts along with music and painting, and made the cuspidor standard equipment in the American home. As for iron manufacturing, even in colonial days it was important enough to be prohibited and too important to be prevented. Of the other manufactures of the New South, the only important one lacking an Old South pedigree is furniture. Even the manufacture of cotton-seed oil had its beginning in the Old South, although quite a bit of it in the process of labeling seems to have undergone a metamorphosis into olive oil. The Old South discovered the coal mines of Maryland, Kentucky, Tennessee, and Alabama and exploited them so far as transportation facilities permitted. And if the petroleum industry be considered a species of mining, we may remember that Louisiana discovered oil before she discovered secession.

The only important change made by the New South in its agricultural inheritance was the substitution on its plantations and larger farms of share-cropping for slave labor and of the country store for the factorage system. Both share-cropping and the country store were Old South institutions now expanded into wider uses. Share-cropping, of course, did not originate in the Old South, but is as old as agriculture itself. The first record of it is found in Genesis 29-31 where it is told how Jacob tended on shares the flocks of his uncle Laban in the land of Padan-aram. It may be noted, incidentally, that Jacob broke his contract, moved away secretly, and took a considerable portion of his landlord's property with him—thereby establishing a precendent that has been followed extensively to this day.

In no phase of the economic life was the New South new. It was not a Phoenix rising from the ashes of the Old; not a revival; not even a reincarnation: it was merely a continuation of the Old South. And not only in its economic life: the New South inherited, also, the *spirit* of the Old. It inherited its racial pride, and if anyone wants to call it racial prejudice, there can be no objection, because pride and prejudice were inseparable companions long before Jane Austen proclaimed their union. The student of history cannot turn moralist either to exalt or to condemn this racial pride, but he must take note of its continuing existence. The New South inherited, also, a laissez faire philosophy of living which manifested itself subjectively in an indifference to progress and objectively in a distaste for reforming its neighbors or to confessing other people's sins. It inherited the Old South conviction that certain questions could not be surrendered to the jurisdiction of public law. The one quality of the Old South apparently uninherited by the New was self-confidence and consequent self-assertion. Says a Confederate arithmetic: If one southerner can whip twelve Yankees, how many Yankees can six southerners whip? Although the premise of this problem seems to have been somewhat unstable, it evidences a spirit of confidence that for a long time seemed lost to the New South. It may be, however, that the aggressiveness and boastfulness so characteristic of the Old South instead of dying out after the war simply followed the trail of cotton and migrated to Texas. From the time they annexed the United States in 1845 until their recent singlehanded and unaided conquest of Germany and Japan, Texans have been noted for their aversion to understatement. But it is possible that when Texans talk "big" they are speaking not as Texans but as southerners. Certainly, that Texan was speaking the language of the Old South when he rose at a banquet and gave this toast to his state: "Here's to Texas. Bounded on the north by the Aurora Borealis, bounded on the east by the rising sun, bounded on the south by the precession of the equinoxes, and on the west by the Day of Judgment."

As to the final factor in our concept, the War Between the States cannot be considered as a mighty cataclysm engulfing the Old South or as a chasm dividing the Old South from the New. The pondering of might-have-beens is normally an exercise taken in vain, but it seems clear that in no essential way did the war alter or deflect the course of southern development. It was an interruption but not a cleavage. It was, in long perspective, only an episode in a continuous southern history: a tragic episode, but even its tragedy was transient. No southerner can be tempted to belittle the war or deplore the remembrance of it. Surely it was worthy of all remembrance—a war of heroism unrewarded, of suffering uncompensated, of hopes unrealized, and of dreams that have no waking. But for the South it marked no end and no beginning: it neither buried the Old South nor brought the New to birth. There is, in very fact, no Old South and no New. There is only The South. Fundamentally, as it was in the beginning it is now, and, if God please, it shall be evermore.

Chapter XV

The Provincial South

LESTER J. CAPPON

IN THE SPRING of 1949 the imprisonment of three veterans for debt in Rutland, Vermont, provoked widespread comment in the daily press and the news magazines.* When one of the prisoners was freed through payment of his debt by a cotton shipper in Memphis, Tennessee, an editorial with the title "Who's Backward Now?" appeared in the Richmond *Times-Dispatch,* from which I quote:

> Try to imagine what would happen if war veterans—or nonveterans, for that matter—were being imprisoned for debt in some Southern State under an old English law discarded in England, itself, as well as in most of the United States, long, long ago. Throughout the North, self-appointed guardians of civil liberties would go trumpeting to the fray. The Southern State in question would be termed medieval and backward and its citizens would be depicted as ignorant, vicious and cruel. . . .
>
> But the State in which war veterans have been, and still are, imprisoned for debt is not a backward Southern State. It is Vermont which is in New England and, therefore, enlightened and forward-looking. . . .
>
> Maybe somebody now will demand a law forbidding backward Southerners to interfere with such fine old institutions as debtors' prisons in enlightened Northern States.[1]

Credit for original publication of this editorial goes to the Buffalo (New York) *Courier-Express* and for reprinting to the *Times-Dispatch,* which editorially awarded the writer "on the faraway shores of Lake Erie . . . one engraved cawn pone, two beakers of bourbon and branch water and one carload of hush-puppies and grits." The editorial has, I am sure, a familiar ring in the ears of southern historians.

The South, which has partaken of much of the standardization of modern America, is still different in many respects from other regions,

*Presented in Williamsburg, Virginia, November 11, 1949.

as it has been throughout its history. It has attracted many a traveler out of curiosity to see for himself so that he might confirm or refute conflicting reports perennially in circulation. Of those who have come to observe, relatively few have tarried to live permanently, and they have found adoption a slow process, which is doubtless as it should be. If there is a southern way of life that persists through controversy and the impact of powerful outside forces, one must live with it and within it to develop understanding. The visitor from the North finds that to some southerners he is still a Yankee, if not a "damn Yankee," although the term "rebel" among northerners has long since been forgotten and southerners have themselves been "Yanks" in two world wars. He may be shocked to see the Confederate flag on parade, but he has much to learn and comprehend. So too has his southern fellow American who still wonders why the people of the North were willing to fight for the Union.

From my southern grandmother, who lived in a northern city as the result of a typical "boy-meets-girl" episode, I heard my first stories of the South, and, as you might guess, they were about the Civil War. For a good many years I have been learning about this southern way of life and seeking to understand it from within. It is a long course, and a slow one, you may conclude from this paper. Some of the shortcomings in our historical interpretation, I believe, stem from an oversimplification of southern problems in the attempt to master their complexity. Thus one historian has built southern history around slavery, another upon states' rights, a third upon an unprofitable agricultural system. In recent years the sociologists have been analyzing and diagnosing the South, especially in terms of regionalism. Much of their work is actually based upon previous research of historians. But the latter have been prone to see the South in its own image, however critical their investigation and conclusions, rather than with a broader perspective that is acquired from knowledge of other sections and "foreign" points of view.

The word "provincial" in the title of my paper might be called a relative term and as such it offers tempting opportunities for semantic discourse. Lest its use here suggest solely a spirit of adverse criticism, let me remind you that the word and its corresponding nouns have a variety of connotations, favorable, unfavorable, and indifferent. Those of our ancestors who were residents of the British colonies before the Revolution were all provincials, whether they lived in royal or proprietary colonies, but with independence "province" was discarded for "state," and it is significant that "we, the people of the United States, in order to form a more perfect union," did not revert to provincials when the new Federal government was established.

This usage provides the basis for one definition of province as "a comprehensive designation for all parts of a country outside the capital or chief seat of government; e.g. of France apart from Paris, or England apart from London."[2] This meaning was extended geographically to the American colonies and accepted by them; indeed, they exploited it somewhat to their advantage in the arguments over taxation without representation. In variations of the meaning of the term, the colonies were "dependent on a distant authority"; but their acknowledgment of that authority was mixed with a generous measure of self-sufficiency, although they spoke of England as "home." American provincial society exhibited many ways and manners suggestive of the countrified shires of England in contrast to cosmopolitan London; yet there was Philadelphia, second largest city of the Empire, with cultural attainments that would have surprised many an educated Englishman who never thought the colonies were worth an inquiry; or there was Charleston which brought to a focus on a smaller stage the culture of plantation society. Nevertheless, what American provincials could demonstrate by their works during the half-century before independence must be assessed in relation to their British heritage and its influence in an American environment and in comparison with achievements in the mother country. Attraction to Great Britain was strong, but the Empire was more closely knit culturally than politically.

The feature of this colonial provincialism with which historians have been chiefly concerned is, in the words of the *Oxford Dictionary,* the "attachment to one's own province, its institutions, interests, etc., before those of the nation or state of which it is a part." This firm attachment, voiced at times in tones of a provincial patriotism, is, of course, at the heart of the phenomenon of an emerging Americanism. The new colonial policy alienated the provinces and fostered a rising American spirit. There had developed imperceptibly a latent feeling of pride in this new world on the part of its inhabitants which the home government may have suspected but did not take seriously before 1763. Intercolonial rivalry tinged with jealousy had always been the rule rather than the exception, and it is not difficult to find expressions of this tenor by members of the Continental Congress as well as by numerous private travelers who were wont to make invidious comparisons.[3] But there was a subconscious, growing bond of union. It was well put years later by Colonel William Few of Georgia, who confessed little knowledge of politics or the principles of free government but, he recalled, "I felt the spirit of an American, and without much investigation of the justice of her cause, I resolved to defend it."[4] That the general government which evolved from this background and appeared in written form should be Federal in structure seems a foregone conclusion. But when the political tie with Great Britain was severed in July, 1776, British provincials did not become Americans overnight. This fact is fundamental in understanding the so-called critical period. We cannot point to the birth of American nationality in any historical event or give it any specific date. And what of the relative strength of state loyalty and sectional interest? Was there a southern provincial attitude in evidence?

By the eighteenth century the colonists inhabiting the region from Chesapeake Bay to Spanish Florida were Virginians or Carolinians or Marylanders, loyal to Great Britain but cherishing that freedom from outside control peculiar to Englishmen. In tracing the gradual emergence of a new nationality one wonders whether these colonies were "Southern" in a sectional sense before they were American. I believe they were not. "Southern" does not always deserve the capital "S." Although the plantation economy and mode of life in the influential tidewater areas of these colonies were similar, forces of cohesion, such as found expression in New England from time to time, were lacking. Promotional tracts of neighboring colonies usually glorified one fair land by detraction of another—Georgia, how ideal except for the threat of South Carolina! One seventeenth-century writer described Virginia and Maryland as "Leah and Rachel, ... the two fruitful sisters,"[5] but this was an exceptional judgment, for their political and economic relations were not as a rule sisterly in the best meaning of the word.

Before the middle of the eighteenth century two rival centers of influence had developed, in Virginia and South Carolina. The Old Dominion was an empire within the Empire, but Williamsburg, its capital, was a city only by virtue of incorporation, in contrast to Charleston, which was large enough to have acquired urban characteristics and, according to the surveyor De Brahm, was "renowned for ... courteousness ... especially to foreigners, with out regard or respect of nation or religion."[6] The older colony might boast of primacy in several respects (this indulgence was to become morbid in the nineteenth century), but Charlestonians have never been overawed by Virginians or others of their compatriots. Both Virginians and South Carolinians harbored mutual feelings of superiority toward their frontier neighbor. This attitude of long duration was most genially expressed by a Virginian, as North Carolinians are well aware. On this frontier, we read in one of William Byrd's milder passages, "Nothing is dear but Law, Physick, and

Strong Drink, which are all bad in their Kind.... And, considering
how Fortune delights in bringing great things out of Small," he remarked
flippantly but prophetically, "who knows but Carolina may, one time
or another, come to be the Seat of some other great Empire?"[7] At the
hands of their more wealthy and aristrocratic neighbors and in the
histories and geographies of the period North Carolinians fared but
poorly. The Tar Heel may have taken a crumb of comfort, however,
from reading in one such work what he already knew, that large families were the rule and, what he may not have suspected, that "many
women from other places, who have been long married without having
the blessing of children, have soon after their removal to Carolina become joyful mothers."[8] It was these Carolinians, by the way, who first
attacked the privilege and corruption of courthouse politics and supported more wholeheartedly democratic government of later years.

Although the southern colonies fitted nicely into the British mercantile system, the planters' mounting debts and customary freedom from
outside political interference turned their thinking toward liberty in
the issues with the mother country. Backed by American merchants,
they supplied their quota of Sons of Liberty and vigorously supported
nonimportation agreements. Charleston had its own tea party, and committees of correspondence were widespread. But when the yoke of
Britain was cast off and the war was won, the principle of life, liberty,
and the pursuit of happiness was only partially secured in republican
governments of the states, and an aristocracy of talent did not quickly
succeed hereditary class rule.

Although the Articles of Confederation assured a weak Federal union
of sovereign states, William Drayton of South Carolina prophesied at
this time what Madison reflected upon ten years later, that sectional
differences would arise between North and South "from the nature of
the climate, soil and produce of the several states."[9] Yet this experiment in federalism was subject to varied interpretations during its born-
ing, as it was to be afterwards in countless constitutional debates and
post mortems. Maryland's insistence on cession of western land claims
by the states before she ratified the Articles paved the way for Jefferson's land ordinances of 1784 and 1785 and the great Northwest Ordi-
nance of 1787; and both northern and southern states contributed to
this national domain. Although the final draft of the United States Constitution and its ratification amounted to a victory for the forces of
conservatism, it was accomplished at the expense of no section. The
amendments to be added shortly eased the fears of the liberals by
guaranteeing certain individual rights against the tyranny of Leviathan
and by stating specifically that the national government was one of

delegated powers. "National," in contradistinction to "Federal," Madison explained years later, "was not meant to express the *extent* of power, but the *mode of its operation*."[10] The three-fifths compromise was a concession to the slaveholding states, though that was to become a moot point in antebellum days. They expressed objections to national regulation of commerce, but their confidence in the rapid growth of population throughout the South and Old Southwest served to allay their fear. The father of the Constitution believed that "a crisis had arrived which was to decide whether the Am[erica]n Experiment was to be a blessing to the world, or to blast for ever the hopes which the republican cause had enspired."[11] Jefferson, living under the old regime in France during these years, envisaged his country as the inspiration for European revolution; and Americans at home rapidly developed a sense of destiny.

In the Union under the Constitution the southern states played a prominent part not only in guarding their sovereign rights but also in strengthening the national structure. The Revolution had been accomplished by young men in their thirties and forties who differed sharply on what was the best kind of Federal government, but those who survived the first quarter of the new century could reflect on the young nation with pride, if with some misgivings too. Jeffersonian Republicans in Kentucky and Virginia who spoke out boldly against highhanded legislation by a Federalist Congress were concerned most directly with infringement of individual rights in their state resolutions.[12] Tidewater South Carolinians were strongly Federalist while that party remained in power and for some time afterward.[13] During the second decade of Jeffersonian rule, when party factions confused the issues and new political leaders were searching for their bearings, the War of 1812 gave a spur to patriotism in some quarters and (to put it mildly) to separatism in others. The close ties of southerners with the West, from the very nature of its settlement and expansion, aroused a nationalistic fervor against Indians and British. It is well exemplified in Nathaniel H. Claiborne, an up-country Virginia public official, who had published even before the battle of New Orleans some *Notes on the War*. "The conduct of the citizens of Tennessee, Mississippi Territory, and Georgia, in this war," he expatiated, "has been such, that when they visit the other states in the Union, ... the ardent patriot through the whole nation extends the right arm of fellowship, and in the language of the heart exclaims, 'you too are my brethren.'" While New Englanders were moving toward their ill-starred Hartford Convention, Claiborne was calling for revenge against the enemy after the destruction of "our infant Rome." He predicted boldly that "if the war continues two years longer, *we* shall become one of the most powerful nations in the world."[14] It may be worth noting that his essay was reprinted without alteration five years later, in 1819. This was a period of articulate patriotism with undertones of sectional complaint. The Virginia dynasty of a quarter-century duration had been mindful of state and local interests, but the vast expansion of the nation required reconsideration of the times and future prospects. Who would deny that national power was more far reaching by the end of this period and that southerners had contributed to this result?

A leading historian of our own day has declared that "nothing is more sacred in a nationalistic age than the nation, hence the sanctity of any development which preserved the Union. . . . an idealistic entity known as the State must be preserved!"[15] A kindred idea is at the root of the academic argument of a past president of the Southern Historical Association that the southern states would have been better off if they had rejected the Constitution and formed a confederacy of their own in 1789.[16] I do not want to indulge in any speculation based upon what might have happened if certain critical events had not transpired, which really did not occur anyway;[17] nor do I desire to labor the point of national consciousness as a theme of our history. But sectionalism can be rightly understood only in relation to the nation, and southern sectionalism developed at a time and under circumstances that have affected profoundly the nation and especially the South itself down to our own day. I have stated that the feeling of being American beyond limited attachment to one's state is discernible before a conscious sectionalism appeared in the South. If, however, this assertion is open to argument, it is evident that the American nation had become well established within the first thirty years of its existence—so substantially, in fact, that the burden of proof in favor of dissolution always rested on the malcontents, even though men disagreed heartily on the nature of the Union. Some of the manifestations of southern sectionalism bespeak a provincial South in attitude of mind and grasp of its problems.

At the risk of traversing an overworked subject I shall venture some comments on the southern way of life. It grew, of course, out of an agricultural economy based early upon the plantation system of a new country with apparently unlimited land for expansion. It developed a society of clearly defined classes on the English model. By the early eighteenth century the pattern was firmly fixed—extensive cultivation of staple crops, slave labor, marketing abroad in exchange for manufactured goods by means of an involved system of credit—and virtually the same economic arrangement prevailed a century later in the American nation. Although the small farmers of the South comprised a large proportion of the population and their standard of living was more restricted than that of the planters, the latter dominated the social and political life of the region. Furthermore, in the westward movement of population the prototype of the older South was established without much modification. The white population was homogeneous to the extent that it was predominantly English, and the language barriers of French and especially German gradually broke down and disappeared. Few nineteenth-century immigrants from the Continent came to the South to intermingle with the colonial stock of ancestral Americans and to challenge their theories of Anglo-Saxon superiority. The Negro population too became an integral part of this civilization in language and tradition, religion and manners, but without prospect of advancement in the social scale.

Life on farm and plantation was isolated, and transportation was generally limited on an average journey beyond one's own county. Even when full allowance is made for improved means of travel, more frequent mail service, and expansion of journalism in the decades after the War of 1812, the Old South never kept pace with the accelerated speed of the outside world. Indeed the southerner was inclined to set his own pace for the pleasure of living. He has always been famed above all other Americans for his hospitality. Hugh Finlay, surveyor of post offices and roads for His Majesty's government just before the Revolution, after stopping at numerous plantations in the Carolinas, had written: "The hospitable Americans kill you with kindness, and detain you from pursuing your journey."[18] The sources of southern history are replete with evidence on this score. Genuine hospitality takes time. Since we have convinced ourselves of a great lack of time in our own day, it is difficult to appreciate the attitude of a society that has left so definite an impression of abundant and conspicuous leisure.[19] Polite manners generally prevailed, sometimes displaying deference mingled with crudity among the unlettered. There was indolence too, encouraged by a warm climate and slave labor, and there was a noticeable lack of thrift; but plantation records and merchants' accounts have revealed business operations that could not have been managed successfully without considerable time and attention. Jefferson contrasted the cool, sober, persevering, but chicaning northerner with the fiery, "voluptuary," unsteady, but generous and candid southerner, and informed the Marquis de Chastellux that "these characteristics grow weaker and weaker by gradation from North to South and South to North, insomuch that an observing traveler, without the aid of the quadrant may always know his latitude by the character of the people among whom he finds himself."[20] This was a philosopher's conclusion, however, which would have pleased neither section. The southerner's love of the outdoors was attested in the popularity of the hunt and bar-becue, the camp meeting and militia muster, court day and the hustings. Oratory rather than literature was the favorite vehicle of rhetoric. The library, whether public or private, had limited appeal for men who were not essentially of a reflective turn of mind. With few cities and widely separated towns, with hopeless poverty in certain marginal areas, yet this was a bountiful land, where life was comfortable and toil was eased for those who could afford at least a Negro servant or two, and where an attitude of "live and let live" encouraged the status quo and resisted interference from without.

Let us recall at this point the definition of provincialism quoted earlier: "Attachment to one's own province, its institutions, interests, etc., before those of the nation or state of which it is a part," and couple with it the corollary, "The manner, fashion, mode of thought, which characterize a particular province, . . . as distinct from that which is (or is held to be) national, or which is the fashion of the capital." A realistic analysis and interpretation of the historical problem at hand involve, as I have suggested, the attitudes of the states comprising the section as well as sectional loyalties; and this is especially true when older states with deeply rooted customs and traditions are part of the region. State and sectional consciousness have both enriched and com-plicated American history, for every section has raised at one time or another critical issues at variance with national trends or interests which themselves may be altered by shifting alignments of sections. The South has had no monopoly of this kind of provincialism. Perhaps if the United States had developed a cultural as well as a political capital, it would have served as a center of gravity and symbol of unity. But, except for the seat of government, still on trial, Washington of-fered little attraction and no prestige comparable to that of the historic towns and cities which were the pride of the several states.

I have already cited some examples of state (or provincial) pride and rivalry in the colonial period. Countless others are in evidence down to the present. The influence of the older states was carried west-ward and gradually transformed into loyalties to new commonwealths. How the Virginian character was diluted during the "flush times" of the Old Southwest was best told by one of them who wrote with gentle satire: "It makes no odds where he goes, he carries Virginia with him; not in the entirety always—but the little spot he came from is Virginia. . . . He may breathe in Alabama, but he lives in Virginia."[21] Although we are chiefly concerned with that provincialism which emanated from southern sectionalism, we must not overlook "the little spot" the Vir-

ginian or the Alabamian came from. Here lies the other pole of provincialism which is more commonly associated with the term. Here
again is a phenomenon peculiar to no single state or section, rural or
urban. When, for example, a New York paper in the 1880's referred
to the rest of the United States as "the provinces,"[22] the writer was
only exposing his own city's provincialism in a common form. But the
most clear-cut illustrations of it are doubtless to be seen in the New
England town and the southern county.

In discussing southern sectionalism in terms of provincialism I do
not aim to argue a case for the North or to berate an agricultural society
in contrast to one with rapidly growing industrial power. A combination of industrial and commercial forces is difficult to withstand, and
the more so under the additional impact of the industrial revolution
which reached America during the transitional period of party politics,
of which it became a part. There was an irresistible ruthlessness about
this capitalist expansion that would not be denied its gains, but exploitation at a new pace was the order of the day in staple-crop agriculture as well as in manufacturing. The itch of manifest destiny made
restless northerner and southerner alike. If money was king of the
industrial realm, the chosen monarch of the South was also a member
of the economic dynasty. And when the new southern nation was established, king cotton was still relied upon to work wonders abroad for
the Confederacy.

During these years when the South fell a generation behind the
North in economic development, the attitude of southern leaders toward
their current problems was in some respects undecided and unrealistic,
though some kept an eye on comparative census figures. They seem to
have been unaware or uncertain of the course of events in a changing
modern world in which their nation had confirmed its status in a second
war for independence. Although southern statesmen had been among
the greatest revolutionaries and builders of republican governments before the rise of nineteenth-century democracy, their successors lost
touch with this democratic movement and accepted it charily. Likewise
they braced themselves against the mounting wave of antislavery feeling
which threatened one of the cornerstones of their society and could not
be diverted from the public mind.

A brief glance at specific cases in economic, political, and social
affairs will substantiate these points. The South had suffered during
the colonial period from lack of a balanced economy and of control
over its own trade. When southerners became convinced about 1800
that their future would be best assured by concentration on cotton
culture, they made little effort, despite previous disadvantage, to get a

foothold in the carrying trade during the early years of expansion in the cotton economy. After the War of 1812 New York merchants forged ahead in overseas and coastwise trade. They caught the Yankees napping, but Boston recovered in time to regain her share. Not so the cotton ports. By 1825 their trade was firmly controlled by the New Yorkers, and it was too late for Charleston, Savannah, Mobile, and New Orleans to compete successfully.[23] Now not only merchant capital, but shipping, banking credit, insurance, and all related business of southern exports went through northern hands taking large profits on southern production and on southern consumption of European goods imported through northern ports. No wonder the protective tariff was doubly a grievance. Although South Carolina forced and won the tariff issue by means of nullification, the trade itself remained out of southern control. A convention of merchants and others at Augusta, Georgia, in 1838 declared: "We look back with surprise to the fact, that a people possessed of such vast advantages, should have so long and so patiently submitted to a state almost of 'colonial vassalage.' "[24] The best corrective for this state of affairs, it appears, would have been manufacturing, which a small minority advocated in vain in successive commercial conventions and elsewhere to build up southern markets and credits beyond. The planting interests and their allies, convinced of king cotton's superior bargaining power, were too shortsighted to invest capital in young industries. Men like millowner William Gregg and ironmaster Joseph Reid Anderson of the Tredegar Company succeeded in spite of this stubborn provincialism[25]—this desire for autonomy without the substance to maintain it.

In politics the colonial aristocracy, though somewhat liberalized by the Revolution and Jeffersonian ideas, maintained its grip on the seaboard states by denying proportional representation to the western counties on a fair basis. It became a more fluid aristocracy, encouraged none the less by the master-servant relationship and easy opportunities for accumulating a landed estate. Upper-class influence carried westward was less watered than the popular meaning of the frontier implies. Nevertheless, the drafting and remaking of state constitutions, especially in the Mississippi Valley, under the influence of Jacksonian equalitarian ideas, broadened the basis for democratic government and swept away old restrictions. It became popular and necessary to seek public office by campaigning. Virginia and South Carolina remained the last bulwarks of aristocratic control in state and county politics, where it had always been held that voters should be educated to the privilege of franchise. But the old guard believed themselves too strongly entrenched to feel the need to apply this rule to the common man who came into his own politically, east and west, without training for responsible government, and who won the franchise as a right, not a privilege.[26] As a voter he could be easily swayed by the captivating oratory of leaders whose appeal on behalf of the established economic and social order he was not prepared to refute.

This aristocratic tradition was strikingly expressed in education for the few and a belated sense of public responsibility for the many, even on a selective basis of talent and ability recommended by Jefferson in his scheme for a comprehensive system of state-supported schools. In most southern states public primary and secondary education had customarily borne the stigma of charity. It was a favor granted, not a fundamental human right to be stoutly maintained. Some noteworthy accomplishment had been made in North Carolina and in a few of the larger cities by 1860, but southern public education was trailing behind in this expression of the democratic movement. Private academies prepared the more fortunate southerners for the colleges and universities which in state support, enrollment, and number of professors compared favorably with northern institutions. Attendance of many southern youths at colleges in the North may have amounted to a reflection upon the faculties in some of the home institutions; at least this annual migration to northern founts of knowledge was frowned upon as tension grew between the sections. More serious, however, was the restriction of academic freedom in the South over the slavery issue.[27] Jefferson's great pronouncement—"we are not afraid to follow the truth wherever it may lead, nor to tolerate any error, so long as reason is left free to combat it"—was now spoken softly, even in the university which he had founded.

During the early halting growth of education in the South there had been little incentive for preparation and publication of its own school books. Besides, others were available from outside sources and especially from New England with its Puritan zeal for common schools. Edward Hooker, Connecticut tutor in South Carolina in 1806, on a trip into the mountains was surprised "to see lying about the seats [of a primitive church] a number of school books, but particularly Webster's Spelling Books."[28] Years later, when Yankee textbooks were discarded for homemade products, some of these outdid the American jingoism of the North with their own brand of provincial patriotism. The principal of the Vineville Academy of Macon, Georgia, for example, in explaining that this book of exercises in reading and declamation was "designed to supersede ... either Foreign or Northern" compilations, announced that "we repudiate that universal civism, that citizenship of the world, which would extinguish our partialities for our own country."[29] Was that country the United States or the South? And South Carolina youths who read in their geography of the early 1830's that trade within the commonwealth must be developed to retain her wealth at home,[30] were ill equipped to wrestle with the economic problems of the forties and fifties.

These actions and reactions of what I have called the "provincial South" are climaxed in the problem of Negro slavery and, more broadly, of the Negro himself in American society, which Ulrich B. Phillips considered the "central theme of southern history." We need not dwell upon the fact that politicians, northern and southern, made political capital of the issue for selfish ends or that often they represented vested interests which stood to gain or lose by the outcome of other measures tied up with slavery and its extension. In the free states the Negro's economic and social status was not an enviable one compared to the white man's, and in many of these states his political rights had been reduced before 1820. In the South the slave code was tightened. The hopes of the Revolutionary generation for emancipation had died with them. Their successors developed an elaborate justification of the system as a positive good on both social and religious grounds, and effectively denounced the "wage slavery" of white laborers in the North. With its political doctrine of minority rights as phrased by John C. Calhoun the South might contend successfully against majority rule under the Constitution, and some new compromise be worked out.

But the humanitarian impulse of this period was another matter. Emancipation in the British colonies in 1833 was a blow to the South. Human slavery was fast becoming an outmoded institution in the occidental world, and a separate "sociology for the South" could not truthfully deny the debasing aspects of the slave trade and slaveownership, economically in respect to the dignity of free competitive labor, white and black, and socially in the psychology of a master race. Yet the antislavery reformers (not to mention the abolitionists), asserting the high principle of individual liberty, were inclined to prosecute this great moral issue with more romanticism than realism, as they would contend again on the next line of advance, political and social equality, during Reconstruction. In the face of the irrepressible conflict and the appeal to a higher law than the Constitution, the South took a revolutionary stand in defense of the old order by repudiating the traditional principle of natural rights. The ominous prediction by the articulate proslavery interests of economic ruin and social disruption if northern reformers won their case unified most southerners on behalf of the accepted way of life, which offered security for one race and, at best, paternalism for the other. But the weakest point in their position was the defiance of the "spirit of the age" which, as James Russell Lowell put it, the South asked the American nation to abandon for the sake of a discredited institution.[31] When war came, emancipation of the slave, joined with preservation of the Union which most northerners regarded as synonymous with American democracy, was a powerful alliance to combat; so too was the southerners' will to fight for their "cause." But the irony of the tragedy was that, although a new union was gained, it achieved no sure decision, beyond emancipation, as to the ulitimate status of the Negro in a white man's society throughout the nation.

The complex factors and chain of events in the development of the Old South that tended to set it apart from other regions and to breed a spirit of inward self-assertion have continued to operate in some measure down to the present. I want to call attention to only one phase of the subject, in connection with the writing of southern history. As southerners themselves complained, the history of the South was too long neglected and poorly written. Before the Civil War it was confined narrowly to state histories in the nature of annals, and the total output was small compared to that in other older regions of the country. William Cabell Rives explained the matter by comparing southerners with the Romans as being "more bent on action than narration," and, referring to the colonial period, he believed they "were less mindful than Northern [men] of their rightful place in history."[32]

Two factors, I think, arising out of provincialism have been influential in southern historiography: the first, a mixed feeling of resentment, especially toward the nineteenth-century New England historians whose writings on the sectional controversy were suspect, if not always biased, and of inferiority because the South had provided no equal of these heirs of the Puritans in scholarship and literary ability; and second, a defensive attitude intensified by the Civil War and its aftermath. The first point is well illustrated in William Gilmore Simms's criticism in 1853 of *The American Loyalists,* by Lorenzo Sabine, who, according to Simms, misrepresented South Carolina's part in the Revolutionary War in his laudation of New England's. The "saints," said Simms, have always regarded themselves as the chosen people. "Reading their own historians only, they are amicable enough to believe all their assurances; and historians thus honored with their exclusive confidence, show themselves quite worthy of this trust when writing; as if they never once forgot they were in possession of the ear of the entire parish. Fortunate historians in the possession of such a parish! Fortunate parish in the possession of such historians! Mutually fortunate parish and historians in the possession of one another!"[33] That much of this historical writing concerning the South, composed elsewhere, was prejudiced and misleading cannot be gainsaid; but the feeling of bitterness and of frustration was not alleviated during the next few decades through great achievement by southern historians. The postbellum generation, in defense of the old regime and glorification of the war for southern independence, was chiefly interested in the heroic story of the Confederacy, told subjectively by soldiers, politicos, and other participants. Edward Ingle, one of the rising group of "scientific" historians of the South, wrote understandingly of his fellow southerners near the turn of the century: "Among some there is a disposition to have their historian assume the *rôle* of an advocate;... and others, not without justification, are not disposed to permit the veil to be lifted by any one whose antecedents are not thought to be a guaranty of a treatment of the subject in accord with tradition."[34]

In spite of the new approach to the history of the South during the first quarter of the twentieth century and the constructive work of its professional historians, the rancor of old grievances was still nourished by amateur writers who could count on a hearing through the support of patriotic societies. Among those zealots none spoke in more strident tones than Miss Mildred Rutherford of Georgia, who led a campaign, without much success, to rid the schools of northern textbooks. Her *Scrap Book* was cut from a fringe of the same cloth as were superpatriot publications in other parts of the country during the roaring twenties. She compiled a formidable list of "firsts" which the South might claim. Her "Don'ts of History" included "Don't say you believe the South was right; say *you know she was right*"; and she trumpeted her section as a "vital part of the Anglo Saxon civilization of this country."[35] Read twenty-five years later in another postwar era, Miss Rutherford's invective sounds ludicrous but not entirely unfamiliar.

While the southern academic historian of recent years has not been an advocate, he has been more than a narrator of facts with which some disciples of the scientific school thought they were exclusively concerned. He has become an interpreter of data and opinion, carefully assembled from an abundance of fresh materials hitherto inaccessible, and on this basis he has a point of view, as what historian has not? His main shortcoming is his inclination to write the history of the South too much detached from the history of the nation without benefit of comparative study, in part because he knows less about other sections than he should to achieve most enduring results. This fault is reflected in his teaching which seldom embraces courses dealing with other sections, although most of his students are southerners who, like American youth elsewhere, need a broadening of perspective.

At the other end of the historical scale the professional historian has not given sufficient attention to the history of communities, at the roots of our culture. He has shied away from local history and its provincialisms—to use the word in yet another meaning—because it bears the implication of antiquarianism. He has been loath to suffer the drudgery of investigating tax returns, census figures, and voluminous county records in order to break new ground and establish new conclusions that cannot be derived from our customary stock in trade. That such research can be rewarding a few southern scholars have already demonstrated. But the study of local history also involves some appreciation and understanding of the elements of folk culture. Although they have been within the province of other disciplines in our modern compartmentalized learning, the historian can find clues and evidence for his investigation in balladry and tall tales, phonetics and linguistics, folk music and art. The South has a rich survival of such culture, but its preservation in recorded form has come none too soon, during the same period that has witnessed the development of modern historical scholarship.

Thus, out of the provincial South in varied shades of its connotation have arisen manifold opportunities for writing and rewriting the history of the region which a magazine editor of Reconstruction days called the *Land We Love.*

Chapter XVI

The South and the West

WILLIAM C. BINKLEY

CUSTOM decrees that upon this occasion the president of the Association shall deliver himself of whatever wisdom he may have on some subject of his own choosing, and the program of last year's meeting suggests that he faces the prospect of future appraisal and classification which may not reflect credit upon him or his wisdom.* Among the many lessons to be derived from Clarence Nixon's scintillating critique of a year ago, by no means the least significant is the implicit idea that presidents, like all historians, must be wary of becoming champions of a cause.[1] His suggestion that past presidential addresses have perhaps given too much emphasis to regional subjects overlooks the fact that this is a regional organization whose primary objective is the promotion of interest and research in southern history. Naturally, therefore, its presidents have sought to examine, to describe, and to explain those elements in the past experience of the region which appealed most strongly to them as historians. Theirs was the task of dealing with what had happened rather than with what ought to have happened. If they have succeeded in presenting interpretations which provide a better understanding of some of the problems of either the past or the present, whether within the region itself or in its relations with other parts of the nation, they have advanced the cause for which the Association was founded.

That the Association's concept of southern history is latitudinarian has been demonstrated, I think, by the contents of its official organ and by the wide range of topics discussed in the programs of its annual meetings. But to assume that all aspects of the region's past could have been covered within the brief space of fifteen years would be to

*Presented in Atlanta, Georgia, November 10, 1950.

forget that if this miracle had been achieved the Association's mission would have been completed and there would be no further occasion for presidential addresses. There is comfort as well as a challenge for potential future presidents in the recent statement of our committee on research possibilities that "no area of southern history has received adequate treatment."[2] That committee, whose membership, incidentally, included eight of the sixteen persons who have served as president of this Association, has prepared a series of suggestions which give special attention to the need for research in certain neglected fields within the region and which, by implication at least, leave the impression that external relationships are either less important or sufficiently exploited. Literal adherence to these suggestions would turn research in southern history into an introversive enterprise; but the committee obviously had no such intentions. Fundamentally, it was seeking to promote the establishment of a better basis for understanding both the problems of internal developments and those of external relationships rather than to discourage the continuation of work already being done in either field. It is only through further study along both lines that the South of today can understand itself or that the rest of the nation can be made to understand the South.

In the area of external relations, for example, on which so much has been written, the question might well be raised whether the traditional emphasis of both the historians and the politicians on sectional conflict between South and North has prevented us from seeing other parts of the pattern. Although it has been more than half a century since Frederick Jackson Turner made us conscious of the importance of the West in American development, one still looks in vain for a systematic study of the part which the South may have played in determining the character of that West. We find carefully prepared essays on the westward transit of civilization and on the sources of culture in the West, which seem to take for granted either a New England origin or a European pattern tempered as it passed through the northeastern states; and we have at least one scholarly study of the "expansion of New England," innumerable monographs on various phases of northern interests and activities in the West, and a recent popularized account of a so-called "Yankee exodus." But where is the rest of the story? Did not southerners also go west? And when they did, is it reasonable to assume that in leaving their native region they carried with them none of its cultural concepts or its attitudes toward political, economic, or social institutions? Were they so completely inundated in a flood of northern migration that they made no impression on the society of the region to which they had moved? Before these questions can be answered on anything more than an instinctive basis, it will be necessary to spend long hours of research in such records as may be available on migration from the South to the West, and then to try to ascertain what these emigrants did in their new environment. For one whose Tennessee boyhood was followed by growth to manhood and professional tutelage in California and a decade of commuting between Texas and Colorado before returning to his native state twenty years ago, this presents an intriguing subject to which he has only recently been able to turn. It will be possible here, therefore, merely to indicate the nature of the problem as it appears after an exploratory examination of widely scattered materials of various types, and to suggest a few tentative generalizations—or hypotheses, if you prefer—with the hope that some of them may stimulate others to take up the research required to test their validity.

The search for the materials upon which to base such a study leads in two directions. For the migration itself we can begin with the nativity statistics of the published census reports after 1850; but in order to obtain a reasonably complete picture of the size, the sources, and the specific destination of the movement of population into the West it will be necessary to dig deeply into the manuscript population schedules for the western states and territories so far as they have been released for research purposes. From this material it would also be possible to identify the individual southerners who formed a part of that movement and whose activities subsequent to their arrival should provide important clues for determining the southern influence. Ideally, of course, this should be done county by county for each census; but because of the brevity of man's life span and the paucity of research funds we may have to be satisfied with the less comprehensive coverage afforded by a judiciously planned sampling procedure. As we turn to the question of what the southerners did in the West, the search leads us toward local and personal rather than general records. The official archives of every western state contain information concerning their political activities; the county records will disclose their economic interests and condition; newspaper files and county histories will throw light on their standing in their community; and collections of letters, diaries, reminiscences, and other personal papers in such depositories as the Huntington Library, the Bancroft Library, the Pacific-Northwest Collection, and some of the state historical societies will yield information on almost every aspect of the careers of many of them. Scattered and diversified though they may be, the materials exist and are waiting to be used.

If these materials are to be used intelligently, such new information as they reveal must be studied with its relationship to the existing frame of reference concerning western development always in mind as something which it will either confirm or cause to be revised. This is obviously not the place to review the history of the West or even the development of historical writing about the West; but since this discussion is based on the premise that parts of the story have not yet received adequate treatment we must at least try to establish a point of departure. The appearance of Turner's famous essay in 1893 is of course the starting point for any consideration of frontier historiography. Its influence is too well known to require elaboration here, and we cannot stop to pass judgment on the merits of the many conflicting interpretations which it has received. For the purposes of this discussion, however, two important facts concerning it call for special mention. The first is that the essay inspired a regional approach to the study of American history. Basically, it was an expression of Turner's protest against an interpretation which did not seem to be confirmed by what he had observed in the evolution from frontier to stable society in the upper Mississippi Valley. Perhaps because it came at a time when the spirit of protest was rampant in the West, its emphasis on American rather than European influences appealed at once to the historians in that region as the vehicle through which they might express their own reaction to the eastern interpretation. Lacking the comprehensive perspective of the master and failing to appreciate fully the significance of his attention to successive changing frontiers, they concentrated their detailed studies upon the region which they knew best and apparently developed the illusion that this region and the West were synonymous. For them, therefore, the southern frontier ceased to be part of the West as soon as it showed characteristics which did not conform to their own regional pattern. And as the differences came to be construed as manifestations of sectionalism the South lost its place in their history of the West.

The second fact is that this essay had very little immediate effect upon the writing of history in or about the South. That Turner himself recognized the role of the South in the early stages of the frontier process is clearly shown by his illustrative references and some of his generalizations. As Avery Craven has pointed out: "He mentions the various frontier stages shown in Virginia and the Carolinas—trapper, herdsman, and exploitive farmer, and includes the fall line and the southern mountains among the natural frontier boundaries that are to be noted. It was at Cumberland Gap that he took his station to watch these stages move, procession-like, into the interior. He notes the Western influence on Southern land legislation, religious developments, and slavery attitudes, and climaxes his political discussion by asserting that the West made Jefferson's democracy into the national republicanism of Monroe and the democracy of Jackson—all three Southern men."[3] When he discussed early western state-making in a later essay, it was in Kentucky and Tennessee that he found his best examples; and as he considered the apparent contradictions which came as "different streams of population occupied differing physical basins," he saw the southern West as an area which needed to be studied more carefully for the light which its differences might shed upon the process as a whole. But the historians in the South were becoming too deeply absorbed with the study of more tangible problems related directly to the sectional conflict and its aftermath to appreciate the implications of this new approach for the history of their own region. There are tantalizing possibilities in the purely speculative question of what would have happened to the writing of southern history if the notable group of young southerners who became known as "the Dunning school" had turned their faces toward Wisconsin instead of Columbia at the beginning of the present century.

It was largely through this predisposition of each section to study its past almost exclusively in terms of its own peculiar interests and development that a provincial frame of reference for the history of the American West was evolved. It is disturbing, if not altogether surprising, for example, to find Turner's successor at Wisconsin saying in 1929: "In the generation that ends at Gettysburg and Vicksburg, the South ceased to be the West, and became enchained to a destiny of its own, in one of the great tragedies of social history. But the West stayed West." Only the Middle West, he continues, remained true to the American standard and thus became "in a peculiar way the heart of the United States."[4] Such sweeping generalization could come only out of inability or unwillingness to understand the diversities which had made other Wests than the one which he knew. It also gives added meaning to the lament voiced at about the same time by another historian, who had recently been transplanted from South Carolina to Southern California, that the story of the West was being written "as if the East-West march across free soil were virtually the whole of it, with southern experience, southern problems, southern motives, southern influence, all a mere adjunct." But it is discouraging to find him likewise reflecting his own provincial attitude in the oversimplified and unsupported generalization that the westward movement in the North "was in the main a movement of discontent, a movement of escape," while that in the South "was chiefly a movement of the contented portions of the old communities, a movement not of escape but of transposition, not of social revolt but of social expansion."[5] That each man was presenting the truth as he saw it does not change the fact that neither saw the whole truth.

In order to orient ourselves once more on the broad lines of Turner's vision of the whole westward movement in time and space and quality, we need to look for a moment at the familiar outline of the geographic stages by which successive Wests arose out of varying backgrounds, attained stable social orders adapted to the requirements of their environment, and receded into Easts as the frontier moved beyond them to repeat the process in newer Wests. For the one hundred years beginning at the middle of the eighteenth century we may pass in rapid review the last colonial West, extending over the eastern piedmont and longitudinal valleys of the Appalachians from New York to Georgia; the Ohio Valley West, which formed the first trans-Allegheny salient reaching out tentacle-like toward the Mississippi River; the two parallel movements which created the Gulf Plains West and the Lake Plains West, filling in the areas on either side of the salient; and the first stages of the trans-Mississippi West, embracing a crescent-shaped region from Minnesota to Texas with outposts being planted on the far-away Pacific Coast. By 1860, on the eve of the Civil War, the entire area east of the Great Plains had attained the rank of statehood, while to the west Texas, California, and Oregon were states and the eight territorial governments covering the remainder of the region symbolized the fact that this was now the West.

But geographic progression alone does not explain the Wests which had passed, nor does it account for the sectional conflict which their differences are supposed to have engendered. Since their quality was determined as much by the character, the background, and the interests of the people who settled them as by the local conditions that had to be met, we must also try to analyze the composition of their population in terms of regional or sectional origin. For the first trans-Allegheny West the census data give little help; but such indirect and incomplete information as can be gleaned from local or unofficial sources indicates that perhaps the most striking fact about the movement of population into the Ohio Valley was the absence of sectional consciousness in its settlement and organization. Whether we look back from Kentucky and Tennessee in 1790, or from Ohio in 1800, or from Indiana and Illinois in 1810, we find that the seaboard states all the way from New England to Georgia have contributed to the lines of migration which converged in almost any portion of the Valley to form settlements. When Tennessee framed its constitution in 1796, for example, it drew in approximately equal proportions from those of Pennsylvania, Virginia, and North Carolina, and three of its first five governors were natives of Pennsylvania. Nearly a quarter of a century later Illinois adopted a constitution drawn from a similar diversity of sources, and all of its first five governors were born in the South. The election of a former slaveholding planter from

Virginia as governor of Illinois and a nonslaveowning merchant from Pennsylvania as governor of Tennessee at the height of the Missouri controversy suggests that the people of this region were much less concerned than Congress about the slavery question. In the 1820's Horace Holley from Yale and Philip Lindsley from Princeton became educational leaders in Kentucky and Tennessee, and the work of such men as Finis Ewing and Peter Cartwright was as important in the religious life of Illinois as it had been in that of the southern fringe of this same West a few years earlier. The Ohio River was the spinal cord of a West which had been built upon the blending of southern and northern elements into a new society differing from that of either of the regions from which its people had come. The South had contributed more heavily than the North in numbers and influence; but there was no disposition to impose uniformity of thought or action. It is possible that the spirit of mutual understanding—the ability to accept and absorb or concede and compromise varying points of view—which characterized this merging of northerners and southerners into westerners furnishes the key to what American development might have been if the process could have continued its normal advance into the regions on either side of the Valley.

The process was interrupted, however, by the parallel development of two other Wests which were entirely different from this one in quality and character. To the south, the opening of the Gulf Plains for settlement immediately after the War of 1812 became the signal for an immense migration into the region from the states of the southern seaboard, and especially from the Carolinas and Georgia. To the north, the completion of the Erie Canal facilitated the rapid spread of emigrants from New England and New York over the area around the Great Lakes. The impelling motive in both cases was the quest for better economic opportunity rather than a conscious determination to extend and preserve a particular social order; but since the population in each case had come almost exclusively from one region, the necessity for concession and adaptation to varying points of view was absent. Consequently, each tended to perpetuate the concepts and institutions of the society from which it had sprung, with only such modifications as the new physical environment required. That there were fundamental differences between the two social orders which were thus reaching out into wider areas is too well known to require discussion here; nor is it necessary to dwell upon the nature of those differences. That they were not completely irreconcilable seems to have been shown in the results when Virginians and Carolinians intermingled with New Englanders and Pennsylvanians in the Ohio Valley to create a new society under frontier conditions. But in these newer movements the absence of such intermingling meant that one essential element of the frontier process was missing; and this would seem to raise a question of whether either region ever became truly West in anything more than a geographic sense.

While no conclusive answer to this question can be given, at least one significant clue appears in the fact that the change in physical environment seems to have had little effect on the basic attitude of the migrants of either group toward their own institutions or toward those of the other group. But as each projected its own social order into a new region it enlarged the area of activities and thus undoubtedly increased the intensity of the sectional conflict already existing between North and South. It was in the westward extension of the South, for example, that the institution of slavery obtained a new lease on life; and correspondingly, the extension of the North took up the abolition crusade with the same determination that had previously characterized the movement in New England. The Ohio Valley, lying between the two extensions, reflected the attitude of the true West in its efforts to find acceptable compromises; but as its northern sector was submerged by the new migration instead of being merged with it, the Ohio River was changed from a spinal cord to a dividing line, and the region lost its identity. Thus the West was gone east of the Mississippi River; and the sectional crisis came before another West had developed sufficiently to take its place.

Across the Mississippi, the basis for a new West had gradually grown out of what seemed to be unrelated beginnings in a vast expanse of territory; but as late as 1860 there was little outward indication of a realization that this region might have a destiny beyond the issues in which it was then involved. The movement had begun as an extension of the Ohio Valley frontier process into the territory immediately west of the river, where the early predominance of southern influences established Missouri as a slave state and then gave way to an incoming migration from other parts of the country which made that state more western than southern in its outlook. While it became the focal point for converging lines of migration from both North and South and at the same time the starting point for another set of lines radiating into new areas farther west, the settlement of the regions on either side of it reverted to the sectional pattern of the earlier developments to the eastward. Arkansas was primarily a continuation of the southern advance, while Iowa and, a little later, Minnesota were occupied by settlers from the northern states; and by 1860 this tier of new states, with the possible exception of Missouri, had been absorbed into either the North or the South. It was in the region beyond the line forming their western boundaries, therefore, that the next West would have to emerge; but because the process of that emergence became ensnarled in the issues of the slavery controversy its real character was obscured at the time and has been misunderstood and misconstrued ever since.

As we turn to a consideration of this newer western development, we must begin by recognizing the fact that we will not find a uniform pattern for the region as a whole. Geographically, there were four distinct areas, each of which presented its own peculiar problems of adjustment. Chronologically, the development ranged from the beginning of the Anglo-American movement into Texas in the 1820's through the occupation and organization of the California-Oregon country around 1850 to the opening of the Kansas-Nebraska region for settlement in the middle 1850's and the movement from both directions into the Rocky Mountain area at about the same time. The differences between these four regions are obvious; and possibly because of that fact it has been difficult to see those elements in their development which were sufficiently consistent with the general pattern to suggest a common denominator. In this case, for example, an examination of the sources of the migration into these regions seems to reveal a typical frontier situation in which the promise of unusual economic opportunities in a new and relatively undeveloped area has attracted settlers from all parts of the country. The nativity statistics of the census of 1860 show that approximately 565,000 persons living west of the line forming the western boundary of the first tier of states across the Mississippi had been born in the states east of that line, and that 45.4 per cent of the total had come from those states lying south of the Mason and Dixon–Ohio River–Missouri Compromise line. A further breakdown of the distribution shows that 15.4 per cent of the total were natives of Kentucky and Tennessee; 30.0 per cent came from the rest of the South; 23.0 per cent from the Northeast and 31.6 per cent from the North Central states. If we remove Texas from this picture, however, the pattern changes to a distribution of 8.9 per cent from Kentucky and Tennessee; 10.6 per cent from the rest of the South; 35.8 per cent from the Northeast; and 44.7 per cent from the Middle West. An analysis of the distribution by areas in the West shows that the southern states had furnished 17.9 per cent of the immigrants into the Kansas-Nebraska region; 16.5 per cent of those to the Rocky Mountain territories; and 21.1 per cent of those who went to California and Oregon; and conversely, the northern states had furnished 15.2 per cent of the immigrants to Texas.[6]

This seemed to mean that four new Wests were being brought into existence under conditions similar to those of the earlier Ohio Valley West and that this blending of people of different backgrounds might bring the creation of another new society whose character was more likely to be determined by its own environment and needs than by the interests or ambitions of the sections from which its members had come. But any possibility that the normal frontier process might soon merge these Wests into a broader common pattern for the region as a whole was already being destroyed by the effectiveness of the crusade against slavery. From the perspective of nearly a century later it is easy to agree with Professor Charles W. Ramsdell that the natural limits of slavery expansion had been reached by 1860,[7] or to accept the carefully considered judgment of Professor William O. Lynch that "most migrating southerners, and northerners likewise, would have sought homes and opportunities just about where they did had slavery not existed between 1783 and 1861."[8] But earnest zealots condemned Daniel Webster for making similar statements in 1850 and then proceeded to confuse the basic issue of constitutional rights by spreading their propaganda that the South had embarked on a deliberate aggressive campaign to establish slavery in all parts of the West. We know now that the real contest over the extension of slavery in the 1850's was being carried on not in the plains of Kansas and Nebraska, or the plateaus and valleys of New Mexico and Colorado, or the legislative assemblies of California and Oregon, but in the halls of Congress and the press and public forums of the East; but at the time, the propaganda sounded so plausible to those who did not know the facts that it had the desired effect of discrediting the South in the eyes of the rest of the nation, and thus contributed directly toward transforming the sectional controversy from a debate to a war.

Our concern here, however, is not so much with the effect of such propaganda on the course of events at that time as with its effect on the work of the historians who have since sought to explain or interpret those events. It would be difficult to read both the abolition literature concerning the designs of an "aggressive slavocracy" and such books as Horace Greeley's *American Conflict* or the general histories by Hermann E. von Holst, James Schouler, James Ford Rhodes, and others without being impressed by the similarities in language and emphasis. Even some of the later works, written since numerous scholarly monographs have provided significant corrective interpretations, continue to reveal a reluctance to abandon the version handed down by the propagandists; and nowhere has the influence of that version been more persistent than in the treatment of the South's role in the development of the newer Wests. Despite the authoritative studies of such scholars as Eugene C. Barker and Justin H. Smith, for example, there are still those who see the colonization and annexation of Texas, the war with Mexico, and the acquisition of California as links in a deliberate scheme to obtain more territory for the creation of additional slave states. For such it has seemed natural to assume that because many of the southerners who migrated to New Mexico, California, and other parts of the Far West before 1860 became prominent in the political or economic life of the region their activities were part of the plot. Thus misunderstanding and misrepresentation have been carried over from propaganda to color the writing of both the local and the general history of the Far West.

On the other hand, it must be admitted that superficial appearances might seem to confirm the misinterpretations. In far-away Oregon, for example, a native of Tennessee who had practiced law in Missouri was one of the leaders in the first move for the establishment of a local government, and the first territorial governor was a native of North Carolina who had come by way of Kentucky and Indiana. In California, fifteen of the forty-eight members of the convention which drew up the first state constitution had come from southern states, while the first governor and one of the first two United States senators of the new state had been born in adjoining counties in Middle Tennessee, and the other senator was a native of Georgia. When in 1859 David S. Terry, chief justice of the California supreme court, who had come from Kentucky by way of Texas, killed United States Senator David C. Broderick, a former Tammany Hall ward heeler, in a duel growing out of a fight for control of the Democratic party organization in the state, it was a simple matter to transform Broderick into a martyr whose life had been sacrificed to wrest California from southern domination.[9] On a broader scale, although less than 10 per cent of the total population of California in 1860 had been born in the South, three of the five men who had served as United States senators from that state up to 1861 and five of its eleven representatives were natives of southern states. In Oregon during the same period, one of its two territorial delegates was southern-born, and he also became one of the state's first two senators; in Washington, one of its four territorial delegates was a southerner; and in New Mexico, where only eight tenths of one per cent of the population claimed southern birth, two of its four territorial delegates had come from southern states, the other two being Mexicans born in the territory. In the case of Colorado, Utah, and Nevada, no southerners had been sent to Congress before 1861; but a total of twelve out of the thirty men who had represented these two states and five territories indicated a southern influence out of all reasonable proportion to its 6.7 per cent of the inhabitants of the region as a whole.[10]

It is perhaps not unreasonable to suggest, however, that instead of proving the existence of a deliberate plan of the South to gain control of the West these facts actually indicate that the issues of the sectional controversy seemed far less important to the people of this new region than to the agitators in the East. If there had been a conscious struggle for supremacy within the region over the question of slavery, it does not seem possible that less than 10 per cent of the population could have elected 40 per cent of the men who represented it in Congress and sometimes even higher proportions of the local officials. Apparently, these men were being chosen by the votes of both northerners and southerners on their own merits rather than on the basis of sectional issues. But Hubert Howe Bancroft, hard at work in the 1880's on his monumental history of the Pacific states, thought he saw otherwise, and his treatment of the California constitutional convention may be used as an excellent illustration of the way he manipulated his materials to support his point of view. Stating that the convention "was understood to be under the management, imaginary if not real, of southern men," he succeeded in finding twenty-seven instead of fifteen southerners by ignoring the official list and by counting the native Californians from below the extension of the Missouri Compromise line as belonging to that group. He then drew upon indirect evidence to explain that the members of this southern majority permitted the adoption of the free-state provision without debate because they intended to define the boundaries of the proposed state in such a way that future division would be necessary, in which case a new slave state could be created. He carefully selected from the official journal those arguments by southerners which seemed to confirm this view, but he completely ignored its record of the voting, which showed clearly that in no instance did either the northerners or the southerners vote as a unit on the numerous boundary proposals which were submitted; nor did he explain that a majority of the southerners opposed every proposal which would have encouraged future division and that their nearest approach to unanimity came in their support of the provision finally adopted, which, in his opinion, represented a victory for the North.[11] Having thus found what he construed as a cleavage over the slavery issue, he proceeded to interpret the political rivalries of the next decade within the state in terms of that conflict; and other writers are still uncritically following his lead.

Fully as important as these misinterpretations of the part played by southerners in the political affairs of the West is the almost complete absence of any serious attention to their contribution toward the development of the economic, social, and cultural interests of the region. Here it becomes necessary to return to that provincial frame of reference which enabled the Middle Westerners to reach the conclusion that their region became "in a peculiar way the heart of the United States." One would like to know, for example, to what extent this concept was itself one of the results of the propaganda campaign through which the South came to be misunderstood. If it was true that southern migration into the West had been for the purpose of extending and perpetuating the institution of slavery, then the outcome of the Civil War had removed the incentive for such migration. It seemed logical to assume, therefore, that since southerners would no longer be interested in going to the newer West the continuing growth of that region must be due to migrations from the Middle West and the Northeast; and this would lead naturally to the conclusion that the society which developed there was essentially a projection of their own with only such modifications as might be imposed by the change in environment. Thus the transit of civilization had at last become a clear, undefiled stream of "true American standards" flowing from New England across the Middle Border into the Far West; and the South, having become "enchained to a destiny of its own," no longer disturbed the western waters.

That this is a vastly oversimplified statement of the evolution of an attitude of mind is of course obvious. That the attitude of mind itself is not sheer fabrication, however, can be seen in the language and emphasis of some of the essays on the sources of culture in the West, in discussions of American thought, and in many of the specialized studies of various aspects of the development of the West. Perhaps the most striking illustration of its persistence is to be found in a recent book entitled *The Yankee Exodus,* in which the author, a native of Vermont now living in Oregon, sets out to show "what a large part of the United States owes its character to the migrations of New Englanders westward since the latter 18th century."[12] Casting his net far and wide, he brings up some two thousand individuals whose fields of operations range from New York to the Hawaiian Islands, and through them he makes New England responsible for contributions varying all the way from the introduction of seedless oranges or the invention of innumerable gadgets to the founding and development of the University of California or the writing of "the fabulously successful novel *Ramona.*" Standing alone, this book conveys a distorted impression; but its importance lies in the effectiveness of its presentation of one part of the picture and in the clue which it provides to the method to be used in obtaining the information needed to correct the perspective.

The application of a similar method to a study of those who left the South would also bring to light other thousands of individuals who made their contributions, and as their activities are brought into the picture it will become increasingly apparent that it was neither North nor South alone, but the interaction of the two, that shaped the character of the West. A significant illustration of such interaction may be cited in the fact that the founding and development of the University of California, instead of being solely the work of New Englanders, was the result of the harmonious cooperation of John and Joseph LeConte from South Carolina with Henry Durant and Daniel Coit Gilman from New England in determining the character of the new institution.[13] Similarly, Helen Hunt Jackson was able to absorb the atmosphere for making *Ramona* into a successful novel because she lived for a year as a guest in the San Diego County home of Cave Johnson Couts, a native of Tennessee whose reputation throughout California for liberal hospitality sounds strangely like that of the traditional southern planter.[14] Evidence of case after case of the activities of explorers, promoters, businessmen, professional men, public officials, and private citizens indicates that the South contributed far more than an interest in slavery and that its participation in the development of the West continued undiminished long after slavery was gone.[15]

This is the story that is waiting to be told. That it needs to be told has perhaps been demonstrated in the many questions which this paper has raised and left unanswered. Its telling will not be a simple task; but if the research which it requires should show that the questions themselves and the hypotheses prompted by them have validity, a contribution will have been made toward a sounder interpretation of the development of American society. If, on the other hand, it shows them to be unsound, we can then accept the existing interpretation with a greater degree of assurance. In either case, a step will have been taken in the search for the whole truth; and that, after all, is the real aim of the historian.

Chapter XVII

The Price of Union

AVERY CRAVEN

T HE HISTORIAN'S JOB is to find order in a disorderly world.* He must seek out the threads, whether they exist or not, which tie events together in a somewhat meaningful way. He must show that there is some sense in what has occurred—some progress or some decline; some relationship between events which rescues them from mere chaos. In his hands well-arranged causes produce inevitable and, therefore, just results. The human mind requires this for its sanity, and the historian must assume the responsibility and provide the assurance that we live in a rational universe.

This is what is meant by the lessons which history teaches. This is what makes history a profession. This is why we must forever be rewriting and reinterpreting our history, and why what one generation has done with history is inadequate for the needs of the next. One age may wish to see the hand of God in all that has happened; another that economic forces have determined the course of human affairs; a third may wish to be shown that society is forever evolving from patterns simple to those more complex. But whatever the demand, the historian has at all times been adequate. The past in his hands makes sense. When he has finished arranging and interpreting events, this is, in spite of all its confusion and contradictions, an orderly world. Men and nations have gotten their just deserts.

With this understanding of the historian's task in mind, it is not surprising that the American Civil War has been seen as an "irrepressible conflict." Some have viewed it, as did Abraham Lincoln, in terms of "the eternal struggle between *right* and *wrong*." It was waged to save the Union, and the Union was worth saving because it was man's great

*Presented in Montgomery, Alabama, November 9, 1951.

experiment in democracy, and because human slavery had no place in such an undertaking. Others have described it as an inevitable struggle between agriculture and industry for the shaping of a nation's economic destiny. They have seen two opposing ways of life, amounting to civilizations, in a predestined struggle for existence. Still others, with states' rights in mind, have insisted that it primarily involved the emergence of nationalism over and against the hindering forces of provincialism. But regardless of differing interpretations, *all* have understood that *progress* was at stake; a more just and equitable social order in the balance; and that victory ultimately rested on the side of justice and soundness. In this way a nation's conscience has been soothed to accept four bloody years of battle and ten years of civil enslavement as necessary and beneficial steps towards a sounder future.

Yet regardless of what historians have thought and said about the causes of the Civil War, the fact remains that the victory of northern arms over the Confederate States of America meant the triumph of one section over another; of one set of economic forces over a rival set of economic forces; of one type of social values over another; and of one set of political ideas and one party organization over those which had been in opposition. Regardless of the part which slavery and states' rights may have played in *producing* the war, its most significant and lasting result was the free and unhampered emergence of a new America— an America with a strangely different temper and spirit from the old, with a new set of values, and with new dominating interests. Freed from southern restraint, the nation rushed forward into the Gilded Age, the era of Robber Barons, the day of Big Business and bigger depressions. To put it more bluntly, the values and interests of the Northeast, as evolved under industry and finance on a Puritan background, took charge to shape and direct the course of the United States into the modern world.

Against just such an outcome in values and interests, the South as a section had long contended and, in the end, had risked her very existence. She had been able until now to force something of economic balance in national life, to retain the respectability of certain rural social values, and to hold in check the drift towards consolidation in Federal government. Unfortunately she permitted the slavery struggle to obscure these facts. That was a fatal blunder.

It is probably true that Negro slavery was the fundamental factor in producing the American Civil War, and it is probably safe to make the assertion that if there had been no such thing as slavery, civil war might have been avoided. But when one talks this way he must understand that, by 1860, slavery had become the symbol and carrier of *all* sectional differences and conflicts. Because of its moral and social implications, it supplied the emotional force necessary for both attack and defense. It produced those fighting terms, "The Abolition Crusade" and "The Slave Power." It colored every issue and often hid behind the words "right" and "rights" the more basic issues. As William H. Seward said: "Every question, political, civil, or ecclesiastical, however foreign to the subject of slavery, brings up slavery as an incident, and the incident supplants the principal question. We hear of nothing but slavery, and we can talk of nothing but slavery."

To the Northeast, and after 1854 to the Northwest, slavery became the sole reason for southern opposition to tariffs, internal improvements at Federal expense, homestead legislation, national banking, and freer immigration laws. It symbolized the political dominance which the South was supposed to hold in the nation through control of the Democratic party. It explained the southern emphasis on states' rights and strict construction of constitutional powers. It came to signify what they called "backwardness" in things social and economic. It was thought to have reduced the Northeast to the status of a conscious minority after Federalist days and to have kept the Northwest from its fullest development following the Mexican War. The Republican party had been created to right these wrongs.

In the South, slavery was magnified into the cornerstone of a perfect society. It was supposed to have solved the labor problem and the far more difficult race problem. It was the source of southern stability and the wide acceptance of personal and social responsibility which characterized the section. Its right to exist where men desired it and to expand into the new territories became the symbol of a section's constitutional rights and its equality in national life. In the end, the southern states were willing to go to war in its defense.

Yet in spite of these facts, it is perfectly clear that the war was waged over antagonisms much broader than slavery and that the purposes back of the so-called Reconstruction program, inaugurated at the close of the war, had far more to do with reordering the South as a section than they had to do with the Negro as a human being. The nearly total abandonment of the Negro to the control of the southern states after 1876, the brazen political-economic bargaining or compromising in the disputed election of that year, and the quick turning of the Negro's Fourteenth Amendment almost exclusively to economic uses were, in fact, only the logical climax of steady developments which had, for a generation, been reducing the South, as a section, to a completely colonial status in relation to the finance-industrial areas. Without ignoring the part which fear, vengeance, love of Union, and interest in the Negro played in

Reconstruction, it must be perfectly clear to every scholar that the establishment of permanent Republican party control, the protection of the already exorbitant tariffs, and the securing of financial arrangements satisfactory to the bankers, the creditors, and the rising industrialists were basic factors in determining the treatment given the South. Many northerners were perfectly frank about the matter. The Negro must be enfranchised, they said, to counteract southern white votes which would most certainly be given to the Democratic party. If this were not done, wrote a friend to Charles Sumner, it would produce evils "fearful to contemplate"—"a great reduction of the Tariff doing way with its protective features—perhaps Free Trade to culminate with Repudiation,— for neither Southerners nor Northern Democrats have any bonds or many greenbacks." The *Nation* opposed "the speedy readmission of the Southern States" because of the effect it would have on government securities, and the New York *Tribune* was equally certain that "the cotton-planters," educated by Calhoun "to the policy of keeping the Yankees from manufacturing," would "vote solid to destroy the wealth-producing industry of the Loyal States." No wonder Governor Horatio Seymour of New York insisted that the radical talk of making the South over into the likeness of New England simply meant an acceptance of its "ideas of business, industry, money making, spindles and looms."

The appearance of such attitudes in Reconstruction should not, however, be a matter for surprise. Southern interference with the emergence of modern America had, in fact, constituted the basic reason for northern complaint. It was not just opposition to specific measures, such as tariffs, homesteads, and internal improvements, but rather the continued insistence on *the locality* in an age when increasing interdependence and improved communication demanded a consolidated nationalism: it was the emphasis on agricultural values and the refusal of southerners to change their minds as the physical world in more than half the nation altered. These were the things that mattered most. The mass production of goods, the widening of credit, the application of steam to transportation, and the greater mobility of ideas, persons, and things were all out of keeping with a restricted central government, with purely local financial agents, and with a leisurely way of life. Constitutional regulations and governmental agents made for a handful of agriculturists and traders in colonial days did not necessarily meet the requirements of thirty millions of people emerging into finance-industrial capitalism and spreading over half a vast continent. The enslavement of human beings did not jibe with the labor requirements of free enterprise or the ethical standards of a competitive society. A "backward" minority had no right to restrain a progressive majority. Men who were already economically dependent had no right to political dominance.

The subjugation of the rural-agricultural South was, therefore, a foregone conclusion long before the indignation against Negro slavery, however real it may have been, provided the moral force which produced an irrepressible conflict. Regions which supply raw materials and markets seem inevitably to be cast for the role of backward dependents in the modern industrial age. Southerners had early realized this fact and their changing status in national life. Their complaints against a growing dependence were as bitter as were those of the North against restraint. Robert J. Turnbull had declared in 1827 that "internal improvements are drawing off our resources to the North, and tariffs are driving us rapidly into Colonial vassalage." He was convinced that the interest of the North and West was "that the government should become more and more National"; while that of the South was "that it should continue Federal." The South would, therefore, have to wage a constant fight for the "preservation" of the Constitution against the "usurpation" of northern "manufacturers." John C. Calhoun had seen the Wilmot Proviso as "a scheme, which aims to monopolize the powers of this Government and to obtain sole possession of its territories." This meant inequality, and rather than yield one inch of southern equality he would "meet any extremity upon earth." "What! acknowledged inferiority!" he cried. "The surrender of life is nothing to sinking down into acknowledged inferiority!"

The protests against economic, social, and intellectual dependence gained added momentum after 1850. The drives for agricultural improvements, direct trade with Europe, the establishment of manufactures, the improvement of southern schools, the establishment of southern periodicals, and the boycotting of northern colleges and summer resorts, all had back of them both the realization of dependence and the desire to make the section self-sufficing. Writers and speakers were constantly pointing with shame to the fact that from the rattle with which the nurse tickled the ears of the southern child to the shroud that covered the cold form of the dead or the marble slab that marked the final resting place, everything with which the southerner worked and played came from the North. The senseless talk of making Kansas a slave state arose, not from any sound hope of slavery expansion, but from a determination to preserve southern equality. In fact, the danger of slavery expanding to any existing territory in 1860 was so slight that the Republican appeal was primarily to an abstract principle, and its popularity due to the fact that it represented northern opposition to all that the South now symbolized.

Its economic program, on the other hand, was emphatically concrete and meaningful. It pointed directly towards modern America.

The South also reacted to Republican success as a symbol of defeat in a long struggle. It is difficult to explain secession strictly in terms of the threat carried by Abraham Lincoln as a President. Secession in terms of thwarted slavery expansion per se does not make sense. States reacted to an accumulation, to emotions, to a discouraged feeling of helplessness, to a conviction that all they stood for and all they valued was endangered. They were trying to protect the ways of a minority against the power of a differing economic-social majority. A movement that took from November, 1860, to April, 1861, to reach its climax represented a reluctant drift, not precipitous action.

As the possibility of civil war became clear, however, patriotic and moral justification for resort to force necessarily pushed aside the material elements in sectional conflict and lifted the struggle to high and lofty levels. All wars are ultimately fought for things too sacred to be yielded. God does not lend his support to unworthy causes. Men are willing to give their lives only for *right* and *rights*. Yet in spite of high-sounding words, the material causes for sectional rivalry and conflict were not overlooked. A few northerners early spoke of a peaceful acceptance of separation, but when faced with the social-economic consequences, drew back, and few "patriots" showed the slightest inclination to yield on a single interest item. As a northern historian has recently written:

Throughout the secession winter, the Northern compromisers generally showed great enthusiasm for concessions on matters that seemed to have no direct bearing upon their particular interests, but they displayed an unfeeling obduracy toward concessions on sujects that touched them closely. In Congress nearly every type of sectional legislation came up for debate; and Northerners, whether radical or conservative, Republican or Democratic, refused to surrender any law which brought special benefits to their constituents. Southerners could cry out against discrimination and Northern tyranny, but Yankee congressmen were unmoved.[1]

More significant was the fact that southern congressmen had hardly left their seats in 1860–61 before the complete overturning of the old economic order began. A homestead act, the passage of which marked the final yielding of the nation's natural resources to private hands, was hurried through. The long-debated protective tariff was started on an upward swing that would ultimately carry it to heights surprising even to the industrialists themselves. The quick passage of a national banking law, soon to be followed by a whole series of fiscal measures favorable to investors and creditors, put an end to financial values that had held since the days of Andrew Jackson. A Pacific Railroad bill, in turn, marked the end of a long controversy over the part which government should play in internal improvements and economic developments. Even the immigration laws, which southerners had so ardently defended, were loosened to permit the importation of wage earners by contractors. The Fourteenth Amendment, with its restrictions on state action, climaxed a legislative program of near revolutionary proportions.

War needs furnished immediate justification for most of this legislation. Yet the whole program was one toward which the North had been driving and against which the South had stood firm for more than a generation. It was a program which embodied every essential ingredient necessary for the rise of the American businessman, his institutions, and his values. It would make possible wealth undreamed of by those who planted. It would build great cities, require transcontinental railway lines, and begin the production of material things in quantity and quality such as mankind had never known. It would be called the Industrial Revolution.

With the exception of speed and degree, however, there was little basically new in the developments which followed in the United States. Much the same social-economic transformation had already taken place in western Europe. England and France had early felt the magic touch of steam power and factory production. These would soon do a more rapid and more thorough job in remaking Germany. The rise to strength and dominance of the city and the factory was a common phenomenon in the nineteenth century. What was unique and peculiar in the American story was its temper and its methods—both the product of the sectional struggle and Reconstruction.

What was done to the South, and how it was done, is a familiar story. It was from one angle the complete elimination of an economic and political rival guilty of thwarting Progress. From another, it was the completing of a glorious mission in the name of patriotism and morality— the wielding of the Lord's "terrible swift sword." Either justified a perfectly ruthless procedure. And, what is equally important, the practical interest end might be served under the banner of the piously abstract. It is therefore always difficult to say whether Thaddeus Stevens and Charles Sumner were motivated by a godlike indignation or by a plain, everyday hatred of a sectional rival. The results, however, were the same. The South, which was once so powerful that some charged it with ruling the nation, was turned over to the mercies of an army of occupation, its political action regulated and supervised, and its social values discredited by the assumption of backwardness. If the section had any contribution to make to a people blundering into the Gilded Age, in terms of rural-agricultural moderation of industrial and financial excesses, or of living as against acquiring, it was neither asked for nor appreciated. Southern emphasis on good manners, on personal and social responsibility, or on the right of men and regions to be different, were old-fashioned in such an age. These things were not progressive. They did not yield profits. They belonged to an era and a section that had produced a Jefferson and a Madison, a Marshall and a Calhoun, a Lee and a Davis, but which had been unable to produce a single Rockefeller, a Morgan, a Hill, or a Carnegie. Until it had been made over in the image of its conqueror, it could be ignored.

Thus for nearly two generations the South would play little part in the larger affairs of the nation. Wrapped up with its own problems of recovery and adjustment, it would share little either in the great economic prosperity of the age or in the shaping of national character. Thus to the already staggering cost involved in the physical and political destruction of an important segment of the nation must be added the equally staggering waste of talent and ability and culture. Balance was being sacrificed; human qualities and values, essential to national greatness, were being discredited and ignored. Southerners were being forced, like the peoples in any conquered and occupied country, to resort to deception, violence, and intrigue. Double standards and nonmoral attitudes were inevitable results.

The cost in northern values was even greater. Doing these things to the South damaged the aggressor more than they did the victim. It gave the leadership in national life to such twisted, unbalanced, vindictive men as Thaddeus Stevens, Edwin M. Stanton, Benjamin F. Butler, Zachariah Chandler, and Charles Sumner. It loosed an "age of hate" and social irresponsibility. Stevens would break up and relay the whole "political, municipal and social" fabric of southern society. Chandler thought that the only rights southern whites possessed were "the constitutional right to be hanged and the divine right to be damned." The good citizens of Boston, assembled in Faneuil Hall, asserted that the "defeated rebels" had "no civil nor political rights" which loyal men were bound to respect. A northern clergyman declared in a sermon that "I would try and condemn to be hung for treason, every rebel who has registered as Colonel, or as a higher rank in the Confederate army, or was of corresponding prominence in civil service." The few he would pardon he would let go under sentence with a rope around their necks with a clear understanding that if they ever touched "their accursed feet" upon "this soil of ours again . . . that postponed halter [would] swing them still."

Action, fortunately, never quite matched such talk. But the emotions stirred did silence conservative voices and permit an extreme course to be taken. Even in cases where public approval was uncertain, bold men who knew what they wanted were able to drive ahead amid the confusion and uncertainty of conflicting forces. A certain ruthlessness in dealing with opposition; a complete disregard of public opinion; a justification of corruption where deemed necessary to reach ends; a harsh indifference to the welfare of the helpless; a sham righteousness assumed in the interest of progress; these were the attitudes that were being woven into the temper of a people about to enter the industrial age. Already one could almost hear a Vanderbilt exclaim: "The public be damned."

The political cost was equally heavy. The Republican party had come out of the war with the reputation of having saved the Union. It was not a deserved reputation. War Democrats had given loyal support, and extreme Republicans had made no end of trouble. Professor William Archibald Dunning always bluntly insisted that the Republican party, as such, had ceased to exist by 1864, and that a Union party composed of War Republicans and War Democrats had taken its place. More than that a goodly number of old Republicans of the liberal Lincoln tradition were soon in revolt against the party's conservative trend, while a considerable group of old Democrats of the John A. Logan and Ulysses S. Grant stamp were becoming the most ardent of Republicans. In the fight against President Andrew Johnson, however, Republicans had ignored the facts in the case, unfairly charged all Democrats with Copperhead leanings, and had returned to the old arrogant assumption that they were, and always had been, the only sound and loyal party.

This assumption, moreover, included loyalty to the Republican economic interests now magnified and adjusted to the needs of the emerging new day. Business thus shared in the luster of loyalty and the great moral benefits from having freed the slave. The Republican party became the party of business; business, in turn, became the heir to all the attitudes which the Republicans had developed in "reconstructing" the "disloyal South." To keep the party in power became an object of more importance than preserving democracy. The emoluments of public office were, of course, a consideration, but the avoidance of southern policies was more vital. Even the appropriation of a presidential election, clearly lost, was justifiable. Sound economic policies—meaning tariffs, payment of debts in gold, and free enterprise—were a part of the Republican faith. The party had an economic mission as well as a divine commission. Henry Wilson declared that in the Republican party there was more of moral and intellectual worth than was ever embodied in any political organization in any land. It had been "created by no man or set of men but brought into being by almighty God himself . . . and endowed by the creator with all political power and every office under Heaven." And its claim to rule rested on both moral and economic grounds. For, as said George F. Hoar, it contained "the best elements in our national life ... the survivors and children of the men who put down the Rebellion and abolished slavery, saved the Union, and paid the debt and kept the faith, and achieved the manufacturing independence of the country, and passed the homestead laws." So, said another, in 1876, "Let your ballots protect the work so effectually done by your bayonets at Gettsysburg and on so many a field of strife."

The Democratic party, on the other hand, was charged with having sympathized with treason. It had sided with "rebels." It had "no high aims, no patriotic intentions." It was "controlled by the foreign population and the criminal classes of our great cities, by Tammany Hall, and by the leaders of the solid South." "Every unregenerate rebel calls himself a Democrat," cried Oliver P. Morton of Indiana.

Every bounty jumper, every deserter, every sneak who ran away from the draft, calls himself a Democrat. . . . Every man . . . who murdered Union prisoners . . . who invented dangerous compounds to burn steamboats and Northern cities, who contrived hellish schemes to introduce into Northern cities . . . yellow fever, calls himself a Democrat. Every dishonest contractor . . . every dishonest paymaster . . . every officer in the army who was dismissed for cowardice calls himself a Democrat. . . . In short, the Democratic party may be described as a common sewer and loathsome receptacle. . . .

The conclusion was obvious. As the Chicago *Tribune* put it: "The War of the Rebellion, on the surface a conflict between the North and the South, was in reality a conflict between the Republican and Democratic parties and principles." It would not be ended until "the Democratic party was dead and buried." *Harper's Weekly* was just as specific. "Reconciliation," it said, "will not result from taking the control of government from New England, the Middle States, and the Northwest and giving it to the Southern and border States. The power must remain where it is, because there the principles of the New Union are a living faith."

Such blunt acceptance of the basic significance of a long-existing power struggle, more than a decade after the abolition of slavery, which is supposed to have been the sole reason for sectional strife, is indeed revealing. It recalls to mind the words of Joshua R. Giddings, back in 1844, when he warned that the annexation of Texas would place "the policy and the destiny" of the nation in southern hands, and then asked:

Are the liberty-loving democrats of Pennsylvania ready to give up our tariff? Are the farmers of the West, of Ohio, Indiana, and Illinois, prepared to give up the sale of their beef, pork, and flour, in order to increase the profits of those who raise children for sale, and deal in the bodies of women? . . . I appeal to the whole population of the western States—of all classes and conditions, and political parties—to say whether they are willing to give up their harbor improvements, and the improvement of our river navigation, for the purpose of improving the southern slave trade, and of perpetuating slavery in Texas?

The basic nature of the conflict had evidently not changed. The only difference, seemingly, was that the sin of slaveholding carried the appeal in 1844, while the guilt of having attempted to break up the Union supplied the emotional force in 1874-76. Such appeals did infinite damage to the two-party system. They created a solid Democratic South and equally solid Republican blocs all over the North. Regardless of actual interests, men continued to vote their emotions. Reform of corruption became difficult; the honest facing of problems impossible. They magnified the service rendered by the soldier to the nation; brought men as unfitted as Ulysses S. Grant to the highest office in the land; and, with the organization of the G. A. R., thrust the military hand deep into the national treasury and made military service a prerequisite to the holding of every office from the presidency to the janitorship in the humblest county courthouse. What the resulting corruption and incompetency cost the United States no one will ever know.

Business, meanwhile, took its cue from politics. Ends justified dishonest means. Private conduct and the private conscience were one thing; what a man did in business was quite another. Men who later were to be called "Robber Barons" were as pious churchmen as were the politicians who waved the bloody shirt. Men who exploited labor as ruthlessly as they wasted a nation's natural resources or bribed a public official were even more honored and rewarded than were the politicians who, ten years after the close of war, were still saving the Union and freeing the slaves. One of the most brutal tricks history has ever played on blundering mankind was to shift the scenes so rapidly that these businessmen, who had so eminently succeeded, by the accepted standards of their day, were scarcely permitted to leave the stage before they were being denounced as "predatory capitalists." Evidently the application of Reconstruction methods and values in business was not acceptable even to the North.

The heaviest cost of union, however, fell on agriculture. In a larger sense the economic struggle had been against the rural-agricultural interests and values united under southern leadership. The disintegration of the early alliance between the West and South, in the 1840's, had marked a turning point in national affairs. This agricultural combination until now had dominated national policy. Through the Democratic party, it had had its way with banks, tariffs, homesteads, and internal improvements. As the West grew and matured, however, differences arose, and the South more and more found herself standing alone on old issues. The question of slavery extension into the territories completed the break and pushed the strictly rural-agricultural issues into the background. Farmers, however much their interests remained the same, were now hopelessly divided.

War and Reconstruction only widened the gap while at the same time they actually increased farmers' common interests. Southern leadership, moreover, was now completely discredited. The nation's agriculturists, who justly laid claim to being gentlemen and who stressed the importance of culture, dignity, and good living in rural areas, were now broken and out of fashion. The homestead act and the heavy land grants to railroads, on the other hand, gave the northwestern farmer new and greater opportunities. Equipped with the new machinery which war necessities had popularized, he swept out across the vast prairie and plains regions to write, in action, one of the great epics of human history. Aided by the heavy flow of foreign immigrants, farmers and cattlemen literally flooded the western world with food. In the three decades after 1870, one generation of men settled more land and turned it into farms than all their predecessors put together. In the same period, they added over 225 million acres to what the census called "improved lands" —an amount far in excess of all that improved since Jamestown.

Into the lap of the astonished world these farmers poured their yields. "Year after year came from widening acreage...torrents of wheat, of pork, of cattle, of corn, swelling the channels of trade....Year after year, more and more freight cars creaked wearily with heavier and heavier loads to cities whose prosperity waxed higher and higher and higher." Dependent urban and industrial groups could go on expanding without worry about cheap food. Common men the western world over could now eat roast beef and white bread, once the food of kings.

But there was another side to it. The farmer was selling in a world market and functioning in a society now dedicated to the proposition that the rise of cities and the spread of industry measure all progress; that governments are instituted among men for the purpose of aiding such developments; and that there is no difference between developing a nation's resources and exploiting them. Slowly, one by one, the European farmers accepted peasantry before the competition of cattle raised on the open range and produce raised on cheap homestead lands. In England this produced what W. H. R. Curtler calls "a minor social revolution" in the ruination "of the old landed aristocracy as a class." A Jena economist, meanwhile, warned the German farmer that he must "let go his hold on the traditions of the past; he must arouse his energies and adapt himself to the demands and circumstances of the time. Agriculture is now revolutionized." Scandinavian farmers suffered almost as much. Only industry, which was increasingly dependent on the outside world for food, raw materials, and markets, profited by what a Berlin writer called "the boundless blessings conferred upon the population of Europe by the shipments from transmarine sources." One day such dependence, phrased in a demand for an "equal place in the sun," would plunge the whole western world into war.

The western farmer himself fared little better in such an order. While he sold in an unprotected market, he bought behind the walls of a tariff that soon reached 50 per cent. He bore the brunt of the businessman's methods in railroads and finances. He overcrowded the range and he glutted his markets. Without knowing it, he was depleting his soils and lowering his water levels. Soon he made the discovery that the new rulers of America no longer believed, as had Thomas Jefferson and John Taylor, that the farmers were "the chosen people of God." He even found out that the term "farmer" might be used to imply inferiority. When he attempted to strike back at the railroads and other corporations, he learned what Reconstruction had done to the American system of government. The attempt to impeach Andrew Johnson had weakened the presidential office itself and had struck a blow at executive independence. Soon, members of Congress would speak of the sweet reasonableness of a chief executive. The refusal of the Supreme Court to test the validity of the Reconstruction program had amounted to virtual abdication. It had even permitted Congress to remove cases from its jurisdiction. It too had lost independence and was being overshadowed by the legislative department. Congress, thus, had grown all-powerful and the welfare of business and finance seemed to be its chief concern. The Senate had become a millionaire's club. It was, charged James B. Weaver of Iowa, filled with men who represented "the corporations and the various phases of organized greed. . . .To an alarming extent," he went on, it could and did "control both the House and the Executive," with the result that while the war had destroyed a "slave holding aristocracy, restricted both as to locality and influence," it was "only to be succeeded by an infinitely more dangerous and powerful aristocracy of wealth, which now [pervaded] every State and [aspired] to universal dominion." The strictly sectional character of this new aristocracy was clearly indicated by Congressman George W. Morgan, who complained "of the tribute money which the shrewdness of New England politicians extorts from the people of the agricultural States for the benefit of certain Eastern monopolies. . . . So well established is the dominion of New England over the people of the other States," he continued, "that they humbly bow their necks to the yoke and meekly pay the tribute." "The lords of the loom" were, as Samuel S. Marshall of Illinois repeated, levying tribute "upon the people of the West at pleasure and without limit."

The real difficulty, of course, was that agriculture, under the new order of things, was not prospering. Another farming region was being reduced to a colonial status. The economic order was out of balance. As one writer said, the railroads had never been so prosperous; the banks had never done a better or a more profitable business; manufacturing enterprises never made more money; yet agriculture everywhere was in a languishing condition. It was a situation which southerners had seen coming and had struggled to prevent. It was part of the price paid for union. Spokesmen for the western farmer had simply taken over the role once played by Turnbull, Calhoun, and Davis. It was a leadership, however, vastly inferior. Ignatius Donnelly, James Baird Weaver, and William Jennings Bryan had little of the logic or the understanding of their predecessors. They too were doomed to defeat. Yet the problem they faced was the old familiar one; only the setting had changed. Farmers were battling to preserve their equality before the onrush of finance and industrial capitalism. Too late, they were discovering the tragic fact that slavery, in spite of its great importance, was only one phase of a far broader problem forced upon a people moving all too swiftly out of a simple past into the complexities of an industrial future.

And so the historian trying to find order in this disorderly world might, if his conscience permitted, suggest that the basic developments which took place in the United States in the nineteenth century, when stripped of their exaggerations, were the product of those great forces which were ushering in the modern world. He might even hint that the American tragedy lay in the way in which changes were brought about and in the ruthlessness, waste, and corruption which resulted. Looking for longer lines and a bit more sense in what happened, he might even argue that the greater interdependence of men and regions on each other which came with major technological, industrial, and financial changes rendered old political and social arrangements and ideas inadequate. Men's minds were left behind in one age while their bodies were being thrust forward into another. The centers of power and influence had altered; population had shifted and concentrated; a new emphasis on nationalism and freedom for the individual had become necessary.

The historian might also suggest that under such conditions, developments everywhere overstressed the importance of industry and glorified the businessman and his values far above their worth. Fabulous returns in early days, moreover, tended to hide weaknesses, and the all too apparent tendency to debase and exploit areas which supplied raw materials, food, and markets. Men failed to see the bitter rivalries that lay ahead as dependent industrial peoples reached out for necessary supplies and places in which to sell surplus goods. They could not know what would happen when the age of expansion neared its close, nor could they understand that the early conflicts on local stages were but a prelude to international wars which, in turn, would call for world organization and better means for using the democratic process and keeping world peace.

Chapter XVIII

The Irony
of Southern History

C. VANN WOODWARD

IN A TIME when nationalism sweeps everything else before it, as it does at present, the regional historian is likely to be oppressed by a sense of his unimportance.* America is the all-important subject, and national ideas, national institutions, and national policies are the themes that compel attention. Foreign peoples, eager to know what this New World colossus means to them and their immediate future, are impatient with details of regional variations, and Americans, intent on the need for national unity, tend to minimize their importance. New England, the West, and other regions are occasionally permitted to speak for the nation. But the South is thought to be hedged about with peculiarities that set it apart as unique. As a standpoint from which to write American history it is regarded as eccentric and as a background for a historian something of a handicap to be overcome.

Of the eccentric position of the South in the nation there are admittedly many remaining indications. I do not think, however, that this eccentricity need be regarded as entirely a handicap. In fact, I think that it could possibly be turned to advantage by the southern historian both in understanding American history and in interpreting it to non-Americans. For from a broader point of view it is not the South but America that is unique among the peoples of the world. This eccentricity arises out of the American legend of success and victory, a legend that is not shared by any other people of the civilized world. The collective will of this country has simply never known what it means to be confronted by complete frustration. Whether by luck, by abundant re-

*Presented in Knoxville, Tennessee, November 7, 1952.

sources, by ingenuity, by technology, by organizing cleverness, or by sheer force of arms America has been able to overcome every major historic crisis—economic, political, or foreign—with which it has had to cope. This remarkable record has naturally left a deep imprint upon the American mind. It explains in large part the national faith in unlimited progress, in the efficacy of material means, in the importance of mass and speed, the worship of success, and the unquestioning belief in the invincibility of American arms.

The legend has been supported by an unbroken succession of victorious wars. Battles have been lost, and whole campaigns—but not wars. In the course of their national history the Americans, who have been called a bellicose though unmartial people, have fought eight wars. And among them there has not been so much as one South African fiasco such as England encountered in the heyday of her power. This unique good fortune has isolated America, I think rather dangerously, from the common experience of the rest of mankind, all the great peoples of which have without exception known the bitter taste of defeat and humiliation. It has fostered the tacit conviction that American ideals, values, and principles inevitably prevail in the end. That conviction has never received a name, nor even so much explicit formulation as the old concept of Manifest Destiny. It is assumed, not discussed. And the assumption exposes us to the temptation of believing that we are somehow immune from the forces of history.

The country that has come nearest to approximating the American legend of success and victory is England. The nearness of continental rivals and the precariousness of the balance of power, however, bred in the English an historical sophistication that prevented the legend from flourishing as luxuriantly as it has in the American climate. Only briefly toward the end of the Victorian period did the legend threaten to get out of hand in England. Arnold J. Toynbee has recalled those piping days in a reminiscent passage. "I remember watching the Diamond Jubilee procession myself as a small boy," he writes. "I remember the atmosphere. It was: well, here we are on the top of the world, and we have arrived at this peak to stay there—forever! There is, of course, a thing called history, but history is something unpleasant that happens to other people. We are comfortably outside all that. I am sure, if I had been a small boy in New York in 1897 I should have felt the same. Of course, if I had been a small boy in 1897 in the Southern part of the United States, I should not have felt the same; I should then have known from my parents that history had happened to my people in my part of the world."

The South has had its full share of illusions, fantasies, and pretensions, and it has continued to cling to some of them with an astonishing tenacity that defies explanation. But the illusion that "history is something unpleasant that happens to other people" is certainly not one of them—not in the face of accumulated evidence and memory to the contrary. It is true that there have been many southern converts to the gospel of progress and success, and there was even a period following Reconstruction when it seemed possible that these converts might carry a reluctant region with them. But the conversion was never anywhere near complete. Full participation in the legend of irresistible progress, success, and victory could, after all, only be vicarious at best. For the inescapable facts of history were that the South had repeatedly met with frustration and failure. It had learned what it was to be faced with economic, social, and political problems that refused to yield to all the ingenuity, patience, and intelligence that a people could bring to bear upon them. It had learned to accommodate itself to conditions that it swore it would never accept, and it had learned the taste left in the mouth by the swallowing of one's own words. It had learned to live for long decades in quite un-American poverty, and it had learned the equally un-American lesson of submission. For the South had undergone an experience that it could share with no other part of America— though it is shared by nearly all the peoples of Europe and Asia—the experience of military defeat, occupation, and reconstruction. Nothing about this history was conducive to the theory that the South was the darling of Divine Providence.

In his recent book, *The Irony of American History,* Reinhold Niebuhr conducts an astute analysis of national character and destiny that emphasizes another set of American pretensions which he calls the illusions of innocence and virtue. These illusions have their origins in both North and South, though at a period before there was any distinct regional consciousness. They were fostered by the two great moral traditions of early national life, New England Calvinism and Virginia humanism of the Jeffersonian school. While they differed upon theology, theocrats and humanists were agreed that their country was "God's American Israel," called out of a wicked and corrupt Old World and set apart by providence to create a new humanity and restore man's lost innocence. I believe that Niebuhr would agree that what I have described as the American legend of success and victory has assisted in fostering and perpetuating these illusions of innocence and virtue. At any rate he demonstrates that these illusions have been preserved past infancy and into national adulthood. Arriving at man's estate, we have suddenly found ourselves in possession of immense and undreamed of power and compelled to use this power in ways that are not innocent and that cover us with guilt. In clinging to our infant illusions of innocence along with our new power, writes the theologian, we are "involved in ironic perils which compound the experiences of Babylon and Israel"—the perils of overweening power and overweening virtue.

Our opposite numbers in the world crisis, the Russian Communists, are bred on illusions that parallel our own with ironic fidelity, even though they are of very different origin and have been used to disguise (perhaps even from themselves) what seems to us much greater guilt of oppression and cruelty. They combine these illusions with Messianic passions that find a paler reflection in one layer of American conscience. Looking upon their own nation as the embodiment of innocence and justice, the Russians take it for granted that America is the symbol of the worst form of capitalistic injustice. Both America and Russia find it almost impossible to believe that anyone could think ill of them and are persuaded that only malice could prompt suspicions of motives so obviously virtuous. Each tends to regard the other as the only force willfully thwarting its dream of bringing happiness to all mankind.

There are many perils, both for our nation and for the world, inherent in this situation—and they do not all come from abroad. We are exasperated by the ironic incongruities of our position. Having more power than ever before, America enjoys less security than in the days of her weakness. Convinced of her virtue, she finds that even her allies accuse her of domestic vices invented by her enemies. The liberated prove ungrateful for their liberation, the reconstructed for their reconstruction, and the late colonial peoples vent their resentment upon our nation— the most innocent, we believe, of the imperial powers. Driven by these provocations and frustrations, there is the danger that America may be tempted to exert all the terrible power she possesses to compel history to conform to her own illusions. The extreme, but by no means the only expression, would be the so-called preventive war. This would be to commit the worst impiety of the Marxists, with whom it is dogma that they can compel history to conform to the pattern of their dreams by the ruthless use of force.

To save ourselves from these moral perils, Dr. Niebuhr adjures us to disavow the pretensions and illusions of innocence derived from our national childhood, along with all self-righteousness, complacency, and humorless idealism. If we would understand our plight and prepare for the role we must play, we must grasp the ironic implications of our history. I realize that Niebuhr's view of human strivings is based on theology, a subject definitely beyond my province. Whatever its theological implications—and I have frankly never explored them—the view has a validity apart from them that appeals to the historian. Yet the ironic interpretation of history is rare and difficult. In the nature of things the participants in an ironic situation are rarely conscious of the irony: else they would not become its victims. Awareness must ordinarily be contributed by an observer, a nonparticipant. And the observer must have an unusual combination of detachment and sympathy. He must be able to appreciate both elements in the incongruity that go to make up the ironic situation, both the virtue and the vice to which pretensions of virtue lead. He must not be so hostile as to deny the element of virtue or strength on the one side, nor so sympathetic as to ignore the vanity and weakness to which the virtue and strength have contributed. Obviously the qualifications of the ironic historian are pretty hard to come by.

Now the South is deeply involved at present in the ironic plight of our country as a full-fledged participant. In fact the headlong precipitancy with which the South has responded to the slogans of nationalism in recent world crises has often exceeded that of other sections of the country. Mass response sometimes suggests the zeal of recent converts. Yet there are aspects of its history and experience that make the South an observer as well as a participant, which set it apart in certain ways from the experience of the rest of the country, and which constitute a somewhat detached point of view. From that vantage point I believe it is possible for the southern historian, and indeed all those absorbed in the study of southern history, to make a special contribution to the understanding of the irony of American history, as well as that of the South's history.

The ironic implications of southern history are not concealed by any legend of success and victory, nor by the romantic legend of the Lost Cause. To savor the full irony of the confident and towering antebellum dream of a Greek Democracy for the New World one has only to recall the words of a speech that Robert Barnwell Rhett made when South Carolina seceded. The orator was picturing the historian of 2000 A.D. writing this passage: "And extending their empire across this continent to the Pacific, and down through Mexico to the other side of the great gulf, and over the isles of the sea, they established an empire and wrought out a civilization which has never been equalled or surpassed—a civilization teeming with orators, poets, philosophers, statesmen, and historians equal to those of Greece and Rome—and presented to the world the glorious spectacle of a free, prosperous, and illustrious people." As a matter of fact, in the eyes of the true believer the coming of the Golden Age did not have to await the year 2000. It had already arrived, full blown, here and now. For as Charles Sydnor has observed, "the affirmation of Southern perfection" meant just that. Blind to evils and imperfections all around them, southerners described what they saw as the ultimate in social perfection. "Fighting to defend their way of life," says Sydnor, "they had taken refuge in a dream world, and they insisted that others accept their castle in the sky as an accurate description of conditions in the South."

The shattering of this dream and the harsh education that followed has not made the South the home of a race of philosophers. Nor does it seem to have made southerners any wiser than their fellow countrymen. But it has provided them with a different point of view from which they might, if they will, judge and understand their own history and American history, and from which to view the ironic plight of modern America.

The meaning of the contrast between the 1930's and the 1940's is a case in point. This transformation took place too recently for anyone to have forgotten, though many seem to have forgotten it entirely. In the thirties and well into the following decade there occurred the most thoroughgoing inquest of self-criticism that our national economy has ever undergone—not even excepting that of the muckraking and progressive era. No corner nor aspect nor relationship of American capitalism was overlooked, and no shibboleth of free enterprise went unchallenged. The prying and probing went on at every level from the sharecroppers to holding companies and international cartels. Subpoenas brought mighty bankers and public utility empire-builders to the witness stand. Nor was this activity merely the work of the wild-eyed and the woolly-haired, nor the exclusive concern of one of the major parties. It was a popular theme of the radio, the press, the screen, the theater, and even the pulpit. Some churches took up the theme and incorporated it into their programs. Universities hummed and throbbed with it. And in 1940 the former president of a public utility holding company, then candidate for President of the United States on the Republican ticket, made the theme a part of his campaign. Some of the outpouring of criticism in the thirties and forties was misdirected, some was perhaps a bit silly. But the electorate repeatedly endorsed with large majorities the party that was the more closely identified with the movement. On the whole the people regarded it as productive of good. It was at least indicative of a healthy and self-confident society, uninhibited by fear.

Then in the mid-forties something happened. It happened rather suddenly. The floodstream of criticism dwindled to a trickle and very nearly ceased altogether. It was as if some giant sluice gate had been firmly shut. The silence that followed was soon filled with the clamor of voices lifted in accusation, denial, or recantation. No reputation was now secure from the charges of the heresy hunters, the loyalty investigators, and the various committees on public orthodoxy and conformity. Choruses were lifted in rapturous praise of the very institutions that had been so recently the objects of attack. And the choruses were joined by many of the former critics.

Surveying this remarkable transformation, the historian of the South can hardly escape the feeling that all this has happened before—or something strongly suggestive of it: that what happened in the 1940's had its counterpart in the 1830's. The earlier development was on a smaller scale, to be sure, and there were certain other obvious discrepancies to be taken into account. The dangers inherent in any such comparison between historical epochs are numerous and forbidding, for certainly no analogy is perfect since no two eras, movements, or events are entirely alike. To suggest that modern capitalism is comparable to slavery as a system of labor would be to indulge in the loose and irresponsible language of polemics and propaganda. With due precaution and full awareness of the risks, however, one may venture a comparison not between the two institutions but between the public attitudes toward them and the transformations that took place in those attitudes.

What happened in the South during the 1830's is too familiar a story to require elaboration here. Before it happened, however, we know that the Jeffersonian tradition protected and fostered a vigorous school of antislavery thought in the South. The great Virginians of the revolutionary generation, nearly all of whom were on record for emancipation, lent their prestige to the movement. Critics of slavery spared no aspect of the peculiar institution. They spoke out against the effect upon the master as well as upon the slave; they exposed the harm done the manners and morals of the South as well as its economy and society. Nor were the critics mere misfits and radicals. They included men of influence and standing: politicians, editors, professors, and clergymen. Antislavery thought appeared in respectable newspapers and infiltrated evangelical sects of the upper South particularly. In the 1820's the slave states contained a great many more antislavery societies than the free states and furnished leadership for the movement in the country. It would be false to suggest that slavery was on the way out, or, in spite of some amelioration, that the reformers made any very substantial alterations. But it is not too much to say that this was a society unafraid of facing its own evils. The movement, you will recall, reached a brilliant climax in the free and full debates over emancipation in the Virginia legislature during the session of 1831-32. The effort to abolish slavery failed there as elsewhere. But as Joseph Robert writes, "The institution was denounced as never before; it was condemned wholesale fashion by legal representatives of a slave-holding people. The vigor and breadth of the assault provide the debate with its most obvious distinction."

In spite of the vigor of the movement and the depth of its roots in southern tradition, it withered away to almost nothing in a very brief period during the middle thirties. By 1837 there was not one antislavery society remaining in the whole South. Of the thousands of voices that had been raised in outspoken protest a short while before there were to be heard only a few whispers. Opponents changed their opinions or held their tongues. Loyalty to the South came to be defined in terms of conformity of thought regarding one of its institutions. Past records and associates were scrutinized closely, and the recency with which one had denounced northern abolitionism became a matter of public concern. The South concentrated its energies upon the repression of heresy and raised intellectual barricades against the ideas of a critical and unfriendly world. The institution that had so recently been blamed for a multitude of the region's ills was now pictured as the secret of its superiority and the reason for its fancied perfection.

The causes behind the transformation of attitudes in the South were numerous and complex. So are the reasons behind the transformation that has taken place in the attitudes of contemporary America. Broadly speaking, however, both of these revolutions in public attitudes were re-actions to contests for power in which the two societies found themselves involved. These great struggles included many clashes of interest and issues quite apart from those concerning morals and contrasting labor systems. Even in the absence of ideological differences the strains of conflict would have been severe in each case. In the 1850's as in the 1950's, however, the crisis tended to be increasingly dramatized as a clash between different systems of labor: as slave labor versus free labor. In both the nineteenth-century war of words and the twentieth-century cold war each party to the conflict, of course, contended that the other practiced the more immoral, wicked, and shameless type of exploitation, and that its own system was benevolent, idealistic, and sound. Our own opinions as to which of the parties in each crisis was the more deluded or disingenuous in its contentions are likely to be pretty firmly fixed already, and the problem is such that it need not detain us.

The point is that there exists, in spite of obvious differences, a dis-quieting suggestion of similarity between the two crises and the pattern of their development. The mistakes of the South, some of which have already been suggested, are readily apparent and their meaning open to all who would read and understand. In the first place the South permitted the opposition to define the issue, and naturally the issue was not defined to the South's advantage. In the second place the South assumed the moral burden of proof. Because the attack centered upon slavery the defense rallied around that point. As the clamor increased and the emotional pitch of the dispute intensified, the South heedlessly allowed its whole cause, its way of life, its traditional values, and its valid claims in numerous nonmoral disputes with the North to be identified with one institution. And that was an institution of which the South itself had furnished some of the most intelligent critics. It was a system known to have reached the natural limits of its expansion in this country already and one which was far gone on its way to abandonment abroad. Yet in its quest for friends and allies the South made the mistake of competing with the North for the favor of the West by insisting upon the acceptance of a system totally unadapted to the conditions and needs of the territories and often offensive to their moral sensibilities. And in looking to Europe for support from England and France, powers that might reasonably have been expected to be drawn to its cause for reasons of self-interest, the South encountered difficulties from the start. Some, though certainly not all, of these difficulties were due to the fact that those countries had already repudiated the system upon which the South had elected to stand or fall.

The knowledge that it was rapidly being isolated in the world community as the last champion of an outmoded system under concerted moral attack contributed to the South's feeling of insecurity and its conviction that it was being encircled and menaced from all sides. In place of its old eagerness for new ideas and its outgoing communicativeness the South developed a suspicious inhospitality toward the new and the foreign, a tendency to withdraw from what it felt to be a critical world. Because it identified the internal security of the whole society with the security of its labor system, it refused to permit criticism of that system. To guarantee conformity of thought it abandoned its tradition of tolerance and resorted to repression of dissent within its borders and to forceful exclusion of criticism from outside. And finally it set about to celebrate, glorify, and render all but sacrosanct with praise the very institution that was under attack and that was responsible for the isolation and insecurity of the South.

Modern America is more fortunate than the antebellum South in having an economic system which, though threatened with abandonment by other countries, has shown few of the serious weaknesses and is covered with little of the moral obloquy from which slavery suffered. And in spite of verbal orthodoxy regarding the doctrine of capitalistic free enterprise, the American political genius has shown willingness to experiment extensively with heterodox cures for ills of the orthodox system. This experimentation has, of course, been accompanied by loud protests of loyalty to the true faith. Again, modern America is not handicapped in the struggle against its powerful antagonist by the economic and military weaknesses that helped to doom the South to defeat.

There is, however, no cause for complacency in this good fortune. Nor does it rule out entirely the analogy that is here suggested. We should not deceive ourselves about the opinions of other peoples. While we see ourselves as morally sound and regard our prosperity as the natural and just reward of our soundness, these views are not shared by large numbers of people in many parts of the world. They look upon our great wealth not as the reward of our virtue but as proof of our wickedness—as evidence of the ruthless exploitation, not only of our own working people but of themselves. For great masses of people who live in abject poverty and know nothing firsthand of our system or of industrialism of any kind are easily persuaded that their misery is due to capitalist exploitation rather than to the shortcomings of their own economies. Hundreds of millions of these people are taught to believe that we are as arrogant, brutal, immoral, ruthless, and wicked as ever the South was pictured in an earlier war of words. And among their leaders are extremists ready with the conclusion that people so wicked do not deserve to live and that any means whatever used to destroy their system is justified by the end. One of these means is the subversive indoctrination of our labor force for insurrection. The malevolent caricature of our society contrasts so glaringly with what we believe to be the demonstrable facts—not to mention the contrast with our traditional illusions of virtue and innocence—that we are driven to indignation. And when we hear faint echoes of the same propaganda from our own allies, who no longer share our dedication to capitalism, our indignation turns into a sense of outrage.

Fortunately modern America has not yet followed the course of the South between 1830 and 1860, but the pattern of response evoked by these exasperations is not a wholly unfamiliar one. There are some unhappy similarities. Threatened with isolation as the last important defender of an economic system that has been abandoned or rejected without a trial by most of the world and is under constant moral attack from several quarters, we have rallied to the point of attack. We have shown a tendency to allow our whole cause, our traditional values, and our way of life to be identified with one economic institution. Some of us have also tended to identify the security of the country with the security of that institution. We have swiftly turned from a mood of criticism to one of glorifying the institution as the secret of our superiority. We have shown a strong disposition to suppress criticism and repel outside ideas. We have been tempted to define loyalty as conformity of thought, and to run grave risk of moral and intellectual stultification.

Opposing each of these dangerous tendencies there is still healthy and wholesome resistance struggling to reassert our ancient tradition of tolerance and free criticism, to maintain balance and a sense of humor, to repel the temptation of self-righteousness and complacency, and to reject the fallacy that the whole American cause and tradition must stand or fall with one economic dogma. But it is too early to say that on any one of these points the healthy resistance is certain of triumph. In fact the fight is uphill and in many instances the issue is doubtful. I am not contending that successful resistance to all the tendencies I have deplored will guarantee peace and solve the problems of the 1950's, any more than I am sure that the same course would have resulted as happily in the 1850's. But I believe I am safe in contending that in view of the South's experience each of these tendencies should be the subject of gravest concern.

In the field of diplomacy and foreign relations modern America suffers from a divided mind, torn between one policy that is reminiscent of the way of the South and another more suggestive of the way of the North in the Civil War crisis. On the one hand are those who would meet the foreign challenge by withdrawing from a critical community of nations teeming with heresies and, by erecting an impregnable barricade, forcibly keep out all alien ways, influences, and ideas.[1] Another modern group that has a counterpart in at least one school of southerners in the 1850's are those who in the 1950's, heedless of world opinion, would brook no opposition, would not cooperate with, nor consult other people's views, but insist that America must be strong enough to carry her way by economic coercion or by force. Suggestive also of the southern way are those who, in competing with our opponents for the favor of uncommitted peoples, would urge upon them institutions and abstract ideas of our own that have little or no relevance to their real needs and circumstances. And there are those also who resent as evidence of disloyalty any defection on the part of our allies from the particular economic faith upon which we have decided to take our stand.

More reminiscent of the way of the North, on the other hand, are those who hold that this is an irrepressible conflict, that a world divided against itself cannot stand, that the issue is essentially a moral one, that we are morally obligated to liberate the enslaved peoples of the earth, punish the wicked oppressors, and convert the liberated peoples to our way of thought. The true American mission, according to those who support this view, is a moral crusade on a world-wide scale. Such people are likely to concede no validity whatever and grant no hearing to the opposing point of view, and to appeal to a higher law to justify bloody and revolting means in the name of a noble end. For what end could be nobler, they ask, than the liberation of man? Fortunately wiser counsel prevails at the moment,[2] counsel which charts a course of foreign policy between the perilous extremes of isolationism and world crusade. But each of the extreme courses still has powerful advocates, and neither can yet be regarded as a dead issue.

We have been admonished lately to heed the ironic consequences of the characteristic American approach to international affairs since the beginning of the present century. The main deficiencies of our policy of the last fifty years, we are told, are our legalistic and moralistic approaches to foreign relations. It is possible and even desirable, I believe, to accept the validity of this critical insight without embracing the strictly amoral, pragmatic, power-conscious policy of national self-interest that has been proposed as an alternative by those who criticize the moralistic approach. It is all too apparent that the association of the legalistic with the moralistic concept results in a torrent of indignation and bitterness against the lawbreaker and a blinding conviction of moral superiority to the enemy. Expressed in military policy and war aims these passions overwhelm reason and find no bounds short of the complete submission, unconditional surrender, and total domination of the defeated people. The irony of the moralistic approach, when exploited by nationalism, is that the high motive to end injustice and immorality actually results in making war more amoral and horrible than ever and in shattering the foundations of the political and moral order upon which peace has to be built.

Those who trace our moralistic aberrations back to the American crusade to liberate Cuba have, I believe, overlooked remoter origins. For there would appear to be valid grounds for seeking these origins in the period of the Civil War. While both sides to that dispute indulged in legalistic as well as moralistic pretensions, it was the South that was predominantly legalistic and the North that was overwhelmingly moralistic in its approach. Although southern historians have made important contributions to the understanding of that crisis, it is doubtful whether anyone has stated more aptly the ironic consequences of the moralistic approach than a northern historian in a recent book called *And the War Came*. "Yankees went to war," writes Kenneth Stampp, "animated by the highest ideals of the nineteenth-century middle class.... But what the Yankees achieved—for their generation at least—was a triumph not of middle-class ideals but of middle-class vices. The most striking products of their crusade were the shoddy aristocracy of the North and the ragged children of the South. Among the masses of Americans there were no victors, only the vanquished."

Ironic contrasts between noble purposes and sordid results, between idealistic aims and pragmatic consequences are characteristic of reconstruction periods as well as war crises. This is nowhere more readily apparent than in the postwar period through which we are now living and with the problems of which we are still struggling. It is especially in such times that moralistic approaches and high-minded war aims come home to roost. As usual, it is only after the zeal of wartime idealism has spent itself that the opportunity is gained for realizing the ideals for which the war has been fought. When the idealistic aims are then found to be in conflict with selfish and pragmatic ends, it is the ideals that are likely to be sacrificed. The probability of moral confusion in reconstruction policy is increased when a nation finds itself called upon to gird for a new world moral crusade before the reconstruction consequent upon the last is fairly launched. Opportunities for moral confusion are still further multiplied when the new crusade promises to be fought in alliance with the public enemies of the previous moral crusade and when the new public enemy happens to have been an ally in the previous crusade.

Americans have in common the memories of an earlier experiment with reconstruction and are generally conscious of some of the shortcomings of that effort. But again, the South experienced that same historic episode from a somewhat different point of view. Once southern historians have purged their minds of rancor and awakened out of a narrow parochialism they should be in a singularly strategic position to teach their fellow countrymen something of the pitfalls of radical reconstruction: of the disfranchisement of old ruling classes and the indoctrination of liberated peoples, of the occupation of conquered territory and the eradication of racial dogma, of the problems of reunion and the hazards of reaction. They should at least have a special awareness of the ironic incongruities between moral purpose and pragmatic result, of the way in which laudable aims of idealists can be perverted to sordid purposes, and of the readiness with which high-minded ideals can be forgotten.

With all her terrible power and new responsibilities combined with her illusions of innocence and her legends of immunity from frustration and defeat, America stands in greater need than she ever did of understanding her own history. Our European friends, appalled by the impetuosity and naïveté of some of our deeds and assumptions, have attributed our lack of historical sophistication to our lack of a history

—in their sense of the word. America's apparent immunity to the tragic and ironic aspects of man's fate—that charmed and fabled immunity that once made America the Utopia of both the common men and the philosophers of Europe—has come to be pictured as Europe's curse. For the fear that haunts Europeans is the fear that America's lack of a common basis of experience and suffering will blind her to the true nature of their dilemmas and end by plunging them into catastrophe. But the Europeans are not entirely right. America has a history. It is only that the tragic aspects and the ironic implications of that history have been obscured by the national legend of success and victory and by the perpetuation of infant illusions of innocence and virtue.

America has had cynical disparagement of her ideals from foreign, unfriendly, or hostile critics. But she desperately needs criticism from historians of her own who can penetrate the legend without destroying the ideal, who can dispel the illusion of pretended virtue without denying the genuine virtues. Such historians must have learned that virtue has never been defined by national or regional boundaries, and that morality and rectitude are not the monopolies of factions or parties. They must reveal the fallacy of a diplomacy based on moral bigotry, as well as the fallacy of one that relies upon economic coercion through the fancied indispensability of favored products. Their studies would show the futility of erecting intellectual barricades against unpopular ideas, of employing censorship and repression against social criticism, and of imposing the ideas of the conqueror upon defeated peoples by force of arms. Such historians would teach that economic systems, whatever their age, their respectability, or their apparent stability, are transitory, and that any nation that elects to stand or fall upon one ephemeral institution has already determined its fate. The history they write would also constitute a warning that an overwhelming conviction in the righteousness of a cause is no guarantee of its ultimate triumph, and that the policy that takes into account the possibility of defeat is more realistic than one that assumes the inevitability of victory.

Such historians must have a rare combination of detachment and sympathy, and they must have established some measure of immunity from the fevers and prejudices of their own times, particularly those bred of nationalism with all its myths and pretensions, and those born of hysteria that closes the mind to new ideas of all kinds. America might find such historians anywhere within her borders, North as well as South. But surely some of them might reasonably be expected to rise from that region where it is a matter of common knowledge that history has happened to our people in our part of the world.

Chapter XIX

The Roles of the South
in the French Intervention
in Mexico

KATHRYN ABBEY HANNA

THERE is a preface to the address this evening.* It is actually a duet performed as a solo. The research behind the story belongs to my husband as much as to myself, since for some years we have been prowling together through archives and writing as a team.

The movement which we call the French Intervention in Mexico from 1861 to 1867 was broader than the term implies, both in concept and expected results. Had it succeeded, the destinies of the Western Hemisphere would have been modified. That it failed was due to a combination of circumstances rather than to the single effort of an individual or a group.

Among the many links between the French Intervention and the South I have chosen to outline four issues in the course of which France exploited or planned to exploit the southerners. These four issues might be simplified thus: (1) Could American disunion be used to initiate the Emperor's grand design for the new world, or, as the French called it, *la Grande Pensée de l' Empereur?* (2) Could a divided United States further *la Grande Pensée?* (3) Would recognition by the Confederacy strengthen the Mexican Empire? And (4) would Confederate migration bolster the wobbling fortunes of that empire?

The South's role in initiating the Mexican Intervention was unpremeditated. Whatever her long-range intentions toward Mexico—and many Mexicans believed them imperialistic—the immediate concern

*Presented in Jacksonville, Florida, November 13, 1953.

was to prevent Union troops from being allowed to cross northern Mexico to attack Texas. Yet the Lincoln administration was convinced that had there been no rupture within the Union there would have been no tampering with Mexico. It rested its case on political deduction; we rest ours on the letters of Napoleon III, his minister of foreign affairs, and his ambassadors.

Americans in the middle of the last century had no conception of how apprehensively Europe viewed the phenomenal growth of the United States. Tocqueville sounded the tocsin in the 1830's against both Russia and the United States as the "two great nations in the world which tend to the same end. . . . each of them seems to be marked out by the will of Heaven to sway the destinies of half the globe."[1] The Russian threat was more easily handled. Russia was monarchical in government and backward in economics. Moreover, she had a common boundary with Europe and could be pressured by international policies; to name one, support of the Turk as an established power.

On the other hand, the United States held herself outside the orbit of European power politics. Far from economically backward, she flourished in ways no European state could emulate. The American republic gave the courts of the monarchs many a bad moment. All had "demagogic centers," as they were called, to which the appeal of democracy was compelling and from which thousands departed to seek broader horizons across the Atlantic. As for American territorial expansion, one French senator, Baron Charles Dupin, in a memorial to Napoleon III insisted that by 1963 the United States would possess a population of 512,000,000 and to feed them would need both Central and South America.[2]

Obviously the situation needed remedy, and Mexico was the logical place to build a check to the United States, as Turkey, it was expected, would serve as a check to Russia. But to initiate such a course was about as easy as seizing a greased pig in a county fair contest. The three powers most interested in America—France, England, and Spain —must consider the vulnerability of their colonies in the west, the great distance at which they must operate, and the danger that a move on their part might touch off the very thing they sought to prevent.

The powers concerned spent the years between the Mexican War and 1861 in uneasiness and frustration: uneasiness concerning the extent of American aggression which the Americans naïvely called Manifest Destiny, and frustration because they did not dare to stop it. Besides the assortment of Mexican exiles who clustered around the French court urging that their country be saved by restoring them to power, the French minister to Mexico frequently reported feelers from Mexicans in and out of office for French assistance. More specific were the arguments of the Marquis de Radepont who had entered Mexico as a foreign observer with General Winfield Scott's American army and stayed to seek his fortune. From 1856 on, Radepont laid siege to Napoleon III. His opening gun was a voluminous memorial on Mexico, "the Turkey of America," which France and only France could save.[3] Later, Radepont advanced his contention for a Mexican throne which he insisted popular acclaim might establish. His was the plan of procedure France attempted to follow in 1861. Napoleon III approved of Radepont; some years later, he said Radepont was one of the few Frenchmen who understood the purpose of the Intervention and he had never regretted giving him his confidence.[4]

As conditions in Mexico worsened, France and England attempted the milk-toast panacea of mediation in 1859. It got nowhere, for it presupposed that a third government would emerge from two warring factions. Benito Juárez, who regarded himself as the rightful head of the state under the Constitution of 1857, scorned the offer of European interference.

Precisely at this dark moment the Democratic party in the United States split in convention assembled, the Black Republicans nominated the antislavery Rail Splitter of Illinois, and life became beautiful for the Emperor of France, awaiting an opportunity to act as agent of Providence for the New World.

During the summer of 1860 M. de Gabriac left the French legation in Mexico for home. He expected to return but events were too portentous for the Quai d'Orsay to leave the post without a minister. Dubois de Saligny, his successor, was carefully briefed on the developing American scene. Saligny had served previously in the United States and in the independent Republic of Texas; he was reported to be a protégé of the Duc de Morny, half brother of the Emperor and speculator in Mexican investments.

Saligny's mission as he understood it was to open the way for French influence in Mexico. Shortly after Saligny reached his destination Juárez defeated the Conservatives and marched back into the capital. Although Saligny recognized the Liberal government, he was so vigorously hostile to it that the Quai d'Orsay advised prudence until it was clear how serious disunion in the United States would become.[5] Saligny did not have to create an occasion for intervention by France because the Juárez government, quite unaware of the designs against it, opened the door by its suspension on July 17, 1861, of interest payments on the foreign debts. Saligny abruptly suspended diplomatic relations when the Mexican Congress refused to rescind the law in twenty-four hours.

Although Napoleon III had determined on his plan, he wanted the cooperation of England and Spain. The spur which France applied to her allies in these negotiations was the need of speed to forestall renewed expansion by a divided Union. The three powers regarded the division of the Union as likely if not certain; this being the case, argued Napoleon III, both parts would spread out in an effort to recoup the loss of each to the other. Assurances by Confederates that once they had their own government more territory would not be desired were passed over with polite incredulity. The best which could be expected from a rupture of the American Union was the opportunity to initiate intervention in Mexico and time to bring it about.[6]

The second role planned for the South was that of contributor to the furtherance of the French Emperor's design. Neither the Confederacy nor the Union ever glimpsed the full scope of *la Grande Pensée de l'Empereur* although at moments each entertained unpleasing suspicions. But the prize for the South was recognition by France, and early in her efforts toward this end the Richmond government endorsed the French Intervention in Mexico, regarding it as bait irresistible to the Tuileries. Actually, the Mexican situation was one of the greatest handicaps to recognition faced by the South.

Napoleon III considered his *Grande Pensée* for the New World as a noble and humane plan. Apologists for the Emperor endorsed its loftiness of purpose but explained that since it was at heart both anti-Union and anti-Confederate, it could never be properly elucidated, even to the French people.

While regarding himself as a true Frenchman, Napoleon III had always been enamored of far places. Since his imprisonment at Ham when he was urged to go to Nicaragua to head the construction of the Canal Napoleon between the Gulf of Mexico and the Pacific, he had interested himself in Central America; and this interest expanded to Mexico. These regions he visioned as areas of potential riches untouched by the material progress of the nineteenth century. Like many others of his day Napoleon III was fascinated by material progress and marked it as the goal of mankind and the ultimate tool of human welfare. The great obstacle to such progress was political instability; therefore, the first job was to draw all men, regardless of faction, into a wholly new order of society, supported from the outside to prevent it from falling into the dissensions which had plagued earlier governments. Once this regime was established, a truly amazing economic blossoming would inevitably result similar to that of the Americans, while France, the inspiration and guide of this wonder, would reap garlands of glory, mountains of francs, and security from the aggressive United States.

Various groups provided the material for the imperial *Pensée*. Rade-pont, the French economist, Michel Chevalier, J. B. Jecker and his associates dwelt upon the untapped wealth of Mexico; Saligny and the Mexican *émigrés* painted the black iniquities of Juárez and his party, and the yearning of all "sane" Mexicans that some good angel like Napoleon III should pull them and their country back from the abyss and call them to a new order similar to his own empire. The Empress Eugénie, fascinated by the project, of which her knowledge was microscopic, egged her husband on. On the periphery of the *Grande Pensée* were other ends to be served, such as the cultivation of the House of Habsburg with whom France still shared delicate issues in Italy.

But if Napoleon III borrowed from the programs of others, the composite result was his own. For example, Radepont's choice for a Mexican monarch was the Duc d'Aumale; that of Napoleon, the Archduke Maximilian of Austria. From the Mexican *émigrés,* reactionary and proclerical, he accepted assertions that Mexico wanted a monarchy. But he never planned to restore reactionary Mexicans to power nor the Mexican Church to its former position. He allowed Saligny to claim validation of the face value of the Jecker bond swindle and, thereby, swell the total of French claims to a figure certain to insure Mexican refusal. Yet once the Intervention started, the Emperor showed little interest in Jecker. In fact, the latter complained that his misfortunes really started when he received support from France.

Napoleon's initial purpose was the establishment of a Mexican monarchy in two or three months. He had been told this was possible and he chose to believe it. By the summer of 1862, when the Union and Confederacy were getting into their war, Mexico's new order was supposed to be moving into high gear; consequently, France prepared to speak from strength on New World matters. Unfortunately this schedule never materialized; France blamed dissension among the allies for this delay and deluded herself that once they had withdrawn in April, 1862, the Mexican express could be put back on the track. Defeat before Puebla on May 5 ended this dream. New order was not to come to Mexico by the *coup de théâtre* method. No stampede of "sane" Mexicans for monarchy was visible. On the other hand, France could not retreat before an army she had scorned as ragamuffins. National honor, let alone the Emperor's prestige, demanded that the stain of *Cinco de Mayo* be wiped out. More French troops were dispatched under a new commander, General Elie Frédéric Forey; additional credits voted by the Corps Législatif; and the fiction of a quick victory was discarded. Indeed, there is much evidence that Napoleon's mind was even opened to other forms of reorganization than monarchy in Mexico.[7]

During the same year, 1862, Confederate agents abroad pressed for recognition. The previous fall, 1861, Napoleon had discussed this issue with Maximilian and the *émigrés*. Everyone agreed that recognition of the Confederacy must serve the protection and advantage of the new order in Mexico. But after *Cinco de Mayo,* the French in Mexico were vulnerable. Juárez was seeking money and arms from Washington, and if he got them, Forey's army could be endangered. If Seward refused aid to Mexico for fear France would recognize the South, France was equally aware of the havoc Yankee arms could cause in Mexico, should Seward retaliate for an accepted Confederacy.

Although Napoleon saw perils in recognition, he considered mediation desirable. Recognition accepted the Confederacy as it was constituted and antagonized the North; through mediation the whole territorial picture might be changed. On October 30, 1862, the Quai d'Orsay informed the French minister at Washington, Mercier, that the Emperor judged the time had come to offer mediation.[8] A few days later, identical notes were sent to England and Russia suggesting that they join France in proposing a truce in the American war. Both courts declined the invitation. Washington was equally opposed. France, however, did not despair; North and South would eventually exhaust themselves. Pending the arrival of that moment, the Emperor and his foreign minister mulled over possibilities. Some of their meditations are set down in a "Note on the Affairs of Mexico and the United States, January 21, 1863."[9]

The theme of this "Note" was the reorganization of the United States and Mexico into a "hyphenated confederation." North and South would never reunite, but complete separation posed vexatious questions. Better a new confederation similar to that existing in Germany, composed of four fairly equal states: the North, the South, the West, and Mexico, administered by a diet similar to that of Frankfurt. Such a confederation would be a monument to France; it would secure her influence in the New World, rid her of the problems of the American Civil War and the Mexican Intervention, and dissolve the great mass in North America so disturbing to Europe. Since Washington was not ready to accept reorganization, the war must go on.

The Confederate government knew nothing about this French scheme for territorial realignment, but several rather disturbing incidents occurred. In August, 1862, M. Theron, French vice-consul at Galveston, wrote Governor Francis R. Lubbock of Texas for appraisal of Texan relationships with the United States and the Confederacy.[10] Lubbock responded tersely; it had been a good thing for Texas to join the United States, and even better to join the Confederacy.[11] Then the worthy governor had a disturbing idea. Why should a curious Frenchman thus dissect the soul of Texas? He sent Theron's letter to Jefferson Davis. At Richmond, M. Tabouelle, chancellor of the French consulate, button-holed Senator William S. Oldham of Texas to discuss Texan resources.[12] The resemblance of these two incidents was more than coincidental in the judgment of Confederate Secretary of State Judah P. Benjamin. Both consuls were expelled although Tabouelle talked himself into reinstatement. Benjamin urged John Slidell to find out what he could; it might be Saligny's work, he added, and almost hit the bull's-eye.[13] As early as 1861 Saligny had mentioned the possibility of possessing Texas.[14]

When Napoleon's letter to Forey of July 3, 1862, appeared in the Yellow Book, Americans both North and South had printed proof that the Intervention was designed to check their expansion. Had they seen his original letter, their alarm would have been greater still, because the Yellow Book version was a pallid expurgation.[15] Even so, the Richmond *Enquirer* questioned Napoleon's authorship and thought, perhaps wishfully, that it was more Yankee propaganda.[16]

Fantastic ideas of territorial manipulation were discarded by the summer of 1863. Gettysburg and Vicksburg gave military preponderance to the Union. Forey finally captured the Mexican capital and a hand-picked assembly of Conservative Notables offered a throne to Maximilian and established a regency without consultation with Napoleon III. The latter by then had planned a different procedure, but he made the best of events. Forey's successor, Marshal François Achille Bazaine, was instructed to attempt a union of all factions and to hold in check the Mexican clergy. The result was never satisfactory. Where the French army rested, the new regime prospered, but civilian officials possessed "neither zeal nor morality" in Bazaine's judgment. With the clergy he was soon almost at swords' points.

Under existing circumstances, Maximilian must be speeded to Mexico. The presence of the new ruler might pull things together so that French troops would see an end to their enterprise and the French treasury a prospect of reimbursement. The latter was to come from the unexploited mines of Sonora about which Midas-like stories had circulated.

Thus in the fall of 1863 there was still a chance that *La Grande Pensée de l'Empereur* might work out even though its course had varied completely from the blueprints and its results were so far disappointing. Hostility from Washington could ruin everything, however, and thus we come to the third role of the South. Undoubtedly, the Emperor spoke the stark truth when he declared to Sir Charles Wyke in November, 1863, that war with the Americans "would spell disaster to the interests of France and would have no possible object."[17]

But war with the United States might not be necessary. If the new empire became, or looked to be, stable and accepted by the Mexicans, the United States might be induced finally to accept it. Could alluring opportunities be available for Yankee capital, these interests, relieved that Mexico was no longer a problem, might bring effective pressure on Washington.

Drouyn de Lhuys, French foreign minister, went out of his way to explain that France had no intention of controlling Mexico or of keeping troops overseas indefinitely. After the Council of Notables proclaimed for Maximilian, William Dayton, American minister to Paris, was impressed with the emphasis which Napoleon III placed on a more democratic expression of popular will as well as hints that recognition of the new government would be a means of hastening French withdrawal.[18]

For his part, Seward contributed to this growing fiction. In the fall of 1863 the war between the North and the South was still serious and the danger of an alliance or at least a friendship between Imperial Mexico and the Confederacy imminent. The policy sent to Dayton in Paris and talked over with Mercier in Washington was hard to pin down and permitted various interpretations as Seward undoubtedly intended. The United States stood for nonintervention in Mexico, the nonintervention which she required of other nations during her current troubles. She had no disposition or right to interfere in the domestic affairs of Mexico, to establish any form of government, or to intervene in the French war. Nevertheless, she felt Mexico preferred a republic and, it must be admitted, the security of the United States depended on the survival of free institutions.[19]

In a conference with Mercier, which the latter reported on September 14, 1863, Seward impressed his caller with rare consideration for France.[20] He had entire faith in the declarations of the Quai d'Orsay, appreciated the tireless efforts of Mercier for friendship between the two countries, and wanted to do all in his power for the same end. The secretary reminded the Frenchman that the United States had never officially protested the establishment of a monarchy in Mexico "for fear that the communication might become a cause of embarrassment" to France. To quiet agitation at home, Seward continued, he might have published some of Dayton's recent dispatches, but he did not. He had even instructed John L. Motley at Vienna to make no comments on French policy. Finally he had written Thomas Corwin, American minister in Mexico, not to recognize a Mexican empire, but at the same time not to try to maintain relations with Juárez.

Small wonder that a few conversations, comparable to the one above, plus contacts which Mercier had in financial New York, sold the French minister on the possibility of ironing out difficulties between France and the United States over Mexico. He planted these views in the mind of the minister from Austria, Count Giorgi, so that the latter stopped predicting immediate war between Paris and Washington. In Paris, rumors that the United States would recognize the Mexican Empire were so numerous in the spring of 1864 that Dayton explained to Seward he had in no way contributed thereto.[21] In fact, no one had promised recognition. France had convinced herself that the empire could be made to look like the will of the Mexican people and that when this had been brought to pass, United States opposition would dissolve.

Unfounded as this belief was, there is no doubt that Paris regarded it seriously. With such a prize as this to be won, recognition of the Confederacy was put away in moth balls. Dayton was able to assure the State Department that rumors of recognition of the Confederacy by France and Mexico and an alliance between the latter empire and the South were "altogether devoid of foundation."[22]

But Maximilian was unaware of French thinking until his visit to Paris in March, 1864. The prospective Mexican Emperor, therefore, continued to operate on the policies endorsed by France in 1861, namely, that a divided Union was a needed protection to his new realm and should be favored. Various southerners were in touch with Maximilian; among them, Matthew Fontaine Maury and ex-Senator William M. Gwin. The latter had plans for developing the Sonora mines; the former urged that California be annexed to Mexico and offered himself as a prospective commander of imperial ironclads to do the job.[23] Such energy must have appalled the hesitant Austrian who knew about southern expansionists. His comments on the South were penned on a letter from José Miguel Gutierrez Estrada, "They have always been and always will be the sworn adversaries of Mexico whatever the form of its government."[24]

As Maximilian's visit to Paris neared, Slidell and his associates readied themselves for the fruition of their labors. To their consternation they were brushed away from the archduke. The rumor, current in Paris, was reported by Slidell to Benjamin that Mercier on his arrival from Washington had brought word from Lincoln that Maximilian's empire would never be recognized by Washington if the Confederacy were accepted by Paris.[25] The truth of the report can neither be proved nor disproved. If Mercier brought such a message, it was given to him orally and in like manner passed to the Quai d'Orsay. Really, this final touch was not needed to prove that Napoleon III had abandoned southern recognition for an effort to win that of the United States for Imperial Mexico.

As soon as Maximilian reached Mexico, his mind turned to the courting of Washington. Count Montholon, minister of France, urged that negotiations be left in French hands and that nothing be attempted before the presidential election of 1864.[26] This was a prudent suggestion, since the platform of the Republican party contained a plank inimical to the Mexican Empire. Montholon and the French in Mexico also believed in future recognition by the United States. After Montholon had been transferred from Mexico City to Washington he continued to assure Paris that he would be able to negotiate to this end.

Meanwhile Richmond had appointed General William Preston to represent the Confederacy in Mexico and draw Maximilian into virtual alliance with the South.[27] En route to his post, Preston received reports from Paris which caused him to tarry in Havana while Captain R. T. Ford went ahead to make certain of his reception. Ford learned that Maximilian, in line with his Paris tutelage, favored strict neutrality. Montholon said to him, "Tell General Preston that he must not think of coming here at present."[28] Preston traveled to Paris and London to find out what had so completely upset the beginning of a beautiful international friendship. He, too, was convinced that Napoleon had been the obstacle and tried his own brand of pressure in an interview with the Mexican *émigré,* Juan Hidalgo. Should the North and the South make peace, he hinted darkly, one condition might be the enforcement of the Monroe Doctrine. Back in Richmond in the early days of 1865 there was proper irritation at France. Preston's threat was echoed in Congress.[29]

The last role of the southerners in Mexico during the Intervention was different. War between North and South was ended and the United States was again intact. Gone were the questions of recognition, mediation, and the nebulous schemes of French rearrangement of territory. Maximilian and his consort, Carlota, sat on the prefabricated throne, but by the spring of 1865 there was a growing fear that it was shaky. The French blamed everything but the unsoundness of *La Grande Pensée* of Napoleon III. Maximilian had not possessed the magic touch, and enthusiasm for his regime was dwindling. His government was anti-French and the Mexicans still without "zeal and morality." The flood of immigration advocated since 1862 was but a trickle, and foreign capital was less and less available. Maximilian and the church were hopelessly in opposition. Finances were in chaos and the French still paid the bills. Exploitation of Sonora mines was categorically abandoned by Paris in November, 1864,[30] although Senator Gwin and the United States did not learn of this for some months. Napoleon III persisted in his efforts to get Maximilian accepted by Washington but the purpose was not to cap a triumph; rather, he wanted a pretext for withdrawing from Mexico.

In France opinion grew highly critical. There was uneasiness over relations with the United States, and European events were disquieting. In fact, the whole situation in the New World and the Old was working toward the point where common sense seconded the advice given by Alphonse Dano, successor to Montholon as French minister to Mexico: either France must accept indefinite military occupation and financial assistance for Mexico or find a way to withdraw at once.

Just at the moment when this downhill momentum was gathering speed, Confederate immigration became a problem. The Confederates migrated to Mexico to make new homes and fortunes under Maximilian's banner. They were not especially pro-French; some were even hostile, probably still smarting under what they considered Napoleon's abandonment of the Confederacy, yet all were willing to fight for the Mexican Empire if war broke out with the United States.

The inevitability of war was a natural assumption. The Confederates were aware that a group of Union generals, among whom figured no less a person than Grant, expected and even desired war with France and were attempting to set the stage for its conduct. With the knowledge of Matias Romero, Juárez's minister to Washington, two efforts had already been made to win Confederate cooperation. The first was a conference between Francis Preston Blair, Sr., and Jefferson Davis in January, 1865. Blair proposed that the Confederate president, accompanied by Major General Francis Preston Blair, Jr., and other Union generals, lead Confederate and Union troops against the Mexican Empire while Grant hovered in the background.[31] When this design fell through, a second effort was made through General Lew Wallace with the active support of Grant. Wallace met with General James E. Slaughter and Colonel John S. Ford at Point Isabel, Texas, in March, 1865. In a twenty-four hour conference, he tried to seduce the Confederate military leaders of the trans-Mississippi to abandon the waning Confederacy, accept attractive terms from the Union, and sign up for an expedition against the French. The United States, blithely confided Wallace, was now in the control of a military hierarchy: Lincoln did whatever Grant suggested. As unsuccessful as the Blair intrigue, the Wallace plot had one original result. The Confederates presented copies of all the letters and reports of the Point Isabel contact to General Tomás Mejía, commanding at Matamoros. Mejía forwarded them to Bazaine who, in turn, relayed them to the Minister of War in Paris.[32]

Thus, when the self-exiled southerners talked of impending war between the United States and France, the French knew the basis of their predictions. When some of the ex-Confederate soldiers asked to join the French Foreign Legion in Mexico, the temptation to accept them was great. France did not want war with the United States, but if it came the southerners would be no small asset. Bazaine wrote home for instructions. The Quai d'Orsay replied that admission of southerners to the

Legion in an organized body would be unneutral, and imprudent as well, because they might raid the frontier to exercise vengeance or even go over in a body to the side of Juárez. Scattering their enlistment through the various corps was satisfactory provided prominent names were not featured.[33] Following this permission, the French Minister of War reported that some Confederates had been accepted;[34] among them were some of Joseph O. Shelby's men who joined the counterguerrillas under the notorious adventurer, Colonel Charles Dupin.

Maximilian was constantly pressured to formulate a policy for Confederate colonization. Finally, early in June, 1865, he made up his mind. Dano reported an audience, called at Puebla.[35] Maximilian told his listeners that he saw a way to use the defeat of the Confederacy to his advantage. He was glad he had resisted the "adventurers" from the Richmond government because he hoped the moment had come to gather the fruits of the neutrality which he and Napoleon III had observed toward the South. The southerners, through their agents, Gwin, Pierre Soulé, and Maury, had asked to settle in the northern provinces. This Maximilian would never allow. "They would be loyal for a while," he asserted, "but I must think of the future. What will happen when a compact Anglo-Saxon group is established on the frontier? They will become rich and will they follow our rule or want to be independent?" Southerners, he concluded, should be kept away from the border and from the Isthmus of Tehuantepec where many had had investments before the war. The only place for them was in central Mexico, scattered about so as to blend with the population. On this basis he would take as many as wanted to come. Here Dano murmured to himself, "Poor Confederates; they will not gain much, especially with the Emperor afraid of them."

Having disposed of the southerners, Maximilian continued his plan. He would use the issue to open negotiations with Washington. On the pretext of sending a note of sympathy for Lincoln's death to President Johnson and the American people, General Juan N. Almonte would go on a mission to the United States. Once he had presented the note, he would reach an agreement with the United States regarding Confederate immigration and eventually establish commercial relations. Meanwhile Luis Robles, Minister of Fomento, would handle the southerners who had crossed the frontier. The Emperor was optimistic: "I have full confidence in the mission because I am going to send the most capable man to fill it."

Like everything connected with the French Intervention, plan and result had little resemblance. Almonte did not go to Washington; in his place was sent Mariano Degollado with the less imposing title of secretary of mission. President Johnson never received him, a fact which

Paris claimed arose from lack of cooperation with the French legation.[36]

Confederates continued to arrive in Mexico throughout the late spring and summer of 1865; how many it is impossible to determine amid conflicting claims, but there were several thousand. France approved of Maximilian's reception of the Confederates provided the United States was convinced that Mexico did not really want them but was merely following her duty to humanity by granting them asylum from the fortunes of war.[37] Nothing was done by the imperial government for some months. By the end of summer, Matthew Fontaine Maury emerged as the leader of colonization, probably because his project fitted imperial views. Optimistically, Maury predicted that 200,000 southern families would establish plantations in Mexico.

On September 5, 1865, Maximilian issued a decree establishing colonization.[38] Maury had written it but, as he informed his wife, the decree "had been injured in the translation."[39] Probably the greatest injury was that Mexico was opened "to immigrants of all nations" whereas its promoter was interested only in providing a "New Virginia" for southerners. But although the base of the decree was broadened, it was tailored to the southern figure in many obvious ways; for example, free passage "for those who have lost their substance," free transportation for goods, and, most of all, provision for bringing former Negro slaves on an apprenticeship basis.

Maury became a naturalized Mexican, was created honorary councilor of state, and appointed imperial commissioner of colonization. A land office was established under ex-Confederate General John B. Magruder. Confederate engineers initiated a system of land surveys, and Confederate immigration agents appeared on both coasts and in the interior. A Confederate newspaper, the *Mexican Times,* made its bow in September, 1865, edited by the former Confederate governor of Louisiana, Henry W. Allen, and subsidized for some months by the imperial government. In a word, Confederates had taken over imperial colonization lock, stock, and barrel. The French were amazed, not to say appalled. The Mexicans, many of whom favored the idea of colonization, changed their opinions once they observed the new American invasion. Landowners were outraged at the surveys of public land. During the years of anarchy they had increased their properties by the simple process of appropriation. It was horrifying to be asked to produce title.

Imperial Mexico was so honeycombed with Juárist sympathizers that it was quick work to send copies of the decrees underwriting colonization across the border to Romero in Washington. The latter packed them off to the State Department accompanied by the acid comment that the

Habsburg archduke and the former enemies of the United States had combined to force Negro slavery on a free people.[40]

This latest caper of Maximilian annoyed the American Secretary of State. He instructed John Bigelow to bring the colonization decrees to the attention of the Quai d'Orsay. Drouyn de Lhuys feigned indifference; immigration was a domestic policy of the Mexican emperor. "We are not the Government of Mexico and you do us too much honor by regarding us as such," he told the American minister.[41] But the dispatch to Dano which almost stepped on the heels of Bigelow as he left the Foreign Office was anything but casual.

Dano shared the views of his superior. He, too, marveled that a man who had feared and distrusted the southerners in June rested the development of his empire in their hands in September. Equally puzzling was the offer to subsidize colonists by a government whose expenditures already were two and one-third times its income.[42] The French minister had criticized Maximilian's policies before, but armed with the dispatch from Paris, he returned to the argument.

Whenever Maximilian met determined opposition from France he weakened, and the interview which Dano reported on January 28, 1866, was no exception. The Mexican emperor admitted that Negroes invited to migrate were under protective legislation and therefore to a degree slaves, but, he added, he was revising the decrees. He confessed it had been a mistake to feature the Confederates in his service; he had foreseen opposition from the United States but—and here he took refuge in that excuse which has been current since the Garden of Eden—Carlota had urged the idea; she had recommended both Maury and Magruder for office. He had a remedy for the mistake, Dano wrote. "His idea, without dismissing the Confederate agents and thus appear to have lied to them, is to render their powers so illusory that they will ask to resign."[43]

Perhaps this decision to double-cross the Confederates was one of the few Maximilian actually carried out. However, a bankrupt treasury and a disintegrating government would have destroyed colonization without neglect from the Emperor. In February, 1866, Maury received permission to visit his family in England. Two months later Maximilian wrote him that "impelled by motives of economy" the imperial commission of colonization had been abolished.[44] "Pleasure and satisfaction" were expressed for Maury's efforts and he was urged to return, an invitation which was declined because, explained Maury to his son-in-law, "if colonization fails, Mexico is no place for me."[45]

With the abandonment of colonization the southerners lost their role in the Mexican Intervention. The debacle of the empire itself absorbed all attention. Most of the Confederates had left Mexico by the end of the empire. A few stayed beyond the triumph of Juárez, but they took on the character of foreign residents whose presence left the international scene untroubled. There was no longer a *Grande Pensée,* to serve whose ends they might be used.

Chapter XX

Tolerating the South's Past

FRANCIS BUTLER SIMKINS

THE AGE of Enlightenment represented the Middle Ages as a Gothic night—an interlude of ignorance and superstition when men were enveloped in a cowl, oblivious to the wonders of knowledge, and concerned only with escape from the miseries of this world and of hell.* Voltaire said that Dante was considered a great poet because no one read him and that a Gothic cathedral was a monument to the stupidity of its builders. The humility of holy men and the faith of the Catholic offended the egotism, skepticism, and common sense of the leaders of the Enlightenment.

Historians of the nineteenth and twentieth centuries have thrown aside the conceits of those who went before them and have learned to appraise the medieval age in terms of its own values. It is now recognized as a period when the Christian church and an imaginative architecture flowered, when artists were humble enough to glorify God rather than themselves, and when universities, chivalry, and vernacular literatures had their beginnings.

The reputation of the region of the United States below the Potomac today suffers from the same forces from which the Middle Ages suffered at the hands of historians during the Enlightenment. The historians of the South often do not grasp the most elementary concept of the sound historian: the ability to appraise the past by standards other than those of the present. They accept a fanatical nationalism which leaves little room for sectional variations, a faith in Darwinian progress which leaves no room for static contentment, and a faith in the American dream of human equality which leaves little room for one person to get ahead of another except in making money. In theory at least, our historians refuse

*Presented in Columbia, South Carolina, November 12, 1954.

313

to tolerate the concept of "all sorts and conditions of men" of which *The Book of Common Prayer* speaks.

Growing out of the uncritical acceptance of the creed of contemporary Americans by the historians of the South are certain concrete dogmas. Among them are: the church and the state should be separate, but not the school and the state; school but not church attendance should be compulsory; universal education is better than folk culture; political democracy is better than aristocracy; freedom is better than slavery; nationalism is better than provincialism; urban standards are better than rural standards; small farms are better than plantations; the larger the number of voters the better the commonwealth; and the two-party system is better than the harmony of one party.

I am not asking the abandonment of any of these dogmas as bases for action in the world of today. These dogmas make up the American Dream on which much of American prosperity and hope is based. I am asking that southern historians not hide the fact that their ancestors did not put these dogmas into practice in the aspects of their lives which explain their regionalism. I am also asking that southern historians not accuse their ancestors of being stupid or unreasonable when they did not do so.

The friendly historians of the region who accept the ideal of human equality seem ashamed of the degree to which the South has not attained this ideal. In defense of their beloved region, the hopeful among them find evidences of the struggle of the lower classes for a greater degree of equality. They present the followers of Nathaniel Bacon as yeomen farmers rebelling against an oligarchy of planters. They give credence to many rumors of slave insurrections, and they often envisage the common people rising against political oligarchies. Their faith in the benefits of two political parties has led them to predict, for the past eight decades, the breakup of the solid South and the coming of a state of rectitude like that of New York or Illinois. They are apologetic over the existence in the South of the sharpest social distinction in all America: that between the white man and the Negro. They hail breaks in the color line as forecasts of the good times a-coming.

Their attitude when proclaimed by publicists and politicians may be justified as part of the policy of accommodation to the dominant ideals of the ruling part of the United States. But such diplomacy applied to the issues of the past convicts historians of naïveté or what the French and the Germans call Anglo-Saxon hypocrisy.

Those who accept national unity as the ultimate goal of all Americans find it difficult to defend a region whose chief distinction is that it attempted to destroy that unity. The friendly historian often chooses states' rights or secession as the theme of his writings. Then, when he starts writing, he deplores the existence of the things which, if they had ever existed, would have deprived him of his theme. He joyously emphasizes the existence of minorities who adhered to the national rather than the sectional cause. He gives the honors to such nationalists as Andrew Jackson and Andrew Johnson instead of to such divisionists as John Randolph and John C. Calhoun. He seems almost to get his inspiration from William T. Sherman who felt justified in imposing a cruel punishment upon the South because it tried to destroy the national unity.

Why do not our historians take their cue from Sinclair Lewis when he condemns America to an esthetic hell because most of its provinces have succeeded in ironing out their provincial differences? Why are they not proud of the fact that Lewis' criticisms apply least of all to the South? If this were not true, the South would not be worth writing about. So let the historians take for themselves the task of understanding and appreciating the sectional variations.

There is a reality about the South which historians with egalitarian standards find hard to understand or appreciate. This reality is that many of the so-called advances in equality turn out to be imaginary. Freedom, for example, to the early Georgians meant revolt against the tyranny of foreign despots who wanted to prohibit slavery and large estates as a means of preventing the colony from having the social and economic inequalities of the other southern colonies. The so-called rising of the Virginians in the American Revolution against oppressors turns out to be, in the light of modern researches, the struggle of an aggressive aristocracy against an official oligarchy, with the common man following noisily the leadership of his social betters. There is much that is artificial and sentimental in Virginia's greatest political philosopher advocating the equality of man and at the same time owning slaves, living in a house which Europeans would call a palace, and tolerating a political machine more oligarchical than that of Harry F. Byrd.

A paradox of southern history is that progress in political democracy was often followed by the desire of the newly enfranchised to destroy certain aspects of equality. Those who got the vote under the Jacksonian reforms of the 1830's were not displeased when their leader was transformed into a planter and a southern gentleman; and when a catty journalist in our day accused Rachel Jackson of smoking a pipe, there was resentment among the descendants of the original Jacksonians. The Jacksonian reforms were followed by the strengthening of the slave code and the disfranchisement of the free persons of color. The freer exercise of the suffrage by the common white man in the 1890's was followed by the Jim Crow laws and the disfranchisement of most of the Negroes.

The southern Negro has never got much beyond the rhetorical stage in his enthusiasm for closing the social gap which has separated him from the southern whites. As a slave, he never carried out a general rising against his masters. The equalities which after the Civil War were supposed to be his never got beyond a narrow political stage. One of the reasons for this is that the Negro never made a determined demand for social equality. In withdrawing from the white churches he surrendered an element of social intimacy with the white man which he had experienced under slavery. In our day he has been invited to attend white churches, but in many cases he does not want to accept this invitation. The most exalted of outside interventionists in the social arrangements of the South recently restored to the Negro the suffrage, but he turned around and joined the political party of the white oligarchy.

Much is written by our historians concerning the Negro's discontent with his caste status and concerning the progress he has made in changing this status. It cannot be denied that there is some reality in these assertions, but it is often forgotten that the white man has more often been discontented with the Negro than the Negro with the white man. Those of us who, through the years, have known southern life intimately are familiar with the constant complaints leveled against the exasperating race. The white man has been able to act on his complaints more effectively than the Negro has on his. In recent decades the white man, for example, sharpened the color line and took business and residential opportunities away from the black man.

It is time that historians who explain or defend the South recognize the existence of social hierarchy in their section. They can be sympathetic toward it without being illogical, remembering that arguments advanced for social gradations by Plato are as logical as arguments advanced to the contrary. They should realize that the arguments of Jefferson Davis and James D. B. De Bow in favor of the gradations in slave society had more influence on the nonslaveholding whites than did the arguments advanced by Hinton R. Helper and other enemies of southern social practices. They should know that the color line was created to sustain the most important fact in southern history. Two biologically aggressive races have dwelt together in large numbers for 335 years without the ruling race losing its integrity of blood. Without this fact there would be no South in the social or psychological sense; the region between the Potomac and the Rio Grande would be just a geographical expression.

The historian of the South should accept the class and race distinctions of his region unless he wishes to deplore the region's existence. He should display a tolerant understanding of why in the South the Goddess of Justice has not always been blind, why there have been lynchings and

Jim Crow laws, why the legend of the Cavaliers exists, and why, as William Alexander Percy puts it, "Even today from Virginia to Texas ten thousand crepuscular old maids in ghostly coveys and clusters" seek to trace their ancestors. Our historian should stop trying to prove that the maidens of the Old South did not always have wasp waists and stand on colonnaded porches attended by bandannaed mammies who did not have wasp waists. At least one southern historian, Francis P. Gaines, has retired from the iconoclastic task of trying to prove that the Old South was not what it is supposed to have been. He has become the keeper of the tomb of the knight whom not even our most energetic fact-finder has accused of being unworthy of the company of King Arthur.

A logical consequence of the disparagement of the sectional values is that the leader who tried hardest to break the national unity has fared so badly at the hands of his biographers. They condemn Jefferson Davis as a prolonged conspirator against the Union. But the facts show that as late as 1860 he, as a United States senator, was advocating appropriations for the army he was to fight in less than a year. A proper sympathy for the sectional values would perhaps lead to a condemnation of Davis because he did not become a conspirator against the Union soon enough. Unlike Caesar or Hitler, Davis was not one of the great revolutionists of history; he was too honorable for that. Unlike William L. Yancey and R. Barnwell Rhett, he was slow in understanding that the North was in a revolutionary conspiracy against the Constitution as he interpreted it and could be answered effectively only by counterrevolution. Allen Tate, the poet, is the only biographer who condemns Davis for not understanding that the aim of the plutocratic democracy of the North was to crush his beloved Southland.

Davis should be praised for at last recognizing the forces arrayed against his section and then heroically defending its concept of truth and justice. Despite physical weaknesses, he maintained a proud but ragged nation for four years against the powers of wealth, progress, and patriotism. After defeat he did not repent.

For his failure to repent, historians will not forgive Davis. He did not respond to the new wave of nationalism which came after the Civil War. He was no pragmatist, no evolutionist. Until his death he remained in spirit the slavemaster, the soldier who found greatest virtue in continuing the battle charge after the enemy has inflicted a grievous wound, and remained the scholastic who accepted the Bible and the Constitution just as they are written. He was as optimistic in his devotion to the antique values of the South as was Don Quixote to the antique values of an older land. If the historians of the South were as tolerant of our past as are the European historians of theirs, they would confer on the defeated President of the Confederacy as many honors as have been conferred on the famous Spanish knight.

Friendly southern historians bolster the pride of the section by exaggerating the way in which the South approximated the achievements of the North. Ignoring the Negro third of the population, they emphasize the degree to which the Old South achieved political democracy and universal education. Remembering prejudices against the large landowner, they emphasize the role of the yeoman farmer in Southern agriculture. Ignoring the prejudices of the section against foreigners, they make much of isolated cases of foreigners who found the South congenial. And, in refutation of the assertion that the region has been a Sahara of talent, long lists have been compiled of southerners who played eminent roles in the building of the nation.

The candid observer must admit that, according to the urban standards of the North and of Europe, Frederick Law Olmsted's harsh judgment on the paucity of southern culture has remained sound for most of the hundred years since this nosy New Englander wrote. Perhaps the reason the *Dictionary of American Biography* has articles on only 724 natives of Virginia compared with articles on 1,763 natives of Massachusetts is that southerners have been indifferent to those in their midst who have had latent talents in music, sculpture, painting, and the other arts. Here in the South Carolina of my youth the only art we recognized was English and Northern literature. We read Walter Scott and James Fenimore Cooper; we did not read William Gilmore Simms. We recognized native greatness only in war and in politics.

It is true that in recent years the South has learned to recognize native eminence in literature and in business. But a southern book to be acceptable to southerners must first hit the New York sounding board. Our distinguished businessmen are often dependent on Wall Street to promote and finance the South's industrial expansion. For mechanical inventions, the most creative of American achievements, the South has been utterly dependent upon the North. Its people do not invent or manufacture the machinery which makes possible southern industry. Industrially the section is still as colonial as Asia or South America.

Our historians should explain or justify these supposed deficiencies of the South by showing that its genius is rural, not urban; that the larger the cities grow the more countrified they become because of the rural origin of their newer inhabitants. Our historians should also explain that our townsmen build country-style houses, that they have little or nothing to contribute to the urban amenities, and that they support few good restaurants, theaters, orchestras, or book stores. As in the days of the English traveler George W. Featherstonhaugh, they talk of hogs, horses, and cows when they are not talking about the mechanical contrivances northerners have sold them.

The true southerner should take pride in the fact that his section's fame is based on tobacco, hogs, rice, and cotton, and that its greatest man is the country gentleman with his cult of hospitality, his sense of leisure, his neglect of the passion for trade, his capacity to refurbish old mansions and to build new ones in imitation of the old, and his creative interest in the rehabilitation of antique furniture. In his capacity as a farmer the southern gentleman has been creative from the days of John Rolfe and George Washington down to the day of our professors of agriculture and of our merchant-farmers. Our professors of agriculture perfect new seeds and varieties of animals; our merchant-farmers establish farms with green pastures which serve as models for professional farmers. If the South has had an internal revolution since 1865, it is in a type of endeavor in which the people have adhered most firmly to the traditions of their ancestors. The revolution has been in agriculture.

Southern historians, trapped by the belief that education is a cure-all, have exaggerated the accomplishments of formal schooling. They like to prove that Sir William Berkeley was inaccurate when he said that there were no free schools in seventeenth-century Virginia. They are dazzled that today we have "a triumphant 'progressive' education which progresses even faster than the North." They gloss over the defects of our much-praised educational system. They should remember that our public schools have affronted the American dogma of the universality of education, treating the Negroes differently from other people and at one time prohibiting them from going to school. They should realize that we of the South indulged to a greater degree than other people in "the education that does not educate" in the sense of changing people, presumedly for the better, in the arts of living and in outlook on life.

The historians would be wise to admit the defects of southern education as measured by the proclaimed goals of American public schools; indeed they might be skeptical of these goals. They might admit that Berkeley was not a complete fool when he inveighed against schools and presses. The defender of this seventeenth-century gentleman can find comfort in high scholarly authority of the twentieth century. Arnold J. Toynbee wrote in 1947: "The bread of universal education is no sooner cast upon the water than a shoal of sharks [the presslords] arises from the depths and devours the children's bread under the educator's very eyes." Southern historians should realize that the faith in the rule of the educated common man has brought us no nearer the millennium than were our ancestors in the eighteenth century.

Southern historians agree with Montesquieu that a political structure should "fit the humor and disposition of the people," and yet they judge the educational achievements of a rural people by standards imported from Prussia by way of New England. In New England the Prussian-type school was loaded with antislavery sentiments and with notions of social reform repulsive to a region of Christians not dominated by hopes of earthly perfection. The leveling tendencies of the new schools ran counter to the Old South's conception of hierarchy. Their content was more suited for those who needed guidance for town life than for a people whose chief task was to subdue a wilderness and to establish farms.

Someone should tell that the South's resistance to formal schooling did not grow out of laziness or stupidity. This resistance was a vital part of the region's attempt to survive as a social and cultural entity. The South unconsciously fought against the idea that the school be allowed to iron out provincial differences in order to make the southern states into undifferentiated units of the republic. Southerners have preserved their folkways and ancestral superstitions. Thereby they have avoided the fate of the people of Hawaii, a people who have deliberately escaped their ancestral heritage in order to be Americanized through the public schools. Such a people lack creative originality.

Our chroniclers of the past should quit being ashamed of the cloud of illiteracy which once hung over their province. They should wake up to the fact that the unschooled Uncle Remus was among the wisest southerners. They have stressed to such a degree the benefits of the schools that they have neglected the triumphs of informal training outside the school. This informal education was good because it was useful. Our colonial and frontier ancestors put the arts of subduing the wilderness first; they learned to use the ax and the rifle extremely well. With some justice they regarded formal education as an adornment of the upper classes.

The dark spot on southern civilization of denying formal education to the slaves can be wiped out by an understanding of what was accomplished in the so-called school of the plantation in which the barbarian captive from Africa was Anglicized. This was a type of training more effective than anything the South has experienced since. The slave was so well inoculated with Anglo-American culture that almost all elements of his African background disappeared. The Negro imbibed the rich heritage of European folklore and became so skilled in English handicrafts and in the intricate practices of plantation agriculture that he was perhaps better educated in the industrial arts than those Negroes who have lived since the time of Booker T. Washington.

The acceptance by our historians of the national faith in equality has led them to neglect the constructive role of class distinctions and aristocracy in southern culture. The masses of the South imitate the classes with so much enthusiasm that most of the section's approved practices and attitudes are of upper-class origin. I can think of only two popular social diversions of lower-class origin. They are jazz music and corn whisky. The aristocratic pretensions of all classes are so strong that everybody thinks of himself as a gentleman. Wilbur J. Cash observes that the yeoman farmers of the Old South adopted from the plantation aristocracy "a kindly courtesy, a level-eyed pride, an easy quietness, a barely perceptible flourish of bearing, which for all its obvious angularity and fundamental plainness was one of the finest things the Old South produced." And the Jeeter Lesters, for all their ignorance and barbarism, possessed aristocratic attitudes, hating manual toil and taking on, as Cash says, "a sort of unkempt politeness and ease of port, which rendered them definitely superior to their peers in the rest of the country."

A majority of southerners believes that the nearest approach to heaven this side of the grave is that aristocratic perfection known as the Old South. This was not only the belief of Walter Hines Page's "mummies," but also of such innovators as Daniel A. Tompkins, Ben Tillman, and Tom Watson. One finds it in the writings of such divergent persons as Thomas Nelson Page and William Faulkner. Then it was, so runs the legend of the Old South, that the Virginia Gentleman lived in a feudal splendor that was justified by the belief that he had ancestors from the novels of Walter Scott; that the Mississippi Gentleman's comparable splendors were justified by the belief that he had Virginia ancestors. These beliefs are supplemented by the assertion that the Confederate soldier because he was always brave was also always virtuous. The fact that all classes in the South cherish the aristocratic concept has brought about a unity of spirit which results in a friendly tie between the masses and the classes.

A host of southern historians would prove, through the collection of multitudes of facts, that things were not what they were supposed to have been. Census reports are used to prove that the number of planters who owned a hundred slaves was small; that plantation houses were more often like factories than like Walter Scott's castles; that beautiful maidens were then not more numerous than they are now. Some historians are at pains to prove that the ancestors were not Virginia gentlemen and that the ancestors of the ancestors were not knights. Numerous investigators accuse the colonial Virginians of being ordinary persons. James Branch Cabell, with a vicious glee, befouls the nests of the ancestors of the ancestors by creating a repulsive age of chivalry.

Some southern historians would change a belief which both friend and foe have taught us to think was the essence of the Old South. They tell us that the distinctions between aristocracy and humble folk were not so great as was once supposed; thereby would they take away from the aristocracy many of the distinctions of superior position. They tell us that the poor whites were not so numerous as was once supposed and that there was a substantial middle class which had no reason to feel inferior to the planter aristocracy. On the other hand, others, touched by twentieth-century concepts of human welfare, would let us know that the glory and glamor of the antebellum aristocracy was paid for by the humbling of the masses of both races.

A small shelf of books has been written by southerners proving that all Confederate soldiers were not brave and loyal Christian gentlemen; that in fact many of them were seditionists, draft dodgers, and deserters. To add to the disillusionment, Vann Woodward advances the belief that many of the brave and loyal veterans of the Confederate army did not possess common honesty. In page after page of interesting but disillusioning data, he parades paladins of the Confederacy from John B. Gordon to Basil Duke as a second generation of scalawags who robbed the land they professed to love.

This revision of southern legends is factually correct, based as it is upon much research in manuscripts and other original documents. But it carries with it the danger of equating facts with truth. The facts that can be unearthed by research in as complex a subject as human behavior are so infinite in extent that one set of facts can be unearthed to refute another set of facts. The masters of reasearch, for example, have for a generation or two been digging up data to prove whether or not the gentry of Virginia are descended from King Charles's Cavaliers. The evidence is so varied, and the English and southern methods of computing aristocratic descent so different, that the reader has not yet been able to draw conclusions.

Sometimes southern historians forget that what is often important to southerners is not what actually happened but what is believed to have happened. Southerners want their historians to do them concrete good by revealing or creating ancestors for them. An ironic fact about southern historical writing is that the only practitioners of the craft able to make a living from their efforts are the genealogists. Their unique vice or virtue is that they are able to dig up useful ancestors where there may have been none before. Such discoveries give a person of declining fortunes a satisfaction not unlike the consolations of religion or philosophy. Such discoveries, on the other hand, give persons of energy and ambition something with which to justify their assumptions of social and civic worth.

Disillusioning researches in the records of the South's past have not generally impressed the southern people. This sort of revelation must go unheeded if the South is to survive as a cultural entity.

Donald Davidson says that the key to southern literary greatness is not the literature of protest but "the literature of acceptance." Obedience to this standard, Mr. Davidson believes, is why the southern imaginative literature of our times is appreciated by the critics and the reading public. William Faulkner, Eudora Welty, and Robert Penn Warren write in the most modern manner; at times their stories are sordid. They tell everything good and bad about the South. They only reject what Davidson calls "the false knowledge" of ignoring or deploring aspects of southern life and character. They are not, like so many of our historians, narrow democrats and nationalists who measure the South's past by the values of educated Americans of today.

The standards of factual accuracy demanded of the southern historian are so exacting that he is often frightened out of writing a book because he must face the holy terror of having his factual errors exposed by well-intentioned reviewers. A strange sense of reticence prevents him from telling a tale which may be a revelation of the truth about the teller and his people. Think of the fate of one of our historians if he were to join Faulkner in asserting that our mulattoes were descendants of Yankee soldiers and carpetbaggers. The southern novelist is more concerned with the meaning of events than with the technical accuracy of their recording. He heeds the legends, the undying superstitions and prejudices of the people. His willingness and ability to use these in his tales is where his genius lies.

Southern historians often ignore the poor whites, rationalize them out of existence, or treat them as fit subjects for social-welfare programs. The novelists, on the other hand, portray them without apology or gratuitous sympathy and endow them with pride and humor. William Faulkner gives us a mob of country folk too chivalric to push aside a lady guard in order to lynch a Negro.

Religion as a constructive force in southern life is generally unappreciated by our historians except for what it has done for education and social progress. Christian Fundamentalists are scolded for their capture of the southern mind in the early nineteenth century and for their interference in science and politics in the twentieth century. The great Baptist church is tactfully ignored because, perhaps, it is an example of the union of southern democracy with absolutism too indelicate and lusty for believers in Jeffersonian democracy. On the other hand, the novelists possess an affecting sympathy for the traditional religion. Ellen

Glasgow in *Vein of Iron* and William Faulkner in *Light in August,* for example, demonstrate a tender understanding of southern clergymen who were persecuted by their congregations.

Vann Woodward in *Origins of the New South* complains of the lack of understanding among southern historians of the strain of violence which runs through southern history. If measured at all by our historians, it is in terms of civics textbooks. Violence, on the other hand, is a dominant theme in southern fiction. There murderous gentlemen and outlaws are presented with compassion and explained in terms of grand tragedy.

The historian of the South should join the social novelist who accepts the values of the age and the section about which he writes. He should learn to identify truth with legend and with faith as competently as he has learned to identify truth with facts. By mixing sympathy, understanding, and a bit of kindness with his history, he might attract the people about whom he writes to read his books. And this could be done without sacrificing scholarly integrity.

Not all historians who rise above the level of scholarly compilations are ashamed of the peculiar standards of their section. Some of them write "the literature of accommodation." The southern historian who has won the greatest applause writes of the heroes of the Confederacy without arguing whether or not they were quixotic. The best recognized historian of the Old South pictures plantation life without assuming that is was a grand mistake. Another historian examines the literature on the poor whites without moralizing against them because they were not as thrifty as their social betters. A recent historian of the New South joins William Faulkner in exposing the true tragedy of the South. It was not the defeat at Appomattox but the truckling of both scalawag and Bourbon, both materialist and idealist, to alien values.

Chapter XXI

A Time of Greatness

BELL IRVIN WILEY

THE LATE Douglas Southall Freeman found that one of the most cherished rewards of his research had been the privilege of living for more than a decade in the company of a great gentleman.[1] For some twenty years I have lived with a group of historical characters who were at the opposite end of the social spectrum from Lee.* But association with them has been so pleasant and inspiring that I look back on it with a feeling comparable to Freeman's.

My associates have been the plain Americans of the Civil War period —the Johnny Rebs and Billy Yanks who carried the muskets and their folk at home who labored in fields and factories and ran the households. If my understanding of them is less profound than Freeman's of Lee, the fault lies in me and not in the records. The conflict of the sixties attracted more attention to plain Americans in newspapers and official records than ever before. It stimulated them to keep diaries, and, separated from their families, they took to letter writing—and their letters were not censored. These circumstances gave me an opportunity to know them more intimately than would otherwise have been possible. I have had the privilege of reading some thirty thousand of their letters and more than a thousand of their diaries, and exploring various other sources that contain direct reflections of their life and character. Most of those who became articulate in these ways were soldiers, but the men who marched in the ranks were representative, in human qualities and social habits, of the great mass of plain people from which they came.

In my association with these lowly Americans of the 1860's I have naturally formed some opinions of them and their conduct in the crisis of the war. I cannot attribute to them all the qualities that Freeman

*Presented in Memphis, Tennessee, November 11, 1955.

325

found in Lee. Freeman once stated that in all his research he had failed to discover evidence of the use by Lee of any obscene or profane word or phrase.[2] I cannot say as much for his humble contemporaries. They were people of many faults, though some had more shortcomings than others, and many individuals among them were his equal in purity of mind and loftiness of character.

For the most part they were earthy people, in whose natures the fear of God was rivaled by the attraction of the world, the flesh, and the Devil. Among those who donned the uniform, evil, or at least that which was adjudged evil by Americans of a century ago, flourished more freely than righteousness. Despite the best efforts of chaplains and occasional outbreaks of revivals, profanity, gambling, drinking, and obscenity were notoriously common in both Union and Confederate camps. Wrongdoing was subject to more restraint on the home front, but the conflict of the sixties, like the wars of our own time, brought a general deterioration of morals.

The plain people had little education, and ignorance nurtured prejudice, credulity, and provincialism. Rumors of the most fantastic sort were commonly believed, and the unfamiliar was disparaged for the mere fact of being strange. Yankee soldiers generally found the southern country unattractive, the women ugly, the men depraved, the children filthy, and the general level of culture far below that of their own section. Confederates had little opportunity to gain firsthand impressions of the North and its inhabitants, but perusal of civilian letters that they picked up on the battlefield confirmed their long-held opinions that Yankee women were brazen and uncouth and that northerners generally were far inferior to southerners.

Fighting men of both sides initially were prone to view their opponents as cowards, and this concept, rooted in prejudice, was remarkably strong. As late as 1864 both Rebs and Yanks when conceding gallantry to their opponents often gave the explanation: "Before the battle they had been treated to liberal doses of whiskey and gun-powder."[3]

Prejudice and provincialism were by no means restricted to estimates of opponents. A Reb who in 1861 went from his native Buncombe County, North Carolina, to the environs of Charleston, South Carolina, wrote back home: "Father, I have Saw a rite Smart of the world Sence I left home But I have not Saw any place like Buncomb and henderson yet."[4] And eastern soldiers, whether Yanks or Rebs, looked down their noses at westerners as being culturally inferior and less effective on the battlefield than themselves, while the back-country folk just as vehemently denounced easterners as uppity snobs and "band box" soldiers who were far more impressive on the parade ground than on the firing line.[5]

Unquestionably the ranks of the plain folk included numerous mean and worthless characters. One does not have to delve very deeply into the records to find Civil War versions of Faulkner's Snopeses and Caldwell's Jeeter Lester clan. Schemers, shirkers, cowards, criminals, and traitors abounded among the masses of both North and South, and records of military and civilian tribunals reveal a wide assortment of knaves and villains, including arsonists, murderers, rapists, thieves, plunderers, pimps, and prostitutes. Depravity at its lowest was recorded by the military court that found a Yankee private guilty of "buggery with a mare."[6]

While freely admitting the shortcomings of the plain folk both individually and collectively, I do not wish on this occasion to spell out their deficiencies. Rather it is my desire to point up and dwell on their virtues. For with all their weaknesses they have always been a good people. The terrible conflict of the 1860's made enormous demands on them and put them to severe tests. The manner in which they rose to meet the crisis evidenced strength, even greatness.

One of the engaging qualities of the lowly folk as they revealed themselves in the crisis of war was humor. Their sensitiveness to the ludicrous and the spontaneousness of their mirth gave them escape from their troubles and made the burdens of war more tolerable. Soldiers and their folk at home joked and teased each other in their letters. A Tennessean who playfully rebuked his wife for presenting him with a daughter instead of a son was put in his place with the reply: "I think you give your boys to some one else."[7] Another Reb, after a year's absence from home, wrote his wife: "If I did not write and receive letters from you I believe that I would forgit that I was marrid I don't feel much like a maryed man but I never forgit it sofar as to court enny other lady but if I should you must forgive me as I am so forgitful."[8] Young women sometimes amused themselves by writing sugary missives to soldiers over false signatures, and a mischievous soldier for a considerable period carried on both ends of an amorous correspondence for an illiterate comrade.[9]

Billy Yanks sometimes advertised for correspondents through the personal columns of the newspapers. Some of these notices are obviously the work of mischief makers. The Chattanooga *Gazette* of March 6, 1864, for example, carried this advertisement: "Any young lady not sufficiently homely to frighten a dog out of a butcher shop nor sufficiently beautiful to bewitch the idle shoulder straps about town can get up considerable fun by commencing a correspondence with *Aaron, Chattanooga Post Office.*"[10] The New York *Herald* of March 8, 1863, under the heading "Matrimonial," printed this notice: "Two young gentlemen possessed of large fortunes, but rather green, wish to open correspondence with young ladies of the same circumstances with a view to matrimony—brunettes preferred—but no objection to blondes provided they are perfect past all parallel. Address Harry Longsworth and Charley B. B., Camp Denison, Ohio."[11]

A Vermont Yank who had not heard from a friend in a long time wrote: "Ans[wer] this as soon as you get it and let me know w[h]eather you are alive are [or] not if you are dead I shall like to know it."[12] And an Ohioan who lacked postage because of arrearage of pay wrote on an envelope addressed to his homefolk:

> Postmaster please to pass this through,
> I've nary a cent, but three months due.[13]

In camp, fun-loving propensities were manifested in pranks and horseplay. Green recruits were sent to supply sergeants with instructions to demand their unbrellas, or were honored by election to the high but fictitious position of fifth lieutenant and then put to catching fleas and carrying water. Visitors who came to camp wearing stovepipe headpieces were hailed vociferously with such greetings as "Come out of that hat! I see your legs," or "Look out, that parrot shell you're wearing's going to explode." Wearers of shiny new boots were apt to be told to "Come up outer them boots; ... I know you're in thar; I see your arms sticking out." Anyone who rode through company streets sporting an elegant mustache was almost sure to be hailed with suggestions to "Take them mice out'er your mouth; take em out no use to say they aint thar, see their tails hangin' out"; or, "Come out 'er that bunch of har. I see your ears a workin'."[14]

Civilians and dull-witted comrades were the usual victims of such horseplay. But officers, especially those who held staff positions, or who were incompetent, overbearing, or given to putting on airs, were considered fair game by pranksters. Indeed, soldiers were able when they set their minds to the task to ridicule intolerable superiors into resignation.

The humor of the common soldier was so irrepressible as frequently to manifest itself in battle. At Chickamauga a chaplain who, as the shooting started, exhorted his charges to "Remember, boys, that he who is killed will sup tonight in Paradise," was urged by a Reb to "come along and take supper with us." When the parson refused the invitation and galloped to the rear, a resounding shout went up from the advancing ranks, "The parson isn't hungry, and never eats supper."[15]

In another battle Rebel George Lemmon in his excitement fired his musket too close to comrade Nick Watkins' head, shooting a hole in his hat. Whereupon Nick turned and said: "George Lemmon, I wish you'd look where you're shooting—I'm not a Yankee."[16] Many similar incidents occurred among the men in blue. In 1863 a Pennsylvania private wrote his homefolk, "We laugh at everything. . . . The roughest jokes I ever heard were perpetrated under a heavy fire."[17]

I do not mean to say that humor, rich and robust as it unquestionably was, held complete sway in camp and cottage. For the plain folk have a streak of sadness in their make-up. The melancholy side of their nature is reflected in folk songs and spirituals which lay heavy stress on violence, death, and mother in heaven. The sorrow and tragedy produced by the deadly conflict of the 1860's naturally intensified this mournful bent and gave rise to an unprecedented volume of gloomy expression.

Death and the prospect of death were favorite subjects of letter writers both at home and in the army. A Virginia woman in 1863 informed her cousin that "Sylas Harvel dide Thursday last and Arthur Wood dide Friday and is beried today and the other one was beried yesterday and they is another one as loe as he can bee to bee alive."[18] Soldiers spelled out to their wives the horrors of the battlefield, lingering over such gruesome details as disemboweled comrades clutching at their intestines, brains spattering the battleground, severed limbs flying through the air, and the hideous shrieks of wounded men caught in flames raging through the underbrush. Typical of many descriptions was that of a Yank who wrote his mother from Fredericksburg in December, 1862: "There was a Hospital with[in] thirty yards of us and during the day I saw thirteen buried. The sight was revolting. About the building you could see the hogs . . . eating arms and other portions of the body."[19] Another Yank wrote to his father after Antietam: "I could have walked on the bodes all most from one end [of the field] too the other. . . . We don't mind the sight of dead men no more than if they was dead Hogs."[20]

Soldiers, with complete disregard of the anxiety sure to result, regaled their homefolk with such doleful statements as:

I saw James Hiner the other day and he was well then. But a man may be well here one day and the next be in eternity.[21]

I am not very well at present but I keep about so far . . . you all must not think and greave after me when I am gone to my grave.[22]

I was much surprised to here of the death of Lewis but he has only gone before and we must follow shortly. We are of but few days and full of trouble.[23]

Dear Wife . . . cis [kiss] Mark for me and think of me as little as you can for I will never see no more pleser in this world.[24]

The sad quality also found expression in popular songs of the period. Rollicking tunes such as "Dixie," "Goober Peas," "Gay and Happy Still," and "Pop Goes the Weasel," while rating high in public favor, never attained the popularity of such lugubrious pieces as "Lorena," "Just Before the Battle, Mother," "Weeping Sad and Lonely," "Who Will Care for Mother Now," and "Tenting on the Old Camp Ground."

The inconsistency of jollity and dolefulness flourishing side by side among the plain folk and in the same personalities was more apparent than real. For the lowly people, forced as they were into close association with sorrow, found relief in bringing tragedy out into the open, and writing, talking, and singing about it. By recognizing sadness as an inescapable part of living, they found it easier to endure.

Another impressive quality of the plain folk was ability to give colorful and forceful expression to their thoughts, and this despite the serious deficiencies of most of them in grammar and spelling. Some of their figures of speech were pungent and vivid. One Reb commented that "the Yankees were thicker [th]an lise on a hen and a dam site ornraier," while another reported that his comrades were "pitching around like a blind dog in a meat hous," and a third wrote that it was "raining like poring peas on a rawhide."[25] An Ohioan reported that Rebel dwellings near Fredericksburg looked like "the latter end of original sin and hard times," and another Yank wrote from Chattanooga that he was so hungry he "could eat a rider off his horse and snap at the stirrups."[26] Still another wearer of the blue characterized a recently received letter as "short and sweet just like a rosted maget."[27]

Choice comments were inspired by the boredom and monotony of camp life. "You wanted to know how I like it," wrote an Ohioan to a friend; "i ain't home Sick i don't no What home Sick is but i no the diferens between home and Soldieren."[28] Efforts to recount battle impressions and experiences also gave rise to vivid passages. An Illinois Yank reported after the battle of Jackson, Mississippi, that "the Balls ... Sung Dixey around our years [and] the grape and Canister moed hour Ranks down like grass before the Sithe"; and a New York soldier wrote after the Williamsburg, Virginia, fight that "the air perfectly whistled, shrieked and hummed with the leaden storm."[29] A Texan who was at Chickamauga noted in his journal that "if ten thousand earthquakes had been turned loose in all their power they could not have made so much racket."[30]

One Yank describing his reactions to combat referred to "the wild joy" that thrilled his every fiber as the conflict raged, while another, after his first experience under fire, gave his father the following account: "Went out a skouting yesterday.... We got to one house where there was Five Secessionist and they broke and run and Arch . . . holoed out . . . to shoot the ornery Suns of bitches . . . and They all let go there fire. . . . They may Say what they please but godamit pa It is Fun."[31]

Camp rations inspired some of the most picturesque comments. A Reb complained that the beef issued to him must have been carved from a bull "too old for the conscript law," while a comrade declared that the cows that supplied the meat for his unit were so feeble that "it takes two hands to hold up one beef to shoot it."[32] Yanks also found much fault with their meat ration which they commonly referred to as "salt horse"; but their choicest remarks were directed at the hardtack which comprised their bread ration.[33] "Teeth-dullers" and "sheet iron crackers" were favorite designations for hardtack, and one Yank suggested that it "would make good brest works."[34] A Kansan claimed that he overheard the following camp dialogue:

SERGEANT: Boys, I was eating a piece of hard tack this morning, and I bit on something soft; what do you think it was?
PRIVATE: A worm?
SERGEANT: No, by G-d, it was a ten penny nail.[35]

Innumerable Yanks reported finding worms in their hardtack. One mathematically inclined campaigner counted thirty-two worms in one cracker, while another declared: "All the fresh meat we had came in the hard bread, and I preferring my game cooked, used to toast my biscuits."[36]

Common soldiers of both sides achieved exceptional pungency in denouncing their officers. An Albamian wrote his wife that "Gen. Jones is a very common looking man who rides just like he had a boil on his stern."[37] Another Reb declared that his colonel was "an ignoramus fit for nothing higher than the cultivation of corn."[38] A Floridian stated that his superiors were "not fit to tote guts to a Bear."[39]

Yanks registered comments even more caustic. A Massachusetts soldier who seems to have been a prototype of Bill Mauldin wrote: "The officers consider themselves as made of a different material from the low fellows in the ranks. . . . They get all the glory and most of the pay and don't earn ten cents apiece on the average the drunken rascals."[40] Private George Gray Hunter of Pennsylvania stated: "If there is one thing that I hate more than anothe[r] it is the Sight of a shoulder Strap, For I am well convinced in My own Mind that had it not been for officers this war would have Ended long ago."[41] But the peak of denunciatory expressiveness on either side was attained by the Yank who wrote: "I wish to God one half of our officers were knocked in the head by slinging them Against A part of those still Left."[42]

A great deal of esthetic sensitiveness was to be found among the humble folk of North and South. Women frequently wrote their loved ones in the army about the abundant flowering of their gardens, the rich coloring of the forests in autumn, and the resplendence of the snow-clad hills. Yanks and Rebs wrote back of clear streams tumbling down from lofty mountains, of wild flowers blooming along the route of march, and of the plaintive singing of the whippoorwill at dusk. "There is a sort of companionship in the stars when one is alone," wrote a Wisconsin soldier to his sister after a night of sentry duty in Kentucky.[43] And a Georgian serving in Virginia wrote his wife:

Here I had a great feast, something that was beautiful. One day we stopped at four o'clock in the evening ... in full view of the Blue [Ridge] mountain and after I got through with my work I took my little Bible and got off in a lonely place ... [and] had a good time. ... You could see the hills commence like potato hills and the farther they went the larger they got, until they would rise up all most to the heavens. Thus it was as far as you could see in the west and from north and south. I was so much delighted with the scene that I forgot the toil and trouble of war and enjoyed myself very well until the sun was about to bid adieu to earth when it was just throwing its last glittering rays on the huge mountains behind which it had to go.[44]

With comparable appreciativeness a Mississippian wrote to his wife of beauties observed in Florida:

I am here today Sitting on this butiful Bay Dischargeing my Duty as a Soldier ... while all Nature Standes out before me as it Ware, in his glory and Majesty and the Spring birdes flutter and singe in the groves of Butiful Live Oaks that Line the Beach of this Butiful bay whoes waters Lye Spread out before me as Smooth as a mirror with not a Solatary Riple on its Braud Busom Save the Floteing Ducks and geese that are seen Skiming its Smooth Surfice and now and then a huge Porpus will pop up its head and Bellow and Sink down again into its native element.[45]

This Mississippian was a rustic whose hand was far more accustomed to the plow than to the pen and whose spelling was so poor that his letters were barely decipherable. Yet his soul was attuned to beauty. And countless others like him were to be found among the lowly inhabitants of North and South.

Another trait often demonstrated by the plain people was generosity. Yanks and Rebs who received boxes of food from home nearly always shared the contents freely with their messmates. Strong and healthy men voluntarily performed guard duty and other camp chores for weak or ailing comrades and nursed them during periods of serious illness. Unmarried soldiers sometimes gave up long and eagerly anticipated furloughs so that comrades whose families were in distress might have leave to go to their assistance. Among lowly civilians generosity manifested itself in good neighborliness and hospitality. Gristmill owners frequently ground corn without charge for needy wives of soldiers. Families incapacitaed by sickness or other misfortune often had their fields plowed, their meals prepared, and their chores performed by kind-hearted acquaintances. Travelers in distress, especially those who wore the uniform, usually received welcome and help when they knocked at the doors of humble cabins. "I found the hill people as a general thing very hospitable [though] a great many of them are in . . . a deplorable state of destitution," wrote a Confederate serving in Mississippi early in 1864;[46] and a Texas Reb who rode through Arkansas about the same time stated: "The country through which we have traveled the past two days, is a poor 'piney-woods' country; but is blessed with as warm hearted inhabitants, as ever the sun shone upon."[47] Such comments were not at all unusual.

The plain folk have ever been a sentimental people, and at no time in the history of this nation has this quality been more amply manifested and richly expressed than during the Civil War. Among the unmarried the war caused an increased interest in courtship and a loosening, though sometimes so slight as hardly to be perceptible, of the strict conventions that governed relations between the sexes. Since a large proportion of marriageable males were in uniform, much of the romancing had to be done by correspondence.

Owing to excessive timidity of many of the young folk and an inclination on the part of their parents to regard any exchange of letters as a portent of serious involvement, romance by mail often moved at a snail's pace. In other instances, in which skillful maneuvering by the feminine correspondent frequently is apparent, love came to full flower with breath-taking speed. In November, 1862, Private Charles Cook of Indiana added a friendly greeting to a tentmate's letter to a girl back home. The postscript brought a quick reply, and before six months had passed Cook wrote his Hoosier sweetheart, "Maggie you are mine and I am yours and may the attachment that has sprung up in each of our hearts . . . be the germ that shall bud on earth and blossom in heaven." By the autumn of 1864 he was pouring out his affection thus: "In the springtime we will plant flowers & they will spring up in the pathway and shed their fragrance around our happy home the tiny humming bird will visit us and feast on the bouquet that Jupiter sips. our paths shall be pleasantness & the end thereof will be peace."[48]

A similar case was that of Sergeant Christian Kuhl of Lee's army and a young widow of Virginia. In the spring of 1864 while home on furlough Kuhl got a glimpse of the widow at church, ascertained her name, and after returning to camp wrote her a letter. She must have responded with enthusiasm, for in less than five months their relationship had reached such a stage that he was able to write: "You need not fear, for I truely love you. And I respect you as a kind-hearted, tender, affectionate, pious, civil, virtuous and Lovely Dove."[49]

Blue and Gray Galahads often resorted to poetry to convey their gentler sentiments. The most frequently used verses were trite rhymes such as

> When this you see remember me,
> Though many miles apart we be.[50]

> My pen is poor my ink is pale
> My love for you shall never fail.[51]

But many correspondents composed their own verses and some of these, despite crudities of form, reveal a genuine sense of poetry.

Sentimentality of the plain folk received some of its richest expression in the letters of soldiers to their wives. As a general rule Rebs used endearing and affectionate phrases much more freely than did Yanks, though letters of the men in blue contain many tender passages. An illustration of the romantic effervescence of southerners is afforded by the following message of an Alabama sergeant to his wife:

The winds are souing sweatly against my little cabin tonight, Carrie, like messengers from a far off spirit land! I hope they are sweetly fanning your brow as it reposes in health upon your pillow. May it bear some sweet message from me to thee! May it kiss thy cheek and dry the tear if perchance sorrow should have planted one there! . . . Sweet dreams to you . . . and heaven's protecting hand guard you. Now I'll to my bunk to court some sweet vision in the form of wife till it shall please Morpheus to take me to his fond embrace and drown my memories till the dawn of another day.[52]

This soldier, like many others North and South, used the medium of poetry in writing to his wife. Occasionally wives would attempt a rhyming response, but the cares of home usually bore so heavily on lowly women as to give little opportunity for poetic expression.

A young Alabama Reb in 1863 began a letter to his wife with these lines:

> Come list my own Dear Mary
> While I sing life's cares away
> And warble with love's early notes
> Bright dreams of life's young day
> When heart to heart we plighted love
> Affection's tender vow
> I loved thee then my Mary Dear
> But love thee better now.[53]

A Georgia Reb, William R. Stilwell, wrote many poems to his wife. One of these, "I Watch for Thee," written at Fredericksburg in May, 1863, opened with this stanza:

> I watch for thee when parting day
> Sheds on the earth a lingering ray
> When the blushes on the rose
> A richer tint of crimson throws
> And every flower[l]et's leaves are curled
> Like beauty shrinking from the world
> When silence reigns o'er lawn or lea
> Then dearest love I watch for thee.[54]

These poetic expressions of soldier husbands are indicative of another trait strikingly apparent among the plain people of Civil War times; namely, devotion to home and family. Long absence from loved ones produced more anguish than any other aspect of the conflict. And homesickness was undoubtedly responsible for many of the hospital cases whose stubbornness and strange characteristics baffled the surgeons. Indeed, it seems hardly an exaggeration to state that many Yanks and Rebs literally died of homesickness.

Soldiers sought to create as much of a home atmosphere as camp life would permit. In winter, they built cabins, equipped them with crude bunks and chairs, hung pictures on the walls, and set up housekeeping. In spring they sometimes planted and tended gardens until forced by resumption of active campaigning to abandon them. Cats, dogs, and other stray animals were adopted, and these were sometimes carried along on the march at considerable inconvenience. American males, in spite of their protests to the contrary, have always been strongly domestic animals.

Love of home manifested itself in many ways. Soldiers repeatedly asked wives and parents to give them full details about home affairs. They wanted to know what crops had been planted, what fruits were ripening, what flowers were blooming, how the horses, cows, dogs, cats, and other domestic animals were faring, and what new pets had been born. They were insatiably curious about the doings of all members of the family circle—what they talked about, how they were amusing themselves, what trips they made, and what they ate, drank, and wore.

Fathers displayed an eagerness that was sometimes pathetic to hear about the doings of their children. Standard inquiries of those who had left infants at home were: "What new tricks has the baby learned?" "Does it look any more like its pappy than it did?" "Have you weaned it yet?" "Does it still suck its thumb?"

Soldier parents were terrified by the thought that their children might forget them, and they often urged their wives to keep alive the memory of the father in young sons and daughters. Some of the tenderest letters were those addressed by Rebs and Yanks to their children. Typical of many was the following note of a Virginia soldier to his son:

I hope you have been a good little boy since I have been from home and when I get back I hope I may find you still a good boy. I hope my son you are trying to learn your books. Tell your Sis Susa I say she must heare your lessons for you. I want you to try and be a good & smart boy. I hope my son you are good to your ma and little sister. I hope my child it will not be very long before I can come home and stay with you. May the Lord bless you my son.[55]

"Be good, mind your mother, don't neglect your books"—this advice reflected the most earnest longings of lowly fathers North and South for their children, regardless of how short they themselves might fall of the standards that they stipulated. Next to godliness—if, indeed, it was next —they desired most that their offspring should have the rudiments of education. And like-minded wives, struggling mightily with raggedness and starvation, made tremendous sacrifices that their children might have better opportunities than themselves; that they might not grow up in ignorance.

Some soldiers were able to assuage their longing for home and family by occasional furloughs, but that Yank or Reb was exceptional who was able to visit his loved ones more than two or three times during his service. For the most part his home yearnings had to be satisfied by writing, dreaming, and pining. A boy soldier from Wisconsin, while stationed at Columbus, Kentucky, wrote his father: "I never look at the [Mississippi] river but I think of home. I go down to the shore nearly every day to wash my feet. When I dip my hand in the water I think that it comes from Wisconsin and I wonder what part of it came from Beef River. . . . Last night . . . I lay in my tent with the lappel thrown back so I could see the North Star and the dipper. Both of them are nearer the horizon than in Wisconsin. But they brought to me in their silence and sameness something of the nearness of home."[56]

Soldier husbands carved rings, beads, and lockets from bones, wood, and other materials obtainable in camp and sent them with affectionate messages to their wives. And the women in turn, sometimes by working late at night, and nearly always at great inconvenience, wove and spun clothing and cooked delicacies of all sorts, packed them in boxes, and sent them great distances to their beloved soldier boys.

The delivery of letters was often haphazard and uncertain, especially in the Confederacy. Inability to communicate with loved ones led to great unhappiness. A Reb who had been out of touch with his wife for several weeks early in 1863 wrote: "I am almost down with histericks to hear from home."[57]

Lack of contact with their loved ones, while not often productive of hysteria, did drive many men to practices that they would not have engaged in at home. The enormous prevalency in camp of gambling, drinking, and similar evils was attributable in large measure to an effort of miserable husbands, sons, and fathers to escape their consuming loneliness.

Another trait often demonstrated by the common folk in the crisis of the Civil War was pride. The greatest fear of the soldier as he faced the ordeal of battle was not that he might be killed or wounded—though concern for his safety was deep and real—but that by showing the white feather he might disgrace himself before his comrades and bring shame on himself and his loved ones. "I did not know whether I had pluck enough to go through [it]," wrote an Iowa Yank to his brother shortly after his baptism of fire at Fort Donelson, "but now I have no fear but I can do my duty, although I know the danger is great."[58] A similar sentiment was registered by a Georgian who wrote his wife after his first fight, "it was a pretty severe anniciation ... but thank god I had nerve to stand it."[59]

On the day after the first battle of Bull Run a Federal soldier wrote proudly to his father: "We got the worst of it but ... I didn't run."[60] And following the terrible fight at Franklin, Tennessee, in 1864 a Rebel informed his brother: "One of Old Abe's boys pluged me in the right foot making a severe wound, [but] I am proud to say that there was no one between me and the Yankees when I was wounded."[61]

When deprivation, sickness, and war-weariness caused spirits to sag, pride in self and family kept soldiers at their posts. Private John Cotton of Alabama wrote his wife in May, 1863: "I want to come home as bad as any body can ... but I shant run away ... I don't want it throwed up to my children after I am dead and gone that I was a deserter ... I don't want to do anything if I no it will leave a stain on my posterity hereafter."[62] And despite enormous hardship and anxiety both of himself and his family, he remained faithful to his cause until the end.

A surgeon of the Army of Tennessee in 1864 related an instance of the power of family pride and a commander's recognition of its influence. "Five brothers all in one company had made good soldiers," he stated, "& one of them deserted, was caught, court-martialed, & sentenced to be shot. The other four brothers went to Gen'l Johnston & begged for his life & promised that he would make a good soldier & never desert any more, & Johnston pardoned him."[63]

The folk at home often manifested a deep concern for the family's reputation. A Mississippian who went on furlough late in the war informed a companion after returning to camp: "Pa [some]time ... is out of heart, but he does not believe in desertion atall. He told me that he did not want none of his boys to desert and ly out in the woods ... [and]

that he had rather for us to stay to our posts and die than for us to run away." The soldier added: "I had rather die than to run away myself."[64]

Much has been made of the fact that soldiers were prompted to desert by letters from relatives urging them to come home. But equally impressive is the fact that countless Rebs and Yanks were urged by their homefolk to remain faithful to their soldierly commitments and keep the family name untarnished. A North Carolina Reb who in June, 1863, took an unauthorized furlough gave the following account of his reception at home: "My old grey headed Farther met me at the gate with Joy. . . . After passing the usial compliments he asked me if I was on furlough. I told him I was not; the old man broke in tears and told me I could not stay with him that I must go and join my Regt . . . [and that if I did not] he certainly would [have me arrested]." The son wrote Governor Vance admitting his wrong and asked for a pass to return to his command.[65]

Yet another quality conspicuously demonstrated by the plain folk during the Civil War was an acute sense of duty. The trait was especially notable among the men in uniform. The words "honor" and "duty" appear with impressive frequency in their correspondence. The duty to which Rebs and Yanks generally seemed to be most sensitive was that involving their associates in arms. With few exceptions they considered themselves honor bound to perform their allotment of camp chores, to share equally the inconveniences and deprivations of army life, and to stand firmly by their fellows in the hour of peril.

The sense of obligation to comrades in arms found frequent and forceful expression in home letters. In 1863 a Mississippi private wrote his wife: "I have never had a mark for any neglect of duty Since I have been in the Service—and I don't intend that I ever Shall if it can be avoided." And he lived up to his pledge until honorably released by a Federal bullet at Franklin.[66] In May, 1864, one of Lee's soldiers wrote his mother: "I have been quite sick with fever for the last 4 or 5 days. They wanted me to go to Richmond but I am determined to see this fight out if it costs me my life."[67] A Georgia Reb wrote a friend shortly after Chancellorsville: "I was very near not going into the fight; I had been sick so long; but when I got to thinking about it, I could not stay behind. . . . If it had killed me, I do not think I could have kept out of the fight."[68] A similar sentiment was registered by an ailing Yank who, in response to his sister's inquiry if he had applied for a discharge, wrote: "I have not, and never shall. I would feel ashamed if I should succeed even in getting it . . . and I would love to join my Reg't soon.

You don't know how sorry I feel I am not there now, as they no doubt will again be thrown into the fight with their decimated ranks, and share the *glory* with them. I really feel ashamed at my situation." [69]

Duty to cause and country, while never as frequently expressed as obligation to companions in arms, was deeply felt by many soldiers of both sides. Patriotic duty as most Rebs seemed to interpret it meant defending their section and their people against invaders who denied them the time-honored right of self-determination and whose intent was to destroy the South's cherished way of life. Many of them saw a parallel between the struggle that they were waging and that conducted by their Revolutionary forefathers, and when hardship weighed heavily on them, they derived much comfort from recalling the triumph over similar sufferings of Washington's army at Valley Forge. Shortly after the costly defeats at Gettysburg and Vicksburg, Sergeant John W. Hagan of Georgia wrote his wife: "I & every Southern Soldier should be like the rebbil blume which plumed more & shinned briter the more it was trampled on & I beleave ... we will have to fight like Washington did, but I hope our people will never be reduced to destress & poverty as the people of that day was, but if nothing elce will give us our liberties I am willing for the time to come." [70] This humble man fought on in the face of increasing adversity, and when his lieutenant played the coward in the early stages of the Georgia campaign, Sergeant Hagan took command of his company and led it heroically through fight after fight until he was captured in the battle of Atlanta. [71]

At the same time Hagan was fighting for his country he was in a very real sense fighting for the protection of his fields and fireside. Because the South was the invaded land, he and most other wearers of the gray probably were more keenly aware of their duty to home than to country, though the two loyalties were often indistinguishable.

Billy Yank's patriotism was also a compound of loyalties to home and country. The dual attachment was forcefully expressed by Sergeant Amory Allen in a letter to his wife. "I would give anything in my possession to be with you," he wrote from Virginia in the dark period following Fredericksburg, "but I am in the service of my country and ... will do nothing that will disgrace you or my Children or my people state or government and if I should live I expect to serve my time out and come home manly and with honor to myself and country ... and I shall never be ashamed or afeared to see or be seen by any body." [72]

Northern homes, with very few exceptions, were never threatened by invasion. Hence the duty uppermost in the minds of Billy Yanks was that which they owed to their country, and it was for the preservation of the Union that the overwhelming majority of them fought. Their letters are filled with testimonials of devotion to what many of them called the best government on earth.

On September 16, 1861, Samuel Croft of Pennsylvania, after a long march over difficult country, wrote his sister: "I did not come for money and good living, my heart beats high, and I am proud of being a soldier, when I look along the line of glistning bayonets with the glorious Stars and Stripes floating over them . . . knowing that the bayonets are in loyal hands that will plunge them deep in the hearts of those who have disgraced . . . that flag which has protected them and us, their freedom and ours, I say again I am proud and sanguine of success."[73] Croft's patriotism was sorely tried by the mismanagement and reverses that bedeviled the Army of the Potomac for the next two years, but he served his country faithfully until he was shot down at Gettysburg.[74]

A second witness is Sergeant Edmund English of New Jersey, the son of an Irish immigrant who on January 8, 1862, wrote his mother: "Though humble my position is—gold could not buy me out of the Army until this Rebellion is subdued. A man who would not fight for his Country is a scoundral!"[75] Sergeant English also experienced periods of discouragement, but his shining patriotism always restored his spirit. In April, 1863, he wrote: "The blind acts of unqualified generals and Statesmen have had no lasting impression on the motives which first prompted me to take up arms or chilled my patriotism in the least. I cannot get tired of soldiering while the war lasts. . . . As long as God spares my health and strength to wield a weapon in Freedom's defense, I will do it."[76] His life and health were spared, and when his three-year term of service expired in 1864 he re-enlisted and fought on to the end of the war.[77]

A third witness is Private Ira Butterfield of Wisconsin who on April 23, 1863, wrote his mother: "I dont want a discharge by a long shot for if I were at home I could not take any comfort as long as there was men in the field doing Battle for me and my priveleges when I went in I goes the whole hog and never take hold of the plow and look back."[78]

The sense of duty manifested by these men and countless others who wore the blue sustained the Union through the first years of bungling, gloom, and disaster. And when the expiration of the original terms of enlistment approached early in 1864, and the nation stood in grave danger because of the threatened loss of their hardiness and experience, they came forward by company, regiment, and brigade to pledge their continued service. By thus freely offering themselves for what they knew would be another season of bloody sacrifice, they gave the nation one of its most glorious moments. To them and their kind the Union will ever owe an overwhelming debt of gratitude.

Another quality demonstrated by the plain people during the terrible war of the sixties was an enormous capacity for hardship. Because of their limited resources, southerners were required to endure far more of suffering than were northerners. But many northerners experienced great misery, and when put to the test they bore their lot with no less fortitude than Confederates.

Soldiers of both sides had their starvation times, though Rebs were far more intimately acquainted with hunger than Yanks. Many men in gray went for days without any food save a few grains of corn picked up from the places where the horses fed and parched over the glowing embers of their campfires. Yanks on the Knoxville campaign of late 1863 and Rebs at Nashville marched for miles over rocky, ice-coated roads in bare feet, leaving traces of blood behind them. Raggedness was the rule among men in gray after 1863. But few of them complained long or seriously of their plight, and some even made jokes of it. A Reb wrote his homefolk from near Atlanta in June, 1864: "In this army one hole in the seat of the breeches indicates a captain, two holes a lieutenant and the seat of the pants all out indicates that the individual is a private."[79]

The sick and wounded of both armies experienced enormous hardship, and in Confederate hospitals inadequate facilities, shortage of food, and dearth of medicine led to unspeakable agonies. Literally thousands of Rebs were subjected to the ordeal of having limbs sawed off without benefit of anesthesia. But the sick and wounded bore their miseries and tortures with remarkable courage and patience. An Alabama nurse wrote her superior from a Virginia hospital in 1861: "The fear that my *womanly* nerves would give way within the hearing of the 'groans of the wounded' almost made me shrink from the position I occupy, but while I grow sick at the sight of the amputated limbs and ghastly wounds, I must testify that a groan has rarely reached my ears and the heroism of our men has developed itself more thoroughly and beautifully in enduring bodily suffering . . . and want of home comforts that of necessity attaches to a war hospital."[80]

Great as was the hardship of Rebs and Yanks, their lot was in many ways better than that of their homefolk. Soldiers could get about, see new country, and behold interesting sights. They were removed from family responsibilities. And they had always the companionship of fellows to whom they were bound by common purpose, common suffering, and long association, and with whom they could sing, joke, play, and commiserate. But wives of common soldiers often were left on isolated farms, encumbered by small children, without adult help, and with limited funds. Such women lived lonely, anxious, and weary lives.

Owing to the South's greater poverty, the absorption of a greater proportion of its manpower in the armed services, the pitiful inadequacy of its relief agencies, and the strangling effects of the blockade, the plight of Confederate women was much worse than that of northern women. The overwhelming majority of soldier wives in the South were rural, nonslaveholding women. The burdens that these lowly women were called on to bear in the crisis of war were so great as to be almost beyond the conception of present-day Americans. Most of them had children, the number usually corresponding roughly to the years that had elapsed since their marriage. Since they received little money from their spouses, whose meager army pay was usually several months in arrears, they had to find the means for feeding and clothing themselves and their dependents. Some of them were able to obtain the assistance of relatives or friends in performing the heavier farm chores, but many plowed the fields, harvested the crops, cut and hauled the firewood, and ran their households. Their labors were greatly increased by the necessity of making at home soap, candles, leather, cloth, dye, and various other essentials that virtually disappeared from the markets by the end of the war's second year.[81]

The manifold responsibilities of home and farm kept lowly wives at work far into the night. Periodically their burdens were multiplied by one or more of their children becoming sick. Professional medical service was not to be had in many communities, and even where available it could do little to combat the ravages of such diseases as diphtheria, pneumonia, and typhoid, all of which took a heavy toll of lives from Confederate homes. Many poor women, whose husbands even in the direst emergencies frequently were unable to obtain furloughs, had to endure alone the agonizing suspense of the death vigil and the heartrending task of burying a beloved child. And for some the sad experience was more than once repeated.

One of the greatest burdens that the women had to bear was anxiety for their soldier husbands, for they were keenly aware that disease and enemy bullets made army life one of constant peril. This worry was common to all classes, but poor women, with numerous children and with no near relatives able to provide substantial assistance, must have viewed widowhood with greater dread than those belonging to more privileged groups.

As a general rule the lowly women seem to have borne up well under the heavy load of hardship. Remarkably few of them seem to have been broken by their cares; and many of them found the time and had the spiritual and physical stamina to keep up a flow of hopeful correspondence with their husbands. One of these stalwart characters, a Virginia woman who by resourcefulness and toil was able to sustain several children, wrote her soldier husband on November 20, 1864: "donte be uneasy about us. We will try and take care of [our]selves the best we can. I donte mind what I have to do [just] so you can get back safe."[82]

William W. Heartsill, a Texas soldier who traveled extensively in the Confederacy and who seems to have found the plain folk considerably more hospitable than the planters, gave the following description of an Arkansas woman in whose house he and three comrades spent a night early in November, 1864: "Here we find really a NOBLE WOMAN, she has unaided, raised a crop of WHEAT, CORN, RYE and POTATOES. Ploughed, hoed, and gathered with her own hands, hauled her own firewood. . . . her husband is in the army, and she keeps him clothed by her own industry, and supports three or four children."[83]

Heartsill added that such women were "very scarce," but they were more numerous than he thought. A North Carolinian wrote Governor Vance in May, 1863, that women of his section were "heroically plowing, planting and hoeing while their babes ly on blankets or old coats in the corn rows."[84] Similar incidents might have been reported from other southern areas and from some of the corn and wheat districts of the Middle West.

Heroines of Dixie is the title of a recent book made up of the diaries, letters, and memoirs of upper- and middle-class Confederate women.[85] But with all due credit to them, these were not the real heroines of the Lost Cause. The real heroines of both South and North were the poor women, the wives, mothers, and sisters of the plain soldiers, who with limited means, against odds that seemed insurmountable, sustained themselves and their dependents while their menfolk in blue and gray struggled on distant battlefields. Such women did not have the time or inclination to keep diaries, and the hard-marching, light-traveling husbands who received their letters usually were not able to preserve them.

Another quality impressively demonstrated by the plain people through their representatives in the armies was the ability to face death unflinchingly and to die gallantly. The Civil War required more raw courage than most conflicts of recent times. For in that war men marched to battle in massed formation with a minimum of protection from supporting arms. Until the latter part of the conflict they disdained to dig trenches and throw up hasty fortifications. Fighting was open, and closing with the enemy was more than a colorful phrase. Contests were decided by desperate charges in which muskets were fired at such close range as to burn the faces of contestants, and the climax was frequently a savage tussle in which men pitched into each other with bayonets, clubbed muskets, rocks, and fists. An Iowa soldier who took part in the fight at Allatoona Pass in October, 1864, wrote: "When the battle was over one of our boys was found dead facing the enemy who had killed him. Both of them lay with their faces nearly touching ... with their bayonets run through each other."[86] And this incident was by no means unique.

The desperateness and the deadliness of Civil War combat is attested by the casualty rates. At Balaklava the Light Brigade, whose charge was immortalized by Tennyson, suffered a loss in killed and wounded of 36.7 per cent.[87] But at Gettysburg the First Minnesota Regiment sustained a loss of 85.5 per cent, nearly all of which came in an assault of the second day.[88] This was the heaviest loss of any regiment in any Civil War engagement, but the First Texas had 82.3 per cent of its officers and men killed or wounded at Antietam, and the total number of regiments on both sides suffering losses of more than 50 per cent in a single battle ran to well over one hundred.[89]

Combat as Johnny Rebs and Billy Yanks knew it was unquestionably a terrible thing. Some were not able to stand up under the ordeal, but the overwhelming majority met the test courageously whenever it came. Their gallantry was so impressive in some engagements as to inspire cheers of their opponents. History has recorded no greater displays of heroism than the Confederate assaults at Malvern Hill, Corinth, Gettysburg, and Franklin and the Federal attacks at Fredericksburg, Kennesaw Mountain, Vicksburg, and second Cold Harbor. In this last fight, men of Hancock's Second Corps, when informed of the order to charge a seemingly impregnable Confederate position, wrote their names on slips of paper which they pinned to their uniforms so that their homefolk might be promptly informed of their fate. About twenty minutes after the assault was launched three thousand soldiers of this battle-scarred organization lay dead or wounded on the field.[90]

In the hard-fought contests of the Civil War innumerable plain Americans who ordinarily would have lived uneventfully and obscurely, without ever knowing the stuff of which they were made, attained the heights of heroism. Official reports of unit commanders which record the details of their gallantry tell of humble soldiers on both sides volunteering to perform perilous tasks, shrieking defiance at their foes, denouncing and even striking officers who played the coward, vying with comrades for the privilege of carrying the colors, taking over command when officers were all disabled, and refusing to leave the field when seriously wounded.[91]

Two examples must suffice to illustrate the gallantry displayed by some of these noble men. Rebel Private Mattix, wounded so severely in the left arm at Murfreesboro that he could not wield his musket, went to his regimental commander and said: "Colonel, I am too badly wounded to use my gun but can carry the flag, may I do it?" Private Mattix knew that carrying the colors was the most dangerous of all combat assignments. He also knew that three color bearers of his regiment had already been shot down in that furious battle. But when the colonel nodded assent, Mattix seized the flag staff with his good arm, stepped in front of the regiment, and kept the colors flying through the remainder of the battle.[92]

Near the close of the fight at Hanover Court House, May 27, 1862, a wounded Yank called out feebly to a regimental commander who was passing by. The officer turned around and stooped low over the prostrate soldier thinking that he wanted to send a farewell message to some loved one. But what the wounded man whispered instead was the inquiry: "Colonel, is the day ours?" "Yes," replied the officer. "Then," responded the soldier, "I am willing to die." And he did die and was buried on the field where he gave his life.[93] This common soldier may never have heard of the Plains of Abraham and the heroic statements made there by the dying Montcalm and Wolfe. But his words were as glorious as theirs, and his valorous death deserves no less than theirs to be immortalized on the pages of history.

The greatness of this heroic Yank, of Rebel Private Mattix, and of their comrades who comprised the rank and file of the Union and Confederate armies was recognized and acclaimed by contemporaries. Joseph C. Stiles, a distinguished minister who accompanied Lee's army on the Antietam campaign, wrote afterward to his daughter: "I could tell you a thousand thrilling incidents indicative of the glorious courage of our [common] soldiers." And he quoted a Federal prisoner as remarking: *"A Confederate soldier! I believe the fellow would storm hell with a pen-knife."*[94] After the battle of Chickamauga a Confederate brigade commander, William B. Bate, reported: "The private soldier . . . [vied] with the officer in deeds of high daring and distinguished courage. While the 'River of Death' shall float its sluggish current to the beautiful Tennessee, and the night wind chant its solemn dirges over their soldier graves, their names, enshrined in the hearts of their countrymen, will be held in grateful remembrance."[95]

In his official report of the Murfreesboro campaign General W. S.

Rosecrans, after noting the splendid conduct of officers, stated: "But, above all, the sturdy rank and file showed invincible fighting courage and stamina, worthy of a great and free nation."[96] A few days after Rosecrans made his report Braxton Bragg, the commander who had opposed him at Murfreesboro, wrote the Confederate adjutant general:

In the absence of the instruction and discipline of old armies . . . we have had in a great measure to trust to the individuality and self-reliance of the private soldier. Without the incentive or the motive which controls the officer, who hopes to live in history; without the hope of reward, and actuated only by a sense of duty and of patriotism, he has, in this great contest, justly judged that the cause was his own, and gone into it with a determination to conquer or die. . . . No encomium is too high, no honor too great for such a soldiery. However much of credit and glory may be given . . . the leaders in our struggle, history will yet award the main honor where it is due—to the private soldier, who . . . has encountered all the hardships and suffered all the privations.[97]

Bragg's prediction that history would award principal honor to the private soldiers has not yet been borne out. The generals and political leaders continue to dominate writings about the Civil War. But Bragg was right in his appraisal of the character of the Confederate private. And what he said about Johnny Reb's individuality, self-reliance, and dependability was equally applicable to Billy Yank.

The Civil War was in large degree a soldier's war. In that struggle the determination, self-sufficiency, and endurance of the individual in the ranks were of utmost importance. Officer casualties were heavy, and in the hurly-burly of combat those who survived often were able to exercise little control over their units. In the crucial, climactic stages of battle the common soldiers were to a large extent on their own, and it was often their courage and tenacity, individual and collective, that ultimately decided the contest.

A considerable portion of the plain folk of Civil War times were colored folk. Some 200,000 Negroes served as soldiers in the Union army, and Federal authorities employed an equal number as military laborers. Confederates used many Negroes as army menials and as workers in mines and factories. But the overwhelming majority of blacks were slaves on southern farms and plantations.

Owing to the subordination and inarticulateness of most of them, the role of the colored folk during the war is much harder to appraise than that of the whites. The historian has to try to determine what they thought and did largely through the comments of whites, who generally were far less familiar than they considered themselves to be with the attitudes and activities of the Negroes.

The war of the sixties was in some respects a more critical time for

Negroes than for whites. With their freedom and future position at stake, the slaves had to walk a tight rope while the whites engaged in desperate conflict. Nearly all of the blacks seem to have had a deep yearning for freedom, but so great was the advantage of the whites in every respect that most of the Negroes continued in the ways of bondage until the invading forces brought them deliverance, though some at great peril attempted to free themselves.

The blacks who entered the Union army experienced much hardship and discouragement. White soldiers often abused and insulted them. The government gave them less pay than the white soldiers until near the end of the war and required of them a disproportionate amount of labor and garrison service. Those few who had the opportunity to participate in battle under reasonably propitious circumstances seem to have given a creditable account of themselves, and some displayed great gallantry. In general the conduct of the colored folk during the war was such as to strengthen among them and their white friends the confidence that, given a fair opportunity, they would develop into a responsible and patriotic citizenry.[98]

In pointing up the sturdiness and patriotism of the plain people in the crisis of the Civil War, I do not overlook or play down their shortcomings. Thousands of able-bodied men from the lower classes avoided induction into military service by going west or taking to the swamps and mountains. Thousands of others deserted from the armies, and many of those who left the service protected and sustained themselves by preying on defenseless neighbors. Among both soldiers and civilians were many who whined and grumbled at the slightest hardship and whose demeanor in general was wholly unadmirable.

Even so, the conduct of the plain folk during the crisis of war seems to have been better than that of the more privileged classes. The lowly people bore their hardships with less complaint. They manifested less of selfishness and greed. They indulged less frequently in unreasoning criticism of their leaders and responded more loyally to demands for ever-increasing sacrifice. The voluntary re-enlistment of thousands of Billy Yanks in the last year of the war stands in happy contrast with the money-mania, high living, and indifferent patriotism manifested by a large portion of the North's upper and middle classes. And the privation cheerfully endured by plain soldiers in gray and their folk at home bespeaks much greater devotion to cause and country than does the hoarding, speculation, trading with the enemy, and refusal to comply with government requests for Negro labor that became so common among the Confederacy's business and planter groups. Governor Vance of North Carolina in the fall of 1862 wrote a textile manufacturer who had refused to furnish cloth for soldier uniforms at a 75 per cent profit: "If the standard of patriotism was no higher in the great mass of the people, we might treat with the enemy tomorrow and consent to be slaves at once and forever."[99] And the Tar Heel governor's correspondence indicated a widespread and persistent tendency on the part of manufacturers to speculation and extortion. After the first year of conflict, both state and Confederate authorities in all parts of the South had the greatest difficulty getting planters to lend their slaves for building of defenses.[100] Lieutenant Colonel Ellison Capers, charged with erecting a battery on the South Carolina coast in February, 1863, wrote his wife: "The most of these wealthy planters are very selfish & the only way to get their negro labor is to take it by force."[101] In August, 1863, Senator C. C. Clay wrote Louis T. Wigfall: "Ga. is full of refugees from Miss., Tenn. and N. Ala., flying with their negroes to some safe place. They cling to their flesh pots, while the country cries to them for help."[102] When near the end of the war the governor of Virginia, in response to an urgent requisition of General Lee, called on planters of the state for five thousand slaves to strengthen the Richmond fortifications, only five hundred were sent.[103]

There were, of course, many examples of unselfishness and patriotism among the middle and upper classes of both North and South. Especially noteworthy was the bravery and patriotism manifested by many men from these classes who served as officers in the armed forces. But, on the whole, the record of the more privileged groups appears less impressive than that of the plain folk.

Lincoln always believed in the soundness and dependability of the great masses of the people, and his faith in them was unquestionably personal. On one occasion he remarked to a friend: "Remember, Dick, to keep close to the people—they are always right and will mislead no one."[104] Because he knew and trusted the lowly folk, he took great pains to show them that their welfare was at stake in the war for the Union. On the other hand, Davis, aloof in temperament and never close to the masses, showed little disposition to take the common people into his confidence or give the Confederate cause meaning for them.[105] The greater effectiveness of Lincoln in appealing to the plain folk must be counted among the many reasons that have been given for northern victory.

In the period that has elapsed since Appomattox, many people, North and South, have gone to considerable trouble and expense to prove their aristocratic background and to establish descent from high officers of the Union or Confederate armies. In view of the splendid conduct of the lowlier folk in the great crisis of the 1860's, it would seem that those who spring from that class should take even more pride in their origins, and search the records with greater zeal to prove their connection with privates, corporals, and sergeants. Certainly they have every right to exult if they find among their Civil War antecedents the names of such men as Private Mattix, Private Sam Watkins, Private William Fletcher, Private John Cotton, Private William Heartsill, and Sergeant John Hagan of the Confederate army or Private Chauncey Cook, Private Samuel Croft, Private Ira Butterfield, Sergeant Henry Crydenwise, and Sergeant Day Elmore of the Union army. For it was these men and their kind whose strength was the bedrock of their respective causes and whose greatness made their war one of the most inspiring in the history of embattled humanity.

Chapter XXII

Facets of the South
in the 1850's

JAMES W. PATTON

IN ENTERING new precincts, the mind instinctively looks for salient incidents to fix its whereabouts and reduce or define its vague anticipations."[1] Thus wrote Frederick Law Olmsted at the beginning of his memorable journey through Texas and the southern back country in 1853.* The "salient incidents" that Olmsted found and depicted were associated primarily with the institution of slavery, concerning which he observed an "epidemic insanity on the subject" and a "paralytic effect upon the popular conscience" that this "great calamity of the South" had produced.[2] As a consequence of slavery and the exigency precipitated by its gathering impeachment, the section, in his opinion, was suffering a mental aberration which threw it into a pathological state and rendered it incapable of rational action or deliberation.[3] A person reading Olmsted might, therefore, conclude that the South of the 1850's was so absorbed with slavery as to exclude from its contemplation all other subjects, sacred or profane, human or divine.

Olmsted was not alone in creating such an impression. Contemporary preoccupation with slavery found expression in a vast and varied body of writing and publication, well-known to students of southern history, and ranging from *The Pro-Slavery Argument* to Hinton Rowan Helper's *The Impending Crisis of the South: How to Meet It*. Nor did this preoccupation end with the destruction of the South's "peculiar institution." Succeeding generations of historians, down to the very present, have continued to deal with slavery and its attendant problems to such an extent as to make these, implicitly at least, the central theme of southern history.

*Presented in Durham, North Carolina, November 16, 1956.

With equal facility one might be led to assume that politics, especially that phase of the subject which related to and culminated in secession, pervaded the southern consciousness to the exclusion of other worthwhile activities and to the detriment of the section's welfare. The constant reiteration and elaboration of such phrases and concepts as state's rights, southern nationalism, "the South as a conscious minority," "the course of the South toward secession," "that aggressive slavocracy," and other comparable terms, whether used sympathetically, objectively, or in condemnation, by public men and newspapers of the fifties or by historians at a later date, all serve to convey the idea that the South was in the grip of a dangerous psychosis which manifested itself in "fire-eating" and similar exploits of sectional defense against an encroaching nationalism that was more integrated with the wave of the century.

But slavery and secession were only two facets of the many-sided life of the South in the 1850's. Thousands of southerners lived and loved, married and raised families, suffered the pains of illness and disease, sought the comforts of religion, acquired and disseminated education, operated farms and business enterprises, travelled abroad, visited friends and relatives, and participated in a variety of amusements and social diversions—and recorded their experiences in letters and diaries without exhibiting any special anxiety over slavery or politics. It is with such people as these and the record of their participation in the life of the South that this paper is concerned.

The volume of records written and preserved by these people is impressive. Extension of popular education had greatly increased the number of literate southerners by 1850. Reduction of postal rates in 1845, followed by introduction of adhesive stamps in 1847 and further reduction of rates in 1851 to substantially the same as at present, facilitated letter writing to an extent unequalled in any previous decade. At the same time continued expansion of the frontier and migration of southerners to Texas and California stimulated correspondence between families who had gone to these new areas and friends and kinsmen who had been left behind.

Admittedly, such people as appear in these records are difficult to encompass in one all-inclusive category. Some of them enjoyed a measure of local prominence in their day, but as a group they cannot be classified as distinguished, since with a few exceptions their names are unknown to history and their writings have never appeared on the printed page. On the other hand they were not of "the meaner sort," for the short and simple annals of this latter group were rarely committed to writing. For want of a better term we might call them well-to-do southerners— persons who were literate enough to have the desire and ability to record their observations and experiences and well enough circumstanced to make possible the preservation of what they wrote. It is equally difficult to draw general conclusions as to this class of people throughout the South, or to attempt the delineation of a composite type that would represent the group as a whole; but certain characteristic themes, comments, and observations occur in their writings with sufficient regularity to merit attention. Three of these, relating to health, religion, and travel, will be considered here.

Perhaps the most recurrent of all these themes is that associated with sickness and death. The southerner of this period was the victim of many diseases, and so were his wife, his children, and his servants. Death was an ever-threatening adversary. Again and again appear such comments as those of Mary Jeffreys Bethell of Rockingham County, North Carolina: "We have had much sickness amongst our negroes this year. Four of them died, little Nat, Lucion, Zilman, and John, all of them Abie's children except Nat. The disease was bloody flux. Our white family, that is our children, had it but it did not go hard with them. . . . Dr. McCain's Jane died with fever this fall. Sister Ann McCain's son Nat died in June of bowel disease. I think he was six or seven years old and quite sprightly and interesting. . . . Delia Smith of Milton, young Ben Watkins, and many others. . . . It is solemn to think how many of our acquaintances have gone into eternity this year."[4] David Gavin of Colleton District, South Carolina, wrote that, "Mr. Ch. Rumph lost another negro woman last night. This makes the sixth this summer with the typhoid fever, four on the Sandhill place and two with his son George on the Drose place." Of his own health Gavin noted, "I have no energy to do anything or attend to any business, . . . Dull, Dull, Dull. I was dull and inactive before Brother John's death, but now it seems that I have less [energy] than ever. I am apparently in better health but fear it is only in appearance or I would be more active and energetic. Alas! This world is a poor place."[5] In Ouachita County, Arkansas, John W. Brown observed that "there has been and is yet so much sickness in the country that if we can get through the season, even without much work, I shall be satisfied."[6] An interesting exception is indicated by a physician's lament in Jackson County, North Carolina, in December 1857, that it was so "notorious [sic] healthy in these coves about this time," that "neither myself nor my co-partner are doing anything save drinking liquor and swapping horses"; but he expected to "get a liberal share" of practice later on.[7]

In addition to the widely prevalent and usually fatal maladies of cholera, typhoid and yellow fever, smallpox, and tuberculosis, pneumonia, and other lung trouble, the southerner was plagued with chills and fever—intermittent, remittent, country, Charleston, breakbone, and bilious—dyspepsia, neuralgia, erysipelas, gum boils, risings in the head, whooping cough, hacking coughs, cramp, croup, "lingering disease," salivation, and especially dysentery, diarrhea, flux, and other bowel complaints. To counteract these he dosed himself liberally with calomel, quinine, morphine, opium, and blue mass; with mixtures, tonics, and embrocations; with spirits of nitre and spirits of camphor; with nitrate of silver, tincture of digitalis, mustard plasters, pepper tea, ginger tea, sweet oil and sugar, turpentine in various forms, and other drugs and preparations too numerous to catalog here. Except in cities these remedies were usually prescribed without the advice of a physician and compounded without the aid of an apothecary. When, for example, Judge William Horn Battle suggested that his wife come from Chapel Hill to Morganton, where he was holding the western session of the North Carolina supreme court in the summer of 1856, she demurred on the ground that: "I am more needed at home now than ever before since I had babies, . . . because there is no one in whose charge I could leave this sickly family. . . . Who would make all the pills?"[8] That a people so afflicted could survive, retain its energies, and reproduce its kind in sufficient numbers to fight a four-years' war beginning in 1861, may well appear as no mean accomplishment to a later generation accustomed to widespread benefits of public health and medical care.

Closely connected with, and to a considerable extent resulting from, the southerner's affliction with the ills of this world was his concern for the affairs of the next, as evidenced by his attitude toward and practice of religion. Some southerners of an earlier generation had not scrupled to flirt with rationalism, anticlericalism, and other so-called "infidel" notions. This tendency, of course, found its most erudite and felicitous expression in the deism of Thomas Jefferson; but it was also manifested in cruder forms, as, for example in the will of Willie Jones, recorded at Halifax, North Carolina, which directed that "no priest or any other person is to insult my corpse by uttering any impious observations over it"; or in the cynical epitaph of Ezekial Polk, composed by himself and still carved on marble in St. James Episcopal churchyard at Bolivar, Tennessee:

> Here lies the dust of old E. P.
> One instance of mortality,
> Pennsylvania born, Car'lina bred,
> In Tennessee died on his bed.
> His youthful years he spent in pleasure,
> His later days in gathering treasure.
> From superstition lived quite free,
> And practiced strict morality.
> To holy cheats was never willing,

To give one solitary shilling:
He can foresee and for foreseeing,
He equals most of men in being,
That church and state will join their pow'r,
And misery on this country show'r,
And Methodists with their camp bawling
Will be the cause of this down falling;
An era not destined to see,
It waits for poor posterity;
First fruits and tithes are odious things,
So are bishops, priests, and kings.

Freethinkers of this sort seem to have been rare in the South of the fifties; at least they did not put themselves on record. Far more typical of the period are such testimonials of evangelical piety as: "I was cast down for several days last week, had many cares and a sore trial. I knew that I had *no* help except in God. I prayed fervently for help and direction. I hope he will hear and answer my prayer, for we are commanded to ask, and we should receive. . . . He has been my support and comfort, for he is our sun and shield, will give us grace and glory, and *no* good thing will he withhold from them that walk uprightly. . . . I am not worthy of his goodness, . . . but I go to him for direction in everything. I tell him my griefs and sorrows; he has never turned me away empty"; or "Use me, O Lord, I beseech thee, as an instrument of thy service; number me among thy peculiar people; let me be washed in the blood of thy dear Son . . . let my life be spent . . . in the light of thy glorious countenance . . . and when my connection with time is over . . . and I stand at the bar of God to hear my final sentence pronounced, Lord Jesus remember me in mercy."[9]

As in many other periods, religious faith often performed its works in camp meetings and revivals accompanied by the usual enthusiasm and hysteria that characterized these events. Mary Jeffreys Bethell wrote glowingly of a camp meeting at Prospect in Rockingham County, North Carolina, which lasted many days, with six preachers, and eighty souls converted; and of another at Lowe's "with a good many tents," four preachers, and seventy professions. "When I am at camp meeting," she added, "and hear good preaching, sweet singing, and fervent prayers, it seems like the gate of heaven to our souls."[10] Joseph Milner, en route to California from Tennessee, stopped at Fort Smith, Arkansas, to hear a revivalist who announced to his hearers "that he had been preaching to them for some time without any good; he had been giving them the silver trumpet, but now he would give them the ram's horn," which he proceeded to do in "the true Arkansas style, thunder and lightning, hailstorm and tempest, hell and damnation."[11]

A Georgia woman described a meeting at Columbus in which a certain Judge Wellborn "is the great light among the Baptists. He is very zealous in his experience which it took him an hour and a half to tell. He said that he had committed every sin except that of murder, but after going home and thinking over the matter, he concluded that his intense hatred for Col. Jones amounted to the same thing, and went forth to ask his forgiveness and give him a talk."[12] A Memphis attorney was less enthusiastic on this subject, however, alleging that his wife "under the influence of Methodist inflammatory harangues . . . and constant reading and thought upon the subject . . . is now not far removed from the spirit of the hair shirt and self flagellation penance. It has injured her health, I am sure, and has destroyed my home. . . . The religion of gloom and austerity and asceticism and perpetual devotion, is the religion of the monk and the nun, and suits them; but it is not the religion for the wife and mother, and does not suit a home."[13]

In certain quarters there was a tendency to regard Episcopalianism with considerable suspicion and even some hostility. Olmsted observed this attitude in reporting on a conversation he overheard at a village inn in northern Mississippi. Doubts were being expressed as to the validity of infant baptism, a ceremony of which had been witnessed earlier that day at "preachin." One of the group quoted a certain "Uncle John" on the subject. Conversation as reported by Olmsted:

"Uncle John is an Episcopalian, aint he?"

"Yes."

"Well, there aint no religion in that, no how."

"No, there aint."[14]

A more thoughtful criticism was that of Judge Mitchell King, a staunch Presbyterian from Charleston, who while summering at Flat Rock, North Carolina, attended services at St. John's-in-the-Wilderness and chanced to examine "the Sunday School Catechism of the Episcopal church." He was "really astonished at its inadaptedness for any really valuable moral, doctrinal, or improvingly pious instruction. It seems to me immeasurably inferior to the smaller catechism of the Westminster Assembly."[15] Louisa Wilson of Forsyth County, North Carolina, on attending an Episcopal church for the first time, observed that the rector "is a right good preacher and I guess a good man, but there's too much ceremony for me."[16]

John Houston Bills of Bolivar, Tennessee, expressed similar views, writing in his diary on March 28, 1858: "Attend Episcopal services. *Passion Week.* Service very long and announced for every morning and evening this week. Too much of a good thing, this keeping of *Lent.*"[17] A year later he was still more irritated, when he wrote: "May 8th. Episcopal Convocation. They preach the succession by the imposition of hands and seduce my daughter Clara from her church and Bishop Otey lays his human sinful hands upon her by way of confirmation. Away with such trifling with the King of Kings—God alone can do good."[18] Bills was also critical of clergymen other than Episcopalians. When in Charlottesville, Virginia, paying court to the lady who was to become his second wife, he attended church in the University chapel, where he reported "the Rev'd. Mr. Ruf[f]ner, who is chaplain to this great University, preaches nonsense, making God the author of sin in all its forms, from the Eating the Apple in the Garden down to throwing High Dye and Back Gammon. He degrades the Deity by perversion of his text, 'The Lord Reigneth.' "[19]

Southerners in general, like the true Protestants they were, did not hesitate to criticize the clergy, including those of their own denominations, when occasion seemed to demand. During a visit of Bishop William Mercer Green to the home of a prominent Episcopal layman in Vicksburg the host recorded in his diary: "The Bishop did not come to breakfast [until] just as we were seated and seemed cross because we did not delay and spoil breakfast to give him a chance to have prayers. He was notified half an hour before and not choosing to come, his prayers must be dispensed with."[20] Sarah Gayle Crawford, travelling from Charleston to Wilmington by boat, complained that: "The Convention of Baptists having just broken up, we had our complement of their ministers returning in this direction. I really never saw so much selfishness and less regard displayed for the accommodations of one's fellow travellers, than was exhibited by these preachers."[21] That criticism of one Protestant denomination by another, though often intense, could nevertheless be attended by a sense of humor, was evident on certain occasions. When William H. Holcombe, a homeopathic physician of the Swedenborgian persuasion living in Natchez, was making plans to take his family on a visit to Illinois, "to show off the baby to his relatives, and particularly to get him baptized into the New Church society," the doctor noted that a woman neighbor "was mightily amused at my suggestion that such a measure would put him under the guardianship of a better class of angels than if a good Presbyterian or Episcopal brother had officiated."[22]

Desecration of the Sabbath, lack of regular church services, and other forms of worldliness were often lamented by pious southerners. Jesse Bernard of Alachua County, Florida, was saddened by the fact that "people here in the South never think of having preaching on Christmas Day."[23] and the Reverend Simeon Colton contrasted his situation in Fayetteville, North Carolina, unfavorably with that of the people of New England where "they can go to meeting every Sabbath and hear two sermons every week."[24] Upon hearing from his son, a cadet at West Point, that they had no regular services on Sunday there, and that the superintendent was "a very godless man," A. L. Alexander of Washington, Georgia, wrote: "I think it both a wonder and a shame that the cadets are systematically and officially taught, by example at least, to violate the Sabbath. ... If Mrs. Polk was still the President's wife, I would certainly address myself privately to her, for *she* was a Christian. But Jefferson Davis [then Secretary of War] would be a hard case, I think, and therefore I am not resolved upon the propriety of doing anything."[25]

The most intense of all religious feelings were those provoked by and directed against the Roman Catholic church. Except in Louisiana and certain coastal cities, this institution was of little consequence in the South of the fifties; but wherever he encountered it, whether on his travels or through such oblique channels as reading Macaulay's *History of England* or Prescott's *Ferdinand and Isabella,*[26] the typical southerner felt that he had truly come to grips with the Man of Sin, "the Mother of Abominations," the seven-headed and ten-horned Beast of the Apocalypse. It was "rank idolatry," whose "baleful influence has been to retard the march of intellect and human liberty."[27] Its "nonsensical mummery" was "displeasing to every feeling but one's curiosity."[28] It stood "stagnant and death dealing in an age of enlightenment and progress—aside from the great stream of Christian civilization and social elevation."[29] It was no place for "anyone who reads the gospels."[30] Its membership was associated in the popular mind with Irish immigrants, "the lowest of their race, who [have] been caressed and treated by Demagogues for their votes until they are spoilt,"[31] and its houses of worship were thought to be a rallying ground for "aliens and papists" whose "foreign and Romish influence" would "ultimately prove our national ruin."[32] It is an interesting commentary upon the period that examination of the letters and diaries of approximately two hundred non-Catholic southerners of the fifties failed to reveal a single statement complimentary to this church.

Southerners of the more favored economic classes, as well as some not so well-favored, did a great deal of travelling in the 1850's. In search of health, recreation, and amusement they made the various summer circuits of the springs. These included the Warm Springs (now Hot Springs), in North Carolina; the White, Red, Blue, Gray, Yellow, Sweet, and Salt Sulphur Springs in Virginia, along with the Healing, Bath Alum, Alleghany, Capon, Orkney, and Shannondale Springs and the Rockbridge Baths, also in that state; and the New England circuit, on which the route usually led through Philadelphia, New York, and Saratoga, to various New England points, and then back to New York and home "after the first frost." On business and financial errands they journeyed to Philadelphia, New York, and other eastern seaboard cities. For higher education they went to northern and eastern colleges. On a variety of missions they traversed the West. To see the sights of the Old World a substantial number toured Europe.

Generally speaking the southerner carried his provincialisms and prejudices with him on these wanderings. He appears to have been unable to evaluate alien cultures objectively or to view the actions of foreign men and women other than in the light of his own experiences. Josiah Gorgas, stationed at the Augusta Arsenal in Maine, found "the manners and habits of the people are so uncongenial here that one cannot help sighing after the frankness of southern manners," and he thought "the 'merry jingle' of sleigh bells is but a sorry compensation for the rustle of leaves, the voice of birds, and the beauty and odor of flowers" as he remembered these in the South.[33] A resident of New Orleans who had previously travelled in the North warned his brother, then a student at Yale: "Never think, for an instant, of marrying in the North. I have looked into this matter thoroughly. You can do better here blindfolded than in the North with your eyes open."[34] A young Georgian, en route home from Princeton, stopped in Washington and visited Congress in May, 1856. "I was unpleasantly struck with the uproar and confusion in the House," he wrote. "The 'Black Republicans' appeared to me to bear the impress of their hearts upon their countenances. It might have been prejudice, but I thought I had never seen a more selfish, narrow-minded set of men."[35] Still another Georgian, just landed in California after a forty-two day sea voyage from New York, wrote his mother: "I assure you it is really pleasant once more to be in an American town. I am sick and tired of these infernal Spaniards."[36]

The product in most instances of a rural environment, the southerner was distrustful of large cities. Since these were to be found mainly in the North, this prejudice could easily assume a sectional as well as a sociological aspect. James Thomas Harrison of Mississippi wrote at length upon the ill-mannered crowds that jostled him in New York. The "impudence and want of politeness" which he found among the free Negroes there he considered to be the result of the example set by their "white brethren." He saw "men who set themselves up for gentlemen" ride "inside of the stage coach and compel ladies to ride *on top* of the vehicle"; and force ladies to stand up for miles in railroad cars, "whilst the dogs squared themselves off on the seats with the most complacent air of triumphal success." Thus encountering "as much of Yankeedom as I wish to see," this southerner vowed never to undertake "to travel here with ladies again and mix up with free Negroes and Sam Slicks of Yankees."[37]

Among southern cities New Orleans naturally evoked the most suspicion. Its metropolitan atmosphere, its Latin population, and its allegedly free and easy—at least non-Anglo-Saxon—moral code lay beyond the limits of the average southerner's experience and in consequence was likely to meet with his disfavor. The Reverend Simeon Colton, returning to North Carolina after attending the Presbyterian General Assembly in the Crescent City, in May, 1858, wrote that he "found New Orleans a better place than I expected," but added that "wickedness to a great extent abounds."[38] The same James T. Harrison of Mississippi who was so critical of New York also had some comments on New Orleans, which though not quite so caustic were equally revealing of his sentiments. Shortly after leaving the city, in February, 1858, he wrote:

The St. Charles was jammed, crammed, and double jammed. There was not room enough to turn around in, and as for the ladies' parlor, it was not only full to overflowing, but even the passages and entrances leading to it, were more than full, for they were packed from one end to the other. There were old maids and young maids, young widows and widows not so young, middle aged widows, and old widows, widows that were widows indeed, widows of all ranks and descriptions, including the halt, the lame, and the blind, the rich and the poor, and all of them desirous of marrying rich, but still, rather than miss, willing to put up with such as the good Lord would send them in the way of a husband. It reminded me of the slave market at Constantinople, as I have seen it described, where the Circassian and Georgian girls were sold, with the exception that the widows in question were not so beautiful.[39]

Southerners who travelled in Europe manifested the same tendency to retain the predilections which they carried with them. It was only natural, however, that because of their predominately British extraction, such travellers would be slightly less ill at ease in Great Britain than on the continent. Except for a few evangelical Protestants who were displeased with the ritualism of the Anglican church and some low-church Episcopalians who were suspicious of Puseyism and other high-church practices which they encountered there,[40] the most of them seem to have felt at home in the religious atmosphere of England and Scotland. They likewise admired the beauty of the English landscape and marvelled at the excellence of British agricultural methods as well as at the farm dwellings and barns and outbuildings for the protection of livestock and storage of farm products. James H. Otey wrote that English farmers "cultivate and dress their farms with more care than we put on our gardens," and in the light of this contrast he wondered that "our slovenly modes of procedure" ever cause our fields to "yield anything at all." In spite of all this, however, Otey gave evidence of a certain amount of provincialism. He thought he could detect "an air of sullen repose" that seemed to hang over all the rural scenery of England, "including every living and inanimate object in it. The trees do not seem to rise up high

towards heaven and wave their branches joyfully in the passing breeze—
the horses drawing the ploughs appear to take slow measured steps and
the ploughman is of course equally sober and sedate in his movements.
In short, there is a dullness or a heaviness which compares unfavorably,
at least in my mind, with the activity and spirit that seems to animate us
in America." A further indication of Otey's provincialism appears in the
fact that though he met Lord John Russell and spoke from the same
platform with him, he seemed to have remembered this occasion chiefly
because "His Lordship is more like Col. J. J. B. White of Yazoo, Miss.
than any man I ever saw."[41]

Edmund Kirby-Smith, later to be much better known than he was at
this time, visited England in 1858. Although admitting that the English
"both individually and nationally have many fine traits of character," he
was nevertheless repelled by their "surly, uncivil, and overbearing" ways;
by their so habitually speaking "contemptuously of us"; so universally
trying "to hold us up to ridicule"; and so invariably filling their newspapers "with extracts to our discredit."[42] In Liverpool Kirby-Smith saw
"more drunkenness, squalid misery, and degradation than it has ever
been my misfortune to witness in any other city in this world," and asked,
"Where are the English philanthropists who have so interested themselves in the sufferings and degradation of their poor black brethren on
the other side of the world?"[43]

The Protestant areas of Germany and Switzerland were generally attractive to southerners who visited there in the fifties. Of Geneva, Kate
Jones wrote, "We have seen only one or two priests, as this is altogether
a Protestant community—which readily accounts for the general prosperity of the country."[44] It is doubtful, however, if there ever existed a
group of travellers so completely incapable of understanding and appreciating the civilization of a foreign country as were the southerners
who went to France, Austria, and Italy in the mid-nineteenth century.
With elementary, sometimes infantile, ideas on the subject of art, resulting
among other things from a puritanical inheritance, the average southerner
was unable to grasp the significance of the treasures in this medium that
he saw in the galleries and museums. His antagonism to the Roman
Catholic faith diluted his pleasure in viewing churches and cathedrals.
Frenchmen, and particularly French women, he often suspected of immorality. The Austrians of Vienna he likewise considered immoral, and
with their country as a whole he associated the twin evils of Roman
Catholicism and a cruel and oppressive government. Italians generally
he tended to regard as rascals. Yet these three countries were visited by
nearly all southerners who made any serious efforts at European travel
during this period.

"Well, is this Paris?" exclaimed Sarah Gayle Crawford of Alabama on arriving at the French capital in September, 1853. "The city of all the world that I most detest—not the city—but the unprincipled population, I abhor. I feel really ashamed of my violent prejudices. Perhaps I will be able to overcome them after a while."[45] That she did not readily succeed in this effort is indicated by her remarks on the Paris Opera which she attended about three weeks later. Although marvelling at the beautiful costumes and loveliness of the dancing girls, she deplored "the blackness and depravity of their young hearts. These young girls are almost without exception of ill-fame—live by the sale and barter of their personal charm. They whirl about to make a greater display of their legs and bodies than there is any necessity for."[46]

Young Henry Maney of Nashville, Tennessee, loved the Paris crowds, which he observed moving on leisurely, "enjoying everything around, smilingly polite, and courteous," quite unlike the "rude, rough, and careless" crowds he had seen in London;[47] but William Elliott, somewhat older, from South Carolina, objected to so much walking and noted that "people with tender feet will suffer in this city."[48] Elliott, who had gone to Paris as a South Carolina representative to the Universal Exposition of 1855, and had completed his duties in that capacity, complained that he lacked occupation. "I can go out at night with impunity, but I cannot stand the 5 hours sitting at the theaters—and the performance lasts even that long. How the singers can stand it a single season—is a mystery to me. They must have lungs of leather and throats of brass."[49] Although of high social standing in his native state, and presumably a man of good taste, Elliott indulged himself in a remarkable example of American gaucherie in describing the visit of Queen Victoria to the Paris Exposition. In a letter to his wife he wrote:

I had three near views of her face and one of her legs—which are by far the best part of her: and I speak by the book, for I had an excellent opportunity of judging—as, being directly behind her majesty (accidentally caught there) when she alighted at the entrance of the Exhibition of the fine arts. On being handed from the open barouche by the Emperor she forgot (as ladies are prone to forget) her train—and *that* remained in the carriage while her majesty's feet were on the pavement. Of course, I looked—and without flattery I saw two delicate *mince* feet—two ditto-ditto ankles—two superb calves (royal George stock) and stockings of flesh colored silk—worthy of the entourages. I think I have seen more of her majesty than any man in France— except perhaps Prince Albert . . . Ralph if he heard this will say, "the Old Sportsman knew how to take a stand," but the truth is—it was but a happy accident that placed me where I was—and I know they who choose to open their eyes as they pass through the world can hardly help seeing some things worthy of being remembered.[50]

John Houston Bills of Bolivar, Tennessee, who visited Europe in

1851 and thereby added anti-Roman Catholicism to his already anti-Episcopalian and anti-Presbyterian tendencies, was thoroughly unimpressed with Paris church architecture. On June 27, he "visited *Notre Dame* church, the largest in Paris. It is on the Island in the Seine. Not up to expectation." About a week later, he "Visited Notre Dame a second time. Think no better of it than the first. The order of architecture is generally Gothic and is boasted of as very fine."[51] Equally unenthusiastic was Bills' commentary on the Cologne Cathedral, which he visited later that summer: "It is as large as West Minster and of the same order of building. Many corpses lying all around. Every succeeding Catholic church I visit but confirms me of the utter worthlessness of their faith."[52]

Neither the social life nor the art treasures of Vienna were appreciated by puritanical southerners who visited that gay capital. There in one hour Edmund Kirby-Smith saw more beautiful women than in all the rest of Europe combined, but along with this he found morality at a lower plane than elsewhere. "Twenty-five out of thirty of the children born here," he was told, "are illegitimate, and intrigue seems to be the order of the day."[53] There are few descriptions that so graphically reveal the inability of a provincial southerner to understand the old masters as that penned by Kirby-Smith after visiting a Vienna art gallery. Though lengthy, it merits quotation in full:

As I stood in the Lichstenstein gallery with lewd and lascivious subjects staring me in the face in every direction, in all the rich coloring and nudity of nature, with the names and characters of the subjects written on the picture frames, and with the scenes and acts so vividly and truly represented that nothing is left to the imagination, the conviction forces itself upon me that whilst the public taste was improved the morals must be deteriorated. Why the veriest broken down old blazé could not walk through some of these European galleries without feeling the blood course through his veins in rapturous excitement; and yet the halls swarm with women of every age and clime and sphere in society. The middle age matron and the young girl just budding into womanhood may be seen side by side commenting on and criticizing the rapes of Io, Danae, and Europa, or the more scriptural subject of Susannah and the Elders.[54]

The civilization of Italy failed signally to evoke any great amount of respect from southerners who visited that land. If their writings are to be believed, they found it a country where "the people are generally lazy and depend mainly on strangers for support";[55] where travellers "must make up their minds to do without comforts, to be imposed upon in every possible way and be cheated";[56] where "full half the men of the country are either priests or soldiers; useless, lazy, eating and drinking up the riches of the land, great fat, greasy monks you turn from in disgust";[57] and where the people "all lie so confoundedly that it is really with the utmost difficulty that you can get at the truth or even near it."[58]

Not even Rome was able to inspire in these southern Protestants a sense of reverence. Its "30,000 priests" with "their looseness of morals" led one to believe it "to be the most corrupt, profligate, and licentious place on the globe";[59] while another was astonished at "what numbers there are to be seen, parading the streets, of these holy loungers, these drones of society that live on the labor of the industrious and are supported by ignorance and superstition."[60] "I have seen enough of Rome in two days to sicken and disgust me with the place," wrote a Georgia woman. "If I could visit the *ruins* only, and forget that I am in modern Rome, perhaps I might wish to prolong my visit—but to look around, see the priests by the scores—at all points—hear the miserable tales of crime and degradation, and almost utter absence of everything like virtue and religion—O! it is enough to make the Christian weep tears of blood. All this too under the cloak of religion."[61] After attending high mass at Milan Cathedral, this same traveller concluded: "It really seems *disrespectful* at least [but] what is regarded by a large portion as most sacred . . . was all *most amusing* and *funny* to me . . . I can't possibly control my countenance, so as to wear a grave expression while witnessing these ceremonies, and after attending services in St. Peter's in Rome, I do not think I shall put my foot into a church or cathedral until I reach home, and can attend religious worship more in unison with what I conceive to be its sacredness."[62]

At least two southerners of this period incorporated their European observations in lengthy, though now largely forgotten, published works. Mrs. Octavia Walton Le Vert's two-volume *Souvenirs of Travel*,[63] based upon an extended trip abroad in 1853 and another in 1855, does little more than copy European guide books and repeat the spiels of cicerones, and is therefore lacking in either analysis or criticism. James Johnston Pettigrew, who went to Italy in 1859 to offer his services to the Piedmontese against Austria but arrived after the Peace of Villafranca had put an end to this struggle, then visited Spain and recorded his reflections on the manners and customs of that country in a 400-odd page volume entitled *Notes on Spain and the Spaniards*.[64] Friendly to the Spaniards, exhibiting a comprehensive knowledge of their country and its history, and at the same time attempting to correct the "erroneous ideas . . . transmitted to us generally by the often-times clever, but always partial writings of English travellers and historians," this book is something of an exception to the general run of southern comments upon Europe in the 1850's.

Pettigrew's reactions are even better expressed in his letters written from Europe during an earlier sojourn there in 1850, 1851, and 1852. A brilliant graduate of the University of North Carolina at the age of nineteen, an assistant professor at the Naval Observatory in Washington, and a Charleston lawyer, all before reaching the age of twenty-one, he was perhaps the most highly educated and best balanced of all the southerners who went to Europe during this period.[65] Going to Berlin in 1850, he studied Roman law at the university there, spent a portion of the next year in Italy, and returned home in 1852 by way of Spain, France, England, and Scotland. A discriminating observer, he revelled in the art galleries of Dresden and other German cities, as well as those of Italy.[66] He formed a good opinion of the country and government of Germany, and especially of the wide-spread literacy that he found there,[67] although his "democratic Republican blood boiled over" on occasions at the sight of the princes, a congress of which he once described as "so many lounging, idle, ugly, worthless people [as] I had never before seen. . . . If you desire to imagine how such a personage appears, figure to yourself a man of rather larger body than ordinary, a countenance not intelligent to say the least, forehead retreating, a military coat, with tremendous epaulettes, and his breast covered with ribbands and stars which he does not deserve. Such were the greater part of them and the more I see of such creatures, the more awfully Republican I become."[68] Like other southerners, he described the Austrian government as "hateful," though he did not extend this characterization to the people of that empire, whom he regarded as "certainly the most warm hearted and generous of all Germany, as every stranger who has been at Vienna and become acquainted can vouch."[69] As he neared Italy, he "felt as I used to do in leaving the Yankee land on the way to the South," and upon reaching Venice he wrote that he was "once more *home,* for the first time since leaving home."[70]

Nonetheless his puritanical, albeit Episcopalian, upbringing caused him to look with disfavor upon the continental observance of the Sabbath and to recoil from the enormous amount of beer drinking that he encountered in Germany;[71] and his exultation over northern Italy did not extend to Naples, of which he wrote: "If the Austrian Government would take possession . . . put the King, his 100,000 soldiers and 40,000 lazzaroni in the crater of Mount Vesuvius and establish the order and security which reigns in Lombardy and Tuscany, they would certainly be entitled to the thanks of every friend of civilization."[72] Although of French extraction, he seems to have been only mildly attracted to that country, and became even less so after what he regarded as Napoleon's treacherous withdrawal from the Sardinian war.[73] Probably the most anti-British of all the travellers here described, he was repelled by the drunkenness which he considered "the besetting sin of England." In London, he observed that: "After 10 o'clock a large portion of the city became a scene of riot; the gin shops in full play and men, *women,* and even *children* reeling about. . . . I thought myself reasonably acquainted with the depravity of human nature, but what I saw and heard was a new phase; it seemed as though a Vesuvius of moral degradation had burst its crater and overwhelmed us with a torrent of filth and slime. . . . The simple fact is, that there is more vice in London than any city in the world; Paris, Lisbon, Naples, and New York together would make but a small show beside this giant city. Dickens gives a faithful portraiture according to my little experience." Having spent two years in the more art-conscious capitals of Europe, he deplored the "utter want of taste" in the London public monuments, regarding, for example, the statue of the Duke of Wellington as resembling "a jockey mounted on the veritable Rosinante much more than a great soldier." And "surely," he wrote, "there can be no better proof of the omnipotence of the creator than the existence of the English climate. Nothing less than an all-powerful being could produce such a monster."[74]

Time does not permit further elaboration of the three topics that have been here treated. That these, as well as many other facets of the South in the 1850's, could be explored much more fully, is obvious; but this paper is designed to be suggestive rather than exhaustive. In so far as the information thus assembled may appear to warrant any definite conclusions, the following may be advanced. There existed in the 1850's a large body of southerners who found much to occupy their minds and to stimulate their activities other than preoccupation with slavery and politics. A typical member of this class was plagued with many diseases and, in consequence, gave a great deal of concern to the state of his health. As an orthodox and evangelical Protestant he believed that he was helping to further the Kingdom of God on earth, and by so doing he hoped to be rewarded in the world to come, although it is doubtful as to whether he thought that similar rewards would accrue to Roman Catholics. When travelling or visiting away from home he manifested a tendency to carry his local or native prejudices with him and often to find fault with conditions that transcended his experiences or ran counter to his predilections.

That these findings are tentative, and that different interpretations might be arrived at by a more comprehensive study, is freely admitted. This observation leads to a more general conclusion, and one which, I think, deserves especial emphasis: namely, that there still exist many opportunities for research in the history of the South during the 1850's and that there are many avenues through which this end may be pursued.

Chapter XXIII

West by South

ROBERT S. HENRY

THE United States of America of 1776 was strictly an Atlantic nation.* It had no more than a precarious foothold in the lands west of the Alleghenies and no claim whatever to the lands beyond the Mississippi or those fronting on the Gulf. By 1850, within the span of a single lifetime, the thirteen original states had grown to thirty, five of which fronted on the Gulf and one, indeed, on the Pacific.

This amazing result was produced primarily by a great migration of peoples of many races, from all sections of the country, and from lands beyond the sea. But even this mighty tide might have been diverted to other ends had it not been for a sequence of actions and events which, at critical times and places, opened the way for the movement west by south through which this nation attained its truly continental proportions.

The leadership which determined the course of events at these critical times and places was almost wholly of the South—a fact which, I believe, makes it the more appropriate to recall to this Southern Historical Association some of the points at which the South made special contribution to the growth of the nation. This growth was territorial, and it was more, for out of it flowed a community of interest in the lands acquired in common for the nation which, in turn, fostered a sense of nationhood.

Each one of the series of events to which I should like to invite your attention was small in itself, but each was big in its consequences. There could hardly have been a smaller "army" than the 130 men whose victory at Vincennes in February, 1779, enabled the American diplomats at the peace negotiations of 1782–83 to claim and secure for the new United States title to the Northwest Territory. And from that territory, secured by the vigor and valor of Virginia, sprang the remainder of the series of

*Presented in Houston, Texas, November 8, 1957.

events which carried the sovereignty of the United States to the Pacific.

The little affair at arms at Vincennes had its beginning in the winter of 1777–78—the same winter in which Washington's Continentals suffered at Valley Forge—when Patrick Henry, governor of Virginia, authorized the settlers on that state's far frontier on the Ohio River to organize a force for defense against threats of British and Indian attack from the Northwest. The force to be raised was a Virginia force, under Virginia command in the person of the twenty-five-year-old George Rogers Clark.

Clark acted on the principle that the best defense is an offense. In the summer of 1778, he moved against the British posts at Kaskaskia and Cahokia in the Illinois country. In July, both posts capitulated. So, shortly afterward, did the more central post of Vincennes, but that fall General Henry Hamilton, the British commander at Detroit, recaptured Vincennes and went into winter quarters there.

Clark, who was at Kaskaskia when Hamilton recaptured Vincennes, resolved upon a winter campaign to retake the post. The "season of the year," he explained, was favorable to the enterprise, since "the enemy would not suppose that we should be so mad as to attempt to march 80 leagues through a drowned country in the depth of winter." As Clark wrote Governor Henry, though the resolution to do so was as desperate "as my situation," he saw "no other possibility of securing the country," and "being encouraged by the idea of the greatness of the consequences that would attend on success," he determined to go ahead.

The capture of Vincennes and its garrison by Clark's half-drowned and half-frozen force was not the end of the war in the Northwest, but when the treaty of peace came to be written it played a decisive part in determining that the Old Northwest was to be American territory, open for American occupation, rather than to become a British bar to further westward settlement.

Settlement, meanwhile, proceeded in the Old Southwest, even though it was handicapped by Spanish possession of the mouths of the Mississippi, the Alabama-Tombigbee, and the Apalachicola-Chattahoochee river systems through which the surplus products of the settlers—whenever there was any surplus—had to find their way to market.

In 1803, under the leadership of the Virginian Jefferson, the United States sought to purchase New Orleans and West Florida so as to make secure the free movement of the commerce of the Western states and territories. The American negotiators sought to buy no more than the lands which included the mouths of the rivers draining the interior. They were astounded by the offer of First Consul Bonaparte to sell the entire province of Louisiana, as it had been ceded to France by Spain. With some misgivings as to constitutional authority, but with prescience, the Americans accepted the offer, and their bold action was approved by President Jefferson and confirmed by the Congress.

The purchase of Louisiana—the second great step in the march of American population west by south accomplished under southern leadership—had to overcome a type of opposition not met by Clark in the Northwest, in the shape of sectional objection from within the United States. This objection on the part of Federalists to the acquisition of new territory beyond the Mississippi was not enough, however, to block the consummation of the purchase of Louisiana—at a price which, including interest on the deferred payments, averaged about four cents an acre.

While it is not directly a part of the story of the movement west by south under southern leadership, it might be pointed out that two young Virginians, Meriwether Lewis and William Clark, led the expedition whose successful exploration of the new Louisiana Purchase helped lay the foundations for the American claim to the Oregon country.

The admission of Louisiana as a state of the Union, proposed in 1811 and accomplished the next year, met with even stiffer resistance from the New England Federalists. One of their number, Josiah Quincy, declared in Congress that in his "deliberate opinion," passage of the enabling act would be "virtually a dissolution of this Union; that it will free the States from their moral obligation and, as it will be the right of all, so it will be the duty of some, definitely to prepare for a separation—amicably if they can, violently if they must." Thus at the first step in the enlargement of the nation through creation of new states to the southwest, and from no less a source than a future president of Harvard College, was heard the threat of secession as a consequence of expansion.

A more serious threat to expansion, however, was the British expedition against New Orleans which, as things turned out, was the concluding act of the War of 1812. It is commonly believed, indeed, that the war had been over for two weeks when, on January 8, 1815, that expedition was defeated by the American forces under Andrew Jackson of Tennessee. But the Treaty of Ghent, signed on Christmas Eve, 1814, not only did not settle the issues of the war; it was not even an agreement to stop fighting until *after* the treaty had been ratified by both parties. Ratification did not take place until February 17, 1815—forty days after Jackson's astounding victory on the field of Chalmette.

The question of whether peace was effective before or after that victory might seem, now, to be of only antiquarian interest. At the time, however, it was widely believed in the United States by Federalists and Jeffersonians alike that British victory at New Orleans was not only inevitable but that such a victory would have profound effect upon the situation of the United States with regard to the territory acquired under the Louisiana Purchase.

These apprehensions would have been intensified if the Americans had known of the secret instructions issued by the British government for the commander of the expedition against New Orleans. These instructions, issued after peace negotiations were under way at Ghent, included a directive to "rescue the whole province of Louisiana from the United States," if the inhabitants were found favorable, either for the purpose of setting up an independent government or of returning the province to the "dominion of the Spanish Crown."

The British plenipotentiaries in the peace negotiations early insisted that the "acquisition of Louisiana was illegal" and repeatedly taxed the United States with a "spirit of aggrandizement" manifested, among other acts, by the "purchase of Louisiana from France against the known conditions on which it had been ceded by Spain to that country." What were these conditions of cession?

Louisiana had been French prior to the general settlements at the close of the Seven Years' War, when the entire territory was ceded to Spain. In 1800, under pressure from the imperious Napoleon, the weak king of Spain had retroceded Louisiana to France in the secret Second Treaty of San Ildefonso. The retrocession, however, was on condition that France, in turn, could not alienate the province to any other power than Spain. Thus France had only a conditional title to Louisiana, subject to the reversionary right of Spain. By 1814 Spain had become the ally of Great Britain—and what would have been more natural than the recovery of His Catholic Majesty's "lost province" and its return to the crown which was, in the British view, its rightful owner?

To the British note calling attention to the "known conditions" upon which Spain had ceded the province to France, the American plenipotentiaries replied that "cession of Louisiana was, at the time, communicated to the British Government, who expressed their entire satisfaction with it, and that it had subsequently received the solemn sanction of Spain herself."

In rebuttal, the British delegation declared that the instrument by which the king of Spain was alleged to have given his consent to the transfer of Louisiana had "never been made public"; that the king was "no party to the treaty by which the cession was made"; and that "if any such sanction has been subsequently obtained from him, it must have been, like other contemporaneous acts of that monarch, involuntary, and as such cannot alter the character of the transaction."

To this the United States delegation replied that despite the contemporary protests of the Spanish minister in Washington, the Spanish government had assented to the transfer of Louisiana to the United States, and that the United States did not admit the "alleged disability of the Spanish monarch."

There thus developed in the course of the peace negotiations the definite possibility that New Orleans and Louisiana, if they should fall into British hands, were to be regarded as a special situation to which special considerations would apply. The Duke of Wellington, writing on November 9, 1814, from Paris where he was attending to the restoration of the Bourbon monarchy while Napoleon was on the Isle of Elba, said that he did not believe the status of the American war justified the British negotiators in insisting as a general principle of settlement upon the principle of *uti posseditis*—which might be freely translated as "takers keepers." But, he added, "if you had territory, as I hope you will soon have New Orleans, I should prefer to insist upon the cession of that province as a separate article."

There was not the slightest doubt in England, or in most of the United States for that matter, that New Orleans would be taken and that, if taken, it could and would be held. In the opinion of the Iron Duke, New Orleans was the only "vulnerable point of importance belonging to the United States which we could hope to take and *hold*." Thomas Jefferson was convinced that the port which he had done so much to bring into the United States would fall, and if it did, that it would be held by the British indefinitely. Extreme Federalists, at the opposite pole of politics, were equally without doubt of British success at New Orleans, which would, as some of them thought, dissolve the Union and open the way for a separate New England Confederation—thus anticipating by forty-five years the use of the word "Confederate" as descriptive of a league of states separate from the United States of America. What might have happened if the British had won at New Orleans is a question which Jackson's decisive victory forever foreclosed.

Within a decade after Andrew Jackson's troops perfected the title to Louisiana, the advance waves of the tide of American settlement setting west by south had passed beyond the western boundary of Louisiana and, under the leadership first of Moses Austin and then his great son, Stephen, had penetrated into the Mexican province of Texas. Later, as part of the great propaganda for abolition of African slavery, it was alleged—and is still by many believed—that this entry of Anglo-American settlers into Texas and all the consequences that flowed from it were the result of the machinations of a malign and aggressive "slavocracy." But the colonization of Texas was but a continuation of the westward migration which, as Professor Eugene C. Barker wrote, "had no purposeful relation to the political history of slavery in the United States." And it is significant, particularly in the light of his later course, that John Quincy Adams, while President of the United States, sought to acquire much of the territory of Texas from Mexico. When Andrew Jackson became President, he too sought to negotiate for the acquisition of Texan territory, with no more success than had attended the efforts of President Adams.

The settlers themselves, meanwhile, undertook to better their conditions after repeated Mexican revolutions had effectively subverted the Constitution of 1824 under which their rights had been protected. Texas had been joined with Coahuila as the state of Coahuila y Tejas, but the Texas settlements were allowed only one representative in the legislative body of the joint state and were otherwise handicapped by distance from the state capital and differences in concepts of government and society. In 1834, therefore, some Texans undertook to secure adjustments in their relations with the joint state, including greater representation in its legislature, while other Texans sought separation from Coahuila and admission to the Mexican Union as a separate state.

The efforts of both groups were treated as revolutionary by General Antonio López de Santa Anna, the perennial dictator of Mexico. Being so treated, they became truly so, despite the reluctance to rebel demonstrated more than once by the Texans. It was not until four days before the fall of the Alamo that the Texan Congress abandoned the effort to restore the Mexican Constitution of 1824 and declared Texas to be a free, sovereign, and independent republic—and the defenders of the Alamo died without knowing that they were fighting for a new nation.

This afternoon we stood for a while on the field of San Jacinto, a small field where, in a brief battle, the tiny army led by Sam Houston of Tennessee and Texas made good the declaration of Texan independence. Once again, at a critical turning point, southern leadership had opened the way for continuation of the movement of America west by south.

San Jacinto was fought in April, 1836. In September of the same year the people of Texas voted overwhelmingly to seek annexation to the United States. Formal proposals to that effect were presented in August, 1837, to be rejected by the Senate and filibustered to death in the House of Representatives in June and July, 1838. Whereupon Houston —as one of the last acts of his first term as president of Texas—withdrew the proposal for annexation and began to turn toward a European alignment. His successor as president, Mirabeau Buonaparte Lamar, was outspoken in opposition to annexation, preferring that Texas should continue as an independent republic. This, too, was the aim of British and French diplomacy, which sought to check American expansion to the west and south by building up a strong and independent southwestern nation, allied commercially and politically with Europe.

Affairs remained in this posture for nearly five years, during which the Texas republic was recognized by France, Belgium, Holland, and Great Britain, while the Texas question seemed to be all but forgotten by the government of the United States. By 1843, however, the disadvantages to the United States that would flow from the establishment upon its southwestern frontier of a strong and growing country which was beholden to, and under the influence of, Great Britain began to be more adequately appreciated. The subject was brought into focus when President Tyler—another Virginian—negotiated with Texas a treaty of annexation. The treaty, signed in April, 1844, provided that Texas should come into the Union as a territory, thus leaving to some future Congress the questions involved in its admission into statehood. The treaty was not entirely satisfactory to Texas, while in the United States it met such opposition that in June it was rejected in the Senate by a vote of more than two to one.

Meanwhile, however, in May the national conventions of the major political parties had met. The Whigs, as was expected, had nominated Henry Clay, who had written in opposition to annexation. The Democrats, unexpectedly, had nominated James K. Polk, who had declared himself unequivocally for it. The comparatively less-known Polk—the youngest man up to that time to become President—was elected over the justly famous veteran Clay.

A month after the election, Congress met for its "lame duck" session. President Tyler, soon to go out of office also, reopened the annexation question by proposing that Congress admit Texas as a state of the Union. The necessary joint resolution was passed by the House and, by the narrowest of margins, by the Senate, and was signed by President Tyler on March 1, 1845. Two days later, on the last day of his term, the invitation to enter the Union as a state was started on the long journey to Texas.

There was a great deal of uncertainty whether Texas, twice rebuffed, would accept the terms of annexation. Officials of the independent republic were, in some instances, reluctant to see that country surrender its sovereign status. This reluctance was intensified by the active efforts of Captain Charles Elliott, the British chargé d'affaires, to secure Mexican recognition of Texan independence. In furtherance of this effort, Captain Elliott journeyed to the Mexican capital. To keep the journey secret, he set out from Galveston on a ship bound for Charleston from which he was transferred at sea to a British war vessel which bore him to Veracruz. In Mexico, he succeeded in persuading that government to agree to recognize Texas upon condition that there would be no annexation to the United States.

Unfortunately for the success of Captain Elliott's plan, as his ship sailed out of Galveston it passed—unknown to either man at the time —the ship coming into Galveston which bore Andrew Jackson Donelson, the American envoy bringing to Texas the offer of annexation. Having the opportunity to choose, the Texas congress voted down the proposal brought from Mexico by Elliott and called a convention of the people of Texas to consider the American offer. This convention on July 4, 1845, voted to accept statehood in the American Union.

Since Texas came into the Union as a slave state, the whole process of Anglo-American settlement, successful revolution against Mexico, and admission to the Union aroused the darkling suspicions of abolitionist writers and speakers. To them, the course of events was evidence of a "long premeditated" plot of a malign, sinister, far-seeing, and aggressive "slavocracy."

Such charges, reiterated with passionate conviction and literary power, and emanating from sources to which much of the country had looked for the writing of its history, have darkly colored the common impression of these events, even unto this day. This impression persists in spite of the fact that as long as fifty years ago it was demonstrated that "the charge of premeditated expansion by the United States for the purpose of extending slavery falls to the ground," as Professor Jesse S. Reeves put it. "Instead of slavery's assisting in the expansion of national territory," he wrote, "it delayed and almost defeated it." And, more than forty years ago, Professor Justin H. Smith, after a thorough examination of the evidence, dismissed the charges of a proslavery plot as a "mere collocation of circumstances and guesses." As Professor Chauncey S. Boucher put it in his presidential address before the Mississippi Valley Historical Association in 1921, the "evidence at every turn" is that instead of there being in the South a "powerful, united, well organized aggressive slavocracy," the South itself was far from being a unit in favor of annexation. The fact that extreme proslavery men objected to the step is a contemporary refutation of the idea that the Texas Revolution and the subsequent annexation of Texas, after nine years of independent existence, were the result of a premeditated conspiracy. But despite responsible refutation during the past half-century, the idea continues to prevail—a prime example of the persistence of historical error once it is established and admitted to the canon.

Equally persistent, and equally erroneous, is the common conception of the Mexican War as a predatory assault by a mighty United States upon a weaker neighbor. War with Mexico followed the annexation of

Texas; the war ended with California and the intervening territory in American possession—hence, it was asserted and believed, the United States precipitated the war for the purpose of securing California. To biased Whig partisans, the war was "Mr. Polk's War." To antislavery extremists, it was an unholy aggression to aggrandize the "slave power." And since it was precisely these elements in the population who were most vocal at the time, and whose voices have been most heard down through the years, the result has been that for the most part America has always approached the Mexican War in a shame-faced, apologetic fashion.

Such an attitude is not called for by the facts. The United States acted within its rights and in accordance with international properties in offering annexation to the independent republic of Texas. That republic acted within its rights and in accordance with the proprieties in accepting the offer. The United States did not force the conflict upon Mexico. The Mexican government insisted upon transferring to the United States the smoldering state of war with Texas which had existed ever since San Jacinto, declaring that it would "consider equivalent to a declaration of war . . . the passage of an act for the incorporation of Texas within the territory of the United States; the certainty of the fact being sufficient for the immediate proclamation of war."

The Mexican view of the situation was that Mexico was bound to attempt the reconquest of what it still regarded a revolted province. Under such circumstances, the United States could not have done otherwise than to protect its newly annexed territory and the people thereof from the repeated threats of active hostilities. The inevitable clash of arms happened to occur in the strip of territory between the Nueces and the Rio Grande, title to which was in dispute between Texas and Mexico. But, for that matter, all Texas, clear east to the Sabine, was likewise in dispute and was subject to the announced intention of Mexican reconquest.

The United States sought to avoid war with Mexico through negotiation of claims, boundaries, and other subjects in dispute—any and all subjects other than the fact of annexation, as to which, in the American view of the case, there was nothing to negotiate. The United States was also prepared to offer substantial monetary payment for California, which by 1845 had virtually freed itself from Mexican dominion and which it was suspected—though as we know now, erroneously suspected —was the object of covetous attention on the part of Great Britain. The American offer of purchase, however, had no effect upon the course of negotiations, since neither it nor any other proposals were permitted to be presented.

The government of President José Joaquín Herrera, in December, 1845, refused to receive an American minister authorized to conduct general negotiations, but the mere fact that Herrera had shown a pacific disposition helped to bring about the downfall of his government when General Mariano Paredes "pronounced" against him. General Paredes came to power as president at the beginning of 1846, upon a torrent of war talk, including the reassertion of the Mexican claim to all Texas and his intent to enforce that claim by reconquest.

In the light of Mexican internal politics, Paredes had little choice between negotiations and belligerency. But strange as such an idea seems to us today, he might well have anticipated Mexican victory in an appeal to arms. That, at least, was the opinion of some foreign observers. Mexico's population was smaller and her resources were less than those of the United States, it is true, but she was in position to put into the field a larger number of experienced soldiers, especially in mounted forces.

And when, in the spring of 1846, Paredes was called upon to decide for peace or for war, he might well have had in mind two even more important portents of possible Mexican victory. The first was the apparent possibility that in the event of war with Mexico, the United States might find itself engaged at the same time in war with mighty Great Britain over the Oregon question. True, Polk had not been elected on the slogan of "Fifty-four-forty or fight"—as Professor Edwin A. Miles has convincingly demonstrated[1]—but there was in the Oregon situation, nevertheless, a distinct possibility of hostilities. That possibility was averted by the willingness of Great Britain to negotiate its differences; but when President Paredes decided for war, the Oregon question was still open and war rumblings still were heard.

President Paredes may have been encouraged to his course, also, by what must have seemed to foreign observers to be a deep and irreparable cleavage on the Texas question within the United States itself, such as would materially impair the nation's ability to wage war with success. The utterances of those who regarded the annexation of Texas as the culmination of purposeful plottings of the slave power led Mexican diplomatic representatives in the United States to report that annexation would result in the certain secession of the New England states, and that New York and Pennsylvania, if they did not actually secede, would at least refuse to support any war with Mexico which might grow out of annexation. The event proved how baseless was the prediction, but when President Paredes made his decision, all that was in the future.

President Polk's expressed desire for the acquisition of California is cited as evidence that war was thrust upon Mexico for that purpose.

That Polk desired California is undeniable, but he wished to acquire it by purchase—as Louisiana had been acquired in Jefferson's presidency, as Florida had been acquired during President Monroe's term, and as John Quincy Adams, while President, had sought to acquire Texas itself. The desire to purchase California, however, was not transmitted to the Mexican government and played no part in bringing on the war with Mexico, which ended with the American forces, and the American flag, on the shores of the western ocean.

And so the movement west by south to round out the national territory was completed, as it had been begun, under southern leadership. Virginia and Virginia's daughter, Kentucky, took the first great step in the Old Northwest as the Carolinas and Virginia moved into the Old Southwest. Under Virginian leadership, Louisiana was purchased and explored. Under Andrew Jackson of Tennessee, the validity of that purchase was confirmed for all time and beyond all doubt. Under Sam Houston of Tennessee and Texas, this imperial domain in which we are met became independent, and, after a decade of independence, it became—under the leadership of Tyler of Virginia, Polk of Tennessee, and Houston himself—a state of the United States. The war which followed, conducted under the civil leadership of President Polk and the military command of General Winfield Scott of Virginia and General Zachary Taylor of Louisiana, was the final step in opening the way from the Alleghenies to the Pacific.

All along the way there were turning points where a course different from that which was pursued could have interrupted, interfered with, or even prevented the progression west by south which resulted in the development of the United States as a continental nation. If George Rogers Clark had not undertaken his "mad" venture that led to victory at Vincennes; if sectional opposition had succeeded in frustrating the purchase of Louisiana; if Wellington's estimate of the invincibility of his veterans had not been proved to be in error at New Orleans; if San Jacinto had turned out the other way; if "Mr. Polk's war" had resulted in the failure which many Americans hoped it would—if any of these things had happened, the United States might well have ended up with its territory truncated, its power impaired, and its possibilities for leadership in the world grievously diminished. But none of these untoward events transpired as America moved, west by south, to its appointed destiny.

Chapter XXIV

The Protestant Episcopal Church: An American Adaptation

WALTER B. POSEY

JAMESTOWN it was called, honoring the king, and there Chaplain Robert Hunt read prayers and gave thanks for a safe voyage.* On June 21, 1607, the Holy Communion, according to the Liturgy of the Church, was celebrated for the first time in America. Thus, the Church of England in the Colonies was introduced in the New World. A piece of wood nailed to two trees served as a pulpit, and an old sail gave slight protection against the sun until "a homely thing like a barn"[1] was built to hold the worshipping congregation. Set here in an unoccupied land, the colonists, bringing their minister, their Prayer Book, and their customs, sought to reproduce a small English parish with the old ways of life. This initial pattern of living became a somewhat concrete mold for transplanted communicants of the Anglican church. Nostalgically they clung to the familiar society, timorously ventured inland, and rarely with any enthusiasm moved far from the eastern seacoast. A century and a half after the first settlement in Virginia, its colonists were tied to England with the matriarchal strings of state and church.

The unquestioning acceptance of the institution of the episcopacy by the members of the English church in the colonies placed them at an incalculable disadvantage as compared to their fellow colonists. An acephalous organization in America could not be effective; supervision coming from the Bishop of London was worth but little, and the scattered parishes were held together by no obvious cord. The church's reputation was not benefited by the thriftless and profligate clergy of England who sought refuge in the colonies. Realization of this defect

*Presented in Nashville, Tennessee, November 6, 1958.

led to the creation in 1701 of the Society for the Propagation of the Gospel in Foreign Parts. Having the approval of both the crown and the bishops, this society provided "the only point of contact, the only bond of sympathy, between the Church of England and her children scattered over the waste places of the New World."[2] Its assistance to the colonists was two-fold: in missionaries who worked chiefly among the Indians; and in funds which supplemented the stipend of regular ministers in South Carolina, Georgia, and New York. To the zeal of this society the colonists throughout the eighteenth century were greatly indebted.

The very real evil in the church and colony situation arose in regard to ordination—an ecclesiastical impossibility outside of England. It was necessary for devout and learned men who were capable of praying for and instructing their neighbors to cross the ocean for the purpose of ordination by "a cross old gentleman at Canterbury." From America a cry for a bishop was seldom silent, but it fell on hearers who had only vague conceptions of the wants and surroundings of the colonists. The fact that other churches were on the scene with their complete equipment caused no real concern to the bishops, whose estimate of their office excluded the role of pioneer missionaries.

A group of Scotch-Irish Presbyterians, twice expatriated, had made a settlement on the eastern shore of Maryland about 1649. Influenced in some degree by the attractive offer of Lord Baltimore, they had turned to America as the land of hope and had found so many of their kin already there that in a relatively short time a native organization of large scope was easy to achieve. By the opening of the eighteenth century, immigrants, from Scotland and Ireland, came in like a flood at Boston, Philadelphia, and Charleston, the chief ports of entry. They swept through the seaboard regions to take possession of the frontiers lying in the rich valleys of Virginia and the Carolinas and to move on to the grasslands of Kentucky and Tennessee. Whole congregations came, bringing their ministers with them. Part of the furniture they brought with them was a sullen hatred for the Anglican church. "They planted in the new settlements the seed of hostility, or, at the best, dislike of the Church and her ways."[3] Whenever and wherever a group of Presbyterians found themselves living together, they gave religious tone to the settlements by organizing a church, selecting from among themselves a pastor whose ordination was the simple laying on of hands by some presbytery in session close by.

The local Baptist congregations, scattered the length of the Atlantic seaboard, functioned in almost complete freedom. No administrative office supervised the action of any church or dictated a program. The democratic form of government matched the democratic nature of its membership and appealed peculiarly to a people of little property or culture. They were generally looked on by other denominations with great disfavor. Originally identified with excesses of the Reformation and opposing themselves to long established usages, the Baptists were not always comfortable companions. The churches frequently provided a man's opportunity for self-government, and to him his voice, heard for the first time, sounded sweet and strong. If a Baptist congregation needed a preacher, it chose a man from among its members and ordained him, if no neighboring preachers were convenient.

The Methodist movement, beginning in a small society of Anglican churchmen who desired a personal religious experience, mushroomed with phenomenal growth in America. Its systems of leaders, classes, and circuits were peculiarly fitted to a widely scattered people. When the Bishop of London declined the requests to send a clergy to the American Methodists, John Wesley sent Thomas Coke as superintendent of the societies. Coke with Francis Asbury, a missionary already in America, surreptitiously assumed the title and function of bishops, organized a compact empire, cut the Methodist societies from the Anglican church, and started the Methodist Episcopal Church on its independent way.

So, except for the Church of England, the manner of securing preachers for a growing population in a widely scattered area seemed as simple as reaching into a bag. Now, it is indeed the truth that many a poor pig was pulled from the poke. But from all denominations there came the constant complaint that the supply of preachers was too meager to spread to the new communities and to possess the places which were available.

To people with vision the signs could early have suggested the forthcoming separation of the American colonists from the mother country. Distance as a factor making for independence was soon augmented by economic stability and security of the transplanted folk. The social, political, and commercial interests of the colony and the parent country became radically different, so that the colonial populace by the mid-eighteenth century shared no common sentiment over old or new loyalties and quite naturally and easily had fallen into groups of divergent interests. The Presbyterians and Baptists in the southern colonies, with few exceptions, were active in supporting the Revolutionary cause, in securing colonial liberties, and in forming a constitution for the new government. For all to see, the Baptists had already demonstrated the peculiar advantages of direct democratic government. The story is told that Thomas Jefferson had studiously observed a Baptist congregation near him.

Despite the loss of members and property, the Presbyterian Church emerged from the Revolutionary War in good condition. Its organizations were intact; its members were exultant over victory; its position was excellent to assume a new role of leadership and to resume the tasks so recently interrupted by war. The Baptist Church, like other denominations, lost buildings and schools during the war, yet found at the close it had had a great increase in membership throughout the colonies. Notwithstanding the prejudice and suspicion which hovered over the Methodists because of their Church of England origins, their societies had enjoyed a remarkable growth between 1775 and 1783. An increase of ten thousand members is sufficient evidence that the Methodists did not lose strength. Being practically an unhoused denomination, meeting in home cabins or forest clearings, it had little physical property to lose.

Upon the Church of England in the Colonies the ravages of war fell heaviest. Among the laity some felt a loyalty to their Prayer Book and not to the crown, and from this rank the church contributed to the American side such men as George Washington, Patrick Henry, John Jay, James Madison, the Morrises, the Pendletons, and the Pinckneys. But with the members of the clergy it was different. In the very act of ordination they had sworn perpetual allegiance to the king; herein lay an obligation which conscience could not easily lay aside. Upon them fell the fury of a patriotic populace; few priests were spared indignities of gown or person. Some fled to England, others to Canada, and others to anonymity, leaving the parishioners without priests, as sheep without shepherds. A small number of clergy, feeling absolved by circumstances, openly joined the cause of the patriots. A large proportion, however, by desire or discretion remained loyal to the government they represented. The missionaries, cut off from the support of the Society for the Propagation of the Gospel, had to abandon their labors. The churches were wrecked, the lands and property confiscated by legislation, the chalices and patens defiled, and the baptismal fonts lay in disuse. The disestablishment was accomplished.

When the independence of the American colonies was recognized by treaty, the Church of England in America ceased to exist. Since it was regarded as the church of the English officials in the colonies, its prestige was temporarily destroyed. Long hidden by the Establishment, the real weaknesses of the Episcopal Church lay distressingly bare in the southern colonies. As a religious denomination it was practically defunct. Its communicants drifted into several channels: into membership of other churches, into casual indifference which required no church affiliation, or into concerned isolation which served as a resting place until their kind reassembled.

Conceived in the same formative years and born out of the same set of circumstances, the government of the United States and the organization of the Protestant Episcopal Church reached actuality in the same fashion. Emerging from like schools of statesmanship, both organizations were molded according to the Federalists' notion of a strong central government made up of component parts. The achievement of neither was as simple as these sentences would indicate. Representative churchmen had met in an advisory convention in 1784, and in the next year they adopted a constitution which would provide a skeleton for the reviving church body. Let it be sufficient here to say that the constitution of the church established a unified church for the country, to act through deputies from the churches in the dioceses, meeting once in three years in a General Convention. The constitution vested the episcopate with separate but limited powers, admitted the laity to a major place in the government, and adopted the English Prayer Book with slight revisions so as to bring it into harmony with the political status. It was indeed bold business to form a constitution before the accession of the episcopate, but practical necessity justified this brief, but complete, reversal of the theory on which the church had been based. "It is our unanimous opinion," a contemporary acknowledged, "that it is beginning at the wrong end to attempt to organize our church before we have obtained a head. . . ."[4] Obviously, quick action was required by the three major problems which faced every thoughtful churchman: the preservation of church worship, the conservation of church property, and the inauguration of an American episcopacy.

After the initial step of securing a constitution, further resolution of the problems lay along uncertain approaches. Prior to any schemes for cooperation and union, representatives from Connecticut had taken steps in 1783 to obtain an American episcopate. Secretly sending Samuel Seabury to England for consecration, they hoped to have a bishop, but the Church of England was not free to comply with the request. Then turning to the Episcopal Church of Scotland, Seabury was consecrated at Aberdeen in November, 1784. He thus became the first bishop in the United States, but his position remained precarious until it was strengthened in 1787 by the English consecrations in Lambeth Palace of William White of Pennsylvania and Samuel Provoost of New York. The General Convention meeting in 1789 had the House of Bishops regularly constituted three months after the inauguration of President Washington. Successful union in the political field gave strength to the cause of union in the ecclesiastical field.

As if to plug a hole or to scotch a weakness recognizable after twelve years, the Protestant Episcopal Church adopted the Thirty-Nine Articles of the Church of England, a detailed statement of theology so capable of varying interpretations that it had been acceptable to High, Low, and Broad churches. True to the Roman Catholic background, the Church of England was characterized by zeal for forms of worship rather than for theological uniformity or reformation of society. These inherited characteristics remained quite evident in the transplanted church in North America. Once having achieved union and organization, the Protestant Episcopal Church concerned itself with the religious life of its parishioners by rite and ritual, but did not officially regard as its province their morals or institutions of public life.

Economic adjustment came slowly to the new republic. Stretching from Portsmouth to Savannah, the new nation lay in uneasy freedom while a remarkable group of men sought to give it body and form. Spent, as if exhausted after the straining effort for independence, men awaited the expected prosperity with disappointment and disillusionment. Hard times in the East magnified the attraction of the new land beyond the mountains from where shone the bright, new day of economic betterment. A restless folk in great waves of migration set out to find, join, or surpass the daring ones who earlier had settled in Pennsylvania, Ohio, Kentucky, and Tennessee. There was much similarity in the motives and attractions which prompted emigration from England to America and the lures which encouraged a tide of settlers to move rapidly from the Atlantic seaboard to the trans-Appalachian area.

From here on it is the limitation of this paper to follow the fortunes of the moving people and the one institution under consideration into the region south of the Ohio River and to note the alterations or mutations in the church patterns which the news scene exacted.

From the Bluegrass section and the Nashville Basin beckoning reports were sent to the tardy migrants east of the mountains. Varying in time but identical in enticement, they read the same: "So Rich a Soil we had never Saw before, Covered with Clover in full Bloom . . . it appeared that Nature in the profusion of her Bounties, had Spread a feast for all that lives. . . ."[5] Drawn by inducements or driven by necessities, a variety of people was put on the move. From Tennessee one observer wrote his mother: "On every pleasant evening during the last two months I can set in my porch and be almost continually in view of flocks of travellers flocking from every quarter of the adjacent territories. A large quantity of the travellers are from old Virginia some of them having a hundred slaves in family, and frequently accomplished ladies. . . ."[6] The clarion call never found better voice than in these plain words: "Any man who has been here is sinning against light and reason to live in No. C. And if the people of your neighbourhood knew what sort of place is here they would run away from their home. . . ." The West was spacious enough to accommodate comfortably also the disgruntled, floating stratum of society. Speaking of the opportunities in Alabama the same writer opened wide the door: "[Here are] the most exhilirating prospects which ever saluted the sight of man, and if in your knowledge you find any poor fellow who has dull spirits, the Hy po, any gripes or Belly ake just send him to this country. . . ."[7]

Uprooted from the normal conditions of life, the immigrants by necessity gave their first attention to building houses and clearing fields. If any single sentiment concerning religion characterized the masses, it was indifference. Less than one third of the population of Kentucky had any church affiliation at the time the state was admitted to the Union. Francis Asbury traveling in Tennessee in 1797 thoughtfully observed, ". . . I think it will be well if some or many do not eventually lose their souls."[8] A similar contemporary observation was made by David Rice from Kentucky, ". . . I found scarcely one man and but few women who supported a credible profession of religion. Some were grossly ignorant of the first principles of religion."[9] When John Stark Ravenscroft, Episcopal Bishop of North Carolina, journeyed to Tennessee in 1829 to organize the diocese, he noted that the majority of the people had "no visible connection with the Gospel."[10] Such illustrations can but indicate the early drift from established patterns of religious life. As grim realities of backwoods life increasingly dulled the luster of easy wealth and prosperity, the pioneer stood in need of hope and comfort to make his continuous toil more bearable.

At no time having a sufficient number of clergymen in the colonies, the Church of England was kept well in the bounds of established communities. In the southern colonies it had enjoyed the support of the wealthy and prominent families, the official favor, and the law, but with all of these considerations the church did not have a hardy growth. Rooted by tradition and hindered by custom, it kept to its familiar paths and refrained from following the tide of immigrants into the new lands. Prior to its disestablishment, the church had turned scarcely a glance toward the West. For the next score of years the Protestant Episcopal Church busily attended its own uncertain resuscitation and cautiously avoided overexertion. The beginning of the nineteenth century saw the national organization completed, with resident bishops in seven of the thirteen states and 206 ministers listed by the secretaries of the General Conventions.

Over the general debilitation serious churchmen shook their heads and made woeful comments in a similar tone. Bishop James Madison of Virginia shared the opinion of John Marshall that the church was "too far gone ever to be revived."[11] Bishop William White of Pennsylvania in restrospect said, "The congregations of our communion throughout the United States were approaching annihilation." The Reverend Devereux Jarratt, having previously served between nine hundred and a thousand communicants, lamented that he could scarcely find forty communicants after the Methodists had done their work. Both Bishop White and Bishop Madison, who knew the Methodists well, were genuinely interested in the plan of reunion initiated by Thomas Coke in 1791. When William Meade presented himself for ordination in 1811, family friends expressed general surprise that a college graduate of great promise would enter the ministry of the Episcopal Church. Joseph Doddridge, a former Methodist preacher turned Episcopalian, in surveying the prospects of Tennessee and Kentucky in 1818 claimed that these states had been largely settled by members of the Church of England, and not one in a thousand had heard the voice of an Episcopal minister. An English priest who had lived in and traveled through the West repeated the lament. "Throughout the western part of the United States there are multitudes who have been baptized and educated in the Episcopal Church. Yet by far the greater part of these, after waiting perhaps for many years in the hope of obtaining the services of a clergyman, have been swept away by the prevailing current of popular sentiment and have united themselves with dissenting denominations."[13]

The weak condition of the church and the dull spirit of the dioceses are best indicated by the records of the General Convention, which met triennially. Two bishops and twenty other clergymen met at the General Convention of 1789, and two bishops, twenty-four other clergymen, and fewer than ten of the laity sat at the Convention of 1811. In 1792 the Convention appointed a committee to plan for the support of ministers in the West.[14] These plans were ineffective, but they showed an awakening spirit concerning the duty of the church. In fact, the needs of the West carried so little significance that the region was omitted from the reports of the state of the church until 1817. The bishops urged congregations to send missionaries to destitute frontiers, but this slight gesture of interest had little effect. Nashville, Louisville, and St. Louis were without an Episcopal clergyman as late as 1822. The Domestic and Foreign Missionary Society of the Protestant Episcopal Church was established in 1820, but it was poorly supported financially. Monetary receipts of the tenth year amounted to thirteen thousand dollars; but, in truth, men and not money was the more urgent need. For nearly a decade the work of the society was directed mainly to American Indian missions, some of which were located in Mississippi, Kentucky, and Tennessee. In 1829 Bishop Thomas C. Brownell of Connecticut at the direction of the General Convention made a survey tour of the West. After traveling six thousand miles, he reported that he had found twenty-three Episcopal clergymen and twenty Episcopal congregations in the nine states through which he had passed. Such a report surely made thinking men question the direction in which the Domestic and Foreign Missionary Society was spending its efforts. A request for a missionary bishop to the western frontiers had been presented to the Convention of 1811, but either the needs or the means seemed sufficiently inadequate to delay the filling of this post until 1835. George W. Doane, Bishop of New Jersey, so well defined the office: "A missionary bishop is a bishop *sent forth* by the Church, *not sought for* of the Church; going before to organize the Church, not waiting till the Church has partially been organized; a leader, not a follower."[15] To this challenging office in the Northwest Jackson Kemper was assigned in 1835, and two years later Leonidas Polk was charged with the duties in the Southwest. The year 1835 brought notable change in the mode of missionary operations. Breaking with tradition, the church acknowledged its role as a missionary society and declared every member to be a missionary. The eastern upper and middle classes, traditionally dominant in the church, had finally compromised with the demands of a growing country.

The High Church party, representing the traditional and authoritative elements in the Episcopal church, had as its aggressive leader in America John Henry Hobart, who had been consecrated Bishop of New York in 1811. Time and space here do not permit a discussion of the High, Broad, and Low Church cleavages that had evolved in England and America through three centuries. As a means for immediate identification, it may safely be said here that the High Church group emphasized the authority of the episcopal office and stressed the supernatural elements in Christianity. In contrast, the Low Church of the nineteenth century emphasized the rational approach to Christianity and gave more attention to morality than to religion. In time the Low Church became partially captured by Evangelicalism so that the lines of demarcation became less clear and geographical divisions less distinct.

The most cheerful signs of a living church were found in the significant men elected bishops of the dioceses of Virginia and North Carolina. Richard Channing Moore, consecrated in 1813 as second Bishop of Virginia, began a movement that breathed life into a church that had been scarred by the Revolution, dulled by unenthusiastic preaching, and left "in a sort of respectable torpor" by the withdrawal of the Methodists. Bishop Moore was, in a manner, of the Evangelical school; he sought to alter the lethargic conditions by use of informal devotion and prayer meetings but regarded them as no substitute for the regular public devotions of the Prayer Book. Because of his efforts to invigorate the church in Virginia, Moore was accused of establishing a Methodist church rather than an Episcopal church. John Stark Ravenscroft, a man of dynamic energy and commanding personality, was elected Bishop of North Carolina in 1823. Having experienced a definite spiritual conversion at the age of thirty-eight, he believed that others should feel a comparable experience. During his brief term of office, Bishop Ravenscroft brought the Episcopal Church in his diocese into harmony with the spirit of modern life, but left on it the impress of the High Church party. His great energy, tireless journeying, and preaching of the doctrine of grace permitted nobody to utter the old reproach that Episcopal clergymen "guarded the decencies but neglected the essentials of religion." Bishop Moore and Bishop Ravenscroft represent a turn in direction of the church; the evangelical spirit with which they worked furnished the recreative power of the Episcopal Church and spread beyond them to many of the bishops working in the West.

To the office of bishop the church attracted singularly gifted ministers and able administrators in the six states in the area west and south of the mountains. From the back country the roll of the first bishops reads like a roll of giants: Benjamin Bosworth Smith was made Bishop of Kentucky in 1832; James Hervey Otey, Bishop of Tennessee, 1834; Leonidas Polk, Bishop of Louisiana, 1841; Stephen Elliott, Bishop of Georgia, 1841; Nicholas Hamner Cobbs, Bishop of Alabama, 1844; William Mercer Green, Bishop of Mississippi, 1850. Prior to the Civil War, each of these states had only one resident bishop. Two were born in Virginia, two in North Carolina, one in South Carolina, and one in Rhode Island. All were college graduates except Cobbs. At the time of their elevation to the office of bishop a majority of these men lived in the West or near the fringe of the frontier and were familiar with the needs of the dioceses and the small parishes. Bishop Cobbs died on the eve of the Civil War; Bishop Otey and Bishop Polk, during the war; Bishop Elliott, in 1866; Bishop Smith, in 1884; and Bishop Green, in 1887. An extensive investigation of much material written by or about these several bishops indicates, with a single exception, no lapses of decorum, breaches of faith or trust, or diversions from the strict path of duty. The stature and long tenure of this episcopal group explains in a large degree whatever success the church had in the new area to which it had moved.

Magnetic as these bishops were in personality and spirituality, they did not, contrary to expectations, draw to themselves or to their church a considerable number of men into the ministry. The supply of ministers which their states needed was ever insufficient and ever acted as a retarding factor in the expansion of the church. In 1840 the Episcopal Church had only 152 ministers in the states and territories west of the mountains—only a few more than the Baptist denomination alone had in the one state of Missouri. In the West it was well nigh impossible to raise a native ministry comparable in size with that of the Methodist Church, the Baptist Church, the Presbyterian Church, and the late-comer, the Disciples of Christ denomination. In 1836 Bishop Otey lamented: "We stand in pressing need of Ministers; and God only knows what is to become of our Church in this region . . . unless we can prevail upon the young and talented, and zealous of our Ministry, to come out to her help."[16] Bishop Smith, in a report to his Kentucky diocese in 1843, said that little progress for the church could be expected until a "native-born and home-bred clergy" supplied the message that would entice "the sons of the soil" to the altars of the church. Within a period of twenty-five years, he had seen only two native sons trained in the diocese, and neither of them had remained there. Despairing over the condition, the Bishop dared to express a wish for some Methodist ministers to see the light and to return to the parent church.[17]

The social position of the clergy was not well defined. By English tradition a clergyman should have enjoyed a unique place, but a general leveling was at work everywhere. In the South particularly the minister was treated by the planter, imitating English aristocracy, as an upper class servant. In the North, as a result of the examples set by the Congregationalists and the Presbyterians, the clergy was paid more respect but of a different character from that of the Church of England tradition. The West did not offer a perfectly congenial atmosphere to the transplanted eastern minister. In 1836 an Episcopal minister named Richard Cox wrote to the Bishop of Maryland that he was determined to leave Vicksburg, Mississippi, because of the wretched accommodations there and the shabby treatment he had received. As always there were two sides to such complaints, and many communities felt that some preachers had been sent without the necessary preparation for the sacrifices "to spend and be spent in the cause of Christ & the Church." Those men "who sorrow after the flesh pots of Egypt have no business here," wrote another Episcopal minister from Mississippi. The married ministers complained over the short tenure of the unmarried preachers who had left at home "affections [to] which they must return to redeem."[18] In Mississippi, where no unmarried preacher had remained permanently, the matter was really serious by 1839.

A college education or its equivalent from the personal tutelage of an ordained clergyman was the general preparation for a candidate for the Episcopal ministry. At the beginning of the nineteenth century the only way for a candidate to obtain in America his theological training was through personal guidance. The shift to institutional training occurred almost simultaneously in several denominations. Despite the high standard of education which the Protestant Episcopal Church sought to maintain, the church did not have a single college under its control before the General Theological Seminary was established in New York City in 1817 and the Episcopal Theological Seminary at Alexandria, Virginia, in 1823. In the Lower South several plans reached a partial fruition; but the span of success was short, and schools established in Alabama, Texas, and Kentucky were feeble efforts.

After years of preliminary discussions about a university for the Episcopalians of the South, Leonidas Polk, Bishop of Louisiana, made the first definite step by urging in 1856 the bishops of the nine southern dioceses to take immediate action for a joint school to be erected in the high area of the southeastern corner of Tennessee. He like Cobbs had seen the need for training ministers in a school conveniently located in the South. Responding to his plea, the dioceses sent delegates the next year to Lookout Mountain where final plans for a university were consummated. To the trustees was conveyed a land parcel of ten thousand acres, and a charter was granted by the state. In the fall of 1860 Bishop Polk laid the cornerstone for the first building of the University of the South. In view of the sectional controversy of that date, the name caused comments and accusations of sectionalism. Bishop Otey in reply denied any aim to build a Southern university, but admitted that it was planned as "an institution of conservatism" which would "still the waters of agitation" and "bind the discordant elements" into a "Union stronger than steel."[19]

Churches catering to the disinherited were in an enviable position in the valleys of mid-America. There the European and English tradition of class distinction was negligible. By ability and endurance the common man raised himself in rank and clamored for political, social, and religious acceptance and recognition. In such a situation a preacher with the gift of exhorting had an advantage over the college-trained minister. Some denominations held rigidly to their educational standards, others shuffled requirements for the ministry, and others, having had no prerequisites, required nothing but zeal. In this early scene the Episcopal minister with his formal worship had little attraction for the masses. The eminent respectability which characterized all activities of the church revealed too well the moderate temper of its communicants and indicated an uncongenial atmosphere for people of less refined sentiments. The sermons, carefully prepared and frequently read, had no stirring appeal to the plain man who wanted his damnation or salvation spelled out in no uncertain terms. He could not find absolute, black on white pronouncements from the words of the Episcopal minister. In his sermons the sinner's guilt and his immediate danger of Hell were not clearly revealed; the suffering of Christ on the Cross was not portrayed in deep color and moving tones; salvation by faith was not made clear. Restrained preaching did not arouse as did the stirring, gesticulating delivery of the Methodist, Baptist, and Disciples of Christ preachers. Bishop Otey, having returned from a long tour in Mississippi, commented on the amount of ignorance and prejudice he had witnessed. "Preaching, preaching, preaching," he said, was all the people seemed to care for. He had found that worship and prayer were secondary and the ordinances were accepted by many as mere signs of church membership. The accepted reputation for coldness of the Episcopal Church is reflected in a remark supposedly made by a local Methodist after a tornado had ripped a hole in St. Michael's Church in Charleston. "God Almighty's been trying to get into that church for a hundred and fifty years," he said, "and at last He's succeeded."

When the great waves of revivalistic flames swept the West during the first half of the nineteenth century, no Protestant group was spared except the Episcopal Church. There is considerable evidence that the revivals of the Methodist type had little effect on the Episcopalians, who like some Presbyterians considered the revivals as a sort of religious anarchy. Having a traditional dread of emotionalism and remembering the English bishops' opposition to the preaching of Whitefield and Wesley, the Episcopalians were frightened into a state of semi-helplessness by the camp meetings of the Methodists and the protracted meetings of the Baptists. As a consequence, the sober Episcopal Church, clothed with a curtain of caution that lowered the spiritual temperature, was regarded by the denominations that had accepted revivalistic methods as a spurious form of Christianity. Proof of the defect seemed evident to them in the lack of numerical strength of the Episcopal Church in the West. From many places the Episcopalians sent grave reports of the revivals. In Tennessee in 1848 an Episcopal minister described the revivals as "the most fearful delusion" and said, "extravagances of the most painful kind are looked upon as the necessary evidences of spiritual awakening. . . ." In the same year from Kentucky came another warning against camp meetings. "Tornadoes of the most awful excitements," wrote the Episcopal minister, "have, during the last year, swept over this part of Kentucky, with a violence I have never before witnessed. . . . How strange! that man can feed upon such unstable food. . . ." Even the newly organized Disciples of Christ Church swept through the valley in a fanatical storm. According to an Episcopal minister in Florence, Alabama, in 1846, the Campbellites had stirred the elements and literally seared the countryside of everything green.[20]

The Episcopal Church was subjected to many criticisms by people who had no understanding of the history of the church or the order of its services. Such critics spoke often of the tyrannical form of government and its unsuitability in western democratic society. Although there is little apparent difference in the governing bodies of the Episcopal and Methodist churches, the Methodists escaped this particular criticism by reason of the extremely democratic faith to which they subscribed. The emphasis on ritual which distinguished the Episcopal service probably enhanced the appearance of coldness to those unfamiliar with it. Bishop Cobbs was disturbed that his church had made so slight a numerical advance by mid-century. He was aware that the great mass of western people doubted the spirituality and piety of the Episcopalians. The church must have appeared to the frontiersman strangely tolerant and latitudinarian in its lack of concern for the moral standards in the emerging law and order of the new sections. This uncritical attitude of the church seemed to the common folk a sanction of the aristocratic and expanding planter society.

The literary beauty of the Prayer Book, in which Episcopalians gloried, offered no "springs of refreshment" to a man of meager education. It was the natural description which an ignorant man was heard to use of the service: "Come, let us go and hear that man preach, and his wife jaw back at him,"[21] referring to the responses made by Mrs. Otey, who was often the only respondent in the congregation. The very nature of the service separated the uneducated from it, as those who cannot read are not inclined to prove their ignorance. Bishop Otey has described well the field in which he labored in East Tennessee in 1856. In a courtroom of a country town, people had gathered through curiosity to see something different and to hear the preaching. Certainly they had not come to participate in the worship. They gave no responses to the prayers, and only a few men participated in the singing. He regarded this neglect of worship as the "prevailing characteristic of our population throughout the length and breadth of the land."[22] His efforts were so unrewarding that he felt that his voice was like one crying in the wilderness.

The general absence of organs stripped the church of the beauty of its music, and unaccompanied hymns strayed far from the original melodies. Chants by poor singers were no substitutes for the proper music; tunes of the approved hymns were forgotten or were mutilated; and the state of church music continued very low. The General Convention of 1789 had approved Tate and Brady's collection of Psalms set to meter and twenty-seven additional hymns for use in the service. It is significant that the General Convention, in response to a demand for more spontaneous singing, increased in 1807 the hymns to fifty-seven and in 1826 to 212. Fearing the extremes to which this last concession might lead, the Convention recommended that one Psalm be sung after the singing of a hymn. The stirring songs used by the Methodists and the Baptists had no counterpart among those used by the Episcopalians.

The use of the Prayer Book and the wearing of vestments in the Episcopal service caused some people to confuse these practices with those of the Roman Catholic Church. Bishop Cobbs felt there was some justification for this confusion since some ministers "under pretence of Antiquity and Catholicity [have] introduced various peculiarities, in matters connected with worship and chancel arrangements."[23] In 1836 a rector in Natchez had shifted to the Roman Catholic faith, and such instances were remembered through the years and were magnified beyond their importance. Five years after the event, a Vicksburg paper carried an article, prepared by a Methodist preacher and a Catholic priest, which described the steps that were leading the Episcopal Church "on her way to Rome."[24] The defection in 1852 of Levi Silliman Ives, Bishop of North Carolina, was indeed of serious moment and was regarded among churchmen as the result of extravagant "ritualism." The repercussions from the action of Bishop Ives were widespread and long-lasting.

In the West the sale of pews was an unsavory practice in any church. It recalled to a man an exclusiveness which might have had unpleasant associations in former places. The best seat for the highest price seemed to many to be a rank violation of democratic methods. Now without property or endowment, many Episcopal churches were dependent on pew tolls for their revenue to maintain the buildings and to support the ministers; slips or open pews were not at all common until after 1840.

By the peculiar necessities of the ritual, a permanent structure was generally the first requirement of a congregation. Often a single individual of wealth and prestige contributed the ground and building and would in time largely support a minister when he arrived. Churches with as few as a dozen communicants were not rare. By serving somewhat in a manner of the "chapel of ease," and affording a place for mediation and prayer, they strengthened their tenuous existence until a missionary arrived. Limited by scarcity of men and money, the church, unable to keep step with the westward migration, had to send its missionaries to centers of population.

Regardless of the permanence of the church building, survival of the congregation was the recurring problem. The migratory nature of the western population frequently disrupted the continuity of an Episcopal parish often struggling for existence. This was no affliction borne exclusively by one denomination, and probably it was less acute among the Episcopalians, who by social and economic status were not migratory folk. Restlessness, however, could not be bound by class distinction, and the Episcopal Church also suffered from the transiency of the times. Congregations that had been years in collecting were broken up in a few weeks. It was the same story regardless of the direction one looks. In 1846 from Jackson, Tennessee, came a complaint that no greater increase in numbers could be expected because of "the floating character of our population, the prejudices of the people, [and] the abounding of sects. . . ." And in the same year from Covington, Kentucky, the church reported that restless and adventurous people showed little interest in the church and were lost by removal.[25] Let us hope that the six clergymen who left Alabama in 1847–48 did so in order to follow their restless parishioners. Bishop Cobbs, four years after his elevation to the office, found himself assisted by only one of the clergy who had elected him and even he had changed parishes.

Episcopal churchmen in the West were very conscious of the criticisms which stemmed from ignorance and misinterpretation of their church. The bishops perhaps better than other men in their dioceses were aware of the needs of the time and the subsequent ecclesiastical adjustments necessary to bring the church in agreement with western life. But the bishops had to move slowly, since their office, a new one in America, was looked on with suspicion by some who remembered well the English corruptions. When they dwelt on points of union, they were accused of aloofness in the presence of the denominational controversies which flourished in Kentucky and Tennessee. Yet in their appraisal of society's needs, they moved straight forward in strengthening the connection between religion and morality. The careers of Bishops Otey, Polk, and Cobbs, to take some significant men on the southwestern scene, illustrate in numerous ways a changing church with fresh emphasis on religion as a vital force in social life. Probably the traveling bishop was the greatest break with the past and the most impressive adaptation of the church to the pressing needs of the area. Episcopalians who had long wondered what a bishop was like grew to know him. As Missionary Bishop of the Southwest, Polk served the states of Alabama, Mississippi, Louisiana, and Arkansas, the Indian Territory, and the Republic of Texas. In the first eighteen months of his episcopacy he spent only four months at home. At the end of a tour he wrote so knowingly to his brother: "I have often felt strongly that a missionary bishop ought not to have a family. He should be literally married to the Church." The parental love which commended good conduct of parish affairs also laid on a heavy hand with reprimands if the occasion demanded. "Take care," said a clergyman speaking of Polk, "that the bishop does not have to take you in hand. If he does, he will make you ache in every bone of your spiritual body." Concerning parochial administration, Polk cautioned his ministers: "Make yourself felt rather than seen in your people's work."[26] Applying religion to life, the bishops in sermons condemned indifference, worldliness, extravagance, and minor irregularities such as theatergoing, dancing, drinking, and card playing. Otey in a pastoral letter on "Christian Manners" made clear the distinction between a Christian and a worldly person. Cobbs, when asked what to preach, answered: "Preach what you can throw your feelings into."[27] Although opposed to the revivalistic methods, these bishops always were attuned to the evangelical spirit. But if the ends justified the means, it was a wise bishop who compromised with himself. In order to meet some religious excitement in Montgomery, Cobbs judiciously multiplied his services and visited from house to house. He thus demonstrated that the church could furnish adequate food for stimulated appetites. The meager salary of a bishop in a western diocese permitted no show of personal extravagances. Indeed, the simplicity of his living made him a part of his surroundings.

The manner in which the Episcopal Church adjusted to the rising problems of slavery is perhaps its most successful adaptation to society in the nineteenth century. Recognizing slavery as an established institution, the church through the Society for the Propagation of the Gospel had early committed itself to a missionary program for the Negroes in America. In its flourishing colonial days, the church had performed extensive work with the Negroes in the low country in the southern colonies. Later, in the old places the program was the same, and in the new lands the church supplied both missionaries and ministers for slaves who belonged to the Episcopal communicants. The churches were equipped with gallery seats for the slaves so that they could worship in the regular services, for they, like the children of the family, were expected to attend all services. Upon the master was placed the duty of furnishing his slaves with the opportunity for baptism and religious instruction. Bishop Polk supplied a chaplain for the instruction of his slaves and day nursery care for their children. On his plantation the Bishop said prayers in the cabins with as much regularity as in his own home. Bishop Cobbs was so indulgent with his slaves that Mrs. Cobbs had to assume the care and control of them. In 1838 George Weller, a missionary at Memphis, baptized at a nearby plantation ten Negro adults and thirty-seven children in a rude log cabin hastily equipped for the service. Before leaving he had gained the consent of the planter to build a chapel for his slaves and to employ a catechist for their instruction. The extreme is found in the case of Dr. William Newton Mercer, a planter with extensive holdings near Natchez. In order to provide for the spiritual welfare of his 1,000 slaves, Dr. Mercer had erected a chapel and a rectory costing nearly $30,000 and in addition paid the salary of the chaplain. Bishop Otey commended the fine situation and once participated in the baptizing of 120 Negro children and adults.

Here and there various societies were organized for aiding missionaries to the Negroes. In 1848 the Society of the Protestant Episcopal Church for Diffusing Christian Knowledge in the Diocese of Mississippi was established with the purpose of assisting masters in giving religious instruction to their slaves. The machinery obviously functioned with greater ease than its title would indicate, for from 1851 to 1861 its 100 members contributed $15,000 to the cause.

Nearly all of the southern bishops owned slaves, either by inheritance or purchase. This fact indicates their acceptance of slavery as an endurable if not justifiable burden. When his wife had the option of inheriting money or 400 slaves, Bishop Polk of Louisiana encouraged her to take the slaves, as he thought thereby he could function better in his state as a man of influence. Evidence of his compromise is found in his reaction to slavery as he had seen it as a younger man traveling in England: "The more I see of those who are without slaves, the more I am prepared to say that we are seriously wronging ourselves by retaining them. . . ."[28] When Cobbs, before his consecration as bishop, left Virginia to move to Ohio, he thought it well to free his slaves, but they declined to be left behind. Cobbs, like many thinking men, saw the terrible plight of the freedman and thought his own responsibility lay in the care of the Negro rather than in throwing him without substance or means of living into a society which had no place for him as a free man. He was persuaded that the services of the Episcopal Church were "eminently suited to the wants and circumstances of the colored people,"[29] because its elementary instruction and constant repetition fastened truth on the memory. In his first convention address, Stephen Elliott,

Bishop of Georgia, spoke of the responsibility of the diocese to the Negro: "The religious instruction of our domestics, and of the negroes upon the plantations, is a subject that should never be passed over in the address of a Southern Bishop." He visited plantations, baptized and confirmed Negroes, and insisted that the Negroes were not opposed to the services and the beliefs of the Episcopal Church. "There should be," he said, "much less danger of inhumanity on the one side, or of insubordination on the other, between parties who knelt, upon the Lord's Day, around the same table, and were partakers of the same Communion."[30] It was the practice of Bishops Otey, Elliott, Cobbs, and Polk to administer confirmation to whites and blacks at the same time, kneeling at the same altar rail. Interpreting the acts of the bishops as reflections of the church's attitudes, serious laymen followed the examples set for them in patriarchial relationship. Between the master and the slave, "It was not the virtue of democracy, the practice of equality, but the virtue of aristocracy, *noblesse oblige,* which was exercised in this relationship."[31] Quite rationally from this premise, the church did not consider slaveholding a sin and never officially sought to make it a subject of discipline.

A similar attitude toward slavery was found in the northern congregations of the Episcopal Church. The pronouncements of two leaders will indicate the position of many churchmen who lived outside the rich farmlands of the South. During the Civil War, John H. Hopkins, Bishop of Vermont, declared that slavery was not in opposition to God's will and that slavery as found in the South was far more desirable than the system of the employer and the hired slave. Samuel Seabury, a Protestant Episcopal clergyman of New York, in a book, *American Slavery . . . Justified,* published just before the Civil War, expressed his acceptance of the point of view of southern slaveholders and insisted that slavery was not forbidden by the New Testament and had been established by Divine Providence. The same sentiment had been expressed as early as 1834 by Bishop Ives of North Carolina in a sermon and then printed: "No man or set of men are entitled to pronounce slavery wrong; and . . . as it exists in the present day it is agreeable to the order of Divine Providence."[32] These attitudes sprang from the sincere convictions that what is is right and that it is not the duty or privilege of man to depreciate or criticize the powers ordained of God. The action taken in 1843 by the Diocese of Louisiana seems now most typical in interpreting the attitude of the church toward slavery. The Episcopal churches, it declared, are "not political crusaders, but simple and guileless teachers" of the Gospel, and they should not "dogmatize on the civil relations or rights of individuals" but rather should be "chiefly concerned with the hearts and consciences of those to whom we go."[33] In 1856 the letter of the bishops to the General Convention advised that with party politics and sectional disputes the ministry should have no dealings.

As sectional differences became more marked by vested interests and as controversies over slavery reached white heat, the Protestant Episcopal Church by virtue of its class solidarity was in a unique position on the eve of the Civil War. Almost unique, I should say, for the Disciples of Christ had reached the same place from the other end of the ladder. The Disciples of Christ, centered in Tennessee, Kentucky, and western Virginia, wore the cool aloofness of border interests. This church had neither stretched itself over a large area nor gathered into its fold people of widely different tastes, cultures, and backgrounds. Strictly from the standpoint of membership, the Protestant Episcopal Church, although a national church, had sectional strength—three-fourths of American Episcopalians were residents of free states in 1850. Denominations whose members were evenly distributed in slave states and free states were split by slavery; sectional churches were able to avoid division. Had the Episcopal Church permitted itself to be involved in the political storm prior to the Civil War, any attempt to adopt in the General Convention a resolution condemning slavery would have been resisted solidly by southern bishops, other clergy, and laity, and would have precipitated a division in the church. A split in the church body was too dear a price to pay for the enforcement of a different social pattern on its southern members. When political secession was first proposed, Bishop Otey wrote to Bishop Polk: "It is God alone that can still the madness of the people. . . . To what quarter shall we look, when such men as you and Elliott deliberately favor secession? What can we expect, other than mob-law and violence among the masses, when . . . the Ministers . . . are found on the side of those who openly avow their determination to destroy the work which our fathers established . . . ?"[34] Polk had hoped for peaceable secession; Cobbs with clearer vision saw that it was impossible, for there was no natural boundary.

When secession became a reality, southern leaders in the Episcopal Church, following the precedents and principles of 1789, maintained that political separation in conformity with the autonomous dioceses necessitated the formation of a new church. On July 3, 1861, delegates to a convention met in Montgomery to draft a constitution for the Protestant Episcopal Church in the Confederate States. Not until September 19, 1862, three days before Lincoln issued the Emancipation Proclamation, was the official announcement made of the acceptance of the constitution by the requisite number of dioceses. The Episcopal Church, true to its traditional policy of noninterference in church and state relation, contributed few elements to encourage division or to hinder reunion. The

General Convention so tactfully ignored the existence of ecclesiastical secession that it was possible for the seceding dioceses to return agreeably to their former status at the end of the war. The devotion of Episcopal churchmen to the catholic aspects of their religion had outweighed whatever concern there may have been for social and political issues which had disturbed and divided other churches.

By 1850 the Protestant Episcopal Church, with a program of evangelism and expansion directed by a devoted and capable clergy and laity, had regained the numerical strength which it had enjoyed prior to the American Revolution. A steady addition of communicants, coming largely from other churches, raised the Episcopal Church to sixth place in membership among American denominations—a position approximately the same as it holds today. This strength was well concentrated in the eastern states, with about 5 per cent of its members living in the Tidewater section at the time of the Civil War and even less in the back country of the southern states. The social and economic status of its members may be inferred from the fact that in value of church property it ranked third. From an upper-middle class the church had a core of strength and influence which provided financial resources and social prestige far beyond the normal expectations of its size. These tangible facts lead safely, so it seems, to the assumption that the Episcopal Church between the American Revolution and the Civil War had suitably adjusted itself to design, purpose, and needs. By rules of arithmetic and other inadequate yardsticks, the church lagged far behind some major denominations in the South. Yet this method of comparison fails to take into account the nature of the church and its inheritance, the type of communicant, and the goal to which both the church and the communicant aspired—a sober, moral impact upon a growing country. Judged by education, devotion, sincerity, refinement, and courage, the galaxy of bishops who served the church in the South had no superior among the ecclesiastical leaders in other churches. In the area to which this paper is limited the Episcopal Church and Episcopalians, wise and expedient, accepted many of the bases of a society somewhat crude and unlettered. Although a modified form of Evangelicalism prevailed in several of the dioceses and limited adaptations were made to current religious practices and demands, this transplanted church remained close to its traditional faith and ritual.

Chapter XXV

The Gentleman from Louisiana: Demagogue or Democrat

T. HARRY WILLIAMS

W AS IT TRUE, the reporter asked, probing deeper with his questions, that the state officials and the legislature of Louisiana were corrupt?* Governor Henry Clay Warmoth exploded. His answer reflected what one suspects was a common complaint of the carpetbagger caught up in the swashbuckling politics of Louisiana but at the same time demonstrated that he himself was rapidly adjusting to the realities of the Louisiana scene. "I don't pretend to be honest. . . . I only pretend to be as honest as anybody in politics, and more so than those fellows who are opposing me now. Here are these New Orleans bankers making a great outcry against the dishonesty of the Louisiana legislature. . . . I tell you . . . these much-abused members are at all events as good as the people they represent. Why, damn it, everybody is demoralized down here. Corruption is the fashion."

One may admit a certain exaggeration in the Governor's remarks, and also in the statement of a later critic that Louisianians are not interested in ideologies or principles but in the fundamentals—the whir of slot machines, the pounding of horses' hoofs at the Fair Grounds, and the clink of ice in a Sazerac cocktail. Nor is it necessary to adopt the judgments of those commentators who say that Louisiana is not an American state but a banana republic, a Latin enclave of immorality set down in a matrix of Anglo-Saxon righteousness, a proposition whose basic assumption is highly dubious both in the light of history and present observation. And yet without question Louisianians have a concept of corruption not found in other states. They seem to accept it as a necessary concomitant

*Presented in Atlanta, Georgia, November 12, 1959.

of political life, and, on occasion, even to delight in it. It is an outlook peculiar to the state, perhaps an expression of Latin realism, and it has made Louisiana politics undeniably different. Corruption, which as defined by purists often means only the compromises that are required to keep the machinery of democracy running, has appeared in all states where it has been worthwhile and at all levels of government and has been practiced by all classes. In the Louisiana attitude toward corruption there is little of the sanctimoniousness often found in Anglo-Saxon communities; indeed, there is even a tendency to admire a "deal" if it is executed with skill and a flourish and, above all, with a jest. Louisianians, more than any other people in America, realize, with a kind of paradoxical honesty, the hard fact that politics is not always an exercise in civics book morality. In 1939 Gallup pollsters asked a sample group in the state, "Do you think elections in Louisiana in recent years have been honestly conducted?" Twenty-five per cent answered "Yes," 60 per cent answered "No," and 15 per cent sagely ventured no opinion. The frankness of the response would not have surprised Governor Warmoth.[1]

But we would be committing a common scholarly error if, in picturing the political anatomy of Louisiana, we emphasized unduly either the color or the proportions of the corruption. Academic people, as well as the general public, expect too much of politics; they are too prone to be horrified by departures from an ideal standard of morality that is largely imaginary. As Pendleton Herring has pointed out, a double code of ethics holds for politics. We judge politicians by a higher standard than we apply to men in spheres of private action. This is wrong and can even be dangerous, Herring tells us, because the politician, whose function is to compromise the conflicting desires of frail mankind, has to treat government as a problem of mechanics rather than as a question of morals. "The politician is concerned not with what should be but with what can be."[2] If strong men are forced out of politics by too puristic standards, lesser men will take their place. We may recall Emerson's warning in this connection: "Better, certainly, if we could secure the strength and fire which rude, passionate men bring into society, quite clear of their vices. But who dares draw out the linchpin from the wagon-wheel?"[3] But Americans have always had a curious bifocal view of corruption. Throughout our history we have tolerated corruption to an extraordinary degree, have even encouraged it for certain ends, and in some of the relations between government and business have put it to broad social and economic ends. Perhaps more research is required in this area of behavior, concentrating on the psychology of the corruptible rather than on the arts of the corruptor. It may be that one of our greatest scholarly needs is an honest history of corruption.

Rather than corruption being the hallmark of Louisiana politics, a zest for politics as a game and an appreciation of politics as a power lever have been the distinguishing qualities. Describing the political scene in the 1850's, one historian writes that to a greater degree than in most states "the active electorate revealed a peculiar enthusiasm for the dramatic clash of personalities, the stratagems of politics, and the winning of public offices."[4] Or, put in less academic terms, the state took its politics raw, like corn whiskey, and loved the diet. This fact was not lost on Governor Warmoth, who was an extremely resourceful and audacious operator, possessing in high degree that quality of ignoring existing rules and making up his own that in a politician we call genius. Coming into office with an insecure power basis and confronted by a constant, cunning, and sometimes unscrupulous opposition, he erected an imposing facade of laws that invested him with imperial authority. He could appoint and remove local registrars of voters, tax collectors, and assessors. He could appoint the board of police commissioners in New Orleans, which controlled the selection of all personnel; constables for all parishes except Orleans, Jefferson, and St. Bernard (which were subject to the Metropolitan Police, a state force accountable to the governor); and all members of the militia. He could fill all vacancies in local offices, including those in the potent parish police juries. He could order the arrest of persons anywhere in the state and direct local enforcement officers to execute the warrant, and authorize officers in one parish to aid those in another. On the noninstitutional level Warmoth invaded the floors of the legislature to lobby for his bills and to berate his own followers, and he required undated resignations from some of his appointees. All in all, it was an extraordinary performance in power, and the example most probably impressed a later leader of greater stature than Warmoth.

In 1893 in the north-central parish of Winn there was born a son, the seventh in what would be a family of nine, to Huey P. Long, Sr. The boy was named Huey P. Long, Jr. He grew up in an environment that physically was no different from other areas in rural Louisiana but that possessed a unique historical heritage. Winn was undeniably poor, a parish of small farms, cutover timber lands, and lumber mills. The people had a wry saying that they made a living by taking in each other's washing. The Longs were as well off as the average, perhaps slightly above, the father in 1900 owning 340 acres of land and other property assessed at $780. Historically Winn had a tradition of dissent not equalled by any other parish. In 1861 the delegate from Winn to the secession convention was one of seventeen members who voted against final passage of the secession ordinance and one of seven who refused to sign it. Although the parish furnished three companies to the Confederate service, most of the inhabitants seem to have sat the war out, many refusing to fight to save the rich man's slaves and some openly supporting the Union. John M. Long, Huey's grandfather, was not in the Confederate army, and Huey's father professed strong Union sympathies. The old man told a reporter, "Didn't Abraham Lincoln free the niggers and not give the planters a dime? Why shouldn't Huey take the money away from the rich and still leave 'em plenty? . . . Maybe you're surprised to hear talk like that. Well, it was just such talk that my boy was raised under and that I was raised under. My father and my mother favored the Union. Why not? They didn't have slaves. They didn't even have decent land." It is not surprising—but of great significance—that in his political career Huey P. Long never seriously employed the Confederate legend in his speeches. He stuck to economics in an era when most southern politicians entertained their audiences of rural poor with the magnificent irrelevancy of how their grandpappies had charged up the slopes at Gettysburg.

The parish added to its record of dissent in the farmers' revolt of the 1890's, emerging as the leading center of Populist strength in the state. In the election of 1892 the Populist gubernatorial candidate, a resident of Winnfield, the principal town, swept the parish by a margin of almost five to one, and the Populists won every election in Winn until 1900. The spirit of social protest represented by Populism carried over into a surprising support for Socialism. A strong Socialist party appeared that elected half of the parish officials in 1908 and its slate of municipal officials in Winnfield in 1912. And in the presidential election of the latter year Eugene Debs received almost 36 per cent of Winn's popular vote. This was rural Socialism, of course, hardly distinguishable from Populism, but it is significant that so many Winn residents were not afraid to wear a label that was not popular in the rural South. No Long apparently was a member of either the Populist or Socialist movement. In fact, Huey Long, while still a schoolboy, once debated two touring Populist lecturers, upholding the merits of the Democratic party. But obviously Long's whole political philosophy was shaped and conditioned by the tradition of his environment. If his program has to be labeled, it was neo-Populism.

It is not so clear, however, where Long derived his later formula of Share Our Wealth. Most commentators have ascribed its origins to the Populism and Socialism that Long heard discussed in his youth, and the plan does have overtones of both these creeds. Long himself said that he got the idea from the Bible, but the appeal to Holy Writ seems to have been window dressing. Indeed, Huey may have come to the Bible late, although the evidence on this point is contradictory. According to one story, in the state campaign of 1920 a friend quoted to him a verse that could be used to damage an opponent. Huey, much impressed, peeled off a bill and said, "Go over to Hirch and Lehmen's store and buy me the best damn Bible they've got." Reliable evidence indicates that Long, a keen student of history and thoroughly familiar with the Reconstruction period, drew the inspiration for Share Our Wealth from the experiment of the Freedmen's Bureau and its forty acres and a mule. And it may be that he took another leaf from the lesson of Reconstruction, for when he finally unseated the old political hierarchy in 1928, in erecting his own power structure he would employ, consciously or unconsciously, many of the techniques and devices of Governor Warmoth.

After the overthrow of Reconstruction, the sources of power in the South fell to, or were taken by, the upper income groups, represented roughly by the planters and the new industrial and commercial interests. In every state such an oligarchy dominated the political scene, exercising its power in the Democratic party through the medium of a machine or a combination of factions. Occasionally rebels rose here and there to challenge the existing hierarchies. These are the men we know by the much abused term of demagogue. As W. J. Cash explains them: although in their rise to power they exploited the aspirations of the masses, they did little for the masses when they got power—partly because they were more interested in place than in programs, partly because, although they built their own machines to perpetuate themselves, they were unable, or unwilling, to destroy the old machine, and hence their tenure was never secure.[5] No demagogue of this type appeared to defy the existing order in Louisiana. For almost fifty years after Reconstruction the oligarchy ruled serenely, made confident and smug by the knowledge that its network of influence and interest enveloped the entire state.

The Louisiana hierarchy contained the usual elements found in other southern states and some peculiarly its own. In addition to the familiar planting groups, there were important business interests: lumber, railroads, and sugar. Above all, there was oil; in the 1920's the Standard Oil Company became a major economic and political force in the life of the state. In New Orleans there were shipping interests and gas and electrical utilities. And in the great urban center there was a genuine big city machine, the Old Regulars or the Choctaw Club, closely allied with the business and financial powers. The Old Regular organization was largely the creation of Martin Behrman, long-time mayor and author of the classic statement, "You can make corruption illegal in Louisiana but you can't make it unpopular." The machine performed some of the desirable functions expected of such associations and many of the undesirable ones. In the words of one friendly observer, "The Old Regulars were used to buying out and trading out and swapping out." By means of padded registration rolls, paid up poll tax receipts, and police pressure, the machine could swing the city to any side or candidate. In a gubernatorial election the machine would endorse a candidate with a strong country following in return for a pledge of control over state patronage in the city. The relationship was not, however, as tight or tidy as it sounds; it was almost wholly informal, and no rigid, state-wide machine existed.

Such was the ruling hierarchy, satisfied with things as they were, discreetly corrupt on occasion, devoted to the protection of privilege. It did not even trouble to make the masses feel important by appealing to them for votes, those that could vote; the small towns and the forks of the creeks rarely heard a candidate for governor. The leaders of the oligarchy were singularly blind to the signs of the time. Although the Progressive movement had touched Louisiana, its impact had been light, and what change had occurred had been mild, almost imperceptible. Riley J. Wilson, the hierarchy's candidate for governor in 1928, thought that Long's proposal to pave the roads was preposterous because it would cost too much money. Nor would the ruling classes accept the inevitability of change even when they saw Long swept into power on a program demanding change. Looking back today, many of them see that they made a fatal error in opposing every idea advanced by Long. But said one dolefully, "There is no reform from within, it comes only by defeat." Others still do not know what happened to them. Old patricians who stood apart from the machine or affected not to see its workings ask, "Why should the voters have repudiated men who believed in honest, economical government?" They do not know that the masses in any state are not impressed by honesty unless it promises to bring a better life. The Louisiana ruling class is a perfect illustration of an elite inviting destruction by its own myopia. As he well knew, Huey Long was fortunate in his enemies. "It has been my good fortune to have blind men like these in politics," he said. "They cannot see something after it has passed over them, and they have been knocked down by it a half-dozen times."

Before the advent of Long on the Louisiana scene, governors were elected by "leaders," who usually were the sheriffs of the parishes. The candidate who lined up the largest number of influential leaders could make a deal with the city machine and take the office. Abruptly and rudely Long destroyed this pattern. Often in his first campaigns he would invade a parish and denounce the boss. There was design in this. As he explained to one man, the boss had 40 per cent of the vote, 40 per cent were opposed to him, and 20 per cent were in-between. "I'm going into every parish and cuss out the boss. That gives me 40 per cent of the votes to begin with, and I'll hoss trade 'em out of the in-betweens."

Whatever the formula, it worked. In the rueful words of one opponent, "Overnight, one might say, the leaders found themselves without followers, and the mob was in control." Long then created his own local organization, the sheriff or leader being his man. "That man was sheriff and leader because Huey wanted him to be," explained one admirer. "He cut out the middleman in politics. He went directly to the people. Sometimes he would appoint two leaders to watch each other, and deal directly with the people. That's a system you can't beat."

If Long had stopped after creating an organization of his own, no matter how effective, he would merely have followed the path of previous politicians of his type. But he did more. As W. J. Cash shrewdly perceived, Long was the first southern mass leader to set himself, not to bring the established machine to terms, but to overwhelm it and replace it with one of his own.[6] Long told a former teacher at Tulane University, "That damn political science class of yours with your talk of ideals held back my political career for years. I'm fighting a crooked machine in the Old Regulars and have to fight fire with fire. You have to protect your own damn fools." He did, indeed, face a powerful and implacable opposition. In fact, during Long's entire political career there was hardly a time when he was not under some kind of threat of removal or impeachment. "I have tried for about sixteen years to have it some other way," he once said, "and it has never been any other way, so now I have stopped trying to have it any other way." He was saying that the oligarchy was ruthless and that he would fight it on its own terms. Writers who discuss the so-called demagogues like to detail the methods by which these men supposedly corrupted politics, but they forget that the demagogues only utilized and sometimes improved techniques used for years by the elite and employed particularly against spokesmen of the masses. For instance, in the impeachment proceedings against Long in 1929 the opposition offered huge sums of money for votes to convict. Huey himself charged that Standard Oil brought enough money into Baton Rouge to "burn a wet mule." In addition, the crudest kind of economic pressure was applied. Long retaliated with promises of jobs and favors. Often quoted is Long's remark that he bought legislators like sacks of potatoes. This was made when one legislator who had announced he would vote for conviction switched to Long's side. Asked how he had secured him, Huey replied, "Just the same way they got him. It's just like going to market and getting a sack of potatoes. They got a fixed price. You bought him that way and I bought him the same way."

Of necessity, Long had first to create an organization to pass his program in the legislature. He went into office with a minority of pledged supporters. In the lower chamber he could count on only nineteen votes, whereas, as many of his measures had to be cast in the form of constitutional amendments, he needed a two-thirds majority or sixty-seven. Gradually the desired control was built up, but in the frank words of one Long leader, "They all didn't come for free." The basis of the Long machine was patronage. Deliberately, Long as governor extended his power over existing boards and other agencies, and through the creation of new agencies to perform new functions he continually enlarged the patronage at his disposal. Eventually he was able to deprive the opposition of almost all political sustenance, and then he finally brought the Old Regulars to their knees. In the last phase of his career he reached out for more and more power, too much power, pushing laws through the legislature that repeated Warmoth's program of control of local government and election machinery and went even beyond it.

Like countless other politicians before and after him, Long built a powerful machine. But being a supreme realist, he knew that there were certain areas of government that had to be immune from politics. That is, some jobs had to go to men who would not be interfered with by anybody. This was necessary both to insure the proper functioning of government and to preserve the life of the machine. He insisted that appointees to certain positions enjoy complete freedom of decision and action. Said one not altogether friendly observer, "He was smart that way. He knew where to fit men into positions—nonelastic men." When a judge told him that Long followers were trying to influence his decision on a case, Huey told him to disregard the pressure, "Remember that a crooked judge is no credit to Huey Long." To some heads of departments he would say, "The only thing I ask you is not to hire any of my enemies." The federal Resettlement Administration feared that Long would try to politicize its program, and sent a man to Louisiana to watch him. This official found to his surprise that it was the opposition that demanded the patronage. One day Huey called him in, assured him that he wanted the program to succeed and would not interfere with it. Then, thinking of his enemies, Long added, "The first time I catch you appointing somebody because one of those sons of bitches tells you to, I'll drive you out of Louisiana."

Political machines have to have money, to sustain the strength of the organization and to perform certain welfare functions expected by their followers. This was particularly true in the 1920's and the early 1930's, before the impersonal welfare of the New Deal and later of the states substituted for the services of the machines and hence undermined their power. Long leaders are completely frank in explaining how the machine raised money for campaigns and for other purposes, notably publicity. Because most of the press was in opposition, Long hit on the idea of disseminating his ideas through printed circulars, some 26,000,000 being distributed. During Long's administration the state engaged in a tremendous road building program. The road contractors and contractors on other public works were called on for regular contributions in elections. So also were the distributors of highway machinery, who enjoyed lucrative relations with the state, and the companies that wrote the state's insurance. For obvious reasons, these interests met their assessments. The number of state employees was deliberately maintained at a high level, the jobs being spread around lavishly, and the occupants had to contribute a percentage of their salaries to the machine war chest. Some officials were required to render monthly payments, but in Long's time lower salaried workers were assessed only before elections. In addition, there were approximately a thousand leaders and subleaders who stood ready to supply money for critical needs. As one of these told the writer, "He would send for me and all these other men to come to his room in the Roosevelt, and he would say 'I need $60,000 to pay the poll taxes,' and we would all shell out and that is how Huey got his money. He didn't have to graft it." Not only do Long leaders frankly detail these financial dealings, they insist passionately that the machine's system of raising money was moral, certainly more moral than the system of the opposition. The opposition, they say, asked for money from the interests under the table and hence was subject to the power of a minority, whereas the Long organization took money openly and hence was free to act for the majority.

And act for the majority the machine did. Huey Long was the first southern mass leader to leave aside race baiting and appeals to the gold-misted past and address himself to the social and economic ills of his people. The record of accomplishment can only be summarized here. In 1928 Louisiana had 296 miles of concrete roads, 35 miles of asphalt roads, 5,728 miles of gravel roads, and three major bridges within the state highway system. By 1935 the state had 2,446 miles of concrete roads, 1,308 miles of asphalt roads, 9,629 miles of gravel roads, and more than forty major bridges within the state highway system. In the field of education, free textbooks were provided (stimulating a 20 per cent jump in public school enrollment), appropriations for higher education were increased, and over 100,000 adult illiterates, of both races, were enrolled in free night schools. Facilities in state hospitals and institutions were enlarged, and the services were modernized and, more important, humanized. The money to pay for this tremendous program came partly from increased taxes, bearing largely on corporate interests, but mostly from bonds, the state debt jumping from $11,000,000 in 1928 to nearly $150,000,000 by 1935.[7] Moreover, the costs were based on sound financial practices, the legislature appropriating no money without collaterally providing the revenues and bond issues being capitalized by taxes. Not the least accomplishment in Long's record was his revitalizing of state politics. He created a new consciousness of politics on the part of the masses. By advancing issues that mattered to the masses and by repealing the poll tax, he stirred voter interest to a height unmatched in any other southern state, and he left Louisiana with an enduring bifactionalism that has many of the attributes of a two-party system.

The secret of Long's power, in the final analysis, was not in his machine or his political dealings but in his record—he delivered something. One man, trying to put through to the writer the impact of Long on the masses, could say only, "They felt the hand of Huey." But how is his record to be evaluated? In looking at various judgments of Long, we discover again that curious tendency of scholars to hold politicians to an ideal and impossible standard. Thus one writer lists Long's accomplishments and concedes them to be impressive, but then says, "Aha, they amount to nothing because he didn't touch the problem of sharecropping and tenancy."[8] Another, forgetting that Long acted in a largely rural state, cries, "Yes, but he did little for labor."[9] Such complaints are like saying, "Why didn't Franklin Roosevelt nationalize the banks?" The answer to such queries is, of course, that seemingly ideal solutions may not be politically possible or feasible at a given moment. The politician does what he can, not what he should do. If he acted otherwise, he would cease to be a politician and the democratic system would cease to exist.

Was Huey Long a dictator? The term was thrown at him freely in the 1930's by a generation impressed with the example of the Fascist leaders in Europe, and it has passed into many of the books. The trouble with the dictator label is that it has a European connotation and does not fit the American scene. Long was an American boss, a very powerful and sometimes ruthless one, who in his last phase had too much power. He probably knew that this was so, because he repeatedly told the men who would be his successors that they could not wield his authority. But he was never more than a boss. As one of his associates shrewdly put it, "Huey wouldn't have acted as a dictator on any issue that might have alienated the majority of the voters."

Certainly he had none of the qualities we associate with the Fascist leader. Not even his worst enemies accused him of having religious or racial prejudices. Once Dr. Hiram Evans of the Klan denounced him as un-American and threatened to campaign against him in Louisiana. Long came into the press gallery at the state senate and said he wanted to issue a statement: "Quote me as saying that that Imperial bastard will never set foot in Louisiana, and that when I call him a son of a bitch I am not using profanity, but am referring to the circumstances of his birth." His knowledge of the philosophy of European dictators was only perfunctory, although his evaluation of them was reasonably accurate. Asked if he saw any similarity between himself and Hitler, he said, "Don't compare me to that so-and-so. Anybody that lets his public policies be mixed up with religious prejudice is a plain God-damned fool." The symbols of Fascism excited in him only an amused scorn. Discussing the NRA in the Senate, he said, "However, Mr. President, I hope that if we give it the sign of the Fascisti, known as the 'blue eagle,' or the 'double eagle,' or whatever they call it, we will at least let the eagle have a chance to live. . . . It is all right that the Germans have the Fascist sign in the form of a swastika; it is all right that the Mussolinites . . . in Italy have their sign in the form of a black shirt, and it may have been all right that the Fascisti in America have their emblem in the form of a double eagle, but at least we ought to have given that emblem the right to have lived and to have thrived. I really believe, Mr. President, that we almost condemned that eagle to death in advance when we published [it] looking squarely into the countenance of . . . Hugh S. Johnson. . . ."

Political observers of the 1930's were led to level the dictatorship charge by Long's actions when as United States Senator but still boss of the state he returned to Louisiana to jam laws through the legislature. Special session after special session was called, and Long would dominate committee hearings and storm onto the floor of either house to shout at his followers. On one occasion forty-four bills were passed in twenty-two minutes. In seven special sessions between August, 1934, and September, 1935, a total of 463 bills was enacted. Some bills started out as one thing in one house and became something entirely different in the other. Thus a House measure to codify existing license laws turned at the last minute in the Senate into a bill to tax Standard Oil, much to the consternation of the Standard lobbyists, who had innocently gone home.

But the observers who were horrified at this seeming travesty of the legislative process missed some things. For one, the most important bills had previously been explained in detail by Long in a closed caucus of his supporters. For another, many measures were passed as constitutional amendments and had to be submitted to a popular vote. Fourteen amendments adopted in one special session were ratified by the voters by a margin of seven to one. Still, one wonders if Long's methods comported with the spirit of democratic government. He apparently wondered too. "They say they don't like my methods," he said once. "Well, I don't like them either. . . . I'd much rather get up before a legislature and say 'Now this is a good law; it's for the benefit of the people, and I'd like for you to vote for it in the interest of the public welfare.' Only I know that laws ain't made that way. You've got to fight fire with fire." But in the later stages of his career he did not have to employ fire. He still faced an un- relenting opposition, it is true, but he had it well in hand. Having been forced to overthrow the oligarchy by ruthless methods, he continued to use the same methods after his victory was assured. Either he feared the recuperative genius of the oligarchy or he had become too fascinated with the exercise of sheer power to give it up. Undoubtedly he had been hardened by the constant attempts of the opposition to destroy him, es- pecially by the try at impeachment. There is some kind of personal and sectional tragedy in the Long story. He might have been, lamented one critic, such a leader as the South had never had. But it was not entirely his fault that he did not become Dixie's peerless Progressive. Perhaps the lesson of Long is that if in a democracy needed changes are denied too long by an interested minority, the changes, when they come, will come with a measure of repression and revenge. And perhaps the gravest indictment that can be made of southern politics in recent times is that the urge for reform had to be accomplished by pressures that left in leaders like Long a degree of cynicism about the democratic process.

Was Huey Long, then, a demagogue? Here again we encounter semantic difficulties. The Greeks gave us the term, and we have ac- cepted their definition. The demagogue was "a man of loose tongue, intemperate, trusting to tumult, leading the populace to mischief with empty words." He was "foul-mouthed, ... a low mean fellow." Implicit in Greek thinking about the subject was the assumption that in politics the masterful leader manipulated the mindless mass with the mere turbulence of his rhetoric. We know that for the American scene, at least, this concept has little validity, yet we permit it to affect our judg- ments of American politicians. Scholars particularly have been influenced by the notion that violent language is the peculiar mark of the dema- gogue. They seem to think that popular leaders have risen to power simply because they could excite and entertain the voters. Certainly Huey Long was a master in the use of scathing invective and also of effective satire, as witness his elucidation of the possible meanings of NRA: National Racketeering Association, National Ruin Administration, Nuts Running America, or Never Roosevelt Again; or his application of damaging and durable nicknames to his aristocratic Louisiana foes: "Kinky" Howard, "Liverwurst" Nicholson, "Shinola" Phelps, "Turkey- head" Walmsley, "Feather Duster" Ransdell, and "Whistle Britches" Rightor. But his skill with words was only one of several factors that explain his success, and a minor one at that. And only a cursory reading of the literature of Louisiana politics will reveal that extreme language was not a Long patent. Among the terms applied to Long—by the best people—were: "an ultra Socialist" whose views went "beyond Marx,

Lenin, and Trotsky," "an impeached thief and scoundrel," "a political freak, cringing coward, and monumental liar," a man with "the face of a clown, the heart of a petty larceny burglar, and the disposition of a tyrant."

Long himself was deeply interested in the application of the term of demagogue and perceptively aware of its limitations. In one especially realistic analysis he said, "There are all kinds of demagogues. Some deceive the people in the interests of the lords and masters of creation, the Rockefellers and the Morgans. Some of them deceive the people in their own interest. I would describe a demagogue as a politician who don't keep his promises." On that basis he denied that he deserved the label. But on another occasion, changing the definition, he accepted it. Referring to his program, he said: "I shall have to admit, it is a demagogy, because in the old Greek parlance that meant the language that was acceptable to the majority. That is not meant as a derogatory term, and I do not take it as such, because when I advocated free school books in Louisiana that was termed demagoguery; when I advocated free bridges instead of toll bridges it was called demagoguery; and when I advocated paved highways instead of dirt roads that likewise was called demagoguery."

Let us dispense with the word demagogue in dealing with men like Long and employ instead a term suggested by Eric Hoffer, mass leader. As listed by Hoffer, the principal qualities required in a mass leader are —and Huey Long had all of them—audacity, an iron will, faith in his cause or in himself, unbounded brazenness, and a capacity for hatred, without which he may be deflected from his goal.[10] To these we may add others. The mass leader must have an abnormal and combative energy. Long was, as Henry Adams said of Theodore Roosevelt, "pure act." The mass leader must know which enemies he should destroy and which ones he should maintain as symbols of the continuing evil he fights against. "Corporations are the finest enemies in the world," Long once remarked. "You got to know how to handle them." After he had broken the power of Mayor Walmsley in New Orleans, an associate asked why he simply did not get rid of Walmsley. "He said, 'No, that would be bad psychology. You always leave a figurehead for your boys to fight against. If you don't, they start fighting against themselves. Walmsley is a perfect target for us to fight. He's impotent and can't do us any harm.' "

The quality above all others that the mass leader must have is audacity —a boundless self-confidence which lets him give full rein to his ideas, a brazen courage which enables him to disregard conventionality and consistency, and a daring imagination which equips him to ignore existing rules and create his own. Examples of Long's audacity are too numerous to be considered here, but a few must be cited. During one of the several financial crises of the early 1930's a run developed on the New Orleans banks, threatening a general collapse. The problem was to close the banks over a weekend until money could be secured from the RFC. Aides feverishly sought for a holiday that could serve as an excuse. Huey easily supplied one. A proclamation by the governor announced that the banks would be closed because, Whereas, on this date Woodrow Wilson severed diplomatic relations with Germany. . . .

The triumphant climax of Long's many savage jousts with Standard Oil came when the legislature, at his bidding, enacted a tax of five cents a barrel on refined oil. From the viewpoint of the Standard Oil this was bad enough, but worse was to come. Another legislature, also at Long's bidding, authorized the governor to suspend any portion of the tax. The suspension would come, of course, only if the Standard conformed to certain conditions, and the full tax could be reapplied at any time. It was a completely effective device to keep the great corporation in line. At the height of the controversy over the tax measure the company sent an emissary, a close friend of Long's, to ask him to desist. Long listened to this man but then remarked that he was not particularly interested in the tax anymore. "Pete, I'll tell you what I'm going to do. Tell the Standard Oil to get the hell out of Louisiana and I'll exappropriate that plant and the legislature will appropriate enough money to buy it and we'll operate it. And from the funds the first year we will educate the top boy and girl in every high school in the state at LSU free, and as the profits begin to grow we will educate the second and third ones and so on. . . . It will take a constitutional amendment but the people will vote for it when I tell them that we will use that money to educate the boys and girls of Louisiana free from the profits." The emissary departed hastily.

It is possible that we have been too apologetic about and too patronizing toward all the southern demagogues. Some of them were hopelessly confused and some were merely clowns. Some did nothing to control the interests they attacked and some sold out to those interests. But the best of them tried to do something for their people. Throw out the crudities they had to employ to arouse a submerged electorate and the race baiting, and these men are the Norrises, the La Follettes, and the Borahs of another section. Even such an object of hatred to the righteous as Theodore Bilbo meets the test for admission to the liberal heaven, a straight New Deal voting record in the Senate. Indeed, many of the southern demagogues, in their genuine concern for the welfare of the masses, in their essential respect for the democratic system, conform in their own peculiar fashion to Eric Hoffer's picture of the good mass leader—the leader who does not hesitate to "harness men's hungers and fears" to weld a following in the service of a cause but who, because of his faith in humanity, does not attempt to use the frustrations of men to build a brave new theoretical world.[11] Or, to shift to another formula, many of the demagogues conform, again in their own manner, to Jacques Maritain's image of the prophet leader, whose main mission is "to *awaken* the people, to awaken them to something better than everyone's daily business, to the sense of a supra-individual task to be performed."[12] Certain it is that without the driving force supplied by the demagogues a static society would not have been renovated as quickly—or as painlessly—as it was.

One night in Long's hotel room in New Orleans, while he seemingly dozed on the bed, a group of visiting correspondents fell to analyzing his political personality. Finally arousing himself, he said, "Oh, hell, say that I'm *sui generis* and let it go at that." In a class by himself he certainly was. He stands without a rival as the greatest of southern mass leaders. He asked the South to turn its gaze from "nigger" devils and Yankee devils and take a long, hard look at itself. He asked his people to forget the past, the glorious past and the sad past, and address themselves to the present. There is something wrong here, he said, and we can fix it up ourselves. Bluntly, forcibly, even crudely, he injected an element of realism into southern politics. Not without reason did Gerald Johnson, who disliked him, say that Huey Long was the first southerner since Calhoun to have an original idea, the first to extend the boundaries of political thought.[13] Above all, he gave the southern masses hope. He did some foolish things and some wrong things. He said some things that he should not have said and some that he did not believe. But this we may be certain he meant: "Nevertheless my voice will be the same as it has been. Patronage will not change it. Fear will not change it. Persecution will not change it. It cannot be changed while people suffer. The only way it can be changed is to make the lives of these people decent and respectable."

Chapter XXVI

Four American Traditions

WILLIAM BEST HESSELTINE

TRADITION, says the lexicographer, is "the handing down of statements, beliefs, legends, customs, etc., from generation to generation, especially by word of mouth or by practice."* Or, as a minor poet put it, "Man yields to custom as he bows to fate. In all things ruled—mind, body, and estate."

Throughout the course of American history, tradition has played a major role—and one that commentators, searching for explanations of the phenomena of American development, have often ignored. More popular as a touchstone to test and explain the American story has been the popular political myth that the central function of the United States has been the evolution of personal liberty and civil rights, through a persistent conflict between Darkness and Light, a never ceasing clash between a so-called liberalism and a pre-defined conservatism. Equally popular, and often related to the political myth, is the dogma that the rivalry of opposing economic forces has given form and color to American life. Thus Charles A. Beard could see the American story as a basic conflict between a rising industrial order and a steadily declining agricultural society. Frederick Jackson Turner perceived the perennial re-creation of new societies on the frontier, and counted their reactions upon the older and established orders. Others, borrowing consciously or unconsciously from Karl Marx, and bolstering their arguments with James Madison's remarks anent economic factionalism, have found a long enduring warfare between the rich and the poor, the "Haves" and the "Have-Nots." For the most part, the commentators on the American past have attended to the conflicts, real and imagined, to the clash of verbal issues, or to the resounding rhetoric of rival partisans, while they

*Presented in Tulsa, Oklahoma, November 10, 1960.

have neglected to examine and assess the unifying forces of American life.

From the American Revolution to the present, the American people have demonstrated a capacity for conciliation and compromise to a degree remarkable among the nations of the world. The Civil War, by virtue of its singularity, illustrates the persistence of the traditive methods of unity rather than supports the supposition that clash and conflict have been the primary characteristics of America. Moreover, those who have sought to resolve the problems of the United States, and to organize the data of the American past in terms of contending dichotomies, have frequently become bemused in the pathetic fallacy of ascribing anthropomorphic characteristics to capital and labor, to agriculture and industry, and have emerged incoherent in their effort to distinguish between progressive and conservative, radical and reactionary. Whatever validity the political terms "right" and "left" may have had in describing the seating arrangements of a French assembly, and however useful they may have been in the rhetorical arsenal of modern pundits and partisans, they have proved defective as viable concepts for examining the history of the American people.

Rather than conflict and clash, the American story has been one of concert and concurrence. The search for the elements of American unity may constitute a more intriguing intellectual challenge than the reporting of pseudodramatic contests or reciting bygone exhibitions of forensic skill. In a land without the geographical unity which has sometimes been the basis of nationalism, without a discrete language or literature, yet containing a multitude of economic activities, the problem of political, social, and cultural unity has been ever-present, and its achievement, with a comparatively minor amount of violence and coercion, a notable accomplishment.

To a large extent, the American story is the result of the persistence of four basic traditions. From the first settlements in the new world, to the latest political contest, there have been developing and changing among the American people at least four bodies of traditional statements, beliefs, legends, customary modes of behavior, and concepts of society. If they have not "in all things ruled—mind, body, and estate," they have infused most aspects of American life and entered deeply into the national character. Described in terms of their exponents, the four basic American traditions are those of the Trustees, the Squires, the Artisans, and the Yeomen.

Each of these basic traditions had its origins in England and came to America with the early English settlements. Time and experience produced divergence from the British models, and gave each tradition new and distinctively American characteristics. The trustee tradition carried echoes of the rise of the English middle classes and drew strength from British Calvinism and the Puritan strain in British thought. The squires of the new world consciously imitated and sometimes overtly imported the concepts of the manorial system. The artisan tradition perpetuated in a new environment some of the legends, sentiments, and customs of the medieval gilds, while the tradition of the sturdy yeomen who stood at Crècy and Agincourt had not passed entirely from the memory of the landless city dwellers who made up the bulk of the earlier migrants to the colonies. In America, and under American conditions, these traditions merged, took on new forms, ceased to be the particular philosophies of severely separated classes, and became the common heritage of the American people.

Although by no means the exclusive philosophies of particular social or economic groups, each of the four traditions at various times in the nineteenth century found its characteristic expression in one or another dominant group in some region of the country. Yet the traditions were never sectional, and they never furnished convenient categories for the arbitrary classification of individuals or groups in the American past. Throughout the nineteenth century, men lived sometimes as manorial lords, and were even addressed as "Squire," yet shared the beliefs and legends of the trustee tradition. The exponents of the artisan tradition could be found on corporation boards, in the manager's office of railroads, as well as in the bicycle shops where tinkering mechanics dreamed of revolutionizing transportation. The traditions, in fact, transcended politico-economic categories to permeate all orders of society and to give significant unity to the American scene.

In nineteenth-century America, the most coherent and often the most aggressive groups were those who adhered to a tradition that described them as Stewards of the Lord, weighted with a tremendous responsibility for properly ordering society. The trustee tradition drew its rationale from Calvinist theology and found its fullest manifestation in New England's Puritan commonwealths. The dogma of election lay at the base of the tradition. Explicit in it was the belief that God's Elect should guide their fellow men in the paths of righteousness. The Elect should so order society that it conformed to the will of the Creator and glorified the Lord. Fortunately, those whom the Almighty elected for salvation, He also prospered. But their prosperity, whether counted in the wealth of the world, the powers of the intellect, or in elevation of spirit, belonged not to men but to their Creator. They were but stewards obliged to use their wealth and their talents to effect a social order which would conform to moral law.

Professor Clifford Griffin has traced the evolution of the concept of stewardship from the Puritan fathers to the end of the American Civil War. The Puritan commonwealths of New England illustrated the theory of the state held by men who conceived of themselves as Their Brothers' Keepers. Griffin has shown, as well, that the trustees were adaptable to new conditions and could maintain their objectives in a changing economic world and adopt even a new vocabulary without altering their basic premises. When a growing population in colonial Masachusetts forced a reconsideration of representative government, the trustees accepted a Halfway Covenant and continued to direct society along the paths of righteousness. When Deism threatened the foundations of the old Calvinism, the trustees adopted what Professor Griffin calls a "stewardship of ethics" which posited the doctrine that new men of the Enlightenment—successors of the predestined Elect—understood the laws of nature and should guide men toward a perfect state. So, too, when Federalism lost power to Republicanism, the trustees turned to moral suasion and formed a host of benevolent societies devoted to Sabbath observance, education of ministers, the spread of religious literature, peace, temperance, and the abolition of slavery—all designed to bring society into conformity to the moral law. And then, when moral suasion made slow progress, the men of the trustee tradition turned once more to the state and demanded Sunday closing laws, compulsory education, the prohibition of alcohol, and the abolition of slavery. They gave allegiance to a higher law than the Constitution.

The Civil War saw the men with the beliefs and legends of the trustees assuming direction of the conflict and diverting it into a moral crusade. At the war's end, they proposed to reorganize the South's economic, social, and political system—"to infuse," as one religious paper put it, the South "with a purer, more liberty-loving civilization." As America passed into the Gilded Age, men adapted the trustee tradition to new economic realities, yet never lost from sight the goal of a society which would conform to God's will for man.

The new rationale of the Stewards of the Lord substituted the possession of special traits of character for the older dogmas of election. The democratic concept of self-made man found a new theoretical basis in Social Darwinism, a new rationale in the so-called Social Gospel, while the possession of wealth was both a testimony of God's favor and an evidence of the social operation of the laws of natural selection. "The way to success," said a writer in the *Baptist Quarterly* in 1873, "lies through competence, industry, enterprise, and honesty." And wealth, when "wielded by educated intelligence, puts in a ... definite and positive claim for rulership and authority."

Yet not even in the Gilded Age did men forget that wealth implied responsibility. Ministers of the gospel reminded men of means that they must give an account of their stewardship. "How does it become us, being the stewards of God, to use what His bounty has intrusted to us?" asked one of them. And, as in the pre-Civil War days, when societies for moral improvement insisted upon a doctrine of benevolence, the custodians of the trustee tradition advocated philanthropy. Henry Ward Beecher proclaimed that God blessed the man who built a library or a hospital, who established a savings bank, or who taught the gospel of thrift to the people. John D. Rockefeller put the teaching into practice, asserting that it was a man's duty to accumulate wealth in order to use it in good works. In 1859, his donations to charity were $28.37, a decade later, $5,489.62. In the end they amounted to millions.

There was more than pious benevolence in the trustee tradition in the last decade of the nineteenth and the first years of the twentieth centuries. The men of the trustee tradition never for long pinned their hopes for a moral society upon voluntary institutions. They were in the forefront of movements for social reformation through the coercive power of the state. They sponsored force bills to make the South accord full political rights to Negroes. They fought the Demon Rum with local option laws and with state and national prohibition. They advocated pure food and drug acts. They policed private morals with local ordinances against prurient literature, and public morals through congressional investigations. They tried to stamp out interstate prostitution and the use of narcotics. They were national humanitarians, calling themselves Progressives, who believed that the government, under their direction, should make a society which would eliminate evil. "My observation and reasoning as I study these problems at home and abroad," said Frank Munsey to Theodore Roosevelt, "leads unerringly to the conclusion that the state has got to swing back a bit from our vaunted Republicanism and take on a more parental guardianship" of the people. "The people," he continued, "need safeguarding in their investments, their savings, their application of conservation. They need encouragement, the sustaining and guiding hand of the state. . . . It is the work of the state to think for the people, and plan for the people —to teach them how to do, what to do, and to sustain them in the doing." The plans for Utopia were still in the making. In the vocabulary of their spiritual ancestors among the Puritan Fathers, they would make a society which would glorify God.

The society, of course, would be world-wide. Late in the nineteenth century Josiah Strong called the nation's attention to its duty as a trustee in world society. Under the direction of men of the trustee tradition, the United States rescued Cuba and inaugurated a new empire with a model colonial system. Under the leadership of men of the trustee tradition, it prepared to fight to make the world safe for democracy. The concept of the trustees that the Elect should rule society, that wealth in money, skills, and talents should be used for the general good, have dominated American participation in world affairs. The twentieth century would see the World Court, the League of Nations, and the United Nations, each an embodiment of the principles of the trustee tradition, while the U.S.I.S., the Point Four Program, and the manifold "aid" activities under the I.C.A. were counterparts of the tract societies, the Bible and missionary societies, and the educational societies of the nineteenth century.

Of the four basic traditions of America, the statements, beliefs, legends, and customs of the trustees were the most oriented to government and the most politically dynamic. The trustee tradition was, essentially, a tradition of leadership, and its devotees and adherents were committed to leading the nation into paths of a preconceived righteousness. Yet the trustees were not alone as leaders. Another tradition, that of the squires, also embodied the concepts of leadership, and its exponents assumed an obligation to guide the people. In their basic compulsions, the squires were less guided by theology—or, at least, less prone to resort to a theological rhetoric to define and defend their position. Rather than presuming to act as the agents of the Lord, the squires found their rationale in the concepts of gentlemanly behavior, in the doctrine of noblesse oblige, in the realization that men favored by wealth, or by talents, had the duty to guide their neighbors. While the obligation of the trustees was to mold society, the squire's duty was to guide the morals and the behavior of the individuals in his care.

The model of the squire was the manorial lord of England whose people—his tenants, his neighbors, and his family—were his personal responsibility. The concept had its origins in feudalism, its examples in the baronial courts. Transferred to America, it was associated with the ownership of land, and with the regulation of the affairs of men in accordance with law. Where the trustee relied upon Divine guidance, upon the correct interpretation of the Scriptures, upon the Protestant ethic, and ultimately upon the higher law, the squire was guided by the ways of the barons, the customs of the manor, the legends of the nobility. He was concerned with the relations of man to man; he devoted himself to the maintenance of law and order and ultimately gave his allegiance to the fundamental law of the Constitution. The law of landlord and tenant derived from the traditions of the squires; John Marshall's decisions wrote the squire's concepts of land into the Constitution of the United States.

Fundamentally, the squire's responsibilities were both to man and to the land. He had a respect for the land and for its use, and gave time and energy to agricultural experiments. Thomas Jefferson tested new plants and improved seeds, John Jay at Bedford worked to "resuscitate agriculture" with gypsum, Edmund Ruffin explored the uses of calcareous manures. John Steele watched with interest German efforts to cross the ass and the ox. John Taylor's *Arator* recited his experiments with new implements, fertilizers, and breeds of livestock. Agricultural societies, farm journals, and agricultural fairs served to emphasize the squire's concern with the good use of the earth, and to instill among his yeoman neighbors his own devotion to the soil. John C. Calhoun declared that there was no better way to advance the nation than to contribute to the improvement of agriculture.

Above all, the tradition of the squires was an apologetic for agriculture. The whole economic structure of the nation, declared John Taylor, depended on the well-being of agriculture; "if the cultivation of land flourishes, all other occupations prosper; if it languishes, they decay." All the virtues were the products of the country—truth, refinement, and culture were, cried a writer in the *Literary Messenger* in 1858, products of the countryside. "Learn the speech of the elements," he advised. "It will be of more benefit than the language of barbarous people." Moreover, agriculture stimulated the mind by giving an insight into the "real affairs of life, with a necessity for investigating the arena of nature." It was, too, said Abel P. Upshur, "the best school of both public and private virtue." And, since landholders were ever ready to defend their country, it was the source of patriotism.

On the other hand, as all squires knew, cities were the breeding places of vice and corruption. Abel P. Upshur was sure that big cities were the birthplace of sedition, riot, disorder, and a threat to rational, regulated liberty. Thomas Jefferson deplored the necessity for sending his grandson to school in Philadelphia. "I am not a friend to placing growing men in populous cities, because they acquire there habits and partialities which do not contribute to the happiness of their after life." George Fitzhugh catalogued the evils of the cities—the police reports, calendars of crime, ignorance, atheism, destitution and starvation, trade unions, mobs, unemployment, disease, gambling hells, noisome factories. The country, sighed Dolly Madison, provided "the happiest and most true life."

As much as he owed an obligation to the land, the squire owed more to his people. He lived among them and was in daily contact with them, and the sense of noblesse oblige guided his conduct. He defined himself as a gentleman and instructed his children in the ways of gentle folk.

The gentleman was characterized by truth, courtesy, bravery, and generosity. John Randolph scorned the criteria of wealth, but placed an emphasis on discriminating taste and judgment. He told the War Hawks of 1811 to "go talk to the good old planters" and learn standards of judgment. In bucolic images he sought for "the better hawk," the "dog with the deeper mouth," the horse which bore its rider best, and the girl with the "merrier eye." Thomas Ruffin's father instructed him in the duty of a gentleman to check unruly passions and sinful desires and to develop the qualities of meekness, gentleness, charity, and good will toward others. Thomas Jefferson advised his grandson that honesty, disinterestedness, and, above all, good humor were requisites for success. The tradition of the squires was a tradition of leadership, but positions of leadership must be deserved. Jefferson told his grandson to apply himself to his studies in order that he might some day become a useful member of society. John Randolph reminded his nephew that "it follows that the richer, the wiser, the more powerful a man is, the greater is the obligation upon him to employ his gifts in the lessening of the sum of human misery."

The duty and responsibilities of a gentleman imposed a code of etiquette upon the men of the squire tradition. Instead of the divine precepts which regulated, at least in theory, the daily lives of the trustees, the squire's relations with his fellow man were defined in rules of etiquette. He prided himself on good manners, on the punctilio of polite society, on behaving as a man of honor. He defended his honor, when need arose, with pistols at dawn. He placed stress on courtesy, on respect for women, on politeness. He expected politeness in return. A code of etiquette proscribed the relations of man and man, of father to son, of master to servant. He expected young men to address their elders in phrases of respect, young women to curtsy, the lesser ranks of men to touch their caps as they passed by and to come bareheaded into the presence of their betters. In a society in which good manners were the highest virtue, bad manners were the greatest sin. Perhaps nothing in the post-Civil War South was more offensive than the ill manners which the freedmen displayed toward their former masters. The former slave, signalizing his new found freedom by impudence and discourtesy, sinned against the fundamentals of social order.

The code of good manners extended to entertainment and to hospitality. The squire's house was open, his table free to visitors who shared his traditions. He erected entertainment into a fine art. With an interest in sports, games, athletic contests, and trials of skill, he endowed them with rules of etiquette and the concepts of good sportsmanship. The tradition of the squires enjoined reading—not for moral profit, but for enjoyment—and he collected books and lined his shelves with volumes of classics in many languages. He patronized music and even art. He cultivated the arts of oratory and of conversation.

The tradition of the squire required the assumption of responsibility for the well-being and the good conduct of his people. The squire who was a slaveholder frequently placed the happiness of his slaves above his own material prosperity. Thomas Dabney, moving from Virginia to Louisiana in the 1830's, refused to put part of his slaves on another plantation because he would no longer be able to attend the welfare of each bondsman. John A. Quitman, faced with bankruptcy, refused to part with his slaves. "I would rather," he declared, "be reduced to abject penury than to sell one of them." The nonslaveholding squire bore the same responsibility to his neighbors and, when in public life, to his constituents. It was a patriarchal tradition, and it took cognizance of the duties as well as the privileges of the patriarchs.

Part of the obligation was the duty of public service. The squire participated in the activities of the county courts, the vestry, the legislature, and the Congress. Calhoun was firm in the belief that men of education and leisure must take part in government. Only by the influence of gentlemen could dignity enter public affairs. "If the capable and worthy retire," he wrote, "the designing, or worthless will take their place." The squire derived his ideas of government from the classics and applied them in his politics. The form of government most to be admired was a republic ruled by an aristocracy of worth, and kept small enough to be both comprehended and controlled. "An overgrown state, like an overgrown man," thought George Fitzhugh, was "not generally equal in wisdom or strength to one of moderate size." Moreover, as his own affairs were regulated by a code of etiquette which had the authority of statutes, public affairs should be regulated by law. It was the duty of a citizen to obey the laws, and above all, the law of the Constitution. Speculation about a "higher law" might be an interesting intellectual exercise, but action based on higher law mandates was treason. Perhaps, indeed, thought James Fenimore Cooper, it would be best if the state had a limited suffrage. The shifting population of the United States caused men to lose their roots and their sense of community responsibility, while the steadily increasing flow of immigrants brought in new elements unadjusted to the American heritage. Cooper found that Connecticut's government by a tight patrician clique was one of the purest democratic communities in the world! "A system must be radically wrong, when the keeper of a tavern . . . can command more votes than a man of the highest attainments, or of the highest character," thought Squire Cooper.

The role of the men of the squire tradition was long in American history. In the beginning there were the planters of the South and the patroons of the Hudson Valley. In the tradition have lived the cattle kings, the wheat kings, the citrus growers of the Rio Grande, the vineyardists of Cincinnati and California, apple men of the Yakima and the Shenandoah. There have been Van Cortlandts and De Lanceys, Masons, and Kings, Middletons and Carters, Livingstons, and Heywards. On the national scene there were George Washington and Thomas Jefferson, James Madison and James Monroe, Andrew Jackson, Zachary Taylor, and Jefferson Davis. In the states the names of the squires who assumed the duty of participating in public affairs were legion. They were the members of colonial councils, of county courts, of state legislatures. They maintained a code of etiquette on the frontier, made and enforced the laws which protected property, and established rules of behavior in new communities. They were bishops of the Episcopal Church and officers in the army. They served on the boards of colleges, on the vestries of the churches, on countless committees for social betterment. They were in the forefront of movements for civic improvement.

Fit representative of the squire tradition was the Tennessee historian, J. G. M. Ramsey, whose varied activities ranged from the practice of medicine to the financing of railroads. He defined himself as a patriot and as an aristocrat. Patriotism, he defined as "something else than party zeal or a selfish scrabble for offices." Aristocracy, he defined more elaborately as being of four kinds. First there was the aristocracy of birth and family, and such aristocrats "can never be brought to believe that because an individual has had a grandfather or an ancestor of elevated character, unquestioned integrity, high-souled honor, stainless reputation, etc., that he is thus placed on a level with the son of a thief, a defamer, or a blackguard." A second kind of aristocracy was one of virtue—"a love of truth, probity, sincerity, candor, justice, humanity, honor, and public and private virtue." And, he remarked, "if to these attributes is added a becoming deference to age, to character, to position, to sex and to private worth the possessor is deservedly esteemed the superior of the ignoble, the supercilious, the vulgar, the rude, the selfish upstart and pretender." In fact, thought Dr. Ramsey, the aristocrat of virtue had "a title of nobility which even the disciples of Black Republicanism would be unwilling avowedly to discard or openly to invalidate." Then, said Dr. Ramsey, there was an aristocracy of intellect— "well cultivated intellect, a well disciplined mind, well balanced thinking power, the ability to investigate, to discriminate, to analyze, to sublimate, to elucidate, to philosophize, to generalize—this ability gives the individual possessing it a genuine claim to true nobility." And finally, Dr. Ramsey admitted, there was an aristocracy of wealth. Now wealth acquired by honest industry was praiseworthy—especially if its possessor "be generous in his public and private benefaction, unselfish and liberal in his charities, a patron of learning and science and the material improvement of the country." But wealth acquired dishonestly "makes the owner purse-proud, arrogant, supercilious and pretentious, intolerant and overbearing to the poorer classes, sycophantic or envious of those superior to them in rank or public esteem."

By his standards of aristocracy and patriotism, Dr. Ramsey raised his children and served his community. His pride in his family led him into the study of history, and his *Annals of Tennessee* was one result. He was a devout Presbyterian, serving on the boards of trustees of church colleges and academies. He made his house into a house of prayer. He made it, too, into a house of culture. At Mecklenburg, which he built exactly at the point where the French Broad and the Holston Rivers converge, he gathered a library of four thousand volumes and documents and manuscripts of Tennessee history. There he entertained statesmen and clergymen, scholars and men of letters. His patriotism, his duty to his community, led him into other activities. He served as a canal commissioner; he promoted railroad connections between the Tennessee mountains and the outside world; he was president of a bank, a school commissioner, the president of the Tennessee Historical Society. He wrote poetry. He was a postmaster. He operated a ferry. He owned and managed a plantation with its slaves. He practiced medicine. In politics he was a States' Rights Democrat. When the Civil War came, he became a treasury agent and served as a volunteer surgeon on the battlefields of the Confederacy.

The war swept away the world of Dr. Ramsey. Mecklenburg with its library and manuscripts was burned to the ground; the colleges which he had served passed into alien hands; his railroad became in time a part of a Yankee-owned system. At the age of sixty-eight he borrowed a horse and a doctor's saddlebags, and with thirty-five cents worth of drugs, he resumed the practice of medicine. Once he returned to Knoxville only to find that its society had changed. There was more commerce, more manufactures, and more business, but with it there was less social stability. "There was an undercurrent of discordant material," he noted. "Antagonisms were visible everywhere and in all pursuits. ... There was less hospitality, less of the generous emotions and manly passions, more of the sordid love of money, less culture, much less refinement, a more vulgar taste. Less evangelical piety—more religious pretention. Less patriotism, and, of course, more selfishness. Less of learning and, of course, more of pedantry. Less deference for age, character, and worth and more boastful effrontery and upstart consequence. The people were ruder and coarser, less gentle, less amiable." Sadly, Dr. Ramsey turned his thoughts to history and dwelt again on the glories of his ancestors.

But though Dr. Ramsey ended in disillusionment and distress, the tradition which he represented did not disappear from American life. Even Dr. Ramsey recognized the possibility. There were, in the Knoxville which distressed him, "some model gentlemen," and he hoped that in time the "passion for money" could "be cultivated into an enlarged public spirit and thus come up to the dimension and proportion of a lofty patriotism." In the generations which followed him, the tradition of the squires received new life and new manifestations. Newer men took up the old tradition and guided their lives by the precepts which Dr. Ramsey embodied. Some of them sought out the old columned houses or modeled new dwellings upon them as symbols of the tradition. Some of them sought to emulate and perpetuate the codes of etiquette by which gentlemen lived. Some of them gave their time and energies to civic improvements—to adhere to Dr. Ramsey's ideals of public and private virtue. The men of the squire tradition had not lived exclusively in the South, and from New England to California, in communities new as well as old, the sense of noblesse oblige, and the concepts of community service, continued to inspire men to assume the responsibilities of leadership.

The tradition of the squires, like that of the trustees, was one of leadership. The squire prepared himself for civic responsibility, rationalized his acts and his ambitions in terms of his duty to his people, his community, and his constituents, prided himself on his public services, and was deeply offended when his people rejected his leadership. His people, all too often for his happiness, adhered to a different tradition and guided themselves by the statements, beliefs, legends, and customs which were handed down from generation to generation of yeomen and artisans.

The yeoman and artisan traditions, unlike those of the trustees and the squires, were traditions of producers rather than of leaders. Neither yeomen nor artisans labored under either a feudal or a Calvinist compulsion to regenerate society or to impose either a moral code or a code of etiquette upon mankind. They were, instead, consoled and uplifted by the knowledge that they fed and clothed the world. They were willing enough to follow squires or trustees, to accept the rules of conduct of the squires or to adhere to the moral code and enlist in the benevolent crusades of the trustees, so long as the leaders pointed the pathway to increased production, to profitable markets, and to progress.

They were equally willing to rebel, to riot, and to strike when the leaders inhibited production or the enjoyment of the fruits of their labor.

The yeoman tradition in America had evolved, under American circumstances, from the ways of life of the freeholders of England. Yeomen of England were "plain honest men," and the term was in common use in colonial America. From England the yeomen inherited a tradition of sturdy independence, and they carried it with them across the continent. The yeoman tradition was in no sense a peasant tradition. The American yeoman was devoted to agriculture and to the processing of agricultural products, but he was never content with subsistence farming. His independence may, indeed, have been a myth, for he was never able to take his gaze from the market place. The value of land, the price of produce, and the cost of supplies were ever present realities to the American farmer, but the yeoman tradition rested firmly on the belief that the tiller of the soil was the primary source of American wealth, that all other ways of life were dependent upon him, and that he who was surrounded by his own farm and enjoyed the fruits of his own industry owed no man anything but love and good will. "There is not another department of society which enables so many men to live as independent principals," intoned Henry Ward Beecher, and the agricultural journals quoted him with approval and rang the changes upon it.

> Surrounded by the friends I love,
>   And free from every fetter
> I am an independent man
>   And wish for nothing better.

Out of the staunch independence of the yeoman sprang the defense of the country's soil. "There is one class of men on whom we can yet rely," said the *Tennessee Review.* "It is the same class that stood on the green at Lexington—that gathered on the heights of Bunker Hill, and poured down from the hills of New England." And the *Prairie Farmer* found place for a poem recounting how, in "Seventy-Six,"

> What heroes from the woodland sprung
>   When through the fresh-awakened land,
> The thrilling cry of freedom rung,
>   And to the work of warfare strung
> The yeoman's iron hand!

Next to the belief that the yeomen were independent stood the firm conviction that the agrarian was happy, healthy, religious, and moral. However much the outside observer, be he a Squire Byrd running a boundary line or a Trustee Dwight screaming his fears of a growing western power, might find the yeomen uncouth and write scornfully of their cultural attainments, the yeomen took pride in their simplicity and pointed the finger of scorn at the followers of "fashion." They condemned the immorality of cities, the cringing life of the merchants, and the deceptions of politicians. They were following a divinely instituted calling, and their every act was one of worship of God and nature.

> No glory I covet, no riches I want,
>   Ambition is nothing to me:
> The one thing I beg kind heaven to grant,
>   Is a mind independent and free.

Inherent in the agrarian tradition was the belief in the moral value of hard work. Farm journals repeatedly urged their readers to "teach the rising generation that industry is the surest road to respectability." Work was divinely ordained, and only by the sweat of one's brow should he eat bread. Labor prevented moral evils, subdued the passions, promoted individuality of character, and increased the wealth of society. "Oh, there is good in labor," said a Wisconsin poet:

> Oh, there is good in labor
>   If we labor but aright,
> That gives vigor to the daytime
>   And a sweeter sleep at night
> A good that bringeth pleasure
>   Even to the toiling hours—
> For the duty cheers the spirit,
>   As the dew revives the flowers.

With such concepts, the American yeomen were primarily interested in production and in the preservation of their independence from all outside interference. They were opposed to every limitation upon their free use of the land. They opposed quitrents, direct taxes, proclamation lines, grants to speculators, to land companies, and to railroads. They favored homesteads, free trade, farm-to-market roads and canals. In defense of their tradition they rioted against the landed families of New York in the 1760's, stood embattled at Lexington and Concord, joined Ethan Allen's Green Mountain Boys, or marched with Campbell and Shelby to turn back the British at King's Mountain. They were the men of Bacon's Rebellion, of Shay's Rebellion, of the Whiskey Rebellion. Jefferson marshaled them in his Republican party; Benton and Jackson led them in the Democratic party. They voted themselves a farm in 1860, fought for it on Seminary Ridge and Missionary Ridge in 1863, and homesteaded it in the 1870's.

Despite their asseverations of sturdy independence and of greater happiness, the men of the agrarian tradition firmly believed that they were the victims of discrimination and stood always on the defensive. Liberal theologians attacked the yeoman's fundamentalist religious beliefs, and conservatives condemned the excesses of his evangelical practices. Educational leaders insisted upon foisting a nonfunctional curriculum upon the rural schools and waged a winning battle against the one-room country school. And although musicologists collected the folk songs of the yeoman, an effete pseudo culture affected to scorn hillbilly songs, revival tunes, and country music. More serious by far was the long line of discriminations placed upon the men of the yeoman tradition. Governments of the colonial period, more concerned with British mercantile interests than with colonial producers, levied taxes, fixed prices, and restricted settlements with no regard for agrarian interests. The Founding Fathers, acting in accordance with the traditions of squires and trustees, drafted a constitution which aroused the suspicions of the yeomen. The Federalists were oriented toward the enemies of the farmers. Squire Jefferson, ever mindful of their votes and conscious of his duty, compromised their interests, and his successors stepped away from them. The West was theirs—but only with a struggle. Whether the discriminations were real or imaginary, the belief that farmers were despised, ignored, or exploited became a part of the agrarian tradition, and yeomen considered themselves weak in the government and fighting a losing battle with the forces and groups which clung to other American traditions.

Although men of the squire tradition assumed the responsibility for voicing the concepts, beliefs, and legends of the yeoman, the agricultural journals became the principal medium for carrying on the tradition and adapting it to changing circumstance. A constant refrain of the farm papers, repeated by the publications of the agricultural societies and emphasized by orators at state and county fairs, was that the farmer was not accorded the respect in society to which his virtue and his contributions entitled him. The *American Agriculturalist,* the *Ploughboy,* the *New England Farmer,* and the *Ohio Cultivator* dwelt at length on the lowly state of the farmer and the low repute of agricultural labor. "There is a belief in this country," moaned the *Farmer's Almanac,* "that agriculture is a vulgar occupation." One result of this belief, thought the farm journalists, was that their young people were leaving the farm.

Against the widespread denigration of the farmer, the journals waged a many-sided campaign. They used, in fact, the real or the alleged lowly state of the agrarian to strengthen the tradition and to bring ideological unity to farming groups. Over and over they recited the virtues of farm life, reiterated the dogmas of the agrarian's independence and moral superiority, and glorified agricultural labor. At the same time they attacked the city dwellers, the bankers, and the politicians. They urged youth to stay on the farm, praised simplicity, and derided "fashion." But above all, they were the exponents of education. Sharing the common American belief that the schoolroom was the entrance hall to the house of prosperity, they demanded agricultural schools, research into better methods of farming, scientific experimentation, and, of course, the reading of books and agricultural journals.

In the 1870's a new agency essayed the task of strengthening the yeoman tradition. The Patrons of Husbandry gathered the farmers to reiterate the dogma that, as the Worcester, Massachusetts, Grange put it in its constitution, "the soil is the source from whence we derive all that constitutes wealth. . . . The art of agriculture is the parent and precourser of all arts, and its products the foundation of all wealth." The songbooks of the Grangers told again how

> 'Tis toil that over nature
>   Gives man his proud control
> And purifies and hallows
>   The temple of his soul.
> It startles foul diseases,
>   With all their ghastly train;
> Puts iron in the muscle
>   And crystal in the brain.

They repeated that

> The farmer's the chief of the nation—
>   The oldest of nobles is he;
> How blest beyond others his station,
>   From want and from envy how free!

and were sure that "the true and honest husbandman" was "the noblest work of God." God, in fact, conferred the obligation to till the soil:

> Awake! Awake! The world must be fed,
>   And Heaven gives the power
> To the hand that holds the bread.

Against the temptations of the city, the yeomen in the Granges could sing advice to their youth:

> Come, boys, I have something to tell you
>   Come near, I would whisper it low;
> You're thinking of leaving the homestead—
>   Don't be in a hurry to go.
> The city has many attractions,
>   But think of its vices and sins;
> But once in the vortex of fashion
>   How soon our destruction begins.

.   .   .   .   .

The farm is the best and the safest,
  And certainly surest to pay;
You're free as the air of the mountain,
  And monarch of all you survey.
Then stay on the farm a while longer,
  Though profits come in rather slow,
Remember you've nothing to risk, boys,—
  Don't be in a hurry to go.

By the days of the Grange movement, the men of the yeoman tradition had come to confront the usury of the bankers and had fallen into debt. In measured numbers the Grange songbooks gave simple advice:

See that your right to the homestead
  Is not encumbered by debt;
Strictest economy practice
  And toil with a vigorous arm,
Make it your strong resolution,
  Never to mortgage the farm.

It was better indeed to wear old clothes:

Friends, don't run in debt; never mind, never mind,
  If your clothes are some faded and torn;
Fix them up, make them do, it is better by far,
  Than the heart be weary and worn.
Who will love you the more for the set of your hat,
  Or your ruff or the tie of your shoe,
Or the shape of your vest, or your boots, or cravat,
  If they know you're in debt for the new?

It was the concepts of the yeoman tradition, often enough expressed in homely verse, that gave basis for the Granger legislation in the states and furnished the background for the Populist movement in politics. The yeomen of America believed, indeed, with William Jennings Bryan that the cities rested upon the broad and fertile prairies and that the destruction of the farm would cause the grass to grow in the city streets. The yeoman tradition was a tradition of production. It bolstered the legend of independence, stressed the dignity of toil, and found virtue in simplicity. It was not a tradition of leadership—the yeoman had no compulsive drive to reform, regenerate, or guide society. It was, however, a tradition of criticism, and men of the yeoman tradition judged the acts of squires and trustees by criteria derived from the soil.

For the most part those who would lead the American people paid lip service, at least, to the criteria and the values of the yeoman tradition. But one orator, appearing at the Wisconsin State Fair in 1859, made short shrift of the yeoman tradition. "I presume," he began, "I am not expected to employ the time assigned to me, in the mere flattery of the farmers as a class. My opinion of them is that, in proportion to numbers, they are neither better nor worse than other people."

The speaker was Abraham Lincoln, and he devoted his time to talking about inventions and the application of machinery to the farm. He spent, in fact, considerable time speculating about how a stationary engine could operate a plow. Abraham Lincoln was no yeoman. His interests stemmed from the artisan tradition, and his approach to the problems of the farm, as to all other problems before the country, were in terms of craftsmanship, mechanical skills, and material progress.

The artisan tradition was also a tradition of work and of production. It was the tradition of those jacks-of-all-trades who amazed European travelers and American observers alike. There was an element of craftsmanship in it, and of the pride of silversmiths and cabinetmakers who signed their work. But more than craftsmanship which a European worker might stress the American boasted of his ingenuity. An English visitor was amazed when a general mended the broken wheel of his wagon, but such versatility was commonplace in America. In Fond Du Lac, Wisconsin, far out on the frontier, lived an "Uncle Dexter" whose nephew remembered how he was a carpenter and joiner and carried on a shop for general repairing and "all sorts of tinkering." He would undertake anything, "from a piano to a penny whistle." In New England the village blacksmith made farm implements, household utensils, cutlery, hardware, ship anchors and fittings. In the country villages and in the growing cities, the artisan tradition inspired men to develop skills, but most of all it inspired them to invent new gadgets, perfect new devices, and improve the methods of work.

The men of the artisan tradition prided themselves on the name "mechanic." Horace Greeley never let it be forgotten that he was a printer and looked back upon the greatest of printers, Benjamin Franklin, as a patron saint. In the line of mechanics were Roger Sherman the shoemaker, General Henry Knox the bookbinder, General Nathanael Greene the blacksmith. Abraham Lincoln asserted that he was "in no sense a farmer" and recounted his days as a craftsman, a sawmill worker, and a railsplitter. Andrew Johnson bored his associates in the United States Senate with tales of his days in a tailor shop and as President could remember that he always made a good fit and got the work out on time.

Spokesmen for the artisan tradition found deep meanings in the labor of the mechanic. Man's superiority over the other animals, said one, "is attributable solely to the influence of the mechanic arts." He went on to elaborate: "The culture of the mechanic arts [is] not only calculated to elicit, expand, and invigorate the inventive faculties of man, to strengthen his natural imbecility, inform his natural ignorance, and enrich his natural poverty, but also to advance his morals, refine his manners, and elevate his character." When, early in the century, Philadelphia workmen faced trial for conspiracy, they had no hesitancy about proclaiming that "the principle is undeniable that labour constitutes the real wealth of a country." The "real patriots," asserted the *Working-man's Advocate* in 1830, are "the mechanics, who have produced this vast national wealth." If the laboring classes were to decline, intoned the *Mechanic's Free Press,* all other classes would fade away. "Aristocracy," echoed the *Advocate,* "will then have to hide its head, and those who produced the wealth of the nation—the farmers, mechanics, and other working men—will rank, as they should do, as the most useful classes of society, and be respected in proportion to their usefulness."

From the beginning, the great problem of America was engineering, and the mechanics knew full well that they were building the land, that they were creating a new heaven on the earth. They looked upon the devices they invented and which they knew how to operate, and told the tale of American progress in terms of new and better machinery. Progress was their most important product. They were the true prophets of progress, and sometimes they looked with skepticism upon the Puritan reformism of the trustees which frequently called itself "progressive." "We plan to raise, beyond the all," said the poet Whittier,

> Thy great Cathedral, sacred Industry—no tomb,
> A keep for life for practical invention. . . .
> Mark—mark the spirit of invention everywhere—
> Thy rapid patents
> Thy continual workshops, foundries, risen or rising.

Inherent in the concepts of the artisan tradition were theories of society and of social organization. When the poet Longfellow invited Elihu Burritt to visit him, the learned blacksmith asked if he could bring his hammer with him. "I can assure you that my hammer is as much predisposed to *swim* on the top of all my ideas, as was the axe to float on the surface of the water at the touch of the prophet." The hammer, in fact, swam on top of all the ideas of the artisan tradition. The social concepts of the artisans were more complex than those of the yeomen, the squires, or the trustees. They ranged from simple demands for the recognition of the importance of labor, through apologetics for a capitalistic society, to grandiose schemes for social reform. Burritt wanted "no higher human reward for any attainment I may make in literature or science, than the satisfaction of having stood in the lot of the laboring man." The *Workingman's Advocate* was sure it would be better to have legislatures composed of farmers and mechanics who could make laws intelligible rather than of "lawyers who involve us in perplexity and mischief." The common people should "therefore, trust in nobody but themselves, and be divinely or charitably and equitably impelled by true nobleness of spirit." The *Mechanic's Free Press* called for the unity of the productive classes for the preservation of American free institutions and argued that "whatever is conducive to the real prosperity of the greatest numbers, must in the nature of things conduce to the happiness of all." When workmen won political victories in Philadelphia, the paper rejoiced that "the balance of power has at length got into the hands of the working people, where it properly belongs, and it will be used, in the future, for the public weal."

Not only were spokesmen for the artisan tradition sure that the mechanics made the wealth of America, they were also convinced that artisans were intent upon the general welfare. They had only contempt for those who would freeze the workingman in his lot or who would separate workers from capitalists. Elihu Burritt visited a cooperative colony and pronounced it a "demonstration how utterly impracticable, unnatural, visionary, and absurd was this chimerical species of Association. Never did I see a place where more self denial and sacrifice of personal comfort, right, and privilege seemed requisite than here. . . . Here, aloof from the world, they flatter themselves that they are going to develop a new character in human nature and society. . . . With no practicable ideas of business or mechanical arts, they are going to compete with shrewd individual genius and enterprise." More attuned to the tradition was Abraham Lincoln who was himself an inventor and a lawyer for inventors. He lectured on inventions and argued that invention was the source of American supremacy. And the inventions came from labor, from which all human comforts and necessities were drawn. There existed—and rightly so—a "certain relation between capital and labor. . . . That men who are industrious, and sober, and honest in the pursuit of their own interests should after a while accumulate capital, and after that should be allowed to enjoy it in peace, and also if they should choose when they have accumulated it to use it to save themselves from actual labor and hire other people to labor for them *is right.*" There was, said Lincoln, no permanent class of hired laborers: "The hired laborer of yesterday, labors on his own account today, and will hire others to labor for him tomorrow. Advancement—improvement in condition—is the order of things in a society of equals."

Industrial capitalists, who were themselves exponents of and pro-

ponents of the artisan tradition, were willing to place their entire reliance on the social theory which Lincoln advanced, and believed that
the reorganization and regeneration of society could spring from more
and better machines. They sponsored inventions and, in time, subsidized scientific research in universities in hopes that the processes of
invention and mechanization would be speeded. Yet, at the same time,
other men of the artisan tradition turned to other forms of social reform
—with the hammer still swimming on the top of all their ideas. The
poet Whittier found a German in Pennsylvania who was "possessed with
the belief that the world was to be restored to its Paradisial state by the
sole agency of mechanics." He proposed to create huge steam engines,
"Niagaras of waterpower, windmills with sail-broad oars like those of
Satan in Chaos," with which he would level out hills and valleys, uproot
forests, drain swamps, cool the tropics with ice from the poles, and dot
the ocean with artificial islands. All he needed was three thousand dollars and ten years' time! Human happiness would inevitably follow upon
this geographical rearrangement.

For some groups in the artisan tradition, faith in the automatic regeneration of society through mechanization dimmed in the decades
after the Civil War. By virtue of the very tools which they invented,
some mechanics became capitalists, and others found themselves unable
to rise through individual merit. Under the analysis of the dispossessed,
it seemed that obstacles of law, of social structure, and of the organization of industry blocked their progress. The panacea seemed to be group
action against the system and group ownership of the tools of produc-
ton. They began to organize.

Group activity had long furnished a kind of spiritual and emotional
satisfaction to mechanics. Essentially they were men of the cities, and
they congregated, partly by necessity but also in part by choice, in their
own communities. They lived in Little Italy, the Irish wards, or clustered
about the openings of the mine shafts. The saloon was, from choice, the
poor man's club. Their games, often of chance, were played around
tables. They danced in dance halls, took outings at congested beaches.
They joined in groups for social activities and for political action. They
were often in gangs in childhood and in their adult years in Tammany,
in the Ancient Order of Hibernians, in marching clubs, and in labor
unions. Andrew Johnson enjoyed gathering fellow tailors, apprentices,
and companions in his tailor shop. Samuel Gompers looked back with
nostalgic reminiscence to the fellowship of the shop wherein he rolled
cigars. "I loved the freedom of that work, for I had earned the mind-
freedom that accompanied skill as a craftsman." The way of life of the

artisans was communal. Their modes of thought made them respond to appeals for the Workers of the World to arise. They could be persuaded to believe that there was a universal brotherhood of the working class.

In the last quarter of the nineteenth century, the organization which embodied the hopes and grievances of the mechanics was the Noble Order of the Knights of Labor. Before it collapsed after the Eight Hour demonstration in 1886, it had done much to formulate in idealistic terms one aspect of the artisan tradition. The Order proposed to "make industrial worth, not wealth, the true standard of individual and national greatness" and to "secure for workers the full enjoyment of the wealth they create." Their enemy was capitalism and the capitalists. Their program called for putting a check "upon the unjust accumulation and the power for evil of aggregated wealth." Their specific demands called for national laws favoring labor and the abrogation of laws and practices benefiting capitalists. In their general political orientation they were nationalists. They proposed national income and inheritance taxes, national postal savings banks, ownership by the national government of telegraphs and railroads. They advocated abolishing the national bank system, but not the substitution of state banks. They envisioned a future economic system in which the tools of production and the control of the markets would be in the hands of producers' and consumers' co-operatives.

Perhaps, indeed, the Knights of Labor was too noble an order for the crude and hard-bitten days of the Robber Barons. Its cooperatives failed to win a share of the national market, and its leaders, perhaps, gave too much attention to accomplishing the Order's idealistic political program. It found skilled workers not yet ready to cooperate with the unskilled. The Knights disappeared, but they left behind a legacy of no small importance. They had given a new emphasis to one phase of the artisan tradition, and they had attracted a host of liberal and humanitarian intellectuals to the idealistic cause. Even though the Knights gave way to the job conscious and realistic American Federation of Labor, a body of intellectuals, college professors of the social studies, journalists, and preachers, continued to apologize for labor, to rationalize its acts, and to clothe the tradition of the artisans in a new and idealistic rhetoric.

Yet this was only one phase of the artisan tradition. Essentially, the tradition of work and of production, the belief that society could be saved by the practice of the mechanical arts, the legends of invention which were supported by the statistics of the patent office, and the established custom of looking to industrial achievement for spiritual satisfaction continued. The artisan tradition was an essential part of the American heritage.

Even though the artisan tradition became, in the hands of labor unions and their apologists, almost an ideological weapon of a social and economic class, these four traditions never became crystallized as embodying the social, political, or economic position of rigid economic classes in American society. Whatever their origins may have been, the traditions of the yeoman, squire, trustee, and artisan were held by rich and poor, by intellectuals and by the uneducated. They were not monolithic, or even mutually exclusive. They were traditions—ways of life and attitudes of mind—and embodied statements, beliefs, legends, and customs to which generation after generation of Americans adhered. Men shifted freely, almost unconsciously, from one to another as economic circumstance, cultural development, or even marriage and age might dictate. They had, indeed, much in common—a common language (if not always a common vocabulary), common roots in Western civilization, a common literature, common family institutions, and a common law. If yeomen and squires seemed to place an excessive emphasis on individual freedom, it was balanced by the group consciousness, almost the group dynamics, of artisans and trustees. The artisan glorification of inventors compared favorably with the trustee's assertion that society should be guided toward perfection by stewards of wealth and talent. Trustees and squires were committed to leadership, but there was no commitment in the artisan and yeoman traditions that imposed a dogma of subservience. Yeomen followed squires so long as the squires led them toward yeoman objectives; and artisans, with a belief in social betterment through mechanical progress, might follow easily the trustees in the mitigation of social evils but could balk at the imposition of puritanical rules of conduct. In the long run the areas of concord between the four traditions proved to be greater than the differences, and each body of legends, beliefs, statements, and customs made its distinctive contribution to American life.

The process, of course, was not simple. Throughout the nineteenth century, the medley of contention and communion produced a recurrent dilemma and challenge to the American politician. Since no group, representing a single tradition, had a majority of the electorate, politicians sought means of appealing to groups which adhered to two or more traditions. Political parties, combining regional interests, faced the problem of appealing to yeomen, trustees, squires, and artisans. Jefferson and Jackson successfully united squires, yeomen, and artisans against the Federalists who clung to the trustee tradition. The Republicans appealed to the artisan, yeoman, and trustee traditions to unite against squires. The Bourbon-ridden Democrats of the1880's united the interests of trustees and squires and regarded artisans and yeomen alike with suspicion. Populism, a movement of the agrarian tradition, appealed to artisans by adopting the slogans and the programs of the Knights of Labor. The problem of the politician was clear: He had to appeal to men of several traditions, combine them against a common enemy, and resolve the conflicts between men of different traditions among his own cohorts. Each political party became an exponent of conciliation, each party platform a formulation of compromises.

The years around the beginning of the twentieth century were years of ferment and contention within each of the four traditions. Perhaps the exponents of the squire tradition were less articulate than they had been, but new writers were beginning to emphasize again the values of the squires and to justify their ways of life. The Populist movement, which sprang out of the yeoman tradition, had proved a political failure, but it continued as Bryanism in the Democratic party and La Follettism among the Republicans. The basic grievances which occasioned the farmers' revolt remained, and protests against them grew in number. Out of the artisan tradition, at the same time, came protests and panaceas as divergent as the writings of Henry George, Edward Bellamy, Gustavus Myers, and Upton Sinclair, but out of it, too, came the glorification of industrial progress embodied in the social theories of Andrew Carnegie, Thomas Edison, and Henry Ford. In the line of the trustee tradition stood muckraking Puritans who were horrified that men were waxing wealthy without benevolence and with no evidence of divine election, while others among the trustees were indeed looking beyond the muck to perceive that industrial wealth was making it possible and imperative that the elected stewards should extend their horizons and create a world society which would glorify God.

The twentieth century inherited the traditions of the trustees, the yeomen, the artisans, and the squires. The concepts and beliefs, the legends and the customs of the traditions infused the institutions of America. The educational structure of the country reflected the influence of the traditions. Exponents of each tradition had long insisted upon the values and virtues of education. The squires had defined the education suitable for gentlemen; the trustees had dotted the land with Calvinistic colleges to indoctrinate the people with proper Protestant principles. The yeomen had echoed the squire demand for agricultural research and experimentation. The artisans had believed that education in the mechanical arts would elevate individual men and save society. By the middle of the twentieth century the schools of the United States had incorporated each demand; and the confusion of vocational courses, the humanities, research in physics and soils, animal husbandry, medieval history, theology, international relations, law, commerce, and photography bore testimony to the American capacity to make adjustments and compromises and to synthesize the traditions which entered the American heritage.

The political institutions of the twentieth century gave the same reflection of the four traditions. The so-called progressive movement, which sometimes showed little regard for industrial and mechanical progress, was partly a voice of the yeoman protest and partly an expression of the trustees' compulsion to reform society. Its rhetoric and its specific panaceas were vote catching devices designed to appeal to the workingmen who adhered to one phase of the artisan tradition. The New Deal enlisted the sense of personal responsibility of the squires and the reformism of the trustees. The programs of individual politicians and of political parties have sought, as did the politics of the nineteenth century, to incorporate the demands and the ideals of the four basic American traditions.

The story of America has not been solely a story of political and economic conflict. Conflicts there have been, but though they have produced much violence there has been little revolution. Essentially, the story of America is the story how men of different traditions have approached the problems and the opportunities of their regions, their states, and their nation. The study of their intellectual achievement is the essential problem of American history. The statements, legends, beliefs, and customs of yeomen, artisans, squires, and trustees have not only infused our institutions but have also entered into the minds of each American until we are, as Jefferson once said, all Federalists, all Republicans. We are, indeed, all yeomen, squires, artisans, and trustees.

Chapter XXVII

Professor James Woodrow
and the Freedom of Teaching
in the South

CLEMENT EATON

ACADEMIC freedom in America is like the honor system; it can only work successfully after a tradition has been created.* There must be martyrs in the cause. Outstanding among these martyrs, the heroes in the struggle for freedom of teaching in the South, were Dr. Thomas Cooper of South Carolina College, Benjamin Sherwood Hedrick of the University of North Carolina, Alexander Winchell of Vanderbilt University, John Spencer Bassett of Trinity College, and James Woodrow of Columbia Theological Seminary and the University of South Carolina. With the exception of the iconoclastic Cooper, Woodrow waged the most prolonged and tenacious fight of all these professors to preserve academic freedom.

The uncle of Woodrow Wilson, James Woodrow displayed much of the fighting spirit and devotion to principle that distinguished his famous nephew. When the controversy over Professor Woodrow's teaching of evolution began, Wilson, then a graduate student at Johns Hopkins University, wrote to Ellen Axson, his sweetheart in Georgia,

If Uncle J. is to be read out of the Seminary, Dr. McCosh [president of Princeton University] ought to be driven out of the church, and all private members like myself ought to withdraw without waiting for the expulsion which should follow belief in evolution. If the brethren of the Mississippi Valley have so precarious a hold upon their faith in God that they are afraid to have their sons hear aught of modern scientific belief, by all means let them drive Dr. Woodrow to the wall.[1]

*Presented in Chattanooga, Tennessee, November 9, 1961.

Woodrow was born in Carlisle, England, in 1828 and brought as a child to this country. His father, a Presbyterian minister, served as a missionary in Canada and then settled at Chillicothe, Ohio. After young James was graduated from Jefferson College at Canonsburg, Pennsylvania, he taught school for several years in Alabama.[2] In 1853 he was appointed professor of natural sciences in the small Presbyterian college of Oglethorpe University at Midway, near Milledgeville, Georgia. Before beginning his work he studied science during a summer at Harvard University under Louis Agassiz. Then, procuring a leave from Oglethorpe, he studied for over two years at the University of Heidelberg, which in 1856 awarded him a Ph.D. degree, *summa cum laude.*

While Woodrow was teaching at Oglethorpe University, he studied theology and Hebrew, and in 1859 was ordained a Presbyterian minister. He preached to humble country churches in the neighborhood of the college, sometimes taking with him Sidney Lanier, his favorite student. Lanier in later life paid high tribute to Woodrow as a teacher who had stimulated in him an interest in science.[3] But the college authorities do not seem to have appreciated this fine scholar and teacher. In appointing a professor in 1858 to fill the new chair of chemistry, they passed over Woodrow and selected another man. Of this episode, he wrote ironically to a friend,

What a convenient objection "Northerner" is! I suppose you know the folly of it as applied to me, as by far the larger portion of my life has been divided between my native land and this State and Alabama, and of this the greater portion has been spent in this latitude. It is a silly reason at best; doubly so, when not true.[4]

In 1861 Woodrow accepted the offer of the "Perkins Professorship of Natural Sciences in Connexion with Revelation" at Columbia Theological Seminary in Columbia, South Carolina. This professorship had been established as a result of a resolution adopted by the Tombeckbee Presbytery of Mississippi in 1857, which declared,

Whereas, We live in an age in which the most insidious attacks are made upon revealed religion, through the Natural sciences, and as it behooves the church, at all times, to have men capable of defending the faith once delivered to the Saints, therefore, *Resolved,* That this Presbytery recommend the endowment of a professorship of the natural sciences, as connected with revealed religion in one or more of our theological seminaries, and would cheerfully recommend our churches to contribute their full proportion of funds for said endowment.[5]

Judge John Perkins of The Oaks near Columbus, Mississippi, had responded to the call by contributing $30,000, later increased to $40,000.

The Presbyterian theological seminary at Columbia accepted the endowment and established the Perkins Professorship.

James Woodrow was elected to be the first professor. In his inaugural address he noted that there was not "a single similar chair in any theological school either in America or Europe, to serve as a model." He listed the points of conflict between revealed religion and science which he proposed to discuss in his lectures. They were (1) the age of the earth, (2) the length of time man has been on the earth, (3) the existence of pre-Adamite animals on the earth indicated by fossils, (4) the flood of Noah, whether it deluged the whole earth or only its civilized portion, (5) the unity of the human race, (6) the introduction of death into the world, and (7) the whole subject of chronology. These questions were raised by the new geology introduced by Sir Charles Lyell. Woodrow did not mention the subject of evolution, for Charles Darwin's *Origin of Species* had been published only two years before and was scarcely noticed in the South before the Civil War. In his address Woodrow stated his belief that nothing would be found in modern science inconsistent with the teaching of the Bible, and he affirmed his belief in the authenticity of the literal word of the Sacred Scriptures. Finally, he made a strong appeal for freedom of inquiry and discussion and declared that in carrying out the duties of the new professorship he would exercise an "untrammeled freedom of inquiry."[6]

The Civil War led to the closing of the Seminary, since the students volunteered *en masse* for service in the Confederate army. The Perkins Professor also volunteered for military service, but was assigned to the position of chief of the Confederate chemical laboratory in Columbia. After the war had ended, Woodrow established a job printing house in Columbia, which published Presbyterian periodicals. He was awarded the state printing contract when Wade Hampton became governor. In addition to his commercial interests he resumed his professorship in the Seminary when it reopened its doors, and he also taught various branches of science in the nearby University of South Carolina.

One of his manifold activities was being treasurer of foreign missions of the Southern Presbyterian Church. In 1871 he was charged with dishonesty in administering this office, whereupon he demanded a trial before the General Assembly of the church to clear his good name. Here he was accused of having too many irons in the fire and of making too much money. He admitted that he had made "a good deal of money," but that, he observed, was not a crime, and he explained how he was able to engage in the numerous activities that he did. Though a small and frail man physically, he was able to accomplish many tasks, he said, by incessant work, by foregoing the pleasures of society, and by giving up rest and recreation. Moreover, his wife, sacrificing normal pleasures, aided him in his work. After hearing his able and sincere defense, the Assembly not only vindicated him from the charges brought against him but commended him for his services to the church.[7]

A large portion of Woodrow's life was spent in controversy. His strong convictions and stubborn fighting spirit made him a formidable controversialist. His appearance gave no indication of this aggressive side of his nature. His portrait which hangs on the walls of the South Caroliniana Library in Columbus is that of a mild-mannered scholar; he wears a long gray beard, and his pale face and blue eyes, looking from behind glasses, give the impression of quiet thought and self-discipline. From his appearance also one would hardly suspect that he was a shrewd and successful business man as well as a professor and ordained Presbyterian minister. He became president of the Central Bank of Columbia, vice president of the Mutual Benefit Building and Loan Association, vice president of the Carolina Land and Investment Company, and president of the Carolina Home Insurance Company. He owned valuable real estate in Columbia, and from 1861 to 1885 he was the proprietor and editor of the quarterly *Southern Presbyterian Review,* and from 1865 to 1893 of the weekly *Southern Presbyterian.*

Woodrow's controversy with religious bigots began while he was a chemist in the service of the Confederacy. In April, 1863, he published an article in the *Southern Presbyterian Review* entitled "Geology and Its Assailants," which gave a premonition of his later fight for the freedom to teach the theory of evolution. In this article he observed that the progress of science had been continuously resisted by the church, for the latter regarded science as its enemy, and ignorant religionists had portrayed geology, not in its true lineaments but in a caricature. He combated the charge that the findings of this science could not be accepted because of the conflict of opinions among geologists; the same conflict of opinion, he observed, existed with regard to history and religion. Instead of true religion being endangered by the study of geology, he maintained, harmony existed between natural science and the Bible. Any attempt to suppress science, he argued, indicated a weak faith in Christianity and a dread that the Bible might be found to be untrue.[8]

The religious enemies of science in the South during the Reconstruction period were led by a dynamic professor of theology in the Union Theological Seminary at Hampden-Sydney, Virginia, Robert Louis Dabney. Dabney was a formidable protagonist, for not only was he a vigorous writer with deep prejudices, but he had the aura arising from his having been on the staff of Stonewall Jackson and his having published a biography of that southern hero. In an article in the *Southern Presby-*

terian Review of July, 1873, Woodrow refuted the allegations of the Hampden-Sydney professor against modern science. He observed that Dabney had been keeping up an unremitting warfare for some years on physical science and that as yet no one had undertaken to confute him. Woodrow's article, often expressed in ironic terms, presented the eminent theologian as an ignoramus with regard to modern science. Science is neither religious nor irreligious, Woodrow maintained; there is no Christian law of gravity; the events of nature must be accepted as produced by natural laws unless proved otherwise, that is by the Holy Scriptures.[9]

Dabney replied in the October issue of the *Review,* raising the question whether chairs of natural science should be introduced into religious seminaries. He held that the amount of instruction in science given in the seminaries would be inadequate for the purpose intended and that "the study of modern geology, especially, is shown by experience . . . to have a tendency towards naturalistic and anti-Christian opinions."[10] Thus, Dabney expressed a deep-seated suspicion of the teaching of science widely held by southern people, a prejudice that underlay in part the violent warfare against state universities as godless institutions which broke out in the 1890's, led by President John C. Kilgo of Trinity College.[11] In opposing such prejudices and upholding the need of teaching modern science, Woodrow published a second article attacking Dabney, entitled "A Further Examination of Certain Recent Assaults on Physical Science."[12]

Woodrow's controversy with Dabney was concerned principally with a defense of the science of geology against the attack of orthodox theologians. He came very slowly, and even reluctantly, to accept the theory of evolution as advanced by Darwin. He was influenced by his old professor at Harvard, Agassiz, the most eminent opponent of the Darwinian hypothesis in America. The outstanding amateur naturalist of South Carolina at this time, the mycologist Henry William Ravenel, also opposed the Darwinian theory of evolution. Like Woodrow, Ravenel was a very devout man, and he had religious scruples against accepting such a revolutionary doctrine. On November 12, 1878, he wrote in his journal that he had talked with Colonel Spratt, who was "embued with the doctrine of the most advanced Evolutionists," but that, however plausible the new theory was, he himself could not accept it.[13]

When Woodrow traveled in Europe in 1872–73, he talked with many scientists and found that practically all of them accepted the new theory; but he rejected it, hoping to be upheld and strengthened in his opinion by scientists in America. He did not take up the subject in his classes, and he told his students that the theory of evolution, whether true or false, did not in the slightest degree impugn the absolute truthfulness of a single word in the Bible. Though he avoided the discussion of evolution, he accepted, as the manuscript notes on his lectures taken by his student Robert McAlpine show, the antiquity of the earth, the unity of the human races, and the limited nature of Noah's flood.[14] He continually maintained that the Bible did not teach science, and that science and the Bible did not contradict each other because they came from the same source, God.

Professor Woodrow did not begin the controversy over the doctrine of evolution that led to his dismissal from the faculty of the Columbia Theological Seminary. When the board of directors of that institution held their first meeting in the fall of 1882 after the Seminary had been closed for two years on account of financial reasons, they adopted a resolution that the faculty of the Seminary was "too honest secretly to impugn the verbal inspiration of any part of the original Scriptures or to covertly teach evolution and other insidious errors that undermine the foundations of our precious faith."[15] Nevertheless, they were disturbed to hear that suspicions had arisen among some members of the synods that Professor Woodrow was unsound in the faith in regard to the theory of evolution. Accordingly, on May 10, 1883, the board passed a resolution requesting him to give in the *Southern Presbyterian Review* his views upon evolution, "as it respects the world, the lower animals, and man." They gave as their reason for this unusual request that skepticism was employing the alleged discoveries in science "to impugn the Word of God."[16]

This request caused Woodrow to review the evidence for evolution, which led him to change his former opinion.[17] He doubtless realized the danger of announcing his adhesion to the theory of Darwin, for only a few years before, in 1878, Professor Alexander Winchell had been dismissed from his chair of geology in Vanderbilt University because he had questioned the Biblical account of the origin of man, and Crawford H. Toy had to resign in 1879 from the Southern Baptist Theological Seminary at Louisville, Kentucky, because he held unorthodox views as to the composition of the Old Testament.[18]

Nevertheless, Professor Woodrow delivered an address before the alumni and the board of directors of the Seminary in May, 1884, in which he boldly stated his belief that Adam's body had probably been created by the process of evolution; however, the soul of man, he hastened to add, was immediately created by God. The study of evolution, he declared, made him admire God's plan of creation more reverently than ever before. Particularly did he emphasize that this new discovery of natural science did not contradict the Sacred Scriptures, every word of which he accepted as truth.[19]

After Woodrow had presented his views on evolution and they had been published in the July issue of the *Southern Presbyterian Review,* the board of directors in their September, 1884, meeting debated what action they should take in regard to teaching such views in the Seminary. One of the members, the Reverend James Stacy, introduced a resolution condemning the belief that the body of Adam was evolved from the lower animals and enjoining the Perkins Professor from teaching such a doctrine in the Seminary. This resolution the board rejected by a vote of 8 to 3 and adopted instead a resolution introduced by the Reverend A. W. Clisby that

This board is in fullest sympathy with the godly jealousy of the church for the infallible truth and absolute inerrancy of the Scriptures of the Old and New Testaments as God's word to man, and we rejoice in the full confirmation by Dr. Woodrow that he stands immovably with us in the same position.[20]

Woodrow was thus victorious in the first round of his battle for the freedom to teach evolution in the Seminary. The fight was then transferred to the associated synods. The board of directors of the Seminary was under the control of the four synods of South Carolina, Georgia, South Georgia and Florida, and Alabama. These ecclesiastical bodies and the General Assembly of the Southern Presbyterian Church were ultimately to decide Woodrow's fate as regards the holding of his professorship.

The first synod to review the Woodrow case was that of South Carolina, meeting at Greenville in October, 1884. Before this body Woodrow defended himself in an able speech. He surveyed the opinions of science professors in the United States on the subject of evolution, pointing out that Alexander Agassiz, the son of Louis, at Harvard, James Dwight Dana and Othniel Charles Marsh at Yale, Alpheus Spring Packard at Brown held to the view of evolution and that the Darwinian hypothesis was being taught at Johns Hopkins University, the University of Virginia, Wofford College (by the young science professor, Warren Du Pré), the University of Georgia, Southwestern Presbyterian University, and Central University in Kentucky; at Davidson College, Professor J. R. Blake taught the nebular hypothesis, and at the University of North Carolina Professor Joseph Austin Holmes was examining the subject of evolution.

In presenting his own beliefs as to evolution, Woodrow made a startling distinction between the creation of Adam's body and of Eve's body. The anatomy of the human male, he maintained, was evolved from the lower animals, but that of the female was directly created by a miracle of God. His reason for making this fantastic distinction was that the Bible had clearly stated the mode of creation of Eve's body but was silent as to the process of the creating of Adam's body. Thus Woodrow must be regarded as a transitional figure, who clung to the old pattern of thought while entering the threshold of the modern world of science.

Woodrow considered his trial at Greenville as belonging to the continuity of the great heresy trials of the past, particularly the trial of Martin Luther at Worms. After citing some of the errors which the Christian church had made in dealing with scientific questions, such as its opposition to the heliocentric theory, he asked the question, "Will you add to this dismal list?" Dramatically, he read the sentence of the Inquisition on June 22, 1663, in the case of Galileo, who was condemned because he believed that, instead of the sun encircling a stationary earth, the earth moved around the sun. Woodrow warned his hearers that the opposition of the church to the teaching of modern science would turn young men against the Bible and the church.[21]

The leading opponent of Woodrow at Greenville was Professor John L. Girardeau, his colleague on the faculty of Columbia Theological Seminary. Girardeau held that the doctrine of evolution was an unproved hypothesis as it related to the origin of man; it was, moreover, contrary to the Presbyterian creed and undermined a belief in the Sacred Scriptures. In his argument before this assembly he directly attacked the principle of academic freedom. The synods of the church, he declared, had a right to dictate what a professor should teach in the Theological Seminary; professors in the Seminary were debarred from teaching views which they sincerely believed but which were opposed to the standards of faith of the church; the liberty of the individual man was different from the liberty of the teacher.[22]

After five days of debate, the Synod passed a resolution disapproving of the teaching of the doctrine of evolution in Columbia Theological Seminary, "except in a purely expository manner, without intention of inculcating its truth."[23] The three other controlling synods of Georgia, Alabama, South Georgia and Florida denounced the teaching of the doctrine of evolution in the Seminary and instructed the board of directors to prohibit such teachings in the Seminary. The synods of Kentucky, Nashville, Memphis, Mississippi, Arkansas, and Texas, with only twelve dissenting votes, also disapproved of Professor Woodrow's views as outlined in his address on evolution and the teaching of them in the Seminary.[24] Confronted with this wide repudiation of Woodrow's views on evolution, the board of directors of the Seminary voted, 8 to 4, to request Professor Woodrow to resign. This he refused to do, asserting that his teachings in the Seminary were in accord with the Bible and the Presbyterian Confession of Faith.[25] The board then voted to dismiss him from his professorship.

Woodrow now appealed to the four synods that controlled the Seminary. Two of these, Georgia and Alabama, upheld the action of the board of directors, but the other two did not. When the board met in December, 1885, they decided that since a majority of the synods having jurisdiction over their action had not approved the removal of Professor Woodrow, legally he held his position on the faculty of the Seminary, and his salary should be paid.[26] At the same time, however, they again requested his resignation. Although he steadfastly refused, he conceded that the proper church authorities had the right to determine what subjects should be taught in the Seminary and he promised, "I will act in accord and with the expressed wishes of the Synod by omitting Evolution from the subjects taught."[27] All through the next year (1886) the board made repeated requests for him to resign, but the intransigent professor continued to refuse.

His tenacious fight to hold his professorship was carried on in various church courts. It makes an astonishingly complex story, full of crosscurrents. In the summer of 1886 he was tried by his own presbytery, the Presbytery of Augusta, Georgia, on the charge of teaching and promulgating opinions, "which are of dangerous tendency, and which are calculated to unsettle the mind of the Church respecting the accuracy and authority of the Holy Scriptures as an infallible rule of faith." Girardeau was once more the chief witness against him. He objected strongly to Woodrow's contention that the dust out of which God created man was "organic matter pre-existing in the body of a brute" (the words used in the indictment).[28] After hearing the arguments on both sides, the Presbytery of Augusta acquitted Woodrow of the crime of heresy. But the decision was appealed by the Reverend William Adams, voluntary prosecutor, to the Synod of Georgia. The Synod reversed the decision of the Presbytery.

Moreover, at a meeting of the South Carolina Synod held at Cheraw in October, 1886, the implacable Professor Girardeau introduced a resolution requesting Woodrow's immediate resignation from the Seminary. This was adopted by a vote of 72 to 42, which was followed up by a telegram from the Synod demanding his immediate resignation. Again Woodrow refused to comply. Angered by such stubbornness, the board, after giving him another chance to resign, dismissed him on December 8, 1886, by a unanimous vote.[29]

But this defeat was still not the end of the struggle. Woodrow appealed to the highest court of the Southern Presbyterian Church, the General Assembly. His case was finally heard at the Baltimore meeting of the assembly in May, 1888. Here he again boldly presented his beliefs on evolution and maintained that they were not in conflict with the Bible or the standards of the Presbyterian Church. By a vote of 139 to 31 the assembly rejected his appeal and declared the doctrine of the church to be that Adam's body was directly fashioned by God out "of the dust of the ground without any natural animal parentage of any kind."[30]

After Woodrow's dismissal, the faculty prohibited students in the Seminary from attending the science courses which he taught in the University. A student named W. W. Elwang defied the will of the faculty and enrolled in Woodrow's class, causing another controversy to arise. The board of directors in their May meeting of 1888, received a protest from a South Carolina presbytery asking,

Will not this prohibiting policy of the Faculty, restraining the students in the Seminary from hearing lectures on scientific subjects by a professor of acknowledged competency, be justly regarded as estopping their free research after truth, and such unwarranted fettering of Christian liberty that many who would naturally prefer to pursue their studies at Columbia Seminary will go elsewhere than wear such shackles?[31]

The board of directors upheld the faculty's prohibition but finally in 1890 made a ruling that all cases of students who asked permission to take Woodrow's courses should be referred to the presbyteries of such students.

The great publicity which was given the Woodrow case did not prevent him from continuing to teach scientific courses in the University of South Carolina. He held his position there at the same time that one of his colleagues, the professor of philosophy, William J. Alexander, was dismissed from his position partly because of his unpopular religious views. In 1891 the board of trustees fired Alexander after he had publicly stated that he was a Unitarian. Woodrow, as far as I have been able to ascertain, did not protest that flagrant violation of academic freedom. One of his staunch supporters in the evolution controversy, the Reverend William J. Flinn, was appointed to fill the post held by Alexander. In that same year Woodrow was elected president of the University of South Carolina and served in that position until 1897. According to Professor Daniel Hollis, the historian of the University of South Carolina, one of his successors considered Woodrow's regime " 'the least progressive of all the administrations of the University.' "[32] His latter days were full of honor, though, and he must have smiled wryly when in 1901 he was elected moderator of the Synod of South Carolina.

Woodrow's bold claim for the freedom of teachers to discuss the revolutionary theory of evolution in their classes came at the beginning of the spread of Darwinism in the South. In the more urbanized and industrialized northern states the Darwinian hypothesis became an issue earlier than it did in the South, and there it was strongly resisted until the

1880's. Louis Agassiz at Harvard opposed the theory of evolution until his death in 1873, and many scientists stood in such awe of his eminence in the scientific world that they did not dare oppose him and risk their own reputations. Although Asa Gray, the Harvard botanist, early accepted Darwin's ideas, Professor James Dwight Dana of Yale College, a prominent geologist, very slowly came to accept the evolution hypothesis —not until 1874.[33] Woodrow himself, we have seen, rejected the revolutionary scientific theory until 1883. By this time the eminent American scientists of the North stood with their allies, intellectuals such as John Fiske, as "a solid phalanx" in the support of the evolutionary hypothesis. But the spread of Darwinism among the mass of the people in the North as well as in the South was slow, extending well into the next century. The Scopes trial at Dayton, Tennessee, in 1925 revealed how tenacious were the religious mores of the rural population of the South in resisting the teaching of evolution in the public schools.

Today the academic community appears to live in a freer and more tolerant atmosphere than in the time of James Woodrow or of Professor Bassett, or in the era of the Scopes trial. Certainly there is little danger at present in teaching evolution in schools or colleges. Yet no final victory will ever be won in preserving freedom of teaching. In the middle of the twentieth century the dangers which threaten academic freedom, though latent, are formidable. Popular hysteria over communism may recur; the discussion of sex poses a danger; a steady movement toward standardization in education is reducing independent thought; and, at the moment, race relations in some parts of the South can not be freely discussed. On these matters there are varying shades of opinion among American professors. They range from radicalism in areas where there is slight danger of a professor's losing his job by speaking out on certain controversial subjects to guarded caution and conservatism where a professor is in real peril of being deprived of his means of livelihood if he disagrees too vehemently with the mores of his community.

The great majority of southern professors, I am confident, believe strongly in protecting academic freedom. Most of them would rush to the defense of a colleague who was in danger of losing his job because he criticized the social order. They would follow the example, I believe, of the faculty of Trinity College in 1903 in rallying to the support of Professor John Spencer Bassett when popular clamor sought to drive him from his position because he had written in the *South Atlantic Quarterly* that Booker T. Washington was "the greatest man, save General Lee, born in the South in a hundred years."[34]

But what is the meaning of academic freedom today? The great issues of intellectual freedom change with each generation. When I was a student at Chapel Hill, I belonged to a group of young liberals who felt that they had emancipated themselves from the shackles of old authority. We were innocents, however, living in a changing world that we did not understand. With all of our exhilarating sense of freedom, especially from religious orthodoxy, we accepted unconcernedly some of the ruling assumptions of the society in which we had been reared. The most illiberal of these assumptions was in regard to the place of the Negro in American life. The young liberals in our universities today are deeply concerned with this question neglected by a previous generation, but perhaps many of them are just as oblivious to other great evils that afflict modern society as we in the 1920's were to the injustice of racial discrimination or as the abolitionists in the 1830's were to the evils of rapid industrialization.

Nevertheless, racial discrimination in our educational institutions is a great evil that we as an association and as individuals can not ignore, for it now has reached the point of interfering with the free trade of ideas in our profession. A recent example of such interference was told me by an able young scholar who was employed by a respectable college in the lower South. The president gave him this advice, "Stay clear of discussing integration and communism and you will get along all right." But can we as individuals or as an association hide our heads in the sand and refuse to express our opinions on these vital subjects? Whatever reputation I may have attained began with the publication of my book *Freedom of Thought in the Old South,* and I can not, either from the standpoint of honor or wisdom, depart from that position. A prominent southern historian observed to me recently that the issue of integration in our association as well as in colleges and schools will be settled in a few years; those of our members who oppose it will in the future be ashamed of their stand. I urge you therefore to stand with the future and not with the conservative past.

Although our association is not a reform or crusading organization, we do not go out of our province in taking a bold and courageous stand on the integration of the races in our educational system. I refer particularly to immediate integration in our colleges and universities and to gradual integration in our schools. It should be a high honor for us to lead public opinion rather than tamely to follow it. We southern historians and teachers of history—I for one certainly—should hope not only to teach and write history but also to influence even in a small degree, the course of future history.

To do this, academic freedom is essential; to many of us it is more precious than money. Yet nearly all of us desperately need to retain our jobs and our right to retirement pay for survival, rights which may be threatened by bold speech. We do not have the economic base for free speech that Professor James Woodrow, a successful businessman as well as professor, enjoyed. The dean of one of the most notable of our southern universities candidly observed to me that the best safeguard for academic liberty was to own a farm. Since few of us are so fortunate, figuratively speaking, as to own farms, we must depend for safety in times of popular hysteria such as the McCarthy era, or possibly today in the lower South, or in the uncertain future, upon the organized support of our colleagues and on the strong traditions of academic freedom which our profession has developed. Tolerance, the great Roman Catholic historian, Lord Acton, has pointed out, is the delicate fruit of a mature society. Academic freedom, likewise, is the product of maturity, a stage of culture that has been reached through growing pains and the struggles of generations of teachers who have preceded us. In the attainment of the large measure of freedom of teaching which we enjoy, the subject of my paper, James Woodrow, played a significant and triumphant role. I salute his memory, and hope that should any of us ever face a similar crisis of academic freedom, we, though lacking a farm, may display his great moral courage.

Chapter XXVIII

The Mobile Frontier

REMBERT W. PATRICK

ELECTION to the highest office in the Southern Historical Association sends the recipient of that honor to the *Journal of Southern History* and to those other important quarterlies—the *American Historical Review* and the *Mississippi Valley Historical Review*—to study the addresses delivered by past presidents of the Southern and other professional historical organizations.* The result is startling. Like the civil servant of another century who resigned from the United States Patent Office because he thought that every tool and machine of value had already been invented, a current president of a historical association is dismayed by the proficiency and coverage of his predecessors. Every great movement, it seems, has already been adequately described, and all possible interpretations have been advanced.

One escape from the predicament of having nothing to say is to talk for an hour on the joys of teaching and to reminisce for another sixty minutes about one's mastery of the art of training eager, youthful minds. But, unfortunately, this speaker has never taken a course in educational methodology. This oversight obviously disqualifies him from writing a treatise on teaching. Although his primary function for a decade has been graduate education, he can not boast of any noteworthy accomplishment. Thus far his graduate students have been of two types: some with extraordinary ability, who would have progressed more rapidly and accomplished more without the interference of their graduate supervisor; and others who should have been preparing themselves for some other profession or learning a trade. The joy of association with students of intermediate ability—ones who could have benefited from a mentor's proficiency in spelling *is* or gained from his explaining the proper usage of *who* or *whom*—has escaped him.

*Presented in Miami Beach, Florida, November 8, 1962.

A second avenue of retreat would be to analyze a current problem, specifically, civil rights in the South. The "statesmen" of the region, however, proclaim that all southerners do enjoy equal justice and equal opportunity. No college professor, especially one subject to investigation by publicity-seeking, irresponsible members of a committee created by a legislature of Caucasoids, should ever contradict the mouthings of politicians. Besides, the task of explaining the daily newspaper and the weekly news magazines to semiliterates belongs to the sociologist and the political scientist; the historian should concentrate on the past.

The fruitfulness of historians, past and present, and the speaker's adopted state have left him no subject other than "The Mobile Frontier." Thousands of articles, monographs, and books have told of the Spanish settlements in the New World, the gold and silver found in Mexico and Peru, the migration of the Puritans to New England, and the influence of the frontier on American history. A number of historians have even chosen the Civil War for their subject. But writers have almost ignored an important facet of American culture. A few dry statistics are sufficient to illustrate this neglect. A billion dollars worth of silver and gold was shipped from the New World to Spain in the sixteenth century; in 1960 American tourists spent $2,500,000,000 in Europe. Not more than 200,000 Europeans, mostly Spaniards, settled in the New World in the 1500's; in 1961 more than 12,000,000 people spent their vacations in Florida. Approximately 25,000 Puritans entered New England in the Great Migration of the 1630's; in one year, 1956, almost 3,000,000 sight-seers visited the Great Smoky Mountains National Park. Between 1790 and 1860 the entire American area west of the Appalachian Mountains increased in population through natural increment and immigration by fewer than 15,500,000 people; in 1961 the number of travelers in Georgia totaled 42,000,000. The largest number of Europeans to enter the United States in any decade was 8,136,016; in 1961 more than 33,000,000 persons made trips in Virginia. More has been written about the Civil War than any other period of American history, but between 1961 and 1965 the expenditures of northern tourists in the South will be larger than the total spent by the northern and southern governments throughout that war.

Like many other historical firsts, the original tourist stems from the prehistoric era. Driven by rumors of larger caves, of better weapons, or of more shapely women with long, thick hair by which the cooperatively unwilling female might be dragged to a crude home, an audacious caveman may have been led to tour hills distant from his own. Certainly the Greeks and Romans visited the other lands bordering on the Mediterranean Sea. Intercontinental tourist Marco Polo recorded his experiences in the Orient while suffering the prisoner's lot in Italy. Forced by shipwreck in 1696, Jonathan Dickinson and his friends became English tourists in Spanish Florida, and Dickinson later recorded the excursion in a remarkably interesting journal.

Both in the Colonial and Federal periods of American history, English and continental Europeans crossed the Atlantic to investigate conditions in the colonies and the new democracy. The reports of these travelers are well known and provide valuable source material for understanding the political and economic conditions, the customs and manners, and the social and intellectual history of our forefathers. Before the Civil War the difference between northern and southern culture attracted Yankee visitors to the South Atlantic states. Ralph Waldo Emerson went as far south as St. Augustine, and Frederick Law Olmsted journeyed through the seaboard slave states. Northern explorers of southern culture were often biased, and at times dishonest, in their comments set down in diaries, letters, and books. Although never within 150 miles of Tallahassee, Emerson, minister and moralist, described the town and its homes for his readers. Olmsted's writing reflected his dislike of slavery, but his reporting was more accurate than southern apologists admit.

These Europeans and northerners toured the South for a purpose, but prior to the Civil War vacation-bent tourists traveled in the South with pleasure-seeking as their primary goal. Many rice planters from the seaboard and some cotton producers from the Piedmont section found excitement for themselves and their families during the social seasons of Charleston and Savannah. Every South Atlantic state boasted of having at least one city or town with magnetic attraction for lonely agriculturalists. Legislative sessions enticed visitors to state capitals, and court sessions brought farmers to the county seats.

Springs or highland health resorts in every state attracted the ill and infirm as well as the pleasure seekers. Most famous of these antebellum spas were the springs of Virginia. The waters of Red Springs were advertised as being "efficacious in all forms of consumption, scrofula, jaundice, and other bilious affectations; chronic dysentery and diarrhea, diseases of the uterus, chronic rheumatism and gout, dropsy, gravel, neuralgia, tremor, syphilis, scurvy, erysipelas, tetter, ringworm. . . ."

In time, the springs of Virginia became more than vacation spots and health resorts. Mothers and fathers went there to peddle their daughters to eligible men, and sons of financially strained parents sought wives whose fathers' money would manure wornout acres and refurbish shabby ancestral homes. Shrewd Colonel William Pope observed that healing and mating were copartners at the spas. He organized the "Billing, Wooing, and Cooing Society," gave it a constitution, and kept its record on long rolls of pink paper. The waters of the springs became famous as love potions, and their effect was swift and fatal to bachelors and widowers who imagined they were drinking to cure dyspepsia or gout. Any southern belle endowed with a soft, alluring beauty and an eager, romantic heart, who returned from the springs to her plantation home without snaring a man or boasting of the opportunity to reject at least one proposal, would shed copious tears and become a disgrace to her family and her sex.

Affluent southerners gave their families vacations in the North and sent their sons to Europe. Stores stocked with dresses, shoes, and bonnets attracted wives and daughters to eastern cities. Despite an increasing antipathy for northerners, southerners willingly gave their children in marriage to the sons and daughters of wealthy "money-grubbing Yankees." As a reward for winning their collegiate degrees and in order to gloss over any remaining provincialism, some fathers gave their sons the grand tour of Europe. Even the most debauched heir, after sowing his wild oats in the bars and bistros along the route from London to Constantinople, was supposed to return to the plantation and marry a white flower of southern womanhood, whose purity would reform him and guide him into the responsibility of his heritage.

In the poverty-stricken post-Civil War South few residents could afford vacations, but the captains of northern industry had funds for travel. Nurtured by war and peacetime profits, the antebellum trickle of northern tourists widened into a stream. During the winter of 1868–69, Ledyard Bill, author of *A Winter in Florida* (New York, 1869), estimated the number of travelers in Florida at 25,000, which was half the total claimed by boastful Floridians. Most numerous of the passengers on a trip up the St. Johns River were pleasure seekers, Bill reported, followed in numerical order by semi-invalids, speculators looking for bargains in land, and individuals contemplating settlement.

Floridians urged the sick to recover, or at worst to die in comfort, in the semitropical climate of their state. One invalid, who had for years kept one jump ahead of death by wintering in various countries, reported the climate of St. Augustine better than that of any part of Europe and superior to that of the islands of the West Indies. In the early 1880's ill and aging General Ulysses S. Grant declared as he watched the rippling river waters reflect the moonlight, "In all my journey round the world I have seen nothing to equal this trip on the St. Johns." Tallahasseeans procaimed their city a haven for individuals afflicted with lung and throat troubles, and Sidney Lanier was paid to write *Florida: Its Scenery,*

Climate, and History (Philadelphia, 1876) to advertise the healing climate of Florida for victims of tuberculosis.

Florida, however, offered advantages to the healthy as well as to the ill. Silvia Sunshine, pseudonym of Abbie M. Brooks, in *Petals Plucked from Sunny Climes* (Nashville, 1880), counseled in her romantic way:

This is the spot for the jilted lover to forget his idol, and the disconsolate lady her imagined devotee; for those fretted by the rough edges of corroding care to retire and find a respite from their struggles; the bankrupt who has been conquered in the battles of brokerage, to visit and be reminded God has given us more treasures to delight us than the dross which passes from our grasp like a shadow, but which all are struggling and striving to win; the store-house of the fathomless deep, where we can contemplate that great image of eternity; "the invisible, boundless, endless, and sublime."

Even the historian, Silvia Sunshine continued, would find no other place so well adapted to meditation and reconstruction of the past. She warned her readers to bring fat pocketbooks to Florida; the northern proprietors who operated the best hotels charged "two dollars for a dinner with the most unblushing effrontery, while the Floridian is satisfied with fifty cents for a square meal." Most astonishing to Silvia was the mysterious manner by which the natives came into possession of a tourist's name and his financial status. "If you are not flush and free with funds," the author wrote, "you can rest from any annoyances, except boarding-house keepers, who have adopted the motto, 'pay as you go, or go away.' "

Tourists often remained or returned to become citizens of Florida. Northerners seeking escape from the piercing winds and frigid temperatures of New England, the Middle Atlantic states, and the Old Northwest sought the mild climate of Florida. The cool and wholesome winds of the Atlantic Ocean and the Gulf of Mexico enticed residents of Alabama, Georgia, and the Carolinas from their flaying sun and torrid heat to the southernmost state of the Union. "The least desirable . . . as a class," a Chicago journalist reported, were from "Alabama . . . mostly very poor, ignorant, shiftless, improvident, conceited, and lazy. . . . The best immigrants from the Southern States are from Georgia; in fact, the average Georgian is a shrewd, thrifty, sober, industrious individual . . . a regular Southern Yankee."

No man would migrate to Florida, not even from hell itself, John Randolph of Roanoke reportedly said, but time proved the irascible Virginian wrong. If not from hell, at least from New England, came Harriet Beecher Stowe with her quiet, little preacher husband to settle at Mandarin. There on the porch of her home, located on a bluff overlooking the St. Johns River, the author of *Uncle Tom's Cabin* staged her appearance just as a steamboat rounded the bend, to give tourists the thrill of seeing the famous woman working on the manuscript of a new book. Later, the sly New Englander collected payment from transportation companies for her performance. She did, however, in *Palmetto-Leaves* (Boston, 1873), describe for her northern readers the delights and difficulties of living in Florida. The state was ideal for invalids, she wrote, for the sweeping winds from ocean and gulf "temper the air, and blow away malarious gases," but she warned visitors to forget their "romantic ideas of waving palms, orange-groves, flowers, and fruit, all bursting forth in tropical abundance. . . ."

Although Mrs. Stowe returned to Connecticut in summer, other northerners became permanent residents of Florida. Historians have given too much attention to the political aspects of Reconstruction and too little to northerners who, of their own free will, chose to migrate to the South. The three Hart brothers of Poughkeepsie, New York, graduates or former students of Ivy League colleges, had served at various southern posts during the Civil War. After the war they chose Florida for economic rather than political opportunity. The brothers bore no resemblance to carpetbaggers; one became a reporter, the second formed a partnership with a former Confederate colonel to cut timber along the St. Johns River and to operate a cotton plantation near Lake City; and the third grubbed out a farm at Federal Point on the St. Johns. Other than voting, none of the brothers engaged in political activity, and all of them wished their fellow northerners would cease meddling in Florida affairs.

Letters of the Hart brothers to their parents and sisters described the movement of tourists and the problems of new residents; they also contained comments on the folkways and mores of the natives. In one letter to his sister, Ambrose Hart gave a unique reason for a man wooing a maid. One day, he wrote, Louisa McLemore of Lake City begged his advice. For two years she had been living without benefit of clergy with a former major of the Confederate army and of late Major Bags had been beating her frequently and severely. Hart visited the major and warned him that he, not being her legal husband, had no more right to beat Louisa than did any other man. Whereupon, Hart reported, the major took Louisa to the altar to gain legal authority over her and the right to punish her whenever she disobeyed him.

Like the Hart brothers, other northerners toured and settled in the South. "Until a few seasons ago tourists from the East made it a rule to go to Florida points," the 1907 edition of *Handbook of South Carolina* asserted, "but now they are beginning to appreciate the value of the climate of the Middle South. The change from the bitter cold of the East and Northwest to the tropical climate of Florida was too great, and an enervating effect on the system was experienced." South Carolina's winter climate, the publication continued, was of "peculiar benefit to invalids, being bracing while sufficiently warm." Even Harriet Beecher Stowe admitted that "for debility, and the complaints that spring from debility, Florida is not so good a refuge, perhaps, as some more northern point, like Aiken."

Wealthy easterners founded large winter colonies at Aiken and Camden, South Carolina. In 1906 the new and quickly overcrowded Hampton Terrace and Colonial hotels at North Augusta and Columbia turned away hundreds of tourists. The Pine Forest Inn at Summerville, the Bon Air at North Augusta, the Tourist Hotel at Batesburg, and a number of hotels at Charleston catered to northern vacationers. Resort hotels appeared in other states: the De Soto at Savannah, the Battery Park and Kenilworth Inn at Asheville, and the Mountain Park in the Great Smokies; and others at Warm Springs, Georgia, and the springs of Virginia. The Jamestown tercentenary drew travelers from all over the United States, while regional fairs and international expositions brought visitors by the thousands. Jekyll Island, Georgia, became a "Mecca for millionaires," and vacationers found peace in quaint St. Marys, where "the coolest of ocean breezes" playing sportively among the pendant moss blew away the God of Mammon. Crowded hostelries demonstrated the economic importance of tourists to many southern places.

The stream of tourism was flowing; and, in the almost half a century following World War I, it widened and deepened into a mighty river with tributaries extending to hundreds of communities. New economic classes waded into the pleasant waters of tourism. The wealthy continued to winter in the South; but people of middle and low incomes, salaried employees and hourly wage earners, couples and large families, and retired individuals and the unemployed acquired the vacation habit. In waves travelers flowed to seashore or mountain, to historic shrine or educational museum, to restful retreat or bustling city, and to sports event or annual festival. Tourism created a new frontier in America— the mobile frontier.

Many and varied causes brought forth the mobile frontier. Wars and restrictions on travel closed formerly popular European resorts to wealthy Americans. More and more they joined their compatriots who had already discovered the attractiveness of the southern climate. Wartime profits and the shift of the United States from debtor to creditor nation produced abundant capital-seeking investment. Fear of Bolshevism, and later of other isms, made investors question the continuation of private enterprise capitalism in foreign countries. The entrepreneur demanded more than a small, safe return on his investments; the semideveloped areas of the South, particularly the Florida frontier, offered opportunity for tremendous profits. Although in new frontiers awaiting capital expenditure for development, the chances of losses sojourned with hopes of profits, the enterprising American speculator pitted his managerial skill against the possibility of failure. He dotted scrub-covered soil with luxurious hotels, pumped sand from shallow bays to form islands, built bridges to breeze-cooled homesites, and opened natural wonderlands to tourists. Capital investment made distant places alluring and provided comfortable accommodations for travelers.

Meanwhile national changes favored those who gambled on the tourist trade. In the twentieth century the United States was transformed from a country of farmers into a nation of industrial workers congregated in cities. Higher salaries and wages for fewer hours of work, and vacation time with pay, gave Americans leisure and money for travel. Planned insurance programs, pension arrangements of industry, and federal-state social security allowed retired couples to wander hither and yon in search of new adventures and the enjoyment of scenic attractions. Families of limited means followed their affluent neighbors in touring and vacationing in the South. The masses traveled in all seasons, but their limited budgets and specified vacation periods forced them to concentrate their journeys in the summertime. In that season, prices at southern resorts were lower than in the fashionable winter season, and soon the number of summer tourists surpassed that of winter, spring, or fall.

New modes of travel and improvements in existing ones contributed to, and were enlarged by, the mobile frontier. For decades the railroads had carried most vacationers to their destinations. Although they offered more comfort and speed in the twentieth century than before, trains lost patrons with each passing decade. The mechanical marvel from Detroit quickly became the vehicle of tourism. Macadamized roads were widened and paved for the automobile; states constructed toll turnpikes and limited-access highways, and federal-state superhighways crossed and crisscrossed the countryside. Bypasses and expressways shuttled motorists around congested city traffic or sped them by it on multilaned freeways. Bulldozers cleared tree-shaded locations for filling stations to service automobiles, and entrepreneurs built motels for the comfort of motorists. Air-conditioned buses blew their smelly gases along highways, and vapor trails gave tails to airplanes cutting through the atmsophere. Train, plane, and bus provided varying degrees of speed at different costs, but the automobile gave the driver command of his schedule, and was less expensive for large families than other means of travel. Today more than 80 per cent of the tourists use automobiles for transportation.

Many natural endowments enabled the South Atlantic states to benefit from the tourist trade. They were situated within a thousand miles of the great population centers of the nation. A maximum of three days by automobile, twenty-seven hours by train, or a few hours by jet airplane brought residents of crowded cities to warm beaches or cool mountains. The Northeast and Middle West were nearer to Florida than to California. The southern seaboard states had a longer coastline and better beaches than any other region of the United States. The southern Appalachian Mountains with the highest peaks east of the Rockies were within easy traveling distance of 75 per cent of the American people.

In addition to favorable location and natural beauty, the southern seaboard had warmth in winter and many days of sunshine throughout the year. In summer the breezes swept in from the water and made the hot beaches enjoyable. Altitude gave the Appalachian Mountains and the Piedmont hills a comfortable coolness even during the hottest season. Abundant rainfall broke into sunny days to water hill and valley and cover them with lush green vegetation.

The Southeast also had historic and romantic appeal for visitors. Annapolis, Jamestown, New Bern, Charleston, and Savannah brought visions of courageous ancestors or honored pioneers, who began a mighty nation with their settlements along the rivers and bays of the Atlantic. Descendants of colonials visited the places where their forefathers had lived. Stately mansions of former tobacco, rice, and cotton planters stimulated daydreams of the Old South with her white-columned homes, beautiful belles accompanied by chivalrous men, and gay dancers whirling to the music of Negro artists. The fragrance of orange blossoms in Florida caused maidens to hope and matrons to reminisce. The legend of Ponce de León's search for a fountain of youth made aging, balding men dream of their vanished youth. They ogled slim but curvaceous girls sunning on the sand with an enjoyment that drew piercing glances or sharp comments from rotund wives. "You can see almost every type of woman in the world at Miami Beach," one Floridian said to another, "And with the bathing suits they wear," his companion replied, "almost all of them."

Despite human and natural resources the Southeast needed advertising to attain the maximum number of tourists. Railroad companies, steamship lines, and hotels deluged the potential vacationer with promotional literature. City fathers discovered that a photograph of a beautiful bathing girl reclining on a warm, sandy beach appealed to northern newspaper editors who would print the picture side by side with one of a bundled-up, potbellied man shoveling snow from cold sidewalks. Cheesecake was discovered and effectively exploited for tourism. State travel bureaus or development commissions advertised their commonwealths in newspapers and magazines. Manuscripts describing the lures of the southern seaboard states and the activities of famous individuals at vacation spots were snapped up by magazine editors and book publishers.

No longer was advertising directed at the ill, old, and infirm; the twentieth-century appeal was to the healthy. The attractions of the Southeast for active people were emphasized—the participation sports of swimming, sailing, hunting, and golfing, and the spectator sports of horse racing, dog racing, *jai alai,* and football appeared in advertisements. Tourists were urged to stay longer or to buy homes for seasonal residence. Brochures detailed the educational values to be derived from visiting historical places and viewing collections in museums. Visitors were encouraged to become permanent residents, and the advantages of operating a business in the Southeast were pointed out to capitalists and corporation executives.

Government and private enterprise developed attractions to hold the interest of the tourist. The National Park Service restored and operated forts and historic monuments and built facilities for picnickers and campers in national parks and forests. States created park boards and financed the acquisition of wooded and waterfront land for its conversion to public use; museums depicting significant historical stories were constructed; old buildings were maintained; and historical markers were placed along the roadsides. Historical societies also erected markers, established museums and libraries, and opened historic homes and buildings to the public. Individuals and corporations sought the tourist dollar with a multiplicity of displays, some of which offered entertainment and educational values while others peddled historical frauds to gullible spectators. Cities vied with each other in providing stadiums, tennis courts, and golf courses; libraries, art collections, and music halls; and commodious coliseums for large conventions. Luxurious hotels gave their guests almost every conceivable service, and racing or betting enthusiasts lacked no opportunity to watch or bet.

The Florida boom of the 1920's contributed to the growth of tourism. The frenzied buying and selling of real estate brought Florida and other areas of the Southeast to the attention of America. After devastating hurricanes in 1926 and 1928 had almost leveled Miami and neighboring cities in southern Florida, critical individuals hung the three-B appellation—Boom, Blow, and Bust—on the state. Within a few decades, however, Florida's appeal was stronger than ever before, and much of today's tourist trade from Delaware through Georgia depends upon the lure of Florida. She has more hotel, motel, and apartment rooms than all other South Atlantic states combined. Millions of tourists stop and spend as they pass through communities while on their way to Florida.

Finally, among the reasons for the magnitude of the mobile frontier in the southern seaboard states were wars and preparation for war. The Civil War sent thousands of invaders into the South, and millions of men received their military training for the Spanish-American and World wars in the Southeast. Relatives visited them during their terms of service, and after war's end veterans returned to look again on the scenes of their boredom or to relive pleasant moments. In large part, climate determined the placement of training camps in the Southeast. The government still locates many army, air force, navy, and marine installations in the region. Missile sites and research and production centers employ military and civilian personnel whose parents make pilgrimages to see their children and grandchildren. Many of these people, who were initially forced into the Southeast by compelling reasons, became tourists at later dates.

Tourism in the Southeast now numbers its followers in the tens of millions. Because of the preponderance of females in this horde, tourists are frequently referred to as "ducks"—large of bosom, broad of beam, flocking together, waddling amiably behind a guide, and quacking all the time. Sufficient data have been accumulated to permit classification of travelers. The primary division is into intrastate and interstate tourists. Looking only at the interstate tourists, and disregarding the businessman making a livelihood, one may divide pleasure seekers into three categories: the transit tourist, who passes through a state; the hopper, who stops at many localities for times ranging from a few hours to days; and the terminal tourist, who seeks a predetermined destination for a long stay. Some states are, therefore, bridge states, and others are terminal states. In the Southeast, Florida and the District of Columbia are terminal areas, but all states and cities are hosts to terminal tourists. There are also novices and repeaters in tourism; the former is usually a hopper and the latter a terminal vacationer.

State bureaus operating under various names have sampled the traveling public and made estimates of the mobile frontier. Of all the South Atlantic states, Florida has probably been the most thorough in her counting methods; her reports of numbers are conservative and those of other states may be inflated. According to state estimates, in 1959 Virginia had 16,000,000 transit and 14,000,000 terminal tourists; in 1960 North Carolina had 12,000,000 of the first and an equal number of the second category; in 1960 Georgia counted 18,000,000 transit and terminal tourists; and in 1959 Florida listed 11,305,890 terminal tourists. All of these sojourners were interstate tourists; Georgia's claim of

24,000,000 intrastate travelers in addition to her 18,000,000 interstate tourists serves to remind us that many people spend one or more vacations or take numerous trips within the state of their residence. A 1957 survey made by the Bureau of the Census estimated that 80,000,000 tourists chose the fifteen states of the South as their terminal destination. The other three regions—North Central, Northeast, and West—listed in the survey lagged behind the South.

The economic contributions of tourism can be determined with reasonable accuracy. Interstate tourists spent $1,767,562,843 in Florida during 1959, and two years later their expenditures totaled more than two billion dollars. Annual income from interstate tourism reported from other states in recent years was Maryland, $325,000,000; Virginia, $237,212,000; North Carolina, $245,000,000; South Carolina, $110,000,000; and Georgia, $143,000,000. In the Great Smoky Mountains visitors spend more than $28,000,000 in one year. Either these expenditure figures are underestimated or the number of tourists is overestimated for all states other than Florida. The Virginia Travel Council claimed that its state received $750,000,000 rather than the reported $237,212,000 in 1959. Maryland reported tourism the fastest growing industry of the state and one-third more productive than agriculture. In 1960 more than 72,000 workers in North Carolina owed their jobs to tourists. U.S. Highway 301 extends 1,100 miles from the Delaware bridge to Sarasota, and tourism is the largest industry in 75 per cent of the communities through which it runs.

On a world-wide basis, travel in 1960 replaced wheat as the Number 1 industry of the world. Within the United States the traveling public spent $22,000,000,000, and the prospect for growth is bright. In 1956 more than two-thirds of all employed Americans received a total of $4,500,000,000 in vacation pay; salaried employees enjoyed on the average almost three weeks of vacation and hourly wage earners a little more than two weeks. Including weekends, holidays, and vacations, the average employed American now has 122 days of leisure a year. Housewives and their children account for more than 50 per cent of all tourism. The 1961 Georgia Governor's Conference on tourism urged statisticians, economists, businessmen, and political leaders, accustomed to thinking of business and agriculture as the two great means of creating jobs and increasing prosperity, to add tourism to their list. Manufacturing and agriculture were often stimulated by effective tourist programs, the Conference reported, but tourism was seldom increased by building factories, and the Conference classified travel as a growth industry destined for a thirtyfold increase within a century.

Statistics on the many aspects of the mobile frontier could be piled to boring heights. In the terminal state of Florida the average stay of the tourist in 1959 was twenty days, and he was out of pocket $171.88, but in the bridge state of Virginia the average was 1.76 days with an expenditure of $4.33. A *Redbook* survey of 1960 found 50 per cent of all vacationists to be terminal ones, 13 per cent hoppers, and the rest a combination of the two. The same source listed the preferences of tourists as sight-seeing, visiting relatives, swimming, resting, fishing, visiting friends, viewing historic sites, boating, attending the theater, dancing, and participating in active sports. Florida has found that interest in beaches, fishing, and scenery is closely followed by the desire to see historical places and art museums and to roam through state and national parks. Eighty-two per cent of her visitors arrived by automobile, 11 per cent by airplane, 4 per cent by train, and 3 per cent by bus. In 1959 54 per cent of Florida's tourists came from New England, Middle Atlantic, and East North Central regions of the United States.

Every South Atlantic state realizes the economic value of tourism and attempts to increase the take from the industry. *Nothin' Could Be Finah Than to See South Carolina, Okefenokee Swamp: Land of "Trembling Earth,"* and *Great Moments in Maryland's History* are illustrative of the titles of brochures published by state agencies. In 1960 the bridge state of Virginia distributed almost half a million advertising folders in terminal Florida. With twenty-seven years of experience, North Carolina boasts of having been the first commonwealth to advertise her attractions. In 1961 the federal government entered the tourist promotional field, but national and state governments spend only a fraction of one per cent on tourism as compared with what they spend on agriculture. Citizens of greater Atlanta plan the world's largest stadium with seats for 106,700 people and a parking area on 290 acres for 35,000 automobiles. Financial institutions have also entered the picture with "Go Now and Pay Later" or "Save Now and Go Later" programs for tourists.

The economic influences of the mobile frontier are determinable, but few students have investigated the cultural aspects of tourism. The out-of-state patronage of bowl football games and horse racing can be counted, but what effect the vacationer has on education, religion, and the arts remains a question.

In education, the example of Florida is suggestive. For more than half a century this tourist state has led the South in elementary and secondary education. Although North Carolina's Governor Charles Brantley Aycock won national recognition for his support of public education at the beginning of the twentieth century, eight years earlier Florida's Superintendent of Education William N. Sheats had initiated a program designed to establish a high school in every county of his state. In salaries of teachers, and in relative number of high schools, Florida ranks above her sister southern states, and in 1950 her white population surpassed, in median years of schooling, the citizens of all other states east of the Rocky Mountains except coequal Massachusetts.

Tourism, however, has not developed institutions of higher education in Florida comparable to the best of North Carolina. In part this backwardness lay in the number of Floridians having interest in educational institutions outside the state where they or their parents went to school; also, in recent years Florida has divided her resources among a number of universities rather than concentrating and developing a superior one. Another reason was the anti-intellectualism of an old, but youthful, state where voters allowed an investigating committee of the legislature to disrupt the student body of a university at examination period by unnecessary prying into the minds of its students and faculty members.

Certainly the support given by tourists keeps alive cultural institutions in the Southeast. Many museums of art or history would close their doors, but for the vacationers. The outdoor dramas—*Lost Colony, Unto These Hills,* and *Horn in the West* in North Carolina—and legitimate theaters in many states would have to lower their curtains if there were no tourists. The example of one small town demonstrates the validity of this contention. Highlands, North Carolina, with a recorded population of six hundred, has Baptist, Christian Science, Roman Catholic, Episcopal, Methodist, and Presbyterian churches; a weekly newspaper and a summer news bulletin; a high school, public library, little theater, and a motion picture house; concerts by outstanding musicians, educational lectures at the Biological Museum, and art exhibits. Residents of Highlands would enjoy none of these cultural treats except for two or three of the churches and the school but for tourists and summer residents.

The mobile frontier has aided in overcoming provincialism. W. D. Patterson, in an article on the "History and the Tourist" in the *Saturday Review* for March 14, 1959, declared:

> For us, foreign travel is a cultural, political, and economic necessity, if our country is to fulfill its destiny and new responsibility of world leadership. . . . For there can be no atom bomb potentially more powerful than the tourist, charged with curiosity, enthusiasm and good will, who can roam the world, meeting in friendship and understanding the people of other nations and races. . . . Parochialism is obsolete, even though it still haunts our minds and hearts. But with the new forces in the sky—and on the oceans—the mosaic of hate, hostility, and alien prejudice on the earth should be transmitted into a pattern of common trust, friendship and oneness among men.

The author was describing world foreign travel, but his words also apply to the South as well as to the rest of the nation. Generally a state with a limited tourist trade is a culturally backward commonwealth.

Tourism has enriched our lives with folklore and story. Bunyanesque tall tales and stories involving comical exaggerations, incredulous ignorance, and clever duplicity abound.

Concomitant with the desirable in tourism has been the deplorable. Tourist attractions fall into three basic categories: natural, man-made, and a combination of the two. At Natural Bridge, Virginia, man has "improved" on nature with hidden loudspeakers blaring forth music and a voice reading from the Book of Genesis. Around beautiful Silver Springs, Florida, unhappy looking Indians make beads, snakes are milked of their venom, and commercialism is rampant. In western North Carolina wide-eyed youngsters watch the recreation of the Old West in action; there are saloons, fist fights, quick draws, shootings, falling corpses, and other acts of "educational value" for children. "I live," a Floridian wrote, "in the biggest, gaudiest sideshow on earth. . . . It's the nation's perpetual vaudeville show." Rather than the Sabal palm, one disgruntled tourist thought Florida should use the open palm for her state tree. National, state, and local governments have done little to refute or regulate the purveyor of faked historical attractions.

Government agencies, however, have policed the faker more than historians have studied tourism. Only one contemporary United States college textbook has a paragraph on the tourist trade. Tourism involves millions of people and billions of dollars, and influences the highest in our culture; national, state, and local governments recognize its contributions to society; newspaper editors editorialize, and organizations hold conferences about it. The mobile frontier has been important long enough for the past-conscious historian to give respectability to the study of its cause, course, and result.

Chapter XXIX

Mississippi: The Closed Society

JAMES W. SILVER

Between 1938 and 1947 three Mississippi professors, Percy Lee Rainwater, John K. Bettersworth, and Vernon L. Wharton, published scholarly volumes which laid great stress on Mississippi's poverty-stricken leadership in secession, Civil War, and Reconstruction to 1890.* It is quite likely that if these studies were put on the market today, their authors would be run out of the state.

The search for historical truth has become a casualty in embattled Mississippi where neither the governor nor the legislature, in their hot pursuit of interposition, indicates any awareness that Mississippians were Americans before they were southerners or that Magnolia State politicians once stood firm against nullification and secession. The state's present-day exploiters of federal munificence, however, should applaud the cleverness of their ancestors in the 1850's who interpreted state rights as requiring the use of national power to destroy local self-government in the territories and to thwart northern state nullification of the fugitive slave law.

The striking parallel between people and events of the 1850's and the 1950's reminds us that Mississippi has been on the defensive against inevitable social change for more than a century, and that for some years before the Civil War it had developed a closed society with an orthodoxy accepted by nearly everybody in the state. The all-pervading doctrine then and now has been white supremacy—whether achieved through slavery or segregation—rationalized by a professed adherence to state rights and bolstered by religious fundamentalism. In such a society a never ceasing propagation of the "true faith" must and has gone on relentlessly with a constantly reiterated demand for loyalty to

*Presented in Asheville, North Carolina, November 7, 1963.

the united front demanding that nonconformists be hushed, silenced with a vengeance, or in crisis situations driven from the community. Violence and the threat of violence have reinforced the presumption of unanimity.

By 1861 Mississippians had been thoroughly prepared for secession by their shortsighted politicians, their chauvinistic press, their political preachers, and their blind philosophers, all operating within the authoritarian society. Even to the present generation the people have been paying for and *eulogizing* their most unwise decision of all time. In fact the romanticism associated with the Old South, the glorification of the Confederacy, and the bitter remembrance of Reconstruction have played their witless and powerful role in preserving a social order based on neither fact nor reason. According to Citizens Council literature, Mississippi is now the innocent victim of a second vicious Reconstruction from which its stalwart citizenry, demonstrating ancestral courage, will emerge triumphant as it did in 1875.

One of today's little sophistries asserts that equality must be earned, can never be achieved by force or law. The forgotten truth is that between 1875 and 1890 *inequality* was effected by force and regularized by law. By the end of the century Negroes had long since learned that Mississippi freedom included neither political nor any other kind of equality. The caste system had once and apparently for all time been substituted for slavery, the Negro was in his place, and the society was once more closed and sacrosanct.

No meaningful challenge to the caste system was possible in Mississippi in the first half of the twentieth century. In public life no white man, demagogue or patrician, proposed to do anything constructive about the Negro. Preferring corrupt and inefficient government to participation by the black man, the whites got a one-party system without competition between recognizable groups, with no continuity of existence even of factions, and no means of checking the wild-eyed—in sum, a series of Bilbonic plagues and Barnett blights. Whether The Man Bilbo was just the "slick little bastard" described by his admirers, or represented "nothing save passion, prejudice, and hatred," as claimed by Fred Sullens, is of small importance as compared with his career as symptomatic of the chaos and bankruptcy of Mississippi politics and its social order. In such a demoralized wasteland the sharpeyed Snopeses have grasped their petty gains, to the greater glory of laissez faire, which ironically has in turn produced the much damned transfer of state functions to the federal government and a diminution of state sovereignty.

Today the totalitarian society of Mississippi imposes on all its people an obedience to an official orthodoxy almost identical with the proslavery philosophy—this in the teeth of the nearly universal dissipation of whatever intellectual sanction white supremacy had among the enlightened at the turn of this century. Every Mississippi politician not only denies the validity of the Fourteenth Amendment but in his heart hungers for the negative days of the Articles of Confederation. Governor Ross Barnett, whose personal constitution stops with the Tenth Amendment, is conveniently ignorant of the incompatibility of state rights and modern industrialization.

On the racial question, the governor's views are now well known. "If we start off with the self-evident proposition," Barrett says, "that the whites and colored are different, we will not experience any difficulty in reaching the conclusion that they are not and never can be equal." It was his appointee to the Mississippi Supreme Court, Justice Tom Brady, who became for awhile the metaphysician of the master racists with the publication of the hastily written and scholastically barren *Black Monday* (1955). In turn this was outmoded by *Race and Reason* (1961) by Carleton Putnam, Roosevelt biographer and successful airline executive, become, by his own admission, expert theologian, psychologist, and anthropologist within a two-year period. To the enchantment of Mississippians, Putnam exposed the Franz Boas conspiracy which, he asserted, had held the scientific world in a climate of terror and fear of persecution for half a century. Mississippians did not read the book (they just sent it to their friends, as instructed by the Citizens Council), else they would have discovered that, even by Putnam's logic, the white race was already doomed inasmuch as more than half the country's Negroes lived in integrated situations. But who would argue with the new messiah? With a flourish of trumpets he was brought to Jackson on October 26, 1961 (proclaimed by the governor as Race and Reason Day) and feted at a $25-a-plate dinner attended by five hundred patriots.

There was no Dickens to point out that there never had been another such day in Mississippi. It could, Barnett believed, "mark the turning point in the South's struggle to preserve the integrity of the white race." Putnam had indeed provided an Article of Faith that Mississippians could live by. Denouncing the "left-wing pseudo-scientists" for creating the fallacy that "has gained complete possession of the Northern and Western mind," he designated Mississippi as "the heartland of the struggle for racial integrity" and in his best Bryan manner exclaimed, "You don't crucify the South on a cross of equalitarian propaganda." Calling on the South to produce more Barnetts, Putnam identified equalitarianism with communism and segregation with Christianity.

In one respect Putnam's racist argument was not anachronistic. At the very time when the Negro was in the lengthy process of becoming a civilized being, he appeared to be and demonstrably *was* a cultural inferior, carefully trained for that status by every controllable factor in his environment. Faulkner has the Mississippian say: "We got to make him a nigger first. He's got to admit he's a nigger." From birth to death the Negro was exposed to an irresistible pressure for deferential behavior, and when he failed to conform he was driven out or even killed. By and large he played the role of Sambo well, giving little indication of any hope or desire to share in the white man's privileges.

One of the privileges he has seldom had in Mississippi is that of voting. In the twentieth century never so much as 10 per cent and normally less than 5 per cent of the Negro voting population has been allowed to register. Governor Barnett has repeatedly asserted that Negroes in Mississippi just don't want to vote, that they could if they so desired. Since 1954, Mississippi law, Barnett to the contrary, has required the voter applicant to read and write *and* interpret any section of the state constitution and (since 1960) to be of good moral character and to have his name and address published in a local newspaper for two weeks. At the moment, a substantial Negro vote would embarass any white candidate in Mississippi. But the future is also plain. As Senator Bilbo once reminded an organizer for the Amalgamated Clothing Workers, "Son, when you can show me that you can control any sizable number of voters in Mississippi, I'll be the damnedest champion you've ever had."

Gradual improvement of white schools has until very recently been shared by the Negroes only to a remote degree. But, as James K. Vardaman had understood, *any* Negro education spelled the eventual doom of the caste system. There may have been rumblings before, but the summer of 1954 brought a shock from which Mississippi's Old Guard will never recover. Having checked with his retinue of Uncle Toms, Governor Hugh White called in a hundred Negroes to get their anticipated endorsement for "separate but equal" school facilities. But a few young Negro radicals arranged for a caucus the night before the big meeting and after a heated debate carried the timid along with them.

Speaker Walter Sillers opened the momentous conference. Governor White spoke of the amicable race relations of the past. As planned, when the preliminaries were over, Charlie Banks got the floor and argued for the abolition of segregation. Five or six others followed suit. A conservative Negro publisher made a last stand for the old regime but was roundly denounced by a woman delegate as being a classic example of the effects of segregation. In desperation, Sillers called on another known friend of the white man, the Reverend H. H. Humes. The old minister was the center of all attention as he walked to the front of the room. "Gentlemen," he told the governor and his friends, "you all should not be mad at us. Those were nine *white* men that rendered that decision. Not one colored man had anything to do with it. The real trouble is that you have given us schools too long in which we could study the earth through the floor and the stars through the roof." At this point, Governor White, mumbling that you couldn't trust Negroes any more, called the meeting to an end. It was also the end of an era, "For the first time," one of the delegates later said, "I was really proud to be a Negro in Mississippi."

Yet in the years since 1954 the state's Negroes have made few gains. The Establishment is entrenched so strongly that without the help of external forces (channeled through the federal government) Mississippi Negro leadership is for the short run in a helpless position. For, with varying degrees of enthusiasm, the makers of the orthodoxy—the press, the pulpit, the politicians, the philosophers, and patriots—have since the Brown decision rushed to the successful defense of their way of life.

Moderation is expressed in the daily newspapers of Greenville, Tupelo, and McComb, and in an occasional weekly; nevertheless, the Mississippi press as a whole mounts vigilant guard upon the closed society. Negro crime and immorality in the North, Negro complicity in communism, even Negro support for Barnett are given the headlines day after day. Shotgun blasts fired into a Negro home become a NAACP plot, the assassination of Medgar Evers is turned into a sacrificial offering to rekindle racial unrest, Mississippi is victimized by hate peddlers jealous of the state's economic progress. The Jackson *Clarion-Ledger* makes a revealing historical comparison: "Never was Hitler, nor Mussolini, nor the Mikado, nor even Kaiser Wilhelm attacked so venomously" as Mississippi—which invariably represents the South, with the South always a solid and unfaltering unit. But this leading state newspaper will find it difficult to approach ever again the imagination of its most famous headline, inspired by the arrest of Byron de la Beckwith, scion of an old Delta family, born on the Pacific coast but who had lived in Mississippi for thirty-eight years: "CALIFORNIAN IS CHARGED WITH MURDER OF MEDGAR EVERS."

To such editors and their heavy-handed associates the Fifth Circuit Court becomes "the nine judicial baboons in New Orleans," President Kennedy "regards himself as a Jesus whose infinite wisdom represents mankind's only real hope of salvation," and Ross Barnett is twisted into a modern combination of David, Horatius, and Leonidas. Tougaloo College, a center of integrationist activity, is rechristened "Cancer College," with a new summer course in "Rapid Hate," and the slanderous *Rebel Underground,* having recommended the execution of the President of the United States, emerges as "an innocuous handbill." By

March, 1963, the Jackson *Daily News* adds up the "price tag" on the federal invasion of Mississippi as coming to $14 million because of 130 bonus accidental deaths on the state's highways attributed to "a frame of mind, an atmosphere or anger, a period of bayonet-point frustration" which lowered the morale of the highway patrol. For the university faculty members who had the temerity to treat James Meredith as a human being, editor Jimmy Ward predicts crushed spirits, bitterness, even self-imposed tragedy.

In times of trial the Jackson papers lose all semblance of perspective. For example, on the day that Judge Sidney Mize ordered Meredith enrolled in the university, the *Daily News* front page carried these headlines:

ROSS RISKS JAIL TO HALT MIXING
Note Bares Negro Plan to Agitate
Hattiesburg Agitation Order [photostat]
We Support Gov. Barnett [editorial]
Negroes Purchased Shot, Says Mayor
President Deplores Shooting in State
Judge Mize Issues Permanent Injunction [bulletin]
Meredith Effigy Hanged at Oxford
Barnett During and After Broadcast [pictures]
Moses' Automobile [picture]
Editor's Column: All Loyal Mississippians
    Support Him [Barnett]

There was still room for a small cartoon about a Mississippi College football game and the index.

The role of the church since 1954 is more difficult to assess than is that of the press. Some churches have taken exceptional action, notably the Mississippi diocese of the Episcopal Church which issued a general call for support of the Supreme Court's decision and eventual integration. And in the past year many preachers and a few ministerial groups have made courageous stands. But the church as a whole has remained loyal to the status quo. Ministers who led the discussion about segregation were for it, prompted no doubt by "an echo from the pew." In annual session, the Mississippi Baptist convention refused to endorse a series of resolutions reaffirming "our intelligent good will toward all men" and calling upon Christians to pray "that we may live consistent with Christian citizenship." A Baptist missionary, second cousin of Governor Barnett, wrote from Nigeria that Mississippians were making her work extremely difficult: "You send us out here to preach that Christ died for all men. Then you make a travesty of our message by refusing to associate with some of them because of the color of their skin. You are supposed to be holding the lifelines for us, and you are twisting them into a noose of racism to strangle our message. Communists do not need to work against the preaching of the Gospel here; you are doing it quite adequately." The missionary's mother expressed regret: "Antonina doesn't understand that Ross has been doing the best he can."

Other groups in Mississippi society, supporters of the orthodoxy, hold a position comparable to their predecessors of the Civil War period. The conservative men of large property holdings considered secession a doubtful though perfectly legal remedy for their troubles; it was a much larger group of active, restless lawyer-politicians, petty planters, and small-town editors, successful enterprisers on the make, who took Mississippi out of the Union in 1861. After World War II another crowd of "new men," bold entrepreneurs enamored as their forefathers had been of the prevailing social order, too busy making money to think deeply about changes bound to accompany progress, pleased with the "right-to-work" principle embedded in the constitution and with a colossal program of state socialism to entice the Yankee carpetbagger industrialist, sat by quietly and acquiesced in the building of the Citizens Council juggernaut.

Constitutional questions, on which so much controversy has centered since 1954, continue to bring a response in keeping with the quality of Mississippi leadership. There seems to be some confusion in the minds of the state's lawyers and jurists as to whether Mississippians must obey the law of the land as interpreted by the federal courts. Dean Robert J. Farley of the Ole Miss law school repeatedly warned in public that lawyers were acting irresponsibly in permitting by their silence the Citizens Council and irreconcilable politicians to interpret the law for them. The chief dereliction, it seems clear, came in *allowing the people of Mississippi to believe that they could get away with an outright defiance of the courts.* "We as Mississippians," declared Justice Brady in 1959, "will not bow down to a court of nine old men whose hearts are as black as their robes." Brady castigated Governor Coleman, who had frowned upon interposition as so much "legal poppycock," as a moderate —"a man who is going to let a little sewage under the door." But the classic statement regarding law and order came in 1963 from the very top of Mount Olympus. Indignant over the "sickening" conduct of Negro parents and ministers in Birmingham in permitting boys and girls to run "afoul" of the law by "using these children for ignoble and loathesome ends and deliberately and contemptuously inciting them to become juvenile deliquents," Governor Barnett declared in a burst of emotion: "What do these degenerates know of freedom? True freedom consists of and is founded upon the observance of law and the power of law to make those who would break the law conform to it. History tells us that freedom can exist only under the protection of constitutional law. These agitators seek to defy constitutional law under the name of freedom." Once again Ross was doing the best he could.

The new legislature convening in January, 1962, was met by a request from the governor to (1) outlaw the Communist party (years before, the FBI had found one Communist in Mississippi), (2) pass "an enforceable sedition act," and (3) compel state employees to take an oath of allegiance to the United States and Mississippi. (Barnett did not explain whether this could be accomplished in a single oath.) In any event, when Mississippi legislators get together their herd instinct drives them to resolving the fate of the world. If they hate Hodding Carter or the President of the United States, or love Elvis Presley, Dizzy Dean, the Mississippi State basketball team, or South Africa, or feel that a former Miss America is an accomplished actress, they are not inhibited from saying so. Senator Hugh Bailey, who had ridden a mule from Canton to Jackson to fulfill a campaign promise, offered a resolution urging the United States to substitute turnip seed for cash in the foreign aid program. Such action, he asserted, "would relieve pressure in this country's economy and give the world's population necessary vitamins, minerals, and bulk." A mere handful of the seed would feed a hundred people and could be mailed overseas for planting.

Legislators spend much of their time devising legal subterfuges to keep the Negro in his place. When it appeared that the number of "smart alecks" telephoning "white ladies" had reached "epidemic stages," the House voted a $10,000 fine and five years imprisonment for cursing into the telephone. Objection to such stiff punishment brought the assurance that judges would know how to use the law. The House unanimously called for a constitutional amendment barring from voting persons guilty of vagrancy, perjury, and child desertion, and concurred in the addition of adultery, fornication, larceny, gambling, and crimes committed with a deadly weapon. A still further addition of habitual drunkenness was defeated when a member suggested that it "might even get some of us." There was some objection, also, to the inclusion of adultery. Reprisal legislation is common, like that bill which the committee chairman said was "concerned with a woman editor who has been writing things which don't go along with the feelings in the community," or another condemning land belonging to Campbell College after Representative McClellan explained, "Jackson has had a cancer in its midst long enough." The cancer will be removed to Mound Bayou in 1964.

One legislator was sorely impressed with the power of the Citizens Council:

It's hard for us sometimes to consider a bill on its merits if there is any way Bill Simmons [executive secretary of the Citizens Council] can attach an integration tag. For instance, a resolution was introduced in the House to urge a boycott of Memphis stores because some of them have desegregated. I knew it was ridiculous and would merely amuse North Mississippians who habitually shop in Memphis. The resolution came in the same week that four Negroes were fined in court for boycotting Clarksdale stores. Yet the hot eyes of Bill Simmons were watching. If we had voted against the resolution he would have branded us. So there we were, approving a boycott while a Mississippi court was convicting Negroes for doing what we lawmakers were advocating. It just didn't make sense.

As is characteristic of a closed society, the schools, too, are pressured by organized voices of the orthodoxy: the Citizens Council, the American Legion, and the patriotic ladies' groups. A case in point was the withdrawal of a film called "The High Wall," donated to the state by the Anti-Defamation League and shown in Mississippi schools for more than six years. The Citizens Council interpreted the film as teaching "children to pity their prejudiced parents who did not enjoy the enriching experience of intermingling with persons of different racial, ethnic and cultural backgrounds." At the end of the film the Council was saddened to find "Americans and Poles walk arm-in-arm into the setting sun." An "alert state senator" sounded the alarm, a private exhibition was given for Council and Mississippi Sovereignty Commission officials who agreed "The High Wall" was "unfit for showing to Mississippi school children," and the menace was removed.

The state Daughters of the American Revolution have time and again gone directly to the legislature, predictably with the encouragement of the governor who comes down hard for cleaning up the books "so that children can be truly informed of the southern way of life." The *Daily News* was acutely disturbed by such "oblique propaganda as 'gives evidence that Negro people have done much to develop themselves.'" The DAR is understandably unhappy when first-graders are no longer exposed to "the story of the squirrel storing nuts," since it "helped to make America a great nation populated by men and women steadfast in their ability to put into effect their early training for adult life." All but the headiest fans of Lord Keynes may look upon such a lament with sympathy. But listen to what the Citizens Council officially suggests for the third and fourth grades:

God wanted the white people to live alone. And He wanted colored people to live alone. The white men built America for you. White men built America so they could make the rules. George Washington was a brave and honest white man. The white men cut away big forests. The white man has always been kind to the Negro. We do not believe that God wants us to live together.

Negro people like to live by themselves. Negroes use their own bathrooms. They do not use white people's bathrooms. The Negro has his own part of town to live in. This is called our Southern Way of Life. Do you know that some people want the Negroes to live with white people? These people want us to be unhappy. They say we must go to school together. They say we must swim together and use the bathroom together. God had made us different. And God knows best. Did you know that our country will grow weak if we mix the races? White men worked hard to build our country. We want to keep it strong and free.

And some recommendations for the fifth and sixth grades:

The Southern white man has always helped the Negro whenever he could. Southerners were always their best friends. The South went to war to prevent the races from race-mixing. If God had wanted all men to be one color and to be alike, He would not have made the different races. One of the main lessons in the Old Testament of our Bible is that your race should be kept pure. God made different races and put them in different lands. He was satisfied with pure races so man should keep the races pure and be satisfied. BIRDS DO NOT MIX. CHICKENS DO NOT MIX. A friend had 100 white chickens and 100 reds. All the white chickens got to one side of the house, and all the red chickens got on the other side of the house. You probably feel the same way these chickens did whenever you are with people of a different race. God meant it to be that way.

With the makers of the ideology in control and economic opportunity at a minimum, it is not strange that large numbers of the most ambitious Mississipians, the ablest and the most adaptable to change, have left the state year after year. Such constant attrition of potential leadership (proven by the eminence achieved by Mississippi exiles) must be a major reason for the people's unwillingness to discard their ancient folkways. One cannot help speculating as to what degree Mississippi's story would have been more heartening if a sizable proportion of those thousands of bright, perceptive *natural leaders* among the men and women who have left the state had in some miraculous way found it possible to remain.

Some of those who have left had no choice. They were victims of a state now deservedly famous for its incredible past of police brutality and for the harassment, even to death, of those who defy the code. The state retains a good deal of the frontier recklessness toward human life found by William Howard Russell who noted that casual Mississippi conversations had "a smack of manslaughter about them." In the year after the Brown decision, four Negroes were openly slain, with no conviction for any crime; it would almost seem that when these atrocities had served their purpose, murder as an instrument of policy was then put in cold storage for a time.

On March 31, 1963, the Voter Education Project of the Southern

Regional Council released a chronological list of sixty-four acts of violence and intimidation against Negroes since January, 1961. The thirty-page indictment of man's inhumanity to man, with its accusations of whippings, shootings, murder, and outrageous debasement of the courts, admittedly came from an interested party, but it is characterized by understatement.

Mississippi acts of savagery have often been publicized throughout the world, some beyond their merit. The following examples of harassment by the closed society have been examined with caution and some thoroughness.

For twelve years Eugene Cox and Dr. David Minter, both southerners, had worked closely together as manager and physician for the white and black families making up the Providence Cooperative, a 2,700-acre farm in Holmes County. On September 27, 1955, at a mass meeting called by leading members of the Citizens Council, Cox and Minter were ordered out of the community, mainly on the basis of evidence recorded in two hours of questioning by Council and county officials of four Negro boys accused of making obscene remarks about a white girl. Allegations of the intermingling of the races at the farm were denied, though it was conceded freely that white and Negro patrons did attend meetings of the credit union together. Threats of violence were made against both men and their families, and, Minter's patients having been intimidated, his medical practice fell off about fifty per cent. An economic boycott was less effective. Professional segregationist Edwin White said, "We just can't afford to have them up there teaching what they are teaching —which will lead to violence unless it is stopped." At the mass assembly Cox admitted his belief that segregation is un-Christian. A planter whose father had been a minister spoke out, "This isn't a Christian meeting." Cox and Minter continued to deny all accusations and offered to make their records available for investigation. White commented, "I do not say these men are Communists, but I do say they are following the Communist line." With threats of arson increasing, and a roadblock arranged by the sheriff, Cox sat up, a rifle across his knees, from midnight to dawn for ten straight nights. Minter stuck it out until July, 1956. Cox left for Memphis a month later. In their joint Christmas greeting that year, they recalled: "Only two members of our church wrote to us. A few others have voiced their faith in us, but above these small voices is the frightening SILENCE. It is frightening—not only for us, but for any Christian and American who may wake up some morning to find himself persecuted because of his beliefs, or for unfounded rumors and 'guilt by association.' "

When James Meredith made his painful entry into Ole Miss, the "forgotten man" who had tried to break down the Mississippi education racial barrier without federal aid was languishing in the state penitentiary at Parchman, having been sentenced to a seven-year term for stealing by proxy $25 worth of chicken feed. Much of the evidence points to the conclusion that Clyde Kennard was "framed," though no one seems to know who did it. Born in Hattiesburg, moved to Chicago at twelve, discharged from paratroop service in Korea and Germany in 1952, Kennard meritoriously attended the University of Chicago for three years. Upon the death of his stepfather, he returned to Mississippi to help his mother run a chicken farm in Forrest County. For years he discussed with the president of Mississippi Southern University his possible admission on a voluntary basis. In 1958 he turned down Governor Coleman's offer of education outside the state but obligingly agreed to delay his formal application until after the 1959 Democratic primary. On September 15 he was officially refused admission in a fifteen-minute interview witnessed by the chief investigator for the Sovereignty Commission. Within minutes Kennard was arrested for speeding, then fined for possession of liquor (probably planted) in his car. By 1961 when the Mississippi Supreme Court disposed of this summary justice, Kennard had been convicted as an accessory in the theft of three bags of chicken feed and sentenced to one year's imprisonment for each $3.57 worth of feed allegedly stolen. At most the penalty, assuming guilt, would normally have been ninety days. The illiterate boy who made the theft, if there was one, continued in his job with the feed co-operative.

Though President William D. McCain refused Kennard's application, and is alleged to have said that he could do more to "develop honesty, culture, and individual integrity as president of Mississippi Southern than he can in a silly martyrdom for one Negro," Kennard himself refused to believe that McCain "had anything to do with what happened to me." The subsequent career of Clyde Kennard is a sad one. It includes surgery for cancer at the University Hospital in Jackson in June, 1962, unconscionable treatment at Parchman in the months following his operation when he was refused periodic checkups recommended by University doctors, the rapid development of his malignancy, an eight-hour operation in the Billings Hospital at the University of Chicago, and his death in the early summer of 1963. Not long before he died, Kennard was planning to return to his chicken farm and, as he saw it, to help Mississippi "co-ordinate" her race relations. One of his last statements was, "I still think there are a few white people of good will in the state and we have to do something to bring this out."

The most likely candidate in Mississippi for the next Medgar Evers treatment is the president of the state NAACP, Aaron Henry, onetime porter and shoeshine boy in the Old Cotton Bowl Court Hotel in Clarksdale and now owner of a drugstore on Fourth Street. He walks the earth with the sure step and upright carriage of a younger version of another Mississippian, Archie Moore, and he is not likely to be run out of Coahoma County. He does not know how many times the windows in his place of business have been smashed, but the last time, in March, 1963, he left for all to see the bricks, the broken glass, and the displays—one of the Declaration of Independence and the other of the Emancipation Proclamation. In 1962 he was convicted of leading a boycott of Clarksdale stores after it had been determined there would be no Negro float in the Christmas parade.

In March, Henry was fined $500 and sentenced to six months in jail by an eighty-year-old justice of the peace for allegedly molesting a white hitchhiker. According to the *Daily News* reporter, the Bolivar County attorney "during the final arguments, took the Mississippi statute and read to Judge Rowe the disturbing the peace law, explained it to him and told him the maximum sentence and fine." Before defining the sentence, the judge said, "The evidence shows this young man could not have described the interior of the defendant's car unless he was in it." There was no other witness.

When Henry accused the county attorney and police chief of plotting the charge against him, they countered with a libel suit in the Coahoma Circuit Court where the jury awarded them damages of $40,000. All these cases are still in the higher courts. On March 13, 1963, Henry's living room picture window was demolished and his home set afire at two in the morning by gasoline bombs thrown by two young thugs who said they were "just having fun" and were not aware of being in the Negro section of town. Not only did they admit the bombing, but a filling station attendant heard them planning the attack and commenting afterwards that Henry "was lucky to be alive." The first man tried was acquitted of arson by an all-white jury which deliberated for fifteen minutes, and an identical charge against the other was dropped. One of those involved later asked Henry's forgiveness, saying he had been tricked into the nasty business.

In May, 1963, the Henry drugstore was rocked by an explosion which ripped a hole in the roof. Sheriff Ross and Deputy State Fire Marshal Hopkins investigated and found that the blast "was caused by a bolt of lightning." Henry wrote: "I am not really sure as to the cause. The hole on top of the roof is much smaller than the rupture in the ceiling. The experts I have talked with contend that lightning does not act that way." It would appear that Henry is not only courageous but more literate than his opposition.

Harassment by the closed society can be savage even when it is not violent. Twenty-eight young Methodist ministers, feeling that they had "a particular obligation to speak," issued by way of the *Mississippi Methodist Advocate* of January, 1963, a "Born of Conviction" statement that still has the state and church in an uproar. They affirmed their belief in the freedom of the pulpit, the brotherhood of man, an unalterable opposition to the closing of the public schools, and an unflinching antagonism toward communism. Within two weeks the Mississippi Association of Methodist Ministers and Laymen, displaying more churchmanship than religion, had repudiated the "Born of Conviction" pastors, submitted their own "declaration of conscience on racial matters" (drawn up by Medford Evans, Citizens Council consultant, and published in the January issue of the *Citizen*), and called for a secret referendum on whether or not Methodists wanted their church integrated. Later these conservatives declared integration a "crime against God." The lament of one of the young ministers, that "the power clique which dominates the conference has aligned itself with the Methodist Ministers and Laymen and with the Citizens Council," was corroborated by subsequent events.

The closed society battered the outspoken young preachers upon the anvil of public opinion. By summer ten had left the state, and at least half a dozen more were shifted to urban pulpits. At least half volunteered the feeling that they had not been sufficiently supported by their superintendents and their bishop. Methodists in general, with professional assistance, were reflecting an opinion that had driven from Mississippi sixty-eight of their seminary-trained men since 1954. Dr. W. B. Selah, for eighteen years pastor of the largest Methodist congregation in the state, who had supported the "Born of Conviction" statement and had declared "there can be no color bar in a Christian church," resigned in protest when five Negroes were refused admission to his church.

The Mississippi Advisory Committee to the United States Commission on Civil Rights made, in January, 1963, a report on the administration of justice within the state. In a period of fourteen months it had held six open meetings in which a hundred or so Mississippians had testified, though "actively opposed by agents and instrumentalities of the State Government." The legislature in 1960 "passed an act," the committee stated, "to intimidate persons who might wish to assert their rights as citizens by altering the requirement of proof for prosecution of perjury solely in cases where the defendant has testified before this Committee."

In its published findings, the committee declared that "in all important areas of citizenship, a Negro in Mississippi receives substantially less than his due consideration as an American and as a Mississippian." They found that "a pattern exists in our State that leads to the denial of Constitutional rights and, in some instances, to brutality and terror. From the moment a Negro adult is hailed as 'boy' or 'girl' by a police officer, through his arrest, detention, trial—during which his Negro lawyer is treated with contemptuous familiarity by the judge and other officers of the court—and eventual imprisonment, he is treated with a pernicious difference. This difference is incompatible with Christian ideals about the dignity of man and with principles of Anglo-Saxon criminal law." Declaring that "justice under law is not guaranteed for the Negro in Mississippi in the way that it is for the white man," the committee reported that "42.3% of the citizens of this State must either accept an inferior station in life and an attitude of servility or endanger themselves and their families by protesting. We find that terror hangs over the Negro in Mississippi and is an expectancy for those who refuse to accept their color as a badge of inferiority; and terrorism has no proper place in the American form of government." The committee found that "in general the press is failing to meet its obligation to our society. The people of Mississippi are largely unaware of the extent of illegal official violence and the press is partly to blame. . . . When a State disregards a large segment of its population, the Federal Government is compelled to intervene in behalf of the victims."

And the federal government *has* intervened at the state's best known institution of higher learning, the University of Mississippi. The University has had its moments of greatness, its faculty and administrators of integrity and virtue, and a long history of genteel poverty. In the presidency of Alfred B. Butts (1935–46) Ole Miss began a precarious climb from the depths of depression despair and the shame of the Bilbo spoliation. For at least a decade after World War II, under the leadership of Chancellor John D. Williams, the University seemed on the verge of living up to the dreams and hopes of its founders and directors of exactly a century before. A tremendous building program on the already beautiful, wooded campus, an expansion of libraries and laboratories, the addition of new departments, and, most exciting of all, the gathering together of an excellent faculty dedicated to good teaching and fruitful research, all of these developments and more were taking place. The new chancellor was adept not only at selling the university to the people but in making it an integral part of many schemes designed to raise the horizons of a long submerged society.

It was increasingly evident in the middle fifties, however, that changes were taking place in the state that would adversely affect the university. In a series of crises from Kershaw (1955) to Kerciu (1963), the administration became more and more appeasement-minded, more and more involved (like a woman constantly professing her virtue) in present-ing the Ole Miss story to the state as if it were a bar of soap.

More serious was a 1955 edict of the Board of Trustees requiring the screening of all speakers brought to the campus, a ruling steadfastly opposed by the chancellor at its inception but stoutly defended some years later when he refused even to pass along to the board a petition of the AAUP calling for an end to the screening. A clergyman was turned away from Religious Emphasis Week when it became known that he had contributed to the NAACP, and the incoming president of the Southern Historical Association was paid his full fee for not delivering a history lecture after the shocking disclosure that his wife had written in the *Saturday Evening Post* of her teaching experiences with Negro students in Atlanta.

The handling of absurd charges of apostasy and subversion against fourteen members of the university community in 1958 was brought off expeditiously and with a flair for public relations. Faculty members in-volved in this tempest, which was kept going in the press for almost a year, were asked to remain silent (which most of them did) while the chancellor affirmed his belief in the Bible, an omnipotent God, immor-tality of the soul, state sovereignty, segregation, and the right of private property. In August, 1959, the board dismissed the allegations against the chancellor and the faculty and stated its policy that "there should prevail at our universities and colleges an atmosphere of freedom in their research, teaching programs and services and that there should be no political or subversive propagandizing in the academic program."

In the past year or so the University of Mississippi has desperately needed the help of all those concerned with its welfare, but, far from being consulted, these friends have been told that things were under control, the situation was returning to normal, enrollment was holding up in great style, just a few professors were leaving. On the anniversary of the insurrection, the director of the University News Service insulted "some few professors" by accusing them of having leveled "bitter attacks" against the university to "make national headlines" for the purpose of securing better positions, and he belittled the intelligence of those who remained by stating that "the vast majority" of these had refused more lucrative job offers elsewhere. In a state where higher education is ex-pendable, this bowing before and in fact anticipating every wind may have had a soothing effect on the legislature, but it also indicated a chronic inability to face reality. After all, General Ulysses S. Grant has been the only man in history to make a positive decision *not* to destroy the university.

Until 1962 the university successfully avoided integration. In that year, on June 26, almost exactly eighteen months after he had first written to the registrar, James Howard Meredith, the "man with a mission and with a nervous stomach," was ordered admitted to the University of Mississippi. Speaking for the Fifth Circuit Court in New Orleans Judge John Minor Wisdom later said that "A full review of the record leads the Court inescapably to the conclusion that from the moment the defendants discovered Meredith was a Negro they engaged in a carefully calculated campaign of delay, harassment, and masterly inactivity. It was a defense designed to discourage and defeat by evasion tactics which would have been a credit to Quintus Fabius Maximus." Tartly reprimanding Judge Sidney Mize of the United States District Court for the Southern District of Mississippi for "continuances of doubtful propriety and unreasonably long delays," Judge Wisdom viewed the case as one "tried below and argued here in the eerie atmosphere of never-never land." He might have added, "of the closed society." The contention of the Board of Trustees and of university officials, accepted as fact by Judge Mize, "that the university is not a racially segregated institution" and that "the state has no policy of segregation ... defies history and common knowledge." There was nothing in the case "reaching the dignity of proof" to make the court think otherwise. "We find that James Meredith's application for transfer to the University of Mississippi was turned down solely because he was a Negro."

Many members of the faculty expressed dismay when Ole Miss officials made uncalled-for affirmations which the court deemed frivolous and when they followed "a determined policy of discrimination by harassment" and assigned as a reason for rejecting Meredith "a trumped-up excuse without any basis except to discriminate." It was hard, too, to comprehend why an administrator would deny that "he understands and interprets the policy of the State of Mississippi as being that negroes and whites are educated in separate institutions of higher learning." More than a hundred years ago Chancellor F. A. P. Barnard had declared that the university's destiny was "to stamp upon the intellectual character of Mississippi the impress it is to wear...."

From September 13, 1962, when Mississippi's long court battle against Meredith reached "the end of the road" in Judge Mize's sweeping injunction and Governor Barnett read his antiquarian interposition proclamation, it was evident to all that the showdown was imminent. In those last hectic days the "power structure" of the state made a rather impressive attempt to control the Barnett juggernaut, but it was too late, and the people were largely unaware of the effort. Moderate statements by Oxford ministers appeared in the Memphis but not the Jackson papers which thundered about taking note "of those who stand with courage in an hour of crisis." The closed society was operating efficiently and almost automatically, as it does in times of great stress, as if it were some malicious Frankenstein monster.

On the Ole Miss campus was circulated a broadside, *The Liberty Bulletin,* urging students to "Place yourself under the direction of Gov. Barnett. Do not engage yourself in force or violence unless he calls for it." *Clarion-Ledger* columnist Hills reported that "the governor will watch with a jaundiced eye any attempt to apply punitive action against Mississippi's patriots. College presidents are standing ready to fight alongside the governor, or else."

In the upper house of the legislature on September 25, Senator E. K. Collins arose to remark, "We must win this fight regardless of the cost in time, effort, money and in human lives." Senator Hayden Campbell thought "they would have to open the doors to murder and rape." Senator Hilbun barked that "these are the same people who won't let our children pray in school." In Washington, Senator Eastland was sure that the next few days would "determine whether a judicial tyranny as black and hideous as any in history exists in the United States."

On Thursday, September 27, the *Clarion-Ledger* carried a sensational headline to the effect that a "gunbattle" was possible at the university. Representative Walter Hester told the UPI it was "likely" that state officials would attempt to fight off the marshals if they tried to enroll Meredith, but he did not prophesy an all-out insurrection. The situation was "extremely tense and there are some people who don't mind dying for an honorable cause." Either Senator McLaurin or Senator Yarbrough told Senator Lambert that "they were going to provoke the Kennedys into sending troops into Mississippi." Months later, Attorney General Patterson called McLaurin and the "CC & Co." a "little band of would-be ruthless dictators seeking to promote all-out riot and bloodshed on the campus by encouraging the people of Mississippi to pick up their rifles, shotguns and slingshots and go to fight it out with the armed forces of the United States." This could result only in "bloodshed, death, destruction and heartaches."

Barnett talked about jailing any federal officer attempting to arrest a state official. The *Daily News* was accused by the campus paper, the *Mississippian,* of distortion, fabrication, "screaming and sensational stories." On the day of the Ole Miss–Kentucky football game the hysteria whipped up in Jackson was unbelievable. The press and radio added their bluster to the normal uproar of a conference game. At the half-time ceremonies that night when he still might have turned the populace aside from its madness, the governor achieved his greatest triumph of oratorical lunacy: "I love Mississippi—I love her people—I love her customs!" Understandably, the man was overcome by his own hoarse eloquence and the reasonless, incoherent, delirious response. He could not go on. The people were bewildered. Television carried the infection statewide, and former Major General Edwin Walker was on his way to Oxford.

The propaganda machine never faltered. The next day, the Sunday that began so peacefully, a joint legislative committee pronounced nine frivolous reasons for denying Meredith admission and cunningly announced that his registration would jeopardize the accreditation of the University to the point of expulsion from the Southern Association of Colleges. In the afternoon and early evening, fatigued students were driving back to the campus, listening to their blaring radios tuned to the appeals of the Citizens Council to "form a human wall around the mansion" to protect the governor from arrest by federal marshals. Thousands of citizens swarmed the streets of Jackson. Few knew that the governor, called by an Episcopal priest the "living symbol of lawlessness," had already sold out his closest advisers. Word came that planeloads of marshals had flown out of Memphis. For some time their destination was in doubt. Unknown to most Mississippians, Meredith was, before supper, unpacking his bag in his room in Baxter Hall on the Ole Miss campus.

It was impossible that he could stay without help from the federal government. When Mississippi officials blocked by physical might on four separate occasions Meredith's court-ordered enrollment, and the Fifth Circuit Court wearily acknowledged that it had come to the end of its resources, the President was faced with the alternative of acceptance of the breakdown of law or the employment of force. The admission of Meredith was not negotiable. Kennedy performed his constitutional obligation in the same spirit George Washington had exhibited in the Whisky Rebellion. Having apparently learned the lesson of Little Rock, he insisted upon the use of civilian federal marshals rather than paratroopers. Certainly there had been no stated objection to marshals accompanying Meredith on those expeditions when they had been overcome by superior state power. Whatever "deals" he may have made with the governor behind the scenes, the President gently and eloquently appealed to the patriotism and sense of sportsmanship of Mississippi citizens in asking them to obey unpopular court decrees. But former Major General Walker having called for 10,000 volunteers to go to the aid of Barnett, and it being general knowledge that hundreds and perhaps thousands were converging on Oxford, there would have been a serious evasion of responsibility had the army high command not prepared for the emergency. Troops were moved to Memphis. The President earnestly hoped that the job could be done by civilians, and the United States Army was not ordered to the University of Mississippi until it became evident that the marshals were fighting for their lives, and the army's first contingent arrived just in time to prevent a disaster.

From the arrival of the marshals at the Lyceum Building shortly before five o'clock until the firing of the tear gas at eight, it became increasingly apparent that there was a serious lack of liaison between federal and state officials on the scene. At six the chancellor (at this time not much more than a spectator himself) believed the deal had been made and the game would have to be played out, and the gathering students and faculty were so informed. By seven all observers knew that for whatever reason, the Mississippi Highway Patrol had abandoned its enforcement of law and order and was in fact in some cases encouraging the restless crowd to demonstrate against the marshals. Twice these agents of the federal government donned their masks as the crowd closed in. The campus chief of police and four highway patrolmen had moved back part of the surly crowd (which promptly surged forward again when the officers left that part of the scene) and were achieving some little success in front of the Lyceum Building when the marshals opened fire with gas and drove what almost instantly became a howling mob back to the Confederate monument. Whether Chief Marshal McShane was justified in giving the order to fire at precisely the moment he did is a question for the professionals to answer. It is relevant, however, that two score of faculty members and their wives later testified that the marshals had undergone for at least an hour a constant harassment of obscene language and an increasingly heavy barrage of lighted cigarette butts, stones, bottles, pieces of pipe, and even acid. It is a small matter whether the gas should have come fifteen minutes earlier or later, but rather ironic that a full-scale insurrection should get underway at the exact moment that the President was appealing to Mississippians for fair play in the name of Lucius Quintus Cincinnatus Lamar.

Before the work was done that night the army brought more troops to Mississippi than General Sherman had had in the environs of Oxford exactly a hundred years before. Several hundred reporters soon concentrated on the Mississippi campus to ferret out the facts about what actually had taken place and to inquire into the background for the state's turmoil. By and large the reportage was accurate and the interpretation sound and temperate. Those who have wished to know have had spread before them a reasonably trustworthy record of events.

This is true for all the world except Mississippi. With its long history of being on the defensive against outside criticism and a predisposition to believe their own leaders can do no wrong, the people have been almost completely sold on a palpable and cynical hoax. The closed society immediately projected (in fact, it had foreshadowed) the orthodox version that the insurrection resulted from federal encroachment, deliberately planned by the Kennedys and callously incited by McShane when he called for tear gas. What did happen in front of the Lyceum Building in that crucial hour before eight o'clock on the night of September 30? Truth cries out that the orthodox Mississippi view is false, that cleverness in shifting the culpability for defiance of law from those creating the violence to those enforcing the law could succeed only among a people suffering from a touch of paranoia.

The genesis of the deception which shifted the blame for the insurrection from Mississippians to federal officials came from the university administration. A singularly inaccurate story blaming the "trigger-happy, amateurish, incompetent" marshals and suggesting examples of diabolical brutality toward male and female students was in the hands of Barnett and Eastland within an hour or so of the firing of the gas. These opportunists took up and grossly exaggerated the cry and called for state and federal investigations. By October 2, David Lawrence was to devote his syndicated column to the "official" view of the university. Long after it was made abundantly clear that many faculty members had witnessed the inception of the riot and knew for a certainty about the fraud against the federal government, the administration did not deviate from its original position but, on the contrary, continued to search for evidence condemning the marshals.

On the morning of October 1, Governor Barnett ordered the Mississippi flag at half-mast because "there had been an invasion of our state resulting in blood." The riot, he said, had been touched off by those "inexperienced, nervous and trigger-happy" marshals who had "deliberately inflamed" the people "in order that the resulting resistance can be cited as justification for military force against a sovereign state." Next day the *Clarion-Ledger* headline, "Eastland, Others Charge [⅜ in.]/ Marshals Set Off Ole Miss Rioting [⅞ in.]" was serenity itself compared to a featured column which elaborated the official view: "Our state is labeled insurrectionist because it does not care to be negroid in totality." The columnist did admit a temporary defeat: "So watch the peace-lovers come to the fore, grab a nigger-neck and start bellowing brother love."

The Mississippi Junior Chamber of Commerce distributed almost a half million copies of a 24-page pamphlet entitled *Oxford: A Warning for Americans,* which put the blame for the insurrection squarely on the shoulders of John and Robert Kennedy. The most specious implication of the pamphlet was that Meredith would have been allowed to enroll peacefully if only the Attorney General had awaited "the completion of the judicial processes," a most unlikely result in a state which had already indulged in so much legal quackery and whose governor had made it so evident that he would never accept the desegregation of the university. John Satterfield, probable author of the pamphlet and certainly an intimate counselor of Barnett, was now apparently defending his own bad advice which in part came straight from John C. Calhoun. Satterfield has tried to place the mantle of respectability on Barnett's unlawful conduct and to cast doubt on the legality and propriety of the United States government's actions. He threw his weight as past president of the American Bar Association and a prime mover in the Citizens Council into the intellectual propaganda barrage directed at Mississippians, who were unlikely anyhow to pay attention to the statement made on October 2 by the incumbent president of the ABA: "The paramount issue was whether or not the judgment of the court was to be upheld. The executive branch had a clear duty to see that the courts were sustained."

Mr. Satterfield maintained an Olympian objectivity compared to Judge W. M. O'Barr, who in his charge to the LaFayette County grand jury investigating the death of two persons on the night of the insurrection, spoke of the United States Attorney General as "stupid little brother" and described the Supreme Court as made up of "political greedy old men" who "together with the hungry, mad, ruthless, ungodly, power-mad men [in Washington] would change this government from a democracy to a totalitarian dictatorship." The grand jury responded appropriately with an indictment of McShane for precipitating the riot, and for good measure taunted university professors (who had previously defended the marshals) for talking too much.

Support for the state administration came, too, just one month after the insurrection, from Mississippi's Women for Constitutional Government. One of the state's more active groups, they were assembled in Jackson by the sister of the speaker of the House of Representatives to adopt a "bill of grievances" against the "unwarranted and unlawful use of military force" and the alleged violation of Mississippians' civil rights resulting from "the collusion of the President of the United States, the Justice Department, and the Federal courts." The high-flown language of "the thousand angry women" obscured, for Mississippians at least, their exquisitely imaginative account of what had taken place at the university.

In the months after the insurrection, many engaged in the pleasant pastime of guessing whether the governor was at the moment taking instructions from the "resistance to the death" counselors (the White Muslim clique in the Citizens Council) or from the more cautious who, as one observer put it, had planned only a little riot, who didn't really want to see anybody killed. The Council sent up trial balloons suggesting the closing of the university, called upon faculty moderates (to Simmons, "gutless liberals") to accept segregation or resign, and conducted a post-card campaign directing the Board to fire "quislings and scalawags [who] betray our state and our people in the time of crisis." The extent of the Council's responsibility for open defiance of university authorities by extremist students who returned from weekends at home with suitcases filled with cherry bombs and minds filled with rebellion is still an open question. The Oxford council, whose leaders were dedicated if not brilliant, distributed a mimeographed list of faculty members who were to be harassed with anonymous telephone calls—which did cause some inconvenience because the sleeping habits of the daring dialers did not mesh with those of their victims.

The Mississippi Municipal Association prepared a model speech to be used in winning friends and thwarting enemies. After touching lightly on the notion that court decisions, after all, are not the law of the land and warning of the danger of centralization, the orator was then to rise eloquently to the defense of Mississippi's official conduct: "This action is not a defiance of the law or the courts. Such action is an exercise of the heritage of freedom and liberty under the law preserved for us by our fathers." Although it was not suggested, the more gifted ambassadors could also have sung some lines from the "Ballad of the Ole Miss Invasion":

> They came rolling down from Memphis and dropping
>   from the skies
> With bayonets for our bellies and tear gas for our eyes
> Some resisted them with brickbats, while others ran and hid,
> Some tangled with the marshals—who can blame them if
>   they did?

For months it was believed that the General Legislative Investigating Committee would quietly abandon its inquiry into the insurrection as it ran into more and more unpalatable material. Having sent investigators from Washington, Senator Stennis made no report and Senator Eastland shifted his effort to the collection of tall tales by disgruntled students against their instructors. The Mississippi Senate of course did not need facts to plead with the country to "join our State in defiance of all who would destroy our freedoms, heritage and constitutional rights." Only one senator called for secession, a few more demanded Kennedy's impeachment, while others galloped up and down the land to warn their countrymen of the coming of the orange-jackets, those federal fiends whose savage brutalities at Oxford had "stopped short of Nazi atrocities only in that there were no deaths."

The legislative committee took six months to put together from the sworn statements of more than ninety witnesses its masterpiece of sententious fiction. For reasons never explained, faculty witnesses and even legislators who had been at Ole Miss with the federalized national guard had not been called upon to testify. There was no minority report. How scores of the world's crack reporters had been kept from seeing the blundering and the repeated brutalities and "planned physical torture" of the marshals, the women students hit by projectiles fired at point-blank range, the deliberate gassing of seven dormitories, the "torture slab," the army truck set on fire by "a folded paper airplane," and dozens of other Alice-in-Wonderland concoctions will remain one of the mysteries of twentieth-century journalism. It was the sad commentary of an eyewitness that the "young gentlemen of the New Confederacy," who were able to glorify insurrectionist conduct as "freedom fighters" in the "Brick and Bottle Brigade"—attacking the armed forces of their own country—would have small compunction about lying to a legislative investigating committee, especially one that made perfectly clear what it wanted to hear.

The legislative report was "verified" in advance by a documentary film, "Oxford, U. S. A.," depicting "how the federal government violated the constitution in the invasion of Mississippi last fall." Just before he sold three copies to the Sovereignty Commission for almost $7,000, the producer asserted the picture was "based strictly on the Constitution" and had been endorsed by Governors Barnett and Wallace. According to billboard advertising, it "EXPOSES FEDERAL ATROCITIES." Actually, about half of the fifty-minute extravaganza is taken up with poorly filmed statements from Barnett, Johnson, Attorney General Patterson, Chief of the Highway Patrol Birdsong, and a legislator who makes some disparaging and untrue remarks about the university and Meredith. The opening action shot shows motorized troops moving into Oxford, which they did—about eight hours after the beginning of the insurrection. By implication the viewer gets the impression that marshals had fired shotguns (which they did not have) at innocent students and even that they had killed the French reporter. Altogether the film is a shabby conglomeration of falsehood, distortion, and political dissemblance unlikely to convince the fair-minded who may be left in the membership of the Citizens Council.

The people of Mississippi have thus once again been victimized, this time by a gigantic hoax perpetrated on them by their own timeserving leaders whose sense of loyalty is only to the false orthodoxy of the closed society.

The closed society is never the absolute society. There always have been and there always will be the dissenters, the doubters who point to the road not taken. In the past year more than fifty professors have departed from the University of Mississippi, many of them literally driven from the state. The best of them, particularly the native Mississippians, would have remained if there had been any prospect of an atmosphere of freedom or a decent chance to fight for one.

No, the closed society is not absolute. In Mississippi there are legislators, editors, lawyers, labor leaders, educators, and ordinary citizens who sometimes protest against the prevailing orthodoxy. The day that Barnett let loose his interposition blast, Ira Harkey pointed out in the Pascagoula *Chronicle* that it was not the Kennedys but "the United States of America, democracy itself, the whole of humanity" that was making demands upon Mississippi. In a series of five short, logical articles, Representative Karl Wiesenburg demonstrated conclusively that Barnett's course was "the road to riot," that the governor had violated his oath of office, that the bloodshed on September 30 was the "price of defiance," and that states have responsibilities as well as rights. The *Mississippi Methodist Advocate* accepted for the church part of the guilt for the riot.

Three days after the insurrection, the Ole Miss chapter of the American Association of University Professors adopted a ringing statement protesting the fraud against the marshals. Without a campaign in its favor more than seventy faculty members signed the document as their way of "standing up to be counted." A professor of anthropology made his protest by putting into writing the conclusions of those in his profession concerning the validity of Putnam's *Race and Reason,* and this was serialized in the Pascagoula *Chronicle.* The exemplary conduct of more than 3,000 federalized Mississippi national guardsmen is worth the scrutiny and praise of all Americans. General W. P. Wilson said, "There were absolutely no incidents of any individual wilfully refusing to report for mobilization." George Fielding Eliot paid high tribute to the state guard: "In its ranks are men who, as citizens, share some of the views and even the prejudices of their fellow Mississippians. But when the call to duty came, they laid all else aside. After that they were soldiers of the United States, summoned by the President to aid in enforcing the laws of the Union as the Constitution provides." One guardsman who had suffered rough treatment at the hands of the hoodlums, went right to the heart of the matter: "It was just the matter of an oath I took."

There are many thousands of "men of good will" in Mississippi, mild-mannered people for the most part, who in their day-to-day affairs do what they can to ameliorate the difficult conditions imposed upon their fellowmen by the closed society. But because of a strong desire to live in peace or because of one kind or another of fear, these men will not openly protest what they know in their hearts are gross evils all about them. These are the individuals who, when one of their own number speaks out or in some little way defies the orthodoxy and is pilloried as a result, shrug their shoulders and say, "Well, he asked for it."

Men of good will are not enough. In his article in the *Saturday Evening Post* after the riot, John Faulkner professed surprise at a plea to return to law and order: "this to us, the responsible people of Oxford, who raised no finger against any man." In high indignation he refused to see the need for penitence: "If all the sin I have to answer for is my part in bringing on what hapepned here Sunday and Monday, then I relinquish my place to someone more needful of forgiveness than I." Perhaps Mr. Faulkner said more than he intended, perhaps he was speaking for all the good men who to whatever degree had abandoned the feeling of accountability for conditions in Mississippi. These same men were shocked to learn, probably at Leslie's drugstore, the price of defiance as well as the fact that some of their neighbors were throwing rocks at other neighbors in the uniform of the United States government. But they were not moved by the riot—they were solidified. They had forgotten, if they had ever known, that it was not Gavin Stevens who had prevented the lynching of Lucas Beauchamp, but Miss Habersham, Chick Mallison, and Aleck Sander.

The more embattled the closed society becomes, the more monolithic, the more corrupt, and the more willing to engage in double-think and double-talk. There is Mississippi's institutionalized hypocrisy that the Negro can freely vote and freely attend the university of his choice. There is the casuistry of Governor Barnett that he is preserving law and order and upholding the Constitution by physically obstructing the execution of an explicit directive of the Fifth Circuit Court of Appeals of the United States. There is the legislature shamefully passing laws which the judges "will know how to handle" or for the purpose of "getting" certain individuals. The idea that this is a nation of laws and not of men, constantly reiterated within the state, has a hollow ring in Mississippi. How few of its leaders can come into court with clean hands!

Hostility to authority and disrespect for law are commonplace in Mississippi. How could it be otherwise in a state which tolerates the cynical disregard of prohibition and collects the black-market tax? How can anything else be expected when the state itself brazenly tells the world it has achieved "separate but equal" school facilities, when in 1959–60 local school expenditures were $81.86 for the white child as against $21.77 for the colored? Or when, as in 1951, the county superintendents of education, looking greedily toward the allocation of equalization funds, reported 895,779 children of educable age (6–20) while the United States census of 1950 listed the number of children from 5 to 19 as only 651,600? What respect can there be for the legal process when one standard of justice prevails when a Negro commits a crime against a Negro, another when a Negro commits a crime against a white, still another when a white commits a crime against a white, and a fourth when a white commits a crime against a Negro?

What can be said about the morality of a social order that sends a teen-age colored girl to a long term in an institution for delinquents because, by walking from school to the courthouse, she is held to have violated an injunction against demonstrations? And, when questioned, justifies the exorbitant penalty on the basis of previous abortions—which up to the time of her sentence the society had ignored? Which is immoral, the girl or the society?

In spite of the closed society the Negro has made *some* gains since his emancipation a century ago. In the same period, the white man, determined to defend his way of life at all costs, has compromised his old virtues, his integrity, his once unassailable character. He has so corrupted the language itself that he says one thing while meaning another. He no longer has freedom of choice in the realm of ideas because they must first be harmonized with the orthodoxy. New currents of thought he automatically distrusts, and if they clash with the prevailing wisdom he ruthlessly rules them out. He cannot allow himself the luxury of thinking about a problem on its merits. In spite of what he claims, the white Mississippian is not even conservative—he is merely negative. He grows up being against most things other men at least have the pleasure of arguing about. All his life he spends on the defensive. The most he can hope for is to put up a good fight before losing. This is the Mississippi way, this is the Mississippi heritage. It will ever be thus as long as the closed society endures.

Although there have been moments of enlightenment, the spiritual secession of Mississippi from history has never ended. For more than a century Mississippians have refused to be bound by the national will. Perhaps this recalcitrance could be borne within the past, as have been many other excesses of democracy. But with the sanctuary provided by the oceans gone, the national interest, the instinct for survival, demand discipline. They demand also that attitudes or "principles" growing out of racial situations not be allowed to intrude themselves into the country's policy making decisions. Since Reconstruction Mississippians have had no real reason to believe that they were not free to handle the race question as they wished, without meaningful interference from the federal government; and, when they now discover that all their bluster and subterfuge and intransigence will avail them nothing, they have little to fall back on except blind rage and fierce hatred.

In committing itself to the defense of the biracial system, Mississippi has erected a totalitarian society which to the present moment has eliminated the ordinary processes by which change may be channeled. Through its police power, coercion and force prevail, instead of accommodation, and the result is social paralysis. Thus, the Mississippian who prides himself on his individuality in reality lives in a climate where nonconformity is forbidden, where the white man is not free, where he does not dare to express a deviating opinion without looking over his shoulder. Not only is the black man not allowed to forget that he is a nigger, but the white moderate must distinctly understand that he is a "nigger-lover."

Mississippi has long been a hyperorthodox social order in which the individual has no option except to be loyal to the will of the white majority. And the white majority has subscribed to an inflexible philosophy which is not based on fact, logic, or reason. Nonwhite Mississippians and all others are outlanders. Close contiguity with a large repressed population and fear of what these "inferior" people might do have held the society near the point of unanimity. Especially in times of stress the orthodoxy becomes more rigid, more removed from reality, and the conformity demanded to it more extreme. Today the advocacy or even the recognition of the inevitability of change becomes a social felony, or worse. Mississippi is the way it is not because of its views on the Negro —here it is simply "the South exaggerated"—but because of its closed society, its refusal to allow freedom of inquiry or to tolerate "error of opinion." The social order that refuses to conform to national standards insists upon strict conformity at home. While complaining of its own persecuted minority station in the United States, it rarely considers the Negro minority as having rights in Mississippi.

Perhaps the greatest tragedy of the closed society is the refusal of its citizens to believe that there is any view other than the orthodox. In recent years there has been a hardening attitude among college students who do not want to hear the other side. In such a twilight of non-discussion, minds not only do not grow tough, they do not grow at all. Intelligent men with ideas are isolated from the rest of the community, and what little interracial communication existed in the past is now destroyed. One reason the Ole Miss faculty failed to protest an ugly situation before the insurrection was that through one means or another freedom of speech had long since been curtailed. This was at least a partial cause for from eight to ten members of the history department leaving in the two years *before* the troubles of last year. The jolt of the

violence on the campus and the obvious fraud against the federal government initiated a spurt of resistance to ignorance, stupidity, and conformity. For the moment many of the faculty developed a healthy scorn
for expediency and security. In the light of Mississippi's history it was
probably already too late to expect anything more than an occasional
stand, such as that put up by the ministers who were willing to count
the cost and pay the price. With the great silence from the men of good
will, and the disposition of the good people to let things run their course,
there can be little hope for anything constructive in Mississippi in the next
decade.

It can be argued that in the history of the United States democracy has
produced great leaders in great crises. Sad as it may be, the opposite has
been true in Mississippi. As yet there is little evidence that the society of
the closed mind will ever possess the moral resources to reform itself, or
the capacity for self-examination, or even the tolerance of self-examination. Inasmuch as a nation marching swiftly in the direction of the fulfillment of the promise of the Declaration of Independence and the
Emancipation Proclamation is at the same time fighting for survival
against communism, it will not much longer indulge the frustration of its
will. Nevertheless, it would seem that for the foreseeable future the
people of Mississippi will plod along the troubled road of resistance,
violence, anguish, and injustice, moving slowly until engulfed in the
predictable cataclysm.

And yet, in spite of all that has been presented in this paper, it
seems inescapable that Mississippians one day will drop the mockery of
the late Confederacy and resume their obligations as Americans. It is
just that there is small reason to believe that they will somehow develop
the capability to do it themselves, to do it, as William Faulkner said,
in time. If not, the closed society will become the open society with the
massive aid of the country as a whole, backed by the power and authority
of the federal government.

Notes

CHAPTER I E. MERTON COULTER

1 *De Bow's Review* (New Orleans), XV (1853), 163.

2 *Ibid.,* 162

3 *The Southern and Western Literary Messenger and Review* (Richmond), XIII (1847), 2. Cited hereinafter as *Southern Literary Messenger.*

4 In writing his history of Alabama in the 1840's, Albert J. Pickett almost gave up in despair as he was unable to find the documents necessary for his story; and William Bacon Stevens was forced greatly to delay his work on the history of Georgia while he sought for historical material.

5 P. M. Hamer, "The Preservation of Tennessee History," *North Carolina Historical Review,* VI (1929), 127.

6 J. G. de Roulhac Hamilton, "The Preservation of North Carolina History," *ibid.,* IV (1927), 4, 5.

7 L. L. Mackall, "Edward Langworthy and the First Attempt to Write a Separate History of Georgia, with Selections from the Long Lost Langworthy Papers," *Georgia Historical Quarterly,* VII (1923), 1–17.

8 *History of Kentucky.*

9 *History of the Commonwealth of Kentucky.*

10 *History of Louisiana,* 2 vols.

11 *History of North Carolina, from the Earliest Period,* 2 vols.

12 *History of Maryland,* 2 vols.

13 Respectively, *History of North Carolina,* 2 vols., and *Historical Sketches of North Carolina, from 1584 to 1851,* 2 vols.

14 T. H. Jack, "The Preservation of Georgia History," in *North Carolina Historical Review,* IV (1927), 241.

15 *A History of Georgia from its First Discovery by Europeans to the Adoption of the Constitution in MDCCXCVIII.*

16 *History of Alabama, and Incidentally of Georgia and Mississippi,* 2 vols.

17 Their works are respectively, *Texas and the Texans: or, Advance of the Anglo-Americans to the Southwest,* 2 vols., and *History of Texas, from its First Settlement in 1685, to its Annexation to the United States in 1846,* 2 vols.

18 *Southern Literary Messenger,* XIII (1847), 2.

19 *Southern Quarterly Review* (Charleston), III (1843), 42.

20 *Collections of the Georgia Historical Society* (Savannah), I (1840), 303–305.

21 A. S. Salley, Jr., "Preservation of South Carolina History," *North Carolina Historical Review,* IV (1927), 148 ff.
22 *North Carolina Historical Review,* III (1843), 263 ff.
23 *Ibid.,* V (1848).
24 For example, see "Judge Law's Oration before the Georgia Historical Society, February 12, 1840," *Collections of the Georgia Historical Society,* I (1840), 1–41.
25 *Southern Literary Messenger,* XII (1846), 110.
26 L. L. Veazey, "History," *Scott's Monthly Magazine* (Atlanta), I (1866), 208.
27 *Southern Literary Messenger,* III (1837), 97.
28 See page 3 of the book, published in Atlanta, by the National Publishing Company.
29 D. S. Freeman, *R. E. Lee: A Biography* (New York, 1935), IV, 213, 235, 236.
30 Published in 1868 and 1870.
31 Published in 1881.
32 *The Last Year of the War* (New York, 1866), 4.
33 *The Southern Side, or, Andersonville Prison* (Baltimore, 1876), 6.
34 B. H. Hill, Jr., *Senator Benjamin H. Hill of Georgia. His Life, Speeches and Writings* (Atlanta, 1893), 405, 406.
35 *Southern Historical Society Papers* (Richmond), X (1882), 253.
36 *Ibid.,* I (1876), 39, 40, VI (1878), 244, 245.
37 *Ibid.,* I (1876), 40, 43, 44, VI (1878), 244, 245, VII (1879), 159, 253, 254; *Handbook of Learned Societies and Institutions, America* (Washington, 1908), 90.
38 *Southern Historical Society Papers,* I (1876), 41.
39 *Ibid.,* 42.
40 *Ibid.,* II (1876), 248, 249, V (1878), 35, VI (1878), 191, 192. In 1878 the Secretary of War finally allowed southerners to have access to these documents. *Ibid.,* VI (1878), 239, 240. During the period when these papers were not open to unrestricted use, it was easy to exclude the southerners.
41 *Ibid.,* I (1876), 44.
42 This Society gathered together the finest collection of Confederate material in existence. It was later turned over to the Confederate Memorial Literary Society, which preserves it in Richmond.
43 Preface, iii.
44 *Reminiscences of the Civil War* (New York, 1903), preface, xi.
45 *Southern Historical Society Papers,* I (1876), 46, VI (1878), 245.
46 *Ibid.,* I (1876), 108.
47 *Ibid.,* 39.
48 *Ibid.,* X (1882), 253; Dunbar Rowland (ed.), *Jefferson Davis, Constitutionalist; His Letters, Papers and Speeches* (Jackson, Miss., 1923), IX, 141, 142, X, 112.
49 See Charles W. Ramsdell, "The Preservation of Texas History," *North Carolina Historical Review,* VI (1929), 1–16; David Y. Thomas, "The Preservation of Arkansas History," *ibid., V* (1928), 263–74.
50 *Publications of the Southern History Association* (Washington), I (1897), 2–4.

51 *Ibid.*, 4–8.
52 *Ibid.*, 1.
53 *Ibid.*, 9.
54 *Ibid.*, 32.
55 *Ibid.*, XI (1907), 303.
56 *Ibid.*, II (1898), 4, 7, III (1899), 180, 181, VI (1902), 457, VII (1903), 69. In 1902 Thomas M. Owen and Joel C. Du Bose began the publication of the *Gulf States Historical Magazine* (Montgomery, Birmingham), which ran for two years, and then failed on account of finances. It was not the organ of an historical association.

CHAPTER II   CHARLES W. RAMSDELL

1 *The Civil War in America* (3 vols.; New York, 1867–70).
2 Second edition, revised (Richmond, 1862).
3 New York, 1866.
4 Boston, 1872–77.
5 James G. Blaine, *Twenty Years of Congress* (2 vols.; Norwich, Conn., 1884–86); John A. Logan, *The Great Conspiracy* (New York, 1886).
6 This statement was literally correct, since the Confederate call to arms in 1861 was to repel invasion, but it ignores the slavery issue as a cause of secession while it indicates that after the war the southerners were more responsive to the attitude of other peoples toward slavery than they had been before the war.
7 *The Constitutional and Political History of the United States* (8 vols.; Chicago, 1876–92), I. This volume was first published in Germany in 1873 under the title *Verfassung und Demokratie der Vereinigten Staaten* while von Holst was teaching in the new University of Strassburg.
8 *History of the United States under the Constitution* (7 vols.; New York, 1880–90), I.
9 *A History of the People of the United States from the Revolution to the Civil War* (8 vols.; New York, 1883–92), I.
10 While this conspiracy theory was of northern origin it had been given support by the Virginian Edward A. Pollard in his *Life of Jefferson Davis with a Secret History of the Southern Confederacy* ... (Philadelphia, 1869), *44 et seq.* Pollard's motive seems to have been to discredit Davis whom he had attacked unceasingly both during the war and afterwards. This *Life* was a scathing assault upon the Confederate president.
11 *American Negro Slavery* (New York and London, 1918); *Life and Labor in the Old South* (Boston, 1929); "The Central Theme of Southern History," *American Historical Review,* XXXIV (1929), 30–43.
12 Washington, 1914.
13 "The Influence of Slavery on the Colonization of Texas," *Mississippi Valley Historical Review,* XI (1925), 3–36; *The Life of Stephen F. Austin* (Nashville, 1925); *Mexico and Texas, 1821–1835* (Dallas, 1928).
14 *The War with Mexico* (2 vols.; New York, 1919).
15 "In Re That Aggressive Slavocracy," *Mississippi Valley Historical Review,* VIII (1922), 13–79.
16 *The South as a Conscious Minority, 1789–1861* (New York, 1930).

17 *The Secession Movement, 1860–1861* (New York, 1931); *Southern Editorials on Secession* (New York and London, 1931).

18 Urbana, Ill., 1923.

19 "The Genesis of the Kansas-Nebraska Act," *Proceedings of the State Historical Society of Wisconsin,* Sixtieth Annual Meeting (1912), 69–87; "The Railroad Background of the Kansas-Nebraska Act," *Mississippi Valley Historical Review,* XII (1926), 3–22.

20 "Some Phases of the Dred Scott Case," *Mississippi Valley Historical Review,* XVI (1930), 3–22.

21 New York and London, 1933.

22 Two vols., New York and London, 1934.

23 It must be remembered that when this was written the work of Gilbert H. Barnes had not appeared.

24 "Coming of the War Between the States, An Interpretation," *Journal of Southern History,* II (1936), 303–22.

25 In a paper, as yet unpublished, entitled, "Lincoln and Fort Sumter," which was read at the meeting of the American Historical Association in Chattanooga, December 27, 1935, I reviewed the evidence which, in my opinion, shows that Lincoln himself determined upon resort to force as the only means by which to extricate his administration from a dangerous dilemma, and, in order to fix the burden of war guilt upon the Confederates, with consummate adroitness maneuvered the Confederates into "firing the first shot" by attacking Fort Sumter. He thus gained a great moral-strategic advantage in that he was enabled to appeal effectively for northern support of the war on the plea that the "rebels" had wantonly attacked the government.

26 *South Atlantic Quarterly,* XXII (1933), 294–305.

CHAPTER III   THOMAS PERKINS ABERNETHY

1 Thomas J. Wertenbaker, *The Planters of Colonial Virginia* (Princeton, 1922), 60–63, 97–100, 122–23.

2 Professor Frank L. Owsley is now making a study of the nonslaveholder in the Old South, which should throw much light upon such communities.

3 Edgar Woods, *Albemarle County, Virginia* (Bridgewater, Va., 1932), 2–7.

4 Samuel C. Williams, *Dawn of Tennessee Valley and Tennessee History* (Johnson City, Tenn., 1937), 364–77.

5 Nell M. Nugent, *Cavaliers and Pioneers; Abstracts of Virginia Land Patents and Grants, 1623–1800* (Richmond, 1934), I, x.

6 Thomas P. Abernethy, *Western Lands and the American Revolution* (New York, 1937), 319 ff.

7 Murray Kane, "Some Considerations of the Safety Valve Doctrine," *Mississippi Valley Historical Review, XXIII* (1937), 169–88.

8 Abernethy, *Western Lands and the American Revolution,* 288 ff.

9 Ben Perley Poore, *The Federal and State Constitutions . . . of the United States* (2 vols.; Washington, 1878), I, 651; hereinafter cited *Federal and State Constitutions.*

10 Lewis Collins, *History of Kentucky* (2 vols.; Covington, Ky., 1878), I, 274–75.

11 Poore, *Federal and State Constitutions,* I, 658, 660, 662.
12 *Ibid.,* II, 1634–35.

CHAPTER V   CHARLES S. SYDNOR

1 The search for unifying themes in southern history is either illustrated or discussed in the following works: Ulrich B. Phillips, *Life and Labor in the Old South* (Boston, 1929), 3; Phillips, "The Central Theme of Southern History," *American Historical Review,* XXXIV (1928), 30–43; Avery Craven, *The Repressible Conflict, 1830–1861* (Baton Rouge, 1939), 26–27; Craven, *Edmund Ruffin, Southerner: A Study in Secession* (New York, 1932), 96; Richard H. Shryock, "Cultural Factors in the History of the South," *Journal of Southern History,* V (1939), 333–46; Howard W. Odum, *Southern Regions of the United States* (Chapel Hill, 1936); Garet Garrett, "The Problem South," *Saturday Evening Post,* October 8, 1938, pp. 23, 85–86, 88–91; John W. Thomason, Jr., "The Old South Myth," *American Mercury,* XLIV (1938), 344–54.

2 Jesse T. Carpenter, *The South as a Conscious Minority, 1789–1861* (New York, 1930), especially pp. 158–60; Andrew C. McLaughlin, *A Constitutional History of the United States* (New York, 1935), 426–614; Dwight L. Dumond, *Antislavery Origins of the Civil War in the United States* (Ann Arbor, 1939), which contains an excellent analysis of the "higher law" views of the abolitionists. Gerald W. Johnson, *The Secession of the Southern States* (New York, 1933), uses biblical terms to contrast the southern and northern viewpoints. The South, looking to agreements made in the past, represented the Law; the North, looking to the future and seeking change, the Prophets.

3 For a convenient summary of the scriptural defense of slavery, see William S. Jenkins, *Pro-Slavery Thought in the Old South* (Chapel Hill, 1935), 200–41.

4 Although theological trends current in North and South probably accounted for some of the differences between the pronouncements of northern and southern theologians concerning slavery, it is not improbable that the slavery controversy in turn accentuated the divergence between the theological thinking of the two sections.

5 A number of citations in proof of the above statement are marshaled in Avery Craven, "The 'Turner Theories' and the South," *Journal of Southern History,* V (1939), 305–307. Additional evidence is available in William H. Russell, *My Diary North and South* (2 vols.; New York, 1863), II, 7–11; [Augustus B. Longstreet], *Georgia Scenes* (Augusta, 1835); James S. Buckingham, *The Slaves States of America* (2 vols.; London, 1842), II, 3–4; George W. Pierson, *Tocqueville and Beaumont in America* (New York, 1938), 640, 642; "South Carolina Morals," *Atlantic Monthly,* XXXIX (1877), 467–68.

6 Thomas J. Wertenbaker, *The Planters of Colonial Virginia* (Princeton, 1922), 155, thus summarizes the opinions of Robert Beverly, Jr., John F. D. Smyth, Hugh Jones, Thomas Anburey, Philip Fithian, and other eighteenth-century writers.

7 Henry D. Gilpin (ed.), *Papers of James Madison* (3 vols.; Washington, 1840), III, 1391.

8   "Social Life in Old Virginia," *The Novels, Stories, Sketches and Poems of Thomas Nelson Page* (18 vols.; New York, 1906–18), XII, 188–89.

9   Horace S. Fulkerson, *Random Recollections of Early Days in Mississippi* (Vicksburg, 1885), 15, 16, 144.

10   Alexis de Tocqueville, *Democracy in America,* trans. by Henry Reeve (2 vols.; New York, 1900), I, 400. See also, Daniel R. Hundley, *Social Relations in Our Southern States* (New York, 1860), 70–71; and Thomas Jefferson, *Notes on the State of Virginia* (Philadelphia, 1794), 236–38.

11   Charles S. Sydnor, *A Gentleman of the Old Natchez Region: Benjamin L. C. Wailes* (Durham, 1938), 107.

12   Quoted in Ulrich B. Phillips, *American Negro Slavery* (New York, 1918), 502. Further evidence of the great power of the master over his slave, and of the state's recognition of this power, can be found in cases summarized in Helen T. Catterall (ed.), *Judicial Cases concerning American Slavery and the Negro* (5 vols.; Washington, 1926–37), I, 150, II, 516–17; and in George M. Stroud, *A Sketch of the Laws Relating to Slavery* (Philadelphia, 1856), 55–71; William Goodell, *The American Slave Code in Theory and Practice* (New York, 1853), 32–34, 126, 167–68.

13   Quoted in Bell I. Wiley, *Southern Negroes, 1861–1865* (New Haven, 1938), 170. See also, Hundley, *Social Relations,* 185.

14   Much evidence of the inacceptability of Negro testimony can be found in Stroud, *Laws Relating to Slavery,* 106, 110; Goodell, *American Slave Code,* 300–309; Thomas R. R. Cobb, *An Inquiry into the Law of Negro Slavery in the United States of America* (Philadelphia, 1858), 226–34.

15   Because the Negro had so little direct influence in shaping the policies of the Old South, no attempt has been made to discover what he thought and did in consequence of his partial exclusion from the courts. But it may be noted that the distance between the Negro and the courts continues to be wide, a condition which has important effects. Comments on current extralegal aspects of Negro life can be found in Hortense Powdermaker, *After Freedom: A Cultural Study in the Deep South* (New York, 1939), 126, 173.

16   Richmond *Enquirer,* March 7, 1826, quoted in Joseph C. Robert, *The Tobacco Kingdom* (Durham, 1938), 56.

17   Sydnor, *Benjamin L. C. Wailes,* 108.

18   The white men were flogged and ordered to leave the state. To accomplish their punishment, society had shifted from the court to lynch law. *Niles' Weekly Register,* LIX (1840), 39, 88. See also, Hundley, *Social Relations,* 229.

The southerner likewise avoided the use of Negro testimony in ecclesiastical and academic courts. Examples can be found in Methodist Episcopal Church, *Journal of the General Conference, 1840* (New York, 1844), 28, 57, 87, 88 (Silas Comfort case); and *Record of the Testimony and Proceedings, in the Matter of the Investigation by the Trustees of the University of Mississippi, on the 1st and 2nd of March, 1860, of the Charges Made by H. R. Branham, against the Chancellor of the University* (Jackson, Miss., 1860). Disciplinary duties and troubles frequently plagued presidents and teachers in colleges of the Old South. This condition may have been caused in part by the fact that misdoings of college boys could not be reported by such of the employees as were Negroes.

19 An Alabama lawyer in 1832 advanced yet another explanation of disrespect for law in the Southwest. He believed that "our magistracy is completely incapable, the mass of the people feel it as well as we," and he thought that this condition had been caused by the choice of judges by legislatures or popular votes rather than by the older system of executive appointment. Pierson, *Tocqueville and Beaumont in America,* 640.

20 W. H. Sparks, *The Memories of Fifty Years* (Philadelphia, 1870), 148.

21 In judging how men would behave in a state of nature, the North seems to have followed Hobbes and the South, Rousseau.

22 William E. Dodd, "The Emergence of the First Social Order in the United States," *American Historical Review,* XL (1935), 217–31.

23 Dixon R. Fox, *Ideas in Motion* (New York, 1935), 58–59.

24 Arthur P. Hudson, *Folksongs of Mississippi and Their Background* (Chapel Hill, 1936), 32–34.

25 William E. Dodd, *The Cotton Kingdom* (New Haven, 1919), 81; Hamilton J. Eckenrode, "Sir Walter Scott and the South," *North American Review,* CCVI (1917), 595–603.

26 Hundley, *Social Relations,* 27; "South Carolina Society," *Atlantic Monthly,* XXXIX (1877), 670–72.

27 Page, "Social Life in Old Virginia," *loc. cit.*

28 Delia B. Page, *Recollections of Home for My Brothers and Children* (Richmond, 1903), 56.

29 It is significant that Tocqueville, when contrasting the manners and concepts of honor of Americans with those prevailing among aristocracies, remarked: "I speak here of the Americans inhabiting those States where slavery does not exist; they alone can be said to present a complete picture of democratic society." *Democracy in America,* II, 246, and 181, 227, 244–47, 250–53. Napoléon Achille Murat considered Virginians "the only real aristocrats of the Union" even though they "boasted much of democracy" and were "coarse, vain, and haughty." *A Moral and Political Sketch of the United States of North America* (London, 1833), 11–14. See also, "The Political Condition of South Carolina," *Atlantic Monthly,* XXXIX (1877), 188–89.

30 Discussions of the manners and code of the Old South can be found in Benjamin B. Kendrick and Alex M. Arnett, *The South Looks at Its Past* (Chapel Hill, 1935), 26–35; Hundley, *Social Relations,* 27–74; "South Carolina Morals," *loc. cit.; I'll Take my Stand: The South and the Agrarian Tradition* (New York, 1930).

31 "Southern and Northern Civilization Contrasted," *Russell's Magazine,* I (1857), 102–105.

32 Several of the southern states have retained even to this day statutes under which insult may justifiably be answered by physical force. Such statutes, of course, abrogate the common law rule that insulting language is no defense to an action for assault. Wex S. Malone, "Insult in Retaliation—the Huckabee Case," *Mississippi Law Journal,* XI (1939), 333–39, especially 338; *Huckabee* v. *Nash,* 183 *Southern Reporter* 500 (Miss., 1938).

33   George C. Eggleston, *The Warrens of Virginia* (New York, 1908), 31.
34   There is no adequate study of dueling in the Old South, but the following citations show that duels were not infrequent and indicate something of southern opinion toward this custom: John L. Wilson, *The Code of Honor; or Rules for the Government of Principals and Second in Duelling* (Charleston, 1858); Lorenzo Sabine, *Notes on Duels and Duelling* (Boston, 1855); Thomas Gamble, *Savannah Duels and Duellists, 1733–1877* (Savannah, 1923); Fulkerson, *Random Recollections of Early Days in Mississippi,* 44–49; *Russell's Magazine,* I (1857), 132–42, 439–54; Don C. Seitz, *Famous American Duels* (New York, 1929); Robert R. Howison, "Duelling in Virginia," *William and Mary College Quarterly Historical Magazine,* Ser. II, Vol. IV (1924), 217–44; Isaac M. Patridge, "The Press of Mississippi—Historical Sketch," *De Bow's Review,* XXIX (1860), 505–507; Francis P. Gaines, *The Southern Plantation* (New York, 1924), 159.
35   Henry S. Canby, "Ellen Glasgow: Ironic Tragedian," *Saturday Review of Literature,* XVIII (September 10, 1938), No. 20, p. 3.
       The southerner's sense of being part of a differentiated society had many effects. For example, he was conscious of family relationships; kinship was one way of telling where a man belonged. The letter of introduction was more than a social formality; the writer of such a letter assumed much responsibility. In estimating a man's worth, the southerner was prone to give great weight to personal endorsements.
36   Henry Hughes, *Treatise on Sociology, Theoretical and Practical* (Philadelphia, 1854); George Fitzhugh, *Sociology for the South; or, the Failure of Free Society* (Richmond, 1854); L. L. Bernard, "Henry Hughes, First American Sociologist," *Journal of Social Forces,* XV (1937), 154–74; Bernard, "The Historic Pattern of Sociology in the South," *ibid.,* XVI (1938), 1–12.
37   Similarly, during the Civil War the code of the gentleman sometimes clashed with military discipline. The gentleman in the ranks saw nothing improper in giving advice to his commanding officer especially when the military heirarchy was contrary to the social hierarchy. It was said that in Richmond from the President on down there was a morbid sensitiveness on the subject of personal dignity. George C. Eggleston, *A Rebel's Recollections* (New York, 1897), 31–36, 222.
38   Sectional differences in customs and attitudes sometimes made it difficult for northern and southern men to understand each other's behavior as individuals. For example, Henry Adams liked his Harvard classmate "Roony" Lee, the son of Robert E. Lee, but he could not understand him. Henry Adams, *The Education of Henry Adams* (Boston, 1930), 57–58.
39   *Congressional Globe,* 25 Cong., 2 Sess., 55 (December 27, 1837).
40   George H. Haynes, "Charles Sumner," *Dictionary of American Biography* (20 vols. and index; New York, 1928–37), XVIII, 208–14. See also, James E. Walmsley, "Preston Smith Brooks," *ibid.,* III, 88.
41   Data about the Brooks-Sumner affair can be found by consulting the index of the *Cong. Globe,* 34 Cong., 1 Sess., Pt. II. On pages 1349–50 (June 2, 1856) is the version quoted above of Brooks's statement to Sumner. The text of Sumner's speech is *ibid.,* Appendix, 529–44 (May 19–20, 1856). See also, his remarks to Stephen A. Douglas in *ibid.,* 547

(May 20, 1856); and "Statement of Preston S. Brooks," Massachusetts Historical Society, *Proceedings,* LXI (1928), 221–23.
42 Joshua 24:15.

CHAPTER VII B. B. KENDRICK

1 The author wishes it understood that while he recognizes the necessity for complete national unity now that the country is at war, he sees no reason to modify any part of the interpretation he has placed upon events preceding the outbreak of war.

2 With regard to Madison it is only fair to point out that, as revealed in his masterpiece, "Federalist, Number 10," no other man of his time perceived so clearly the influence of economic interests upon political principles and actions. Apparently his own intellectual honesty led him to believe that the Constitution would always be interpreted strictly and that the United States government would remain federal in a sense opposite to central or national.

3 It is interesting to speculate on the position Jefferson would have taken on the Constitution had he been in the country in 1787–88. It seems that consistency and his keen distrust of the "economic royalists" of his time would have demanded that he oppose it, had he been present. That he could have opened Madison's eyes (as he did later) to the danger latent in the Constitution is also probable. Together Jefferson and Madison, in all likelihood, could have prevented southern ratification.

4 The terms "good" and "bad," "right" and "wrong," are employed throughout this paper in no moral sense. Whether such moral or ethical "goods" as the greater glory of God, democracy, human happiness as a whole, or even the "greatest good for the greatest number" were promoted or retarded by the Constitution no one can say with certainty. In general, historians, even including southern historians, have proceeded on the assumption that all these ethical "goods" were served by the Constitution. Using the words as terms in social dynamics then, rather than in morality or ethics, it may be stated that the Constitution was "good" for the development of a system of capitalism in which control is concentrated in relatively few hands, and "bad" for a system of agricultural and other small tangible personal property interests in which control is widely dispersed.

5 In this connection it may be stated with some dogmatism that relations with Canada would not have been so pleasant had that dominion once been a part of the United States and afterwards have established its independence.

6 Splendid examples of the two types of argument are Hamilton's memorandum in support of the constitutionality of the Bank of the United States and Jefferson's in opposition.

7 That Jefferson himself was not unaware of what was going on is attested by a letter he wrote in 1822 to Albert Gallatin and another in 1824 to Martin Van Buren. In the former he said: "Do not believe a word of it [that the lion and the lamb are lying down together]. The same parties exist now as ever did." In the letter to Van Buren he wrote: "Tories are Tories still, by whatever name they be called."

8 It should be pointed out in this connection that the source of inspiration

for the rising northern literati (especially those of New England) came to be the antislavery crusade. In addition to the preachers whose service of God was more and more equated with opposition to slavery, the theme song of the orators, poets, essayists, and novelists was subsequently expressed by Mrs. Howe in the lines:

In the beauty of the lilies
Christ was born across the sea,
With a glory in his bosom that transfigures you and me;
As he died to make men holy, let us die to make men free,
While God is marching on.

Under such circumstances a "holy" war was inevitable. Sooner or later moderate men would be in a hopeless minority and be castigated as Copperheads—the "Appeasers" of that day. The comparison *is not* mine.

9 Conversely, democracy as a way of social and political life may well be doomed when ownership and management is highly concentrated in the impersonal corporate form.

10 That there will be a fierce struggle for control between the New Deal and imperialist interventionists at or near the end of the war may be predicted with a high degree of certainty. It will be interesting to see which side will secure the support of southern politicians.

CHAPTER VIII   A. B. MOORE

1 Paul H. Buck, *The Road to Reunion, 1865–1900* (Boston, 1937), 12.
2 *Ibid.*, 22
3 Quoted in *ibid.*, 57.
4 See *American Historical Review*, XXVI (1921), 489-90.
5 Buck, *The Road to Reunion*, 25.
6 James L. Sellers, "The Economic Incidence of the Civil War in the South," *Mississippi Valley Historical Review*, XIV (1927), 190.
7 *Nation*, XXVIII (1879), 398–99.
8 Quoted in Walter L. Fleming, *The Sequel of Appomattox* (New Haven, 1919), 148.
9 Buck, *The Road to Reunion*, 149.
10 Walter P. Webb, *Divided We Stand; the Crisis of a Frontierless Democracy* (New York, 1937), 22.
11 *Ibid.*, 23.
12 *House Document*, 76 Cong., 1 Sess., No. 271, p. xiii.
13 National Emergency Council, *Report on Economic Conditions of the South* (Washington, 1938), 55.

CHAPTER IX   J. G. DE ROULHAC HAMILTON

1 Thomas Jefferson to Ebenezer Hazard, February 18, 1791, in Albert E. Bergh (ed.), *The Writings of Thomas Jefferson* (20 vols.; Washington, 1904), VIII, 127.
2 William W. Hening (ed.), *The Statutes at Large; Being a Collection of all the Laws of Virginia* [1619–1792] (13 vols.; Richmond, 1809–1823), I, iv.

3   William C. Torrence, for example, said in his paper, "Public Archives of Virginia," American Historical Association, *Annual Report,* 1906 (2 vols.; Washington, 1908), I, 134, that outside pressure as much as anything else spurred Virginia to care for its archives.

4   Hening (ed.), *Statutes at Large, I,* 303–304.

5   *Ibid.,* II, 509.

6   *Ibid.,* II, 42–45.

7   *Ibid.,* XII, 497, XIII, 23.

8   Act of 1715, chap. xi.

9   Act of 1716, chap. i. See also, Bernard C. Steiner, "Restoration of the Proprietary of Maryland," American Historical Association, *Annual Report,* 1899 (2 vols.; Washington, 1900), I, 231–307.

10 Stephen B. Weeks, "Historical Review of the Colonial and State Records of North Carolina," William L. Saunders and Walter Clark (eds.), *Colonial and State Records of North Carolina* (30 vols.; Raleigh, etc., 1886–1914), XXX.

11 *Revisal* of 1715, chap. xxxviii.

12 J. R. B. Hathaway discovered such a register for Berkeley Precinct, with entries as late as the Revolution. See *North Carolina Historical and Genealogical Register,* III (1903), 199–220, 263–410.

13 *Colonial and State Records of North Carolina,* VII, 488.

14 *Ibid.,* XIII, 127.

15 *Ibid.,* IV, 572.

16 *Ibid.,* IV, 423.

17 *Ibid.,* VI, 301.

18 *Ibid.,* IV, 721.

19 *Ibid.,* V, 18.

20 *Ibid.,* V, 156–57.

21 "Resolved, That the Books, records and Papers of the Secretary's office being lately by the Governor's Order removed to Cape Fear near the Southern Extremity of this Province renders it Extremely expensive & difficult for the Generality of People to have the necessary recourse to that office." *Ibid.,* VI, 412.

22 *Ibid.,* VII, 963.

23 *Ibid.,* XXIV, 951.

24 The Title, No. 106, appears in John F. Grimké (ed.), *The Public Laws of South Carolina . . . to 1790* (Charleston, 1790), vii.

25 Title No. 256, *ibid.,* xii, 11.

26 Title No. 423, *ibid.,* xx.

27 Title No. 650, *ibid.,* 148. For a fuller discussion of the policy of South Carolina, see Alexander S. Salley, "Preservation of South Carolina History," *North Carolina Historical Review,* IV (1927); 145–57.

28 William G. Stanard, "The Virginia Archives," American Historical Association, *Annual Report,* 1903, (2 vols.; Washington, 1904), I, 647–51; Wilmer L. Hall, "The Public Records of Virginia," *Virginia Libraries,* IV (1931), 2–22.

29 Salley, "Preservation of South Carolina History," *loc. cit.*

30 Theodore H. Jack, "The Preservation of Georgia History," *North Carolina Historical Review,* IV (1927), 240.

31 *Ibid.,* 239–51.

32   James A. Robertson, "The Preservation of Florida History," *North Carolina Historical Review,* IV (1927), 352.

33   Mitchell B. Garrett, "The Preservation of Alabama History," *ibid.,* V (1928), 3–19; "Report of Public Archives Commission," American Historical Association, *Annual Report,* 1904 (Washington, 1905), 493–95.

34   The territorial and state capitals were, successively, "Old Concord"; Natchez in 1819; Washington, 1820; Columbia, 1821; and Jackson since 1823. Dunbar Rowland, *First Annual Report, Department of Archives and History of Mississippi* (Jackson, 1902); William H. Weathersby, "The Preservation of Mississippi History," *North Carolina Historical Review,* V (1928), 141–50.

35   They were: Biloxi, 1699; Mobile, 1701; New Biloxi, 1719; New Orleans, 1722; Donaldsonville, 1825; New Orleans, 1831; Baton Rouge, 1850; Opelousas and Shreveport, 1862; New Orleans, 1862; Baton Rouge, 1879.

36   Grace King, "The Preservation of Louisiana History," *North Carolina Historical Review,* V (1928), 363–71.

37   Charles W. Ramsdell, "The Preservation of Texas History," *ibid.,* VI (1929), 1–16.

38   David Y. Thomas, "The Preservation of Arkansas History," *ibid.,* V (1928), 263–74.

39   Knoxville, Kingston, Knoxville again, Nashville, Knoxville, Murfreesboro, and then, from 1826, Nashville, have served as capitals. R. A. Halley, "The Preservation of Tennessee History," *American Historical Magazine,* VIII, 49–63.

40   Philip M. Hamer, "The Preservation of Tennessee History," *North Carolina Historical Review,* VI (1929), 127–39.

41   Irene T. Meyers, "The Archives of Kentucky," American Historical Association, *Annual Report,* 1910 (Washington, 1912), 336.

42   There are innumerable places in the South known to have been the site for as many as four or five houses.

43   For a quotation from a New York newspaper, giving an account of this discovery, see Charles Campbell (ed.), *The Bland Papers* (2 vols.; Petersburg, 1840–43), I, ix n.

44   William P. Palmer *et al.* (eds.), *Calendar of Virginia State Papers and Other Manuscripts* [1652–1869] (11 vols.; Richmond, 1875–93), I, xx. In the same connection, Palmer also said: "The abodes of the numerous patrician class, who so long inhabited ancestral homes scattered over Virginia, from Arlington House and Hungar's, on the Eastern Shore, to Temple-farm on the Western; from the region about Green-spring and Stafford house, to Green-way court, the extreme limit of the Northern neck; and from Bacon-castle and Varina, to the cliffs of Tuckahoe and Dungeness, must have abounded with historical material, accumulated through the correspondence and diaries kept by their intelligent occupants. Many of the latter, it should be remembered, were connected by ties of blood, with influential families in the old country. Others having occupied important posts under the government, had established intimate relations with leading men of state, and had maintained familiar intercourse with their friends abroad. In the course of their correspondence, matters of public concern, were not only discussed, but in the

scarcity of printed newspapers, their letters abounded with incidents of private history, and recorded the current news and talk of the day. . . . Even at this late day, there are doubtless remaining in the lofts of old mansions, and in the possession of descendants of those who once occupied others long since passed away, many valuable papers now regarded as worthless rubbish." *Ibid.,* xviii.

45 *Papers of the American Historical Association* (5 vols.; New York, 1886–91), II, 20–21.

46 "And yet, unless wariness be us'd, as good almost kill a Man as kill a good Booke; who kills a Man kills a reasonable creature, God's image; but he who destroyes a good Booke, kills reason itself, kills the Image of God, as it were in the eye. Many a man lives a burden to the Earth; but a good Booke is the pretious life-blood of a master spirit, imbalm'd and treasur'd up on purpose to a life beyond life."

47 *Calendar of Virginia State Papers,* I, x.

48 The facts of this case are to be found in the *Annual Report of the Attorney General of Virginia,* 1916 (Richmond, 1917), 279–91. Mr. Morgan's letter contained the following interesting paragraph: "Should the case, however, come to trial, issues will be raised as to the late war and the status of participants therein, which, it seems to me, better should not be raised in view of the fifty years of peace and unity which have elapsed since the termination of the war. I do not wish that through any act of mine, differences long settled should be recalled. Rather than revive the memories of ancient strife, long since consigned to oblivion by the good sense and good feeling and patriotism of the people of the United States, I greatly prefer to waive such personal rights as I believe I have in this matter."

The New York *Times,* in various issues, referred to the case. Commenting editorially, it took the view that the will could not be regarded as stolen property, expressing the opinion, as justification of the remarkable argument, that it would probably have been destroyed later if it had not been taken. It expressed its belief that "Morgan and Lossing probably did not know" that such southern papers were stolen, and that there was no proof that the will had been stolen. The editorial continued: "The Southern states were slack and slovenly in their guardianship of these relics in ante-bellum days. . . . When Union soldiers appeared at the various county seats they had a better appreciation of the value of what they found, and had not false modesty about appropriating these souvenirs as prizes of war." Issue of February 22, 1914.

49 Louise P. Kellogg, "The Services and Collections of Lyman C. Draper," *Wisconsin Magazine of History,* V (1922), 256.

50 Worthington C. Ford, "Manuscripts and Historical Archives," American Historical Association, *Annual Report,* 1913 (2 vols.; Washington, 1915), I, 77–78.

51 Hening (ed.), *Statutes at Large,* I, iv.

52 For this statement of purposes, see *North Carolina Historical Review,* IV (1927), 6.

53 J. G. de Roulhac Hamilton, "The Preservation of North Carolina His-

tory," *North Carolina Historical Review,* IV (1927), 3–10. Governor Jarvis, in an address to the North Carolina Literary and Historical Association, gave a delightful account of how all this came about.

54　See Weeks, "Historical Review of the Colonial and State Records of North Carolina," *loc. cit.*

55　The counties are: Accomac, Charles City, Elizabeth City, Essex, Henrico, Northampton, Rappahannock, Richmond, Surry, Warwick, and York. See Lyon G. Tyler, "Preservation of Virginia History," *North Carolina Historical Review,* III (1926), 529–30.

56　William H. Browne *et al.* (eds.) *Archives of Maryland,* I (1883), vi.

57　"Report of the Public Archives Commission," American Historical Association, *Annual Report,* 1900 (2 vols.; Washington, 1901), II, 19.

58　Jack, "The Preservation of Georgia History," *North Carolina Historical Review,* 243.

59　See *ibid.,* 245–46, for an excellent description of Candler's work on this project.

60　Salley, "Preservation of South Carolina History," *loc. cit.*

61　Ramsdell, "The Preservation of Texas History," *loc. cit.*

62　Weathersby, "The Preservation of Mississippi History," *loc. cit.*

63　King, "The Preservation of Louisiana History," *loc. cit.* See also, Benjamin F. French (ed.), *Historical Collections of Louisiana* (5 vols.; New York, Philadelphia, 1846–53), II, 8–11.

64　Ford, "Manuscripts and Historical Archives," American Historical Association, *Annual Report,* 1913, p. 79.

65　William P. Trent, "The Study of Southern History," Vanderbilt Southern History Society, *Publications,* I (1895), 23–24.

CHAPTER X　　WENDELL H. STEPHENSON

1　William P. Trent, "The Study of Southern History," Vanderbilt Southern History Society, *Publications,* I, 1, 5–7, 14–19.

2　John M. Vincent, "Herbert B. Adams: A Biographical Sketch," *Herbert B. Adams: Tributes of Friends, with A Bibliography of the Department of History, Politics and Economics of the Johns Hopkins University, 1876–1901* (Baltimore, 1902), 9–23; Richard T. Ely, "A Sketch of the Life and Services of Herbert Baxter Adams," *ibid.,* 27–49; John M. Vincent, "Herbert B. Adams," Howard W. Odum (ed.), *American Masters of Social Science* (New York, 1927), 97–127, a rewriting of Vincent's earlier sketch; John S. Bassett, "Herbert Baxter Adams," Allen Johnson and Dumas Malone (eds.), *Dictionary of American Biography* (20 vols. and index; New York, 1928–37), I, 69–71.

3　See "The Historical Library," *Johns Hopkins University . . . Register for 1896–97* (Baltimore, 1897), 104–108; *Eighth Annual Report of the President of the Johns Hopkins University . . . 1833* (Baltimore, 1883), 50, and the *Annual Report* for each year from 1883 to 1900.

4　"Historical Library," *loc. cit.;* William Birney to Herbert B. Adams, January 12, 14, May 8, 1891, in Herbert B. Adams Correspondence (Johns Hopkins University Library, Baltimore, Maryland); James C. Ballagh, "The Johns Hopkins University and the South," New York *Evangelist,* March 29, 1900, reprinted in Johns Hopkins University

Circulars (Baltimore), XX, No. 149 (January, 1901), 23. In slightly modified form, Ballagh's article appeared in *Twenty-Sixth Annual Report of the President of the Johns Hopkins University ... 1901* (Baltimore, 1901), 31–32. See also, William K. Boyd, "Southern History in American Universities," *South Atlantic Quarterly,* I (1902), 240.

5 *Sixteenth Annual Report of the President of the Johns Hopkins University ... 1891,* pp. 10, 60; *Twenty-Sixth Annual Report of the President of the Johns Hopkins University ... 1901,* p. 81; John S. Bassett to Adams, June 21, October 23, November 14, December 15, 1899, April 1, November 2, 1900, Adams Correspondence; *id.* to John M. Vincent, February 5, 1900; January 15, 1901, *ibid.*

6 *Twenty-Sixth Annual Report of the President of the Johns Hopkins University ... 1901,* p. 83; *Twenty-Seventh Annual Report of the President of the Johns Hopkins University ... 1902* (Baltimore, 1902), 58.

7 See the bibliographical portion of *Herbert B. Adams: Tributes of Friends, with a Bibliography of the Department,* 1–160; Boyd, "Southern History in American Universities," *South Atlantic Quarterly,* I, 241.

8 Trinity College was a Hopkins "colony" before Bassett's appointment to the faculty. Stephen B. Weeks received the doctorate at Johns Hopkins in 1891, taught at Trinity for the next two years, and inaugurated some of the historical activities which Bassett continued. As a North Carolina historian and bibliographer and as editor and researcher for the United States Bureau of Education, Weeks made significant contributions to southern historiography.

9 Some of these have been published in W. Stull Holt (ed.), *Historical Scholarship in the United States, 1876–1901: As Revealed in the Correspondence of Herbert B. Adams* (Baltimore, 1938); others are in Adams Correspondence. For a brief sketch of Bassett, see William K. Boyd, "John Spencer Bassett," *Dictionary of American Biography,* II, 38–39.

10 Trinity College *Catalogue for the Year 1896–97* (Durham, 1897), 50, 63; *1897–98* (Durham, 1898), 53; *1899–1900* (Durham, 1900), 61; *1906–1907* (Durham, 1907), 73.

11 Bassett to Adams, September 26, 1897, Holt (ed.), *Historical Scholarship in the United States,* 246.

12 The speech, originally published in the *Trinity Archive,* January, 1898, pp. 177–87, is quoted in Nannie M. Tilley, *The Trinity College Historical Society, 1892–1941* (Durham, 1941), 51–59.

13 John S. Bassett, "The Problems of the Author in the South," *South Atlantic Quarterly,* I (1902), 203.

14 *South Atlantic Quarterly,* II (1903), 297–305.

15 John S. Bassett, *The Southern Plantation Overseer As Revealed in His Letters* (Northampton, Mass., 1925), iv.

16 The notable exception was John S. Bassett (ed.), *The Writings of "Colonel William Byrd of Westover in Virginia Esqʳ"* (New York, 1901).

17 William P. Trent to Adams, January 8, 1898, in Holt (ed.), *Historical Scholarship in the United States,* 250.

18 *Id.* to Charles D. Warner, June 11, 1892, quoted in Franklin T. Walker, "William Peterfield Trent—A Critical Biography" (Ph.D. dissertation, George Peabody College for Teachers, 1943), 135.

19   *Id.* to Adams, June 9, September 30, November 14, 1890, March 5, April 17, 1891, Adams Correspondence; William P. Trent, *William Gilmore Simms* (Boston, 1892), vi–vii, 37–41, 50–51, 56, 104–105, 286–87, *passim.*

20   William P. Trent, *Southern Statesmen of the Old Régime* (Boston, 1897), *passim*, 181, 199, 261–62.

21   William P. Trent, *Robert E. Lee* (Boston, 1899), 32–34.

22   *Catalogue of the State Agricultural and Mechanical College; Alabama Polytechnic Institute, 1892–93* (Montgomery, 1893), 64. A similar statement had appeared in the catalogue as early as the issue of 1887–88 (Auburn, n. d.), 45; the quotation remained in the catalogue until 1920.

23   George Petrie to Adams, April 21, 1900, Adams Correspondence. An enclosure listed the books Fleming had read.

24   *Catalogue of the Alabama Polytechnic Institute . . . 1900* (Montgomery, 1900), 67; *1901* (Montgomery, 1901), 77.

25   Alfred W. Reynolds, "Auburn Historians (1896–1941)," *Auburn Forum,* II, (1941), No. 7, pp. 9–10, 21.

26   The Adams Correspondence contains several letters from Franklin L. Riley, the most significant of which have been published in Charles S. Sydnor (ed.), "Letters from Franklin L. Riley to Herbert B. Adams, 1894–1901," *Journal of Mississippi History,* II (1940), 100–10. A larger assemblage of Riley letters is available in the Thomas M. Owen Correspondence, Department of Archives and History, Montgomery, Alabama.

27   *Historical Catalogue of the University of Mississippi, 1849–1909* (Nashville, 1910), 53–57; Sydnor (ed.), "Letters from Franklin L. Riley to Herbert B. Adams," *Journal of Mississippi History,* II (1940), 105.

28   Bassett to Adams, January 24, 1898, May 27, June 17, 1900, April 21, 1901, in Adams Correspondence; *id.* to *id.*, April 3, 1899, in Holt (ed.), *Historical Scholarship in the United States,* 269–70; William K. Boyd to Bassett, n. d., but probably early fall, 1900, November 27, 1900, April 7, 18, 28, 1901, John S. Bassett Correspondence (Division of Manuscripts, Library of Congress).
      Boyd serves here as an appropriate transition; an appraisal of his work is reserved for a later study. Pertinent data are available in Bassett Correspondence; and in William K. Boyd Memoir and William K. Boyd Correspondence (Manuscript Department, Duke University Library, Durham, North Carolina). See, also, *In Memoriam: William Kenneth Boyd, January 10, 1879—January 19, 1938* (Durham, 1938); Tilley, *Trinity College Historical Society, passim.*

29   J. G. de Roulhac Hamilton (ed.), *Truth in History and Other Essays by William A. Dunning* (New York, 1937), xi.

30   For "a picture of the master," see *ibid.*, xi–xxviii; for sketches, Charles E. Merriam, "William Archibald Dunning," in Odum (ed.), *American Masters of Social Science,* 129–45; J. G. de Roulhac Hamilton, "William Archibald Dunning," *Dictionary of American Biography,* V, 523–24; *American Historical Review,* XXVIII (1922–23), 174. It is a factor of some significance that Dunning's father, a carriage maker with artistic and classical tendencies, inspired an interest in Reconstruction problems.

See dedicatory page, in William A. Dunning, *Reconstruction, Political and Economic, 1865–1877* (New York, 1907).

31 James W. Garner, *Reconstruction in Mississippi* (New York, 1901), vii–viii.

32 Edwin C. Woolley, *The Reconstruction of Georgia* (New York, 1901); J. G. de Roulhac Hamilton, *Reconstruction in North Carolina* (Raleigh, 1906); Charles W. Ramsdell, *Reconstruction in Texas* (New York, 1910); William W. Davis, *The Civil War and Reconstruction in Florida* (New York, 1913); Thomas S. Staples, *Reconstruction in Arkansas, 1862–1874* (New York, 1923). Hamilton's dissertation traced Reconstruction in North Carolina through 1868; he continued working on the subject and published at New York in 1914 a much longer volume on the whole period.

33 Walter L. Fleming, *Civil War and Reconstruction in Alabama* (New York, 1905); C. Mildred Thompson, *Reconstruction in Georgia, Economic, Social, Political, 1865–1872* (New York, 1915).

34 Ramsdell, *Reconstruction in Texas*, 7.

35 Dunning, *Reconstruction, Political and Economic*, xv.

36 The status of Reconstruction writing is treated in Howard K. Beale, "On Rewriting Reconstruction History," *American Historical Review*, XLV, 807–27. For an interesting roundtable discussion of Reconstruction, see Albert B. Moore, "The Sixth Annual Meeting of the Southern Historical Association," *Journal of Southern History*, VII (1941), 66–68.

37 One is surprised to find, for example, that Garner discovered "a feeling of genuine admiration . . . for the Northern teacher" in Mississippi, and concluded that, when the Radicals relinquished control of government, "the public school system which they had fathered had become firmly established, its efficiency increased, and its administration made somewhat less expensive than at first." Garner, *Reconstruction in Mississippi*, 359–70.

38 For biographical and bibliographical data, see *American Historical Review*, XXXIX (1933–34), 598–99; Fred Landon, "Ulrich Bonnell Phillips: Historian of the South," *Journal of Southern History*, V (1939), 364–71; Wood Gray, "Ulrich Bonnell Phillips," William T. Hutchinson (ed.), *The Marcus W. Jernegan Essays in American Historiography* . . . (Chicago, 1937), 354–73; Fred Landon and Everett E. Edwards, "A Bibliography of the Writings of Professor Ulrich Bonnell Phillips," *Agricultural History*, VIII (1934), 196–218; David M. Potter, Jr. (comp.), "A Bibliography of the Printed Writings of Ulrich Bonnell Phillips," *Georgia Historical Quarterly*, XVIII (1934), 270–82. Philip C. Newman, "Ulrich Bonnell Phillips—The South's Foremost Historian," *ibid.*, XXV (1941), 244–61, possesses little if any merit. Transcripts of the Ulrich B. Phillips Papers are in possession of the writer.

39 William E. Dodd to Adams, July 16, 21, 1900, in Adams Correspondence.

40 *John P. Branch Historical Papers of Randolph-Macon College*, I (1901–1904), No. 1 (1901), inside front cover, 1, No. 2 (1902), 65.

41 *Ibid.*, I (1901–1904), No. 1 (1901), 24–63, No. 2 (1902), 111–54, No. 3 (1903), 217–56, No. 4 (1904), 325–73, II (1905–1908), No. 1 (1905),

47–142, No. 2 (1906), 78–183, Nos. 3–4 (1908), 253–353, III (1909–1912), No. 1 (1909), 27–93.

42 *Catalogue of Randolph-Macon College . . . 1903–1904* (Lynchburg, 1904), 46; *1905–1906* (Richmond, 1906), 52.

43 As early as 1900 Edwin E. Sparks gave a course in Reconstruction history, later expanded to secession, Civil War, and Reconstruction, 1860–72. A course in Confederate history appeared in 1906, and another on slavery expansion the following year. Meanwhile, Jameson had been teaching classes in social and economic history of American Slavery. *University of Chicago Annual Register, 1899–1900* (Chicago, 1900), 183, and other catalogues for the years 1900–1908.

44 Interest in church history manifested itself in courses on the religious history of the South, the break-up of the churches in the two decades prior to the Civil War, church and state in the Old South, and the rise of democratic churches in the South from 1740 to 1800. Sometimes his program ran to rigly specialized fields, as the South and the Declaration of Independence, the South and the tariff, the South and the Mexican War, the South and the Missouri Compromise, the South and the Compromise of 1850. The secession movement appeared in the catalogue several times; once the title was phrased as a direct question, "Did the People of the South Wish to Secede in 1861?" Two seminars in South Carolina history appeared: South Carolina and the War with Mexico, and the influence of the state in southern history during the period 1833–61. Twice he listed courses on the peculiar institution: slavery in the Southwest, and the slavery question in the Northwest. Southern influence in the Northwest illustrated his interest in the impact of his native region on that in which he lived. As Civil War offerings he listed the internal history of the Confederacy, later narrowed to studies in Confederate internal administration, Jefferson Davis and the Confederacy, and political and social problems during the Civil War. Once he prescribed economic influences in Reconstruction history. See University of Chicago catalogues for the period 1908–1933.

45 Dodd to William K. Boyd, May 21, 1915, in Boyd Correspondence. See also, *id.* to *id.*, May 7, June 13, 1915, *ibid.*

46 *Id.* to *id.*, March 12, 1916, *ibid.*

47 *Ibid.*

48 William E. Dodd, *Woodrow Wilson and His Work* (Garden City, N.Y., 1920), 61–68.

49 Dodd to Boyd, April 15, 1908, in Boyd Correspondence.

50 William E. Dodd, *Lincoln or Lee* (New York, 1928), 3–4.

51 *Ibid.*, 94

52 Thomas M. Owen (ed.), *Report of the Alabama History Commission to the Governor of Alabama, December 1, 1900* (Montgomery, 1901). This *Report* was published as Alabama Historical Society, *Publications, Miscellaneous Collections,* I. For an appraisal of Owen's work, see R. D. W. Connor, "Dedication of the Archival Section of the Alabama World War Memorial Building," *American Archivist,* IV (1941), 77–83.

53 Philip A. Bruce to Adams, July 8, 13, 1895, in Adams Correspondence.

CHAPTER XI   FLETCHER M. GREEN

1   Alexis de Tocqueville, *Democracy in America,* trans. Henry Reeve (4th ed., 2 vols.; New York, 1845), I, 1–2, 5.
2   Thomas S. Goodwin, *The Natural History of Secession; or, Despotism and Democracy at Necessary, Eternal, Exterminating War* (New York, 1865), 40–41.
3   Elhanon W. Reynolds, *The True Story of the Barons of the South; or, The Rationale of the American Conflict* (Boston, 1862), 34–35.
4   Richard Hildreth, *Despotism in America: An Inquiry into the Nature, Results, and Legal Basis of the Slave-Holding System of the United States* (Boston, 1854), 8.
5   See also, Hermann E. von Holst, *The Constitutional and Political History of the United States* (8 vols.; Chicago, 1876–92), I, 348–49.
6   George Sidney Camp, *Democracy* (New York, 1841), 155. Harper and Brothers were so anxious to spread the influence of this first general analysis of the principles of democracy by a native American that they brought it out in their Family Library.
7   *Niles' Register,* XXXVII (1829), 145.
8   Salisbury *Western Carolinian,* July 17, 1821.
9   Milledgeville *Southern Recorder,* May 31, 1832.
10 Salisbury *Western Carolinian,* October 22, 1822.
11 *Proceedings and Debates of the Convention of Virginia* (Richmond, 1830), 68–71, and *passim.*
12 For Brownson's opposition to majority rule, see his "Democracy and Liberty," *United States Magazine and Democratic Review,* XII (1843), 374–87, and his "Unpopular Government," *ibid.,* XII, 529–37.
13 *United States Magazine and Democratic Review,* XLI (1858), 227–28.
14 Conventions were held in Virginia in 1829–30, Mississippi in 1832, Georgia in 1833 and 1839, Tennessee in 1834, North Carolina in 1835, and an abortive or revolutionary one in Maryland in 1836. There is a close parallel in the action of the northern states. Beginning with Connecticut in 1818, Massachusetts, New York, Delaware, Vermont, and Pennsylvania, all held general constitutional conventions by the end of the 1830's; and in Rhode Island there was an unconstitutional convention in 1842 that went beyond the extralegal action in the southern states.
15 Among northern states, New Jersey and Rhode Island retained property qualifications, and Connecticut, Massachusetts, Pennsylvania, and Ohio retained the tax-paying requirement.
16 Samuel E. Morison and Henry Steele Commager, *The Growth of the American Republic* (2 vols.; New York, 1937), I, 82, state that "Jefferson did not mean to include slaves as men."
17 Louisiana in 1844 and 1852, Kentucky in 1849, and Maryland and Virginia in 1850.
18 Frederick Grimké, *Considerations upon the Nature and Tendency of Free Institutions* (Cincinnati, 1848), 311, 314; Camp, *Democracy,* 220–21.
19 For descriptions of the equality of all classes at the polls, see Hamilton W.

Pierson, *In the Bush; or Old-Time Social, Political, and Religious Life in the Southwest* (New York, 1881), 131–46, and Lester B. Shippee (ed.), *Bishop Whipple's Southern Diary, 1843–1844* (Minneapolis, 1937), 22–23, 52.

20 "Joseph Johnson," *Southern Historical Magazine,* I (1892), 185–87.

21 Gustavus W. Dyer, *Democracy in the South before the Civil War* (Nashville, 1905), 80–82.

22 Kemp P. Battle, *Memories of an Old Time Tar Heel* (Chapel Hill, 1945), 93.

23 Albert Gallatin Brown, *Speech of . . . in the House of Representatives* (Washington, 1852.)

24 White population is used as a basis for all these calculations except that free population is used for the six states that permitted Negroes to vote. South Carolina is excluded, since the presidential electors of that state were chosen by the legislature. Population figures are taken from the United States Census reports; the votes from Thomas H. McKee, *The National Conventions and Platforms of All Political Parties, 1789–1900; Convention, Popular, and Electoral Vote* (Baltimore, 1900).

25 *Proceedings and Debates of the Convention of Louisiana, Which Assembled at the City of New Orleans, January 14, 1844* (New Orleans, 1845), 316–19.

26 James M. Garnett, "Popular Education," *Southern Literary Messenger,* VII (1842), 115.

27 *Proceedings and Debates of the Convention of Louisiana . . . 1844,* p. 909.

28 Edgar W. Knight, *The Influence of Reconstruction on Education in the South* (New York, 1913), 94, 98.

29 See, for instance, Charles J. Faulkner, "Speech," *United States Magazine and Democratic Review,* XLI (1858), 218.

CHAPTER XII ELLA LONN

1 Naturally, this summary is intended to be suggestive rather than exhaustive.

2 Paul H. Buck, *The Road to Reunion, 1865–1900* (Boston, 1937), 306.

3 "It is reassuring to find that the older parts of the United States, undisturbed by economic changes and the terrific ordeal of civil war, maintain their patriotism and that it responds instantly to challenge." New York *Herald-Tribune,* February 25, 1944.

4 Holland Thompson, *The New South; A Chronicle of Social and Industrial Evolution* (New Haven, 1919), 90–104; Victor S. Clark, "Manufactures in the South from 1865 to 1880," in Julian A. C. Chandler and others (eds.), *The South in the Building of the Nation* (13 vols.; Richmond, 1909–1913), VI, 253–304; *Eleventh Census of the United States* (1890), *Manufacturing Industries* (Washington, 1895), Part III, 168, 172.

5 Preston W. Slosson, *The Great Crusade and After, 1914–1928* (New York, 1931), 262–63, 265; Ida M. Tarbell, *The Nationalizing of Business, 1878–1898* (New York, 1936), 270, 281.

6 A comparison of the number of cities of 25,000 and over in the South

Atlantic and South Central regions in 1900 with the number in 1940 shows an increase from 29 to 67. The failure of the earlier census to separate the Southwest from the West renders it impossible to include the cities west of the Mississippi River. More striking than the growth of the larger cities in the four decades is the number of southern cities which sprang into existence by 1940, such as Chattanooga, Jacksonville, Miami, Houston—places which had been mere towns forty years earlier. See *Twelfth Census of the United States (1900), Population* (Washington, 1901), Part I, lxvii, 1x; *Sixteenth Census of the United States (1940), Population* (Washington, 1942), Part I, 28, 32.

7 H. M. Douty, "Development of Trade Unionism in the South," *Monthly Labor Review,* LXIII (1946), 555, 557, 566, 570–71, 575–77.

8 Some government employees founded the Grange, which enjoyed an outstanding growth from 1871 to 1874, at which latter date it numbered almost 15,000 local granges with a membership of 1,500,000. Allan Nevins, *The Emergence of Modern America, 1865–1878* (New York, 1927), 168–77; Solon J. Buck, *The Agrarian Crusade; A Chronicle of the Farmer in Politics* (New Haven, 1920), chaps. iii, vi, viii, x. John D. Hicks gives a lower total membership but a larger number of local granges —800,000 and 20,000 respectively. See his "The Granger Movement," James Truslow Adams (ed.), *Dictionary of American History* (5 vols.; New York, 1942), II, 410.

9 Tarbell, *Nationalizing of Business,* 135–45.

10 *Farmers in a Changing World—A Summary* (United States Department of Agriculture, Yearbook Separate No. 1727 [Washington, 1941]), 7, 23, 70, 77.

11 According to a recent pamphlet issued by the Department of Agriculture, the exact number is 681,790. See Foreward by Secretary Claude R. Wickard, in *Negro Farmers in Wartime Food Production* (Washington, 1943), 1. For the migration of the Negro, see Slosson, *Great Crusade and After,* 253–59. For a specific case of race rioting in Chicago, see *The Christian Century,* LXI (May 31, 1944), 672.

12 Marion Talbot and Lois Mathews Rosenberry, *The History of the American Association of University Women, 1881–1931* (Boston, 1931), chaps. i, v.

13 See Mark Mohler, "The Episcopal Church and Reconciliation," *Political Science Quarterly,* XLI (1926), 571–82. Bishop Perkins of Vermont was the presiding bishop.

14 "An Epochal Conference," *Christian Century,* LV (April 20, 1938), 488, and "Methodists Unite," *ibid.,* LV (May 11, 1938), 583–86.

15 For the episode at Decorah and Ossian, Iowa, see *Emigranten* (La Crosse, Wis., 1859–64), June 22, 1861.

16 Wood Gray, *The Hidden Civil War; The Story of the Copperheads* (New York, 1942).

17 Richmond *Examiner,* April 3, 1864.

18 Mattson's statement appears in a long letter to his wife, dated Fort Snelling, October 3, 1861, in the Hans Mattson Papers (Minnesota Historical Society, St. Paul). The letters of Colonel Heg have been translated. See Theodore C. Blegen (ed.), *The Civil War Letters of Colonel Hans Christian Heg* (Northfield, Minn., 1936).

19   "Address of Paul F. Rohrbacher," *Pennsylvania at Gettysburg* (2 vols.; Harrisburg, 1893), I, 405.
20   In a letter from a soldier in the Fifteenth Wisconsin Regiment ("The Scandinavian Regiment") to the editor of *Emigranten*, sent from Camp Randall in Wisconsin and appearing in the issue of that Norwegian paper of December 23, 1861.
21   The quotation from the Swiss officer is found in Rudolf Aschmann, *Drei Jahre in der Potomac-Armee; oder, Eine Schweize Schützen-Compagnie im Nordamerikanischen Kriege* (Richtersweil, Switzerland, 1865), Introduction, iii.
22   Wilhelm Kaufmann, *Die Deutschen im Amerikanischen Bürgerkriege* (München, 1911), 493.
23   Francis Marshal [Pierce], *The Battle of Gettysburg* (New York, 1914), 37-39. He claims that the two forces in these fifty battles were within two per cent of being equal.
24   Mary A. Gay, *Life in Dixie during the War* (Atlanta, 1894), 119–23, 135–45. Miss Gay clearly felt guilty because she had had to press the boy on when he complained of feeling ill. She had taken some trunks of bedding, glass, and china to Atlanta to a friend for safe-keeping. At the close of the day when she found the railroad connection to her home at Decatur cut by the raid, she felt obliged to walk the six miles to Decatur because she knew that her mother would be worrying over the delayed return.
25   Buck, *Road to Reunion*, 128.
26   Morris Schaff, *The Battle of the Wilderness* (Boston, 1910), 89–90. See also, Morris Schaff, *The Sunset of the Confederacy* (Boston, 1912), 168, 265–75; and *Personal Memoirs of U. S. Grant* (2 vols.; New York, 1885–86), II, 479–80, 483–95.
27   Buck, *Road to Reunion*, 255.

CHAPTER XIII   THOMAS D. CLARK

1   The figures quoted above are taken from *Pettingill's Newspaper Directory and Advertisers' Handbook*, for 1868 and 1885, and from *Ayer's American Newspaper Annual and Directory*, for the year 1929. Listing of papers in each volume is alphabetical by states.
2   John D. Allen, "Journalism in the South," William T. Couch (ed.), *Culture in the South* (Chapel Hill, 1934), 153–58.
3   Elmo Scott Watson, *A History of Newspaper Syndicates in the United States, 1865–1935* (Chicago, 1936), 5, 7–13.
4   Organizations of both new counties and new papers accounted for this fact. A good example of shrinking newspaper territory is the history of the Stanford (Ky.) *Interior Journal*. This paper once served nine Kentucky counties.
5   W. P. Walton, editor of the Stanford *Interior Journal*, January 21, 1876.
6   Much of this editorial matter was quoted in home-set editorials, but more of it was supplied by the syndicated pages. This was perhaps the most valid service rendered by the "patent sides" features.
7   Forest *Register*, February 11, 1871.
8   Butler (Ala.) *Choctaw Herald*, April 16, 1885.

9   Winnsboro (S. C.) *News and Herald,* June 30, 1887; Ackerman (Miss.) *Choctaw Plaindealer,* February 24, 1893, quoting the Baltimore *Sun.*

10 Greensboro (Ga.) *Herald,* January 21, 1869; Abbeville (S. C.) *Press and Banner,* December 24, 1869; Yorkville (S. C.) *Enquirer,* July 13, 1882; Dalton *North Georgia Times,* February 5, 1885; and Fayetteville (N. C.) *Observer,* December 6, 1888.

11 Sparta (Ga.) *Ishmaelite,* April 20, 1881.

12 Characteristic of these letters were those from "Beeswax" to the Sandersville (Ga.) *Herald,* September 25, 1874; "J. L. S." to the Greensboro *Herald,* March 15, June 1, August 10, September 14, and December 7, 1882; R. G. Hammill to the Louisville (Miss.) *Winston County Journal,* May 26, 1905; and James D. McClean to *Our Southern Home* (Livingston, Ala.), August 20, 1902.

13 "Exoduster" stories appeared in nearly all southern papers from 1870 to 1918. Some of the more exciting were those which appeared in Georgia weeklies describing the activities of R. A. ("Pegleg") Williams. Greensboro *Herald,* December 22, 1899, January 19, 1900. Other accounts of Negro migrations: Newberry (S. C.) *Herald and News,* February 21, 1889, January 2, 1890; Athens (Tenn.) *Post,* January 30, 1874; Abbeville (S. C.) *Medium,* March 3, 1880, January 5, 1882; Fayetteville *Obesrver,* June 24, 1889, October 3, 1889; Pittsboro (N. C.) *Chatham Record,* April 17, 1879; and Hazlehurst (Miss.) *Weekly Copiahan,* February 14, 1880.

14 Characteristic stories of this type are to be found in the Yorkville *Enquirer,* October 28, 1881; Troy (Ala.) *Messenger,* January 12, 1882; and Sparta *Ishmaelite,* January 4, 1882.

15 Marietta (Ga.) *Journal,* December 15, 1881.

16 *Ibid.*

17 Newberry *Herald and News,* December 19, 1886, and Fayette (Miss.) *Chronicle,* January 14, 1887.

18 Toccoa *News,* September 8, 1882.

19 Characteristic arguments on this subject are to be found in the Marietta *Journal,* June 22, 1882; Pittsboro *Chatham Record,* January 30, 1882; Fayette *Chronicle,* May 4, 1894; Greensboro *Herald,* September 9, 1875; Eufaula (Ala.) *Times and News,* February 3, 1881; Selma (Ala.) *Southern Argus,* December 1, 1869; and Yorkville *Enquirer,* July 6, 1876.

20 Calhoun (Ga.) *Times,* January 6, 1887; *Our Southern Home,* November 20, 1901; Abbeville *Press and Banner,* April 1, 1883; Marietta *Journal,* February 9, 1882; Pittsboro *Chatham Record,* July 3, December 5, 1879; and Fayetteville *Observer,* August 28, 1881.

21 Pulaski *Citizen,* December 7, 1882.

22 Elberton *New South,* March 1, 1881.

23 *Ibid.*

24 *Ibid.*

25 Greensboro *Herald,* October 5, 1900.

26 Fayetteville *Observer,* February 7, 1889.

27 Yorkville *Enquirer,* May 8, 1884.

28 Winnsboro *News and Herald,* March 10, 1887.

29 Macon (Miss.) *Beacon,* August 27, 1892.

30   Troy *Messenger,* March 2, 1882.
31   Eufaula *Times and News,* July 17, 1888.
32   Fayette *Chronicle,* July 8, 1887.
33   Ellaville (Ga.) *Schley County News,* April 22, 1897.
34   Hartford (Ky.) *Herald,* August 27, September 10, 19, October 22, 1881.
35   Marietta *Journal,* March 23, 1882.
36   *Ibid.,* November 3, 1881; Stanford *Interior Journal,* February 11, 1876.
37   Gibson *Enterprise,* January 17, 1884.
38   Elberton (Ga.) *Gazette,* March 12, 1879.
39   Ackerman *Choctaw Plaindealer,* February 3, 1888.
40   *South Carolina Statutes at Large* (Columbia, 1902), No. 590, p. 1093.
41   Quoted by the Edgefield (S. C.) *Chronicle,* July 22, 1902.
42   Lynching stories were too numerous to be cited in any significant body
     of material in so brief a space, but the following references reflect varied
     editorial attitudes: Sparta *Ishmaelite,* August 31, 1906; Ellaville *Schley
     County News,* April 27, 1899; Louisville *Winston County Journal,*
     March 24, 1901; Fayetteville *Observer,* September 26, 1889; and Aiken
     (S. C.) *Journal and Review,* May 7, 1890.
43   Perhaps no other social subject received more publicity in the country
     weeklies. Some revealing attitudes are to be found in the following:
     Woodville (Miss.) *Republican,* May 28, 1904; Newberry *Herald and
     News,* January 23, 1890; Winnsboro *News and Herald,* May 4, 1887;
     Forest (Miss.) *Register,* February 18, 1871; Lenoir (N. C.) *Topic,*
     February 20, 1884; Macon *Beacon,* October 15, 1881; Dalton *North
     Georgia Citizen,* July 27, 1871; and Marietta *Journal,* February 19, 1881.
44   Linden *Reporter,* June 20, 1902.
45   Quoted by Abbeville *Medium,* February 11, 1880.
46   Butler (Ala.) *Courier,* September 6, 1882; Fayette *Chronicle,* Febru-
     ary 12, 19, 1904; Linden (Ala.) *Reporter,* September 26, 1902; and
     Pulaski (Tenn.) *Citizen,* February 17, 1881.
47   Enterprise (Ala.) *Weekly Enterprise,* April 10, 1901.
48   Demopolis (Ala.) *Marengo Democrat,* October 18, 1901.
49   A pattern of this type of epithet was the reference by the Forest *Register*
     (April 21, 1872) to the Negro senator, Bob Gleed, from Lowndes
     County. He was called "flatnosed, thick-lipped, long-heeled, goat-
     scented." Adjectives were added to these for the next fifty years.
50   Characteristic of southern newspaper salutations was that which appeared
     in the Winnsboro *Herald and News* when P. M. Brice and J. O. Davis
     assumed its editorship on January 4, 1888. "The policy," they wrote,
     "will be conservative in all things. It is superfluous perhaps to state
     that it will continue in the future, as in the past, to hold steadily to the
     principles of the Democratic Party."
51   Quoted by Louisville (Miss.) *Winston County Journal,* December 12,
     1892.

CHAPTER XIV   ROBERT S. COTTERILL

1   Broadus Mitchell, *The Rise of Cotton Mills in the South (Johns Hopkins
     University Studies in Historical and Political Science,* Ser. XXXIX, No. 2
     [Baltimore, 1921]), 57.

CHAPTER XV   LESTER J. CAPPON

1 Richmond *Times-Dispatch,* May 29, 1949.
2 *The Oxford English Dictionary* (10 vols. in 14, and supplement; Oxford, 1888–1933), VII, 1523.
3 Cited in Evarts B. Greene, *The Revolutionary Generation, 1763–1790* (New York, 1943), 185–87, 300–301.
4 "Autobiography of Col. William Few of Georgia," *Magazine of American History,* VII (1881), 346.
5 John Hammond, *Leah and Rachel, or, the Two Fruitfull Sisters Virginia and Mary-Land: Their Present Condition, Impartially Stated and Related* (London, 1656), 6; Peter Force (comp.), *Tracts and Other Papers Relating Principally to the Origin, Settlement, and Progress of the Colonies in North America, from the Discovery of the Country to the Year 1776* (4 vols.; Washington, 1836–46), III, No. 14.
6 John G. W. De Brahm, "History of the Province of South Carolina," P. C. J. Weston (ed.), *Documents Connected with the History of South Carolina* (London, 1856), 196.
7 John S. Bassett (ed.), *The Writings of "Colonel William Byrd of Westover in Virginia Esqʳ."* (New York, 1901), 80, 47.
8 Daniel Fenning, *A New System of Geography* (2 vols.; London, 1764–65), II, 669.
9 Quoted in Merrill Jensen, *The Articles of Confederation: An Interpretation of the Socio-Constitutional History of the American Revolution, 1774–1781* ([Madison, Wis.], 1940), 187.
10 James Madison to Thomas Cooper, December 29, 1826, in Max Farrand (ed.), *The Records of the Federal Convention of 1787* (rev. ed., 4 vols.; New Haven, 1937), III, 474.
11 Madison to J. G. Jackson, December 27, 1821, *ibid.,* III, 449.
12 Adrienne Koch and Harry Ammon, "The Virginia and Kentucky Resolutions: An Episode in Jefferson's and Madison's Defense of Civil Liberties," *William and Mary Quarterly,* 3rd Ser., V (1948), 174.
13 Ulrich B. Phillips, "The South Carolina Federalists," *American Historical Review,* XIV (1908–1909), 731–43.
14 Nathaniel H. Claiborne, *Notes on the War in the South* (Richmond, 1819), 6, 12, 16; originally printed in *The Crisis,* no copy located.
15 Richard H. Shryock, "The Nationalistic Tradition of the Civil War: A Southern Analysis," *South Atlantic Quarterly,* XXXII (1933), 299.
16 B. B. Kendrick, "The Colonial Status of the South," *Journal of Southern History,* VIII (1942), 9–15.
17 For example, Winston Churchill's entertaining article, "If Lee Had Not Won the Battle of Gettysburg," *Scribner's Magazine,* LXXXVIII (1930), 587–97.
18 Frank H. Norton (ed.), *Journal Kept by Hugh Finlay, Surveyor of the Post Roads on the Continent of North America* [1773–74] (Brooklyn, 1867), 62.
19 "We were quite cloy'd with the Carolina Felicity of having nothing to do," wrote Byrd in his "History of the Dividing Line," Bassett (ed.), *Writings,* 81.

20   Worthington C. Ford (ed.), *Thomas Jefferson Correspondence, Printed from the Originals in the Collections of William K. Bixby* (Boston, 1916), 12–13. See also the characterizations in Charles Stedman, *The History of the Origin, Progress, and Termination of the American War* (2 vols.; London, 1794), I, 5.

21   Joseph G. Baldwin, *The Flush Times of Alabama and Mississippi* (New York, 1853), 73. Some present-day Virginians refer to southwestern Virginia as "the Southwest."

22   Edward A. Freeman, "Some Points in American Speech and Customs," *Longman's Magazine,* I (1882), 89.

23   Robert G. Albion, *Square-Riggers on Schedule: The New York Sailing Packets to England, France, and the Cotton Ports* (Princeton, 1938), chap. iii.

24   *Minutes of the Proceedings of the Second Convention of Merchants and Others, Held in Augusta, Georgia, April 2d, 1838* (Augusta, 1838), 16.

25   Lester J. Cappon, "Government and Private Industry in the Southern Confederacy," *Humanistic Studies in Honor of John Calvin Metcalf* (University of Virginia *Studies,* I [Charlottesville, 1941]), 156–58.

26   Charles S. Sydnor, *The Development of Southern Sectionalism, 1819–1848* (Baton Rouge, 1948), chap. xii, has an excellent discussion of political democracy.

27   Clement Eaton, *Freedom of Thought in the Old South* (Durham, 1940), chap. viii.

28   "Diary of Edward Hooker," American Historical Association, *Annual Report,* 1896 (2 vols.; Washington, 1897), I, 895.

29   M. M. Mason, *The Southern First Class Book ...* (Macon, 1839), iii.

30   Thomas P. Lockwood, *A Geography of South Carolina, Adapted to the Use of Schools and Families ...* (Charleston, 1832), 129.

31   "The Question of the Hour," *Atlantic Monthly,* VII (1861), 120.

32   William C. Rives (ed.), *Journal of an Exploration in the Spring of the Year 1750, by Dr. Thomas Walker* (Boston, 1888), 11.

33   [William Gilmore Simms] *South-Carolina in the Revolutionary War ... by a Southron* (Charleston, 1853), 11.

34   Edward Ingle, *Southern Sidelights* (New York [1896]), 4.

35   Mildred Lewis Rutherford (ed.), *Miss Rutherford's Scrap Book, Valuable Information about the South,* I, No. 2 (February, 1923), 17–20, 23–24, I, No. 3 (March, 1923), 16–18, I, No. 4 (April, 1923), facing p. 1, I, No. 7 (July, 1923), 16. It also contained commercial advertisements—"only such as can heartily be endorsed," for example, White Rock Spring Water and Azalea Hills real estate.

CHAPTER XVI   WILLIAM C. BINKLEY

1   "Paths to the Past: The Presidential Addresses of the Southern Historical Association," *Journal of Southern History,* XVI (1950), 33–39.

2   "Research Possibilities in Southern History," *ibid.,* XVI (1950), 54–63.

3   "The 'Turner Theories' and the South," *ibid.,* V (1939), 296–97.

4   Frederic L. Paxson, *When the West Is Gone* (New York, 1930), 63–65, 79.

5   Nathaniel W. Stephenson, "An Illustration of the Frontier as Seed Bed,"

Proceedings of the Pacific Coast Branch of the American Historical Association, 1928 ([Washington, 1929]), 57–58.

6 These figures are derived from the statistics on distribution of free native population, in *Eighth Census of the United States, 1860: Population* (Washington, 1864), 616–19.

7 "The Natural Limits of Slavery Expansion," *Mississippi Valley Historical Review*, XVI (1929–30), 151–71.

8 "The Westward Flow of Southern Colonists before 1861," *Journal of Southern History*, IX (1943), 327.

9 See, for example, Hubert Howe Bancroft, *History of California* (7 vols.; San Francisco, 1884–90), VI, 722–39, and Jeremiah Lynch, *A Senator of the Fifties: David C. Broderick of California* (San Francisco, 1911). Information on the other side of the story appears in "Memoirs of William M. Gwin" (MS in Bancroft Library, University of California).

10 It should perhaps be noted that these percentages are of the total inhabitants, including those born in the region, while the ones appearing earlier in this paper refer only to those migrating into the region from the eastern states.

11 Bancroft, *History of California*, VI, 282–96. An excellent critical discussion of Bancroft's treatment of the boundary question is in Cardinal Goodwin, *The Establishment of State Government in California, 1846–1850* (New York, 1914), 136–74. For the official journal, see J. Ross Browne, *Report of the Debates in the Convention of California, on the Formation of the State Constitution, in September and October, 1849* (Washington, 1850).

12 Stewart H. Holbrook, *The Yankee Exodus: An Account of Migration from New England* (New York, 1950). The quotation is from the jacket.

13 See, especially, William D. Armes (ed.), *The Autobiography of Joseph LeConte* (New York, 1903).

14 The information on Mrs. Jackson's visit appears in an obituary notice of Couts's grandson, in Carlsbad (Calif.) *Journal*, September 2, 1948 (clipping in Bancroft Library). For typical comments on his hospitality and his activities, see Benjamin Hayes, "Emigrant Notes" (MS in Bancroft Library), 502, 554, and correspondence between Benjamin D. Wilson and Couts in Benjamin D. Wilson Papers (Huntington Library).

15 This statement is based on an examination of approximately a thousand manuscript "Dictations" obtained in the 1880's by the agents of Hubert Howe Bancroft in interviews with prominent individuals throughout the Far West to be used in the writing of his history. They now constitute part of a collection in the Bancroft Library designated as Biographical and Reference Notes.

CHAPTER XVII   AVERY CRAVEN

1 Kenneth M. Stampp, *And the War Came: The North and the Secession Crisis, 1860–1861* (Baton Rouge, 1950), 160.

CHAPTER XVIII   C. VANN WOODWARD

1 Recent examples are the admission of the Post Office Department that it is burning tracts mailed from the Iron Curtain countries, and the action

of port authorities in excluding alien seamen for political reasons in enforcing new immigration laws. Both instances, of course, suggest antebellum counterparts.

2   This was written in October, 1952.

CHAPTER XIX   KATHRYN ABBEY HANNA

1   Alexis de Tocqueville, *Democracy in America* (2 vols.; New York, 1841), I, 471.
2   Memorial of Baron Charles Dupin to Napoleon III, November 9, 1863, No. 18 (Memoires et Documents, Ministere des Affaires Etrangères, [Mexique]), X.
3   "Plan for the Regeneration of Mexico," sent with letter of October 4, 1856, by Aimé Louis Victor de Bosc, Marquis de Radepont to Alexandre, Comte Walewski (Correspondance Politique, Mexique, Vol. 46).
4   Napoleon III to Radepont, September 4, 1864, in Radepont Papers (Harvard University Library), No. 15.
5   Edouard Thouvenel to Dubois de Saligny, April 11, 1861, Confidential (Correspondance Politique, Mexique, Vol. 54).
6   Thouvenel to Auguste Charles Joseph, Comte de Flahaut, October 11, 1861 (Correspondance Politique, Angleterre, Vol. 720); Thouvenel to Adolphe Barrot, April 22, 1862 (Correspondance Politique, Espagne, Vol. 860).
7   Aynard de Clermont-Tonnerre to Radepont, August, 1862, Radepont Papers, No. 13.
8   Thouvenel to Edouard Henri, Baron Mercier, October 30, November 6, 13, 1862 (Correspondance Politique, Etats-Unis, Vol. 128).
9   (Correspondance Politique, Mexique, Vol. 60.)
10 B. Theron to Governor F. R. Lubbock, August 10, 1862 (Correspondance Politique des Consuls, Etats-Unis, Vol. 14).
11 Lubbock to Theron, September 9, 1862, *ibid.*
12 Alfred Paul to Edouard Drouyn de Lhuys, December 12, 1862, *ibid.*, (Vol. 12).
13 Judah P. Benjamin to John Slidell, October 17, 1862, in *Official Records of the Union and Confederate Navies in the War of the Rebellion* (30 vols., Washington, 1894–1922), Ser. II, Vol. III, 556.
14 Jurien de la Gravière to Thouvenel, December 9, 1861 (Correspondance Politique, Mexique, Vol. 57).
15 Napoleon III to General Elie Frédéric Forey, July 3, 1862 (Memoires et Documents, Mexique, Vol. 10). Signed Napoleon III, this letter is marked "corrected for the Yellow Book" and contains the corrections therefor.
16 Richmond *Enquirer*, February 6, 1863.
17 Charles Wyke to Stefan Herzfeld, November 27, 1863, in Archiv Kaiser Maximilian (Wiener Staats Archiv) quoted in Egon Corti, *Maximilian and Charlotte of Mexico* (2 vols.; New York, 1928), I, 289.
18 William L. Dayton to William H. Seward, September 7, 1863, Confidential (Dispatches National Archives, Washington, France, Vol. 53).
19 Seward to Dayton, September 26, 1863 (Instructions, National Archives, Washington, France, Vol. 17).

20 Mercier to Drouyn de Lhuys, September 14, 1863 (Correspondance Politique, Etats-Unis, Vol. 130).

21 Dayton to Seward, March 21, 1864 (Dispatches, France, Vol. 54).

22 *Ibid.*

23 Mathew F. Maury to Maximilian, November 11, 25, 1863, Archiv Kaiser Maximilian (Wiener Staats Archiv).

24 Daniel Dawson, *The Mexican Adventure* (London, 1935), 336.

25 James M. Mason to Benjamin, March 16, 1864, in *Official Records, Navies,* Ser. II, Vol. III, 1048.

26 Charles, Marquis de Montholon to Drouyn de Lhuys, June 28, 1864 (Correspondance Politique, Mexique, Vol. 62).

27 Commission to Preston, Benjamin to Henry Preston, January 7, 1864, *Official Records, Navies,* Ser. II, Vol. III, 154.

28 Captain Walker Fearn to Benjamin, June 30, 1864 (Diplomatic Correspondence, Confederate States of America, Manuscripts Division, Library of Congress).

29 Resolution of Henry S. Foote, November 28, 1864, in "Journal of the Congress of the Confederate States of America," *Senate Documents,* 58 Cong., 2 Sess., No. 234 (Serial Nos. 4610–4616), Vol. 7, p. 308.

30 Drouyn de Lhuys to Montholon, November 29, 1864 (Correspondance Politique, Mexique, Vol. 62).

31 Matias Romero to Minister of Foreign Affairs, January 10, February 4, 21, 1865, in *Correspondencia de la Legacion Mexicana en Washington ...1860–1868* (10 vols.; Mexico City, 1870–92), V; John Bigelow, Diary, October 14, 1866–April 16, 1867, in Bigelow Papers (New York Public Library), entry of March 2, 1867; John G. Nicolay and John Hay, "Abraham Lincoln: A History, Blair's Mexican Project; the Hampton Roads Conference," *Century Magazine,* XVI (1889), 838–51.

32 General François Achille Bazaine to Maréchal Randon, April 28, 1865 (Correspondance du Général en Chef avec le Ministre de la Guerre (Archives Historiques, Ministère de la Guerre).

33 Drouyn de Lhuys to Alphonse Dano, August 21, 1865 (Correspondance Politique, Mexique, Vol. 64).

34 Ministre de la Guerre to Drouyn de Lhuys, September 29, 1865, *ibid.*

35 Dano to Drouyn de Lhuys, June 11, 1865, *ibid.* (Vol. 63).

36 Drouyn de Lhuys to Dano, August 16, 1865, *ibid.* (Vol. 64).

37 Drouyn de Lhuys to Dano, July 15, 1865, *ibid.*

38 Imperial Decree of September 5, 1865, *Diario del Imperio* (Mexico City), September 9, 1865.

39 Maury to Mrs. Maury, September 12, 1865, in Maury Papers (Manuscripts Division, Library of Congress, Vol. 23).

40 Romero to Seward, October 5, 1865, in Relaciones Exteriores de México (Archivo General de Relaciones Exteriores, Mexico City), Legajo 10–21–33.

41 Begelow to Seward, November 5, 1865 (Dispatches, France Vol. 59).

42 Dano to Drouyn de Lhuys, September 29, 1865 (Correspondance Politique, Mexique, Vol. 64).

43 Dano to Drouyn de Lhuys, January 28, 1866, *ibid.* (Vol. 66).

44   Maximilian to Maury, April 19, 1866, in Maury Papers (Vol. 25).
45   Maury to S. Wellford Corbin, October 21, 1865, *ibid.* (Vol. 23).

CHAPTER XXI   BELL IRVIN WILEY

1   *R. E. Lee* (4 vols.; New York, 1934–1935), I, viii.
2   Statement of Freeman to the writer, January 15, 1933.
3   Bell Irvin Wiley, *The Life of Johnny Reb: The Common Soldier of the Confederacy* (Indianapolis, 1943), 313, and *The Life of Billy Yank: The Common Soldier of the Union* (Indianapolis, 1952), 349–50.
4   J. B. Lance to his father, November 10, 1861, in Lance Letters (Louisiana State University).
5   Wiley, *Life of Johnny Reb,* 340; *Life of Billy Yank,* 312–23.
6   *General Order No. 5,* Headquarters Department of the Tennessee, Jackson, Tennessee, November 4, 1862, in Adjutant General's Office Records (National Archives).
7   Mrs. Alfred W. Bell to her husband, September 5, 1862, in Bell Letters (Duke University).
8   William R. Stilwell to his wife, April 28, 1863, in Stilwell Letters (Georgia State Department of Archives).
9   J. W. Gaskill, *Footprints Through Dixie: Everyday Life of the Man under a Musket* (Alliance, Ohio, 1919), 186; William B. Johnson, *Union to the Hub and Twice around the Tire: Reminiscences of William Benjamin Johnson* (n.p., n.d.), 17.
10   Chattanooga *Daily Gazette,* March 6, 1864.
11   New York *Herald,* March 8, 1863.
12   W. C. Jackson to Dudley Tillison, April 27, 1863, in Charles Tillison Letters (Vermont Historical Society).
13   Gaskill, *Footprints through Dixie,* 154.
14   Wiley, *Life of Johnny Reb,* 162–63, 345–46; *Life of Billy Yank,* 171–72.
15   Sam Watkins, *"Co. Aytch," Maury Grays, First Tennessee Regiment; or a Side Show of the Big Show* (Jackson, Tenn., 1952), 114.
16   R. H. McKim, *A Soldier's Recollections* (New York, 1910), 37.
17   Donald Gordon (ed.), *M. L. Gordon's Experiences in the Civil War* (Boston, 1922), 34.
18   Martha A. Sloan to Nancy J. Melton, undated but about 1863 (Hench Collection, University of Virginia).
19   William Hamilton to his mother, December 24, 1862, in William Hamilton Letters (Library of Congress).
20   Joseph H. Diltz to his father, October 10, 1862, in Diltz Letters (Duke University).
21   J. C. McLaughlin to his sister, August 15, 1864 (Hench Collection).
22   James K. Wilkerson to his sister, August 29, 1864, in Wilkerson Letters (Duke University).
23   Henry Converse to his brother, March 21, 1863, in Converse Letters (American Antiquarian Society).
24   J. M. Guess to his wife, undated but 1862, (Miscellaneous Collection, Confederate Memorial Hall, New Orleans).

25 Spencer G. Welch, *A Confederate Surgeon's Letters to his Wife* (New York, 1911), 121; John Rogers to his brother, June 24, 1861, in Miscellaneous Confederate Letters (Emory University); J. W. Anderson to his mother, January 21, 1862, *ibid.*

26 James Rich to his wife, undated but 1863 (typescript in possession of Dr. A. M. Giddings, Battle Creek, Michigan); Michael R. Dresbach to his wife, August 22, 1864, in Dresbach Letters (Minnesota Historical Society).

27 Charles Babbott to his father, January 1, 1863, in Babbott Letters (Hayes Memorial Library, Fremont, Ohio).

28 Seth H. Cook to Curtis Babbott, December 10, 1862, *ibid.*

29 Robert W. Rickard to Simon Rickard, August 14, 1863, in Rickard Letters (Illinois State Historical Library); Felix Brannigan to his sister, May 15, 1862 in Brannigan Letters (Library of Congress).

30 W. W. Heartsill, *Fourteen Hundred and 91 Days in the Confederate Army* ... (Jackson, Tenn., 1954), 154.

31 Felix Brannigan to his sister, May 15, 1862, in Brannigan Letters; unidentified Pennsylvania private to his father, September 11, 1861 (in private possession).

32 Robert L. Partin (ed.), "An Alabama Confederate Soldier's Report to his Wife," *Alabama Review,* III (1950), 29; P. L. Dodgen to his wife, May 17, 1863, in Dodgen Letters (typescript, Georgia State Department of Archives).

33 Wiley, *Life of Billy Yank,* 239–40.

34 *Ibid.,* 237.

35 *Ibid.*

36 Charles A. Barker to his mother, August 2, 1863, in Barker Letters (Essex Institute, Salem, Massachusetts); Samuel Storrow to his parents, November 26, 1862, in Storrow Letters (Massachusetts Historical Society).

37 Partin, "An Alabama Confederate Soldier's Letters to his Wife," *Alabama Review,* 32.

38 W. C. McClellan to his brother, November 9, 1861 (in private possession).

39 James Hayes to his wife, January 20, 1863, in Hayes Letters (typescripts, Georgia State Department of Archives).

40 Charles A. Barker to his homefolk, March 30, 1862, and August 17, 1863, in Barker Letters.

41 George Gray Hunter to his brother, February 20, 1864 (in possession of William A. Hunter, Harrisburg, Pa.).

42 John Hope Franklin (ed.), *The Civil War Diary of James T. Ayers* (Springfield, Ill., 1947), 34.

43 "A Badger Boy in Blue: The Letters of Chauncey H. Cooke," *Wisconsin Magazine of History,* IV (1920–21), 323.

44 William R. Stilwell to his wife, September [no day], 1862, in Stilwell Letters.

45 J. B. Sanders to his wife, March 18, 1864, in Sanders Papers (Mississippi State Department of Archives and History).

46 William L. Nugent to his wife, January 22, 1864 (typescript in private possession).

47   Heartsill, *Fourteen Hundred and 91 Days,* 186.
48   "Letters of Privates Cook and Ball," *Indiana Magazine of History,* XXVII (1931), 247, 251, 260–61.
49   Christian Kuhl to Mrs. C. A. Beattie, April 19, August 28, 1864 (Hench Collection).
50   Wiley, *Life of Billy Yank,* 185.
51   Wiley, *Life of Johnny Reb,* 203.
52   Hiram T. Holt to his wife, May 10, 1863, in Holt Letters (typescripts in possession of Professor Robert L. Partin, Alabama Polytechnic Institute).
53   W. A. Roberts to his wife, December 5, 1863, in Roberts Letters (Duke University).
54   William R. Stilwell to his wife, May 9, 1863, in Stilwell Letters.
55   J. M. Estis to his son, November 22, 1864 (Hench Collection).
56   "A Badger Boy in Blue: The Letters of Chauncey H. Cooke," 333–34.
57   E. K. Flournoy to his wife, March 21, 1863, in Flournoy Letters (Alabama State Department of Archives and History).
58   Ruth A. Gallaher (ed.), "Peter Wilson in the Civil War," *Iowa Journal of History and Politics,* XL (1942), 269.
59   S. G. Pryor to his wife, October 6, 1861, in Pryor Letters (typescripts, Georgia Department of Archives).
60   W. O. Lyford to his father, July 22, 1861, in Lyford Letters (in possession of Charles N. Owen, Glencoe, Ill.).
61   James A. McCord to his brother, December 3, 1864 (in possession of Colonel Thomas Spencer, Atlanta, Ga.).
62   Lucille Griffith (ed.), *Yours Till Death: Civil War Letters of John W. Cotton* (Tuscaloosa, 1951), 65.
63   Enoch L. Mitchell (ed.), "Letters of A Confederate Surgeon of the Army of Tennessee to his Wife," *Tennessee Historical Quarterly,* V (1946), 167.
64   Charles L. Stephens to Amelia Stephens, March 5, 1865, in Stephens Letters (in possession of Mrs. Addie Stephens, Cedar Bluff, Miss.).
65   James McLure to Governor Zebulon Vance, June 16, 1863 (typescript in possession of Professor Hugh Lefler, University of North Carolina).
66   Weymouth T. Jordan (ed.), "Matthew Andrew Dunn Letters," *Journal of Mississippi History,* I (1939), 115.
67   Ed G. Higgaron to his mother, May 29, 1864 (in possession of Miss Louise Baker, Aberdeen, Miss.).
68   Micajah J. Martin to Joseph T. Martin, May 8, 1863, *Virginia Magazine of History and Biography,* XXXVII (1929), 228.
69   George D. Harmon (ed.), "The Military Experiences of James A. Peifer, 1861–1865," *North Carolina Historical Review,* XXXII (1955), 409.
70   Bell Irvin Wiley (ed.), *Confederate Letters of John W. Hagan* (Athens, Ga., 1954), 28.
71   *Ibid.,* 35–53.
72   "Letters of Amory K. Allen," *Indiana Magazine of History,* XXXI (1935), 364.
73   Samuel W. Croft to his sister, September 16, 1861, in Croft Letters (typescripts, Washington and Jefferson College).

74 *Id.* to *id.,* various dates, 1861–63; W. R. Botsford to David Croft, July 19, 1863, *ibid.*
75 Edmund English to his mother, January 18, 1862, in English Letters (Henry E. Huntington Library).
76 *Id.* to *id.,* April 12, 1863.
77 *Id.* to *id.,* various dates, 1863–65.
78 "Correspondence of Ira Butterfield," *North Dakota Historical Quarterly,* III (1929), 141.
79 Sebron Sneed to his wife, June 7, 1864, in Sneed Letters (University of Texas).
80 Lucille Griffith (ed.), "Mrs. Juliet Opie Hopkins and Alabama Military Hospitals," *Alabama Review,* VI (1953), 111.
81 The experiences of Confederate women are treated in detail in Francis B. Simkins and James W. Patton, *The Women of the Confederacy* (Richmond, Va., 1936); Mary Elizabeth Massey, *Ersatz in the Confederacy* (Columbia, S. C., 1952); and Bell Irvin Wiley, *The Plain People of the Confederacy* (Baton Rouge, 1943).
82 Mrs. William A. Hammer to her husband, November 20, 1864 (Hench Collection).
83 Heartsill, *Fourteen Hundred and 91 Days,* 222.
84 C. D. Smith to Zebulon Vance, May 4, 1863 (typescript in possession of Professor Hugh Lefler, University of North Carolina).
85 Katherine M. Jones, *Heroines of Dixie* (Indianapolis, 1955).
86 William B. Johnson, *Union to the Hub and Twice around the Tire,* 51.
87 William F. Fox, *Regimental Losses in the American Civil War, 1861–1865* (Albany, N. Y., 1889), 37.
88 *Ibid.,* 26, 36, 402, 556–58.
89 *Ibid.,* 26, 36–37, 556–57. Fox lists sixty-three Union and fifty-two Confederate regiments suffering losses of more than 50 per cent in a single engagement.
90 Wiley, *Life of Billy Yank,* 361. Thomas L. Livermore in *Days and Events* (Boston, 1920), 302, tells of another instance, at Mine Run, of Federal soldiers pinning names and addresses on their uniforms in anticipation of a bloody battle.
91 For instances of heroism, see Wiley, *Life of Johnny Reb,* 80–83; *Life of Billy Yank,* 91–94.
92 *The War of the Rebellion: A Compilation of the Official Records of the Union and Confederate Armies* (129 vols. and index, Washington, 1880–1901), Ser. I, Vol. XX, Pt. 1, p. 867; cited hereinafter as *Official Records,* all citations to Series I unless otherwise noted.
93 *Ibid.,* Vol. XI, Pt. 1, pp. 732–33.
94 Joseph C. Stiles to his daughter, September 30, 1862, in Brock Papers (Henry E. Huntington Library).
95 *Official Records,* Vol. XXX, Pt. 2, p. 387.
96 *Ibid.,* Vol. XX, Pt. 1, p. 199.
97 *Ibid.,* 670–71.
98 This summary of the activities of Negroes during the war is based largely on Bell Irvin Wiley, *Southern Negroes, 1861–1865* (New Haven, 1938) and Benjamin Quarles, *The Negro in the Civil War* (Boston, 1953).

99 Zebulon Vance to F. and H. Fries, October 10, 1862, in Vance Executive Papers (North Carolina State Department of Archives and History).
100 Wiley, *Southern Negroes,* 121–25.
101 Ellison Capers to his wife, February 26, 1863, in Capers Papers (in possession of Raynor Hubbell, Griffin, Ga.).
102 C. C. Clay, Jr., to Louis T. Wigfall, August 5, 1863, in Wigfall Papers (typescripts, University of Texas).
103 Wiley, *Southern Negroes,* 122.
104 Allan Nevins, "Sandburg as Historian," *Journal of the Illinois State Historical Society,* XLV (1952), 362.
105 Davis' deficiencies in public relations are treated in the writer's *The Road to Appomattox* (Memphis, 1956).

CHAPTER XXII   JAMES W. PATTON

1 Frederick Law Olmstead, *A Journey Through Texas* (New York, 1859), 1.
2 *A Journey in the Back Country* (2 vols.; New York, 1907), I, 205, II, 231.
3 Broadus Mitchell, *Frederick Law Olmsted, A Critic of the Old South* (*Johns Hopkins University Studies in Historical and Political Science,* Ser. XLII, No. 2 [Baltimore, 1924]), 68.
4 Mary Jeffreys Bethell, Diary, December 12, 1853. (Unless otherwise noted, all manuscript sources cited herein are in the Southern Historical Collection, University of North Carolina Library, Chapel Hill, North Carolina.)
5 David Gavin, Diary, October 18, 1855, and June 12, 1858.
6 John W. Brown, Diary (microfilm), August 20, 1852.
7 R. A. Edmonson to Dr. J. M. Lyle, December 21, 1857, in Lyle-Siler Papers.
8 Lucy M. Battle to William H. Battle, July 14, 1856, in Battle Family Papers.
9 Mary Jeffreys Bethell, Diary, January 5, 1855, January 12 and February 3, 1858; William S. Pettigrew, March 23, 1850, in Pettigrew Papers.
10 Mary Jeffreys Bethell, Diary, October 16, 1856.
11 Joseph Milner, Diary, March 25, 1849.
12 Julia A. Powers to her sister, June 25, 1858, in Lewis N. Whittle Papers.
13 Henry Craft, Diary, May 20, 1860.
14 *A Journey in the Back Country,* I, 145–46.
15 Mitchell King, Diary, October 5, 1856.
16 Louisa Wilson to Mrs. Julia C. Jones, June 13, 1859, in Jones Family Papers.
17 John Houston Bills, Diary, March 28, 1858.
18 *Ibid.,* May 8, 1859.
19 *Ibid.,* May 18, 1851.
20 James Roach, Diary, March 18, 1858.
21 Sarah Gayle Crawford, Diary (microfilm), May 31, 1849, in Gayle-Crawford Papers.

22 William H. Holcombe, Diary, June 4, 1855.

23 Jesse Bernard, Diary, December 26, 1858.

24 Simeon Colton, Diary, December 4, 1851.

25 A. L. Alexander to Edward Porter Alexander, September 5, 1853, in Edward Porter Alexander Papers.

26 Everard Green Baker, Diary, September 27, 1849, and Thomas Miles Garrett, Diary, June 15, 1849, respectively, expatiated on their unfavorable impressions of the Roman Catholic Church derived from reading Macaulay and Prescott.

27 Daniel A. Horn to his father and mother, June, 1850, in Daniel A. Horn Papers; Joseph B. Cottrell, Diary (microfilm), November 9, 1853; Everard G. Baker, Diary, September 27, 1849.

28 Joseph B. Cottrell, Diary, September 20, 1855; Jane Caroline North, Diary, September 5, 1853, in Pettigrew Papers.

29 Rev. John T. Wheat to his wife, June 22, 1859, in Wheat-Shober Papers.

30 Jane Caroline North, Diary, October 5, 1851, in Pettigrew Papers.

31 John W. Brown, Diary (microfilm), April 20, 1854.

32 David Gavin, Diary, November 9, 1855; E. V. Levert to F. J. Levert, March 24, 1852, in Levert Papers; James Nunn, Diary (typed copy), October 13, 1854, in Edgar W. Knight Papers.

33 Josiah Gorgas, Diary (microfilm), January 12, 1857. Gorgas actually was born in Pennsylvania, but he had married a southern wife and by this time had become identified with the southern way of life.

34 Randall L. Gibson to Hart Gibson, April 22, 1854, in Gibson-Humphreys Papers.

35 George A. Mercer, Diary, May 16, 1856.

36 Thomas Butler King to his mother, January 8, 1851, in Thomas Butler King Papers.

37 James T. Harrison to his wife, August 15, 1853, in James T. Harrison Papers.

38 Simeon Colton, Diary, May, 1858.

39 James T. Harrison to his wife, February 17, 1858, in James T. Harrison Papers.

40 [Mary Lewis?], Diary, July 4, 1857, in Lewis Papers, and Mrs. Joseph L. Locke to Mrs. William B. Bulloch, July 18, 1853, in Bulloch Papers are good examples of these two attitudes.

41 James H. Otey to Thomas Maney, July 8, 1857, in John Kimberly Papers.

42 Edmund Kirby-Smith, Diary, June, 1858.

43 *Ibid.*, May 31, 1858.

44 Kate Jones, Diary, August 14, 1851.

45 Sarah Gayle Crawford, Diary (microfilm), September 12, 1853, in Gayle-Crawford Papers.

46 *Ibid.*, October 1, 1853.

47 Henry Maney to his sister, December 26, 1851, in John Kimberly Papers.

48 William Elliott to his wife, July 31, 1855, in Elliott-Gonzales Papers.

49 *Id.* to *id.*, September 20, 1855, in *ibid.*

50 *Id.* to *id.*, August 27, 1855, in *ibid.*

51 John Houston Bills, Diary, June 27 and July 4, 1851.

52 *Ibid.*, July 13, 1851.

53 Edmund Kirby-Smith, Diary, July 9, 1858.
54 *Ibid.*, July 10, 1858.
55 Helena Kirchoff, Diary, March 28, 1851.
56 *Ibid.*, April 15, 1851.
57 Henry K. Burgwyn to his wife, October 10, 1851, in Henry K. Burgwyn Papers.
58 *Ibid.*, April 15, 1851.
59 Kate Jones, Diary, July 29, 1851.
60 William B. Crawford, Diary (microfilm), September, 1852, in Gayle-Crawford Papers.
61 Kate Jones, Diary, July 29, 1851.
62 *Ibid.*, July 22, 1851.
63 (Mobile, 1857).
64 (Charleston, 1861).
65 Pettigrew knew enough German to attend lectures at the University of Berlin. He kept diaries in both Italian and Spanish and corresponded in Italian with Jane Caroline North, who married his brother. He also knew and wrote in French.
66 James Johnston Pettigrew to William S. Pettigrew, August 11, 1850, and May 26, 1851; *id.* to James C. Johnston, August 21, 1850, in Pettigrew Papers.
67 *Id.* to James L. Petigru, March 2, 1850; and to James C. Johnston, April, 1850, in Pettigrew Papers.
68 *Id.* to Annie B. Pettigrew, June 16, 1850, in Pettigrew Papers.
69 *Id.* to William S. Pettigrew, November 20, 1850, in Pettigrew Papers.
70 *Id.* to James C. Johnston, March 15, 1851, in Pettigrew Papers.
71 *Id.* to *id.*, February 4, 1850; *id.* to William S. Pettigrew, March 1, 1850, in Pettigrew Papers.
72 *Id.* to James C. Johnston, April 2, 1851, in Pettigrew Papers.
73 *Notes on Spain and the Spaniards*, 6–16.
74 James Johnston Pettigrew to James C. Johnston, July 19, 1852, in Pettigrew Papers.

CHAPTER XXIII   ROBERT S. HENRY

1 " 'Fifty-four Forty or Fight'—An American Political Legend," *Mississippi Valley Historical Review*, XLIV (September, 1957), 291–309.

CHAPTER XXIV   WALTER B. POSEY

1 Quoted in William Meade, *Old Churches, Ministers and Families of Virginia* (2 vols.; Philadelphia, 1872), I, 166.
2 Quoted in Charles C. Tiffany, *A History of the Protestant Episcopal Church in the United States of America* (New York, 1900), 281.
3 Samuel D. McConnell, *History of the American Episcopal Church* (New York, 1890), 158.
4 Tiffany, *Episcopal Church*, 333.
5 Archibald Henderson, *Conquest of the Old Southwest* (New York, 1920), 234.

6   James Campbell to Elizabeth McDonald Campbell, November 18, 1818, in Campbell Papers (Duke University Library, Durham, N. C.).

7   John J. Jones to Daniel Shine, April 16, 1820, in Shine Papers (Duke University Library).

8   Francis Asbury, *The Journal of the Rev. Francis Asbury* ... (3 vols.; New York, 1821), II, 286.

9   Robert H. Bishop, *An Outline of the History of the Church in the State of Kentucky ... Containing the Memoirs of Rev. David Rice* (Lexington, Ky., 1824), 68.

10 *Journal of the Proceedings of the Third Convention of the Clergy and Laity of the Protestant Episcopal Church in the State of Tennessee ...* (Nashville, 1831), 12.

11 Meade, *Old Churches,* I, 30.

12 Leonard W. Bacon, *A History of American Christianity* (New York, 1921), 210.

13 Henry Caswall, *America, and the American Church* (London, 1851), 225.

14 For this and similar material, the best source is the official journals of the General Convention, published triennially.

15 James T. Addison, *The Episcopal Church in the United States, 1789–1931* (New York, 1951), 133–34.

16 *Spirit of Missions* (New York), I (1836), 82.

17 *Journal of the Fifteenth Convention ... in the Diocese of Kentucky ...* (Louisville, 1843), 13; *Journal of the Thirtieth Convention ...* (Frankfort, 1858), 35.

18 Richard Cox to William R. Whittingham, November 28, 1836; George Weller to Whittingham, December 4, 1839, August 18, 1840, in Whittingham Papers (Duke University Library).

19 William M. Green, *Memoir of Rt. Rev. James Hervey Otey* (New York, 1885), 65.

20 *Spirit of Missions,* XI (1846), 376, XIII (1848), 102, 105.

21 Green, *Otey,* 9.

22 *Journal of the Proceedings of the Twenty-Eighth Convention ... of Tennessee ...* (Columbia, Tenn., 1856), 11.

23 *Pastoral letter of the Rt. Rev. N. H. Cobbs to the Clergy and Laity of the Diocese of Alabama* (Tuscaloosa, 1849), 5.

24 George Weller to William R. Whittingham, July 25, 1841, in Whittingham Papers.

25 *Spirit of Missions,* XI (1846), 169, 382.

26 William M. Polk, *Leonidas Polk, Bishop and General* (2 vols.; New York, 1915), I, 164, 214.

27 Greenhough White, *A Saint of the Southern Church: Memoir of the Right Reverend Nicholas Hamner Cobbs* (New York, 1897), 162.

28 Polk, *Polk,* I, 140.

29 *Journal of the Proceedings of the Fifteenth Annual Convention ... of Alabama ...* (Mobile, 1846), 14.

30 *Journal of the Nineteenth Annual Convention ... in the Diocese of Georgia ...* (Columbus, Ga., 1841), 7; *Journal of ... the Twenty-Fifth Annual Convention ...* (Marietta, Ga., 1847), 13.

31 H. Richard Niebuhr, *The Social Sources of Denominationalism* (New York, 1929), 248.
32 [Samuel Wilberforce], *A History of the Protestant Episcopal Church* (New York, 1849), 304.
33 *Journal of the Fifth Annual Convention of the Diocese of Louisiana ...* (New Orleans, 1843), 8.
34 Green, *Otey*, 91.

CHAPTER XXV   T. HARRY WILLIAMS

1 It may be contended that there is some exaggeration in the above statements. Of course, any generalizations concerning the whole people of a state are subject to qualification. What I have described as the Louisiana attitude toward corruption is especially prevalent in south Louisiana, which contains, however, a substantial majority of the state's population. Some observers would argue that tolerance of corruption has been replaced in the last decade or so by a stricter view, and this may be true. Certainly today most people would say that elections have been conducted honestly—and point to voting machines as the reason.

Much of the information in this paper was obtained from interviews, many of them tape-recorded, with dozens of Huey P. Long and anti-Long leaders. Some of these men have no objection to being quoted by name, while others do object. Because of the difficulty of segregating such sources, no documentation of the interviews has been attempted. The writer is firmly convinced that the scientifically conducted interview is a valid source for the history of the recent past. Indeed, it may be the only source in a technological age when few people write letters or keep diaries.

2 Pendleton Herring, *The Politics of Democracy* (New York, 1940), 146–47.
3 Ralph Waldo Emerson, *Complete Works* (Concord ed., 12 vols; Cambridge, Mass., 1903–1904), VI, 258.
4 Roger W. Shugg, *Origins of Class Struggle in Louisiana* (Baton Rouge, 1939), 150–51.
5 W. J. Cash, *The Mind of the South* (Garden City, N. Y., 1954), 252–53, 255–56.
6 Cash, *Mind of the South*, 387–88.
7 The size of the debt is differently computed, depending on what items are included. Long claimed that he was not responsible for over $42,-000,000 in bonds issued against the Port of New Orleans under previous governors and sold as state obligations. The maturities fell due in his administration.
8 Cash, *Mind of the South*, 289.
9 Allan P. Sindler, *Huey Long's Louisiana* (Baltimore, 1956), 105.
10 Eric Hoffer, *The True Believer* (New York, 1951), 111–14, 153.
11 Hoffer, *True Believer*, 147–48.
12 Jacques Maritain, *Man and the State* (Chicago, 1951), 141.
13 Gerald W. Johnson, "Live Demagogue, or Dead Gentleman," *Virginia Quarterly Review*, XII (January, 1936), 9.

CHAPTER XXVII CLEMENT EATON

1 Woodrow Wilson to Ellen Axson, June 26, 1884, in Ray Stannard Baker, *Woodrow Wilson, Life and Letters* (8 vols.; New York, 1927–39), I, 209–10.

2 John E. Pomfret, "James Woodrow," *Dictionary of American Biography* (20 vols. and index; New York, 1928–37), XX, 495–96.

3 Charles R. Anderson and Aubrey H. Starke (eds.), *The Centennial Edition of the Works of Sidney Lanier* (10 vols.; Baltimore, 1945), VII, 19 n.

4 James Woodrow to John Kimberly, March 18, 1858, in Kimberly Papers (Southern Historical Collection, University of North Carolina, Chapel Hill).

5 *Southern Presbyterian Review*, XII (April, 1859), 182.

6 *Ibid.*, XVI (January, 1862), 14–50.

7 Marion W. Woodrow (ed.), *Dr. James Woodrow As Seen by His Friends* ... (Columbia, S. C., 1909), 508–54.

8 *Southern Presbyterian Review*, XVI (April, 1863), 549–69.

9 *Ibid.*, XXIV (July, 1873), 328–77.

10 *Ibid.*, XXIV (October, 1873), 539–86.

11 The attacks on state universities were also motivated by the jealousy of religious colleges because of state aid to such institutions. See Clement Eaton, "Edwin A. Alderman—Liberal of the New South," *North Carolina Historical Review*, XXIII (April, 1946), 206–21; Paul N. Garber, *John Carlisle Kilgo, President of Trinity College, 1894–1910* (Durham, N. C., 1937).

12 *Southern Presbyterian Review*, XXV (April, 1874), 246–91. For a discussion of the Woodrow-Dabney controversy, see Fred K. Elder, "James Woodrow," *South Atlantic Quarterly*, XLVI (October, 1947), 483–95.

13 Arney R. Childs (ed.), *The Private Journal of Henry William Ravenel, 1859–1887* (Columbia, 1947), 393.

14 Robert McAlpine, Notes on Dr. Woodrow's Lectures, October 29, 1870 —January 30, 1872, in James Woodrow Papers (South Caroliniana Library, Columbia).

15 Minutes of the Board of Directors of the Theological Seminary, Columbia, S. C. (Columbia Theological Seminary Archives, Decatur, Georgia), II, 397; hereinafter cited Minutes of the Board of Directors.

16 *Ibid.*, 421.

17 Footnote by Woodrow in John B. Adger, "Calm and Candid Review of Some Speeches on Evolution," *Southern Presbyterian Review*, XXXVI (July, 1885), 381.

18 Virginius Dabney, *Liberalism in the South* (Chapel Hill, 1932), 193–94. See also Andrew D. White, *A History of the Warfare of Science with Theology in Christendom* (2 vols.; New York, 1914), I, 129, 313–19, and Howard K. Beale, *A History of Freedom of Teaching in American Schools* (New York, 1941), 36.

19 *Southern Presbyterian Review*, XXXV (July, 1884).

20 Minutes of the Board of Directors, II, 447–49.

21 Woodrow, *Dr. James Woodrow*, 21–84.

22 John L. Girardeau, *The Substances of Two Speeches on the Teachings of Evolution in Columbia Theological Seminary* (Columbia, 1885), 1–35. See also George A. Blackburn (ed.), *The Life Work of John L. Girardeau, D.D., LL.D. . . .* (Columbia, 1916).

23 F. D. Jones and W. H. Mills, *History of the Presbyterian Church in South Carolina Since 1850* (Columbia, 1926), 175. See also William C. Robinson, *Columbia Theological Seminary and the Southern Presbyterian Church . . .* (Decatur, Ga., 1931).

24 Minutes of the Board of Directors, II, 460.

25 *Ibid.*, 469.

26 *Ibid.*, 500.

27 *Ibid.*, 505–506.

28 *Record and Evidence in the Case of the Presbyterian Church in the United States versus James Woodrow* (Columbia, 1888), 10. A copy of this scarce pamphlet is in the Yates Snowden Collection (South Caroliniana Library).

29 Minutes of the Board of Directors, II, 557–77. The Woodrow controversy seems to have injured the Seminary, for the Board reported that at the opening of the fall semester of 1887 only fourteen students registered.

30 T. Watson Street, "The Evolution Controversy in the Southern Presbyterian Church with Attention to the Theological and Ecclesiastical Issues Raised," *Journal of the Presbyterian Historical Society*, XXXVII (December, 1959), 243.

31 Minutes of the Board of Directors, II, 591–92, 601, III, 53–57, 62–68, 74.

32 Daniel W. Hollis, *University of South Carolina* (2 vols.; Columbia, 1951–56), II, 178.

33 Bert J. Loewenberg, "The Reaction of American Scientists to Darwinism," *American Historical Review*, XXXVIII (July, 1933), 687–701.

34 John S. Bassett, "Stirring up the Fires of Race Antipathy," *South Atlantic Quarterly*, II (October, 1903), 299-305.

Contributors

THOMAS PERKINS ABERNETHY (1937) retired in 1961 as Richmond Alumni Professor of History at the University of Virginia. He was born in Lowndes County, Alabama, August 25, 1890, and holds the B.A. (1912) from the College of Charleston, and the M.A. (1915) and Ph.D. (1922) from Harvard University. He is the author of *The Formative Period in Alabama* (1922), *Frontier to Plantation in Tennessee* (1932), *Western Lands and the American Revolution* (1937), *Three Virginia Frontiers* (1940), *The Burr Conspiracy* (1954), and *The South in the New Nation, 1789–1819* (1961). The last-named was awarded the Phi Beta Kappa prize by Beta of Virginia in 1961.

WILLIAM CAMPBELL BINKLEY (1950), Professor Emeritus of History, Tulane University, was Holland N. McTyeire Professor of History at Vanderbilt University when he delivered his address. He was born in Newbern, Tennessee, April 30, 1889, and holds the A.B. (1917), M.A. (1918), and Ph.D. (1920) from the University of California. His books include *The Expansionist Movement in Texas, 1836–1850* (1925), *Official Correspondence of the Texan Revolution* (2 volumes, 1936), and *The Texas Revolution* (1952). He has also served as President of the Mississippi Valley Historical Association and Managing Editor of the *Journal of Southern History* and the *Mississippi Valley Historical Review*.

LESTER JESSE CAPPON (1949), Director of the Institute of Early American History and Culture at Williamsburg, Virginia, was Book Publications Editor of the Institute at the time of his address, and previously Archivist and Associate Professor of History, University of Virginia. He was born in Milwaukee, Wisconsin, September 18, 1900, and holds the B.A. (1922) and M.A. (1923) from the University of Wisconsin, and the M.A. (1925) and Ph.D. (1928) from Harvard University. His books include *Bibliography of Virginia History Since 1865* (1930), *Virginia Newspapers, 1821–1935, A Bibliography* (1936), *Iron Works at Tuball* (1945), *Virginia Gazette Index, 1736–1780*, with Stella F. Duff (1950), and *The Adams-Jefferson Letters* (1959). He has also served as President of the Society of American Archivists.

THOMAS DIONYSIUS CLARK (1947), Professor and Chairman of the Department of History at the University of Kentucky, was born in Louisville, Mississippi, July 14, 1903. He holds the B.A. (1928) from the University of Mississippi, the M.A. (1929) from the University of Kentucky, and the

Ph.D. (1932) from Duke University. He wrote *Pills, Petticoats, and Plows* (1944), *The Southern Country Editor* (1948), *Frontier America* (1960), and *The Emerging South* (1961), among other books, and is editor of *Travels in the Old South* (3 volumes, 1956, 1959) and *Travels in the New South* (2 volumes, 1962). He was Editor of the *Journal of Southern History* (1948–52), and has also served as President of the Mississippi Valley Historical Association and of Phi Alpha Theta.

ROBERT SPENCER COTTERILL (1948) is Professor Emeritus of Southern History, Florida State University. He was born in Battle Run, Kentucky, August 12, 1884, and holds the B.A. (1904) from Kentucky Wesleyan College, the M.A. (1907) from the University of Virginia, and the Ph.D. (1918) from the University of Wisconsin. His books include *History of Pioneer Kentucky* (1917), *The Old South* (1936), *A Short History of the Americas* (1939), and *The Southern Indians: The Story of the Civilized Tribes Before Removal* (1954).

ELLIS MERTON COULTER (1935) was Visiting Professor of History at Louisiana State University, on leave from his position as Professor of History at the University of Georgia, when he delivered the first presidential address. He is now Regents Professor Emeritus of History, University of Georgia. He was born near Hickory, Catawba County, North Carolina, July 20, 1890, and holds the B.A. (1913) from the University of North Carolina and the M.A. (1915) and Ph.D. (1917) from the University of Wisconsin. His many books include *Civil War and Readjustment in Kentucky* (1926), *College Life in the Old South* (1928, 1951), *Georgia, A Short History* (1933, 1947), *William G. Brownlow* (1937), *Thomas Spalding of Sapelo* (1940), *The South During Reconstruction, 1865–1877* (1947), *Travels in the Confederate States: A Bibliography* (1948), *The Confederate States of America, 1861–1865* (1950), *Auraria, The Story of a Georgia Gold-Mining Town* (1956), and *James Monroe Smith, Georgia Planter: Before Death and After* (1961). He has served as President of the Agricultural History Society and is coeditor of *A History of the South* (1947——).

AVERY ODELLE CRAVEN (1951), Professor Emeritus of History, University of Chicago, was born in Randolph County, North Carolina, August 12, 1886. He holds the B.A. (1908) from Simpson College, the M.A. (1914) from Harvard University, and the Ph.D. (1923) from the University of Chicago. He is the author of *Soil Exhaustion as a Factor in the History of Virginia and Maryland* (1926), *Edmund Ruffin* (1932), *The Repressible Conflict* (1939), *Democracy in American Life* (1941), *The Coming of the Civil War* (1942), *The Growth of Southern Nationalism, 1848–1861* (1953), and *Civil War in the Making, 1815–1860* (1959). He has served as President of the Mississippi Valley Historical Association and of the Agricultural History Society, and as Pitt Professor, Cambridge University.

CLEMENT EATON (1961), Professor of History at the University of Kentucky, was born in Winston-Salem, North Carolina, February 23, 1898, and received the B.A. (1919) and M.A. (1920) from the University of North Carolina and the Ph.D. (1929) from Harvard University. He has written

Freedom of Thought in the Old South (1940), *A History of the Old South* (1949), *A History of the Southern Confederacy* (1954), *Henry Clay and the Art of American Politics* (1957), *The Growth of Southern Civilization, 1790–1860* (1961), and *The Leaven of Democracy* (1963). He has served as a Fulbright appointee in England and Austria, and will lecture in Italy in 1964–65.

FLETCHER MELVIN GREEN (1945), Kenan Professor of History at the University of North Carolina, was Professor of History at the time of his address. Born in Gainesville, Georgia, July 12, 1895, he holds the Ph.B. (1920) from Emory University, and the M.A. (1922) and Ph.D. (1927) from the University of North Carolina. His books include *Constitutional Development in the South Atlantic States, 1776–1860* (1930), *Essays in Southern History* (1949), *The Lides Go South—and West* (1952), and *Ferry Hill Plantation Journal* (1961), co-author, *Travels in the New South: A Bibliography* (1962). He has also served as Secretary and Treasurer of the Southern Historical Association, and as President of the Mississippi Valley Historical Association, the Historical Society of North Carolina, and the North Carolina Literary and Historical Association.

PHILIP MAY HAMER (1938), editor of the Henry Laurens Papers, was Chief of the Division of Reference, National Archives, at the time of his address. Born in Marion, South Carolina, November 7, 1891, he holds the B.A. (1912) from Wofford College, the M.A. (1915) from Trinity College (now Duke University), and the Ph.D. (1918) from the University of Pennsylvania. He was Professor of History at the University of Tennessee, 1920–35. His books include *The Secession Movement in South Carolina, 1847–1952* (1918,) *Tennessee, A History* (2 volumes, 1933), *A Guide to Records in the National Archives* (1948), *Federal Records of World War II* (2 volumes, 1950), and *A Guide to Archives and Manuscripts in the United States* (1961). He has served as President of the East Tennessee Historical Society, Executive Director of the National Historical Publications Commission, and President of the Society of American Archivists.

JOSEPH GRÉGOIRE DE ROULHAC HAMILTON (1943) was retired in 1948 as Kenan Professor of History and Government and Director of the Southern Historical Collection, which he founded, at the University of North Carolina. He was born in Hillsboro, North Carolina, August 6, 1878, and died on November 10, 1961. He held the M.A. (1900) from the University of the South and the Ph.D. (1906) from Columbia University. His books include *Reconstruction in North Carolina* (1914), *Party Politics in North Carolina, 1835–1860* (1916), *North Carolina Since 1860* (1919), *The Correspondence of Jonathan Worth* (2 volumes, 1909), *The Papers of Thomas Ruffin* (4 volumes, 1918–21), *The Papers of Randolph Abbott Shotwell* (3 volumes, 1929), and *The Papers of William Alexander Graham* (4 volumes, 1957–61). He served also as President of the North Carolina Literary and Historical Association and the Historical Society of North Carolina.

KATHRYN ABBEY HANNA (1953), of Winter Park, Florida, has served as Associate Professor and Professor of History at the Florida State College for Women, and in the Extension Division, University of Florida, and as Lecturer in the Adult Education Series, Rollins College. Born in Chicago, Illinois, November 5, 1895, she received the A.B. (1917), M.A. (1922), and Ph.D. (1926) from Northwestern University. Her books include *Florida, Land of Change* (1941), *Lake Okeechobee,* with Alfred Jackson Hanna (1948), *Florida's Golden Sands,* with Alfred Jackson Hanna (1950), and *Confederate Exiles in Venezuela* (1960).

ROBERT SELPH HENRY (1957), retired Vice President of the Association of American Railroads, was born at Clifton, Tennessee, October 20, 1889, and holds the B.A. (1911) and LL.B. (1910) from Vanderbilt University. His books include *The Story of the Confederacy* (1931), *Trains* (1934), *The Story of Reconstruction* (1938), *This Fascinating Railroad Business* (1942),*"First With the Most" Forrest* (1944), *Headlights and Markers,* edited with Frank J. Donovan (1945), *The Story of the Mexican War* (1950), and *As They Saw Forrest* (1956).

WILLIAM BEST HESSELTINE (1960), Vilas Research Professor of History at the University of Wisconsin at the time of his death on December 8, 1963, was Professor of History at the time of his presidential address. Born at Brucetown, Virginia, February 21, 1902, he held the B.A. (1922) from Washington and Lee University, the M.A. (1925) from the University of Virginia, and the Ph.D. (1928) from Ohio State University. His books include *Civil War Prisons* (1930); *Ulysses S. Grant, Politician* (1935); *The South in the American Nation,* with David L. Smiley, originally *A History of the South* (1936, 1943, 1960), *Lincoln and the War Governors* (1948), *Confederate Leaders in the New South* (1950), *Pioneer's Mission: The Story of Lyman Copeland Draper* (1954), *Lincoln's Plan of Reconstruction* (1960), and *The Blue and the Gray on the Nile,* with Hazel C. Webb (1961). He also served as President of the State Historical Society of Wisconsin.

BENJAMIN BURKS KENDRICK (1941) was Professor and Chairman of the Department of History at the Woman's College of the University of North Carolina at Greensboro at the time of his address and until his death on October 28, 1946. He was born in Woodland, Georgia, October 16, 1884, and held the B.S. (1905) from Mercer University, and the M.A. (1911) and Ph.D. (1914) from Columbia University. His books include *The Journal of the Joint Committee on Reconstruction* (1914), *The United States Since 1865,* with Louis M. Hacker (1932), and *The South Looks at its Past,* with Alex M. Arnett (1935).

ELLA LONN (1946) was retired in 1950 as Professor of History at Goucher College and died on August 10, 1962. She was born in La Porte, Indiana, November 21, 1879, and received the Ph.B. (1900) from the University of Chicago and the M.A. (1909) and Ph.D. (1911) from the University of Pennsylvania. She was the author of *Reconstruction in Louisiana After 1868* (1918), *Desertion During the Civil War* (1928), *Salt as a Factor in the Confederacy* (1933), *Foreigners in the Confederacy* (1940), *The Colonial Agents of the Southern Colonies* (1945), and *Foreigners in the Union Army and Navy* (1951).

ALBERT BURTON MOORE (1942) was retired in 1958 as Professor of History and Dean of the Graduate School at the University of Alabama. He was born in Belk, Alabama, November 22, 1887, and holds the B.S. (1911) and M.S. (1912) from the Alabama Polytechnic Institute and the M.A. (1915) and Ph.D. (1921) from the University of Chicago. He has written *Conscription and Conflict in the Confederacy* (1924), *A History of Alabama and Its People* (1927), *A History of Alabama* (1935), and has contributed to the *Dictionary of American Biography* and the *Dictionary of American History*. He has served as President of the Conference of Southern Graduate Deans, Regional Director of the Survey of Federal Archives, and President of the Alabama Historical Association. He is Executive Director of the Alabama Civil War Centennial Commission.

FRANK LAWRENCE OWSLEY (1940) was Professor of History at Vanderbilt University at the time of his address and Friedman Professor of Southern History at the University of Alabama at the time of his death on October 21, 1956. He was born in Montgomery County, Alabama, January 20, 1890, and was awarded the B.S. (1911) and M.S. (1912) by the Alabama Polytechnic Institute and the M.A. (1917) and Ph.D. (1924) by the University of Chicago. He wrote *States Rights in the Confederacy* (1925), *King Cotton Diplomacy* (1931, revised 1959), and *Plain Folk of the Old South* (1949), and contributed to the Agrarian Manifesto, *I'll Take My Stand* (1930).

REMBERT WALLACE PATRICK (1962) is Julien C. Yonge Graduate Research Professor of History at the University of Florida. He was born in Columbia, South Carolina, June 9, 1909, and holds the B.A. (1930) from Guilford College, and the M.A. (1934) and Ph.D. (1940) from the University of North Carolina. His books include *Jefferson Davis and His Cabinet* (1944, 1962), *Florida Fiasco* (1954), *The Fall of Richmond* (1960), and *Aristocrat in Uniform* (1963). He has also served as Editor of the *Florida Historical Quarterly* and Regional Vice President of the American Association of State and Local History.

JAMES WELCH PATTON (1956) is Professor of History and Director of the Southern Historical Collection at the University of North Carolina. He was born at Murfreesboro, Tennessee, September 28, 1900, and holds the B.A. (1924) from Vanderbilt University and the M.A. (1925) and Ph.D. (1929) from the University of North Carolina. His books include *Unionism and Reconstruction in Tennessee* (1934), *The Women of the Confederacy*, with Francis B. Simkins (1936), and *Messages, Addresses, and Public Papers of Luther Hartwell Hodges* (3 volumes, 1960——). He has also served as President of the South Carolina Historical Association and of the North Carolina Literary and Historical Association.

WALTER BROWNLOW POSEY (1958) is Chairman of the History Department, Agnes Scott College, and Professor of History at Emory University. He was born in Smyrna, Tennessee, October 22, 1900, and holds the Ph.B. (1923) from the University of Chicago, and the M.A. (1930) and Ph.D. (1933) from Vanderbilt University. He has written *The Development of Methodism* in the *Old Southwest, 1783–1824* (1933), *The Presbyterian Church in the Old Southwest, 1778–1838* (1952), and *The Baptist Church in the Lower Mississippi Valley, 1776–1845* (1957).

CHARLES WILLIAM RAMSDELL (1936) was Professor of History at the University of Texas at the time of his address and until his death on July 3, 1942. He was born in Salado, Texas, April 4, 1877, and held the B.A. (1903) and M.A. (1904) from the University of Texas and the Ph.D. (1910) from Columbia University. His books include *Reconstruction in Texas* (1910), *History of Bell County* (1936), *Laws of the Last Session of the Confederate Congress* (1941), and *Behind the Lines in the Southern Confederacy* (1944). At the time of his death he was coeditor of *A History of the South* (1947———).

JAMES WESLEY SILVER (1963) is Professor of History at the University of Mississippi. He was born in Rochester, New York, June 28, 1907, and holds the B.A. (1927) from the University of North Carolina, the M.A. (1929) from The George Peabody College, and the Ph.D. (1935) from Vanderbilt University. His books include *Edmund Pendleton Gaines: Frontier General* (1949), *Confederate Morale and Church Propaganda* (1957), *A Life for the Confederacy* (1959), *Mississippi in the Confederacy* (1961), and *Mississippi: The Closed Society* (1964).

FRANCIS BUTLER SIMKINS (1954) is Professor of History at Longwood College. He was born in Edgefield, South Carolina, December 14, 1897, and holds the B.A. (1918) from the University of South Carolina and the M.A. (1920) and Ph.D. (1926) from Columbia University. He has written *The Tillman Movement in South Carolina* (1926), *South Carolina During Reconstruction,* with Robert H. Woody (1932), *The Women of the Confederacy,* with James W. Patton (1936), *Pitchfork Ben Tillman* (1941), *A History of the South,* originally *The South Old and New* (1947, 1953, 1963), and *The Everlasting South* (1963).

WENDELL HOLMES STEPHENSON (1944), Professor of History at the University of Oregon, was Professor of History at Louisiana State University at the time of his address. He was born in Cartersburg, Indiana, March 13, 1899, and holds the B.A. (1923) and M.A. (1924) from Indiana University and the Ph.D. (1928) from the University of Michigan. His books include *Alexander Porter, Whig Planter of Old Louisiana* (1934), *Isaac Franklin, Slave Trader and Planter of the Old South* (1938), *The South Lives in History* (1955), *A Basic History of the Old South* (1959), and *Southern History in the Making: Pioneer Historians of the South* (1964). He has served as Managing Editor of the *Journal of Southern History* and the *Mississippi Valley Historical Review,* President of the Agricultural History Society and of the Mississippi Valley Historical Association, and as coeditor of the Southern Biography Series. He is also coeditor of *A History of the South* (1947———).

CHARLES SACKETT SYDNOR (1939) was Professor of History and Dean of the Graduate School of Arts and Sciences at Duke University at the time of his address and until his death on March 2, 1954. He was born in Augusta, Georgia, July 21, 1898, and received the B.A. (1918) from Hampden-Sydney

College and the Ph.D. (1923) from Johns Hopkins University. His books include *Slavery in Mississippi* (1933), *A Gentleman of the Old Natchez Region: Benjamin L. C. Wailes* (1938), *The Development of Southern Sectionalism, 1819–1848* (1948), and *Gentlemen Freeholders: Political Practice in Washington's Virginia* (1952).

BELL IRVIN WILEY (1955), Charles Howard Candler Professor of History at Emory University, was Professor of History there at the time of his address. He was born in Halls, Tennessee, January 5, 1906, and holds the B.A. (1928) from Asbury College, the M.A. (1929) from the University of Kentucky, and the Ph.D. (1933) from Yale University. His books include *Southern Negroes, 1861–1865* (1938), *Plain People of the Confederacy* (1943), *The Life of Johnny Reb* (1943), *The Life of Billy Yank* (1952), *The Road to Appomattox* (1956), *They Who Fought Here* (1959), and *Embattled Confederates* (1964).

THOMAS HARRY WILLIAMS (1959) is Boyd Professor of History at Louisiana State University. He was born in Vinegar Hill, Illinois, May 19, 1909, and holds the B.E. (1931) from Platteville State Teachers College and the Ph.M. (1932) and Ph.D. (1937) from the University of Wisconsin. He has written *Lincoln and the Radicals* (1941), *Lincoln and His Generals* (1952), *P. G. T. Beauregard* (1955), *A History of the United States,* with R. W. Current and Frank Freidel (1959), *Americans at War* (1960), *Romance and Realism in Southern Politics* (1961), *McClellan, Sherman and Grant* (1962), and *The Union Sundered and the Union Restored* (1963). He has served on the Historical Advisory Committee, Department of the Army, and he received the Truman Award in Civil War history in 1963.

COMER VANN WOODWARD (1951), Sterling Professor of History at Yale University, was Professor of History at Johns Hopkins University at the time of his address. He was born at Vanndale, Arkansas, November 13, 1908, and holds the Ph.B. (1930) from Emory University, the M.A. (1932) from Columbia University, and the Ph.D. (1937) from the University of North Carolina. He has written *Tom Watson, Agrarian Rebel* (1938), *Origins of the New South, 1877–1913* (1951), *Reunion and Reaction* (1951), *The Strange Career of Jim Crow* (1955), and *The Burden of Southern History* (1960). He has received the Bancroft Prize, the Literary Award of the National Institute of Arts and Letters, the Scholarship Award of the American Council of Learned Societies, and the Sydnor Award of the Southern Historical Association. He has also served as Harmsworth Professor, Oxford University.

*   *   *

GEORGE BROWN TINDALL (editor) is Associate Professor of History at the University of North Carolina and was a member of the Institute for Advanced Study during the preparation of this volume. He was born in Greenville, South Carolina, February 26, 1921, and holds the B.A. (1942) from Furman University, the M.A. (1948) and Ph.D. (1951) from the University of North Carolina. He is the author of *South Carolina Negroes, 1877–1900* (1952).